MAFIA MOVIES

A Reader

Second Edition

EDITED BY DANA RENGA

MAFIA MOVIES

A Reader

Second Edition

UNIVERSITY OF TORONTO PRESS
Toronto Buffalo London

ISBN 978-1-4875-0023-8 (cloth)
ISBN 978-1-4875-2013-7 (paper)

First Edition 2011
Second Edition 2019

♾ Printed on acid-free paper with vegetable-based inks.

Toronto Italian Studies

Library and Archives Canada Cataloguing in Publication

Title: Mafia movies : a reader / edited by Dana Renga.
Names: Renga, Dana, 1971– editor.
Series: Toronto Italian studies.
Description: Second edition. | Series statement: Toronto Italian studies | Includes filmography. | Includes
    bibliographical references and index.
Identifiers: Canadiana 20190091746 | ISBN 9781487520137 (softcover) | ISBN 9781487500238 (hardcover)
Subjects: LCSH: Mafia in motion pictures. | LCSH: Gangster films – United States – History and criticism. |
    LCSH: Gangster films – Italy – History and criticism.
Classification: LCC PN1995.9.M23 M34 2019 | DDC 791.43/6556—dc23

University of Toronto Press acknowledges the financial assistance to its publishing program of the Canada
Council for the Arts and the Ontario Arts Council, an agency of the Government of Ontario.

 Canada Council
for the Arts
Conseil des Arts
du Canada

 ONTARIO ARTS COUNCIL
CONSEIL DES ARTS DE L'ONTARIO
an Ontario government agency
un organisme du gouvernement de l'Ontario

Funded by the   Financé par le
Government   gouvernement
of Canada   du Canada   Canadä

 MIX
Paper from
responsible sources
FSC® C016245

Dedicated to JoAnne Ruvoli (1968–2018)

Contents

Part Four. Italy's Other Mafias in Film and on Television: A Roundtable

Part Five. Double Takes

The Godfather

Gomorrah

Photos follow pages 144 and 368

Acknowledgments

I am grateful to my friends and colleagues at The Ohio State University for providing me with a welcoming, collegial, and intellectually stimulating home. I couldn't imagine a better place to teach and write on what I love. I extend a special thanks to the students in classes I have taught over the last decade that engage with mafia cinema and television. Our discussions are always exciting and inspirational, and your feedback helped shape the 2nd edition of *Mafia Movies*.

I am grateful to Allison Cooper, Alan O'Leary, Catherine O'Rawe, and Elena Past for conversations and counsel on the 2nd edition. Versions of the introduction and contributing chapters (although not their own!) were read and commented on by Allison Cooper, Piero Garofalo, Danielle Hipkins, Elizabeth Leake, Giancarlo Lombardi, Alan O'Leary, and Catherine O'Rawe. Thank you all for providing valuable and constructive comments and making the volume so much better. A special recognition is due to all of the contributors for their smart and insightful analyses.

Research assistants Julie Parson and Jessica Henderson deserve applause for attention to detail in copy editing and for compiling the filmography and list of suggested readings.

At the University of Toronto Press, high praise is due to my first editor, the wonderful Ron Schoeffel, who enthusiastically supported the project from its inception. He, together with Mark Thompson and Anne Laughlin, are stellar editors, while Toronto's copy editors are admirable for their thorough and productive close readings.

I wish to acknowledge the amity and encouragement of friends and family in the United States and Britain. I extend abundant affection to my partner and best friend Richard Samuels for his love, intellectual curiosity, and excitement in talking all things mafia movies.

A portion of 'Italy's Other Mafias in Film and Television: A Roundtable' appeared in *The Italianist*. 'Introduction: The Banda della Magliana, The Camorra, The 'Ndrangheta and the Sacra Corona Unita: The Mafia Onscreen Beyond the Cosa Nostra,' Dana Renga; 'Historicizing Italy's Other Mafias: Some Considerations,' John Dickie; '*Romanzo criminale*: Roma Caput Violandi,' Allison Cooper; '*Romanzo criminale: la serie*,' Catherine O'Rawe; 'Toxic Tables: The Representation of Food in Camorra Films,' Amy Boylan; 'The New Mafia in *Una vita tranquilla*,' Giovanna De Luca; 'Soap Operas,' Giancarlo Lombardi, 'Response #1,' Robert Gordon; 'Response #2,' Danielle Hipkins; 'Response #3,' Robin Pickering-Iazzi; 'Conclusion,' Allison Cooper, *The Italianist*, copyright © Italian Studies at the Universities of Cambridge, Leeds and Reading, reprinted by permission of Taylor & Francis Ltd, http://www.tandfonline.com on behalf of Italian Studies at the Universities of Cambridge, Leeds and Reading. I thank *The Italianist* for their permission to republish.

PART ONE

Setting the Scene

1 The Corleones at Home and Abroad

DANA RENGA

PAULIE: Ton', what's your favorite scene?

TONY: I can't have this conversation again ... Don Ciccio's villa, when Vito goes back to Sicily. The crickets, the great old house. Oh, it's f**in beautiful. Maybe 'cause I'm going over there, you know?

The Sopranos (David Chase, 2000)

In 2008, two mafia-related media events received national attention in the United States. On the lighter side, the famous horsehead scene from *The Godfather* was revisited in an Audi commercial featured during the Super Bowl. Four days later, indictments in New York led to mass roundups and arrests in both the United States and Sicily, one aim of which was to breach the intimate relationship between the Sicilian mafia and the notorious American Gambino crime family. The first event was much discussed on websites and in the print media for quite some time (the video has been viewed millions of times on YouTube). The second disappeared from the public eye within days. The commercial, although clearly a spoof, was done exquisitely and, except for one minor detail, more or less replicates the scene from *The Godfather*, albeit without the brutality of decapitation. American audiences have grown so accustomed to the offer promised by Coppola that it has supplanted the criminal organization itself.

Clearly, the myth of the mafia is still alive and well in the American imaginary, both on- and off-screen.[1] What is not so clear to most Americans is that various Italian-American mafias are still making a living off various illicit activities, albeit in a much less centralized and structured fashion than about twenty years ago.[2] Of course, the same is true of the various Italian mafias as a regular look at Italian newspapers offers up stories of corruption, clan wars, raids, drug busts, political scandals, and homicides, all mafia-related. The 'octopus' (*piovra*), as it is called in Italy, has pervaded almost every facet of Italian cultural life. Italians acknowledge that the mafia exists, is insidious, and can affect the average citizen's daily life. On the whole, Italian filmmakers demonstrate the extent to which the mafia extends into politics, on both national and international fronts. They associate the origins of the mafia with the origins of the Italian state, and they represent *mafiosi*, anti-mafia martyrs, politicians, and the everyday man or woman who lives daily under the mafia's shadow. American filmmakers, however, tend to glamourize organized crime and to create sympathetic mobsters that many of us would like to invite over to dinner. The trend towards crafting alluring criminal antiheroes is now palpable in recent Italian cinema and television.[3] As a result, most Americans retain a romanticized view of the mafia and tend to associate it with the severed horse's head in Jack Woltz's bed, the expression 'I'm gonna make him an offer he can't refuse,' or the famous melody composed by Nino Rota, all examples from the epic *The Godfather*.

Coppola's trilogy positioned the town of Corleone as the birthplace of *mafiosità*, even though filming took place in the nearby towns of Forza d'Agro and Savoca. Mafia ethos in the film equals honour, just vendetta, and traditional gender roles – 'In Corleone, a woman is more dangerous than the *lupara*,' Michael is told, and from Michael's fictional stay in the town that bears his name during the late 1940s up until about 1994, nothing was further from the case as Corleone and surrounding areas witnessed hundreds of mafia-related murders of 'excellent cadavers,' mafiosi, and bystanders alike. Just a few years ago, however, the town of Corleone engaged in a process of reinvention, focusing on mafia tourism and a proposed name change to 'Cuor di Leone.' Pasquale Scimeca's film *Placido Rizzotto* from 2000 treats the story of the eponymous character murdered in 1948 by the Corleonesi, the mafia clan that shares the city's name, as a result of his anti-mafia activity with the trade union. The film marks an important turn in this reinvention: mafioso Luciano Leggio retains none of the glamorous and paternal properties associated with the Corleone clan in the Coppola trilogy,[4] and Placido's martyrdom opens the doors for new advertising opportunities. It is now possible to buy products such as pasta or wine from the anti-mafia association Libera Terra that promise 'the taste of legality.' The Placido Rizzotto cooperative owns and operates the popular bed-and-breakfast Portella della Ginestra, which was the summer residence of the notorious Don Giovanni Brusca (made famous for murdering anti-mafia prosecutor Giovanni Falcone) and another residence in the former dwelling of 'boss of bosses' Toto Riina, run by the Pio la Torre cooperative. While on site, vacationers can sip a wine called 'Placido Rizzotto linea I cento passi.' *I cento passi* (*The Hundred Steps*) is the title of the film that treats the murder of anti-mafia activist Peppino Impastato, and for only seventy euros a night sightseers can participate in the myth of a mafia vanquished. It is not my contention that Libera Terra consciously sets out to capitalize on mafia culture in the same way that, for example, numerous tour companies in New Jersey have by offering 'tours of Sopranoland.' Nonetheless, it is compelling how many pivotal events and notorious figures of Sicilian mafia history since the Second World War have been bottled, as it were, and decanted into a wine glass. Those events and figures are treated in this volume of essays: the bandit Salvatore Giuliano and the infamous Portella della Ginestra May Day massacre in 1947; the murders of anti-mafia crusaders Placido Rizzotto in Corleone in 1948, Peppino Impastato in Cinisi in 1978, Pio la Torre in Palermo in 1982, and Giovanni Falcone in Capaci and Paolo Borsellino in Palermo in 1992. As witnessed by the lawsuit brought against Time Warner by the Italian American Defense Association, the Italian-American community was up in arms about the prejudicial identification of the IADA with the mafia on *The Sopranos*; now Italy uses the mob to market itself to Italian Americans. Corleone and its surroundings have become minor tourist attractions, and all the while the Cosa Nostra, 'our thing,' the general term for the Sicilian mafia, continues to operate effectively.

This is not the case for all of Italy's mafias. The Camorra, the mafia of the Campania region and the city of Naples, is capturing the international imaginary, no doubt in part due to the mammoth success of the film, book, play, and especially the television series *Gomorra*. Yet it is doubtful that engaged art will influence the battle against the mafia. One reviewer questions: 'As they say in the world of fashion journalism, is the Camorra the new mafia?'[5] In today, out tomorrow, around for hundreds of years. A case in point: not too long ago, accounts of mafia violence in Naples went largely unnoticed in the international community, but Naples in the new millennium recalls the

Palermo of twenty to thirty years ago. News coverage of piles of rotting or burning garbage, election rigging, attacks on immigrants and subsequent rioting, gangland killings, many orchestrated by 'baby gangs,' and troops occupying various Neapolitan cities evoke Sicilian author Vincenzo Consolo's description of Palermo from 1988:

> Palermo is rank, infected. In this fervent July, the bitter sweet stench of blood and gelsomino wafts in the air, a strong odor of creolin and fried oil. The smoke of the garbage burning at Bellolampo is stagnant over the city like an enormous compact cloud. Here, Palermo is a Beirut destroyed by a war that has lasted now for 40 years, the war of mafia power against the poor.[6]

In recent news, Naples and its surroundings is quite different from the region visited by Tony Soprano that represented a mythical font for the American Cosa Nostra. Tony, in fact, conflates the two geographies, evidenced by a discussion about the merits of *The Godfather: Part II* right before his departure to Naples, as cited in the epigraph above.

Mafia Movies: Design and Objectives

The second edition of *Mafia Movies: A Reader* expands on the first in terms of amplification of scope and diversity of structure. Seven new essays have been added to Parts One and Two that treat important films and television series that were either omitted from the first edition or produced following its publication. A section is included that focuses on Italy's other mafias besides the Cosa Nostra, and the essays there engage with representations of the Camorra, the Calabrian 'ndrangheta, the Sacra Corona Unita of Puglia, and the Banda della Magliana in Rome. This component takes the shape of a roundtable and addresses, to various extents, more than twenty popular films and television series not discussed elsewhere in the volume. Also new to the volume is a section titled 'Double Takes' that offers six readings each of four of the most widely taught mafia visual texts: *The Godfather*, *The Sopranos*, *Romanzo criminale*, and *Gomorra*. The twenty-four brief interventions offer perspectives on performance and star studies, adaptation, mise en abîme, masculinity, gender, politics, and urban space. This section also includes close analyses of key scenes and episodes.

The essays in this volume offer unique perspectives on mob movie and television classics and sleeper films alike that engage with the Italian American and Italian mafias. The authors are interested in exploring the myth of the mafia that is so widespread in America and tracing its history and function as it passes across time and through various cultures. Overall, the volume questions whether there exists a unique American or Italian cinema treating the mafia and explores how filmmakers from the two countries approach the subject in dissimilar fashions, especially in terms of stereotyping, gender roles, and representations of violence. At first glance, it might appear that American directors are mainly interested in making films that romanticize and idealize mob life, while Italian filmmakers are concerned with socially conscious filmmaking. A key aim of this volume is to get the reader to think beyond these paradigms and to consider to what extent American films might play with generic hybridity or critique the very organizations they seem to endorse. We also want the reader to ponder the ways in which Italian directors branch out from 'engaged' or 'political cinema' into other genres (women's film, gothic, the western, film noir, comedy) or, in more recent films, might be indebted to the Hollywood tradition and glamorize criminality.

Many readers will be familiar with several of the Hollywood blockbusters treated here that take us inside the gangster lifestyle and that push viewers to align with characters played by Joe Pesci, Marlon Brando, James Gandolfini, Robert DeNiro, Al Pacino, Steve Buscemi, and Johnny Depp. Hollywood has had a long and evolving interest in representing the Italian American mafia, beginning with Wallace McCutcheon's *The Black Hand* in 1906, the first mafia movie to tap into widespread prejudices against Italian immigrants and to align Italian ethnic identity with illegality – a fictional and ill-founded association that lives on in contemporary popular culture.[7] Essays in the first section explore these and other stereotypes in films and television series made over the last century by auteurs and showrunners such as David Chase, Francis Ford Coppola, Martin Scorsese, Terence Winter, and Brian De Palma, along with some less-studied films by Abel Ferrera and Martin Ritt, the shorts of D.W. Griffith, and the television series *The Untouchables*, and chart the way that filmmakers have engaged with the spellbinding figure of the mafioso. In this section, 'family' stands out as a key theme, in particular the distinction between the 'family' that one is born into and the 'Family' into which the mafioso enters through a symbolic ritual.[8] In many American films and television series, generational conflicts are foregrounded and gender roles, with few exceptions, are far from elastic. Also, many American (and Italian) films and TV series engaging the Italian American mafia can be read as racist, homophobic, sexist, and ableist (for example, *The Godfather* films, *Mean Steets*, *Goodfellas*, *Gomorra: la serie*, *Romanzo criminale: la serie*, and *Boardwalk Empire*). The authors writing about these and other texts acknowledge their inherent biases, while pushing further to explore, for example, the racial tensions, gender discrepancies, and political projects inherent in the narratives. Furthermore, many men and women in the mafia a come off initially as types: the cool-headed don, the trigger-happy soldier making his way up the ranks, and the jealous or excluded wife or kept *goomah*, slang for the Italian *comare*, or mistress. Upon further examination, however, such clear-cut descriptions unravel – in several texts, women yield significant power in mafia ia families or masculinity is time and again revealed as fragile.

The volume includes chapters on films by the Italian directors best-known for their work on political cinema, such as Pietro Germi, Elio Petri, Francesco Rosi, and Damiano Damiani. Also included are pieces engaging with popular and exportable films and television series by Italy's most commercially successful faces, such as Paolo Sorrentino, Michele Placido, Claudio Cupellini, and Stefano Sollima. Several essays treat representations of the Sicilian mafia; others are dedicated to engagements with the Camorra or the Sacra Corona Unita. With few exceptions, Hollywood films focus on figures at different levels of the mob hierarchy. Italian mafia movies, more often than not, tell the story of peripheral or problematic figures: on the one hand, those involved in the 'system,' to borrow Roberto Saviano's wording from the bestseller *Gomorrah*, such as bandits, politicians, businessmen, or members of the police force; and on the other, figures who have stood up to the mob and, in most cases, paid with their lives for their efforts. While many American mobsters come off on screen as dapper, handsome, and even charming, Italian mafiosi, for the most part, are typically represented as excessively violent, ailing, or somewhat humdrum – for example, Zi' Bernardino in *Gomorrah* can be seen as an anti–Don Vito Corleone in that he is unkempt and suffering from throat cancer. More recently, however, Italian screen products have focused on conventionally attractive and fascinating gangsters who warrant the viewer's sympathy, which raises interesting questions about audience reception, given that Italy's mafias are more powerful than ever. Up until about twenty years ago, Italian mafiosi had not enjoyed the media cachet associated with the likes of Al Capone, John Gotti, or Joe Bananas. Over the last ten or fifteen years, Italian gangsters have developed controversial fan pages on social media sites and have often become the focus of blogs, remediated videos, or debates in the media.

As we see in this volume, mise en abîme is key to the mafia film genre; films cite one another ad nauseam, and real-life *mafiosi* mimic what they mafia on screen. As a result, the reader will note that several chapters point out the elastic confines of the mafia movie genre. For example, local mob boss Giovanni in Scorsese's *Mean Streets* finds a model in Lucky Luciano, the women in *Mob Wives* self-consciously perform the role of mafia wife imparted from the movies, and many episodes of *The Sopranos* cite mafia movies, from *The Godfather* trilogy to *Goodfellas* to Italian classics. The film, the novel, and television series *Gomorrah* all point out how *camorristi*, the mafiosi belonging to the Camorra, ape Hollywood stereotypes in order to lend themselves legitimacy, a self-reflexive motif already apparent in the cover design for John Dickie's *Cosa Nostra,* which is borrowed from Quentin Tarantino's *Reservoir Dogs*. Saviano's chapter 'Hollywood' first describes Walter Schiavone's (the brother of Sandokan, a long-time boss of the Casalesi clan in the Campania region) mega-mansion, now a rotting and burnt-out skeleton, which was dubbed 'Hollywood' and modelled after Tony Montana's villa in Brian De Palma's 1983 film *Scarface*, and then details various mafiosos' reverence for and emulation of gangster characters in *Pulp Fiction, Donnie Brasco, The Godfather, The Crow,* and *Il camorrista*. In the media age, Saviano tells us, it is only natural that mobsters turn towards Hollywood prototypes and mimic 'mob' behaviour. This came full circle when in 2008, Bernardino Terracciano, who plays a mob boss in Garrone's *L'imbalsamatore* (The Embalmer) and the infamous Zi' Bernardino in *Gomorrah* were arrested together with six other suspected *camorristi*. One of the most striking mise en abîmes in *Gomorrah* is the brief scene shot on location in 'Hollywood' when wannabe *cammoristi* Marco and Ciro act out the famous fatal scene from De Palma's film. Marco reclines in the empty abandoned pool, another replica from the movie, and tells Ciro 'the world is ours,' a mantra that was originally borrowed from Howard Hawks's *Scarface* from 1932 and that in these three films leads Tony Camonte, Tony Montana, and Marco and Ciro to their bloody ends. With the mafia, then, it all comes down to representation – with real consequences, however. Thus life imitates art, but only up to a point, and indeed, several essays in this volume grapple with this dichotomy in an attempt locate the brutal, violent reality of the mafia within the new millennium imaginary.

The fascinating role of women in, against, and around the mafia is also a key theme running through the essays of both sections, as authors investigate what it means to be a woman in a 'men-only society' in which violence and fear have become such a normal part of daily life that resistance seems futile. In recent television serials, women are front and centre and hold signficicant sway over mafia operations.[9] Jane and Peter Schneider's introductory essay looks closely at gender relations and associated cultural productions of violence in the Italian and Italian American mafia. Although organized around the notion of the mafia woman's 'submerged centrality' – her role is central in that she is frequently a silent witness and raises her children to follow mafia values yet is regularly denigrated and closed off from the inner workings of the secret society – this chapter also introduces many of the key themes that run throughout the following essays, such as the nature of blood symbolism, including intermarriage and recruitment rituals, the hierarchy and structure of the organization, the central role of *omertà* (silence before the law), and the *pentito* phenomenon, that is, the trend over the past twenty years or so for mafia men and women alike to turn state's evidence and become collaborators of justice.

Beyond *The Godfather*: More Than One Hundred Years of Gangsters, Wiseguys, and Sopranos On Screen

It was an abortion, like our marriage, something that's unholy and evil. I wouldn't bring another one of your sons into this world! It was an abortion, Michael. It was a son, a son, and I had it killed because this must all end. I know now that it's over. I knew it then. There would be no way, Michael, no way you could ever forgive me, not with this Sicilian thing that's been going on for 2,000 years.

Kay, *The Godfather: Part II* (Francis Ford Coppola, 1974)

You know you talk about these guys like it's an anthropology class. The truth is, they bring certain modes of conflict resolution from all the way back in the old country, from the poverty of the Mezzogiorno, where all higher authority was corrupt.

Meadow, *The Sopranos* (David Chase, 2004)

Above, Kay and Meadow voice two predominant misconceptions about the Italian mafia in general and mafia ethos at large: first, that the association has been around since the time of ancient Roman settlements, a widespread belief that, until quite recently in Italy, made it nearly impossible for prosecutors to identify it as a hierarchical organization with a specific history and an accompanying set of rules and power positions; and second, that *mafiosi* have traditionally been thought of as protectors of the poor or those disabused by a corrupt government. Instead, over the last twenty years or so, historians, anti-mafia activists, and critics have aligned the birth of the Cosa Nostra with the birth of the Italian state in the 1860s and have been privy to testimonies, documents, and first-hand insider reports that reveal a scrupulously organized and well oiled machine with a strict sets of rules and business interests. *The Godfather: Part II*, however, tells a different story,[10] one that suggests that ethnic family solidarity and organized crime are the natural by-products of a feudal and backward Sicily. Coppola's film begins in 1901, the earliest period treated in the films in this section, to tell the story of Vito Corleone's tragic childhood in Sicily, immigration to America, and gradual ascent up the ladder of organized crime in New York's Little Italy. As John Paul Russo notes, Don Vito is aligned with plenitude, nature, and the old country and its accompanying values – vendetta, the don as protector, and a close-knit family – while Michael as don shares none of these attributes. The empty chair that opens the film signifies Michael's difference from his father as well as Coppola's distance from his film of just two years earlier: Michael represents a new, internationalized multi-ethnic mafia that could not be more different from the organization Don Vito headed in Little Italy after murdering Black Hand extortionist Don Fanucci in the earlier part of the twentieth century. Two chapters treat films that reflect growing anxieties regarding the Italian mafia in America at the beginning of the last century, in particular the threat of the *Mano nera* or Black Hand and the vengeful, hot-headed, and morally depraved Sicilian up to no good in the urban centre. Films made at this time capitalize on the anti-Italian sentiment that arose as a result of mass migration of southern Italians into the United States between the 1880s and the 1920s and offer a visual equivalent to the eugenics movement, so widespread at the time, that defined southern Italians as culturally backward and lacking in intelligence and a solid work ethic. Vincenzo Maggitti's chapter positions Wallace McCutcheon's *The Black Hand* (1906) as launching the mafia movie genre in the United States and argues that McCutcheon latched onto nativist fears of the other at the dawn of modernity. Inspired by an actual kidnapping case, the Biograph one-reeler is meant to be educational, to warn law-abiding citizens of the threat of Italian immigrant *mafiosi*, labelled 'Black Hand' due to a common signature on ransom notes, while at the same time tapping into a sensationalist discourse running awry in the media. Although it is true that the Italian mafia arrived in America with waves of Italian immigrants before and after the turn of the last century,[11] McCutcheon's film, in that it comes off as an amalgam of fiction and documentary, would have us believe that drunken, illiterate, and violent Italians were waiting around every urban corner, intent on stealing our children and disrupting our moral order. Both McCutcheon's film and several of D.W. Griffith's Biograph shorts made between 1908 and 1912 suggest that Italians must assimilate into American culture and leave behind backward codes of *omertà*, amoral familism, and brutish force brought over from the old country, as did Joe Petrosino, an Italian immigrant and NYPD officer who was dedicated to bringing down Italian criminals and went so far as to travel to Sicily in 1909 with the aim of infiltrating the crime syndicate abroad. Instead, he was gunned down in a piazza in Palermo, and thus became one of the first 'excellent cadavers' in the American fight against organized crime. JoAnn Ruvoli looks at the ideological discourse at work in several of Griffith's shorts and identifies various stereotypes associated with non-assimilated racial difference – moral turpitude, excessive emotion, and a thirst for vendetta at all costs – in order to position one of his later and best-known shorts, *The Muskateers of Pig Alley* (1912) as an early embodiment of Michael Corleone's famous dictum: 'It's not personal, it's strictly business.'

By the Prohibition Era, mafia syndicates were well established in many American cities, where they branched out of blackmail, kidnapping, and thievery into the more lucrative markets of embezzlement and black-marketeering. Three chapters treat works that depict aspects of the Chicago mafia, known as 'The Outfit,' and the legendary figure of Al Capone. Norma Bouchard argues that Mervyn LeRoy's *Little Caesar* (1931) and Howard Hawks' *Scarface* (1932) solidify the cliché of the 'Hollywood Italian' (to borrow from Peter Bondanella) – a cliché that has been running through Hollywood cinema since *The Black Hand*. To be sure, these two quite popular pre-Hays Code films represent Italian gangsters, and both are loosely modelled on Capone's life and present the audience with overly ambitious gesticulating buffoons driven by ego and destined to succumb to the forces of good. Thanks to the invention of sound in film, audiences were privy to what was considered a more 'realistic' depiction of gangster life, one where markers of 'Italian-ness' and ethnic culture bar the immigrant from integrating into the American mainstream.

By the time the popular and controversial television series *The Untouchables* premiered in 1959, several Italian-American organizations were well established in the United States and quite active in protesting the Italian-American-equals-gangster formula that was prominent in the popular media and had been so for several decades. Without a doubt, the popularity of the television series was augmented by the media sensation of the Kefauver hearings of 1950 and 1951, during which close to one thousand people were subpoenaed to testify before a committee of senators whose aim was to better understand the extent and activities of organized crime in the United States. Americans were fascinated, finally able to put real-life names to fictional faces. Jonathan J. Cavallero looks closely at competing discourses of ethnicity in and around the ABC series, particularly in terms of how the network responded to protests from several Italian-American organizations. The series focuses on Eliot Ness, the famous agent of Chicago's prohibition bureau, and his band of 'Untouchables' who battled Capone's crime syndicate in the two-part premiere 'The Scarface Mob,' and after his arrest in 1931, held forth against a series of fictional and true-to-life Chicago mobsters. Cavallero's institutional analysis reveals that even though writers responded to criticisms by aligning Italian and Italian-American characters with both sides of the law (i.e., we all have a choice, and criminality is not predestined based on ethnicity), 'good' Italians are still portrayed as inferior to the likes of Eliot Ness and other 'white' gunslingers. Conversely, Norma Bouchard's chapter on Brian De Palma's *The Untouchables* from 1987 questions why this film, which, unlike other mob movie classics, not only paints a very negative image of the Italian gangster but also presents the 'good guys' as no better than those they are attempting to put away, met with little or no protest and was extremely popular. Unlike the TV series, De Palma's film focuses only on the years that precede Capone's incarceration, and as Bouchard argues, in its postmodern appropriation of such well-known genres as the western and the early mob movie, the film highlights the fictional status of these mobsters as such and invites the viewer to sit back and enjoy the visual spectacle of a good guy/bad guy narrative that is much distorted from its original.

Quite often in earlier gangster cinema, integration into American culture went hand in hand with the rejection of mob mores, an example being the tale of Joe Massara in *Little Caesar*, and markers of alterity were exploited and derided on screen. Other films, however, tell a different story, one that weds the rise to power in organized crime syndicates with traditional American values such as hard work, loyalty, and prosperity, with families all the while holding onto their ethnic identity. In the decades that followed the end of Prohibition, mafia families expanded beyond local business interests such as bootlegging, prostitution, and racketeering into the more global and legitimate realms of gambling, the film industry, and the stock market. Thus we see a generational conflict emerge: first-generation *mafiosi* held on to traditional 'Old World' values, while many second-generation Italians distanced themselves from their ethnic origins through higher education or by entering mainstream businesses. Significantly, or perhaps as a result, in this changing landscape we are frequently brought inside mafia families to witness private battles for control of mob hierarchies. Abel Ferrara's *The Funeral* (1996) is most troubling for its portrayal of the enduring legacy of the culture of vendetta. Set in 1930s New York, the film is an exemplum of power and violence gone awry once they have turned inwards. Lara Santoro reads the film from a gendered perspective and argues that female characters problematize mob mores and challenge their male counterparts. By investigating and questioning spaces that in the mafia ethos are traditionally thought of as 'male' and 'female' (above all, the inner sanctum of the home versus the public domain of business), Santoro exposes the Tempio brothers as sadistic and deranged killers. Ultimately, the brothers destroy each other and the women are left alone to possibly forge a different path away from mafia influence.

Fratricide is also central to Martin Ritt's *The Brotherhood* (1968). Often referred to as a forerunner to *The Godfather*, Ritt's film, as Robert Casillo points out, announces many of the other's themes, in particular in how it plays out the tension between various types of blood symbolism and kinship ties in mafia families apparent in the *double entendre* of the title – here, agnatic kinship (consanguinity) and ritual friendship (blood brotherhood) in the threatening presence of vendetta.[12] The clash between Old and New World mentalities looms large in both films, and even though *The Brotherhood* takes place in the 1960s while *The Godfather* is set during the decade following the Second World War, in drawing sharp parallels between agrarian and traditional Sicily and the urban centre as the locus of mafia expansion, both films show that family loyalties only go so far, as they are by demand subsumed to the larger interests of the Family.

Of course, Coppola's *über*film is often cited, and criticized, for its admiring portrayal of mob life, and commentators frequently point out how Don Vito's paternalistic, Old World ways are discordant with his position as head of a violent crime syndicate. Anthony Julian Tamburri investigates this paradox, and looks towards visual clues in the film that allow for a more complex reading, one that challenges the prevalent view that the film glorifies mob violence. Tamburri warns the viewer to read beyond the obvious (i.e., Don Corleone is a benevolent immigrant grandfather, a man of the soil; his successor Michael represents a new type of businessman that critiques both capitalism and the war in Vietnam) to discern an aura of the macabre within the machinations of America's favourite family; and let us not forget that the film makes a very loose reference to the 'Five Families' that have been in control of the American mafia since 1931 up to the present day.[13]

In its gritty depiction of life on the streets in New York's Little Italy in the early 1970s, Martin Scorsese's *Mean Streets* (1973) offers a counterpoint to Coppola's presentation of the dignified mafioso. By focusing on a group of idiosyncratic 'mafia wannabes' trying to scrape their way up and around the mob hierarchy, Scorsese's film, as Pellegrino D'Acierno argues, can be read as a demystification of the mafia movie. Today considered seminal to the genre, this film, which was shot in only twenty-seven days, offers a frenzied, nihilistic, and carnivalesque portrait of gangster life. A series of meta-cinematic references remind the viewer of the self-reflexive nature of the genre and disavow sympathy with mobsters or the mob lifestyle. As D'Acierno tells us, *Mean Streets* could be retitled *Cinema Streets*. Filmed more than twenty years after *Mean Streets*, Scorsese's *Casino* (1995) is set in 1970s Las Vegas. Claudio Bisoni's chapter on the film focuses on masculinity and ethnicity, in particular how both concepts are performed and constructed. For example, rather than presenting ethnicity as intrinsic, in *Casino* ethnicity is represented as a superficial 'narrative stereotype.' The two main male protagonists grapple for power in the Nevada desert, believing that they are autonomous and capable of forging their own destinies. As Bisoni shows, however, none of the characters in *Casino* are free agents; all are pawns in a panoptic capitalist system. The characters in *Casino* will never live up to the Rat Pack legacy the film self-consciously references. At its core, *Casino* strips the mafia of its mythology while making clear that the organization's sole purpose is to accumulate capital.

While in *Mean Streets* gangsterism was presented as somewhat local in nature, *The Godfather: Part III* offers a radically different portrait of New York mob life in the 1970s, one that leaves the street and goes global to uncover ties between the mafia and big business, Italian politics, and the Vatican, in particular with the Banco Ambrosiano scandal of 1982. John Paul Russo looks at the film in light of the first two of the series and wonders why Coppola was so intent on punishing and killing off Michael, therefore bringing the saga to an abrupt and frustrating conclusion. Coppola's final message is clear: Michael's unquenchable thirst for power costs him dearly when his daughter is gunned down in front of his eyes on the steps of the Teatro Massimo in Palermo, and years later his solitary death on the island is dramatically different from that of his own father, who passed away while playing with his grandson in a vegetable garden.

Conversely, John Huston's black comedy *Prizzi's Honor* (1985) offers a parodic take on issues of honour, familial loyalty, and vendetta so ingrained in the gangster genre. As Rebecca Bauman notes, Huston turns the genre on its head by depicting two women who challenge the sexual politics of mob life. On the one hand, we have the hired killer and ethnic outsider Irene, whose strong-willed, career-oriented nature is in line with contemporary depictions of the New Woman in Hollywood cinema; on the other, we have Maerose Prizzi, who, like Connie Corleone some years later, works behind the scenes to manipulate power structures within the mafia and to secure a solid place for herself at the top of the mob hierarchy. Although Huston does not offer an alternative to mob life for these women (one is killed off, the other is at ease with the system in which she now flourishes), he does present a more ambiguous study of gender than do several of the genre's predecessors.

Another mob comedy that underscores the constructedness and crisis of masculinity is Harold Ramis's truly innovative *Analyze This* (1999), a film that points towards an 'evolution of the gangster picture.' In his essay, Louis Bayman pays attention to genre and looks at how Ramis's film parodies the concept of the mobster as a stable figure. Rather than the legendary, determined, seductive, and captivating personality from, say, the 1930s, the more contemporary gangster is a banal and domestic figure who suffers from erectile disfunction and is in dire need of male companionship and comfort. As the protagonist works through his feelings, the therapist falls victim to the criminal's allure. Thus, *Analyze This* prefigures the television series *The Sopranos* in depicting an everyday mobster seeking help and enlightenment through therapy and a therapist who struggles with (1) loyalties to an ethical code and to upholding the law and (2) a captivation with criminality.

Yet another take on the mafia wife is offered in Martin Scorsese's *Goodfellas* (1991) through Karen, wife of real-life gangster-turned-informant Henry Hill, who is granted some agency through having her own voiceover in the film but is still pigeonholed in the reductive yet all too realistic role of mafia wife and mother. Scorsese's film is one of several in this volume that touches on the consequences of the Racketeering Influenced and Corrupt Organizations statute (RICO), passed in 1970, which allowed the government to prosecute entire organizations and not just individual *mafiosi* for illegal activities. Much more so than in past years, federal agents went undercover to infiltrate criminal organizations, and many mafiosi turned state's evidence, tempted in part by the Organized Crime Control Act (1970), which among other things, established what is commonly referred to as the Witness Protection Program. So in depictions of 1970s mob life and beyond, a new type of mafioso emerges on screen: one whose loyalties only go so far or who is easily seduced into other ventures (drugs, for example.) Scorsese's representation of Hill and his gang of 'goodfellas,' as Fulvio Orsitto tells us, captures this new gangster impeccably: he, together with his wife, is an average Joe seduced by mob life, and believes he is following the American Dream, which turns into 'the American nightmare.' Scorsese felt a compulsion to tell this story as he had lived it years before, and he takes the viewer on a violent and defamiliarizing Dantesque journey through New York mob life from 1955 to 1980 that pushes the limits of the mob genre in order to suggest that we all, like Henry, could possibly be drawn to the allure of money and power associated with the mob take on capitalist enterprise. Indeed, this is exactly what happens to the eponymous character of Mike Newell's *Donnie Brasco* (1997), whose connection to made man Lefty Ruggiero trumps his loyalty to the FBI, which, as Robert Casillo tells us, is portrayed in the film as an impersonal bureaucracy little interested in one of its own. The film, based on the true story of Joe Pistone, whose infiltration into the Bonanno crime family from 1976 to 1981 led to two hundred indictments and one hundred convictions, grants us insight into the codes of conduct, homosocial relations, and common jargon (such as the many variances of the phrase 'fuhggedaboudit') omnipresent in mob life. Newell, who takes considerable liberties in his adaptation, plays on viewer sympathies and foreshadows the type of mobsters we see in *The Sopranos* just a few years later: cold-blooded killers are cast as the everyday man, with real fears, illnesses, and enduring friendships. Indeed, Pistone looks on Lefty, for whose death he feels responsible, as a surrogate father. Betrayal also lies at the heart of Scorsese's *The Departed* (2006), which, according to Margherita Heyer-Caput, plays out the anxieties surrounding a lost (departed) ethnic identity in the context of late capitalism. Set in contemporary Boston, the film focuses on the deceptions of three men who all, in different ways, turn their back on their ethnic past in order to seek acceptance, power, or material wealth in and around South Boston gang life. Although the film treats the Irish-American mafia, Heyer-Caput shows that Scorsese harkens back to the story of real-life mafioso Frank Costello (born Frank Castiglia, 1891–1973), who renounced his Sicilian roots in order to integrate into the more established Irish-American mob syndicate. Ultimately, Scorsese leaves us wondering whether such a thing as a universal ethnic identity is possible in the postmodern age.

Ethnicity once again is at the fore of one of America's most popular mob TV series, David Chase's *The Sopranos* (1999–2007), which takes us away from the urban centre and into the New Jersey suburbs. The two chapters that engage with the program look closely at the mechanics of alignment both within the economy of the show and between the viewer and Tony to consider why domestic and foreign audiences alike went wild for a balding, slothful, and cold-blooded killer. Franco Ricci investigates the complicated psychodynamics of attraction and repulsion that categorize the relationship between Tony and his therapist Dr Melfi and places the crux of the series' narrative drive in the battle between the word, traditionally associated with masculinity, and the more feminized image. Tony is essentially divided: he is outwardly masculine, yet traumatized since childhood, 'petrified,' as it were, by female power. It is not until he is able to exorcise all feminine qualities within himself, thereby conforming to the rhetoric of masculinity demanded by mafia life,[14] that he, and we, are able to let him go. Paradoxically, Melfi finally renounces Tony as a patient only after banishing her interest in the dark side of her own ethnicity and reaffirming the power of the written word. Lombardi reads the season's much-anticipated and debated final season in terms of Chase's deliberate thwarting of viewer expectations. Narrative uncertainty is central to Chase's project, yet as Giancarlo Lombardi notes, the final season is carefully constructed so that we are ready to begin to turn our backs on Tony and all that he represents. The elaborate mise en abîme of the Sopranos, friends, and colleagues watching Christopher's movie premiere, whose plot borrows greatly from their own lives, breaks all codes of traditional Hollywood alignment constructed around the driving principle of visual pleasure and leaves them, and us, deeply uncomfortable. The fade to black that ends the series and that caused so much dissension and outright anger among the show's millions of fans engenders Chase's profound and paradoxical critique regarding future representations of the mafia on bigger and smaller screens: Don Vito has been unmasked, and we are all now frighteningly aware of what he, and others like him, are capable of. Nevertheless, we do not want to let them go, cannot stop watching, and anxiously await someone to fill his shoes.

Following the colossal success of *The Sopranos*, several American television series aired that focused on alluring criminal antiheroes and invited viewers to forge relationships with them. HBO's *Boardwalk Empire* (2010–14) centres on Nucky Thompson, a Prohibition-era Atlantic City gangster and corrupt politician with a traumatic past that haunts him. In his chapter, Paolo Russo pays close attention to the meticulously researched representation of history in the series (in particular in Season One) so that it encompasses the racism, corruption, politics, Prohibition, gangster *personae*, and activism that characterized the 1920s, a period of 'age-defining conflicts.' Through an analysis of *Boardwalk Empire*'s macrostructure, Russo demonstrates how engagements with history are fundamental to narrative development and to the advancement of fictional plot lines. The series' emphasis on history brings to light the complexity of its characters. For example, Nucky's crises stem from a conflict between his attraction to a corrupt criminal milieu and his remorse for the aftermath of his decisions and actions as a gangster. In the final essay in this section, Jacqueline Reich and Fatima Karim perform a gendered analysis of the reality television show *Mob Wives* (2011–16), which focuses on women married or related to men with mafia connections. Reich and Karim make a case for the docusoap's progressive agenda, as the mob wives construct their own 'feminist narratives.' They also analyse how *Mob Wives* reappropriates the image of the Italian American mafiosa commonplace in earlier mafia movies such as *The Sopranos* and *Goodfellas*. As they argue, viewers regularly construct sympathetic allegiances with villainous men like Don Vito Corleone, Henry Hill, and Tony Soprano, allegiances that are prompted by costume, performance, music, and dramatic action. Why is the same not possible for female antiheroes, they ask, especially in a series where the confessional is a fundamental narrative device that allows viewers to get to know protagonists and, thus, to understand and potentially forgive them? Reality TV is frequently political and invariably engages with contemporary culture. As the authors make clear, *Mob Wives* captures two core features of American political culture: its consumerism, and the cult of the celebrity. Of course, these elements are characteristic of mafia film and television production more broadly, as many of the contributions to this anthology make clear.

Resistance and Myth in the Italian Mafia Movie: From the Corleonesi to the Camorra

Sleep my dear Chevalley, sleep is what Sicilians want, and they will always hate anyone who tries to wake them.

Prince Fabrizio, *Il gattopardo* (*The Leopard*, Luchino Visconti, 1963)

Who should we fight against? Against the rich and powerful bosses? Against the field guards? Against the corrupt? Or against ourselves? … If we want to build a future, we have to do it with our own hands. Our enemy is not the bosses, but ourselves … We are not born master or slave, we become it.

Placido, *Placido Rizzotto* (Pasquale Scimeca, 2000)

The history of Sicily is frequently summed up in the illustrious quotation from Giuseppe Tomasi di Lampedusa's 1958 novel *The Leopard*: 'If we want things to stay as they are, things will have to change.' Uttered by Tancredi Falconeri to his uncle Prince Fabrizio di Salina on the eve of Unification, the oxymoron points towards a broader understanding of the perseverance, power, and reach of the mafia in Italy. As Elizabeth Leake argues, Luchino Visconti's eponymous film from 1963 can be thought of as the mother of all Italian mafia movies, even though there is nary a mafioso in sight. Instead, Visconti's film, borrowing heavily from Tomasi's novel, performs a double operation: it encodes *mafiosità* at the individual level, thereby furthering the Sicilian-equals-mafioso identification that had been at the heart of debates around the 'southern question' for a century, and it firmly positions the mafia as inside and not ancillary to the Italian state. Like Tancredi, who embodies the operation of transformism at work during Italian Unification, the Cosa Nostra has proven to be extremely adaptable: capitalizing on the wide economic and cultural gulf that separated the island from the mainland, it was able to insinuate itself into the withering feudal system, which was soon after replaced by a modern state when the new nation transitioned from monarchy to republic. The deeply impoverished peasants were the organization's first victims, and from there, the mafia enterprise quickly and adeptly expanded beyond petty crime and brigandage in and around Palermo and into politics, legitimate business, and the Church. How did this happen so quickly? And more crucially, why today are Italy's many mafia bigger and stronger than ever before? In *The Leopard*, at least, one answer lies in Sicily's deep-rooted and much-debated mistrust of outsiders (the government and the police force, for example), which stems from thousands of years of colonial rule and translates into Prince Fabrizio's declaration regarding a generalized desire to sleep, meaning to withdraw from history, and to follow the all too common practice of *omertà* instead of looking inwards, as Placido Rizzotto urges, and finding the courage to stand up to the 'honoured society.'

In fact, it was not until 1925, three years after Mussolini came to power, that the government moved against the mafia: he sent 'Iron Prefect' Cesare Mori to the island to wage a war against the mafia, which to him represented opposition and chaos; incidentally, this was quite a well-crafted PR move.[15] The regime famously took credit for defeating the mafia, but in fact, Mori's violent and erratic campaign did little to impede its basic operations. Mafiosi sat tight, maintaining discretion or even entering politics, and when the war ended, they were prepared to get back to business as usual. After the war, the public viewed the mafia as more or less untouched by fascism, and this perhaps influenced a rather sympathetic or romantic portrayal of the Cosa Nostra in what is broadly considered to be Italy's first film on the subject: Pietro Germi's *In nome della legge* (In the Name of the Law, 1949). Danielle Hipkins's gendered reading shows that Guido, the new sheriff in town intent on establishing law and order, is initially aligned with the weak and ineffective state through his identification with Teresa, the corrupt land baron's wife, which leads to his feminization and marginalization. Only after being granted the approval and support of his surrogate (mafia) father is he able to assert his masculinity, which had previously been compromised through his association with the gothic heroine, and win the respect of the townspeople. In this decidedly Oedipal battle, it might appear good has trumped over evil, but mafia law still rules the day.

Italy's most engaged political filmmakers have frequently turned towards the subject of the mafia and have taken issue with Tomasi's problematic statement. This is the case with Francesco Rosi's *Salvatore Giuliano* (1961), which treats the story around the eponymous bandit, commonly referred to as Italy's Robin Hood, who was active in the Movement for Sicilian Independence following the Second World War. He was considered responsible for the Portella della ginestra May Day massacre of 1947 and was murdered in 1950 in his native Montelepre, where, the narrator tells us, the population is dominated by '*omertà*, passion, and fear.' However, as Laura Wittman points out, the film that bears his name is not really about Giuliano at all – in fact, we only see him up close after his death – but about Sicily and the web of corruption and impenetrability that has haunted the island for centuries. Rosi's enigmatic, non-linear narrative comments on the ambiguity surrounding Giuliano's life, death, and deeds and is meant to prompt scepticism, to get us to think beyond the 'whodunnit' of the bandit's death, and to lead us on an investigation into the serious face of power, what Rosi labels the 'holy trinity': 'the mafia, bandits, and the police.' Michael Cimino's American production *The Sicilian* (1987) offers a drastically different portrait of the bandit, one that, as Chiara Mazzucchelli points out, aligns Giuliano with the New World/American values of capitalism and self-reliance and thus sets him apart from his native Sicily, which Cimino imbues with an overwhelming sense of Lampedusian slumber (in fact, Giuliano wrote to President Harry Truman entreating him to annex Sicily to the United States). Cimino constructs Giuliano as a mythic hero who cooperates with the mafia only under duress, and thus Giuliano becomes a tragic figure as he attempts to bring about change in a land where nothing changes. Cimino's straightforward take on a historically complex and unresolved tale is in line with the Coppola trilogy in its construction of Sicily as America's subordinate other.

Corleone, just twenty miles from Montelepre, is the home of Placido Rizzotto, the title character of Pasquale Scimeca's film from 2000. Rizzotto has returned from fighting with the Partisan Resistance at the end of the Second World War to find that his town has become a Cosa Nostra stronghold. While Giuliano's alliances are still up for debate, Rizzotto was clearly united with the subaltern classes. As head of the local labour union, he engaged Michele Navarra and Luciano Leggio, contemporary and future *capo dei capi* of the Corleonesi, in a battle to reclaim land illegally appropriated by the mafia; for this, he paid with his life. Scimeca's film, as discussed by Amy Boylan, offers a 'different view of Corleone' from that of Coppola: the mobster who lived by the rules of rustic chivalry and old-fashioned courtship has been replaced by one who uses excessive violence, such as rape and the *lupara Bianca* – that is, murder where the body disappears – to achieve his goals. Although quite regional in subject matter, Scimeca's film elevates a previously little-known figure to the status of national martyr by proposing a subtle comparison between the battle against the mafia and the battle against Italian fascism. In doing so, the director reminds the viewer of the vital role that cinema can play in witnessing, remembering, and commemorating those who have fallen.

Films like *Salvatore Giuliano* made in the 1960s and 1970s, however, leave the viewer with more questions than answers regarding the nefarious reach of the *piovra* with the goal of prompting us to continue our research long after the screen goes dark. Many films of this period can beclasified as 'political cinema' or *film inchiesta*, the investigative film, which presents both facts and conjecture around a well-known event, whch the viewer is then left to interpret. Yet due to the convoluted and impermeable nature of the Italian legal system, and of Italian cultural life at large, clarity is frequently wanting, as is the case with Francesco Rosi's depiction of Charles 'Lucky' Luciano, the notorious Italian-American mob boss whose career spanned several continents. Luciano infamously consolidated his power in America on the night of the 'Sicilian vespers,' between 10 and 11 September 1931, when he ordered the murder of around forty mafiosi. In 1936, he was arrested and imprisoned on prostitution charges; in 1946, he was repatriated to Italy under circumstances that are still up for debate today; in 1962, he died of a heart attack in the Naples airport. In *Lucky Luciano* (1973), Rosi is not interested in getting to the bottom of the facts surrounding the relationship between Luciano, the FBI, the Narcotics Bureau, and the Italian authorities (Luciano was instrumental in the heroin trade of the 1950s and 1960s that linked the American and Italian mafias). Instead, as Gaetana Marrone puts forward, Rosi offers a deliberately ambiguous exposé of what facts are known about the Luciano case in order to prompt us to rethink previously accepted ideas or challenge the official point of view (that Luciano's release in 1946 was part of a deal made with the US government because he helped facilitate the allied invasion in Sicily, for example). Rosi knows there are no simple formulas for eradicating the mafia. His films show this through his journalistic approach, which is deliberately alienating, anti-lyrical, and non-conclusive.

Neat conclusions and happy endings are absent from the novels and short stories of Leonardo Sciascia, whose writings during the 1960s and 1970s on the unbreakable bonds between the government, the Church, big business, and organized crime have garnered him international acclaim. Three film adaptations of his novels are included in the volume. The first, *Il giorno della civetta* (The Day of the Owl), published in 1961 and adapted to the screen in 1968 by Damiano Damiani, turns the narrative conventions of the thriller genre, known in Italy as the *giallo*, upside down. In Damiani's Sicily, reason and the law, personified in Captain Bellodi, who hails from the north and is dead set on exposing the local mafia don as a murderer, are trumped at every turn. As Piero Garofalo demonstrates, Bellodi ultimately fails, the reasons for which are shown by the film's director, who unmasks the intricate system of corruption based on favouritism and personal justice that extends from the mafia to the Christian Democratic Party. The director borrows heavily from the western genre, turning the unnamed Sicilian town into a 'land outside of time,' from which the law-abiding sheriff is banished and where mafia law stands in for an absent and negligent state.

In 1966, Sciascia pushed his blatant critique of the all-too-easy collusion of organized crime and regional and national politics even further in *A ciascuno il suo* (To Each His Own), which was adapted the following year by Elio Petri. This time, his 'detective' is a local, a teacher who takes an interest in a double homicide out of pure intellectual curiosity. Daniela Bini shows that while both works critique the ineffective leftist intellectual, and by extension the impotent and compromised Communist Party in Italy, Petri's didactic film is much more politically engaged. Here, Professor Laurana is intent on bringing the guilty to justice. Writing is central to both works, yet in Petri, the words seem to leap from the page and lead the viewer on an investigation into a powerless legal system. Ultimately, our protagonist is unable to understand the world around him and is easily distracted by a femme fatale who leads him to an untimely demise. Petri's expansion of the figure of the femme fatale raises questions regarding the imbrication of eros and thanatos in a mafia context.

The opening scenes of Rosi's *Cadaveri eccellenti* (Illustrious Corpses, 1976) (originally published by Sciascia in 1971 as *Equal Danger*) establish connections between death, power, and cultural decay that run throughout the film. In the novel, Sciascia leaves the sociopolitical scene purposefully ambiguous; Rosi, however, grounds it in present-day Italy, creating a poignant exposition of the abuses of power so common during the 'leaden years' or period of intense terrorism in Italy, which lasted roughly from 1968 to 1980. The film touches on many acute contemporary problems such as fear of a coup d'état, the 'strategy of tension,' terrorist attacks designed by extreme right-wing groups to create a generalized sense of panic and chaos, and the 'historic compromise' by which the Communist Party would back the Christian Democrats so as to foster a stronger and more stable government. Alan O'Leary informs us that 'mafia' in the film is meant to be read metaphorically for corrupt absolute power at large and that the cameras, documents, and tape recorders so omnipresent in the film are tools used to survey the general public – all of which remind the viewer of the organizations' tentacular reach.

In comparison, Alberto Lattuada's dark comedy *Mafioso* (1962) would initially have the viewer think that the Cosa Nostra was exclusively confined within Sicily. Nelson Moe, however, demonstrates the director's interest in deconstructing the stereotypical dualism that positions the north as modern, industrial, and technological and the south as primitive, uncivilized, and traditional; he does so through the trope of precision in the film, a vital trait for both the floor manager of a Milanese Fiat factory and a cold-blooded killer. Nostalgia turns into nightmare during the protagonist Antonio's much-awaited return to his native Calamo in Sicily from Milan as he slowly realizes that he has gone from being a big shot in the north to just another cog in a very large and ever-expanding wheel. When, early in the film, he enthusiastically declares to his blond wife and daughters that the bridge connecting Sicily to the mainland will be built in the very near future, we cannot help but pick up on Lattuada's prescient irony of almost half a century earlier. While up north, Antonio might embody modern values and support his wife's semi-emancipation, he is 'Sicilian at heart,' meaning he falls back without difficulty into the ubiquitous honour politics of his small town and becomes just another *picciotto*, or low-ranking mafia soldier, an easy target to be exploited. Lattuada's film, especially in its focus on regional identity, codes of honour, and internal migration, undoubtedly inspired Lina Wertmüller's *Mimì metallurgico, ferito nell'onore* (The Seduction of Mimi) of ten years later.

The second comedy treated in this section of the volume, by Thomas Harrison, posits that the mafia is a synecdoche for Italy at large by tracing Mimi's identification trajectory throughout the film. Although Mimi's abrupt shift from outspoken member of the Communist Party at home and in the northern city of Turin in the context of the 'Hot autumn' of 1969 to *picciotto* for the mafia of Catania might seem implausible, Harrison demonstrates that Mimi's political activism is always trumped by a patriarchal clan mentality, which is the basis of the mafia family. This is made clear when the supposed liberal-minded Mimi screams, after having learned of his wife's infidelity, 'Screw communism, I am a cuckold!' Mob thinking, in particular the thirst for revenge, the de rigueur subservience of women, and the hyperbolic emphasis on personal honour, finds its roots in the traditional family unit, whose structure is the blueprint for the mafia hierarchy.

While Mimi, victim of his wounded honour, conforms to societal pressures and reaffirms the primacy of amoral familism (which is a linchpin of mafia psychology), other figures fight for the right to live, and to live without fear – basic civil liberties methodically attacked by the organization. Marco Tullio Giordana's *The Hundred Steps*, released the same year as *Placido Rizzotto*, tells the story of passionate anti-mafia activist Peppino Impastato, born in Cinisi in 1948 into a family with ties to the Cosa Nostra, who was violently murdered thirty years later on the order of *capofamiglia* Gaetano (Tano) Badalamenti. As George de Stefano argues, Giordana's film reminds us that Peppino's struggle against the mafia is also against his father, whom he outrightly refuses to 'honour,' identifying instead with his mother Felicia, with whom he has a deep yet ambivalent relationship coloured by Oedipal undertones. Felicia represents a counterpoint to the traditional mafia wife and mother, whose primary task is to instil mafia values, such as the transmission of the cult of vendetta, in her children. In the film, as she did in real life, Felicia supports her son's rebellion and after his death becomes actively involved with her surviving son Giovanni in the anti-mafia campaign. Peppino's murder represents another case of *lupara bianca*, the aim of which is to deprive the family of the basic rite to bury and, it follows, to properly grieve the dead. And although his death is overshadowed on the national scene by the murder of ex-prime minister Aldo Moro by the Red Brigades, Giordana celebrates his martyr status by concluding his film with a fictionalization of an anti-mafia rally held in his name days after his death.

The figure of Aldo Moro, one of the chief architects of the aforementioned Historic Compromise, haunts Gabriele Salvatores's *Io non ho paura* (I'm Not Scared, 2003) which is set in a remote village in Apulia during the summer of that Peppino and Moro were assassinated. Although the film does not directly reference the Sacra Corona Unita, the mafia of southeastern Italy, the *topos* of kidnapping, one of the branch's most historically lucrative endeavours, links the group of desperate villagers to the organization at large. As Michael O'Riley tells us, the film is about missed opportunities and unfinished projects, both within the economy of the film between the southern peasantry and the northern bourgeoisie and in the broader cultural context of Antonio Gramsci's southern question by which the northern proletariat would assist and thereby mobilize the agrarian south. Ultimately, Salvatores's small-time crooks are motivated by the promise of capitalism, which remains elusive. The final images of an unrealized union between the two child protagonists suggest that not much has changed in terms of regional politics, economic disparity, or state intervention since the films of Lattuada and Wertmüller.

Just one year after Peppino and Moro were murdered, Giorgio Ambrosoli, the lawyer responsible for liquidating corrupt international banker Michele Sindona's accounts, was gunned down outside his Milanese flat on orders from Sindona. As Carlo Testa points out, Michele Placido's representation of Ambrosoli in *Un eroe borghese* (A Bourgeois Hero, 1995) highlights the crusader's isolated position in his battle against the mafia and its accompanying 'spiderweb' of egregious corruption. Testa outlines the various key players in the Ambrosoli case, including Italian banks and bankers, the Catholic Church, high-ranking politicians across the political spectrum, the Italian and Italian-American mafia, and the Freemason Lodge called 'Propaganda 2,' and argues that Placido's ethically committed film is faithful to an 'ideal of understatement' that encapsulates Ambrosoli's selflessness.

Many are the fallen in the battle against the mafia. Yet, it was not until the murder of Judges Giovanni Falcone and Paolo Borsellino within less than two months of each other in 1992 in Capaci and Palermo, respectively, that the anti-mafia crusade came to occupy centre stage in the international media. For the first time since its inception 130 years earlier, there emerged a heightened though temporary awareness of the organization's homicidal potential, which generated an immediate albeit short-lived governmental crackdown against organized crime. The fallout from the murder of these two 'excellent cadavers' haunts Ricky Tognazzi's film *La scorta*, released the following year, even though neither judge is mentioned therein. Instead, the film focuses on the peripheral yet indispensable group of *scorta*, or bodyguards, charged with protecting a judge loosely based on real-life magistrate Francesco Taurisano. The circumstances under which these men work – there are only two bulletproof vests for four men, and there is no armoured car at their disposal – shock the modern viewer and remind us of the perils in which those who are committed to the anti-mafia struggle place themselves in on a daily basis. As Myriam Ruthenberg notes, this is a film about male bonding under the most stressful of circumstances that offers a new take on the family/mafia family dichotomy. The alternative family formed by these men through communal rituals such as dining is based on an ethical commitment to the community at large and leaves the viewer with a sense of hope that communal solidarity will eventually translate into actual changes in the sociopolitical arena.

Marco Turco's 2005 documentary *In un altro paese* (Excellent Cadavers), based on the homonymous book by Alexander Stille from 1995, shatters any optimism conveyed in Tognazzi's film. As Maddalena Spazzini tells us, the documentary begins with the assassinations of Judges Falcone and Borsellino, then traces their efforts in the anti-mafia campaign – in particular their work with the Maxi-trial and appeals process during the mid 1980s and early 1990s that led to the conviction of 360 mafiosi, before concluding on a much more sombre note. The film presents a clear indictment of the collusion between the mafia and government politics; it also insinuates that, though Palermo is by no means the war zone it was in the early 1980s (when there were three mafia-related deaths per week), the organization succeeded in further entrenching itself in the government at all levels. (Stille, the film's narrator, tells us that over 80 per cent of Palermo businesses are forced to pay bribe money to the mob.) In its juxtaposition of extremely graphic images of mafia-related deaths, many of them taken by photojournalist and anti-mafia activist Letizia Battaglia, and newsreel footage that functions to humanize Judges Falcone and Borsellino, among others, Turco's exposé strips all vestiges of glamour from the mafiosi of the Cosa Nostra. The overarching public reaction following the murder of several 'excellent cadavers' in the early 1990s prompted the ever-adaptable mafia to be less public and to enter into new, more legitimate lines of business.

At first glance, the comedy *La mafia uccide solo d'estate* (*The Mafia only Kills in Summer*, Pierfrancesco Diliberto, 2013) might seem an unlikely candidate to position alongside other examples of engaged or political films that focus on the anti-mafia struggle. Millicent Marcus addresses how the film represents an important modernization project with regard to how the Sicilian mafia is represented and how spectators are positioned to engage with the ongoing presence of organized crime. In particular, Marcus considers how the film's generic hybridity – it is a mix of comedy, romance, testimonial, and, to some extent, biopic – catches viewers attention while prompting them to bear witness to a history of mafia violence. She positions the film as an example of trauma cinema that 'enacts a therapeutic function' and calls for a civil society founded on social justice and anti-mafia activism.

With the documentary *La mafia è bianca* (*The Mafia Is White*), released in the same year as Turco's film, Stefano Maria Bianchi and Alberto Nerazzini denounce the mafia's infiltration into and misuse of the health care system in Sicily, in particular by handpicking many of the directors of private and very well government-funded clinics. Robin Pickering-Iazzi positions this film as being in line with several other recent documentaries about the mafia. He discusses the particularly challenging task of discerning the contours of an 'invisible mafia,' which is not one that we see on the street corner, in the midst of illegal activity, but one that has seamlessly manoeuvred itself into regional politics and a corrupt health care system. While public hospitals are underfunded, understaffed, and literally falling apart, private clinics are flourishing, with a large portion of the profits going into the pockets of the likes of Bernardo Provenzano, ex-boss of bosses who was on the run for forty-three years until his arrest in 2006. Ultimately, Bianchi and Nerazzini position the viewer as witness to an unseen crime, in the hope of fostering debate and, eventually, rebellion.

Set in a boy's reformatory in contemporary Palermo, Marco Risi's *Mery per sempre* (Forever Mary, 1989) offers a look into a taboo subject in the mafia milieu: the threat of homosexuality and transvestism in a subculture governed by phallocentric values. Risi, as noted by George de Stefano, attempts to break down the classic male/female binary by proposing a new type of father figure in Virzì, a teacher sent from the north but Sicilian in origin who accepts the title character's sexual difference and attempts to get his pupils to think outside the narrow framework demanded by allegiance to mafia values. Virzì's teachings temporarily stand in for mafia law, but paradoxically, only within the walls of a prison-space. The film implies that once the boys leave, heteronormative practices in the mafia context, including rape and compulsory dependence on *omertà*, will win out over any sort of enlightened perspective.

Point of view is fundamental to Catherine O'Rawe's chapter on Roberta Torre's *Angela* (2002). Based on a true story, Torre's film is extraordinary in its attempt to give voice and vision to the daily ins and outs of a woman working with and married to the mob. O'Rawe questions whether it is possible to make a 'woman's film' in the hypermasculinized mafia context, and explores genre and performance to conclude that this film does not succeed in representing the female condition, even though it is centred on Angela and relates her experiences as a mafia wife and drug courier in present-day Palermo, her affair with another mafioso, and her arrest and court proceedings. At the end of the film, we do not 'know' Angela at all. Instead, due to the generic constraints of the mob movie genre and the actual physical constraints with which mafia women must live daily, the title character is in the end fundamentally left adrift in a no (wo)man's land and deprived of any agency.

Very few Italian mafia films focus on women perpetrators. Exceptions are *Angela*, *Galantuomini* (*Brave Men*, Edoardo Winspeare, 2008), and two episodes of the first season of *Gomorra: la serie*. In more recent Italian mafia movies, female criminals with mafia ties are often punished through death, rape, or elision from the narrative. This is not the case for male antiheroes, who are represented as redeemed. For example, Fabio Grassadonia and Antonio Piazza's 2013 film *Salvo* centres on the eponymous character, who is at first depicted as a monstrous mafia killer but is transformed into a vulnerable defender of a blind young woman. Redemptive love saves him, although he ultimately loses his life protecting the object of his affection. *Salvo* is in line with many recent Italian television and movie depictions of sympatic perpetrators that focus on a suffering and conventionally attractive criminal who is less bad than the other perpetrators around him. Boylan notes that the film's depiction of an infernal Sicilian landscape underscores the bleakness and and hopelessness of mafia life.

Paolo Sorrentino in *Le conseguenze dell'amore* (*The Consequences of Love*, 2004) borrows heavily from the tradition of Italian film noir – in particular, its use of colour, shadow, and angulation – to critically present the mafia. Mary Wood analyses noir conventions in Sorrentino's film in order to pin down the director's representation of the new millennium mafia in the context of globalization, where almost everything, as a result of both corrupt media and international commerce, might well be tinged by the organization. Sorrentino's main protagonist is on the surface a reserved man exiled from Sicily to live a solitary life in Lugano, Switzerland, as punishment for having lost the Cosa Nostra billions of dollars. If the mafia is everywhere, how can we see it? Wood answers this question by examining the film's style, in particular during moments when the narrative is disrupted and the viewer is made aware of the split between Titta's cool and controlled exterior, which is central to the mafia's code and culture, and his more hidden attributes – humanity, generosity, memory, and most importantly, that which leads him to his demise: love – that are at odds with the mafia essence.

Sorrentino's film demonstrates how far the Cosa Nostra has advanced in terms of a 'modernization project,'[16] in particular its global reach, immense wealth, and relative autonomy. In his contribution, John Dickie offers a series of considerations that help to historicize Italy's other mafias, in particular the Camorra and the 'ndrangheta, paying particular attention to their periods of visibility on the Italian political scene, their successful internationalization efforts, and the role of women in the Camorra. Dickie's discussion raises themes that recur throughout the volume, such as the mafia's infamous adaptability and international reach, the elasticity of gender roles within the Camorra, and the mafioso's (and mafiosa's) fascination with self-fashioning and ease at reinvention so as to present the best face to the public. In a similar vein, Robert Gordon briefly addresses the protean nature of Italy's other mafias as well as the critical responses to them. The Camorra, the 'ndrangheta, the Sacra Corona Unita, and the Banda della Magliana all have diverse origins, histories, business models, and anatomies, and Gordon wonders how studies of media representations of these mafias might reflect such idiosyncrasies while contributing to a cohesive field of study. In her short piece, Danielle Hipkins raises questions regarding the impact of mafias other than the Cosa Nostra beyond regional borders. For example, are absences of discussions about and representations of the mafias north of Rome the result of a national repression of wounds that are still too fresh? As Hipkins argues, many of the films and television series discussed in this volume compel viewers to reflect on the traumatizing potential of Italy's mafias and to consider our position within, around, and against these organizations.

Although the Camorra is often grouped together with Italy's other mafias, its workings and history are remarkably different from those of the Cosa Nostra;[17] most notably, its structure is vertical instead of hierarchical. This is described by Roberto Saviano in *Gomorrah* as an intricate 'system' of both corrupt and legitimate connections with national and international commerce, industry and politics, one that resembles a spider's web more than a triangle. As of 2006, the Camorra was responsible for four thousand deaths over the previous thirty years – as the author points out, one death every three days. Furthermore, some historians trace the inception of the Camorra to the prison system of 1500s. Also, while the Cosa Nostra was originally rural in nature, the Camorra was a product of the urban centre, a motif played out in Francesco Rosi's *Le mani sulla città* (*Hands over the City*, 1963), which addresses the Camorra's long-standing monopoly over the construction sector. Another apt example of 'political cinema,' Rosi's film exposes the corrupt system of quid pro quo based on kickbacks and patronage that involved regional politicians and real estate speculators in the postwar period of accelerated urban planning and expansion known as the 'sack of Naples.' Anna Paparcone points out that although the word 'Camorra' is never mentioned in the film, Rosi superbly captures the essence of the association: seamless collaboration between economic and political sectors. Sweeping aerial shots of the city remind the viewer that every new development project has already been planned to the advantage of the wealthy and unscrupulous, who prey on the disenfranchised, who are easily manipulated into voting for the next mafia-backed ticket.

The complete negligence of the state in the new millennium is exposed by Antonio and Andrea Frazzi in *Certi bambini* (2004), which is unique in its focus on how the contemporary Camorra preys on children – a recent phenomenon resulting from the status of minors as immune from prosecution. As Allison Cooper notes, social institutions in and outside of the film are morally bankrupt and have failed the populace; subsequently, the children of the film's title easily turn towards local members of the Camorra, who are tempting surrogate fathers willing to step in when other families and institutions have failed them. Rosario, the film's eleven-year-old protagonist, journeys through the slums of Naples, introducing the viewer to the ins and outs of the everyday life of a soon-to-be-initiated *camorrista*, one that involves petty crime, pedophilia, a visit to a pre-pubescent girl prostituted by her mother, and, finally, cold-blooded murder. The Frazzi brothers' message is clear: in a dystopian society where civilization is thwarted or lacking, the appeal of ritualized violence generally wins out.

Nostalgia and crisis are key concerns of Amy Boylan's contribution, which looks at depictions of food and foodways in four feature films and one documentary on the Camorra. In the films discussed by Boylan, *non*-nourishing and contaminated substances are central to daily life, family life is under siege, and dining becomes toxic. The 'food crises' depicted in the texts analysed shed light on the Camorra's significant sway over how food is produced, distributed, and consumed while having the power to transform affective relationships. The Camorra makes a killing off of trafficking in toxic waste and is viewed as an eco-mafia – that is, an organized crime network that engages in activities that harm the environment, such as toxic dumping. The crisis of rubbish disposal in Naples also plays a key role in *Una vita tranquilla* (*A Quiet Life*, Claudio Cupellini, 2010), the film on the Camorra that is the focus of Giovanna De Luca's essay. De Luca looks at how the mafia of Campania has been deterritorialized and then reterritorialized beyond the Italian border and examines the trope of 'gattopardism' at work in the film (and in the mafia at large). Giancarlo Lombardi's essay focuses on representations of the Camorra in soap operas, in particular in Italy's longest-running serial drama *Un posto al sole* (*A Place in the Sun*, 1996–), whose action unfolds in Naples between the sunlit and affluent neighbourhood of Posillipo and the depressed Camorra stronghold of Quartieri Spagnoli. Lombardi argues that even in formal terms, *Un posto al sole* points towards the Camorra's ongoing and seemingly unending nature. The film's contemporary focus – many narrated events are borrowed from the daily news – combined with its open-ended structure underscores its commitment to social realism.

Matteo Garrone's hit *Gomorrah* (2008), based on Roberto Saviano's best-selling eponymous novel, was filmed on location in the Camorra strongholds of Scampia and Secondigliano. Pierpaolo Antonello writes that while Saviano's text, which is a composite of detective fiction, horror novel, pulp fiction, and reportage, does to some extent mythologize the very mobsters it intends to denounce, the film does no such thing. Instead, Garrone's raw 'anthropological look' at the Camorra strips its members of any vestiges of the glamour or mystique they attempt to cultivate through their obsessive imitating of mafia movie icons. The film ends by presenting a list of facts regarding the Camorra's international reach – the number of people killed, the extent and profitability of the drug trade, and the vast expanse of toxic waste and dramatic increase in cancer in the region. The final message that 'the Camorra invested in the reconstruction of the World Trade Center' speaks directly to the American viewer and reminds us that the mafia is all about self-presentation, remessaging, and repackaging. With the mafia, as with most advertising campaigns, the extent to which one cares depends on the extent to which one's public image is damaged. Ironically, in attempting to wake us up, to remind us of the international grasp of the Camorra, Garrone has us return to a more real yet very displaced reality.

Unlike the bleak outlook presented in Garrone's film, the series of the same name is fast-paced, has a contemporary and engaging score, and stars charismatic and attractive actors who commit barbaric acts that make Omar Little from *The Wire* (2002–8) and Walter White from *Breaking Bad* (2008–13) look like choirboys. In her short essay, Robin Pickering-Iazzi notes that gangsters are active agents in the construction and performance of their mafia *personae*, which regularly undergo transformation. As she points out, several examples of mafia cinema and television suggest that mafiosi and their actions are potentially redeemable. This is certainly the case with *Gomorra: la serie* (2014–), as Giancarlo Lombardi shows in his chapter on the most watched series in the history of Italian pay-TV, one that has been distributed in more than two hundred countries.[18] Lombardi focuses on how the series endows 'deeply flawed protagonists' with sympathy, in particular *Gomorra: la serie*'s brooding antihero Ciro Di Marzio. As Lombardi notes, generational struggle is a trope central to the series as *camorristi* struggle for power both within the principal crime family and also on the streets with other clans. Lombardi also explores how viewer allegiances might shift throughout the series as different characters take centre stage, sewing discord while almost always gaining redemption.

Italy's mafias are not confined to the south of Italy. The Banda della Magliana, considered Italy's fifth mafia, was active mainly in and around Rome from the mid-1970s through the early 1990s. Not a mafia per se, the Banda is said to have conspired with the Cosa Nostra, the Camorra, Italian terrorist organizations, and the Italian state and was allegedly involved in several of the most traumatic events of the 'leaden years,' or years of terrorism in Italy, including the kidnapping of Aldo Moro and the Bologna train station bombing that killed eighty-five people and wounded more that two hundred. In 2014, the 'Mafia Capitale' scandals were exposed that pointed towards an intricate web of Mafia–Church–State corruption in the nation's capital dating to at least 2000 and involving some of the original members of the Banda della Magliana. International attention again turned to Rome as a hotbed of mafia activity. Ever since Mafia Capitale made the headlines, it has not been uncommon to read news accounts about gang activity in and around the seaside town of Ostia outside of Rome or to learn of mafia involvement in election rigging in the capital. The Banda della Magliana is the subject of the 2005 Michele Placido film and television series (2008–2010) titled *Romanzo criminale*, both based on Giancarlo De Cataldo's novel from 2002. Chapters by Allison Cooper and Catherine O'Rawe focus on the representations of the Banda della Magliana in the film and series. Cooper notes the unusual setting of Italy's capital for a mafia movie and suggests that Rome can be read as a synecdoche for the violence and corruption inherent in Italy's political system through the centuries. O'Rawe performs a gendered reading of the successful series, identifying the trope of nostalgia that underpins the representation of the historical period and pointing towards a desire to inhabit an idyllic yet irretrievable 'white male past.' Both film and series are in line with other recent depictions of Italian organized crime whereby villains come off in highly sympathetic terms – for example, in *Suburra: la serie* (2017–), Italy's first made-for-Netflix series. In *Suburra: la serie*, *Gomorra: la serie*, and the *Romanzo criminale* texts, gang members are hardened criminals whose offences include murder, kidnapping, money laundering, extortion, armed robbery, prostitution, and drugs and weapons trafficking. At the same time, these men are bound by loyalty and friendship and are coded as feeling gangsters who love, suffer loss, and cry. The mafia in Italy is an ongoing and apparently unending wound to the nation that has none of the cultural cachet that typically delineates cultural traumas. Concomitantly, many recent and popular Italian films and television series that focus on criminal antiheroes humanize perpetrators and lend pathos to them. Such tensions generate fascination and foster debates surrounding how criminality is represented on big and small screens while speaking to the enduring legacy and undoubtedly rich future of mafia film and television.

NOTES

1 See Nelson Moe, 'Il padrino, la mafia e l'America,' in *Traffici criminali: Camorre, mafie e reti internazionali dell'illegalità*, ed. Gabriella Gribaudi (Turin: Bollati Boringhieri, 2009); George De Stefano, *An Offer We Can't Refuse: The Mafia in the Mind of America* (New York: Faber and Faber, 2006); Chris Messenger, *The Godfather and American Culture: How the Corleones Became 'Our Gang'* (Albany, NY: SUNY Press, 2002); Peter Bondanella, *Hollywood Italians: Dagos, Palookas, Romeos, Wise Guys and Sopranos* (New York: Continuum, 2004).

2 Although many commentators argue that the Italian-American mob heyday is in decline, organized crime in the United States is far from defeated. See Bob Ingle and Sandy McClure, *The Soprano State:*

New Jersey's Culture of Corruption (New York: St Martin's Press, 2008); or Selwyn Raab, *Five Families: The Rise, Decline and Resurgence of America's Most Powerful Mafia Empires* (New York: St Martin's Press, 2006).

3 See Robin Pickering-Iazzi's introduction to *Mafia and Outlaw Stories from Italian Life and Literature* (Toronto: University of Toronto Press, 2007).

4 For that matter, in some historical accounts Leggio seems to have co-opted Don Vito's look and demeanour for his court appearances in 1975. See John Dickie, *Cosa Nostra: A History of the Sicilian Mafia* (New York: Palgrave Macmillian, 2004), 260.

5 Cosmo Landesman, 'Gomorra,' *Times Online*, 12 October 2008, accessed 7 November 2008, http://entertainment.timesonline.co.uk/tol/arts_and_entertainment/film/film_reviews/article4907928.ece.

6 Vincenzo Consolo, *Le pietre di Pantalica* (Milan: Mondadori, 1988), 170.

7 See Fred Gardaphè, 'A Class Act: Understanding the Italian/American Gangster,' Ben Lawton, 'Mafia and the Movies: Why Is Italian American Synonymous with Organized Crime?' and others in *Screening Ethnicity: Cinematographic Representations of Italian Americans in the United States*, ed. Anna Hostert Camaiti and Anthony Julian Tamburri (Boca Raton, FL: Bordighera, 2001).

8 See Renate Siebert, 'The Family,' in *Secrets of Life and Death: Women and the Mafia*, trans. Liz Heron (London: Verso, 1996).

9 In the chapter 'Death,' in *Secrets of Life and Death*, Renate Siebert applies Hannah Arendt's thesis regarding 'the banality of evil' that played out under the reign of Hitler to the type of 'crude, gratuitous, passionless evil' at work in the mafia (74).

10 Although the essays are arranged chronologically by release date in two sections, the introduction does take some liberties and groups them thematically. Michael Cimino's film *The Sicilian* is discussed in the Italian film section as it treats the story of a Sicilian bandit.

11 See 'The Mafia Establishes Itself in America,' in Dickie, *Cosa Nostra*, or Thomas Reppetto, *American Mafia: A History of Its Rise to Power* (New York: Henry Holt, 2004).

12 See Anton Blok, 'Mafia and Blood Symbolism,' in *Risky Transactions: Trust, Kinship and Ethnicity*, ed. Frank K. Salter (New York: Berghahn Books, 2002), 109–28.

13 For a complete history of the Genovese, Bonanno/Massino, Lucchese, Gambino, and Colombo families, see Raab, *Five Families*.

14 See Siebert, *Secrets of Life and Death*, where she argues that the *mafioso* must renounce all feminine qualities in order to enter into 'the most holy of mothers' (56).

15 See Christopher Duggan, *Fascism and the Mafia* (New Haven, CT: Yale University Press, 1989), for the most thorough discussion of the period. Pasquale Squitieri's film *Il prefetto di ferro* (The Iron Prefect, 1977) fictionalizes Mori's time in Sicily.

16 Felia Allum and Percy Allum, 'Revisiting Naples: Clientelism and Organized Crime,' *Journal of Modern Italian Studies* 13, no. 3 (2008): 340–65.

17 For a discussion of the Camorra's recent evolution and expansion, see Felia Allum, *Camorristi, Politicians and Businessmen: The Transformation of Organized Crime in Post-War Naples* (Leeds: Northern Universities Press, 2008). For a more general history of the Camorra, see Isaia Sales, *La camorra, le camorre* (Rome: Riuniti, 1988); or Tom Behan, *See Naples and Die: The Camorra and Organized Crime* (London: I.B. Tauris, 2002).

18 Emanuele Coen, '"Rapporti ambigui e psichologie complesse": Comencini svela I seggreti di Gomorra 3,' *L'Espresso*, 25 September 2017, accessed 18 March 2018, http://espresso.repubblica.it/visioni/cultura/2017/09/19/news/francesca-comencini-ecco-le-donne-di-gomorra-3-1.310253.

2 Gender and Violence: Four Themes in the Everyday World of Mafia Wives

JANE SCHNEIDER AND PETER SCHNEIDER

At the end of *The Godfather*, Kay confronts her husband, Michael Corleone, pleading to know the 'truth' of his involvement in a series of vicious murders – their brother-in-law, Carlo Rizzi, among the victims. Reflecting on this pivotal moment, Chris Messenger, in *The Godfather and American Culture*, quotes Michael's response as it was scripted in Puzo's novel. 'Of course it's not. Just believe me, this one time I'm letting you talk about my affairs and I'm giving you an answer. It is not true.'[1] Michael's dissimulation, Messenger proposes, and Kay's willingness to be taken in by it, folding herself in his arms with relief, capture the leitmotif of their marriage. He is the active force in a patriarchal relationship that renders her passive, with no agency of her own. She can ask her urgent questions only when he deigns to grant her an audience; otherwise she is shut off – from the spaces where he works, his friends, his endeavours. Her situation is a 'parody of powerlessness, of the inability to reach dialogue.' Kay '"empties" her mind of all she knows ... to become the perfect avatar of popular fiction's lack of memory and consequences.'[2]

Although iconic, Kay can hardly be taken for the typical 'mafia wife.' Nor was she intended to be. Puzo rooted her in an educated milieu, far removed from the social world of Sicilian American mafiosi, and Coppola compounded this alienation by casting Diane Keaton in the WASP-like role. Yet 'the parody of powerlessness ... (the) inability to reach dialogue' resonates deeply with what we know of other mafia wives. Without claiming to depict 'the' mafia wife as a generic type, this chapter reviews the organizational constraints and cultural practices that bear on this role in both Sicily and the United States, garnering evidence from autobiographical accounts, the depositions of collaborators with the justice system, and our own experiences as anthropological fieldworkers in the Sicilian interior in the 1960s and 1970s.

First, a note on the limitations of these sources. Except for journalist Nicholas Pileggi's depictions of the American mafia, most investigative reports have little to say about women's roles. Joseph Bonanno refers to his wife in *A Man of Honor*,[3] but the autobiography is too obviously self-serving to credibly represent her viewpoint. More promising are the autobiographical accounts of women themselves – the daughters, wives, and mistresses of mafiosi – but these, too, pose challenges. Reviewing accounts by Brooklyn mafia women, Valeria Pizzini-Gambetta notes how such narratives have multiplied thanks to 'the morbid interest shown by the publishing market.'[4] The narrators, she warns, inevitably seek to moralize or glamorize organized crime, cover certain tracks, or pursue a personal vendetta.[5] Similar cautions apply to the wives, daughters, and mistresses of American mafiosi interviewed by journalist Clare Longrigg, although her essays on their lives are supplemented with data culled from other sources.[6]

Regarding the Sicilian mafia, the depositions of justice collaborators, dubbed *pentiti* by the Italian press and media, are the most important inside sources. Yet *pentito* testimony is no more straightforward than Sicily's developing anti-mafia process. In 1984, Tommaso Buscetta and Salvatore Contorno, important players in the losing faction during a struggle for turf and influence in the Palermo region, produced analyses that enabled the successful prosecution of hundreds of organized crime figures in the 'maxi-trials' of the mid-1980s. As they and other collaborators began to identify collusive persons 'above suspicion' in politics, the professions, and finance, however, powerful elites orchestrated a chorus of voices delegitimizing their testimony. A later conjuncture, characterized by 'mass collaboration,' followed the dramatic 1992 murders of anti-mafia judges Giovanni Falcone and Paolo Borsellino, after which the number of *pentiti* multiplied exponentially. The overwhelming number of collaborators soon swamped available resources, which and led to several scandals, further stoking distrust of the justice system.

Overall, Sicilians appreciate the *pentiti* for rupturing the mafia's *omertà* (i.e., code of silence) and for their help in arresting fugitives and in arms and explosive seizures. But many also devalue them as opportunistic, as dedicated to the pursuit of personal advantage or, worse, the pursuit of revenge in ongoing cycles of vendettas. Some also express reservations about the other party to the collaborations, the magistrates, whom they accuse of shaping *pentito* testimony for their own careerist or political ends.[7] Among the most forceful critics are various wives, sisters, and mothers of mafiosi who have rejected their menfolk for turning state's witness. Their statements to the press and media are considerably more audible than the barely present women's voices in the testimonies of the men.

Finally, there are our sojourns as anthropological fieldworkers in a town in the Sicilian interior from 1965 to 1967 and during the 1970s, before the mafia was widely criminalized, during which we were exposed to the daily rounds of a kin group of mafia wives and Peter Schneider participated in a series of mafia banquets. Although these events revealed a great deal about gender relations within mafia families, our understanding of them was limited by our underappreciation, in those years, of the extent of the mafia's institutionalization. Subsequent research by historians, the police, and journalists, and the depositions of the justice collaborators, point rather to a well-formed fraternity, one that includes an initiation ritual in which novices hold the burning image of a saint while their sponsor pricks their finger, mixes the blood and ashes, and exacts an oath of loyalty and secrecy until death.[8] Such boundary-maintaining, identity-creating, and male-exclusive practices, unknown to us at the time and in any case invisible to outsiders, affected mafia wives in ways that in retrospect we can only imagine.

Given the limitations of what are otherwise the richest available materials for understanding the relationships and practices of mafia women, it is comforting to encounter considerable convergence around some general themes – a few contrasts between the United States and Sicily notwithstanding. Four themes concerning wives are sketched out below: substantial endogamy or in-marriage among mafia-related households, bequeathing to each mafia woman a dense web of relations based on kinship and friendship – relations that support but also evaluate and criticize her and her family's behaviours; married men's somewhat adolescent and at times homoerotic spheres of play outside the home in which absent wives are denigrated; wives' substantial contributions to and rewards from the enterprises of organized crime; and the heavy psychological and cultural burden for wives of *omertà*.

Endogamy: Marrying within the Group

Many wives of Sicilian mafiosi come from mafia families; in the words of Antonino Calderone, one of the earliest *pentiti*, they have 'breathed that air since their birth.'[9] As is well-documented in Renate Siebert's *Le donne, la mafia*,[10] the youth of these families are guided through social occasions and parental persuasion into marriages intended to build alliances and consolidate kinship networks. Based on research in rural Sicily in the 1970s, we found that families associated with the mafia were more likely than families at large to arrange cousin marriages for their offspring – unions that required a dispensation from the Catholic Church, which prohibits cousin marriage. Especially favoured were 'patrilateral parallel cousin' marriages, between the son and daughter of two brothers.[11] Perhaps, needless to say, such arrangements reinforce alliances between families.

Frequent intermarriage within mafia circles nurtures genuine friendships – relations of solidarity and cooperation – among women, even when they live in different towns or cities. Such relations are further enhanced through women's frequent encounters at life cycle celebrations – baptisms, funerals, and weddings. Wives, sisters, and in-laws help one another prepare hearty meals for these events, as well as for the grand feasts that follow grape harvests, sheep-shearings, and saint's day festivals. The circles thus formed, although grounded in kinship, are not at all closed; unrelated women can be absorbed as friends, especially if they are invited to become co-parents with a mafia couple – a form of fictive kinship that is widely practised in Sicily and among Sicilian Americans. Within mafia circles, the individual who becomes the godparent links the families of the couple in support of the newborn's future. Not infrequently, however, the biological parents invite as co-parents people of professional or higher status whose relationship to the mafia is contingent or collusive rather than direct. Thus does the mafia wife enlarge her circle of friends. Thus, too, does she serve as an arbiter of her family's reputation, presenting 'a respectable and reassuring image' of herself, her husband, and her children to, for example, doctors, lawyers, and priests.[12]

Most Sicilian men see it as their duty to provide, as 'good family men,' for the economic well-being, security, reputation, and respectability of their closest kin, and mafiosi are certainly no exception. This capacity to provide, however, risks being interrupted by their line of work. Perhaps they will be incarcerated or forced to live on the run; perhaps they will end up prematurely dead. Here, the mafia operates as a mutual aid society, taking special care not only of actual widows and orphans but also of the figurative 'widows' and 'orphans' of prisoners and fugitives. In the case of prisoners, the benefits involved – sums of money, legal assistance, dowries for daughters who are about to marry – in part ensure that the arrested mafioso will not collaborate with the authorities. At one time, a mafioso did not usually 'sing' when imprisoned because he could rest assured that his family was being looked after in his absence. Women's friendships are crucial to this mutual aid. During the 1970s, we accompanied a mafia wife on a visit to an imprisoned mafioso's 'widow' – an encounter that resembled in many respects the obligatory visits that women make to relatives and close friends during times of illness or mourning. Times of emergency, precipitated by the sudden death, flight, or jailing of close male kinsmen, are especially demanding of reciprocities among mafia wives.

Several *pentiti* depositions refer to the understanding that mafiosi expect one another to 'treat their wives with respect'; members who commit adultery or 'fool around' may be punished. Buscetta, for example, testified (at the New York 'Pizza Connection' trial, as observed by P. Schneider) that he was *posato* – suspended from participation in his mafia 'family' for a period of six months because he had 'betrayed his wife'. Sanctions aside, the high rate of marriage between the children of mafiosi constitutes an obvious hazard for errant husbands who would cuckold their brothers-in-law or father-in-law. Kinship alliances further protect women from the virility and charisma of powerful bosses; should any of these figures seduce a mafia wife, he will likely have to confront an interlinked system of patriarchal authority with the possible threat of an honour killing.

By the same token, a mafioso might be *posato* for failing to pursue a vendetta against his wife and her lover, should she be found to have one; his reputation depends upon her comportment, so if she slips and he looks the other way, he too must pay a price.[13] Much is often made of women's additional obligation to transmit 'mafia values' to their children, teaching them respect for the father's authority and silence before outsiders. In our experience, this emphasis on women's social-izing role is somewhat exaggerated, neither clarifying distinctions between mafia families and Sicilian families in general, nor allowing for mothers' understanding that not all of their offspring will necessarily join 'the company'. As noted below, recruitment privileges talent as well as kinship.

In his confession to Judge Falcone, Calderone suggests that living with a 'woman of easy cus-toms' should constitute an obstacle to a man's nomination to the mafia, but then goes on to cite and interpret several exceptions. Yet even if the rigour of the rule is unclear, it appears that in Sicily most mafiosi do not acquire mistresses, or do so only with extraordinary discretion. In the United States, by contrast, having a mistress is routine for some men at all levels of organized crime, who attract women through offers of glamour, thrills, and economic well-being.

American mafia wives are also less likely than their Sicilian counterparts to come from mafia families; some, indeed, have non-Sicilian roots. Take for example Lynda Milito, author of *Mafia Wife,* one of the richest autobiographies to be written,[14] who is Jewish and was married to a Brook-lyn mafioso. Comparing several women tied to the Brooklyn mafia, Pizzini-Gambetta concludes that 'territorial endogamy' – being 'born and raised' in a neighbourhood historically shaped by a mafia presence – trumps ethnic background as a defining characteristic.[15] Not unlike Sicily, growing up in the milieu paves the way for a dense web of kinship, friendship, and mutuality among women, reinforced through their overlapping participation in key life cycle events. Of all the mafia movies, Martin Scorsese's (1990) *Goodfellas* comes closest to capturing this reality, undoubtedly because it so closely follows the ethnographic reporting of journalist Pileggi. The character Karen, whose background is Jewish, comments on the closeness of mafia women, who, to quote Robert Casillo's exegesis, 'did everything together – anniversaries, christenings, going to the hospital for new babies, vacation'; they even patronized the same stores and restaurants, which were owned by members of the mafia.[16]

Mafia Violence and the Denigration of Women

Paralleling the biological family of a mafioso is his performed 'Family' – an exclusively male local-ized sodality known in Sicily as a *cosca*, after the bundled head of an artichoke, and in the United States as a 'crew' or 'borgata'.[17] Threaded into a translocal fraternity – 'the mafia' – through a shared founding myth, initiation rite, esoteric signs of belonging, edgy nicknames, and an ideology of *amicizia* or friendship, multiple territorial Families offer material and emotional support in furtherance of their members' criminal business activities. The above-noted assistance to the 'widows' and 'orphans' of prisoners is an example. Paradoxically, although the crew or *cosca* maintains an ethic of brotherly mutuality, it is fraught with internal tensions, in part for the obvious reason that mafiosi deploy violence and the menace of violence in their line of work. Capable of killing one another, they appear to live by the maxim that security resides in keeping one's enemies under close surveillance while recognizing that friends can become enemies overnight. Mafiosi kill for revenge but also in the paranoid anticipation of another's revenge. Standard justifications for the pre-emptive strike include the idea that the victim was 'scum' and plotting treachery.

Interwoven with the tensions generated by the mafia practice of violence are tensions inherent in the very formation of the respective Families, each of which is rooted in – and, in Sicily, named for – a particular town or urban neighbourhood. New members are recruited from that locale, partly through kinship but also if they are seen as having 'criminal talent.' Young men aspiring to join must be 'sponsored' by a member and will thereafter be recognized, as if in a system of feudal vassalage, as that man's man. For their part, already 'made' members, eager to add to the density of their respective followings, exude generosity and charisma in attracting followers, for whose future behaviour they will be held responsible. But should they draw 'too many' young recruits, or 'too many' of their own kin, they awaken suspicion among co-equals. Hierarchical relations between elders and juniors, magnetic personages and impressionable novices, aggressive upstarts and others who envy, fear, or admire them, intensify disputes over territorial authority and resources, turning struggles of interest into struggles for respect and affection. Although the bosses of the various crews or *cosche* communicate latent power and want their dominion to be acknowledged – although they presume to regulate violence within their respective territories and construct translocal alliances – their authority is always fragile and can implode. As Casillo observes, commenting on *Goodfellas*, it is 'only a matter of time before this gangster society ... collapses from within, incapable of containing its own transgressive violence.'[18]

Mafia wives are of course made anxious by this cauldron of tensions even if, as we discuss below, they are constrained from talking about it. Of interest here is the role they play, by their absence, in the widespread mafia practice of 'horsing around,' whose purpose, it seems, is to suppress conflict and build trust. Women excluded from the fun and games; indeed, solidarity-building rituals revolve around the ridicule of femininity. Siebert considers the 'narcissism' of the fraternal organization to be its defining feature.[19] Through rituals, feasts, and hunting trips, the members shore up and continuously reassert a form of masculine identity that repels affection and dependency as womanly signs of weakness. Underscoring women's exclusion, participants in these activities are affectionate with one another, at times evoking homosexual relationships. Taking advantage of women's absence, they celebrate their fraternal bonding in scatological hilarity.

No wonder that mafiosi are good cooks, able to sustain a lavish and much mythologized banqueting tradition, anchored by characteristic toasts such as 'blood and milk for a hundred years,' in the total absence of women. As noted by Fred Gardaphè, a compelling message of the *Godfather* movies is that 'real men know how to cook.'[20] The late *pentito* Giovanni Brusca referred to men who cook in the 'confession' he made to journalist Saverio Lodato. The mafia, he wrote,

is made up of persons all of whom from the start have to kill, and have to know how to kill ... But we also had our good times, in our own way naturally. The grand banquets, great feasts in the countryside were the principal occasions for socializing ... Women were never admitted ... Different men brought different dishes: baked pasta, meat, fish, cakes and sweets ...We had some excellent cooks ... They cooked for all their comrades when they were in prison.[21]

Brusca, one of the most notoriously brutal members of the mafia in Sicily, further elaborated on the horseplay that women's exclusion made possible:

When everything was ready we sat down and there began a game of offering food and drink ... The bloodthirsty killer (became) a jovial and spirited person, full of sympathy for the young men. We also talked about women ... The banquets almost always ended in general bacchanalia, with the men throwing around sacks of water and plates and glasses going flying ... not one remained intact.[22]

During the 1960s, Peter Schneider had occasion to witness a series of rustic banquets, organized to celebrate a peace among competing meat wholesalers and butchers, which took place in a succession of rural towns over several months. Not all of the assembled guests were mafiosi. Indeed, as the numbers snowballed from banquet to banquet, they came to include ever more public officials and professionals – the mafia's interlocutors. All, however, were men. Men, indeed, revealed a striking ability to carry on without women by preparing each of the lavish, multi-course feasts on their own. Most important, as each of the extravagant meals drew to a close, the revellers settled into an hour or more of carnivalesque entertainment that parodied both the Catholic Church and the absent sex. Ringleaders donned tablecloths as mock priestly garments, rang a bell, and conducted a mock mass, nicknamed the *messa minchiata* after the slang word for penis, *minchia*, which was chanted in place of 'amen'. On the fifth of the five occasions, one of them, who had previously participated in erotic imitations of women doing the striptease and in ribald commentary on the wives and daughters of those present, dressed up in pink silk women's underwear with lace trim, a pink satin nightgown, and a hooded black satin cape, using plump oranges for breasts.[23]

Culturally and psychologically, these banquets insulated the celebrants from other members of society. The antics on display during them seemed the prerogative of a privileged few, the more so as they drew prestigious guests – local mayors, veterinarians, and (ironically) priests – into the company. Moreover, by ridiculing women and rendering irrelevant the moral registers of family, community, and religion, the fun and games created an exalted 'hothouse' effect that valorized the aggressive and often grotesque acts of the mafiosi, up to and including murder and the disposal of bodies. Again, the Scorsese movie *Goodfellas* rings true. In Casillo's words, the movie offers a 'realistic and ironic interpretation in which self-interest conquers honour and loyalty, brutality replaces heroism, and the largely law-abiding, work-oriented productive values of everyday society are flouted by the transgressive, parasitic consumerism of its criminal antagonists.' Furthermore, the more the group 'adheres to the subcultural ideal, the greater its contempt for the world outside, its values, customs, and institutions,' including the world of Catholicism and women. The larger society, then, is a 'field for plunder.'[24]

Yet the Wives Contribute

The social world of mafia women appears at first blush to be quite separate from the social world of mafia men, defined as it is by male-exclusive traditions – hunting and feasting in Sicily, hanging out in bars, casinos, nightclubs, and strip joints in the United States. In both the United States and Sicily, however, mafia wives have a stake and some involvement in their husbands' business interests, a circumstance that has intensified with their husbands' increased involvement in narcotics trafficking and with women's growing exposure to educational and other rights.[25] To begin with, men's illicit earnings often underwrite lavish domestic consumption. American mafia women are particularly renowned for their materialism and are even caricatured as 'princesses', driven by a consumerist desire for clothes, and jewellery, and lavish home decor. Sicilian mafia wives also enjoy fur coats and jewellery, 'American kitchens', and nice cars. The mafia's entwinement with the construction industry contributes to material acquisition in both places, as when free construction labour is deployed in enlarging houses and building swimming pools.

Mafiosi typically place certain assets in their wives' names, sheltering them from the claims of creditors and the confiscatory powers of the state. In addition to this, a mafia wife must tolerate the endless hours her husband devotes to hanging out and talking on the telephone, and aid and abet his hunger for gossip by communicating messages when called upon. She may be asked to ensure the safety and comfort of fugitives whom her husband feels obliged to hide. With some exceptions, her sons will join a crew or *cosca*, and her daughters will marry into one, so she knowingly prepares them for these futures.[26] In Sicily in the summer of 2009, the police arrested an eighty-year-old woman for running a drug ring. For years, she would lower a basket from her apartment balcony to her traffickers waiting below, collecting the profits of her deceased son's illicit drug trafficking business as well as a host of *pizzini* – little notes she would pass on to other traffickers.

Perhaps most important, wives must host and defer to their husbands' friends. When Louie Milito, Lynda's husband, made it into a capacious house on Staten Island, he immediately purchased a 'godfather table' long enough (twelve feet with extensions) to accommodate his crew members and friends at their frequent 'meetings'. Lynda, who reports that they talked for hours, mouthing off 'like a bunch of yentas', stayed in another part of the house; as in *The Godfather*, when men visited the don at home, he asserted dominion over domestic space, closing doors on his wife.[27] Louie also hunted, skinned animals, and endlessly watched Coppola's movie with fellow mafiosi. It 'was like a searchlight had lit up on something he had always believed in' – that mafiosi are 'not just lowlife gangsters and mental defectives, but men who live by respect and honour. After the movie they kissed and hugged each other more than before.'[28]

Here's what Joseph Bonanno said about his (deceased) wife, Fay. Her favourite room was the kitchen; 'she loved making a meal … she loved company'. Asking who was coming on a particular night, she encouraged Bonanno to make it ten or twelve guests. As the woman of a man of honour, she had to keep a 'stiff upper lip and bravely carry on', notwithstanding the perpetual 'conferences at [their] house between [Bonanno] and other men'. Because the conversations were confidential, Bonanno would 'close the door or take [his] friends to another room where [they] could talk in private', joining the rest of the company when they were through. She scoffed at them for being 'big shots', and doing nothing but 'talk, talk, talk'.[29] Although Fay did not like Bonanno's long absences from home, she feigned ignorance about his extramarital relations, trusting that (so he claimed) these were only about sex, not love.[30]

Notwithstanding these many reciprocities between mafia wives and their husbands, the former are far from full partners in the men's affairs. As Calderone has observed, 'men of honour' are necessarily guarded in what they communicate to their wives and daughters; this is not so much from lack of trust as to shield them from knowledge that could make them judicially vulnerable – in effect, it is to give them the protection of deniability.[31] Based on her Brooklyn study, Pizzini-Gambetta concludes that women who are unconnected to the mafia but who engage in criminal activity know more about its workings than do the sisters, daughters, and wives of mafia men. 'To marry a mobster,' she writes, 'appears to be an obstacle to a career in crime for women.'[32] Even when assets are placed in a wife's name, she is unlikely to be given transparent information regarding their provenance. They are simultaneously innocent and not innocent of criminal activity – deliberately ignorant, yet knowledgeable about their husbands' pursuits – and this creates many tangled judicial questions regarding women's culpability.[33] Meanwhile, there is the irony of men usurping roles for which women are stereotyped: cooking, hosting, and gossiping.[34] In the next section we consider the psychological burden of *omertà* that mafia women bear.

Omertà: The Burden for Mafia Women

Usually glossed as 'silence before the law,' the concept of *omertà* more broadly valorizes keeping to one's own affairs and ignoring, or pretending to ignore, the *embrogli* – the complicities and disputes – of others, in part out of fear of coming to know too much.[35] Quoting one of novelist Louisa Ermelino's characters, Gardaphè quite effectively conveys the meaning that 'a man doesn't meddle in business that is not his.'[36] In the case of women, this psychologically demanding practice of turning a blind eye poses a particular challenge, given that, as the arbiters of family reputation, they depend on evaluative gossip, especially from other women. Feigning ignorance may offer an escape from the twisted threads of responsibility, but it can be an awkward impediment to the candid conversations on which true friendships are based.[37]

This moral complexity is especially well illustrated by the Milito autobiography, *Mafia Wife*. The author is impressively open about her confused emotions in relation to her husband, Louie, who was at times gentle and loving, at other times abusive and scary. She was both afraid to stay with him and unwilling to leave him. Louie surely produced handsome revenues for her and her family, stealing from the trunks of cars, stealing the cars themselves and resetting their odometers and VIN numbers before selling them at auction, ripping coin boxes out of pay phones, loan-sharking, and investing in various businesses and properties with partners in organized crime. Along the way, Lynda acquired a real estate licence, making herself almost financially independent; but she also helped out with the shady ventures, keeping the books, acting as a lookout, conveying messages, and 'laundering' cash. Not having a caring family of her own, it was hard for her to imagine alternatives; although she hoped Louie would go straight, she generally accompanied him on his crooked path, even as she 'knew' he participated in several homicides.

Lynda's narrative, divided into twenty-four chapters, is chronological. Part One, about growing up and meeting Louie, covers the years 1947 to 1964. Part Two, from 1964 to 1979, embraces an expansive period in their lives: increased earnings and investments, the big house on Staten Island, a son and daughter to raise and educate, Louie being initiated and beating a few raps. In Part Three, which begins in 1980, the dark clouds gather. Louie is imprisoned for three years in 1985; in his jail cell he learns of the murders of a handful of his close associates and the spectacular assassination of his Gambino Family boss, Paul Castellano, followed by the rise of John Gotti. On 8 March 1988, shortly after his release, Louie disappeared never to be seen again. An epilogue recounts Lynda's struggles with her mental health and her new but troubled relationships with men.

Sammy 'the Bull' Gravano's eventual revelation of his part in Louie's disappearance is the source of the most intense pain. Building suspense towards this horrifying outcome, Lynda informs her readers of Louie and Sammy's close friendship when growing up in Bensonhurst, of her own dislike and deepening distrust of 'the Bull,' and of her inability to communicate to her husband her perception that Gravano was shifty and dangerous. 'Having this man in my house was like having a disease in my brain.'[38] Alas, Louie yelled at her when she showed the slightest disrespect towards Sammy.

At the same time as it chronicles distressing events, Milito's book shows how *omertà* distorts relationships among women. The men of the mafia are constantly gossiping among themselves about 'real issues' of wheeling and dealing, betrayal and loyalty, 'war and peace,' whereas women's gossip – moral talk, talk evaluating others – is inhibited by the fact that they know things they are not supposed to know and are in the dark about things they *should* know. After Louie became a made member of the mafia – a life passage he camouflaged by pretending he had cut his finger when in fact it had been pricked in an initiation ceremony – he refused to allow Lynda to bring friends home unless she warned him and vouched for them in advance; he was teaching her, she claims, 'not to get too close to people, not even a woman, and the result is I still have no real close female friends now and probably never will.'[39] This lament is poignantly illustrated by her relationship to Debra Gravano, Sammy's wife. Their children were close in age. Debra drove all four of them to the same private school, the Staten Island Academy, and took them sledding and skating in the winter. 'To this day,' writes Lynda,

> I think of Debbie as a good and kind person … we had much in common. We both took a lot of shit from our husbands and didn't have whatever it takes to get out from it. We talked just about every day, *but not about that* … [We never discussed] the life … the people we knew in it … what Sammy and Louie did when they were together. We knew better than to talk about certain things.[40]

What did they talk about, then? Nothing, really, she writes. '[We talked about] our kids, their schools, movies, TV, the new malls going up out on Long Island … I guess we both found comfort in it.'[41]

These reflections on mafia women – their dense relationships of kinship and friendship *within* the world of organized crime; their denigration by men who, in building their own sodalities, horse around at women's expense; their emotional and material contributions to criminal activity notwithstanding how much they are not supposed to 'know'; and their cramped interactions with others, including other women, because of *omertà* – speak to the 'parody of powerlessness' or the 'inability to reach dialogue' that Messenger attributes to Kay in *The Godfather*. Kay's surrender of autonomy, willing ignorance, and naive escape from responsibility are extreme to the point of caricature; that said, mafia wives in general encounter pressures that curtail their spheres of action. Making the point with special force are the responses of Sicilian mafia women to *pentitismo*, recently analysed by women magistrates, activists, and scholars allied with the anti-mafia process.[42]

In a few well-known instances, mafia women have publicly identified the assassins of their loved ones. A few women have also become justice collaborators – for example, Rita Atria, who, having lost her father and a brother to mafia violence, joined her sister-in-law in opening up to the magistrate Borsellino. Declaring herself unprotected and desperate after Judge Borsellino was murdered, Atria tragically committed suicide, only to have her grave desecrated by her mother, who had disowned her for collaboration.[43]

The mother's response is far more typical than the daughter's. Understandably, mafia women denounce as traitors unrelated collaborators whose testimony leads to the arrest or conviction of their close kin. Understandably, too, a woman who bravely identifies a relative's killer may later retract her testimony under threat of death to herself or other family members.[44] More complicated and especially telling are cases like that of Rita's mother, where women punish breaks of silence among their own. Perhaps these women resent the loss of income and respected social status entailed when a husband or brother turns state's witness. Surely they fear the psychological and economic consequences of entering witness protection, especially if they have small children; the state's program is designed to remove them from precisely that supportive milieu of localized family and friends. Over and above these compelling concerns, the female relatives of collaborators have to anticipate living in abject fear of treachery and reprisal. When the Di Filippo brothers became *pentiti*, their wives declared them so *infame* (dishonourable) that it would have been better if they were dead. Said one, '[F]or the children he is dead, it's as if they never had a father.' Meanwhile a sister made a public statement on behalf of herself and her parents: 'We cannot open our shutters for the shame of it.'[45] Although in this particular instance, the wives eventually joined their husbands in witness protection, and took back their renunciations,[46] such powerful words are testimony to women's entanglement in a web of remembered benefits, wilful ignorance, supportive relationships, and fear.

NOTES

1 Quoted in Chris Messenger, *The Godfather and American Culture: How the Corleones Became 'Our Gang'* (Albany, NY: State University of New York Press, 2002), 101.

2 Ibid.

3 Joseph Bonanno and Sergio Lalli, *A Man of Honor: The Autobiography of Joseph Bonanno* (New York: Simon and Schuster, 1983).

4 Valeria Pizzini-Gambetta, 'Mafia Women in Brooklyn,' *Global Crime* 8 (2007): 80.

5 Ibid., 92.

6 Clare Longrigg, *No Questions Asked: The Secret Life of Women in the Mob* (New York: Hyperion Miramax Books, 2004).

7 Ibid. See also Jane Schneider and Peter Schneider, *Reversible Destiny: Mafia, Antimafia, and the Struggle for Palermo* (Berkeley, CA: University of California Press, 2003), 194–99.

8 Letizia Paoli, *Fratelli di mafia: cosa nostra e 'ndrangheta* (Bologna: Il Mulino, 2000); Schneider and Schneider, *Reversible Destiny*, 84–5.

9 Pino Arlacchi, *Men of Dishonor: Inside the Sicilian Mafia* (New York: William Morrow, 1993), 145.

10 Renate Siebert, *Le Donne, la Mafia* (Milan: Il Saggiatore, 1994).

11 Jane Schneider and Peter Schneider, *Culture and Political Economy in Western Sicily* (New York: Academic Press, 1976), 73–9.

12 See Alessandra Dino, 'Women and Mafia,' 2004, accessed 27 June 2004, http://members.lycos.co.uk /ocnewsletter/SGOC0504/Dino.pdf.

13 Ombretta Ingrascì, *Donne d'onore: storie di mafia al femminile* (Milano: Bruno Mondadori, 2007), xix, 34.

14 Lynda Milito and Reg Potterton, *Mafia Wife: My Story of Love, Murder, and Madness* (New York: Harper Collins, 2003).

15 Pizzini-Gambetta, 'Mafia Women in Brooklyn,' 89–91.

16 Robert Casillo, *Gangster Priest: The Italian American Cinema of Martin Scorsese* (Toronto, ON: University of Toronto Press, 2006), 288, 538–9n54.

17 For a review of sources on which the following description is based, see Schneider and Schneider, *Reversible Destiny*, ch. 4.

18 Casillo, *Gangster Priest*, 273.

19 Siebert, *Le Donne, la Mafia*, 25–47.

20 Fred L. Gardaphé, *From Wiseguys to Wise Men: The Gangster and Italian American Masculinities* (New York: Routledge, 2006), 41. See also James Fentress, *Rebels and Mafiosi: Death in a Sicilian Landscape* (Ithaca, NY: Cornell University Press, 2000), 218.

21 Saverio Lodato, *'Ho ucciso Giovanni Falcone': la confessione di Giovanni Brusca* (Milan: Mondadori, 1999), 180–84.

22 Ibid.

23 For a fuller description of the banquets, see Schneider and Schneider, *Reversible Destiny*, 96–8.

24 Casillo, *Gangster Priest*, 288–9.

25 Ingrascì, *Donne d'onore*, 49–67.

26 Arlacchi, *Men of Dishonor*, 145; see also Teresa Principato and Alessandra Dino, *Mafia donna: le vestali del sacro e dell'onore* (Palermo: Flaccovio, 1997); Siebert, *Le Donne, la Mafia*.

27 Milito and Potterton, *Mafia Wife*, 204. See also Messenger, *The Godfather and American Culture*, 206, who notes how, in the *Godfather* movies, it is the men who are always 'at home.' Compare, though, the situation of Tony Soprano, whose household is dominated by Carmela's female power and who, if he entertains his friends at home, does so in the basement. Gardaphé analyses this recent, suburban incarnation of the American mafia in a chapter called 'Fresh Garbage: The Gangster as Today's Trickster – David Chase and Tony Ardizzone,' in *From Wiseguys to Wise Men*, 149–67.

28 Milito and Potterton, *Mafia Wife*, 126.

29 Bonanno and Lalli, *A Man of Honor*, 313.

30 Ibid., 314.

31 In Arlacchi, *Men of Dishonor*, 145.

32 Pizzini-Gambetta, 'Mafia Women in Brooklyn,' 91.

33 See especially Principato and Dino, *Mafia donna*; Dino, 'Women and Mafia.'

34 We are grateful to Jason Pine for observing this irony – a complement to men's parodic performance of women's sexuality during their banquets and feasts.

35 Anton Blok, *The Mafia of a Sicilian Village, 1860–1960: A Study of Violent Peasant Entrepreneurs* (New York: Harper and Row, 1974); Jason A. Pine, 'Omertà: The Melodramatic Aesthetic and Its Moral/Political Economy in Naples' (PhD diss., University of Texas–Austin, 2005).

36 Quoted in Gardaphé, *From Wiseguys to Wise Men*, 112.

37 Jane Schneider, 'Women in the Mob,' Review Article, *Global Crime* 7, no. 1 (2006): 127–33; Siebert, *Le Donne, la Mafia*.

38 Milito and Potterton, *Mafia Wife*, 133.

39 Ibid., 129.

40 Ibid., 174; emphasis added.

41 Ibid., 197–8.

42 See, in particular, Ingrascì, *Donne d'onore*; Principato and Dino, *Mafia donna*; Anna Puglisi, *Sole contra la mafia* (Palermo: La Luna, 1990); Anna Puglisi, *Donne, mafia e antimafia* (Trapani: DG Editore, 2005).

43 Alison Jamieson, *The Antimafia: Italy's Fight against Organized Crime* (London: Macmillan Press, 2000), 132–33.

44 Puglisi, *Donne, mafia e antimafia*.

45 Quoted in ibid., 230–1. See also Clara Cardella and Marilena Macaluso, 'Vite sotto protezione,' in *Pentiti: I collaboratori di giustizia, le istituzioni, l'opinione pubblica*, ed. Alessandra Dino (Rome: Donzelli Editore, 2006), 85–113; Puglisi, *Donne, mafia e antimafia*, 64–7.

46 Ingrascì, *Donne d'onore*, 142–3.

PART TWO

American Mafia Movies and Television: The Corleones at Home and Abroad

3 Wallace McCutcheon's *The Black Hand*: A Different Version of a Biograph Kidnapping

VINCENZO MAGGITTI

The Black Hand (1906), a film based on a kidnapping case in New York City in February 1906, stands out among contemporaneous movies as the film that launched the mafia movie genre. In addition to being the genre's *ur*film, *The Black Hand* participates in the nascent medium's construction of a narrative language and also exploits (as did other films of the period) the film's potential as a pedagogical tool. In other words, it aimed not only to entertain but also to instruct audiences. In particular, it sought to raise public awareness of the dangers lurking in the big cities in order to encourage people to seek the assistance of the police and other institutional organizations. This educational impulse was founded on the premise that there was an inherent connection between immigrants and illegality. The prevailing mentality held that social ills were exacerbated by the rising tide of immigrants, whose lifestyle seemed to include criminality as one of its main cultural components. The social issues addressed by movies in the United States during the silent period are of all different types; they include public health and class struggle, to name just two. The enactment of social concerns in filmic images highlighted the complex relation between fiction and documentary that characterized cinema's earliest history.[1]

   The Black Hand is a piece of filmic evidence of the early success enjoyed by what is today called an 'instant movie,' that is, a cinematographic version of real events (often tragic ones, such as murders or disasters), shot in order to feed the public's imagination with a visual narration of the facts. It was released on 29 March, on the heels of an attempted ransom for a kidnapped child that had only just been covered by the press. The movie follows one of the unspoken 'rules' of the new medium by taking its inspiration from the printed page; however, *The Black Hand* reaches farther than other 'instant movies' into the cinematic territory of newsreel (the filmic equivalent of today's TV news) by adopting some of its devices and mixing them with fictional elements. Newsreels were usually shown in nickelodeons in addition to features. They covered all different kinds of events, but they were at times staged in front of the camera because shooting on location was not always possible. Of course, with the advent of television, newsreels became obsolete.

   The criminal drama fictionalized in *The Black Hand* shows a group of gangsters signing an extortion letter with a name whose subsequent success among the mob has been explained as a 'rebound' effect from its frequent use in the printed media. As John Dickie argues in reference to the Sicilian mafia, *Mano Nera* (Black Hand) 'offers further illustration of this brand-name inflation in the United States.'[2] The name – which allegedly originated in Spain, where the expression was used to designate local anarchist groups[3] – spread among extortionists in turn-of-the-century

New York via immigrants from southern Italy, where 'scrounging letters' (threatening letters that demanded money while often also pleading poverty) had long been used in the criminal underworld. The media success of the appellation, whose popularity shadowed the already generalized term 'mafia' for any gang activity, gave way to a linguistic abuse that makes difficult and contradictory any attempt at a philological reconstruction of the name. Things got worse, at least from an ethnic point of view, in the 1950s, when the Kefauver Committee's congressional investigation into organized crime in New York City established the presence of a criminal entity called 'the mafia,' whose activity was no longer run by extortionists who only preyed on their countrymen in the Italian districts of big cities. This criminal code now belonged to the past, and Hollywood had already recognized the 'period' flavour of the colourful descriptor with a movie by Richard Thorp (*Black Hand* – released in 1950), starring Gene Kelly as a young Italian-American who sought vengeance against the 'Black Hand' for the death of his father.[4]

These films attempted to reflect the reality of the Italian immigrants' experiences in the United States, one in which victims and gangsters were likely to share the same neighbourhood and often place of origin (western Sicily). Given New York's sizable Italian American population, the movies would outline the contrasting experiences of the hard-working versus hardly working immigrants by projecting stereotypically opposite characters so as to avoid alienating a potential target audience. Nor could the issue of ethnicity be ignored. Indeed, the ethnic status of the 'Black Hand' phenomenon was deemed so relevant that in 1904, the New York Police Department created a special Italian squad. The head of this division (comprised of only five men) was Sergeant Joe Petrosino, who had found in his job as a policeman a way to climb 'from poor dago to upstanding detective.'[5] It was difficult for such a small squad to keep several hundred thousand Italians under control, besides which, the idea had 'the unintended effect of ghettoizing the problem.'[6] Anticipating modern anti-mafia tactics, Petrosino was sent to Sicily to find out more about the connection between immigration and criminal organizations. On 12 March 1909, he was killed in an ambush in Piazza Marina, a central square of Palermo. Because he had been a high-profile detective in the fight against organized crime, his death produced a cinematographic surge in movies about the 'Black Hand' (including one of the first four-reelers, *Adventures of Lieutenant Petrosino*, in 1912). All of these films were in direct debt to McCutcheon's foundational text.

Besides inventing a genre, *The Black Hand*, an eleven-minute Biograph one-reeler, has secured place in American cinema history by being 'an early example of a film based on an actual incident … shot on the same New York streets where the real crime occurred.'[7] Actually, there are two other locations, each of which depicts, in both a theatrical and a conventional array, Italian immigrants' way of life in New York at the beginning of the twentieth century. One of these is the shop of the assimilated butcher, Mr Angelo. In the film, this is the character based on Pietro Miano, the real-life target of extortion. The heavenly-sounding 'Angelo' – he has a thriving business and a nice, clean shop – serves as an allegory for successful integration into the host society. The other scene depicts the extortionists, whose hideout looks like a dungeon where they do nothing but drink and gamble. The letter they concoct and send to the butcher is given full scope in a still frame that synchronizes the reading by the character and the viewers. Beginning with a misspelled statement ('Bewar!! we are desperut'), the letter reveals the extortionists' lack of education, which was not necessarily typical of these scrounging letters – frequently, as Reppetto documents, these letters were exquisitely crafted and civil.[8] The letter is visibly ink-stained, pointing to a complete lack of civility, and makes use of two common threats: kidnapping and destruction of property.

The core of the movie is the kidnapping sequence, which works as a bridge to other contemporary movies that address the same subject and raises questions about the relationship between documentary realism and fictional mise en scène in what Scott Simmon has fittingly defined as a 'docudrama about urban crime.'[9] The documentary approach to drama in the film is properly testified by the choice of shooting the kidnapping sequence on a real city street, 7th Avenue, which had the practical advantage of being very close to the Biograph studios on 14th Street.[10]

Kidnapping was a favourite subject in the early cinema of both England and the United States: numerous important directors began their careers with features on the topic. In *Rescued by Rover* (1904), one of Cecil M. Hepworth's first films, the dog Rover saves his owners' child by leading the father to the kidnapper's hiding place. Perhaps more dramatically, in his debut film for Biograph, *The Adventures of Dollie* (1908), D.W. Griffith had Dollie (who had been kidnapped by a gypsy) rescued from a raging river by a fisherman in the same spot where the inciting incident had occurred. These movies share some basic traits with *The Black Hand*: the choice of gypsies as abductors, which clearly exploits ethnic discrimination, and the use of a similar plot structure, which contributed both to the codification of cinematic language and to cinema's development as a narrative medium. In all these films, the use of suspense facilitated the audience's acceptance of relatively unfamiliar editing techniques, such as cutting back and forth to different social environments.

The Black Hand handles the abduction sequence as an event recorded, as if by chance, by a camera positioned semi-surreptitiously in a bustling snow-clad New York street. The first part of the sequence, apparently shot on Seventh Avenue, allows the audience to linger on the frame for a substantial length of time before any action takes place, in a manner typical of newsreels, especially those recording 'vistas' of urban spaces, such as railway stations and commercial streets. One of the abductors, who was visually introduced to the spectator in the opening scene (in which the kidnappers wrote the extortion letter), approaches the camera with the hesitant step of someone who is looking for something on the sidewalk, perhaps a coin that has slipped from his pocket. The missing object is later revealed to be a ruse to attract the attention of Maria, the butcher's daughter, who is walking alone just a few steps behind the kidnapper. She kindly assists him in his search and is rewarded with a small bag of candies before being whisked away in a van. Meanwhile, life bustles along on the avenue, faithfully recorded on the reel. The result, according to Peter Bondanella, is 'a very sophisticated use of a stationary camera to frame a number of important narrative details as people walk in and out of the camera's eye.'[11] The details framed by the camera, however, cannot be entirely ascribed to narrative perspective. The uncertain and progressive surfacing of the characters within the frame from the wave of anonymous passers-by empowers the spectators to choose where to focus their attention. Thus, the use of authentic locations disrupts the narrative flow in a rather unpredictable manner by shifting from the patent theatricality of the studio scenes to the documentary realism of the location shots. This visual shift is vividly highlighted by the visible reaction of bystanders to the camera's presence, as well as by the off-camera intervention of policemen, who attempt to stop the kidnapping, which is recorded in Biograph's publicity for the film release. Thus *The Black Hand* unintentionally creates a contrast between the different sets and provides a unique example of the narrative coexistence of documentary and fiction at the dawn of film history. This mediation occurred before the cinema industry committed itself almost entirely to the commercial aspect of storytelling rather than continuing the trend towards experimentation that was discernible, for example, in the Lumiére brothers' offerings.

While the documentary impetus is significant, it is not the *Black Hand*'s sole cinematic reference. The film's two other sets perfectly fit the indoor venues of the butcher's shop and the kidnappers' hideout, which is actually the back room of a junk shop. While the former symbolizes Mr Angelo's assimilation into American society, the latter symbolizes the worthless integration of the criminals. In the two introductory scenes, the senders and addressees of the scrounging letter are clearly indicated and contrastingly visualized for the audience. The shop and the hideout are also used to stage the police interventions.

The first scene is at the butcher's, where two policemen, hiding in the walk-in freezer, wait for a gang member to come collect the ransom. Though apparently devised as a way to highlight the suspense of the scene – the freezer's unlikely window allowed the spectators to see the policemen in hiding – the ambush did happen under similar circumstances; indeed, newspapers asked their readers for a deeper suspension of disbelief than moviegoers, reporting that the policemen had had to spend eleven hours in the cold before the man turned up. Moreover, the butcher's wife is given a chance to play an active role when, escaping the control of the armed man, she lifts the door latch to the icebox (which cannot be opened from the inside) to let the policemen out to catch their man. Her character has a negative counterpart in the criminals' den, where a woman who is dressed like a gypsy acts as a strict ward for little Maria, pushing her under a blanket and roughly ordering her to hush. In addition to the excitement of the arrest, the scene also provides the audience with a moment of comic relief when the policemen are shown jumping about to warm up before returning once again to the freezer. The dénouement, when the gang is finally arrested and Maria is returned to her loving family, is structured on a similar pattern. Following the instructions slipped to her by the police, the girl participates in her own rescue by opening the door and window. The difference, and not a small one, is that the audience is made aware of an invisible space, suddenly charged with expectations – what had looked like just a wall is transformed, as if by magic, into a diegetic space.

In terms of cinematic composition, both scenes are at the extreme opposite of the abduction sequence. They are reminiscent of the theatrical, *ante litteram* 'special effects' introduced by Georges Méliès, the French director of *Le voyage dans la lune* (1902), who coveted the fantastic side of cinema, driven by the desire to surprise film audiences. Instead of witnessing the sudden appearance of a ghost conjured up by a magician, as in many of Méliès's reels, the spectator of *The Black Hand* sees the police as a magic force that can defeat criminal gangs. In the context of a cinema that is concerned with reality, however, the relationship between cinematic spaces is deeply affected by these elements.

The fictional construction of the 'working places' of the butcher and the kidnappers is underscored through what can be defined as a double mise en abîme, for the presence of a closed space that becomes relevant to the stage where the main scene is taking place. The two stages already depict a closed space, where opposite activities – representing good versus evil – are being carried out; however, the use of multiple entrances to the sets links them to a tradition of staging that dates back to Elizabethan theatre, whose influence on cinema has been often remarked upon by scholars. Thus, the interaction between the two spaces leads to a mutual revelation of their falseness, functional to the documentary sequence, which takes on the realistic task of the movie and allows the other two sections to be entertained as fiction. The dreadful possibility, however, of falling victim to the same crime (kidnapping), so impressively exalted in its realism, still lingers for the audience after the happy ending dissolves.

The Black Hand 'logo' fell into obscurity after the mafia embarked on more financially rewarding activities than petty larceny blackmailing. Apart from Thorp's 1950 movie, the Black Hand brand surfaces only sporadically in the intervening years. In 2007, the new edition of *The Godfather* videogame is called *The Godfather: Blackhand Edition*, in reference to the connection between Fanucci, the local mafioso, and the Black Hand who was active at the time when Vito Corleone was still in Sicily, building up his reputation. With this retrospective and nostalgic glance that postmodern remediatization provides for the beginnings of mafia films, a circle has been drawn – but in 1906, the main story had yet to unfold.

NOTES

1 The most interesting book on this topic is still the one by Noël Burch, *La lucarne de l'infini: naissance du langage cinematographique* (Paris: Nathan, 1991), in which he argues that the nineteenth-century bourgeoisie's desire for visual narrative reproduction is linked to the development of cinematographic language.

2 John Dickie, *Cosa Nostra: A History of the Sicilian Mafia* (New York: Palgrave Macmillian, 2004), 172.

3 I have found this retrospective link in Thomas Reppetto's *American Mafia: A History of Its Rise to Power* (New York: Henry Holt, 2004).

4 In a contemporary review of the movie (*The New York Times*, 13 March 1950), Bosley Crowther described the main character as 'a young Italian-American who aspires to help his neighbours rid themselves of the bands of terrorists and extortionists which are fearfully known as "The Black Hand."'

5 Dickie, *Cosa Nostra*, 172.

6 Reppetto, *American Mafia*, 37.

7 Larry Langman's book, *American Film Cycles: The Silent Era* (Westport, CT: Greenwood, 1998), 74, contains a chapter about Black Hand movies, whose title 'We Are Desperut' comes from the misspelled letter textualized in the 1906 movie.

8 'Black Hand letters had become endemic in New York. Usually phrased with exquisite Old World courtesy – "Honored Sir, we respectfully request" – the message was always the same: "Pay or die."' Reppetto, *American Mafia*, 36.

9 *Treasures III: Social Issues in American Film 1900–1934*, curator: Scott Simmon; music curator: Martin Marks, National Film Preservation Foundation, San Francisco, CA, 2007, DVD, Disc 1.

10 This urban detail has been included in Giorgio Bertellini, 'Black Hands and White Hearts: Southern Italian Immigrants, Crime and Race in Early American Cinema,' in *Mob Cultures: Hidden Histories of the American Gangster Film*, ed. Lee Grievson, Esther Sonnet, and Peter Stanfield (New Brunswick, NJ: Rutgers University Press, 2005), 207–37.

11 Peter Bondanella, *Hollywood Italians: Dagos, Palookas, Romeos, Wise Guys and Sopranos* (New York: Continuum, 2004), 177.

4 'Most Thrilling Subjects': D.W. Griffith and the Biograph Revenge Films

JOANNE RUVOLI

Between 1908 and 1913, D.W. Griffith directed more than four hundred one- and two-reel films for the American Mutoscope and Biograph[1] Company. Film historians have recovered nearly all of these films and have inventoried them in the ambitious twelve-volume study titled *The Griffith Project*. Scholars have focused on portrayals of race in Griffith's later features such as *Birth of a Nation* (1915) and *Intolerance* (1916), yet in the earlier Biograph films, too, Griffith was developing a nativist ideology that positioned non-whites as villains in family melodramas. Writers like Anne Friedberg have examined the representations of Griffith's villains in the Biograph films as 'racially stereotyped figures with exaggerated, telegraphed gesticulations – they were gypsies, Italians (usually Sicilians), Mexicans or blacks,' whom Griffith constructed as 'necessary catalysts for family melodramas of threat and reconstitution.'[2] While Friedberg focuses on Griffith's use of insane characters as villains, Gregory Jay's study of American Indians in Griffith's Biograph collection explores similar threats posed to the American middle class and Griffith's use of Native American characters in 'white America's construction of a national identity.'[3] Griffith's representations of Sicilians who commit crimes of vengeance in these popular short films naturalize in a similar way the threat that urban ethnics were thought to pose to national identity and provide an important backdrop to subsequent gangster melodramas.

Twisted handlebar mustaches, wide-brimmed peasant hats, embroidered skirts, straw-bottomed bottles of wine, stiletto knives, crucifixes, and portraits of Saint Anthony: these stereotypical accessories proliferate and superficially mark Sicilian and Italian ethnicity in Griffith's Biograph one-reelers. Griffith and his team of filmmakers, including cameraman G.W. Blitzer, connect Sicilian ethnicity with murderous violence in early films like *In Little Italy* (1909), *The Cord of Life* (1909), and *At the Altar* (1909). Other Griffith one-reelers such as *Lure of the Gown* (1908) and *The Italian Barber* (1910) refrain from depicting characters as outright criminals but continue to portray Sicilian and southern Italian men and women as overly emotional, morally depraved, and violent. In these films, the Sicilian characters seek revenge in ways that threaten the middle-class family unit. As with other ethnically coded types that dominate early cinema, such as the vamp played by Theda Bara and the seducer played by Rudolph Valentino, Griffith's vengeful Sicilians exploit the era's cultural anxieties about how the surging waves of immigration and increased urbanized modernity could threaten the dominant American culture and its middle-class family unit.

By the time Griffith was producing a film a week in 1908, immigration to the United States was approaching peak numbers and the US Congress had already begun 'to regulate the immigration of aliens' with recently enacted laws in 1903 and 1907 that sought to exclude 'objectionable applicants' based on physical, mental, and moral grounds.[4] As Mathew Frye Jacobson details, the unprecedented influx of job-seeking immigrants to the industrialized cities fuelled 'a growing nativist perception of these laborers … as a political threat to the smooth functioning of the republic.' Like the Celts, Slavs, Jews, and Mediterranean immigrants, southern Italians and Sicilians fractured the white supremacists' concept of 'monolithic whiteness' and challenged their ideas about which groups were 'fit for self-government.'[5] Griffith's films were one more contribution to the images of non–Anglo-Saxon immigrants 'swarming' and 'invading' the cities at the turn of the century. Magazine writers and reformists such as Jacob Riis popularized scenes of the ethnic urban slums for middle-class 'civic and reformist groups,' who were 'eager to "visit" the darker half of New York and glean the "truth" of the destitute new immigrants.'[6] Robert Zecker's analysis claims that Riis's popular photographs were specially chosen and posed for maximum effect. The Riis images dwelled upon both 'the "racial" and ethnic melange of the city' and 'on scenes of vice and dissipation' of the poor immigrants.[7] The movement for immigration restriction also offered Griffith many visual and narrative sources to draw from for his films, including the phrenological work that resulted in mugshots, '"scientific" IQ tests' designed to identify 'objectionable' immigrants, and eugenic studies.[8] Each of these sources targeted Italians, and specifically Sicilians, as racially distinct and unfit for citizenship.[9]

The publicity materials for the Griffith Biograph films borrow from the rhetoric of the immigration restriction movement and sensationalize the ethnicity of each film's villain to emphasize his difference. The *Biograph Bulletin*'s description of the film *In Little Italy* highlights Tony's Sicilian origin as the main motivation for his vengeful actions:

> One of the most dominant traits in the Sicilian's nature is indefatigability of purpose where a score is to be reckoned. No amount of hindrance or disappointments can shake his bulldog sedulity, for he will wait days, weeks, and even years to accomplish his plan and this Biograph story portrays this propensity most vividly, making it one of the most thrilling subjects yet released.[10]

For *The Cord of Life*, the *Biograph Bulletin* similarly focuses on Antonine's ethnicity by calling him 'a fascinorous Sicilian profligate' and subtitling the catalogue description of the film 'Thrilling Episode of a Sicilian's Vengeance.'[11] In *At the Altar*'s publicity material, Grigo's ethnicity signifies the degree of his depravity in the film's catalogue description: 'Napoleon I said, "Vengeance has no foresight," which may be true, but it has cunning, and never more than when wrought by this Sicilian.'[12] The language used by the *Biograph Bulletin* does more than highlight each character's Sicilian origins; it emphasizes differences by defining ethnicity in such a way that it remains incompatible with assimilation. Similar opinions about the 'racial distinctness' and 'Italians' innate criminality' were commonly found in the press even predating the 1891 lynching of eleven Italian prisoners in New Orleans, which pushed public opinion about Sicilians into the open.[13] The *Biograph Bulletin*'s language echoes the popular perceptions that ran in newspapers at that time, such as those found in this editorial: 'These sneaking and cowardly Sicilians … who have transplanted to this country the lawless passions, the cutthroat practices, the oathbound societies of their native country, are to us a pest without mitigation. Our own rattlesnakes are as good citizens as they.'[14] Even before audiences saw these films, advertising would have reminded viewers of the long-standing perceptions of Sicilians as unassimilable immigrants.

Melodramas depend on the unquestioned vilification of the antagonists, and Griffith relied on the stereotypical compression of type to achieve the blatantly perceived danger. As Christine Gledhill explains, in Hollywood's domestic melodramas, the 'central protagonists become objects of pathos because [they are] constructed as victims of forces that lie beyond their control and understanding.'[15] In Griffith's racial imaginary, non-Anglo-Saxons such as Sicilians, Native Americans, and blacks are 'forces' that are beyond control or understanding and therefore threaten the sympathetic families in these films. Griffith repeats the familiar plot structure in the 1909 films *In Little Italy, The Cord of Life,* and *At the Altar*, in which Sicilians are the antagonists. First, when rejected, a Sicilian man cannot control his fury and vows revenge. Next, he constructs a violent response against a docile couple. Finally, at the end of each film, he needs to be brought to order by an official institution represented by the police. The melodramatic formula transforms the prejudice that exists against non-whites into 'thrilling' entertainment.

In these three films, each violently emotional Sicilian acts outside of conventions and is portrayed as unable to govern himself or his rage. When the widow Maria from *In Little Italy* chooses to marry a mild-mannered barber and rejects the attentions of Tony, a lower-class Sicilian labourer, the intertitle declares, 'The unsuccessful suitor, crazed by jealousy resolves to be revenged.' From the beginning, Tony is inappropriately passionate and forces kisses upon Maria. He gesticulates wildly and shakes with a violent fury that frightens even the men in the saloon who witness his vow of revenge. With Tony's actions, Griffith plays on nativist fears that immigrants did not 'possess sufficient sexual self-control.'[16] In *At the Altar*, Grigo, another Sicilian, vows revenge when the landlady's daughter Minnie rejects him and chooses instead to marry a sweet Italian violinist. Like Tony from *In Little Italy,* Grigo cannot bear to watch the happy couple prepare for the wedding, and retreats to his empty room where he cries hysterically over Minnie's photo, jealously rips it up, and stomps on the pieces while beating his chest. When Minnie refuses the Sicilian's attentions, he aggressively grabs at her, forcing her to kiss him until the entrance of her parents stops him. Instead of a romantic rebuff, in *The Cord of Life,* a Sicilian named Antonine asks his cousin Galora for money and it is Galora's refusal that sets off a vendetta that rivals those in *In Little Italy* and *At the Altar*. As in the other two films, the Sicilian Antonine viciously vows revenge on Galora's wife and baby by shaking his fist erratically and slashing Galora's apartment door with his 'stiletto' knife. In Grifftith's narrative, once he is jilted, nothing but force will stop the Sicilian villain from his violent retribution. A melodramatic ethnic type with 'the titillating feature of Italians' supposedly ethnically determined lawlessness,' the Sicilian villain cannot be dissuaded by logic, conversation, empathy, or the rules of society.[17]

The object of attack in each of these three melodramas is what Giorgio Bertellini has called the 'good' Italians. In his study of the 'Black Hand' films that were produced about the same time and that also feature Italian and Sicilian characters, Bertellini argues, 'Often the story line divided immigrant characters into two clear-cut groups … The distinction between "good" and "bad" Italians was a profitable narrative compromise.'[18] Griffith's law-abiding, heteronormative couples become the targets of the Sicilians' vengeance, but for them it is not enough just to have revenge – each villain has to assault the social stability surrounding the family and proudly take credit for the violence. The victimized couples appeal both to immigrants in the audience who aspire to Americanization and to Anglo-Saxon nativists who see bourgeois values reflected in the marriages and economic status of the domestic scenes. Griffith usually associates the Sicilian villains with the public streets of the urban enclave. Like the subjects of the Riis photographs, they frequent the saloons, slink through the crowded hallways of the tenements, or hang back in the doorways of alleys and streets. Griffith constructs them as lone men with no other group or family affiliation, in contrast to the women and children, who are usually attacked in their private apartments. Griffith stages the final sequence of *In Little Italy* as Maria's defence of her children and her wounded fiancé in the domestic space. The children fear Tony, too, and help Maria as she uses the accessories of middle-class living, a china cabinet and a blanket trunk, to keep him outside in the street. In *The Cord of Life,* too, Antonine invades the family's domestic space, hanging Galora's infant from a cord outside the apartment window so that when the sash is opened the baby will fall to its death. As in the other films, *At the Altar*'s Grigo seeks to destroy the couple's domestic union. He builds a machine that will automatically shoot a gun and hides it under the altar of the church so that it will shoot the couple as they kneel for their wedding vows.

In each film, the Sicilian is rejected by women or the family and seeks revenge against the domestic sphere. Lee Lourdeaux claims that Griffith uses the details of the domestic scene and religious iconography to exploit 'Anglo fears of ethnic anarchy' and 'symbol[s] of immigrant fertility.'[19] In these early Biographs, Griffith presents his ideas about ethnic manhood, which will become more obvious in his full-length features. While the Sicilian villains are violent and depraved men, the ethnic men of the victimized couples are generally wounded like the barber in *In Little Italy*, in need of assistance like Galora in *The Cord of Life*, or unaware like the violinist fiancé in *At the Altar*. In Griffith's 'good' group of Italians, the men are ineffectual and are not able to save their women, which is a requirement for white manhood according to Griffith's chivalric upbringing in the Southern United States. Ultimately, the police have to be called in to save the day.

Griffith ends each of these films with varying combinations of the chase and the ride-to-the-rescue, which he later elevates to the grand scale of nationhood when the klansmen ride in *Birth of a Nation*. The last segment of *In Little Italy* alternates between Tony chasing Maria and the police's journey through the streets. In a sequence of very short shots, Griffith cross-cuts between Maria's indoor domestic space, the Sicilian's attempts to break in, and the constable's race to apprehend the villain. In *The Cord of Life*, the jilted Sicilian Antonine first stalks Galora in slow-chase style through the streets. Galora slowly advances on the camera until he is in medium close-up, with Antonine in the background wielding a knife. The focus humanizes Galora by showing his sympathetic facial expressions, while the Sicilian villain is kept in the menacing distance. After the police stop Antonine from attacking Galora, Galora and the uniformed cops all must run back to the apartment to stop the baby from falling to its death. In *At the Altar*, Griffith once again turns the last segment of the film into a long ride-to-the-rescue by cross-cutting between Minnie and her fiancé at the church about to kneel in front of the hidden gun and a policeman running through the city streets to stop them in time. In each film, the 'good' Italians who are the victims of the Sicilians' vengeance call for help from the police. In Griffith's ethnic imaginary, this not only reinforces their infantilizing need to be rescued but also proves their loyalty to and faith in the American justice system. As Bertellini has pointed out in other films, 'confidence in the American police force' is a clear indication of the 'assimilated and Americanized immigrants.'[20] Unlike the cinematic gangsters who will appear in subsequent years, Griffith's immigrants do not take matters into their own hands. Each of these films end with the couple or family reuniting, usually in the domestic space. With the Sicilians in restraints or dead, the police have restored order.

In perhaps his most famous Biograph film, *The Musketeers of Pig Alley* (1912), Griffith takes the basic melodrama of the Sicilian revenge films and adapts the narrative to the gangsters making headlines in the newspapers. Called the 'prototypical gangster film,' for many critics *The Musketeers of Pig Alley* is the first gangster feature. Although there are no overt references to Italian and Sicilian immigrants or the mafia, many of the film's circuits of revenge follow the paths between the domestic tenement, the urban street, and the saloon that dominate the earlier Sicilian revenge films. At its core, *The Musketeers of Pig Alley* is a story of a man jilted by a woman, his violent organized response, and the restoration of order by the police. When Griffith subtracts the constraints of ethnicity from the formula of revenge he constructs a more complex and appealing gangster melodrama. Comparing *The Musketeers of Pig Alley* to the earlier films featuring Sicilian villains reveals the limits and boundaries that Griffith's nativist ideology constructs around ethnicity.

The Musketeers of Pig Alley takes place in a generic ghetto described in the opening intertitle simply as 'New York's other side.' Griffith's streets are filled with a hodgepodge of multi-ethnic types – a Jewish peddler, a Chinese messenger – but the action revolves around characters with no overt ethnic markers. In the film, a seamstress called the Little Lady is engaged to a man called the Musician and rejects the amorous attentions of a gangster named Snapper Kid. There are no melodramatic victims or villains as defined by Gledhill. Every character has some agency and is constructed with understanding and sympathy. Without the uncontrollable ethnic qualities of the Sicilian, Snapper Kid's reaction to being rejected is placid and unemotional. He later saves the Little Lady from being drugged by a rival gang, and when confronted with a gang shootout, he shows a psychologically complex combination of fear and bravado, which Griffith presents in what has become an iconic extreme close-up of his expressive face.

The engaged couple again is set in the domestic space of the apartment, in contrast to Snapper's back alleys and saloons, but the Little Lady rejects him without threat of harm and, later, instead of calling the police on him, lies to give him an alibi so he can go free. The Musician, similar to the victimized men in the earlier films, is robbed by Snapper Kid, but instead of being wounded or ineffectual he steals his wallet back from the gangster and protects his fiancée without needing to summon help from the police. Unlike the 'good' Italians of *In Little Italy*, *The Cord of Life*, and *At the Altar*, the Musician and the Little Lady are not targets of a villain's personal rage and violence, and because they show no ethnic or immigrant markers, they do not need to prove their American qualities by calling the police. Instead, they show complicity with Snapper Kid, who lies about his involvement, and with the police who wink at the alibi they provide for him. Everyone is an insider and part of the system.

Similarly, contrasting Snapper Kid to the earlier Sicilian villains shows how Griffith's racial imaginary works to construct heroic whiteness. Zecker claims that the Little Lady 'accept[s Snapper Kid] as an essentially decent person who can be cleansed of the sins the slums have imposed on him,'[21] but in Griffith's terms Snapper does not need to be reformed. The film rewards him at the end for being all the things Griffith associates with Anglo-Saxon manhood. He has chivalrously saved the girl, self-governed his emotions and sexuality, gained the trust of the couple, and been accepted as part of several groups, including the gang, the saloon, and the police. In contrast to the lone alienation of the Sicilians, he is the ultimate insider, and in the last shot Griffith shows Snapper accepting graft from an anonymous hand at the saloon.

With Griffith's ethnic mythos removed, violence pivots on the rivalry between the gangs and the exchange of money instead of personal vendetta. In *The Muskeeters of Pig Alley*, it's not personal; it's all business, which is a concept future mafia films will explore. Everyone exchanges money – the couple, the gangster, the saloon owner – and instead of apprehending a vicious individual for his personal violence, the police restore order to the circuits of money. In contrast to the Sicilian revenge melodramas, Griffith transforms his 'most thrilling subject' of ethnic vengeance into the systemic business transactions of the American gangster.

NOTES

1 All Biograph films except *The Musketeers of Pig Alley* were screened at the Library of Congress.
2 Anne Friedberg, '"A Properly Adjusted Window" Vision and Sanity in D.W. Griffith's 1908–1909 Biograph Films,' in *Early Cinema: Space, Frame, Narrative*, ed. Thomas Elsaesser (London: BFI, 1990), 326.
3 Gregory S. Jay, '"White Man's Book No Good": D.W. Griffith and the American Indian,' *Cinema Journal* 39, no. 4 (2000): 3.
4 'The New Immigration Law,' *American Journal of International Law* 1, no. 2 (1907): 452, 453.
5 Mathew Frye Jacobson, *Whiteness of a Different Color: European Immigrants and the Alchemy of Race* (Cambridge, MA: Harvard University Press, 1998), 41–2.
6 Robert Zecker, *Metropolis: The American City in Popular Culture* (Westport, CT: Praeger, 2008), 43.
7 Ibid., 47.
8 Ibid., 51.
9 Jacobson, *Whiteness of a Different Color*, 56.
10 Quoted in J.B. Kaufman, '219 Biograph: *In Little Italy*,' in *The Griffith Project*, vol. 3, ed. Paolo Cherchi Usai (London: British Film Institute, 1999), 146.
11 Quoted in Kristin Thompson, '96 Biograph: *The Cord of Life*,' in *The Griffith Project*, vol. 2, ed. Paolo Cherchi Usai (London: British Film Institute, 1999), 11.
12 Quoted in Steven Higgins, '106 Biograph: *At the Altar*,' in *The Griffith Project*, vol. 2, ed. Paolo Cherchi Usai (London: British Film Institute, 1999), 32.
13 Jacobson, *Whiteness of a Different Color*, 56.
14 Quoted in ibid.
15 Christine Gledhill, 'The Melodramatic Field: An Investigation,' in *Home Is Where the Heart Is: Studies in Melodrama and the Woman's Film*, ed. Christine Gledhill (London: BFI, 1987), 30.
16 Lee Lourdeaux, *Italian and Irish Filmmakers in America: Ford, Capra, Coppola, and Scorsese* (Philadelphia, PA: Temple University Press, 1990), 31.
17 Zecker, *Metropolis*, 75.
18 Giorgio Bertellini, 'Black Hands and White Hearts: Southern Italian Immigrants, Crime, and Race in Early American Cinema,' in *Mob Culture: Hidden Histories of the American Gangster Film*, ed. Lee Grieveson, Esther Sonnet, and Peter Stanfield (New Brunswick, NJ: Rutgers University Press, 2005), 216.
19 Lourdeaux, *Italian and Irish Filmmakers in America*, 32.
20 Bertellini, 'Black Hands and White Hearts,' 217.
21 Zecker, *Metropolis*, 77.

5 Ethnicity and the Classical Gangster Film: Mervyn LeRoy's *Little Caesar* and Howard Hawks's *Scarface*

NORMA BOUCHARD

The landing of millions of destitute Italians on American shores between 1876 and 1914, or what Humbert Nelli describes as the 'Immigrant Tide,'[1] was certainly not lost on the world of early cinema since directors of the silent era frequently depicted ethnic minorities. From 1907 to 1913, D.W. Griffith released a number of films with Italian subjects, including *The Greaser's Gauntlet* (1908), *In Little Italy* (1909), *The Violin Maker of Cremona* (1909), *Pippa Passes* (1909), *At the Altar* (1909), *Life's Cycle* (1909), *Italian Blood* (1911), and *The Musketeers of Pig Alley* (1912).[2] It was also at this time that Italians began to be associated with lawlessness and criminality. Films such as *The Black Hand: The Story of a Recent Occurrence in the Italian Quarter of New York* (Wallace McCutcheon, 1906), *The Organ Grinder* (Kalem Studios, 1909), *The Detectives of the Italian Bureau* (Kalem Studios, 1909), *The Criminals* (Thomas Ince, 1913), *The Padrone's Ward* (Powers Company, 1914), *The Last of the Mafia* (Sidney Goldin, 1915), and *Poor Little Peppina* (Sidney Olcott, 1916) linked Italian immigrants to the Black Hand, or *Mano nera*, a neighbourhood-based form of criminality where gang violence was mostly exerted within the immigrant communities themselves by way of thievery and extortion.[3] Yet, while these films did much to create a repertoire of signifiers whereby Italians were associated with violence, kidnapping, and extortion, they did not exclusively bind Italian ethnicity to crime. As Kevin Brownlow has argued in his *Behind the Mask of Innocence* and as films such as Griffith's *The Fatal Hour* (1908) and *The Musketeers of Pig Alley* (1912) indicate, other ethnic groups, including Jews, Chinese, Irish, and blacks, were often the target of equally negative, discrediting representations. However, matters changed in the 1920s, when the convergence of a number of social, cultural, and aesthetic developments led to the 'invention'[4] of the Italian-American ethnic subject as the paradigmatic urban criminal. Let us consider more closely these developments before examining the means by which classical cinematic style naturalized and bestowed verisimilitude on the signifiers of Italian ethnicity that were then consolidated in the most important gangster films of the classical era: Mervyn LeRoy's *Little Caesar* (1931) and Howard Hawks's *Scarface* (1932).

In his study of American nativism titled *Strangers in the Land*, John Higham writes that between 1905 and 1915[5] an unprecedented number of immigrants arrived on American shores. Their composition and destination were different from what they had been in the past. Most of the new immigrants were of eastern and southern European descent. as opposed to the previous flow, which had come from the northern nations of the Old World. Rather than seeking agricultural work in rural America, they tended to settle in cities, an environment that was believed to lead to faster assimilation than its rural counterpart.[6] Their presence added a distinct racial dimension to the anti-Catholic and anti-radical currents of American nativism. In 1911, the Immigration Commission published what is known as the Dillingham Report, which outlined the differences between older and newer immigrants in its forty-one volumes. The report was echoed in a number of influential publications, ranging from the newspapers *Century* and *Saturday Evening Post* to books like *The Passing of the Great Race* (1916). Authored by patrician nativist Madison Grant, *The Passing of the Great Race* prophesized the death of a Nordic, Anglo-Saxon racial stock as a result of the influx of southern Europeans and consequent miscegenation. The First World War also increased the general state of anxiety towards the new immigrants, since in the minds of many the war was raising questions, if not doubts, about the loyalty and allegiance of foreign-born people. The nativist trend culminated in 1924 with the passing of the infamous National Quota Act, or Johnson-Reed Act, which restricted the number of immigrants allowed to come into the United States to a mere 2 per cent. But besides the presence of sociological and political factors that spread perceptions of Italian immigrants as undesirable others, new events added to the demonization of this ethnic group.

In 1917, the same year the bill to restrict immigration of illiterate minorities was passed, the US Senate passed the Volstead Act to prohibit the manufacture, sale, and consumption of alcohol in the United States. Having become law in 1920, the Volstead Act ushered in the era of Prohibition that would last until 1933. While Prohibition appeased the Temperance Union and the Protestant constituencies, it led to a number of social problems, chief among them a rise in criminal activity since the American thirst for alcohol did not subside. Liquor continued to be illegally imported, manufactured, and consumed. Racketeering and black market operations flourished while gangsters, often with the cooperation of local officials, acquired much visibility. WASPs, Irish, Jews, Poles, and Italians populated the new landscape of criminality in the Prohibition era, thus one finds the names of Arnold Rothstein, Big Bill Dwyer, Dion O'Bannion, Abner 'Longie' Zwillman, Dutch Schultz, Bugs Moran, and Meyer Lansky alongside those of Frank Costello, Lucky Luciano, Johnny Turrio, and Alphonse Capone. Immigrants of Italian descent – already the target of nativist biases and the object of much media attention because of both gang warfare and news of a formidable accumulation of wealth by the likes of Capone – found their way into the popular art forms of the Hollywood film industry. Within a brief time span, the studios released several gangster films: *Little Caesar, Chinatown Nights* (William Wellman, 1930), *Doorway to Hell* (Archie Mayo, 1930), *The Public Enemy* (William Wellman, 1931), and *Scarface*. While Chinese Americans and Irish Americans were featured in *Chinatown Nights* and *The Public Enemy*, Italian Americans were at the centre of *Doorway to Hell, Little Caesar*, and *Scarface*. Of these three films, the last two enjoyed the most success. As Peter Bondanella recalls, '[I]n 1931, the year of *Little Caesar*, twenty-five gangster films were made. The following year, in 1932, the year *Scarface* appeared, forty gangster films were produced, one-tenth of the entire industry's production.'[7] But *Little Caesar* and *Scarface* did much more than feed the audience's daily appetite for stories of urban forms of gangsterism. As narratives loosely based on the life and deeds of Capone, also known as Al Capone or 'Scarface,' narrated through a repertoire of markers of *italianità* or 'Italian-ness,' *Little Caesar* and *Scarface* achieved the paradigmatic construction of the Italian ethnic subject as the 'true' urban criminal.

Little Caesar, directed by Mervyn LeRoy, traces the ascent and demise of Cesare Rico Bandello, or Rico, an ambitious individual who moves east to 'be somebody.' Through an excessive use of violence, Rico reaches the top of the criminal hierarchy. He enjoys a brief period of success before his disruption of social norms and illegitimate pursuit of the American Dream is recontained. At the end of the film, Rico falls into the gutter. The prophecy from Matthew 26:52 that opens the film – 'For all they that take the sword shall perish with the sword' – turns into reality. and Rico becomes a Depression-era tramp before being gunned down and killed by the police. While *Little Caesar* does not provide a particularly accurate representation of the legendary Capone – the American-born son of southern Italian immigrants who moved from Brooklyn to Chicago, was indicted for tax evasion under the Hoover administration, and died of syphilis in Palm Island, Florida – the film nevertheless draws upon a repertoire of markers of 'Italian-ness' to fasten Italian ethnicity to urban criminality. Thus, at the very opening of the film, Rico, accompanied by his friend Joe Massara, commits a robbery. Unfazed by the murder of the gas station attendant that ensues, he enters a diner where he consumes a meal of spaghetti and engages in a dialogue marked by loud, demonstrative behaviour, a strong accent, and a poor command of the English language. Since these rapid sequences of events act to vilify markers of Italian ethnicity, they establish an immediate connection between the world of criminality and the immigrant cultural background. Such a connection is further consolidated by the world that Rico inhabits. This is a world where criminals abound. Most of them bear Italian names – Pete Montana, Sam Vettori, Tommy Passa, Peppi, Ritz Colonna, and Otero – and gather in a place called Club Palermo. While markers of ethnicity such as food customs, speech patterns, and family or place names create an association with the Italian immigrant and the world of crime, other signifiers of ethnic identity are used to belittle a perceived Italian cultural heritage of elderly wisdom and motherly counsel. For example, the words of Ma' Magdalena, an older fruit and vegetable seller who tells Rico to be 'a good boy,' are of no consequence, as Rico is never redeemed but instead dies while uttering a most defiant question: 'Mother of Mercy! Is this the end of Rico?' Likewise, the advice to make a confession proffered by the mother of Tony Passa to her beloved son results in nothing but Tony's death. In a scene that might betray a Protestant bias against Roman Catholicism, Tony is killed by the impulsive and revengeful Rico on the stairs of the church. This action, among many others, further demonizes Rico, marking him as a character who violates the American social norms of acceptable upward mobility and who knows nothing of the Anglo-Saxon value of restraint. Rico falls into poverty and eventually dies on the streets. The title of the film, 'Little Caesar,' provides an ironic comment on the overambitious Rico, played by the diminutive actor Edward G. Robinson; it also belittles one of the more illustrious markers of 'Italian-ness' – the Roman cultural heritage – by associating it with a conceited, pompous, and even megalomaniac gangster. Yet despite the film's negative use of ethnic markers, it could be argued that *Little Caesar* shows how at least one of the Italian criminals, Rico's friend Joe Massara, leaves the world of crime and is redeemed. It should be noted, however, that from the very first scenes of *Little Caesar*, Joe, played by Douglas Fairbanks, is coded as the least 'ethnic' of the Italian characters – in full command of the English language, tall, and very Nordic-looking – and his redemption and ultimate integration with the norms of American society takes place as a result of his union with Olga. A Russian immigrant played by the actress Glenda Farrell, Olga already possesses all the markers of Anglo-conformity. It is Olga who refuses to run away from the vindictive Rico, as Joe would prefer doing, and it is she who calls the police. She implicitly demonstrates how, once again, Italian ethnic culture is a barrier to both integration and assimilation into the American system of values in that the driving force comes from outside. Thus, notwithstanding the successful ending to Joe's life story, the film establishes an early repertoire of the Italian ethnic subject as urban criminal through the negative use of markers of Italian ethnicity with regard to both the criminal himself and the vast major-ity of the world that surrounds him. This repertoire will be further enriched by the second story about Al Capone, Howard Hawks's *Scarface*.

At the outset of the film, a powerful marker of 'Italian-ness' is evoked as Tony Camonte, a figure more accurately based on Al Capone than Rico Bandello was, sets out to murder his rival 'Big Louie' Costillo. In a play of chiaroscuro, a dark silhouette approaches his victim moving from the right to the left of the screen while whistling an aria from the opera *Lucia di Lammermoor* by the famed Italian composer Gaetano Donizetti. As the narrative progresses, the character of Tony is further developed through additional markers of his immigrant ethnic background. A coarse, even vulgar man, Tony has a poor command of English, and his sentences are marked by a heavy accent and the occasional Italian phrase, evident when he yells '*sta' zitt!*' ('shut up!') at his mother. Even as he begins to ascend the ladder of urban criminality, his immigrant background surfaces: he buys dozens of shirts so that he only has to wear them once, and he purchases ostentatious jewellery while settling into a gaudily furnished home. Like Rico Bandello, Tony inhabits a world of urban criminality where Italians are always present, as characters such as Johnny Lovo, Guino Rinaldo, his secretary Angelo, and even the organ-grinder demonstrate. Yet it is perhaps through the representation of Tony's Italian family that the film binds the gangster most firmly to an eth-nic Italian world. Introduced early in the film, Tony's family is a stereotypical representation of 'Old World Italian familialism.'[8] Tony's mother, dressed in a southern Italian peasant outfit and expressing herself in broken English, is often shown in a farmhouse kitchen as she serves Tony pasta and fills his glass with wine. Within the family structure, Tony, who has no father, is a patri-arch who has the role of protecting his sister Cesca's honour, while Mrs Camonte is the matriarch who guards the family's morality. Yet the structure of Italian familialism is weakened to the point of being unable to provide a viable social model for American society. Tony is a degraded image of a patriarch whose protection of female honour only leads him to murder Cesca's new husband Guino. Tony's actions towards his sister are further represented as a form of incest exemplified in the scene where he rips off her clothes after seeing her dance with another man at the Paradise Club. As Peter Bondanella has noted, in the representation of Tony's desire for Cesca, the film might even actualize a long Anglo-Saxon tradition of associating Italian cultural heritage with Renaissance duplicity and perverse forms of sexuality evocative of the Borgia family.[9] But the film also neutralizes the other dimension of Old World familialism represented by Mother Camonte, whose role as the custodian of the family's morality fails since she has a son who is a gangster and a daughter whom she cannot protect from her 'no-good' boy. Because of the repeated construc-tion of the gangster as an Italian ethnic subject bearing the markers of an ethnicity to be feared for its propensity to violence and even loathed for its transgression of the incest taboo, it comes as no surprise that towards the end of the film, the editor of the daily *Evening Record*, Mr Gar-ston, responds to concerned readers' accusations of running too many stories about gangsters by inviting them to 'put teeth in the Deportation Act' so as to rid the city of those who are not even citizens and run them out of the country.

However, the construction of the Italian as the urban gangster that was created by these films' narrative manipulation of markers of 'Italian-ness' was also aided by specific developments in the Hollywood film industry. By the 1920s, the studios had refined their ability to manufacture screen realism not only through a sophisticated use of lighting and colour but also through editing style and the introduction of sound. Editing techniques of carefully matching cuts according to subject, forms, and action created a spatial and temporal continuity devoid of any ambiguous meaning, in tandem with the introduction of sound, further enhanced the effect of realism. Gunshots, explosions, car chases, and tough urban vernacular could be not only read and seen but also heard, thus promoting the illusion that the cinematic image was an accurate portrayal of reality rather than its fictional transposition. And precisely as Susan Hayward comments, because 'the name of the game [w]as verisimilitude, "reality,"'[10] the classical gangster proved to be most successful at its 'invention' of an Italian ethnicity. To be sure, there were protests and outcries, beginning with a letter written by Fiorello La Guardia, the mayor of New York City, who wrote of *Little Caesar*: 'Mr. Hays would not dare to produce such a picture with a Jew as that character – he would lose his job if he did.'[11] Overall, however, Americans of Italian heritage could not organize effective campaigns to counter their image, and as the history of narrative cinema demonstrates, the idea of the Italian-as-gangster would endure for generations to come. After 1934, when the Production Code became mandatory and its Section 10 was enforced – namely, that 'no picture shall be produced that tends to incite bigotry or hatred among people of different races, religions, or national origins'[12] – the perception of the Italian as criminal was not lost. While gangster films now had to achieve a balance between positive and negative representations of members of ethnic groups, the 'invention' of Italian ethnicity had become essentialized. The idea of the Italian as the paradigmatic urban gangster had gained broad consensual support among cinematic audiences worldwide, ultimately structuring public images of Italian American ethnicity among 'Italian America's own sons and daughters,' as Fred Gardaphé's *From Wiseguys to Wise Men* concludes,[13] and as works such as Francis Ford Coppola's *The Godfather*, Martin Scorsese's *Goodfellas*, and many others amply testify.

NOTES

1 See Humbert Nelli, *From Immigrants to Ethnics* (Oxford: Oxford University Press, 1983).

2 For additional discussion of representations of Italians in American silent cinema, see Peter Bondanella, *Hollywood Italians* (New York: Continuum, 2004); Kevin Brownlow, *Behind the Mask of Innocence* (Berkeley, CA: University of California Press, 1990); Robert Casillo, 'Moments in Italian-American Cinema: From *Little Caesar* to Coppola and Scorsese,' in *From the Margin: Writings in Italian Americana*, ed. Anthony Tamburri, Paul Giordano, and Fred Gardaphé (West Lafayette, IN: Purdue University Press, 1991), 374–96.

3 Thus, for example, in *The Black Hand: True Story of a Recent Occurrence in the Italian Quarter of New York* (Biograph Company, Wallace McCutcheon, 1906), two Italians kidnap Maria, the daughter of a butcher. The butcher calls the detectives to the rescue, and his daughter is saved. Similar themes are also to be found in *The Last of the Mafia* (Sidney Goldin, 1915), *Poor Little Peppina* (Sidney Olcott, 1916), and *The Criminals* (Thomas Ince, 1916).

4 I am borrowing here from the definition of ethnicity provided by Werner Sollors, 'Introduction: The Invention of Ethnicity,' in *The Invention of Ethnicity*, ed. Werner Sollors (New York: Oxford University Press, 1989), xi: 'The forces of modern life embodied by such terms as "ethnicity" … can indeed be meaningfully discussed as "inventions." Of course, this usage is meant not to evoke a conspiratorial interpretation of a manipulative inventor … but to suggest widely shared collective fictions that are continually reinvented.'

5 See John Higham, *Strangers in the Land: Patterns of American Nativism 1860–1925* (New York: Athenaeum, 1970). Of particular interest in Higham's volume is the chapter titled 'The Loss of Confidence,' 158–93.

6 As Humbert Nelli recalls in *From Immigrants to Ethnics*, 'Contemporaries were convinced that Italians would become Americanized more rapidly in rural areas than they would be in a city' (47). Nelli's study also documents efforts to promote the relocation of Italians to farms.

7 Bondanella, *Hollywood Italians*, 183.

8 Casillo, 'Moments in Italian-American Cinema,' 378.

9 Bondanella, *Hollywood Italians*, 192–3.

10 Susan Hayward, *Cinema Studies: The Key Concepts* (New York: Routledge, 2000), 64.

11 Quoted in Jonathan Munby, *Public Enemies, Public Heroes* (Chicago, IL: University of Chicago Press, 1999), 105.

12 Bondanella, *Hollywood Italians*, 197.

13 Fred Gardaphé, *From Wiseguys to Wisemen: The Gangster and Italian American Masculinities* (New York: Routledge, 2006), xv.

6 Playing Good Italian/Bad Italian on ABC's *The Untouchables*

JONATHAN J. CAVALLERO

During its four-year run, *The Untouchables* (1959–63) became one of the most popular and controversial shows in television history. Its two-part premiere (*The Scarface Mob*) on CBS in April 1959 was meant to be only a television special for the Westinghouse Desilu Playhouse (Desilu was a combination of Desi Arnaz's and Lucille Ball's names), but when it averaged an astonishing 56.3 audience share for Part One and an even better 64.8 audience share for Part Two, ABC swooped in to pick up the show as a series. Despite CBS's objections about selling the program to a competing network and despite the fact that Al Capone had been jailed at the end of Part Two, Desilu Productions agreed. During its first full season, *The Untouchables* collected two Emmy Awards, finished second in overall ratings behind only *Gunsmoke* (1955–75), and dominated its 9:30–10:30 Thursday night-time slot.[1] Viewers marvelled at the show's perceived realism and were shocked and titillated by its violence. Yet despite its initial ratings bonanza and sufficient if inconsistent critical acclaim, *The Untouchables* would be cancelled after only four seasons. *The Untouchables* offers a compelling case study in the history of Italian American representation. It was the most controversial show of its time and the target of perhaps the most significant and effective protests of a television program by Italian American groups. Many explanations have been offered for the show's fate, but ultimately, the protests and scrutiny that surrounded the program led to alterations in its content and changed the way audience members viewed the series.

At the time, *The Untouchables'* move to ABC continued a trend for the struggling network. Throughout television's early years, ABC had lagged far behind CBS and NBC, in large part because the Federal Communications Commission had awarded more affiliates to the two big networks. This allowed ABC to embrace a different programming strategy – one that minimized its news programming and educational ventures and instead focused on action-oriented shows that promised potentially larger audiences.[2] With fewer affiliates, ABC shifted its attention to stations in smaller, often more rural markets; it also turned to detective stories and westerns to counter early television's bias towards New York–based programs and viewers. This allowed for more violent and explicit content and helped create a more profit-driven (rather than educational) model of television. In the end, the powers that be became disturbed by the profit-driven role of television rather than the content of specific programs. *The Untouchables*, though, was highly popular and perhaps the most violent show on TV at the time, so it became an important locus point around which competing discourses on both the content and the sociocultural role of television itself circulated.

Protests of *The Untouchables* began almost immediately. The second episode of the first season, 'Ma Barker and Her Boys' (1.2, or season 1, episode 2), drew objections from the FBI, which reminded Desilu that it was FBI agents – not Treasury Department officials like Eliot Ness – who had taken down the infamous gang. In response, Desilu added a statement at the end of the episode crediting the FBI's efforts, establishing a trend that would come to define the series. The producers would offer historically inaccurate representations in order to maximize dramatic impact. Then when protests about the program developed, rather than defend their artistic licence and recognize the show as a dramatic re-creation of historical events (or even a fictional program that exploited historical figures), the producers would respond with disclaimers during the credit sequences or concessions in the content of individual narratives. None of these strategies significantly challenged the perceived realism of the series as a whole. *The Untouchables'* popularity rested in part on the illusion that the program was more or less accurate, and the network and producers maintained the show's popularity by allowing that myth to go relatively unchallenged. However, the supposed willingness of the general public to accept the show as historical fact made 'setting the record straight' exceedingly important for law enforcement agencies and protest groups. Both worried that *The Untouchables* (and, by extension, television generally) had the ability to shape the public's memory of the past and consequently affect perceptions in the present.

The prevalence of jokes that renamed the program 'Wops and Robbers,' 'The Italian Hour,' and 'Guinea Smoke,' and the program's frequent resort to Italian American criminals were of particular concern to Italian American groups.[3] The Order Sons of Italy in America (OSIA) and the Federation of Italian-American Democratic Organizations (FIADO) worried that the perpetuation of the gangster stereotype on one of TV's most popular (and seemingly true-to-life) programs would threaten their public image and minimize their social, educational, and professional opportunities.[4] Many scholars have framed these protests as a silly game of political theatre that ultimately destroyed one of TV's most exciting series, rejecting claims of defamation by arguing that the portrayal of some Italian Americans as criminals was a historically truthful representation. Tise Vahimagi, for instance, writes that the 'Italian element of corruption' was an 'accurate reflection.'[5] For his part, Kenneth Tucker contends that the show's 'downward plunge resulted from the ire of Italian Americans.'[6] Such assessments carry three major problems. First, they remove the program from the sociocultural and historical contexts that surrounded its production and reception in favour of one that emphasizes the moment the programs depict. Second, they perpetuate the idea – apparently universally accepted – that a fictional television program is capable of capturing a historical truth. And third, they minimize the diversity of opinions and tactics that existed within Italian Americana as a whole and even within Italian American protest groups.

This is not to suggest that the Italian American protesters' opinions should go unquestioned. Certainly, their collective belief that representations on a period drama would automatically lead to discrimination in the present are questionable at best. Still, *The Untouchables* was a powerful voice within the cultural discourse of the time, and the desire of some Italian Americans to offer a dissenting opinion should not be quashed or minimized but rather investigated in order to discern the motives for such protests, the strategies these protests used, and the stated and unstated goals they sought to achieve. Laura Cook Kenna, for instance, has offered a more productive approach by relating the protests to other political debates that were circulating during the 1950s and 1960s. Rather than framing the Italian American protests as exploitative attempts to capitalize on the popularity of the program, she demonstrates that anti-defamation arguments were spurred by concerns that besides damaging Italian Americans' reputations, the show, with its focus on ethnic criminals, would lead to greater restrictions in US immigration policies.[7]

OSIA was the first to boycott the show's advertisers in late 1959, and within a year they had won the right to review scripts in pre-production, persuaded the producers that no fictionalized Italian American criminals should appear on the series, and were promised that Enrico Rossi, an invented Italian American member of the Untouchables, would have a more prominent role. In many ways, Rossi replaced the character of Joe Fuselli, another fictionalized member of the Untouchables who had appeared in *The Scarface Mob*. An Italian ex-con whose expertise in the Sicilian and Neapolitan dialects led to an invitation to join Ness's squad, Fuselli becomes one of Ness's most trusted men. When Capone's gunmen try to assassinate Ness, Fuselli sacrifices his own life to protect that of his boss. As Fuselli dies in his arms, Ness sheds a tear. With Fuselli dead, the producers (perhaps anticipating the controversy that would surround the show's representation of Italian Americans) introduced Rossi in 'The Empty Chair,' the first episode to appear on ABC. Rossi was (and is) *the* character on which defenders of *The Untouchables*' representation of Italianness rely. He, like Fuselli before him, continued a strategy evident in many previous gangster productions. Producers placed members of the same ethnicity on opposite sides of the law in order to head off suggestions that criminality was the product of ethnic background; in this way, they framed membership in the mafia or some other criminal organization as a personal choice.

'The Empty Chair' begins with Rossi working as a barber who resents the fact that gangsters are receiving special treatment from his boss. As the boss and Rossi discuss it, Frank Nitti and one of his henchmen enter through a back door and murder members of a rival gang as they sit in the barbershop's chairs. Nitti flees the scene, but Rossi catches Nitti's henchman and slices him with a straight razor. When Ness shows up to investigate, Rossi begs for the opportunity to 'do more than testify' against Nitti. Ness agrees, labelling Rossi a 'rare and valuable find,' and Rossi joins the elite crime-fighting unit. In this and other episodes, Rossi offers an inside view of the criminal underworld. He knows the 'word on the street,' and he is able to go undercover rather easily. In one particularly interesting scene from 'The Empty Chair,' Rossi sells tomatoes at an open-air market. The scene begins with a long shot of the market taken from a fire escape. Metal bars dominate the image's foreground, offering the impression that the ethnic neighbourhood is a kind of prison from which few individuals escape. In other episodes, such as 'Syndicate Sanctuary' (1.13), Rossi plays a similar undercover role by becoming the inside man at a mafia-run gambling parlour. Walter Winchell's voiceover suggests that Rossi is able to infiltrate the mob because he was 'the newest member of the Untouchables and unknown to the syndicate.' Judging from the olive skin tones, dark hair, and prominent noses of his fellow employees, one suspects his ability to go undercover also had something to do with his ethnic appearance.

Rossi was meant to offer a more balanced representation of American Italians. That said, *The Untouchables* was also suggesting that Rossi understood the gangsters in a way outsiders could not, and his value to Ness was often measured by his unique status as a law-abiding Italian who wanted to bring down the mafia. The character had 'positive' character traits, but he was facing a slew of Italian American criminals, with new ones appearing almost every week. Against numbers like these, Rossi seemed to be an exception rather than the rule.

Furthermore, the casting of Greek American actor Nicholas Georgiade is notable, especially given that he had appeared in *The Scarface Mob* as a Capone gang member. After the first season, Desilu cast Italian American actor Paul Picerni in the role of Untouchable Lee Hobson in a further effort to counter claims of defamation. Picerni, like Georgiade, had appeared in *The Scarface Mob*. As Tony Liguri, an associate of gangster Frank Nitti, Picerni spoke Italian and ran Capone's Montmartre Café, where he dressed in dark suits and tuxedos, manhandled women, and was portrayed as a womanizer.[8] As Untouchable Lee Hobson, Picerni wore three-piece grey suits that matched those of his fellow lawmen, spoke English, and pushed aside mobsters and their associates. In 'The Rusty Heller Story' (2.1), Picerni, in his first appearance as Hobson, is prominently positioned behind Ness's right shoulder, while Georgiade as Rossi is behind Ness's left shoulder. Later in the episode, when a Greek criminal remembers 'the Old Country,' Rusty Heller states, 'Well, now I remember why I'm glad Columbus discovered America.' By prominently featuring the character of Rossi, referencing Italians like Columbus in the dialogue, and casting an Italian American in the role of a non-ethnic, assimilated American (which implicitly suggested that the differences between some Italian Americans and white Americans were not so great), the producers were attempting to represent Italian Americans in a way that was more acceptable to Italian American groups. During the second season, FIADO won additional concessions, which included promises that the program would not focus disproportionately on Italian Americans or on any other ethnic group and that a disclaimer labelling the show 'fictional and designed for entertainment' would appear at the end of each episode.[9]

However, concerns about the show came not just from Italian American organizations but also from concerned viewers, parents, and the US government. As early as July 1961, ABC's Cleveland affiliate had stopped airing the program because of 'pressure from parents and others.'[10] A month earlier, special hearings had been convened in Washington to discuss the prevalence and potential effects of television violence (especially on *The Untouchables*).[11] Soon after, viewers became leery of the use of violence on TV and the rapidly increasing number of western and detective series.[12] *The Untouchables*' response was to soften Ness's character – to make him more vulnerable and self-doubting in seasons three and four – which ultimately contributed to the show's demise.[13]

Nonetheless, *The Untouchables* remains an important program, especially in terms of Italian American representation. While many contemporary Hollywood films like *Marty* (Delbert Mann, 1955), *The Wrong Man* (Alfred Hitchcock, 1956), and *Full of Life* (Richard Quine, 1956), and even movies that included gangster characters like *Pay or Die* (Richard Wilson, 1960) and *The Brothers Rico* (1957, directed by Phil Karlson, who also helmed *The Scarface Mob*), mildly challenged the traditional gangster stereotype, *The Untouchables* became a popular series (at least in part) by exploiting notions of Italian criminality, brutishness, clannishness, intellectual inferiority, sexual promiscuity, and accented speech. Even characters like Fuselli, Rossi, and Hobson were often ex-criminals or intellectually inferior. As Tucker has shown, 'Untouchables Lee Hobson and Rico Rossi offer incorrect conjectures and overlook clues while pursuing a case, whereas Ness discerns the vital evidence or makes the correct deduction as to where the captive has been sequestered or the cache of liquor hidden.'[14]

But – as was the case with many Hollywood-style productions – *The Untouchables*' representations were not easily pigeonholed. 'The Noise of Death' (1.14), for instance, was targeted by OSIA for its representation of a fictionalized Italian American criminal. Joe Bucco (played by J. Carrol Naish) is a mafioso who wishes to retire, but his attempts to cut ties with the secretive mafia society make him a target of its violence. By the end of the episode, Bucco has been killed by members of the mob; yet he had never betrayed them despite ample opportunities to protect himself by going to Ness. In contrast to OSIA, *Daily Variety* saw redeeming aspects in the narrative: 'Naish comes through beautifully,' said the paper, 'creating a rounded portrait of the self-made Italian immigrant who's a likable and interesting man warranting respect despite his dirty trade and record.'[15] The episode seemed to suggest that behind all the repulsive criminality of the mob, an enviable degree of loyalty existed.

It is interesting that Joseph Petracca, a television writer who authored or co-authored seven episodes of the series during its first and second seasons, is absent from discussions about Italian Americans and *The Untouchables*. Petracca's scripts usually focused on non-Italian criminals, although Italian American characters like gangland mistress Rita Rocco in 'The St. Louis Story' (1.16) were sometimes featured in minor roles. Petracca did co-author one script that focused on an Italian American living in an Italian American neighbourhood. 'Nicky' (2.3), which Petracca penned with Harry Essex, concentrates on the son of a small-time mobster named Mario Bousso, who is killed during a Ness-led raid. Vowing revenge for his father's death, Nicky targets Ness. His attempt to kill the leader of the Untouchables is thwarted, and he is arrested. Ness, realizing that he may have killed Nicky's father, withdraws his complaint against the seventeen-year-old. The judge warns Ness that the boy will likely make another attempt on his life and that he will almost certainly join a gang like his father had done. Ness says he's counting on that because he wants to uncover the identity of the gang's leader. As the narrative progresses, Ness learns that Nicky's father was intentionally murdered by another gangster before the raid even started. After going to work for his dad's former boss, Gus Marco (alias: Giuseppe Marconi), Nicky learns that his father was involved in illegal activities. Eventually, Nicky realizes that Marco and his associates were behind his dad's death. His epiphany comes just in time, and his efforts help save Ness from an ambush. As the episode concludes, Walter Winchell's voiceover returns: 'For the record, Nicky Bousso graduated from Carnegie Institute of Technology in 1938.'

For the most part, 'Nicky' conforms to the stereotypical representation of the Italian gangster offered in most previous instalments of the series. However, the episode stands out in its emphasis on the Boussa family's working-class status. During the episode, we see Nicky Boussa's little sister sewing in the family's small apartment, and we hear Nicky talk about how his family needs the money he will earn from washing Marco's cabs. These moments imply that Mario Bousso may have entered the rackets not for self-serving purposes but rather as a means of providing for his family. Furthermore, Winchell's concluding voiceover indicates that the judge and Ness were wrong to think that Nicky would automatically turn to a life of crime. He may have dabbled temporarily in that world, but the audience is left with the impression that the Boussos are a good family with much to offer American society. The day-to-day struggles of paying the bills seem to have compromised their morality, but only temporarily.

Ultimately, the producers' willingness to negotiate with OSIA and others speaks to the power of the groups' boycotts but also indicates that the producers recognized that the show's violence placed them in a precarious position with government officials concerned about the development of television. It is probably also true that the show's producers, including the Cuban-born Desi Arnaz, were sensitive to issues of discrimination and stereotyping and did not wish to contribute to the marginalization of ethnic groups, even if they were simultaneously interested in protecting the popularity of their program. In the final analysis, the show's content needs to be read in the context of its time. The protests, anxieties about the mafia's influence on American society and television's influence on its viewers, political debates about immigration, ABC's programming strategies, and the challenges those strategies posed to the future development of television, all influenced contemporary viewers' interpretations of the program. If we are to fully understand *The Untouchables'* significance in terms of Italian American media representations, all of these factors need to be taken into account.

NOTES

1 Tise Vahimagi, *The Untouchables* (London: BFI, 1998), 17–25.

2 James L. Baughman, *Same Time, Same Station: Creating American Television, 1948–1961* (Baltimore, MD: Johns Hopkins University Press, 2007), 72–4.

3 Laura Cook Kenna, 'Dangerous Men, Dangerous Media: Constructing Ethnicity, Race, and Media's Impact through the Gangster Image, 1959–2007' (PhD diss., George Washington University, 2008), 62; Kenneth Tucker, *Eliot Ness and the Untouchables: The Historical Reality and the Film and Television Depictions* (Jefferson, NC: McFarland, 2000), 58.

4 This was especially true since the general public and the US government seemed particularly concerned about the mafia's threat to American values in the 1950s and 1960s. See Lee Bernstein, *The Greatest Menace: Organized Crime in Cold War America* (Amherst, MA: University of Massachusetts Press, 2002). The live broadcast of the Kefauver committee hearings on organized crime in the early 1950s focused public attention on Italian American gangsters and garnered a then unheard of television audience of between 20 and 30 million viewers daily. See Selwyn Raab, *Five Families: The Rise, Decline, and Resurgence of America's Most Powerful Mafia Empires* (New York: St Martin's Press, 2006), 96–102.

5 Vahimagi, *The Untouchables*, 2.

6 Tucker, *Eliot Ness and the Untouchables*, 69.

7 Kenna, 'Dangerous Men, Dangerous Media,' 54–6.

8 Tucker, *Eliot Ness and the Untouchables*, 49–50.

9 Kenna, 'Dangerous Men, Dangerous Media,' 65.

10 Baughman, *Same Time, Same Station*, 286.

11 Kenna, 'Dangerous Men, Dangerous Media,' 8.

12 Vahimagi, *The Untouchables*, 83.

13 As of 2011, only seasons one, two, and three are available on DVD. Season four has yet to be released.

14 Tucker, *Eliot Ness and the Untouchables*, 59.

15 Quoted in Vahimagi, *The Untouchables*, 30.

7   Prelude to *The Godfather*: Martin Ritt's *The Brotherhood*

ROBERT CASILLO

Directed by Martin Ritt, scripted by Lewis John Carlino, and released by Paramount in 1968, *The Brotherhood* is widely regarded as the closest cinematic adumbration of *The Godfather* (1972). Ritt's film calls to mind Coppola's masterpiece in its exploration of mafia familism, tradition, social codes, and Old World origins manifest in a contemporary Italian American criminal family – the Ginettas – torn by the ultimately irreconcilable claims of the ethnic past and the corporate present. *The Brotherhood* anticipates *The Godfather* in striving for an ethnically authentic atmosphere through location shots in New York and Sicily; scenes of Italian American weddings, dances, dinners, and amusements; sprinklings of Sicilian idiom; and liberal indications of mafia lore and criminal expertise. Perhaps most significant from the ethnic point of view, *The Brotherhood* looks forward to *The Godfather* in focusing on the tensions between older and younger members of the second-generation American mafia. As in *The Godfather*, an Italian-American criminal family serves to dramatize the crisis of ethnic loyalty experienced by many second-generation Italian Americans, albeit less violently.[1] Both films thus exemplify and contribute to a new subgenre of the gangster film, namely, the mafia film, which dramatizes the practices of Italian American criminal organizations or 'families.'

During the early twentieth century, loosely organized bands of extortionists known as the Black Hand probably far surpassed the mafia in notoriety. Not only was the Black Hand in permanent eclipse by the mid-1920s, but the name of the mafia had by then largely vanished from public discourse. Many prominent criminals of the 1920s and 1930s were Italian American, whether as actual underworld figures or as cinematic portrayals, but they were generally seen as gangsters rather than as mafiosi, that is, as leaders of multi-ethnic gangs rather than as members of exclusively ethnic and familial organizations grounded in Old World attitudes and traditions. Because of the rigorous enforcement of the Hollywood Production Code after 1934, filmmakers grew increasingly reluctant not only to specify the ethnicity of criminals and criminal groups but also to produce biographies of major underworld figures – a trend that weakened only after the Second World War.[2] Following several decades of neglect, the word 'mafia' acquired far greater notoriety than before as a result of the Kefauver Committee hearings of 1950–51 that, notwithstanding their failure to prove the existence of such an organization, revived fears of an Italian American criminal conspiracy supposedly transplanted directly from Sicily.[3] Though many gangster films of the 1950s imply that the US government and economy have been infiltrated by organized crime, the depicted criminal syndicates with few exceptions remain multi-ethnic. The disclosure of an

Italian American underworld summit meeting at Apalachin in 1957, followed by the revelations of the McClellan Committee and mafia informant Joe Valachi in the early 1960s, sparked interest in specifically Italian American criminals and criminal figures. Yet *Party Girl* (Nicholas Ray, 1958), *Al Capone* (Richard Wilson, 1959), *The Scarface Mob* (Phil Karlson, 1959), *Some Like It Hot* (Billy Wilder, 1959), and *The St. Valentine's Day Massacre* (Roger Corman, 1967) do not treat the mafia as such.[4]

Kirk Douglas, who produced and starred in *The Brotherhood*, conceived of his role as that of a vigorous, middle-aged head of a mafia family, and accordingly required that Carlino rewrite the first version of the script, in which the character had figured as an aged patriarch. Douglas also insisted that key scenes be played not on sound stages but on location in New York City and in Sicily. Despite respectable reviews, *The Brotherhood* failed at the box office. Its failure was attributed to its lack of convincing Italian American actors, along with an inability to capture the ethnic spirit except in a 'purely anthropological' manner, as Paola Casella notes. Although *The Brotherhood* nowhere refers specifically to the mafia, it was protested by Italians of American descent.[5]

When, soon after the release of *The Brotherhood*, Paramount made plans to film Mario Puzo's *The Godfather*, it hesitated for fear of another failure. However, Paramount executives Robert Evans and Peter Bart blamed the shortcomings of *The Brotherhood* on the fact that it relied chiefly not on non–Italian American but on Jewish talent, with a corresponding loss of authenticity. The success of *The Godfather* as a film depended on securing the directorial services of the relatively inexperienced but highly intelligent Francis Ford Coppola, whose ethnic background would enable him to render what Evans described as the 'grit' of Italian America and its criminal families. On the whole, the studio approved of Coppola's decision to cast Italian American actors wherever possible, as Evans did not want the standard 'Hollywood Italian.' The wrath of Italian American organizations was appeased by eliminating specific references to the mafia.[6]

For all its limitations, *The Brotherhood* remains interesting ethnically and generically. Early on, we witness the wedding of Vince Ginetta, younger brother of middle-aged mob boss Frank Ginetta, played by Kirk Douglas, and Emma Bertoldo, daughter of mob boss Dominic Bertoldo. Dominic, like Frank, belongs to the five-man board of a major New York criminal syndicate masquerading, as in many 1950s gangster films, as a legitimate business operation. Unlike the Sicilian Ginettas, Dominic is Neapolitan. The wedding guests include Frank's business associates, two of whom are non-Sicilians (apparently Irish and Jewish), and an aged group of 'Moustache Petes,' that is, Sicilian traditionalists from the early days of Italian American organized crime, whom Frank treats cordially. Their leader is the courtly Don Peppino.

Despite Martin Scorsese's claim that the 'actors [in *The Brotherhood*] did a very good job,' Kirk Douglas exemplifies what Scorsese denounces as the 'Mama mia' style of acting.[7] Imagining that excessive gesticulations, shouting, clowning, sentimentality, and angry outbursts connote *italianità*, Douglas merely reverts to stereotype, and his moustache cannot save him. Yet Scorsese justly praises the Jewish American actor Luther Adler as Dominic, in yet another of Adler's fine Italian American characterizations over a long career. Reserved and understated, and with nothing of the 'Hollywood Italian,' Adler's Dominic combines wary cunning and obliging good nature, patience and exaggeration, family loyalty and worldly interest. Besides having the requisite Mediterranean appearance, Irene Pappas as Frank's convent-educated wife captures the seriousness, matriarchal dignity, and loyalty that Sicilian crime bosses demand in their wives. Having portrayed the gangsters Trock Estrella in *Winterset* (Alfred Santel, 1936) and Johnny Vanning in *Marked Woman* (Lloyd Bacon, 1937), Eduardo Ciannelli is suitably demonic as Don Peppino. The only other Italian American actor in the film is Alex Cord (born Alex Vespi in 1933), whose understated performance as Vince helps offset Douglas's excesses.

Nonetheless, Frank Ginetta constitutes an original character by comparison with most of the earlier portrayals of Italian American crime bosses. The stereotypical boss is obsessed with sartorial display and wants very much to be in style; also, in aspiring to the conventional image of the American businessman, or at least wanting to conform to modern custom, he is clean-shaven and is sometimes shown being shaved. Not infrequently, the crime boss is a psychopathic killer with an inferiority complex, like Rico Bandello in *Little Caesar* (Mervyn LeRoy, 1931), while in other instances the unreflectively titanic egos of Tony Camonte (*Scarface*, Howard Hawks, 1932) and Johnny Rocco (*Key Largo*, John Huston, 1948) exemplify an insane drive for prepotency. Not infrequently, the gang boss is a misogynist given to violence against women, as is Rico Angelo (Lee J. Cobb) in *Party Girl*, or else he exhibits hints of homoerotic perversity, as with Rico, Vanning, and Lagana in Fritz Lang's *The Big Heat* (1953). Even when a crime boss like Rico or Camonte has family ties, they are warped or perverse.

Counter to stereotypes of the mob boss, Frank sports an old-timer's moustache and wears modest clothes reminiscent of the days of Sicilian crime boss Salvatore Maranzano.[8] Whereas the typical cinematic crime boss sees no limit to wealth and power, but always wants 'more of more,' to quote Johnny Rocco in *Key Largo*, Frank remains content with his existing operation. Although Frank's business is violent, he kills economically and shows sadism only in executing Dominic. And finally, unlike his screen predecessors, Frank has a rich family life reminiscent of Don Vito Corleone, maintaining close ties with his relatives in the United States and Sicily. One expects a cinematic crime boss to favour loose women, but Frank remains devoted to his wife both sexually and emotionally in the manner of an old-fashioned Sicilian don.

The struggle between Frank and Vince exemplifies conflicts often experienced by second-generation Italian Americans. Largely acculturated but only partly assimilated, members of the second generation felt pressured by family and neighbourhood to remain loyal to the ethnic culture developed in the group's urban enclaves. Such insularity often made it highly difficult to cooperate with the political, social, and economic institutions of mainstream America. Rather than valuing education for economic and social advancement, many second-generation Italian Americans shared their parents' fear of it as a threat to family and group solidarity. Some second-generation members, however, especially the younger ones, desired occupational and social mobility as a means of assimilation or 'fitting in.' Having lost respect for their Italian-speaking fathers and their narrowed horizons, they rejected the Italian language and sometimes even ethnic cuisine. For them, education often afforded a way into the mainstream.[9]

For all his success, Frank Ginetta remains loyal to the ethnic past, worshipping his father's memory, maintaining his business, and avenging him in Sicilian style. Besides speaking Italian to Vince, he uses southern Italian expressions such as *cedrul'*, referring to a stupid person. His imperfect assimilation is further indicated by his dysfunctional and inappropriate personalism, as when, during a syndicate meeting, he proposes to rely on his hand-picked henchmen rather than the syndicate crew. Upon being told that syndicate members must suppress their personalities and 'be like the furniture,' Frank declares mockingly, 'Okay, I'm a chair.' His preference for personal pleasure over commercial discipline is shown in his casual report of losses at the racetrack – self-indulgent and reckless behaviour unlike the coldly calculating and collective mentality of his syndicate colleagues, whom he finds hard to tolerate. For all his appreciation of Vince's education and accounting skills, he tells him that tradition trumps learning. Ultimately, without refuge in the United States, Frank escapes to Sicily, where he adopts the role of traditional Sicilian patriarch before submitting to execution by his brother. The climactic murder, which follows a large-scale familial feast, not only ironically counterpoints Frank's daughter's wedding celebration at the opening but also underscores that close identification between violence and banqueting that has often accompanied cinematic portrayals of the Italian American gangster.

Vince Ginetta embodies the second-generation Italian American male hungry for assimilation at virtually any cost. His self-contained and nearly affectless demeanour suit him well for the WASP business world, and his education has enabled him to enter a profession whose high-level numeracy typifies capitalist objectivity and impersonality. With his basic detachment from family and ethnic loyalties, and his abstract and matter-of-fact demeanour, Vince objects to his brother's use of Italian as well as to his friendship with the Moustache Petes. Their enthusiasm for bocce ball has no effect on Vince's icy neutrality. In contrast to his brother's filial piety, he refers to their father as a 'nuthin', the owner of a 'peanuts and candy store operation'. Thanks to his daily study of the *New York Times*, Vince has a perspective on the international context of the syndicate far beyond the grasp of his insular-minded brother.

Another striking feature of *The Brotherhood* is its genuine flavour of *sicilianità*, especially in the scenes on location. No other film went so far in this direction before *The Godfather*. In an early scene, as Vince is driven through Palermo to his meeting with Frank, a young man on a motorbike rides along the highway with an old woman clinging to his waist – a grotesque symbol of modernity burdened by traditionalism. Subsequently, Vince encounters local peasants with their donkeys, a long-standing unofficial symbol of Sicily that Coppola employs in *The Godfather: Part III* (1990). Frank and Sicily have deviated from the path of modernity; and it is telling that Vince discovers his brother holed up in a ruined medieval castle, a symbol of Sicily as a historical dead end. It is true that, when Frank tells Vince that his death must occur in traditional style following a celebration including 'all the relatives', the film falsely implies that the extended family has been the Sicilian norm, when in reality the nuclear family has predominated owing to the island's poverty. However, *The Brotherhood* is also about Sicilian ideals and myths and, from that perspective, Frank's celebration of the extended family rings true.

The film's American scenes similarly strive to capture a richly authentic mafia atmosphere. The initial execution is followed by the stuffing of a parakeet into the victim's mouth, indicating his violation of *omertà* (the mafia code of silence). After receiving word of the assassination at the wedding party, Frank praises the presiding priest in terms equally applicable to his henchmen: 'Father, you did a wonderful job.' This exchange anticipates the climactic baptism scene in *The Godfather* with its ironic interpenetration of Catholicism and criminality quite typical of the mafia.[10] When Emma learns of Frank's desire to join the mafia, she exemplifies the mafia wife's typical refusal to know of her husband's 'business' affairs. In murdering Dominic, Frank hog-ties him mafia-style with a rope attached to his neck and ankles, so that he strangles himself in attempting to get free. Frank's denunciation of Dominic as a 'camorrista bastard' reminds us that the children of Italian immigrants sometimes maintained their parents' regional hatreds, the Camorra being the mafia centre of Naples and surrounding areas. However, there is no basis for Don Peppino's claim that forty-one Moustache Petes were exterminated by Lucky Luciano's henchmen in a single 'purge'.[11]

The Brotherhood treats the conflict between kinship and business within the mafia. This conflict appears in *The Brothers Rico* (Phil Karlson, 1957) and *The Godfather* series, yet in some respects *The Brotherhood* shows a clearer grasp of the issue. According to Dwight C. Smith, *The Brothers Rico* misrepresents the mafia as an impersonal organization claiming primacy over blood relationships; in his view Italian American crime organizations or 'families' are based not on impersonal business-like or rationally bureaucratic arrangements but on kinship ties both actual and fictional, and thus harmonize or reconcile business and familial loyalties. Smith relies on Francis A.J. Ianni, who, unlike those criminologists who view Italian American organized groups as centralized, hierarchical, and bureaucratic organizations characterized by business impersonality, describes them as family businesses in which kinship ties provide the operating principle and bond. Ianni's study has influenced Thomas J. Ferraro, who sees the Corleone family in *The Godfather* as exemplifying the idea of the mafia organization as a family business founded on blood relationships.[12] Yet while it is unnecessary to refute Donald Cressey's mistaken comparison of the mafia to a modern-day business corporation, Ianni's, Smith's, and Ferraro's views remain problematic, since the mafia normally supersedes kinship loyalties and other blood relationships. As Howard Abadinsky shows, a major test of loyalty within the fictitiously constituted kinship group that makes up a so-called mafia family is to require a member to kill a blood relative, so as to demonstrate his stronger ties to the criminal organization.[13] Something similar happens in *The Brotherhood*, in which the syndicate uses the threat of the death penalty in order to force Vince Ginetta to kill his brother and thus demonstrate his freedom from kinship ties. This is not to suggest, though, that *The Brotherhood* provides an altogether reliable portrait of the mafia organization and its operations, as the criminal group to which Vince Ginetta devotes himself and for which he murders a blood relative qualifies as a cartel or business association, its members drawn from various ethnic groups, rather than as an artificial kinship group typical of the mafia, whose members would be if not exclusively, then almost entirely, of Italian background.

NOTES

1 Jo Ann Tedesco, 'Sacraments: Italian American Theatrical Culture and the Dramatization of Everyday Life,' in *The Italian American Heritage: A Companion to Literature and the Arts*, ed. Pellegrino D'Acierno (New York: Garland, 1999), 365; Marilyn Yaquinto, *Pump 'em Full of Lead: A Look at Gangsters on Film* (New York: Twayne, 1998), 123; Gabriel Miller, ed., *Martin Ritt: Interviews* (Jackson, MI: University Press of Mississippi, 2002), 179; Ian Cameron, *A Pictorial History of Crime Films* (London: Hamlyn, 1975), 67–8; Paola Casella, *Hollywood Italian: Gli italiani nell'America di celluloide* (Milan: Boldini and Castoldi, 1998), 207–12.

2 Yaquinto, *Pump 'em Full of Lead*, 48, 49, 51; Dwight C. Smith, *The Mafia Mystique* (New York: Basic Books, 1975), 63–4, 116; Francis A. J. Ianni, *A Family Business: Kinship and Social Control in Organized Crime* (New York: Russell Sage Foundation, 1972), 2–4.

3 Smith, *The Mafia Mystique*, 121, 122, 126, 131–44, 147, 148–50, 291–2, 296, 299–300; William Howard Moore, *The Kefauver Committee and the Politics of Crime, 1950–52* (Columbia, MO: University of Missouri Press, 1974).

4 Carl Sifakis, *The Mafia Encyclopedia* (New York: Facts on File, 1987), 18–20; Smith, *The Mafia Mystique*, 152–5, 162–4, 173–8, 185, 219, 223, 225, 228–30, 233–5, 240.

5 Gabriel Miller, *The Films of Martin Ritt* (Jackson, MI: University Press of Mississippi, 2000), 92–3, 106; Casella, *Hollywood Italian*, 247.

6 Harlan Lebo, *The Godfather Legacy* (New York: Simon and Schuster, 1994), 4, 25, 26; Yaquinto, *Pump 'em Full of Lead*, 141; Willliam Malyszko, *The Godfather* (London: York, 2001), 66, 67; Jeffery Chown, *Hollywood Auteur: Francis Ford Coppola* (New York: Praeger, 1988), 63, 65; Gene D. Phillips, *Godfather: The Intimate Francis Ford Coppola* (Lexington, KY: University Press of Kentucky, 2004), 88, 89; Peter Cowie, *The Godfather Book* (London: Faber and Faber, 1997), 10–11, 19, 39–40, 70.

7 David Ehrenstein, *The Scorsese Picture: The Art and Life of Martin Scorsese* (New York: Carol Publishing, 1992), 41.

8 Like mob boss Joe Masseria, whom he defeated in the Castellamarese War (1930–31), Salvatore Maranzano is usually seen as a 'Mustache Pete,' whose criminal methods and ambitions exemplified the mafia as an Old World institution centred in and largely limited to the immigrant community. Maranzano was ultimately assassinated on orders from Lucky Luciano, who, with Frank Costello and others of their rising generation, is often claimed to have typified in his methods as in his manners and style of dress the new Americanizing wing of the mafia.

9 Robert Casillo, *Gangster Priest: The Italian American Cinema of Martin Scorsese* (Toronto: University of Toronto Press, 2006), 24–35.

10 Ibid., 472n15.

11 Humbert S. Nelli, *The Business of Crime: Italian and Syndicate Crime in the United States* (New York: Oxford University Press, 1976), 180–3.

12 Ianni, *A Family Business*; Smith, *The Mafia Mystique*, 265, 315–16, 319–20; Thomas J. Ferraro, "Blood in the Marketplace: The Business of Family in *the Godfather* Films," in Ferraro, *Ethnic Passages: Literary Immigrants and Twentieth-Century America* (Chicago: University of Chicago Press, 1993), 18–52.

13 Donald R. Cressey, *Theft of the Nation: The Structure and Operation of Organized Crime in America* (New York: Harper, 1969); Smith, *The Mafia Mystique*, 42–3, 306–12; Howard Abadinsky, *The Criminal Elite* (Westport, CT: Greenwood, 1983), 6, 81–2, 95–7, 100, 101–3, 108, 109, 121, 149, 158, 159.

8 Michael Corleone's Tie: Francis Ford Coppola's *The Godfather*

ANTHONY JULIAN TAMBURRI

Italian Americans occupy a strong, if often contested, place in American media; and this twentieth-century plight of Italian America may readily be traced back to 1905, at the onset of the motion picture industry. Films such as F.A. Dobson's *The Skyscrapers of New York* (1905), Wallace McCutcheon's *The Black Hand* (1906), and D.W. Griffith's *The Avenging Conscience* (1914) are early vessels for such stereotyping. *Skyscrapers* first offered 'Dago Pete,' a small-time crook who steals his boss's watch while shifting blame onto a co-worker; the second film underscored the stereotype of the 'Black Hand'; and the Italian in this third film is an ill-reputed blackmailer.[1]

From large-scale 'godfather' to neighbourhood 'crook,' the mafia theme has left its mark on the American imaginary vis-à-vis Italian Americans. These celluloid representations and their filmmakers have been hotly debated and, in many cases, vilified. More recently, however, some scholars have reconsidered such representations through a different lens: one that interrogates the visual in search of its *prima facie* irony, thereby offering alternative readings of the signs therein. Thus, the signifying potentiality of images in a film such as *The Godfather* (1972) may indeed be greater than what the naive spectator perceives. In this sense, I have in mind, first, the existence of peripheral signs, and, second, its sister concept of 'liminal ethnicity.'[2]

Of the many things it may signify, *The Godfather* is, at first blush, the story of an Italian immigrant family's 'American' story, its success due to its rise to power, albeit within a criminal structure. To some, this is, indeed, the problem with the film. It glorifies organized crime and underscores the connection of Italian *equals* organized crime. Yet in looking at the film with a greater interpretive flexibility, we may consider it more of a condemnation, rather than an adulation, of the Italian *qua* mafioso. Through a re-reading of seemingly insignificant signs (Vito Corleone's general style of dress and Michael's tie), we see that such signs (peripheral and literally centred, as in Michael's tie) can have much greater semiotic valence than one might initially invest in them.

It is this very sense of semiotic complexity that subtends the visual rhetoric of Coppola's *The Godfather*. From the film's opening scene, the spectator is confronted with a series of signs that are aptly polysemic. The initial appearance of Don Corleone constitutes a clash of possible meanings: Is he the doting father, cuddling a fragile cat, during his daughter's wedding, or the mean-spirited head of a criminal organization? What do we make of Amerigo Bonasera, with that potentially wonderfully hopeful, inspirational name, as it seems only to clash with his profession as undertaker?

There, indeed, exists a series of seemingly conflicting signs apparent throughout the film; and the spectator is consistently challenged to decode said signs as possessing one or the other *interpretant*. Such *coincidentia oppositorum* – the presence of competing imagery and sign functions – is surely part of a rhetorical strategy that provokes the spectator to (re)construct his/her own story: that this may indeed be the trials and tribulations of a mafia family, that their story is a metaphor for making it in America, as some have wanted to see in the film,[3] or, in fact, something else still. Indeed, John Paul Russo deconstructs Coppola's *The Godfather* series in a keen essay, demonstrating how it has succeeded in insinuating itself into the United States' collective imaginary.[4]

Whatever the case may be, the figure of the Italian as mafioso has been a popular one. More than just a criminal, let us not reject the possibility of this figure being, for some, transformed into a countercultural icon, one who, while initially part of the downtrodden, can eventually rise to 'beat the system,' even though the system is a so-called legitimate social structure. This we can infer from Amerigo Bonasera's conversation with Vito Corleone, when Bonasera, in recounting his daughter's ordeal, states, 'I went to the police, like a good American' – an act that clearly had no positive result since he left in the courtroom 'like a fool.' The obvious meaning here is that one needs to work around the system, the way, some would say, that Vito Corleone did. This seems to be the case, to some extent, with Puzo's and Coppola's *The Godfather*, the prototype for the modern-day gangster. Don Corleone has, in this sense, beaten the system, or so it seems. Coppola, especially, has created a wonderfully rhetorical device that plays well into this primary reading of the film. This is, to be sure, what Marco Greco saw as the 'pasta and mobster crap' that Americans associate with Italians par excellence.[5] We therefore would not err in stating that films such as *The Godfather*, *Mean Streets* (Martin Scorsese, 1973), and *Goodfellas* (Martin Scorsese, 1990) may indeed provoke a more intense reading that allows the spectator to grasp more firmly the films' inner semiotic underpinnings. With brief regard to these three films, let us not forget that the mob figure was presented as both a physically violent and, often, a sentimentally devoid individual – a pathetic and despicable human being.

At this juncture, then, I would remind the reader of certain scenes in *The Godfather* that may readily set up a signifying slippery slope that can easily guide the spectator down a semiotic path divergent from an initial reading of Don Corleone as, for example, a self-involved, thuggish mafioso who killed and had people killed on his way to the top. The first scene that comes to mind is Vito Corleone's meeting with Sollozzo, when he ultimately refuses to engage in drug trafficking. What is significant is not just the conversation but also the scene's visual aspects. There are seven men present. Six are dressed in dark suits, white shirts, and ties, typical for 'businessmen' of this era.[6] Vito Corleone, in comparison, wears a brownish suit with greenish stripes; his shirt is olive green; his tie is red-coloured with numerous designs. Thus, contrary to the six other men wearing business suits, Don Corleone is dressed like any Italian immigrant grandfather; no respectable business*man* during this immediate post–Second World War era would be seen without a white shirt and dark suit, especially when attending an important meeting, as was this one with Sollozzo.[7]

This visual sign of Vito Corleone *qua* immigrant grandfather is underscored immediately when he goes to buy fruit, just before being gunned down. Having dispatched Luca Brasi to acquire information from Sollozzo, the director switches scenes. Vito Corleone, in exiting his office, turns to Fredo and says, '*Andiamo*, Fredo, tell Paulie to get the car. We're going.' Then, once outside, Vito says to his son, '*Aspetta*, Fredo, I'm going to buy some fruit.' Both statements involve clear code switching, something readily identified with immigrants, biculturalism, and, accordingly, a desire to hold on to one's cultural identity.[8] In addition, the scene is much too reminiscent of immigrant New York for the informed spectator not to take notice, while foreshadowing the sequel that dramatizes Don Vito's arrival in NYC and earlier life on those same streets.

Furthermore, from the perspective of the camera behind both Vito and Fredo, we cast our eyes on a winter street scene of an open fruit and vegetable market, with a fire burning in a steel barrel drum nearby, the quintessential heat source of the era. More than a gangster film, at this juncture, it seems we are viewing an immigrant saga.[9] The question begged here is, of course, 'Would a genuine underworld crime boss, such as the mythical Don Corleone, be out buying his own fruit and vegetables, and unguarded to boot?'

Another major scene that casts Vito Corleone more as grandfather than as don includes him playing with his grandson, Anthony, in the proverbial Italian American vegetable garden. As he engages Anthony in a make-believe game, Don Corleone feigns being a monster. This scene and all of its signifying capability is one of the more polysemic in the movie vis-à-vis Vito Corleone. Besides the initial fear he instils in Anthony, two important issues stand out. First, this is the last image we have of Don Corleone, as he runs through the tomato plants, first chasing then being chased by his grandson; second, as he lays dying, unbeknownst to his grandson, Anthony begins to spray him with what we can only assume to be insect repellent – given the date of the scene, it is probably DDT. Such a combination of events is too significant to ignore; it is as if the future generation – the sign of which is Anthony – here now rebuffs that old *monstrous* world of organized crime.[10]

Such a reading of Vito Corleone's trajectory compels us to rethink Michael Corleone's own metamorphosis throughout the film. From war hero to 'Don Corleone,' as Clemenza calls him at the film's closing, there is one seemingly insignificant sign that also undergoes a metamorphosis: Michael Corleone's tie. Michael wears five different ties throughout the film: red and white; brown; black (at his marriage to Apollonia and at his father's funeral); pinkish-red (when he goes to Las Vegas to 'buy out' Moe Greene); and a black, grey, and off-white striped tie. It is indeed this striped tie that we first see when, after his return from Italy, he visits Kay at her school. At that moment, Michael is dressed not so much like the businessman one might expect, having taken over his father's 'business'; rather, he is in the quintessential garb we might readily associate with that of the funeral director of the time: derby hat, black overcoat, dark-grey pants, and the aforementioned striped tie, this last item especially the proverbial calling card of the funeral director's so-called classic uniform.

Once Michael returns from his Las Vegas hotel-shopping trip, he basically wears only one tie: the black, grey, and off-white one.[11] He wears it, in fact, with a charcoal, striped suit. It is at this time in the movie, after the above-mentioned passing of the baton, that Michael's metamorphosis completes itself. Also, at this point, we witness the most dramatic example of what I consider the film's challenging *coincidentia oppositorum* that subtends *The Godfather*. The famous baptismal scene is a wonderfully efficacious rhetorical montage of both cinematic narrative and the aforementioned structuring of opposites.

The alternating scenes of the highly ornate church setting of the sacrament of baptism and the individual murders ordered by Michael underscore in this section the film's semiotic antinomy: the movie's most significant juxtaposition of scenes. It pits the highest of Catholic celebrations – the cleansing of original sin – with the most despicable of human acts – murder. Having now acquired his role of godfather to his nephew, Michael must complete the cleansing of his newly inherited 'business' through Carlo Rizzi's murder. That accomplished, Michael himself has been truly baptized as 'heir to his father, heir to his sin,'[12] thus becoming, in the most clichéd manner possible, a 'godfather' twice over.

Such antinomical structuring is present once Michael returns from his Las Vegas trip. Discussing with this father the 'business' in the family garden, numerous things stand out. First, while Vito Corleone is dressed as *everyman*'s grandfather, Michael, in business garb, is wearing his black, grey, and off-white tie. Second, as Vito Corleone offers him advice about the business and his safety, their conversation is peppered with questions and facts about the family, Michael's children especially, which distracts the spectator's attention from one subject (cold-blooded business) and shifts it to another (the general welfare of family members). Third, at one point, Vito becomes a *forgetful grandfather*, repeating himself, to some degree, while his son now adamantly reminds his father, 'I'll handle it, Pop.' This is followed by a pregnant silence, as Vito gets to his feet and eventually goes into his famous speech about how he did not want this for Michael; he saw Michael as the one 'to hold the strings, senator Corleone, governor Corleone, something.' With the spectator distracted by this doting father's unfulfilled wishes for his youngest son's future, the conversation ends with Vito slipping back into his *godfather* role, firmly reminding his son that 'whoever comes to [him] with this Barzini meeting, he's the traitor. Don't forget that!' The spectator, at this point is brought back to the reality of the film's basic premise: the brutal life of organized crime.[13]

Vito's apparent grandfatherly dress and behaviour is certainly a counterpoint to his Don Vito *persona*. Similarly, Michael's metamorphosis, signalled by what appears to be his favourite tie, is a counterpoint to his initial war-hero status. These two antinomical examples can only underscore the possibility of an interpretive strategy on the informed spectator's part and/or a rhetorical device on Coppola's part, even if we cannot divine authorial intentionality.[14] Such a reading is underscored by what we may now identify as a logical bracketing. First, let us not forget that Michael Corleone is dressed in the same suit, shirt, and tie throughout the last twenty-seven minutes of the film. Second, this is the moment he defines his strategy for the takeover, and eventually, he completes the task. Third, the film closes with Michael Corleone, in its penultimate scene, literally framed within the door jamb, surrounded by Clemenza and two others, with Clemenza, as mentioned above, uttering the final two words of the film, 'Don Corleone,' both a greeting and, dare we say, announcement of Michael's ultimate success. He is, at this point, both godfather and – dressed, as he is – undertaker, having now buried, so to speak, his five enemy 'capo-regimes.'

In closing, then, there remains one more sign to invest with meaning. At a little more than midway through the movie, Don Corleone must now call upon Bonasera for that favour he thought he would never have to ask. When he arrives at Bonasera's funeral parlour with his son's corpse, we see Bonasera dressed in full garb, wearing, at centre screen, his funeral director's tie – a black, grey, and off-white striped design similar to Michael's. It is also the same tie Michael wears during the last twenty-seven minutes of the film, when he ultimately solidifies his position as heir to Don Vito Corleone. Thus, we think back to the beginning of the movie, which opens with Bonasera, a true undertaker, whose conversation with Don Corleone emphasizes the role of a just vendetta, as Don Corleone reminds Bonasera that the murder of his daughter's violent would-be rapists would not be 'justice,' since justice signifies otherwise – an eye for an eye, which this would not be. That said, thinking back to the film's opening conversation signals to the spectator that there are indeed various signs that can be manipulated throughout and it may be the spectator's responsibility to invest these various signs with meaning. Now, at the end of the movie, having witnessed various semiotic machinations along the way, we end our viewing with the final confirmation of Michael Corleone, godfather par excellence, dressed in his undertaker's garb. The closing of the door in Kay's face – literally, the final scene – is only an addendum to Michael's framed portrait, as it reminds us that Michael's lie to Kay regarding his role in Carlo's murder is only symptomatic of his manipulation of sign functions (which can be read as meaning or truth), as Bonasera had tried to do with Don Vito Corleone at the film's opening.

NOTES

1 For an acute reading of this period of United States cinema, see Ilaria Serra's *Immagini di un immaginario: L'emigrazione italiana negli stati uniti fra i due secoli (1890–1924)* (Verona, Italy: CIERRE, 1997), 102–59.

2 See my *Italian/American Short Films & Music Videos: A Semiotic Reading* (West Lafayette: Purdue University Press, 2002).

3 For the most complete study on how Puzo's and Coppola's works have impacted the collective American imaginary, see Christian Messenger, *The Godfather and American Culture: How the Corleones Became 'Our Gang'* (Albany, NY: SUNY Press, 2001).

4 See his 'The Hidden Godfather: Plenitude and Absence in Francis Ford Coppola's *Godfather I* and *II*,' in *Support and Struggle: Italians and Italian Americans in a Comparative Perspective*, ed. Joseph L. Tropea and James E. Miller (Staten Island, NY: AIHA, 1986), 255–81.

5 See Will Parriniello's documentary *Little Italy* (1995).

6 Clemenza's shirt is the only one with beige stripes.

7 See George De Stefano's keenly crafted discussion in his 'Don Corleone Was My Grandfather,' in *An Offer We Can't Refuse: The Mafia in the Mind of America* (New York: Faber and Faber, 2006), 91–135. De Stefano nicely points out how the Corleones can indeed remind Italian American viewers of their own families.

8 See, for example, Carol Myers-Scotton, *Social Motivations for Codeswitching: Evidence from Africa* (Oxford: Clarendon, 1993).

9 While Vito points out to the *fruttivendolo* what he wants, a poster is visible advertising the 11 January 1946 boxing match between Jake La Motta and Tommy Bell. This, together with the code switching, surely emphasizes Vito's *italianità* over his criminality.

10 In retrospect, this scene proves most ironic from the perspective of *Godfather III*, where Anthony will totally rebuff the family business and do only as he pleases, which is to sing in the opera, despite his father's wishes to the contrary.

11 The only divergence is at his father's funeral, where he wears a solid black tie.

12 See James Thomas Chiampi's insightful semiotic reading, 'Resurrecting *the Godfather*,' MELUS 5, no. 4 (1978): 18–31.

13 Two scenes separate this father–son conversation and the above-described baptism scene: one is Vito's death; the other is Vito's funeral. These two scenes overall, I submit, underscore the film's *coincidentia oppositorum*, as they, too, though ever so briefly, distract the spectator from the film's basic storyline of organized crime.

14 Umberto Eco deals nicely with this in 'Intentio Lectoris,' *Differentia* 2 (1988): 147–68. We might also
    consider how Vito's dress and his connections to family, garden, traditions, and so on situate him more
    as representing 'old mafia' (i.e., the Old World with its coincidental values) that ultimately conflicts with
    the 'new mafia' and the way in which Michael positions himself.

9 Nihilism and *Mafiositá* in Martin Scorsese's *Mean Streets*

PELLEGRINO D'ACIERNO

Released in 1973 when the American mafia was already in decline and mafia movie madness, as induced by *The Godfather* phenomenon, was just beginning its takeover of the American pop-cultural imaginary, Martin Scorsese's *Mean Streets* effects a 'mobbing down' and demystification of the mafia movie. *Mean Streets* disrupted and thus redefined the conventions and codes of the classical Hollywood gangster movie, while at the same time redefining the mafia movie as it was in the very process of receiving its maximum and most ennobling mainstream codification in the first two instalments of Coppola's trilogy: *The Godfather* (1972) and *The Godfather: Part II* (1974). These movies straddle *Mean Streets* or, to put it the other way round, *Mean Streets* punctuates them, presenting itself, in terms of film history, as an interlude of farce between the first two magisterial acts of the Corleone family's tragedy. It is perhaps best described as an out-of-the-box mafia movie, and its embedding of an auteurist film within a gangster movie marks it as a masterpiece of the 'cinema of difference,' as an art film in the European mode despite its struggle with genre. Its countering of mainstream cinema and deeply postmodern feel identify it as a defining work of New Hollywood cinema, which emerged in the late 1960s and 1970s under various aliases such as American New Wave, independent film, and 'film school brats' cinema.

Scorsese describes his authorial intentions in the following way: '*Mean Streets* was an attempt to put myself and my old friends on the screen, to show how we lived, what life was in Little Italy. It was really an anthropological or a sociological tract.'[1] Certainly, *Mean Streets* is a personal film in both the autobiographical and the cinematic sense, and it is, in its way, an ethnographic 'tract' – an insider's view of 'coming of age in Little Italy,' as it were – through which the spectator is given a thick description of Little Italy as a subcultural universe and an urban space. But there is too much derangement and wildness, too much cinematic mayhem in *Mean Streets* to permit the spectator to view it as a social problem film that deploys a vérité style to document the brutalizing urban conditions at work in the underworld of Little Italy.

Therefore, Scorsese's statement only goes so far in keying a reading of *Mean Streets*. A more implicit statement of intentions can be found in his switching (at the recommendation of his confidant Jay Cocks) of the working title of the screenplay *The Season of the Witch* (borrowed from Donovan's song) to *Mean Streets* (which alludes to Raymond Chandler's celebrated passage that encapsulates the ethos of the big-city detective who manages to remain untainted by it): 'Down these mean streets a man must go who is not himself mean, who is neither tarnished nor afraid. He is the hero, he is everything.' The title shift effects a rekeying of the screenplay, co-authored by

Scorsese and Martin Mardik, who had originally placed their narrative under the sign of *The Season of the Witch* to suggest, following Donovan's song, the uncanniness of a world gone awry. The retitling transposes the film into the key of the hard-boiled world of the Chandleresque, thereby marking *Mean Streets* as a city film in the noir tradition.[2] But Scorsese, instead, makes us go down 'these mean streets' in the company not of an honourable detective but of a band of street punks who lose themselves in order not to find themselves. Their sense of 'honour' is, at best, tactical, and is only vaguely connected to the strict code of honour and respect of authentic *mafiositá*.

Regarding the autobiographical dimension, Scorsese inscribes himself within the filmic text in two ways: he inserts himself literally or indexically by speaking the voiceovers related to Charlie and by appearing as an extra in the role of the trigger-happy hit man, Jimmy Shorts. He inserts himself metaphorically or by transference by rendering the main protagonist, Charlie, into his double, endowing him with a version of his own sacramental consciousness derived from growing up as an Italian American Catholic and situating him within a 'once a Catholic always a Catholic' spiritual crisis that mirrors his own. But this doubling also places him outside the character of Charlie, his autobiographical persona, who remains hopelessly confined to Little Italy and locked into an irresolvable identity crisis, whereas Scorsese uses *Mean Streets* as a way out of the punkdom and 'Dagotude' imposed by the Little Italy subculture. In this sense, Scorsese uses *Mean Streets* and his alter ego Charlie to perform a self-analysis – a 'wild psychoanalysis,' as Freud would say[3] – conducted from the director's chair, upon himself, his environment, and, as a corollary, upon cinema itself.

Embedded in *Mean Streets*, then, are a number of parables of cinema: (1) Scorsese's extra-filmic conversion from street boy to auteurist director, a conversion in the course of which Charlie and his (Scorsese's) friends are sacrificed as celluloid scapegoats: Jimmy Shorts shoots Charlie and Johnny Boy in the climactic final scene, whereas Scorsese 'shoots' the film; (2) Scorsese's transposition of the most improbable of formats – the mafia movie – into a medium through which to raise profound spiritual and ethical questions about the response to, and the responsibility for, others and to narrate Charlie's religious crisis: Charlie's street theology is his tactic for transcending the meanness of the streets, whereas it is Scorsese's tactic for carnivalizing the dogmatic Catholicism of the Church and the priests and for working through his own religious crisis; (3) Scorsese's more extensive carnivalization not only of the gangster film genre, but, more importantly, of the 'sacred' language game of the dominant cinema, which he constantly transgresses by introducing innovative and disruptive stylistic gestures through which he inscribes his auteurship upon the film. Among other things, these parables of cinema serve to locate the real intentionality at work in the film itself: the consecration of cinema as the eighth sacrament.

Mean Streets narrates the (mis)adventures and street follies of a merry but highly dysfunctional band of four Little Italy street hustlers who, as mafiosi and mafia wannabes, are more disconnected from than connected to the mob. They are decidedly 'unusual suspects' for a mafia movie: Charlie, a mafioso in training and a street priest who finds himself in a series of double-binds dictated by conflicting psychic demands; Johnny Boy, part trickster, part fool, and all self-victimizer, who is completely out of control and hopelessly in debt to the neighbourhood loan sharks; Tony, a tavern owner who claims to be a exemplar of the 'safe' life, while keeping caged panthers in the backroom of Volpe's Bar as primary objects of his affection; and Michael, a loan shark and a disappointed don. In a standard mafia movie they would, at best, be cast as supernumeraries or extras. In *Mean Streets* they are compelling punk existentialists suffering from interminable identity crises (individual and collective) that impart a volatile complexity to them; they are not made men but young men in the unmaking.

Disconnection also informs their supposed connectedness to one another as friends and street brothers, and in the course of the film, they move from being brother keepers to enemy brothers, with Michael aligned against Johnny Boy and Charlie, who, for most of the film, successfully manages to mediate the hostilities among them. When the chips are down, Tony also aligns himself with the duo, although he remains out of harm's way, risking only his car. Inevitably the labyrinthine means streets, down which they drift mostly at night and in the spirit of revelry, turn into the one-way-street of catastrophic violence. Michael contracts a hit on Johnny Boy, and Michael, in his role as killjoy, imposes the mafia script that takes the travestied form – albeit near-deadly – of a bungled hit.

There is a carnival spirit running through *Mean Streets* that distinguishes it from the generic gangster movie, which induces, through displays of hyperviolence and gunplay, a 'gangster high' by which the law-abiding spectator is made to overidentify with the gangster figure. The dominant images of *Mean Streets* are the feast and communion. It is no accident that the film's action takes place during the street feast of San Gennaro. Contaminated and propelled by the boisterous rhythms of the San Gennaro Festival, the band of brothers perform their own Feast of Fools that involves transgressions that violate and parody the 'sacred' laws and scripts of the systems (the Catholic Church, the mafia, the neighbourhood, the family, the brotherhood) in which they are caught. The group engages in interaction rituals and rites of male bonding, often involving excessive drinking, heterosexual bravado, plain-old moviegoing, and cruising in cars, that establish their solidarity. Their primary interaction is the *passatella* or dissing, and the film unfolds as one long game of ritual insult.

Nonetheless, the contact of communion brings with it the threat of contamination by strangers and even by those intimates – namely, Johnny Boy and his cousin Teresa, Charlie's secret lover – who are bearers of otherness. The group's relationships to others – racial, gendered, ethnic – are antagonistic, especially towards those they mark stigmatically as outsiders to the neighbourhood, such as the rich kids from Riverdale whom they regard as easy marks in the firecracker scam, or as sexual others such as the homosexuals who infiltrate their macho world, threatening their masculine protocols. Women fare no better, to cite a few examples: Charlie cannot cross over the colour line in his pursuit of an African American go-go dancer named Diane; Johnny Boy, who is programmatically misogynistic, picks up two young Jewish girls at the Café Bizarre whom he marks as 'bohemians' and easy lays and whom Charlie identifies pejoratively as 'Christ killers'; Charlie, in a display of macho bravado in Tony's bar, attempts to engage a barfly while she is in the company of another man. The band's obsessive need to establish identities in terms of territorialization is an expression of their own status as deterritorialized subjects. Although they seem to inhabit the comfort zone of the neighbourhood, their identities do not fully belong to them. Despite their ostensive familiarity and even intimacy, they remain strangers unto themselves and unto to each other.

Nowhere is this more in evidence than in Charlie's conflicted relationship with Johnny Boy and Teresa, which is mediated by Giovanni, the local don and Charlie's uncle and father figure. Giovanni lays down the law of the Father/law of the mafia: 'Honourable men go with honourable men.' Although he is also Johnny Boy's godfather and, thus, bound to his family through the honorific system of *compareggio*, he stigmatizes Johnny Boy as being 'half-crazy' and, thus, as someone who is incapable of comporting himself as a serious person. Similarly, he stigmatizes Teresa, who suffers from epilepsy, as being 'crazy in the head.' In ruling out Johnny Boy and Teresa, he instructs Charlie to disengage himself from them: 'You live next door. Keep an eye open. But don't get involved.' This is precisely what Charlie cannot do, for they hold him hostage as his others, placing him in a series of double-binds. He is bound to Teresa by his ambivalent desire for her as a Madonna/whore figure and separated from her by his uncle's interdiction and by the interferences of Johnny Boy; he is bound to Johnny Boy by his mission as street priest – saving Johnny Boy from himself is a form of self-redemption – and estranged from him by his chaotic and self-destructive behaviour as a clown. Furthermore, as rival brothers, they are entangled within a perverse triangular desire for Teresa, as evidenced by Johnny Boy's sexually offensive comments to and about her. Therefore, their doubling is both sexual, involving as well suppressed homosexual desire as suggested by, among other things, their sharing of a bed, and spiritual, becoming ever more authentically so whenever Johnny Boy puts into crisis Charlie's street theology and mummery of Catholicism. Here we approach the fundamental theme of *Mean Streets*: the otherness that emerges within the sameness of the band of insiders. At the film's end, the three of them are expelled from the familiar world of the neighbourhood, discovering themselves to be its others, strangers unto themselves and to one another.

Mean Streets is primarily concerned with witnessing the disintegration of the friendships among this contentious band of four Little Italy street types who are their own worst enemies and at once friends and enemies to one another. They are neither gangsters nor tragic heroes, but rather 'trouble boys,' more adept at troubling themselves and one another than their marks. Moreover, the narrative of *Mean Streets* does not rise and fall but rather drifts through disjointed episodes (thirty-three scenes) towards a sacrificial crisis that expresses itself in a bungled hit resulting in a car crash that leaves its three injured survivors alive – albeit stigmatized and removed from the fold of the neighbourhood and facing the exile of to-be-continued everyday life.

At the same time, *Mean Streets* effects a demythologization of the mafia movie. Although the mafia is in play, it is presented in the diminished form of a small-time local operation and as a cultural framework that conditions the mentality of its protagonists and the construction of their masculinity. Scorsese's weak version of the mafia is personified by Zio Giovanni, an old-style don whose role model is Lucky Luciano and who watches Fritz Lang's *The Big Heat* on TV for pointers. Although 'godfathering' is thematized in the film, with Giovanni taking his nephew Charlie under his wing and grooming him to take over a restaurant, the spectator is not 'godfathered' into the crime family and made to internalize its code of honour and its will to vendetta. In other words, unlike *The Godfather*, to which it is inevitably compared, *Mean Streets* does not tender to its spectator 'an offer that can't be refused' – namely, overidentification with the omnipotent mafia figure and his will to power as expressed through territorializing strategies and thrilling but calculated violence.

Although critics have consistently applied the 'anti-Godfather' tag to *Mean Streets*, the designation diminishes the paradigm shift effected quite astonishingly by Scorsese, whose low-budgeted, shot-on-the-run (completed in twenty-seven days!) independent film would become the founding text of a sub- or counter-genre. As an out-of-the-box mafia movie, *Mean Streets* is the first fully realized instalment of the 'cinema according to Scorsese': his declaration of cinematic independence and his profession of his abiding apostleship to cinemaphilia. Indeed, Scorsese makes his spectator go down those gritty 'mean streets' of Little Italy that are, at some level, 'Cinema Street,' as the various citations of other films (Fritz Lang's *The Big Heat,* John Ford's *The Searchers*, and Roger Corman's *The Tomb of Ligeia*) and the various self-reflexive gestures – scenes of cinematic seeing that make us aware that 'we are at the movies' – declare.

Members of Martin Scorsese's cinephilic generation who, like myself, rushed to see *Mean Streets* in the first days of its release after its debut at the New York Film Festival in 1973 are still reeling from the visceral impact that initial screening had upon us and from our delirious first encounter with the 'Scorsese effect.' That 'effect' also afflicted Pauline Kael, who epitomized the power of the film in the following way: 'In Scorsese's vision, music and the movies work within us and set the terms in which we perceive ourselves. Music and the movies and the Church. A witches' brew.'4 Kael's 'witches' brew' points the way to the sort of delirious reading the film demands. Such a reading must confront head-on the contagion of violence in which the group of four rival 'brothers' are caught and delineate the specific forms of violence through which they define their identities and practise the street politics of friendship Little Italy style. But it must do much more. It must confront the implications of Scorsese's profanation of religious experience by lowering the sacred into the streets. That profanation is immediately announced by a voiceover, spoken by Scorsese, that is superimposed over a blackout belonging to Charlie's dreaming consciousness: 'You don't make up for your sins in church. You do it in the streets. You do it at home. The rest is bullshit and you know it.' Here is the 'mean streets' scripture in a nutshell, the validity of which is to be tested throughout the course of the film. Later, the spectator is made privy to Charlie's dialogue with God when he questions confessional Catholicism and attempts to cut a private deal with God: 'I mean, if I do somethin' wrong, I just want to pay for it my way.' 'Profane' means *pro fanum* (in front of the temple), and Charlie brings the profane language and mindset of the streets into the sacred precinct of the Church: 'Now, ya don't fuck around with the infinite.' This is exactly what Scorsese does in the remainder of *Mean Streets* by having Charlie enact his punk imitation of Christ and perform his superficial street liturgies.

The carnivalizing reading, however, only takes us so far. The more fundamental problem lies in accounting for the uncanniness and convulsiveness that runs through the film. As a way of locating the disturbances that produce the 'Scorsese effect,' one might use the figure/concept of the syncope. Syncope has three main meanings: physical (a blackout); rhetorical (an ellipsis); and musical (syncopation). Scorsese represents the crisis states of the characters, who are subject to fits, rages, and violent outbursts of all sorts, through scenarios of the syncope such as Teresa's epileptic fit and the staggering drunk's refusal to die à la Rasputin. The film begins with an uncanny blackout – the syncope in the strict sense – that, as we learn from the succeeding shot, belongs to Charlie's dreaming consciousness, with the accompanying voiceover, which awakens him abruptly from his sleep, functioning as the nightmare's caption. This fracturing of his consciousness leads him to undertake an identity check before a mirror, after which he falls back into a fitful sleep, syncopated by The Ronettes' 'Be My Baby' on the soundtrack that introduces the dangerous desire that will 'rock'n'roll' his identity crisis. But syncope/syncopation works at a number of other levels as well: the formal ruptures (e.g., the fits and starts of the three beginnings, the jump cuts, and the climactic dead-end montage); the broken language of the motor-mouthing characters whose fracturing of language ultimately results in the total loss of meaning in two keywords: 'mook' and 'D.D.'; and the 'jukebox' effect of the soundtrack.

The cinema of the syncope is centred in Johnny Boy, who functions as the catalyser of negativity, an evil eye, in the Italian sense. All of Johnny Boy's madcap scenarios lead to and from the scene in which he attempts to shoot a light out in the Empire State Building from a tenement rooftop in Little Italy. It marks Johnny Boy's transformation from trickster to psychopath. It is the most riveting image in the film and one of the greatest instances of urban alienation in the cinema. As a gesture of street nihilism, it constitutes a physical assault on the 'Big City' – the skyscraper as a concrete representation of what Lacan calls the 'big Other' – a futile attempt at territorialization by a city boy trapped in his local (Little Italy) and underworld identities and an act of rage against the social substance he is alienated *within* and separated *from*. Like his blowing up of the mailbox we witness at the outset, it is an empty gesture, rebellion without rebellion, the wildness that stems from being nowhere and everywhere a prisoner: I shoot at the Empire State Building, therefore, I am. As an empty gesture, it bears upon Charlie's concluding empty gesture, which may be read as either a genuine act of self-sacrifice or a cultural suicide dictated by the nihilism of 'these mean streets.'

NOTES

1 See David Thompson and Ian Christie, eds., *Scorsese on Scorsese* (London: Faber and Faber, 1989), 48.

2 Which title best corresponds to what is represented in the film? For an exhaustive reading of this issue, see Robert Casillo, *Gangster Priest: The Italian American Cinema of Martin Scorsese* (Toronto: University of Toronto Press, 2006).

3 For a definition of 'wild psychoanalysis,' see J. Laplanche and J. B. Pontalis, *The Language of Psychoanalysis* (New York: Norton, 1973), 480–1.

4 Pauline Kael, 'The Current Cinema: Everyday Inferno,' *The New Yorker*, 8 October 1973, 157.

10 Thematic Patterns in Francis Ford Coppola's *The Godfather: Part II*

JOHN PAUL RUSSO

Thematic patterns of opposition that Francis Ford Coppola embedded in *The Godfather* (1972) receive their definitive treatment in *The Godfather: Part II* (1974). The major pattern is the desire for plenitude (self-fulfilment, life-enhancement, expansion of power) and an absence at the heart of things (fear, secrecy, negation, death). At the pole of plenitude are its representations of the home, food, *festa*, celebrations of cohesiveness, and the fundamental desire for at-one-ness with the world. According to the myth of the mafia adopted in the film, at variance with the real mafia either in the United States or in Sicily,[1] a godfather's world in preindustrial Corleone extends to the mountain's rim and no farther. In Tönnies's classic distinction, the 'family' is a synecdochic condensation of *Gemeinschaft*, clan or small community, in which associations are based on personal ties, favouritism, and vertical hierarchy, as opposed to *Gesellschaft* or impersonal civil society, in which contractual bonds are formed on the basis of attaining ends rather than as ends in themselves.[2] From the Sicilian latifundia to the New York neighbourhood, the godfathers' desire for plenitude governs under the form of paternalism, clientelism, structured hierarchy, and social custom. These two thematic clusters govern the structure of the film.

Since plenitude aims to eliminate desire, it depends upon a lack or absence, a deeply felt sense of emptiness or dissatisfaction; the goal of desire is to reverse or correct this lack or absence. In *The Godfather: Part II*, absence is associated with the 'business' and its modes of procedure, secrecy, and violence. In many respects Don Vito Corleone's situation is halfway between that of the feudal don and the casino owner. The old dons were not primarily businessmen; their plenitude was satisfied by what they received: in goods, in respect, in the acknowledgment of their power over the local territory. It could be as simple as the cup of coffee that Don Vito claims to have been denied by Amerigo Bonasera in *The Godfather*. This is not the case with his son Michael, the racketeers, and the Nevada casino owners. In *Gesellschaft* culture one tends to level everything and make structures meritocratic, to rationalize, and to impersonalize. Contracts, laws, and money are the same for everyone; there are ideally no special clientelistic intimacies and favouritisms or even loyalties. The secretive nature of the godfathers' activities bears some superficial similarities to advanced corporatism, which otherwise operates by different rules: only illegal corporatism allows for 'front' and 'dummy' companies, laundered money, and bribery of government officials, judges, and police. Other aspects of the clandestine 'business' taken over from Sicily are extortion (selling 'protection'), retribution, and strict surveillance.

As with *The Godfather*, in *The Godfather: Part II* a wide gulf separates the Corleones' family life and mafia business; in contrast to *The Godfather*, however, in *The Godfather: Part II* that gulf narrows to the point of disappearance, with the triumph of absence by the end. In support of this thematic conflict, and contributing to the central form of the film, is the structural conflict of five alternating Vito and Michael sequences. For the Vito sequences, Coppola and Puzo resurrected the don who died in *The Godfather* and wrote his life from boyhood to his mid-thirties. There are clear parallels between him and his son. Vito and Michael have their first big kill at about the same age: Vito is twenty-eight or twenty-nine when he kills the local Black Hand Fanucci, circa 1920. Michael, whom we see as a baby in his arms after this murder, shoots Sollozzo and Captain McCluskey when he is twenty-six or twenty-seven in 1946–47.[3] They cement their power at a similar age, too: Vito is in his mid- to late thirties when he avenges the death of his father, mother, and elder brother by killing Don Ciccio in 1925–26; Michael wipes out the last of his major enemies in 1958 when he is thirty-eight.

These parallels only serve to show more serious generational differences. Vito's inner life remains a mystery. In a moment of crisis, Michael even asks his mother, 'What did Papa think … deep in his heart?' This lack of knowledge has the effect of distancing, isolating, and mythifying the father, another reason why Coppola presents him in just one-fifth of the film. By contrast, a great deal is known about Michael; his sequences constitute four-fifths of the film, giving it an asymmetrical balance in his favour and thereby maintaining his centrality as protagonist. Vito remains in New York; Michael operates on an international stage: Las Vegas, Miami, Havana, Lake Tahoe, New York, Sicily, trains, cars, and planes. Vito is surrounded by his family and retainers. Separated from his wife and friends, Michael tries in vain to hang on to the remnants of his family. He has failed in his goal to become 'legitimate.'[4] At the end of the film, both godfathers have arrived in their mid-thirties, worked with the same values, and stand at the summit of power, yet face entirely different futures.

One of the finest mise en scènes in *The Godfather: Part II* displays the bewitching appeal of natural plenitude contrasted with absence.[5] In a flashback – it seems absolutely right that such an image should be a memory of Sicily in the 1920s, foreign to Michael's contemporary world – Vito has arranged to visit Sicily, ostensibly for a family reunion, but mainly to avenge the deaths of his father, mother, and brother. The clan gathers at the estate of Don Tommasino; they dine at a long table loaded with food; gifts are exchanged; they go for a tour of the olive oil factory, descending into a deep cellar, which takes on a journey into memory. Surrounded by huge oil casks, forming a small circle in the centre of the picture, the family and its henchmen drink a wine toast. Wine is a natural symbol of the earth's fructifying power and is associated with irrational, superhuman strength, Dionysian loss of individuation, and pleasure. The darkness invests the casks with a surreal appearance, and there is just the murmur of warm family voices. This scene is one of the shortest in the film, an almost subliminal image that flashes momentarily across Michael's consciousness; no time is given to focus on an individual, only on the group. Equally potent as a ritual and as an embedded memory, the cellar scene represents the family's most profound wishes – for survival and plenitude. It shows their most complete communion with nature, the past, and themselves, with the god of wine as presiding deity. Vito is invincible, and immediately afterward, to underscore the point, he kills Don Ciccio, consuming, as it were, his victim by disembowelling him.

How different are the film's final shots taken outside the family compound on Lake Tahoe. Alone, Michael stares over the menacing lake in the cold autumn twilight, but he is also looking inward. The camera focuses on his impassive face: it is one of the most chilling conclusions in American film history. The build-up to this shot is accomplished by collision montage, a Coppola specialty with which he brings the lines of his film together, though here in a muted form; dozens of brief scenes or shots lead to this climax.[6] In one of the first scenes, within the boat house, like an earthly, profane counterpart of his patron St Michael the Avenging Angel, Michael sits in an enormous chair, the symbol of authority, itself surrounded by empty sofas and easy chairs. He is alone, having annihilated all his enemies. The plush room is deeply shadowed in reds, leathery browns, and burnished golds, like the lair of a predatory animal.

In a contrast that could not be more vivid, the camera dissolves from Michael to a birthday party for his father in New York in 1941. Instead of being immersed in empty silence, the younger Michael sits among family members and friends at the dinner table awaiting Don Vito. This birthday is a ritual of fulfilment, a reminder of aging and of the pressing awareness of the need for a successor. The immediate object of attention is Don Vito's empty chair, again, the authority symbol; the camera is positioned so that the audience views events from the perspective of the all-seeing, absent godfather. The birthday falls on 7 December, which is the day of the attack on Pearl Harbor, an event of massive violence and (secret) surprise, two of the godfather's specialties. The connection between the don and the 'Day of Infamy' is further strengthened by the fact that he represents a quasi-feudal past and attacks the state; his loyalty is to his family, not his country. Sonny says jokingly, imagine the Japanese 'having the nerve to bomb Pearl Harbor on Pop's birthday,' as if their father stood on the level of world events. Michael destroys the cheerful mood by telling them he has just enlisted. Soon they leave to greet Don Vito, all but Michael, the future godfather, who remains quietly seated and alone, the sign of his election.

The second flashback is Michael's recollection of the family visit to Sicily in 1925. He is a little boy held up in his father's arms at a train window for all to see, a revelation of the successor. 'Wave goodbye, Michael,' says Don Vito in a soft, haunting voice, truly out of the depths of Michael's memory. The voice of the father, the ancient homeland, the gathered clan, all are at the furthest possible distance from his present state.[7] The train pulls away shrouded in steam, mist, mystery.

The camera cuts to Michael seated alone, now outside his house by the lake. Moments earlier we had seen the lake and mountains in eerie twilight; now the light is fading and suddenly the screen darkens quickly, as we move from realistic to symbolic time. The vastness and desolation of the landscape are the mocking symbols of his spiritual emptiness, as is the total silence. 'Because he wished to indicate that Michael was a lost soul,' Coppola decided against any non-diegetic sound.[8] Michael's 'hand covers his mouth and nose; only his right eye and the deep wrinkles around it are clearly visible,' writes John Hess; 'it's the two eyes which give us "perspective," and Michael never had any.'[9] Now that he is the godfather of godfathers, he knows the secret. He has become, in Coppola's words, 'a living corpse': this is why he referred to the film as 'The Death of Michael Corleone,' the ultimate absence: death-in-life.[10]

'The mythology of the classic gangster film, like that of the Western,' notes Thomas Schatz, 'concerns the transformation of nature into culture under auspices of modern civilization … Nature in the gangster film is conspicuous primarily in its absence.'[11] Coppola's godfather trilogy does not conform to this critique because the godfathers emerge from a rural southern Italian background as well as from America's Little Italy and retain a close relation to nature. *The Godfather: Part II* contains abundant imagery from pre-cultural 'nature'; the images are never touristic as in *The Godfather: Part III*, but serve to enhance the psychological action. In the opening scene, Vito's father's funeral in Corleone in 1901, the procession winds through a dry river bed on its way to a cemetery among the Sicilian mountains bathed in the intense sunshine. The body of Vito's elder brother, shot to death by Don Ciccio's men, is found among the rocks. The unforgiving landscape conveys the hardness of life and the toughness needed to survive. In the concluding shots at Lake Tahoe, the cold light, uncanny waters, and otherworldly mountains seem like the symbolic reflection of Michael's gaze turned inward, as outside becomes inside.

A signature metaphor of *The Godfather: Part II* is secrecy, one of the subthemes of the absence cluster. Elias Canetti writes that secrecy lies at the centre of power and is, therefore, necessarily full of duplicity. 'The act of lying in wait for prey is essentially secret'; 'the watcher must be capable of endless patience.'[12] Such watchers are Vito and Michael. They hide from the law, from other underworld families, from friends and brothers; they conceal their innermost selves from their wives. Concealment from social and moral scrutiny, a squad of lawyers, physical defence in fortress-like compounds, these are the order of the day. The godfather's very existence depends on secrecy. Tracking down and assassinating a godfather is the greatest triumph – or catastrophe – because he is the linchpin of the entire structure. Elaborate precautions are taken to protect him. No one knows more than what is absolute necessary, and women know least of all, but not even the 'boss of bosses' can know all the secrets and is vulnerable to that extent. The men are bound to the code of *omertà* ('solidarity,' 'complicity,' 'silence,' etymologically from 'manliness'),[13] violation of which means exile or death. The faces of the godfathers are impenetrable masks. Their secrets are buried within them, speech does not give them away, and questions are viewed with suspicion. The godfathers 'act' through four or five 'buffers' and 'button men.' Vito and Michael outwit their enemies by learning their secrets. Hyman Roth knows only what he needs to know – knowing more could be dangerous: 'I didn't ask who gave the order,' he says, 'because it had nothing to do with business.' Pentangeli must be convinced to commit suicide lest he give away his secret, which could convict Michael of perjury. Sonny's intemperate speech rules him out as a godfather and costs him his life. Everyone knows his secret.

Kay refuses to return with Michael to Nevada and wants to keep the children. In a bitter argument Michael says he will do everything in his power to prevent her from taking them away. With the children in mind she divulges her secret: her miscarriage was an abortion; the three-month-old fetus was male. 'Like our marriage,' she taunts him, the abortion was 'unholy, evil,' but it was the 'only way' she could do something that he 'could *not* forgive' – 'not with this Sicilian thing that's been going on for two thousand years' (the mafia traces in Sicily no further back than the mid-nineteenth century). In having an abortion, she has taken on a role usually reserved for a man and has murdered a (potential) godfather.

Nino Rota's soundtrack contains two major themes of extraordinary power that are expressive of absence and plenitude: the Waltz Theme and the Love Theme. The Waltz Theme opens *The Godfather: Part II* (and the two other films in the trilogy as well), where it resembles much less a waltz than a lament. It is the unforgettable trumpet solo in the dark key of C minor; it is a falling cadence, plaintive and haunting, that might suggest a lonely Sicilian shepherd blowing on a reed pipe (but scoring the music for an actual reed pipe instead of a trumpet would have been folkloristic). This theme also recalls the horn solos and brass band dirges at Sicilian funerals, underlying its links to absence. By contrast, the Love Theme is a lilting dance rhythm associated with continuity and, ultimately, plenitude. Even so, on occasion Rota delicately tinges his Love Theme with a shade of melancholy. The Love Theme was taken by Rota from another film for which he did the music, Eduardo De Filippo's *Fortunella* (1958).[14] As Italian composers know, sometimes a theme or an aria works better in a new setting, as Rota's does here.

NOTES

1 Coppola has persuaded some critics that 'the Mafia is not a substitution for American business, but the very thing itself.' Fran Mason, *American Gangster Cinema: From Little Caesar to Pulp Fiction* (New York: Palgrave Macmillan, 2002), 130.

2 Ferdinand Tönnies (1855–1936) was a German sociologist.

3 In *The Godfather*, Vito's date of birth on his tombstone is 1887; in *The Godfather: Part II*, he is nine years old in 1901.

4 In *The Godfather: Part III* this becomes a virtual self-parody; in his late fifties he is still trying: 'Just when I thought I was out, they pull me back in.'

5 Other examples of mise en scène are Michael's conversation with his sibylline mother by the household fire, with its flames flickering as she speaks; his return to Lake Tahoe in winter, when he sees Kay at a distance quietly sewing on a machine, the traditional distaff image technologized; and the film's final shots of Michael at Lake Tahoe, discussed below.

6 Jeffrey Chown, *Hollywood Auteur: Francis Coppola* (New York: Praeger, 1988), 73–4.

7 *The Godfather: Part II* is imbued with an epic dimension: transoceanic migration, the rise and fall of a family, betrayal, revenge, generational change. It is not only about the great migration; it is much more about the great assimilation.

8 Peter Biskind, *The Godfather Companion* (New York: Harper Perennial, 1990), 117.

9 John Hess, "*Godfather II*: A Deal Coppola Couldn't Refuse," in *Movies and Methods: An Anthology*, vol. 1, ed. Bill Nichols (Berkeley, CA: University of California Press, 1976), 85.

10 Quoted in Robert K. Johnson, *Francis Ford Coppola* (Boston, MA: Twayne, 1977), 148. Studio executives thought the ending too bleak; Coppola stood his ground. He had finished with Michael, and hence his reluctance to add a sequel.

11 Thomas Schatz, *Hollywood Genres: Formulas, Filmmaking, and the Studio System* (Philadelphia, PA: Temple University Press, 1981), 82–3.

12 Elias Canetti, *Crowds and Power*, trans. Carol Stewart (New York: Continuum, 1978), 290.

13 Wayland Young, "The Montesi Affair," *Encounter*, September 1957: 30.

14 With a script by De Filippo and Federico Fellini. See Franco Sciannameo, *Nino Rota, Federico Fellini, and the Making of an Italian Cinematic Folk Opera: Amarcord* (Lewiston: Mellen, 2005), 12.

11   The Sexual Politics of Loyalty in John Huston's *Prizzi's Honor*

REBECCA BAUMAN

When John Huston's *Prizzi's Honor* was released in 1985, it was the first major mafia-themed comedy in American cinema since Billy Wilder's *Some Like It Hot* (1959). Just as Wilder's film had satirized well-known conventions of 1930s gangster films, *Prizzi's Honor* demonstrated its humorous engagement with the mafia film canon in its references to the *Godfather* films and would anticipate a new subgenre: the mafia comedy. These comedies flourished in the following decade, ranging from Marlon Brando's self-parody in *The Freshman* (Andrew Bergman, 1990) to the absurd antics of *Jane Austen's Mafia!* (Jim Abrahams, 1998), to the comic predicament of a mobster undergoing psychoanalysis in the box office hit *Analyze This* (Harold Ramis, 1999). Huston's film foreshadows these comedies with its odd characters, snappy dialogue, and parodic references; but the film's amalgamation of generic conventions also include melodrama and film noir.[1] *Prizzi's Honor* thus commingles comedic and dramatic elements, marking it as a point of transition between the mythologizing seriousness of the *Godfather* films and the broad satire of the mafia comedy of later years. The result of this pastiche of cinematic inheritances is a uniquely postmodern take on mob movies in which the film's generic status is always in flux.

In fact, *Prizzi's Honor* is less recognizable as a mafia comedy than as a serio-comic vision of gender as locus of the battle between traditional and modern values in 1980s America. Billed as a black comedy, the plot of *Prizzi's Honor* centres on the situational absurdity of husband-and-wife contract killers assigned to assassinate each other.[2] This introduction of the female mobster opens the way for a variety of comic predicaments, and the film seemingly celebrates the new breed of liberated female who challenges the male domain of the mafia world. However, when the tale of star-crossed mobsters ends with the triumph of family loyalty over the relationship between male and female equals, the film suggests a preservation of patriarchal values that challenges the shifting social landscape of the era.

Like Mario Puzo's *The Godfather*, *Prizzi's Honor* is a literary adaptation, taken from Richard Condon's eponymous novel from 1982. Like Puzo's novel, Condon's story is concerned with the clash between Old World traditional values and the capitalist New World, with the mafia family struggling to bridge both realms. Thomas Ferraro, comparing these novels in his essay 'Blood in the Marketplace,' observes that in both cases capitalist enterprise is inextricable from familial bonds; the family *is* Family.[3] In the film versions this dialectic is further explored, particularly with Francis Ford Coppola's extended meditation on the Corleone family drama in *The Godfather: Part II*. In Coppola's film, the threat to the family unit arises when the balance between

Family and family is thrown off-kilter, and the modernization of American business practices perverts the ethnic loyalty of the mafia family structured around the patriarchal figure of the don. *Prizzi's Honor* also establishes the mafia underworld as a microcosm of the American business world, only here the threat to family loyalty comes in the form of the female hit woman: an ethnic outsider who operates under an alternative set of business practices. The concept of the female interloper has a precedent in *The Godfather* in the figure of Kay Corleone; as Robert Casillo suggests, 'Michael's mistake was to have married an Anglo-American woman.'[4] The contamination of the traditional family is doubly reinforced in *Prizzi's Honor* by having the wife constitute a threat to the domestic *and* business spheres of the mafia family. Accordingly, Huston uses ironic references to the *Godfather* films to update this dialectic of competing business practices and to more explicitly bring gender conflicts to the fore.

By definition the mafia excludes women, with fidelity to the male-centred society taking precedence over private, male–female relationships.[5] *Prizzi's Honor* affirms this in the opening credits, which set the stage for the protagonist Charley Partanna's eventual choice between his loyalty to the mafia and his romantic allegiance to his wife. The sequence begins with Don Corrado Prizzi observing the infant Charley in the hospital nursery and declaring himself the surrogate father of the child, confirming his patriarchal position as godfather. The next scene shows an eager boy Charley unwrapping a Christmas present of brass knuckles, and then moves on to Charley as a young man undergoing the mafia initiation ceremony. This brief sequence serves the purpose of exposition and also establishes Charley's fixed identity within the organized crime family as something preordained, immutable, and bound to an ancient masculine code of honour. The blood he exchanges with the don in his initiation marks an oath that will ultimately be the 'other woman' in his future love triangle with Irene.

The opening credits are followed by the marriage of Don Corrado's granddaughter – a wedding whose placement in the film is reminiscent of Connie Corleone's nuptial celebration that opens *The Godfather* but with only a trace of its predecessor's ethnic flavour. This scene serves a similar function in establishing a host of characters and emphasizing the prominence of familial bonds. As the camera pans over a range of guests seated in a church during a solemn Catholic marriage mass, we are confronted with the sight of Don Corrado sleeping during the proceedings. Here Huston dispels the mystique enshrined in the reverential depiction of Don Corleone in the opening moments of *The Godfather*, attesting to a newer breed of mafia family. The camera then falls upon Charley Partanna and his father, the don's *consigliere*, and the don's sons Dominic and Eduardo. As in *The Godfather*, the private world embodied in the religious and romantic marriage ceremony demonstrates an inextricable fusion of the 'family' of blood relations and ethnic bonds and the 'Family' of the mafia crime world.

In this wedding sequence we are also introduced to Irene Walker, the beautiful blond 'outside man' hired to perform a hit while the Prizzis are gathered at the reception. Charley espies her seated above him in the church balcony, and her physical distance implies both an angelic presence and an estrangement from the proceedings: she is a heavenly apparition who instantly bewitches the hapless hero as well as a foreign presence once removed from the inner world of the Prizzi family. Irene's difference will continue to be emphasized over the course of the film; her outsider status is associated with both her gender and her ethnicity. Irene is not simply a woman operating in a strictly masculine world of power and domination; she is also a non-Italian, a 'Polack' who had married a Jew and who thus can never be absorbed into the family fold.

Irene's difference has its Sicilian counterpart in the character of Maerose Prizzi, who also occupies a liminal position within the Prizzi family structure but whose ethnic identity aligns her more closely to Charley, her childhood companion, to whom she remarks, 'We grew up together, Charley. We're the same people.' Maerose's appearance at the wedding is only a momentary reprieve from her banishment by her father Dominic, who is punishing Maerose for having 'dishonoured' the family with her sexual transgressions. Both women are outsiders: Irene operates her business in tandem with but never inside the Prizzi power structure, and Maerose dwells in the shadows of the family that has shunned her. They are also successful careerists: Irene is an accomplished assassin and swindler who began her career 'on her back' but has transformed herself into a sophisticated femme fatale. Maerose is a Manhattan-based interior designer who lives independently in her own well-appointed apartment. She, too, has graduated beyond the more traditional realm of the Brooklyn-based family, whose values are embodied in the ornate Gothic mansion inhabited by Don Corrado.

Through these independent women, *Prizzi's Honor* offers new female representations in the life of the mafia film. The classic gangster films of the 1930s often depicted feisty women, but their position was always ancillary to the male mobster's drama. In contrast, the women of *Prizzi's Honor* extend beyond the typical categories of moll or long-suffering mafia wife and anticipate such formidable female characters as Karen Hill of *Goodfellas* (Martin Scorsese, 1990) and Carmela Soprano of *The Sopranos* (David Chase, 1999–2007). In so doing, *Prizzi's Honor* demonstrates that it is synchronous with a tendency in American cinema to depict 'strong women' in roles during an era in which women were advancing in the business world like never before. The New Woman in Hollywood in contemporary films privileged career advancement over romantic fulfilment, as evidenced in stories that focused on women's self-empowerment such as *Places in the Heart* (Robert Benton, 1984), or on women who navigate myriad obstacles to achieve success in male-dominated corporate America, as in the comedies *Nine to Five* (Colin Higgins, 1980) and *Working Girl* (Mike Nichols, 1988). But while Hollywood appeared to extol these new role models, it also produced a backlash of films that revealed a profound male anxiety over female empowerment. In these films, the successful businesswoman is a castrating threat who must be vanquished by the male protagonist and supplanted by a less threatening female love interest who fulfils the traditional roles of mother and wife. This would reach its apotheosis in *Fatal Attraction* (Adrian Lyne, 1987), in which the seductive femme fatale is a savvy careerist whose desire makes her psychotic and who must be killed in order to preserve the traditional family unit.

In the case of *Prizzi's Honor*, the nuclear family sacred to the American Dream is ironically represented in the mafia family with its accompanying arcane rituals, rigid hierarchy, and ethos of ethnic preservation, all of which are upheld by a code of honour that is invoked to justify immoral criminal activity. The loyalty of the Prizzis is not just an imported version of Sicilian 'rustic chivalry' but is part and parcel of their successful business operations; this is what makes them an American family. Thus, the New Woman who operates outside the family business in the interests of self-preservation is symbolic of a dangerous modernity. Irene, an independent contractor, goes against corporate loyalty and represents a new breed of American business operations: the rise of the 'Me'-generation economics. Even Maerose, another self-made woman, defends Irene's entrepreneurial spirit as almost patriotic: 'She's an American! She had a chance to make a buck so she grabbed it.' This professional independence, as much as her sexual and ethnic difference, will configure Irene as subject to punishment.

Caught in between is Charley, who is smitten with the New Woman yet challenged by her confidence and independence. *Prizzi's Honor* also suggests that strong female characters endanger the icon of American hypermasculinity that is the Italian American gangster. Jack Nicholson deftly portrays Charley as a new breed of mobster, one who blends the traditional attributes of the mafioso with a New Age sensibility. He is at ease with violence and holds no scruples about the Prizzi's various illegal practices; he never questions the family's interests until they directly conflict with his own. Yet he is also a hopeless romantic who believes in love at first sight and even reads self-help magazines that encourage him to ponder his own emotional needs (prefiguring the introspection and dependency of Tony Soprano).

In fact, throughout the film, Charley is continually seen in moments of submission to female authority, and although he is a rising force in the Prizzi hierarchy, both Irene and Maerose wield the upper hand intellectually and sexually. Irene demonstrates that she is significantly more adept at her profession than Charley when she offers a superior plan for the kidnapping of the bank president. It is she who ruthlessly murders an innocent bystander, a woman no less, while Charley looks on. She also adopts the masculine position in their courtship: she telephones Charley after their first meeting, plans their subsequent dates, and even orders for them at lunch. Maerose, too, outwits and seduces the men who surround her. Bent on revenge, she enrols Don Prizzi in her bid to return to her father Dominic's good graces and then stages an elaborate charade of having been raped by Charley in the hope of provoking her father's heart attack. When Dominic is finally killed in a gangland assassination, it is suggested that Maerose is behind the hit, adding patricide to her list of tactics. In the meantime, she has two-facedly encouraged Charley to marry Irene, but only after successfully luring him to make love: 'C'mon Charley, let's do it. Right here on the Oriental, with all the lights on.' Charley succumbs as easily to her as he does to Irene's more honeyed manner of seduction.

Yet this more vulnerable aspect of Charley is precisely that which must be exorcised if he is to retain his role within the Prizzi family. As Renate Siebert notes, in the mafia, 'the man is compelled to show proof of his masculinity over and over again; it can never be regarded as secure.'[6] By reinstating himself within the good graces of the Prizzis, Charley is reasserting his stature in the standard sexual hierarchy. The final test of his masculinity comes in a confrontation with the don and his own father in the don's private office. As in *The Godfather*, the sanctuary of the don's study is an exclusive realm barred to women, yet it is one in which the decisions that shape the fate of women are handed down. Here Don Corrado demands the sacrifice of Irene, and Charley pleads for her life by attacking the male-structured world of the mafia itself with a critique that could be intended for the solitary figure of Michael Corleone of *The Godfather* trilogy: 'Is that what you want for me, to grow old like you with nothing but bodyguards and money to keep me company?' It is Charley's most articulate moment, but one that cannot stand against the more persuasive rhetoric of the don, who invokes the promise of the initiation sequence from the opening credits: 'You swore an oath of blood … that you would always put the Family before anything else in your life.'

Charley and Irene's marriage is dissolved by a violent end to the femme fatale in a tongue-in-cheek scene that restores Charley to a position of dominance. Irene suspects that Charley is determined to kill her, and she decides to 'ice' him first. As the couple appears to prepare for lovemaking, they are both actually preparing for murder. The next few shots appear in slow motion: Irene, dressed in creamy satin lingerie, bursts out of the bathroom wielding a pistol, while Charley leaps from his reclined position in the marital bed and flings a stiletto into Irene's neck, pinning her to the wall. With this one move Charlie has switched from a passive position to one of power and, not incidentally, has bested Irene using a 'traditional' weapon versus her 'modern' handgun. Huston holds the macabre vision of the impaled Irene for an extended period as a dramatic crescendo of music swells, resulting in an emphatic blend of shock and irony – the love scene cum splatter film. The perversity of this murder participates in a tradition of memorable violence in mafia cinema, while the brutal disposal of the female protagonist within the domestic intimacy of the bedroom is depicted in a manner both comically absurd and profoundly disquieting.

The final moments of the film intend to justify this gruesome image. Having sacrificed love to honour, in the last scene Charley dutifully telephones Maerose to rekindle their romance. Maerose's response, a disingenuous oh-golly enthusiasm, constitutes a double return of two prodigal offspring. Maerose submits to the original love object condoned by her father and solidifies her reassumption into the family fold, and Charley returns to a romance within the ethnic boundaries he had earlier traversed. Moreover, he has secured his position in the Prizzi kingdom by uniting himself with the Prizzi princess. Tricia Welsch contends that this development relegates Maerose to a subordinate role as mafia wife: '*Prizzi's Honor* reflects [a] 1980s audience's anxiety about either accepting or killing off its visibly powerful female figure (Irene) by reassigning her power to a more traditional female character.'[7] This would suggest that despite her fiercely independent personality, Maerose is destined to be a Mamma Corleone living in resigned fidelity to the authority of the mafia husband. Consequently, this ending would constitute a solution to the threat symbolized by Irene and a preservation of the ideals of family business and masculine privilege – a reactionary and deeply misogynist dénouement, as many critics have observed.[8]

Yet it is not insignificant that the New Woman is replaced by an equally commanding female, one who straddles the modern world of freedom and self-interest along with the traditional world of the patriarchal family. The ending is in many respects Maerose's personal triumph: she has captured her man, disposed of her hated father, and come out smelling like a rose in the process. Rather than challenging the dominant authority from the outside, Maerose adopts mafia tactics to achieve her goals from within, suggesting that even *she* might be the inevitable heir to the Prizzi throne. While the prodigal son has been reincorporated into the family, we are left to wonder what role will befall the most powerful Prizzi of all, the prodigal daughter. Maerose's pre-eminence thus can be read as an intermediary measure that anticipates the inevitable rise of an alternative female authority (and, by association, of late capitalism) precisely because Maerose herself incorporates elements of both the traditional paradigm and the modern one. This attempt to balance the dialectic between the two helps explicate the strange juxtaposition between Irene's brutal murder and the happy ending of Charley's reunion with Maerose. The film's oscillations between dramatic and comedic moments thus serve the purpose of helping prepare the audience for an ambiguous and challenging conclusion.

NOTES

1 For more on the hybrid nature of the film's generic references, see Tricia Welsch, 'Yoked Together by Violence: *Prizzi's Honor* as a Generic Hybrid,' *Film Criticism* 22, no. 1 (1997): 62–73.
2 This plot device is recycled in the Brad Pitt and Angelina Jolie vehicle *Mr. and Mrs. Smith* (Doug Liman, 2005).

3 Thomas J. Ferraro, 'Blood in the Marketplace: The Business of Family in the *Godfather* Narratives,' in *The Invention of Ethnicity*, ed. Werner Sollors (New York: Oxford University Press, 1989), 176–208.

4 Robert Casillo, 'Moments in Italian-American Cinema: From *Little Caesar* to Coppola and Scorsese,' in *From the Margin: Writings in Italian Americana*, ed. Anthony Julian Tamburri, Paolo A. Giordino, and Fred L. Gardaphé (West Lafayette, IN: Purdue University Press, 1991), 387.

5 See Renate Siebert, *Secrets of Life and Death: Women and The Mafia*, trans. Liz Heron (London: Verso, 1996).

6 Ibid., 23.

7 Welsch, 'Yoked Together by Violence,' 67.

8 A number of academic interventions have focused specifically on the theme of misogyny and the representation of women in this film, notably Mas'ud Zavarzadeh, 'The New Woman as Mafia Hit Man: John Huston's *Prizzi's Honor,' North Dakota Quarterly* 56, no. 1 (1988): 154–64; Welsch, 'Yoked Together by Violence'; Dawn Esposito, 'Gloria, Maerose, Irene, and Me: Mafia Women and Abject Spectatorship,' *MELUS* 28, no. 3 (2003): 91–109. Surprisingly few contemporary reviewers of the film made note of this issue.

12 Between Postmodern Parody and Generic Hybridization: The Gangsters of Brian De Palma's *The Untouchables*

NORMA BOUCHARD

Given the rage for all things gangster after the phenomenal success of Francis Ford Coppola's *The Godfather* in 1972, followed by the equally acclaimed *The Godfather: Part II* in 1974, it comes as no surprise that Brian De Palma was to find in the gangster of the post–Hays Code era a genre of many expressive possibilities. A director with a well-known penchant for the cinematic representation of violence afforded by the crime film, as documented by *The Fury* (1978) and *Dressed to Kill* (1980), among others,[1] De Palma fully embraced the genre and within a short period of time released *Scarface* (1983), *Wise Guys* (1986), and finally *The Untouchables* in 1987. The film, which premiered on 3 June 1987, narrates a well-known episode in the history of Chicago criminal activity: the struggle of Eliot Ness against the famed Prohibition gangster Al Capone during the late 1920s and early 1930s. In 1928, Ness, then a young agent working with the US Department of Justice, was charged with putting an end to Capone's many breweries and supply routes. Ness assembled a small squad of law-abiding men to investigate Al Capone and disrupt his criminal activities by employing tactics ranging from phone tapping and confiscation of delivery vehicles to literally destroying the mobster's breweries. Capone, who was quite adept at corrupting law enforcement officials, tried in vain to bribe Ness's agents. Ness, who cultivated his connections with the media, turned Capone's failure into an occasion to publicize his work and make a name for himself. The press soon nicknamed his group 'The Untouchables,' but ironically, Ness himself was never able to put an end to the gangster's operations. The demise of Capone's criminal empire would be the result of an investigation by agents of the Treasury Department, who were able to assemble the evidence necessary to convict the mobster of tax evasion on 17 October 1931. For the following twenty years Ness lived in relative obscurity, but in 1956 Oscar Fraley persuaded him to co-author a book about his fight against Al Capone. The book was published as *The Untouchables* in 1957 and was extremely well received, eventually earning a spot on *The New Yorker* bestseller list.[2]

In *The Untouchables*, De Palma re-creates with much accuracy the period of the 1930s when Eliot Ness, determined to see the end of Al Capone, assembles a group of like-minded law enforcers: Jimmy Malone, George Stone, and Oscar Wallace. In a film that would become a model for many retro, nostalgic gangster films to follow, De Palma's set designs, costumes, and character roles reproduce a bygone era with an accuracy that even encompasses broader ideological forces such as gendered models of masculinity and femininity. Indeed, as Esther Sonnet and Peter Stanfield note, the men's suits and hats designed by Giorgio Armani become powerful markers to illustrate a world of 'prefeminist civic authority and male power.'[3] Women are exemplified only partly, and then only in the sphere of domesticity inhabited by Ness's wife and their young children. However, De Palma's fidelity to the historical record of Ness's struggle against Capone in Prohibition-era Chicago and against broader sociocultural forces ends here.

De Palma's films have been profoundly shaped by avant-garde cinema and independent film-making; he has long been fascinated with the likes of Jean Luc Godard and Alfred Hitchcock.[4] His work has always been characterized by self-conscious and self-reflexive aesthetic concerns. Such concerns were arguably even stronger in the case of a film about Al Capone and Eliot Ness, whose struggle was recorded in the history of Chicago and in Ness's and Fraley's co-authored book and has given rise to endless visual representations. After Ness and Fraley's book was published in 1957, the rights to it were purchased by Desi Arnaz and Lucille Ball, who turned the story into a two-part television series, *The Scarface Mob*.[5] That two-parter was so successful that ABC extended a contract to Arnaz to expand it into a mini-series titled *The Untouchables*. The series, which featured some 118 episodes, ran for four years, from 1959 to 1963. It fuelled the imagination of millions of Americans, who from the comfort of their homes could now experience the world of the Chicago mob on television. To be sure, the series did generate controversy, not only for its graphic depictions of violence but also because it associated gangsters with Italian ethnic heritage (see chapter 6 of this volume).[6] Yet the longevity and appeal of the series also demonstrated that the American public's appetite for gangster stories had not been satiated. This fact was not lost on Hollywood, whose never-ending quest for commercial opportunities was reinforced by a major development in the industry, namely, the replacement of the Hays Code by the letter-rating system in 1968, which made it possible to present violence and explicit sexuality to degrees that were previously unthinkable. Thus it comes as no surprise that from the 1970s well into the 1990s the American film industry would open the floodgates for gangster movies, beginning with Francis Ford Coppola's *The Godfather*, a film that, as Dal Cerro reports, was responsible for generating a strong wave of gangster movies.[7]

Faced with this tradition of on-screen forms of urban criminality, De Palma, in making a period film like *The Untouchables,* confronted the challenge of postmodern belatedness as well as a long history of déjà vu spanning from *The Scarface Mob* and *The Untouchables* to *The Godfather* and beyond. De Palma's solution, as he himself admits, was a heightened degree of awareness regarding the expressive possibilities of the period gangster for 1980s postmodern culture. In his words: 'It is an American myth [Al Capone]. People have made this picture before. Our way of doing it has to explore the mythic possibilities.'[8]

Indeed, behind the facade of historically accurate sets and well-designed period costumes, *The Untouchables* is a film that consistently unfolds upon its own generic conventions to reflect on its narrative and iconographic codes. This approach ultimately undermines the possibility of the gangster film to represent a world of reference and reality existing outside the confines of the celluloid spectacle. To begin with, De Palma's representation of Al Capone and his public downfall at the hands of Ness follows the conventions of the classical Hollywood gangster films of the 1930s, such as *Little Caesar* (1931), *The Public Enemy* (1931), and *Scarface* (1932). As mandated, if not always enforced by the Hays Office, De Palma characterizes Al Capone in a manner that does not invite the spectator's identification or sympathy. He is arrogant, vulgar in his consumption, and brutally violent in his illegitimate quest for the American Dream. The indiscriminate slaughter of a little girl at the beginning of the film immediately casts Al Capone as a monster, and this trait is reinforced in the scene where he takes revenge on one of his men by killing him with a baseball bat. As the camera tracks upwards, a pool of blood widens next to the man's smashed head, further distancing the viewer from any possible romantic association with the all-powerful mobster. But it is perhaps in the ending chosen by De Palma that the allusion to the Hays Code–era gangster is at its clearest. In violation of the historical record, De Palma presents the end of Al Capone's criminal career as occurring at the hands of Ness, thus paying homage to classical gangster film endings such as those found in *Little Caesar*, *The Public Enemy*, and *Scarface*.

But De Palma weaves the gangster movie of classical Hollywood with another genre – films that star the G-Man character, a sort of 'gangster-as-cop.'[9] These latter films originated in the early post–Hays Code era when studios created the character of a policeman who uses mob tactics to enforce the law of the land against gangsters. In *The Untouchables*, as in 1930s G-Man films that preceded it – films like *G-Men* (1935) and *Bullets or Ballots* (1936) – the law enforcers engage in legally sanctioned acts of violence that are comparable to those of the gangsters and indeed are often undistinguishable from them.[10] The cop Malone, a character to whom De Palma gives much prominence, sets the tone for these acts when he unabashedly declares, 'He pulls a knife, you pull a gun. He sends one of yours to the hospital; you send one of his to the morgue. That is the Chicago way; and that is how you get Capone.' Thus it comes as no surprise to see the 'forces of good' dropping mobsters from buildings, smashing breweries, and conducting forceful inter-rogations, along with carrying out kidnappings, applying psychological torture, and taking part in violent shootouts. De Palma's recoding of the characters of Ness, Malone, Stone, and Wallace within the iconography of the G-Man cycle of the 1930s is such that all distinctions between gangsters and law enforcers are blurred and even the morality preserved in the domestic, feminine space of Ness's home has to momentarily disappear from screen as the confrontations within this hypermasculine world head towards a climax. Yet De Palma does not limit himself to bartering and trafficking with the codes of the gangster film in its Code, post-Code, and G-Man variations. In *The Untouchables* he creates a visual pastiche to further interrupt the audience's suspension of disbelief. In a play of postmodern self-reflexivity, he evokes the well-known cinematic codes of the western as well as montage techniques from Soviet cinema of the 1920s. Through a visual sequence that is bound to shatter the illusions of even the most naive of viewers, Ness and his group travel to the Canadian border to stop a shipment of whiskey. Casting the narrative in the form of the western, De Palma initially presents the viewer with a spectacle of horsemen against the rugged landscape of the Canadian Rockies. When the trucks carrying the whiskey arrive on the bridge, Ness and his group join the Canadian mounted police in a scene whose sound and images are highly evocative of a 'cowboys and Indians' movie. An even more powerful example of the iconographic tradition of cinema is provided towards the ending of the film, when De Palma stages a gun battle between Ness's men and Capone's henchmen. Shot at Union Station in Chicago, the scene is a hybrid of the spaghetti western duel – shot in slow motion – and one of the most memorable and discussed scenes in Sergei Eisenstein's *Battleship Potemkin*: the famous episode on the Odessa Steps. As in Eisenstein's classic story of a mutiny of sailors oppressed by a brutal tsarist regime, De Palma makes no attempt at creating the illusion of a smooth transition between scenes that is typical of a continuity editing style. Like Eisenstein did, he creates a montage of accelerated shots of various lengths, shapes, and volumes whose splicing confuses spatial relationships in a way that jolts the spectator, ultimately simulating a visual experience of critical distance. But De Palma does more than just evoke Eisenstein's formal practice of montage. In *The Untouchables*, he directly quotes several units of content from the episode on the Odessa stairway, including the baby, the mother, the guns, the passer-by, and the stairway itself. However, in yet another parody and replay, De Palma also reverses his legendary source. Rather than representing the shooting of the Cossacks' guns, as Eisenstein had famously done, De Palma cites from the code of the western. He allows the 'forces of good,' that is, the 'Untouchable' cowboys, to rescue the baby as George Stone throws a gun to Ness and proceeds to stop the carriage with his foot before firing the film's most precise shot. Finally, the men kidnap Capone's bookkeeper Payne (Jack Kehoe); following Payne's testimony, a judge sentences Capone to eleven years in jail.

This conclusion, which, as I mentioned before, provides yet another citation of the medium – the prescribed downfall of the criminal that occurs in the classical gangster films of the 1930s – leaves no question as to De Palma's success in making a film that transforms the sense of belatedness and déjà vu of Ness's and Capone's stories into a creative, original endeavour. That said, there is also no doubt that the final extirpation of the gangster in *The Untouchables* could potentially strike a wrong chord with audiences, who, just a few years before the release of De Palma's film, were presented with a powerful revision of the genre's narrative and iconographic codes: Francis Ford Coppola's *The Godfather* and *The Godfather: Part II*. As scores of critics have noted, the *Godfather* films empowered Italian American subjects by visualizing ethnic criminals as honourable, wise, and respectable men whose trajectory from rags to riches was predicated on their ability to retain Old World values while showing the business of Italian American crime as an economy not simply parallel to that of legitimate capitalism but equal to American business itself. Since these traits rendered *The Godfather* a powerful platform from which to wage an identity politics battle for Italian American audiences, one wonders about the reception of a film such as *The Untouchables*, in which Al Capone has none of the positive traits of Don Vito Corleone or his son Michael. De Palma's Al Capone remains a vulgar, despicable character fated to meet his disgraceful public downfall instead of passing away peacefully in his old age while playing in a tomato garden with his grandson, as is the case of Vito Corleone, or becoming the head of the most powerful crime family in America, as occurs with the Dartmouth graduate and war hero Michael Corleone. *The Untouchables* also does not refrain from drawing upon a vast repertoire of stereotypical representations of Italian American ethnicity and equally applies epithets of 'wop' and 'dago' to all Italians, regardless of their affiliation with the world of crime or law enforcement.[11]

Nevertheless, *The Untouchables* was received with much critical acclaim and remains De Palma's second-highest-grossing film to date. What is the reason for this success? What led 1980s audiences to praise a film that provided yet another negative image of Italian Americans while glorifying and legitimizing the excessive gangster-like tactics of American law enforcement officials? I would venture that De Palma's self-reflexive practice is the key to explaining the success of his film, inasmuch as such a practice provides visual pleasures to Italian American and other ethnic audiences. In other words, by foregrounding the fictionalized nature of the medium in citations and replays of Code-era gangsters, G-men, and westerns, as well as Soviet cinema of the 1920s, *The Untouchables* makes it more difficult for the medium to claim to be representing a world of reference and reality, a world independent of the celluloid spectacle. As such, it is a film that offers a means to enjoy gangster films for what they are – images and commodities produced and distributed by Hollywood popular culture. In this sense, then, De Palma's postmodern rendition of the gangster not only allows broad visual pleasure – the pleasure of recognition – but also facilitates a cultural critique of historically situated and embodied ethnic subjects. Thus,

Italian American audiences might find, in the pastiche of the retro gangster film of the 1980s, the opportunity for a political reading that is often unavailable in the classical gangster film.

NOTES

1 De Palma makes clear his position towards graphic violence in Paul Mandell, 'Brian De Palma Discusses *the Fury*,' in *Brian De Palma Interviews*, ed. Lawrence F. Knapp (Jackson, MI: University of Mississippi Press, 2003), 46–53; Lynn Hirschberg, 'Brian De Palma's Death Wish,' in *Brian De Palma Interviews*, ed. Knapp, 82–91.

2 The release of the book was most timely because it coincided with a series of investigations of crime syndicates carried out by the Senate Crime Investigation Committee and the FBI, which had been going on since the early 1950s. The committee's findings seemed to confirm the existence of large criminal organizations headed by Italians.

3 Esther Sonnet and Peter Stanfield, 'Good Evening Gentlemen, Can I Check Your Hats Please? Masculinity, Dress, and the Retro Gangster Cycles of the 1990s,' in *Mob Culture: Hidden Histories of the American Gangster Film*, ed. Lee Grievson, Esther Sonnet, and Peter Stanfield (New Brunswick, NJ: Rutgers University Press, 2005), 166.

4 See Laurence F. Knapp, *Brian De Palma Interviews* (Jackson, MI: University of Mississippi Press, 2003), vii–xvi.

5 For additional discussion of *The Scarface Mob*, compare John McCarty, *Bullets over Hollywood: The American Gangster Picture from the Silents to 'The Sopranos'* (Cambridge: Da Capo Press, 2004).

6 At a time of ethnic revival and pride in one's heritage, the chairman of the Senate Communication Subcommittee, John Pastore, and even the singer Frank Sinatra took issue with what they perceived to be ethnic slander against Italians. The controversy was such that villains of other ethnic backgrounds were eventually incorporated into the original script, including a group of Russian mobsters.

7 See William Dal Cerro, 'Hollywood Versus Italians: Them – 400: Us – 50,' *The Italic Way* 27 (1997): 10–32. The titles of these films are too many to recall here, but it will suffice to list a few representative releases from the mid-1970s to the 1980s: *Mean Streets* (Martin Scorsese, 1973), *Crazy Joe* (Carlo Lizzani, 1974), *Capone* (Steve Carver, 1975), *Silver Bears* (Ivan Passer, 1978), *Gloria* (John Cassavetes, 1980), *Once Upon a Time in America* (Sergio Leone, 1984), *Prizzi's Honor* (John Huston, 1985), *The Big Easy* (Jim McBride, 1987), and *Sweet Revenge* (Mark Sobel, 1987).

8 This statement is reported by Vincent LoBrutto in his book *By Design: Interviews with Film Production Designers* (Westport, CT: Greenwood, 1992), 188.

9 Thomas Schatz, *Hollywood Genres: Formulas, Filmmaking, and the Studio System* (New York: McGraw-Hill, 1981), 99.

10 For additional discussion on the G-Man cycle, see Fran Mason, *American Gangster Cinema: From Little Caesar to Pulp Fiction* (New York: Palgrave Macmillan, 2002), 31–50.

11 Malone uses derogatory terms while addressing his friend George Stone, whose real name is Giuseppe Petri. Malone also calls one of the killers sent by Al Capone a 'dago,' a 'wop,' and a 'bastard' who brings a knife to a gunfight.

13 The Bandit, the Gangster, and the American Army Shorts: Michael Cimino's *The Sicilian*

CHIARA MAZZUCCHELLI

After the spectacular debacle of *Heaven's Gate* in 1980 and the lukewarm reception received by *Year of the Dragon* five years later, Italian American director Michael Cimino tried to regain the trust of Hollywood studios by adapting Mario Puzo's 1984 novel *The Sicilian* for the big screen in 1987. This successful biographical novel recounts the life and deeds of Sicilian bandit Salvatore 'Turi' Giuliano, who became an outlaw in 1943 and hid in the mountains around Palermo for seven years until he was killed in 1950 at the age of twenty-seven. With a story that follows the career of a bandit acclaimed by many as the Sicilian Robin Hood who dared to challenge the established authority of both the government and the mafia, Puzo had once again, after *The Godfather*, won the public's acclaim.

Interestingly, more so than Puzo's novel, Cimino's cinematographic adaptation is as much about 'the Sicilian' as it is about 'the American.'[1] In fact, in the film, the Sicilian bandit is portrayed as a promoter of progressive American values over conservative Old World mores. The director himself confirmed this suggestion in an interview: 'My point of view on [Giuliano] is that, even though he was a Sicilian, in many ways he was not. Somewhere in his heart he never came to terms with his being Sicilian, he was full of longing and desire for America.'[2] The film's thesis is very clearly defined: the bandit is a visionary with the ambition to introduce American ideologies to the Old World. However, in Sicily he cannot thrive because on the island – and, by extension, in the Old Country – it is impossible for him to challenge the status quo, let alone subvert existing power relations. It follows that only in a modern country like the United States can an idealist like Giuliano express himself freely and eventually thrive as an individual. This chapter posits that, although on the surface it might appear that *The Sicilian* concerns itself with a specific moment in Sicilian history, the movie reinforces hegemonic notions of Americanness by solidifying the common myth that positions America as the land of freedom and opportunities, with Sicily as its most perfect antithesis.

The representation of the conflict between Sicilian and Anglo-American world views is not new in American culture. It cannot be disputed that Sicily exerted a powerful hold on the American imagination, especially after the appearance of Mario Puzo's *The Godfather* (1969). With its publication, Puzo established himself as an active participant in the creation of a hegemonic discourse that constructed Sicily as America's other. In that novel – and in its film adaptations by Francis Ford Coppola – Sicily's primitive economy and feudal social arrangements conflict with the American industrial and democratic scene of Puzo's time. By the 1980s such representations had become so common that, regarding Americans' perceptions of Sicily, Chris Messenger pointed out:

> The island is symbolically akin to the American Deep South, a region traditionally scapegoated but also rendered earthier, more dramatic, and alive in its melodramatic representation. In the [American] popular fantasy, lives there are more grotesque, poverty and illiteracy endemic, and fierce prejudices give rise to clan warfare. In literary terms, the Sicilians are positively Faulknerian in their mythic intransigence, patriarchal domination, and tragic, unyielding sense of honor.[3]

With its palatable exotic setting and its winning storytelling formula, Puzo's historical novel was sure to appeal to American readers.

By the time Puzo's *The Sicilian* was published, Giuliano's life had already stimulated the interest of many, and Cimino was not the first director to be inspired by the bandit.[4] Francesco Rosi's *Salvatore Giuliano* (1961) is a *film-inchiesta*, or film as investigation, and explores 'the Byzantine interconnections between bandits, the mafia, the Allied occupation forces, and politicians.'[5] Rosi is more concerned with showing the uses and abuses of power in Sicily after the Second World War than with telling the tale of the rise and fall of Giuliano. In fact, the viewer catches only a brief glimpse of the bandit a few times in the film, and only after he is already dead. Rosi's attention is obviously drawn to the circumstances that caused Giuliano to become an outlaw, and in that regard, he provides a lucid analysis of the injustices experienced in Sicily by the peasant masses.

Rosi's work stands in stark contrast to Cimino's insofar as the latter shows little if any concern for the cycle of oppression maintained by the mafia and the government in Sicily, let alone for the plight of the peasants, who are confined to marginal roles. Indeed, when we do see them, they are usually in a group shot, either neatly performing their duties in the fields or passively listening to communist activist Silvio Ferra.[6] The focus in Cimino's film is always fully on Giuliano, who is portrayed as a heroic figure, fearless, proud, and self-confident. In fact, the film seems to suggest that, although Giuliano is the spokesperson for the disenfranchised, he does not think like a Sicilian peasant. His self-determination especially contrasts with the profound fatalism that, according to Leonardo Sciascia, characterizes Sicilian culture and grew out of a history of colonization: 'One can safely say that insecurity is the primary component of Sicilian history, and it affects the behavior, the way of being, the take on life –fear, apprehension, distrust, closed passions, inability to establish relationships outside of the private sphere, violence, pessimism, fatalism – of both the collectivity and single individuals.'[7] Giuliano does not exhibit any of the characteristics that Sciascia attributes to Sicilians at large. Determined to escape his fate as a subaltern subject, he fights for democracy and equality regardless of class divisions, thus proving that he is anything but a passive Sicilian peasant. In the leading role, Christopher Lambert delivers a performance that is coherent with the director's intention of highlighting the bandit's heroic qualities rather than depicting the collective hardship of Sicilian farmers. The actor's declamatory acting style, body language, and facial expressions, frequently shot in close-up, elevate Giuliano to the status of icon, as is made clear in the repeated shots of Giuliano on horseback that recall an equestrian portrait of Napoleon.

Giuliano's rebellion against a society that denies its members legitimate opportunities for socio-economic advancement is inspired by the stories of Sicilian immigrants' success in the United States. And indeed, a significant detail regarding the roots of Giuliano's ideology is to be found during a sequence in which the bandit and his gang interrupt a dinner at Prince Borsa's house and rob him and his rich guests of their valuable belongings. In the privacy of the Duchess's bedroom, the bandit engages in a revealing discussion with the American noblewoman. The bulk of the conversation between the two revolves around Sicily and America, and in this way is revealed Giuliano's infatuation with the Duchess's home country. While he expresses love for his native island, he also plainly avows: 'I wouldn't mind being an American. I'd like to be free.' Giuliano's American Dream meets the test of the Duchess's upper-class cynicism when she suggests that the only two contributions Sicilians have made to the United States are pizzerias and the mafia. To show the Duchess that he is much more cognizant of American culture than the average Sicilian who moves to New Jersey, Giuliano turns the focus of the conversation to contemporary American music and declares that he hates Glenn Miller and prefers Count Basie.

Excited and amused by the bandit's knowledge of Americana, the Duchess puts on some music and, brought closer together by jazz, the two start dancing to the tune of Miller's 'A String of Pearls.' At this point, Cimino cuts back and forth between the dining room, where Giuliano's men are collecting the spoils, and the Duchess's bedroom, where the two are engaged in foreplay. In a revealing scene, Cimino shoots past the Duchess's naked back to show Giuliano standing on the bed, wearing a white tank top and a pair of American Army shorts. Besides expressing his Americophilia, the fact that Cimino's Giuliano wears American Army underwear seems to suggest that he is a soldier whose mission is to spread the values of American liberal democracy and civil liberties in Sicily. *The Sicilian* ultimately chronicles the rise and fall of a leader who, motivated by American ideology, has the ambition to turn Sicily from a feudal oligarchy into a people's democracy, and possibly, as the bandit suggests, to even 'join the States as the forty-somethingth state.'[8]

However, the realization of equality, freedom, and opportunity is hindered in Sicily by the defenders of the status quo. Giuliano explains the power structure at work on the island to a monk by drawing three circles in the dust: one stands for the Church, another for the rich landlords, and another for the mafia. All three elite groups fear a peasant revolt. However, the three circles do not have the same diameter, so to speak. The almighty mafia, in fact, contains and subsumes all other forces as everything is, in one way or another, decided by it. The organization of 'Friends' – as mafia affiliates are constantly referred to in the film – is represented by Don Masino Croce, the boss who initially takes an interest in Giuliano as a potential heir to his Family business. However, as the story unfolds it becomes clear that Don Masino has taken on the role of defender of strictly conservative Old World models against the onslaught of the American values of democracy and equality as represented by Giuliano.

The 'boss of bosses' is all that the bandit is not. He is old, rich, powerful, and disenchanted. 'Life is hard,' he proclaims, a pessimistic statement that would have been more appropriately uttered by one of the many peasants in the film. He regards peasants as unfit for participative democracy. Assisted by his network of 'Friends,' Don Masino makes sure that hierarchies are respected and that century-old arrangements remain unchanged. In these compelling differences between Don Masino and Giuliano we can read the dramatization of the clash between the Old World and the New. The don, who represents the mafia system, aims to maintain the status quo; Giuliano, animated by ideals of freedom and opportunity for all, wants to upend that status quo.

The promotion of American values in Sicily as pursued by Giuliano entails a great many illegal activities, including murder.[9] According to Cimino, the violent aspects of the bandit's life appeal to American viewers by reminding them of the history and legends of the American frontier: 'I think that (Giuliano) exerts a natural, understandable charm on Americans. Giuliano was an attractive character, but he was on the other side of the law, and is therefore very similar to some legendary characters of the story of the American West. By consequence, he is for Americans a familiar type of character.'[10] In *The Sicilian*, Giuliano becomes part of the iconography of American history and folklore, alongside other famous American outlaws such as Jesse James, Butch Cassidy, and Billy the Kid. But there is more to Cimino's film than the appeal of the western. By introducing the mafia as Giuliano's main opponent, Cimino was returning to subject matter that American cinema had explored since the beginning of the 1900s and that had been popularized by Italian American directors such as Francis Ford Coppola, Martin Scorsese, and Brian De Palma. Indeed, *The Sicilian*, like all mafia movies, 'contain[s] everything that concerns and excites us – family, sex, and romance, power, betrayal, and violence,'[11] and the smooth-talking and family-loving Don Masino closely resembles the more popular Don Corleone. However, by pitting an Americanized bandit *against* a Sicilian gangster, *The Sicilian* complicates the genre conventions of both the western and the gangster film.

Giuliano's criminal activities come to a close at a time when he is planning a future in the United States with his wife and the baby she is expecting. Before that future comes, his dreams are shattered by betrayal. Giuliano's death, planned by Don Masino and made possible by his cousin Aspanu, points to the impossibility of introducing democratic change in a society in which stasis or emigration are the only options for the subaltern. The fact that the bandit fails in his attempt to escape to America becomes a parable for the impossibility of changing things in the Old Country. Giuliano's failure to exert control over his social condition signals the end of hope for the subaltern to move up in the Old World's rigid hierarchy. Individual fulfilment can only be obtained within a more flexible social context, one that allows, or claims to allow, upward social mobility regardless of birth status.

In conclusion, while recounting a story set among the shambles of wartime Sicily, Cimino opens for himself the possibility to explore the differences between America and Italy and the relationship between the two. By presenting the Sicilian bandit as the spokesperson for American values of democracy, social mobility, and freedom, the film reinforces the mythology of the United States as a site of empowerment for otherwise marginalized groups. Through a cinematographic trip back in time and place to Sicily in the mid-1900s, Cimino succeeds in dramatizing the never quite resolved tensions between the Old World and the New. The film explores the possibilities offered by the gangster genre, which, despite its long history in the film industry, seems never to exhaust its creative potential and appeal.

NOTES

1 According to Fred Gardaphé, Cimino made this film for both commercial and personal reasons. See Fred Gardaphé, 'Re-Inventing Sicily in Italian American Writing and Film,' *MELUS* 28, no. 3 (2003): 62.

2 Quoted in Massimo Benvegnù and Roberto Lasagna, *America perduta: i film di Michael Cimino* (Alessandria,: Edizioni Falsopiano, 1998), 176–7. My translation.

3 Chris Messenger, *The Godfather and American Culture: How the Corleones Became 'Our Gang'* (Albany, NY: SUNY Press, 2002), 111.

4 Francesco Renda claims that Giuliano is 'the most written about, or one of the most written about, protagonists of Italy's First Republic' (9). According to Renda, some fourteen historical biographies and

monographic essays of the bandit's life had been published worldwide before Italian director Rosi's film *Salvatore Giuliano* was released in 1961, and thirty-seven studies appeared after Rosi's work. This does not include the numerous oral stories and ballads in the Sicilian dialect that celebrate his exploits as a social justice fighter. See Francesco Renda, *Salvatore Giuliano: Una Biografia Storica* (Palermo: Sellerio Editore, 2002), 9. My translation.

5 Peter Bondanella, *Italian Cinema: From Neorealism to the Present* (New York: Continuum, 2003), 169.

6 Silvio Ferra is not a character in Puzo's novel. The fictional Ferra might represent the real-life communist leader Girolamo Li Causi, who was most likely the real target of the massacre of Portella Della Ginestra, which took place on 1 May 1947, when Giuliano's band opened fire on a crowd of communist farmers gathered to celebrate May Day, killing eleven people.

7 Leonardo Sciascia, *La corda pazza: scrittori e cose della Sicilia* (Milan: Adelphi, 1991), 13. My translation.

8 Other critics have made similar observations about *The Sicilian*. See Ben Lawton, 'America Through Italian/American Eyes: Dream or Nightmare?,' in *From the Margin: Writings in Italian Americana*, ed. Anthony J. Tamburri, Paolo A. Giordano, and Fred L. Gardaphé (West Lafayette, IN: Purdue University Press, 2000).

9 According to Renda in *Salvatore Giuliano*, Giuliano was officially responsible for 430 murders, which included innocent bystanders, farmers, labour leaders, and policemen (33).

10 Benvegnù and Lasagna, *America perduta*, 176–7.

11 George De Stefano, *An Offer We Can't Refuse: The Mafia in the Mind of America* (New York: Faber and Faber, 2006), 11.

14 Martin Scorsese's *Goodfellas*: Hybrid Storytelling between Realism and Formalism

FULVIO ORSITTO

'I just know it from what I saw in the streets, and when I saw it, when I lived it, I always said: this is the way it should be on film.'

Martin Scorsese, in *Getting Made* (2004)

'As far back as I can remember, I always wanted to be a gangster ... to me, being a gangster was better than being President of the United States.'

Henry Hill, in *Goodfellas* (1990)

As illustrated in these two quotations, Martin Scorsese's *Goodfellas* (1990) continuously oscillates between the director's need to provide a realistic portrayal of the Italian American mafia and the necessity he apparently feels to explore and display the mythical aspects of the crime under-world in order to represent what seduces Henry Hill (the Irish-Italian protagonist of the film), and what ultimately leads him into a life of crime. In this chapter, I explore Scorsese's realistic treatment of the mob (which is evident in the obsessive attention he pays to costumes and music and in his accurate rendition of the small details of gangsters' everyday lives), while simultaneously focusing on the director's propensity for expressive stylization (i.e., the use of voiceovers, point-of-view shots, freeze frames, camera pans, and numerous citations). Scorsese's skilful blend of realistic elements and stylized storytelling is crucial for crafting such an unusual portrait of the mob – a portrayal whose uniqueness is strengthened by the director's unprecedented attention to gangsters at the ground level. Moreover, while illustrating the transition from Old to New World values, Scorsese adeptly shows the transformation in the Weltanschauung of the modern mafioso. Ultimately, my goal is to demonstrate how *Goodfellas* represents a pivotal change in the mafia film genre, paving the way for a new kind of gangster film.

Scorsese's film is an adaptation of *Wiseguy* (1985), a novel by New York journalist Nicholas Pileggi, who specialized in crime reporting. Based on the reminiscences of Henry Hill (who was only eleven when he started working for the local mobsters and who later decided to cooperate with federal law enforcement authorities), Pileggi's *Wiseguy* presents the reader with an account of twenty-five years of mob life, from 1955 to 1980. Scorsese recalls having been fascinated by Pileggi's realistic approach to the mob since he first read the book in 1985 (while directing *The Color of Money*), especially the author's description of the details and minutiae of the gangsters' daily lives.[1]

One of the things that appealed most to the director about Pileggi's work was the writer's ability 'to get under the skin of the people that Scorsese had grown up with' and his portrayal of 'the Mob almost as a race apart.'[2] Moreover, *Goodfellas* represents Scorsese's return to the subject of his 1973 film *Mean Streets*, this time from a 'distanced, older, wiser and subtler perspective.'[3] For his new account of the Italian American crime underworld, instead of employing the realistic style used in *Mean Streets* (which had more in common with Italian neorealism and the French New Wave than with the typical gangster film),[4] Scorsese decided to translate Pileggi's realism into cinematic language by adopting an unorthodox approach, one that would combine realistic content with formalistic storytelling. Otherwise, in Scorsese's words, 'why make another gangster film?'[5]

A critical success, *Goodfellas* earned Scorsese a Venice Leone d'Argento as well as a French César and a BAFTA Award. *Goodfellas* helped redefine the boundaries of the classic American gangster film with its innovative content (given its focus on the lives of gangsters at the ground level) and its stylized storytelling, which deliberately avoids any resemblance to Francis Ford Coppola's romanticized and epic tone, which is better suited to the larger-than-life figures that inhabit the *Godfather* saga. Although a classic tale of the rise and fall of a criminal in the Italian American underworld, this film represented a new kind of gangster film. With its postmodern pastiche of elements, influences, and citations, *Goodfellas* paved the way for the films of directors such as Quentin Tarantino. However unconventional, the film garnered high critical acclaim, grossed more than $50 million at the box office, and became an instant classic.

Compared to Coppola's *Godfather* films, Scorsese's style in *Goodfellas* is not operatic. It is also grittier: stylized but also down and dirty, with jump cuts that grow in frequency towards the end of the film as Henry descends deeper into decadence and depravity. Paying an almost Viscontian attention to details such as songs and costumes, and contributing personally to the screenplay, Scorsese manages to evoke the daily life of a group of wiseguys. With regard to storytelling, he privileges several forms of expressive stylization that are crucial to establishing the uniqueness of *Goodfellas*. A case in point is his use of the voiceover.

Often exploited as a device to patch little cracks in the screenplay, the voiceover assumes a new and fundamental role in Scorsese's *Goodfellas*. In some senses, voiceover had become something of a cliché in cinematic storytelling until Scorsese reinvented it with a series of small but significant adjustments. He uses it as a *fil rouge* to lend narrative coherence to a series of events seen through the eyes of Henry Hill. At the same time (thanks to Ray Liotta's portrayal of Henry), he uses it to establish a particular sense of intimacy between narrator and audience. As confirmed by McBride, 'sympathy is not the issue here, empathy is,'[6] and since we are to embark on a perilous journey into the depths of the underworld, Henry immediately presents himself as our guide, certainly not a fatherly Virgil-like figure, but rather a brotherly demon, a modern-day Charon (from the Greek χάρων, 'of keen gaze') whose fierce and feverish eyes are perfectly embodied by Ray Liotta's intense gaze. The paternal figure in *Goodfellas* is embodied instead by Paul Sorvino's Paulie Cicero, whose last name reminds us of the great Roman orator and who seems to parody another Dantesque figure, the unmoved mover, whose 'power is that he remains unmoved while compelling others to move.'[7]

Scorsese uses the voiceover as a tool to help us explore 'a forbidden world with conventional blinders removed'[8] – a world narrated subjectively, with detachment, yet a world we feel we can belong to. Using the oldest of Dante's tricks – the one the poet uses to begin *The Divine Comedy*: 'when I had journeyed half of *our* life's way, I found *myself* within a shadowed forest'[9] – the director reminds us that, even though this is not our story, we all are sinners and can all empathize with a character seduced by money and power like Henry. The use of elements typical of the documentary tradition – voiceover, but also titles with the dates and locations of major scenes – enables Scorsese to pursue his quest for realism, allowing him to accomplish the kind of anthropological study of the mob he was aiming for.

In various interviews, the director has candidly confessed his intention to treat the subject 'like a *staged* documentary'; he was attempting to preserve at least 'the *spirit* of a documentary.'[10] What differentiates Scorsese's use of voiceover from its classic use in motion pictures is that he uses it as if his film were a documentary. Additionally, Henry is not the sole narrator of the film – he shares that task with his wife, Karen. Though it has two narrators, *Goodfellas* does not quite achieve the plurality of perspectives that typically characterizes documentaries; even so, it manages to achieve a dual point of view. In this regard, it behaves more like a 'quasi-documentary' (even though, consistent with his superordinate status, it is Henry who delivers most of the voiceovers). The intimacy resulting from the dual voiceovers contributes (paradoxically) to the film's realism, especially to the unconscious impression that the actors are *behaving* more than acting.

The director's conscious attempt to re-create what he saw in the streets comes to life in the film. The opening scene anticipates the protagonist's ambiguous relation to the mafia that develops throughout the film and that culminates in his final decision to cooperate with federal authorities. Scorsese introduces Henry in a scene where he is driving a car with Batts' body inside, implying that he is an accomplice to the crime but not directly involved in any act of physical violence. From the start of the film, Henry appears as a voyeur, an impression corroborated by the director's decision to freeze the frame and show him looking at the body in the trunk of the car. Immediately following the beginning titles, Scorsese cuts to a close-up side view of young Henry's right eye. In this scene, through the window blinds of his room, he watches the neighbourhood gangsters, echoing, as an obvious doppelgänger, Scorsese's own voyeuristic experience.[11] In Casillo's view, the shot is symbolic of the character's 'moral blindness, as well as his distance from the world he observes.'[12] However, one could push this analysis a step further and argue that the protagonist's distance from the inhabitants of this underworld contributes to his perception of the gangster as a mythical figure, a role model to be imitated. In Henry's words, becoming like them means 'being somebody in a neighborhood full of nobodies.' Such a position would allow him to pursue his own version of the American Dream and thereby acquire social mobility and the freedom to do as he pleases.

The mythologizing of gangsters is further achieved through the juxtaposition of wiseguys and possibly the greatest myths of Scorsese's cultural background, towering cinematic figures. A good example is young Henry's initial description of Jimmy Conway's character (Robert De Niro), who is instantly associated with the silver screen and labelled by the protagonist as 'the kind of guy who rooted for the bad guys in the movies.' An equally relevant example is Tommy DeVito (Joe Pesci), the most ruthless of gangsters, who shoots at a young bartender because he is pretending to act like one of the characters in *The Oklahoma Kid* (Lloyd Bacon, 1939). This scene also constitutes a brilliant example of mise en abîme in mimesis, since Pesci's character actually mistakes the lines of that film's villain (played by Humphrey Bogart, an actor known for playing the bad guy) for those of the Oklahoma Kid (played by James Cagney, famous for impersonating gangsters rather than cowboys).

Moreover, at the very end of the film, Scorsese places a micro-sequence of Tommy shooting at the audience that is, at the same time, a quotation from *The Great Train Robbery* (Edwin S. Porter, 1903), the archetype par excellence of the American crime genre, and also a reference to a previous sequence seen from Henry's point of view, in which Karen points a gun at his face. A very effective summary of their marriage, this sequence is based on the implicit symbolic association between the pistol and Henry's sexual organ, providing Karen with both sexual excitement and economic rewards.[13] Scorsese narrates Karen's attempt to punish her husband for his infidelity by having her handle his gun and by deconstructing the same weapon in three consecutive detail shots. Nonetheless, the scene ends with Karen overpowered and thrown to the floor, with Henry pointing the firearm at her. By linking this scene to the final micro-sequence starring Tommy, Scorsese, besides giving us the obvious postmodern pastiche, provides us with an emblematic shot that symbolizes the constant return of the irrepressible. Indeed, with such an iconic assertion, the director states that 'the crime film – embodied in Tommy DeVito as *revenant* – will renew itself as long as the criminal life seduces ordinary people like Henry and Karen.'[14]

The most evident illustration of the protagonist's relationship with the seductive power of the crime underworld (also the most extreme example of Scorsese's tendency towards expressive stylization) is the impressive forward-tracking shot that follows the two characters as they enter the Copacabana Club. This scene, which constitutes the apex of Henry's seduction by gangster life (and the beginning of Karen's), follows the two characters through a labyrinth of corridors and rooms until they reach the dining area near the stage. The decision to execute the entire scene in one take underscores the lack of separation between Henry and the underworld – a world he desires to belong to. The camera enters a world where doors magically open to the protagonist, providing us, as the audience, with an effective metaphor for Henry's ascent to power (which, ironically, corresponds to a descent into the lower floors of the club and, later, into substance abuse). This scene also successfully symbolizes the protagonist's social mobility, since he enters from the back door and winds up at the centre of the club.

Henry is now a successful wiseguy, a goodfella. He works hard, and what he gets in return is a reward, which consists of being able to double-park in front of a fire hydrant without getting a ticket and getting into the club through the back doors. This is the reason why, in Scorsese's own words, this scene 'had to be done in one sweeping shot, because it's his seduction of her, and it's also the lifestyle seducing him.'[15]

Henry thinks he is living the American Dream. What Scorsese portrays, however, is the American Nightmare, or what could be the darkest side of the American Dream. Without indulging in a kind of naive morality, the director shows us how Henry and other wiseguys completely reject the American ideal of a routine, alternating between work and leisure. This storyline constitutes an important revision of the classic figure of the mafioso. Pino Arlacchi shares Scorsese's interest in the issue of gangster demythification, and reflects upon the myth of the mob boss reinforced by the *Godfather* saga. Arlacchi recalls that

> the traditional *mafioso* had no love of ostentation. His power, like his consumption, was characteristically discreet and reserved. To say little, to keep a low profile, to disparage the extent of one's influence – these were the rules the mafia followed in its appearance in public life … The *Mafioso* made no display of superfluous consumption, because none was necessary to establish his respectability.[16]

Arlacchi argues, however, that after the 1960s 'the *mafioso*'s ideology and lifestyle have been radically transformed by his identification with market forces,' so that it was possible to identify a new category of mafia entrepreneurs who adopted capitalist values and regarded profit and power 'not as means to the satisfaction of material needs, but as the goals of life.'[17] This new type of mafioso greatly differed from the old man of honour. A perfect example of this clash between old and new values is illustrated through Tommy's relationship to business and family, work, and domesticity, by his 'contamination of the sacred space of the domus by the bloody world outside.'[18] Pesci's character does not hesitate to stop by his mother's place while Batts is still alive in a car trunk, and after his mother prepares Tommy and his friends something to eat, he even asks to borrow her kitchen knife to finalize the killing. In this scene, the director gives us another postmodern mise en abîme, exemplifying the new mafioso's attitude towards Old World values and previously inviolable domestic spaces. This new attitude is characterized by playfulness and palpable sardonic irony, even if the audience is unaware that Tommy's mother is actually played by Scorsese's mother.

Goodfellas represents a crucial change in the mafia film genre. Perhaps even more effectively than the first two chapters of the *Godfather* saga, this film manages to portray the transition from Old World values to a mafia driven primarily by capitalism. Moreover, Scorsese displays a crucial transformation in the Weltanschauung of the modern mafioso, whose world is now dominated by an anguished sense of danger and uncertainty. After losing stable, spatial boundaries, the mafiosi enter a new phase where not only their lives but also their memoirs, their autobiographies, and their court statements are filled with 'pessimism, fatalism and a feeling of persecution.'[19] The same string of emotions is evident in Henry Hill's life and becomes even clearer towards the end of the film, when the protagonist confirms that he is only capable of basing his actions on purely hedonistic impulses. By verifying his addiction to desire (a compulsion more ancestral and profound than the drug habit he develops), Henry concludes *Goodfellas* – a film characterized by extreme and graphic violence, by innovative storytelling, by an innate postmodern tendency towards pastiche and symbolism, and, in general, by a great degree of complexity – with a remarkable degree of almost Calvinian 'lightness.'[20] In fact, at the peak of his dark humour, Scorsese has Henry complaining that, in his new location, he cannot find decent spaghetti with marinara sauce.

NOTES

1 *Getting Made: The Making of Goodfellas*, Columbia Pictures, 2004, Two-Disc DVD Special Edition of *Goodfellas*.
2 Andy Dougan, *Martin Scorsese: The Making of His Movies* (New York: Thunder's Mouth Press, 1998), 93.
3 Joseph McBride, 'Goodfellas,' *Variety*, 10 September 1990, accessed 15 May 2009, www.variety.com /review/VE1117789056.html?categoryid= 31&cs=1.
4 The stereotypical depiction of mobsters – which began on the silver screen in the 1930s, with films such as *Little Caesar* (Mervyn LeRoy, 1931), *The Public Enemy* (William A. Wellman, 1931), and *Scarface* (Howard Hawks, 1932) – continued in the following decades on both radio and TV, thanks to popular shows such as *Dragnet,* which debuted as a radio drama in 1950 and was later aired on TV.
5 *Getting Made*, 2004.
6 McBride, 'Goodfellas.'
7 Robert Casillo, *Gangster Priest: The Italian American Cinema of Martin Scorsese* (Toronto: University of Toronto Press, 2006), 298.

8   McBride, 'Goodfellas.'

9   Dante Alighieri, *Inferno: A Verse Translation by Allen Mandelbaum* (New York: Bantam Books, 1982), Canto I, 1–2. Emphasis mine.

10 Gavin Smith, 'Martin Scorsese Interviewed,' in *Martin Scorsese Interviews*, ed. Peter Brunette (Jackson, MI: University Press of Mississippi, 1999), 146.

11 Another facet of Henry's doppelgänger condition is his marginality, indicated by the special place he holds both in and outside of the system (since he is only half Italian) and by his status as voyeur. This is a peculiarity that – with a typical postmodern slippage – echoes Scorsese's own special position of voyeur with respect to the Italian American crime underworld he attempts to describe.

12 Casillo, *Gangster Priest*, 274.

13 Ibid., 296.

14 Ibid., 270.

15 Scorsese interview with Andy Dougan, in Dougan, *Martin Scorsese*, 94.

16 Pino Arlacchi, *Mafia Business: The Mafia Ethic and the Spirit of Capitalism* (London: Verso, 1986), 117.

17 Ibid., 119.

18 Casillo, *Gangster Priest*, 315.

19 Arlacchi, *Mafia Business*, 126.

20 According to Italo Calvino, lightness is an antidote to 'the weight, the inertia, the opacity of the world,' *Six Memos for the Next Millennium* (London: Vintage, 1996), 4.

15 Redemption in Francis Ford Coppola's
The Godfather: Part III

JOHN PAUL RUSSO

Francis Ford Coppola resisted filming a third *Godfather* and succumbed only because of financial duress. He 'asked for six months to develop a story and script. [Paramount head Frank] Mancuso gave him six weeks.'[1] Coppola and Mario Puzo rented a suite in a Reno hotel: 'We'd work for hours, and when we ran out of ideas, we'd go down to the casino.'[2] Coppola was attempting not only to unify a complex narrative quickly but also to connect it (however loosely) to the two earlier *Godfather* films shot a decade and a half earlier. His difficulties with *Apocalypse Now* might have shown that such an approach is too uncertain for a large-scale work.[3] On top of all this, Coppola wanted to bring the saga to a definitive conclusion. While *The Godfather: Part II* concluded on a note of despair, with Michael Corleone's death-in-life existence at Lake Tahoe in 1958, Coppola planned to end *The Godfather: Part III* (1990) with his actual death some thirty-nine years later in Sicily. Why was Coppola in such a hurry to kill the golden don? The epic potential of the materials could be expanded in many ways: forwards, backwards, sideways; films filling in the gaps in Michael's life; films working out the fate of other family members; films taking up new characters and moving in new directions. He might have given thought to Zola's Rougons-Macquart series, some twenty novels that capture an epoch, or to Balzac's even larger *Comédie Humaine*, which attempts to capture all the aspects of humanity. In his attempt, Coppola might have succeeded in his goal of making the *Godfather* films a 'metaphor for America' – or the Italian American experience.[4] As it stands, we have two masterpieces and a curiously unsatisfying coda.

Religion in all its forms – spiritual, institutional, popular, ceremonial, commercial – informs *The Godfather: Part III*. The central action links the Corleone family to the Vatican banking scandal, which began in the early years of John Paul II's papacy and led to the collapse of the Banco Ambrosiano in 1982, a period the film compresses into 1978–79. Religious ritual in *The Godfather* and *The Godfather: Part II* had marked the stages of life and emphasized the disparity between formal ideals and human depravity. In *The Godfather: Part III*, religion takes on an even more varied role. There are, for example, touristic views of the Vatican, crowds waiting for the white smoke of election, and the plot based on the rumour that reformist-minded John Paul I was poisoned after little over a month on the papal throne. Then, in the person of Archbishop Gilday (gilded, gliding, slippery), who heads the Vatican bank, the plot involves the Church in a giant swindle, making a forced parallel between the operations of the Vatican and those of the mob underworld. 'It's the Borgias all over again,' Michael expostulates; actually, it is the Rome of modern scandal and canard. Puzo and Coppola gothicize the Church and perpetuate the old, 'northern' prejudice at variance with their otherwise southern Italian perspective, but they also capitalize the Church, which permits their laboured broadsides against corporate business. Finally, the film contains perhaps the only moment of genuine spirituality in the entire trilogy: Michael's confession scene with Cardinal Lamberto, soon to be elected pope.

Religious ritual informs Michael's efforts towards familial reconciliation in the deftly handled opening sequence of *The Godfather: Part III*. A lonely trumpet solo plays Nino Rota's tragic *Godfather* theme. The camera pans across the desolate estate at Lake Tahoe; autumn leaves blow across the grounds under cold, cloudy skies; a statue of the Madonna stands neglected. As the orchestra enters quietly, flotsam clogs the docks, and the camera moves into the dusty interior of the house with a doll and toy cart, at which point, in voiceover, Michael begins: 'My dear children, it is now better than several years since I moved to New York, and I haven't seen you as much as I would like.' But these images of the house in decline are now set definitively in the past; with a sense of *incipit vita nova* (here begins the new life), Michael invites his children, Mary and Anthony, to his investiture into the Order of St Sebastian in New York (at a personal cost of $100 million) to demonstrate his long-sought public acceptance and to unite the family.

Michael states that 'the only wealth in this world is children, more than all the money and power on Earth.' Perhaps the key line in the film, this is no pious sentiment, but an intensely realized commitment to the next generation that might redeem the past. The camera pans across his desk with the photograph of the children, until he himself appears in a reverse shot completing the letter we have just heard with the words, 'I look forward to a new period of harmony in our lives.' This is followed by a cut to the ceremony at old St Patrick's on Mott Street, in Little Italy. Michael kneels at the altar, with Mary, Anthony, and his sister Connie seated in the front pew and Michael's *consigliere* B.J. Harrison, family members, and friends behind them. 'Perhaps you might prevail upon your mother to come to this celebration,' continues the voiceover. While Gilday officiates in Latin, the language of the sacred, Michael recalls his brother Fredo, whom he had ordered to be murdered, the sacrilege of Cain. The camera cuts to Fredo in the boat on Lake Tahoe, saying his Hail Mary to catch a fish, the symbol of Christ; then, back to the ceremony; then to Michael watching from the Lake Tahoe house while Fredo is shot. Back at the church, Joey Zasa, a mafioso from another family, enters with his bodyguard, and just as the ceremony ends, Michael's ex-wife Kay files in with her husband, a judge – the children persuaded her to come. Zasa shows disrespect by entering in the middle of the ceremony, and Kay shows even more by missing the entire thing. Mixing religion, family, and mafia business, the scene is Coppola at his best – the free, indirect style applied to film. He excels in these fluid movements, here indicating the central theme of Michael's attempt to put his life in order together with his reflections and memories, from present to past and back again. In just minutes, it appears that *The Godfather: Part II* and *The Godfather: Part III* have been sutured.

The following scene, which is set in Michael's New York apartment immediately following the investiture and which comprises one-fifth of the script, oscillates between the party's festivities and the godfather's office. It introduces the romance between Mary and her cousin Vincent, Kay's enduring resentment of Michael, the machinations of the rival Don Altobello, and the Vincent–Zasa feud. The basic pattern of a large family event at the outset of the film was set in *The Godfather* with Connie's wedding reception in a sunny Long Island garden, contrasted with Don Vito's 'business' in his dimly lit home office. The decline of the family in *The Godfather: Part II* was indicated by a Holy Communion party for Anthony at Lake Tahoe, concocted merely as an excuse for business, which was conducted inside the house. The repetition of this dual pattern a third time takes away surprise and saps the film of energy. One indication of the further decline of the family is that the Corleones have lost the ability to host a good *festa in famiglia*; there is plenitude, but only in the nature of consumption, not in personal and familial fulfilment. The lighting of the party and the office, two interiors as opposed to interior/exterior, is almost the same: the two worlds are now virtually indistinguishable. As a whole, the party scene comes off in a slapdash fashion. Coppola fails to establish a coherent sense of space – instead of feeling claustrophobic, the audience is just confused.

In the scene in the godfather's office, Michael refuses his nephew Vincent's request to work for him and insists that he make peace with Zasa, with whom Michael had found him a job. When Zasa and Vincent greet with a ritual kiss, recalling Judas and Christ, Zasa whispers 'bastardo' and Vincent responds by biting hard into Zasa's ear. Biting the ear just enough to draw blood indicates a challenge, but Vincent bites deeply, abusing the ritual and raising the level of hatred between the two. This act may also demean Vincent in the eyes of the viewer and create sympathy for Zasa. Later, after Michael suffers his first diabetic attack and the family is vulnerable, Vincent plans to eliminate Zasa, jumping to the conclusion that he must be the source of Michael's problems – the first sign that Vincent does not possess the intellectual competence to be a godfather. The assassination occurs during a religious procession of the Madonna in Little Italy, a sacrilege that links this scene to the broader religious thematic of the film as a whole. Beneath a death-like, whitish-grey sky (which minutes before had been clear and sunny), Zasa runs down an empty street and is shot by Vincent, who is disguised as a policeman on horseback. This scene suffers in comparison to its model in *The Godfather: Part II*. In the earlier film, the crowds were thick and jostling, the atmosphere tangible with festivity; in the later one, the crowds are so thin that the atmosphere seems joyless. In the earlier film, young Vito Corleone crosses the rooftops in a movement counter to the street procession (thereby crossing or violating its spirit) and kills the local don, Fanucci, inside Fanucci's apartment building, where Vito had unscrewed the bulb in the hallway lamp, once again underscoring the transition from light to dark; in the second, most improbably, the assassins are participants in the procession, wearing masks and white robes and carrying machine guns, yet despite the element of surprise, they miss their prey and are all gunned down. It is an additional irony that the earlier scene, though shot on a Hollywood set, looks far more realistic than the later one actually shot on the streets of New York.

The film's emotional climax takes place in the Vatican, where Michael has gone to warn Cardinal Lamberto that he is the victim of a swindle, with the Vatican bank as the mediator and guarantor. In retrospect, it seems strange that a respected cardinal would take counsel from a mafia don. Yet this secret knowledge will soon be helpful to Lamberto when he is elevated to the papal throne. During their conversation in a cloister, Lamberto takes a stone from a fountain and cracks it open: it is dry. So, he says to Michael, Christianity has surrounded Europeans for centuries and has not penetrated to the core. At this point Michael suffers the onset of a second diabetic attack, which is checked by a glass of orange juice, orange being the symbol in the *Godfather* saga of danger and approaching death. Michael looks weak, vulnerable, and even undignified. As he recovers, Lamberto asks him if he wants to make his confession. Taken aback, Michael says he has not confessed in thirty years and is 'beyond redemption.' Yet at Lamberto's gentle urging, Michael proceeds, revealing one mortal sin after another. When he confesses the murder of Fredo, he breaks down in tears. 'Your sins are terrible, and it is just that you suffer,' responds Lamberto. 'Your life could be redeemed, but I know that you don't believe that. You will not change.' Even so, Michael's contriteness is acknowledged by distant church bells, tolling for Paul VI.

When Connie later chastises Michael for telling secrets to a 'stranger' (Lamberto), Michael pursues the confessional mode. 'All my life I kept trying to go up in society,' he tells her, 'where everything higher up was legal, straight. But the higher I go, the crookeder it becomes. How in the hell does it end?' This statement mirrors Coppola's belief that 'it's the same everywhere,' his irritable penchant for making loose, indiscriminate connections between capitalism, religion, the mafia, government, Italy, and America. When Michael pithily states that 'politics and crime – they're the same thing,' that everyone is corrupt, it is a cynical excuse for his own corruption, not a universal truth. The earlier films contained a few sententious one-liners, some of which have passed into common usage. However, in *The Godfather: Part III,* the pressure to write these (mostly for Michael) pushed Puzo and Coppola to clutch at truisms, resulting in statements like 'never hate your enemies – it affects your judgment'; 'even the strongest man needs friends'; 'your enemies always get strong on what you leave behind'; 'when they come at you, they'll come at those you love'; 'power wears out those who have it'; 'it's dangerous to be an honest man'; and 'every family has bad memories.' If Michael had exhibited this shoddy thinking from the start of the trilogy, he would never have had the brains to become a godfather.

Religion also informs the opera within the film. Why did Coppola and Puzo choose Mascagni's *Cavalleria Rusticana* to counterpoint the conclusion of *The Godfather: Part III*? Just as Coppola's trilogy has a high degree of realism, this opera exemplifies *verismo* or 'naturalism'; its music enhances the 'immediacy' of the action, 'making it feel more direct and unmediated, rather than extending or distancing its events in traditional operatic fashion.'[5] On the one hand, as if appropriate for a mafia film, the opera is set in Sicily and is based on the story and play by the Sicilian Giovanni Verga. Its themes are love, betrayal, religion, sacrilege, revenge, and violent death. There is a challenge scene with a ritual biting of the ear, an action that connects the opera back to the main plotline and that Coppola underscores heavily by cutting to Vincent, who nods and smiles. Taking place on Easter Sunday, the opera conveys the idea of redemption, which the film's preceding scenes had stressed, most notably in Michael's confession.[6] On the other hand, the opera plot does not sufficiently mirror the film and so cannot comment upon it in a compelling fashion. *The Godfather: Part III* is not a film about love, betrayal, and revenge, but about Michael's search for inner peace. Moreover, its gravely nostalgic intermezzo had recently been used by Scorsese in *Raging Bull* (1980) and seems redundant. Coppola also re-employs some of the symbolism from the earlier films – for example, the cannoli with orange citron that Connie uses to poison Don Altobello is an association with the victim that goes back to *The Godfather* ('leave the gun, take the cannoli,' spoken in the scene where Pauli is shot in the car off the highway).

Coppola excels in his staged presentation of the opera itself, holding his own against Franco Zeffirelli's 1982 filmed version. From the opera's sixty-eight minutes, he excerpts about fourteen and preserves the main plotline, the Easter hymn alone being out of sequence. However, five separate film plotlines and sub-plotlines are intercut with the opera, a degree of traffic that the piece simply cannot bear. In Eisensteinian montage, content and technique inform and enhance each other; Coppola had taken this approach with technical skill in the finale of *The Godfather*. In *The Godfather: Part III*, collision montage turns into concatenated confusion. Adding to the blunder is the scene where the risen Christ walks on stage to bring the redemption theme to an effective climax – yet even the Son of God's presence fails to connect cinematically or spiritually with Michael. Lamberto appears to have been right after all: he 'will not change.'

When Coppola most needed time and resources in the making of this film, he had none to spare. His interviews present the spectacle of someone looking for excuses for the end result: 'But I always sort of resented that the trilogy took up so much of my life, and that it's about shooting people.'[7] This exaggeration betrays him. The films took up a maximum of four years of his creative life, yet he *resents* his greatest artistic achievements, the only films for which he may be remembered or that made him any real money. What foolish scruple could have led to the terrible reduction of the epic scope of these pictures to 'shooting people'? Coppola disparages the early *Godfather* films as moneymakers, as if their success prevented him from doing something really important, like *The Rain People* and *Rumble Fish* (two of his three 'favourite' films).[8] The money he made allowed him to work independently until he squandered it on ill-planned projects.

Around 1997 Coppola said that, while he was filming *The Godfather* and *The Godfather: Part II*, he thought it might 'ruin' him: 'And in some ways it did ruin me. It just made my whole career go this way instead of the way I really wanted it to go, which was into doing original work as a writer-director.'[9] What could have been more original than the first two *Godfathers*? What artists in their early thirties would not feel blessed by such results? 'The great frustration of my career is that nobody really wants me to do my own work.' Who are these hobgoblins? Studio executives, fans, critics, family members? Who is stopping him? 'Basically, *The Godfather* made me violate a lot of the hopes I had for myself at that age.'[10] It is possible that such an attitude towards his achievement in the first two films carried over into the making of the third *Godfather* film, marring the final panel of the triptych.

NOTES

1 Jon Lewis, 'If History Has Taught Us Anything ... Francis Coppola, Paramount Studios, and the *Godfather Parts I, II, and III*,' in *Francis Ford Coppola's the Godfather Trilogy*, ed. Nick Browne (Cambridge: Cambridge University Press, 2000), 47.

2 Michael Schumacher, *Francis Ford Coppola: A Filmmaker's Life* (New York: Crown, 1999), 417.

3 The problems of an ever-changing film script were compounded by severe weather, enormous cost overruns, and the protagonist Martin Sheen's heart attack during production.

4 Cited by Stephen Farber, 'Coppola and *the Godfather*,' *Sight and Sound* 41 (1972): 223.

5 Alan Mallach, *Pietro Mascagni and His Operas* (Boston, MA: Northeastern University Press, 2002), 66.

6 Don Vito assassinated Don Ciccio on Palm Sunday in 1927.

7 Gene D. Phillips, *Godfather: The Intimate Francis Ford Coppola* (Lexington, KY: University of Kentucky Press, 2004), 142.

8 Schumacher, *Francis Ford Coppola*, 409; Peter Cowie, *Coppola* (New York: Scribner's, 1989), 228. Coppola's third favourite film is *The Conversation*.

9 Cited in Michael Sragow, 'Godfatherhood,' in *Francis Ford Coppola: Interviews*, ed. Gene D. Phillips and Rodney Hill (Jackson, MI: University Press of Mississippi, 2004), 169.

10 Ibid.

16   Narrating the Mafia, Las Vegas, and Ethnicity in Martin Scorsese's *Casino*

CLAUDIO BISONI

This chapter considers the ways in which the cinematic representations of the mafia and Las Vegas are intertwined in Martin Scorsese's *Casino* (1995). First, I trace out the connection between Scorsese's film and the Rat Pack movie *Ocean's 11* (original title *Ocean's Eleven*, Lewis Milestone, 1960) in order to highlight how masculinities and ethnicities of the Rat Pack are revisited, implicitly, in *Casino*. Second, I describe how the actions of Sam and Nicky, the film's two male protagonists, are characterized on a narrative level. Third, I return to the question of the protagonists' ethnicity. Though one central character is Jewish and the other Italian, and they are involved to differing extents in organized crime, I suggest that in *Casino* ethnicity has a secondary role: it affects how the characters construct their social performances but does not directly influence their fate. Instead, ethnicity is an effect of that unique declination of the society of spectacle that Las Vegas represents. Ultimately, what really counts in *Casino* is the embodiment of that common interest which unites the mafia and Las Vegas as the gambling city par excellence: the colour of money and capitalist gain.

In *Casino* the escapades of organized crime syndicates in Las Vegas are narrated against a historical backdrop. The protagonists in the film, the screenplay of which Scorsese wrote with Nicholas Pillegi, are the two criminals Sam 'Ace' Rothstein and Nicholas 'Nicky' Santoro, the former Jewish and the later Italian American, whose illegal activities in Las Vegas's underworld are based on the true lives of organized crime associate Frank 'Lefty' Rosenthal and his childhood friend Anthony 'The Ant' Spilotro. The film is set during the 1970s, in the wake of the golden age of mafia involvement in gambling the decade prior, when Las Vegas was home to Sam Giancana and Jimmy Hoffa and the Rat Pack.[1]

Casino does not resemble a Rat Pack film. Nevertheless, what I term a 'Rat Pack legacy' is present, albeit in a subtle manner, in the beginning of the film, primarily as a result of the soundtrack (which features Louis Prima, Dean Martin, and Sammy Davis Jr). Also, Don Rickles (a friend of Sinatra) has a role in the film. Finally, setting is key, principally certain exterior locations beyond the casinos, which not by chance appear almost identical to those that feature in the HBO biopic *The Rat Pack* (Rob Cohen, 1998).[2]

In performances by The Summit (the original name of the Rat Pack), Sinatra and Martin – in Vegas as well as in Chicago – chat habitually on stage about the jobs they did for the mafia.[3] In other words, humorous comments and jokes made by the two Italian Americans celebrate, in a politically less-than-correct way, the amorality of showbiz, and they brandish their connections with the mafia (be they true or exaggerated) as an essential component of their masculinity and their social capital within show business itself. Conversely, in the quintessential Rat Pack movie *Ocean's 11*, the protagonists are outlaws but the links between casinos and the mafia are never made explicit.[4]

Casino inverts *Ocean 11*'s restraint, basing itself specifically on the 'skimming' operation through which the Kansas City mafia gains enormous profits from gambling in a city where it cannot set foot without being arrested. Scorsese shoots the world of gambling with lively visual style, characterized by eccentric framing (such as the iconic shot from the perspective of the inside of a rolled-up banknote used to snort a line of cocaine) and visually pleasing cinematography (including virtuoso camera movements and a use of illumination centred on intra-diagetic lighting and radiant colours). These camera movements shift the spectator from the interiors of gambling halls, lit by bright-coloured lights, to the behind-the-scenes spaces of The Tangiers (the casino that Ace manages). Akin to *Goodfellas*, the film's narrative is accompanied by two voice-overs, one from Ace himself and the other from Nicky. The two voices swap as one passes the baton to the other; at times they contradict each other, while elsewhere they describe the same events from different points of view – for example, when the men narrate the film's two count room sequences. The count room is an extremely important set in the film: it is 'the most sacred room in the casino' (in Ace's own words), the place where we see the material gains of an entirely legal activity, that is, the accumulation of economic fortune generated by the work of the gamblers. Everything criminal happens before or after this moment, before or after what happens in that sacred and secret place where riches are magically conjured up by exploiting the desires of the consumers/players. In the first count room sequence, a Steadicam transports viewers from the gambling hall to the count room. Ace's voiceover accompanies the action as far as the armoured door, where it is then substituted by Nicky's. In the second sequence, a similar movement accompanies Nicky's voice. The same action is thus repeated and observed from two different yet complementary perspectives. Ace is responsible for the money ending up in that room; Nicky is responsible for how the room is emptied out. This division of duties corresponds to a division of roles; at the same time, it is consistent with two different types of masculinity. Ace is in charge of populating the casino and extracting money from the clients: his actions are on the side of accumulation (of capital, money, energy, and social respectability). Nicky takes care of the holes in the desert where bodies are made to disappear, and of cleaning out the casino's safes: his work sits on the side of violence, the dispersal of capital, consumption, crime, and excess. Nicky's character moreover embodies a brutal form of masculinity connected to physical force. Ace represents a more problematic masculinity: he is rarely ever the agent of direct physical violence, but he is defended (when possible) by Nicky. He values clothing, locations, and modes of behaviour that contradict the mafia's street code; in other words, he utilizes this code to gain protection while simultaneously distancing himself from it.

None of *Casino*'s characters are free to behave autonomously or to pursue their own desires. For example, Ginger, Sam's wife, is not free, since the fulfilment that she finds in drugs, money, and material goods derives from the economic exploitation of her husband and ultimately leads to her self-destruction.[5] Neither is Nicky, who believes he can transform Las Vegas into an arena for his very own gold rush and is ultimately punished for his unrealistic goals. And in the end, neither is Ace. For the first part of the film, Rothstein's success is equated with a metaphor of visual control. He literally makes The Tangiers work, and to do so he commands a chain of controlling gazes, each one watching over the next.[6]

This game of overlapping gazes has been described in Foucauldian terms as a panoptic disciplinary mechanism and as a totalitarian apparatus of control.[7] It is certainly a system of gazes that reflects and feeds a power system, and Ace is not in control in this system: from the outset, external forces significantly limit his agency. He does not have access to the count room, and as Nicky's voiceover reminds us, 'nobody knew all the details' about the casino's construction and management: '[I]n the end, we fucked it all up. It should've been so sweet, too. But it turned out to be the last time that street guys like us were ever given anything that fucking valuable again.' Everything that Ace and Nicky own is theirs only because somebody gave it to them.

Ace is akin to Henry in *Goodfellas*: he is characterized by a strong sense of in-betweenness. He mediates between various power systems (the criminal underworld, the world of state institutions that regulate gambling by law). Ace is not criminal, nor is he Italian American enough to really be a part of the mafia and benefit from its unconditional protection: he can only be someone who acts on behalf of organized crime. Nor is he respectable enough to negotiate on the level of the Las Vegas establishment that controls the gambling commission. He is therefore reprimanded by the world of crime for having excessive desires for social integration and also by the citizens of Las Vegas for being no more than a friend to the mafia. Ultimately Ace fails, but not because he is swallowed up by the glamour of Vegas, and not because of his mania to control both the casino's operations and Ginger, which leads him to make erratic decisions. Instead, he fails because the nature of his desires is fundamentally contradictory: he yearns for riches, beauty, and social respectability, but he wants to attain these with a cocaine-addicted hustler and a sociopathic serial killer by his side.

Casino narrates a system of surveillance and games of control between characters. In this way, *Casino* parallels *Goodfellas*, where, as Robert Kolker notes, the interpellation of the spectator is achieved through the voiceovers of Henry and Karen Hill: 'They are, of course, fictional voices, which are mediated by another narrator, the controlling voice of the film itself. That "voice" is a synthesis of the screenplay and direction, of the cutting of the film and its mise en scène.'[8] The same can be said of Nicky and Ace's voiceovers in *Casino*, where the characters' actions, as depicted through images and mise en scène, are integrated, at times ironically and contradictorily, with the comments of the voiceovers and the use of the soundtrack, which comments further on protagonists' actions.[9]

On the level of mise en scène, the mafia is represented in *Casino* as an external force to the spaces of Las Vegas, a force that nevertheless is able to condition the lives of the protagonists who work and live there. Scorsese depicts the Italian American mafiosi as 'greaseballs' (in Nicky's words), who get together in the backroom of a produce market to eat spaghetti cooked by their mothers and talk business while listening to Dean Martin's 'You're Nobody till Somebody Loves You.' In other words, these aged mafiosi reflect the iconographic cliché of the Italian American gangster that Scorsese himself helped create in his trilogy of gangster films (*Mean Streets*, *Goodfellas*, *Casino*). At the same time, the characters' power appears stable: they decide who lives and who ends up buried in the desert that surrounds the city.

The question of ethnicity is central in Scorsese's films and contributes to what can be called a semi-documentary accuracy that emerges from the behaviour, habits, dress styles, and speaking patterns of the Italian American characters populating his films.[10] What then does the representation of Italian American and Jewish ethnicity bring to *Casino*'s representation of gangsters?

According to Larissa M. Ennis, during the 1990s progressive identity politics began to threaten the integrity of a North American white masculinity, which led to a backlash, with men reacting by projecting themselves as victims of a multiculturalist threat.[11] The 1990s saw the release of a cycle of gangster films that can be read as symptoms of this 'white' fear. *Goodfellas* in particular can be defined as a film that 'participates in the contemporary practice of making white men into victims, presenting men who lose their gangster community.'[12] Space constraints prevent a more detailed discussion of this interpretative hypothesis in relation to *Goodfellas*. It is nevertheless worth emphasizing that for Ennis, *Casino* (as well as *Donnie Brasco*, *King of New York*, and *The Godfather: Part III*) belongs to this cycle of gangster victim films of which *Goodfellas* is most exemplary. On the contrary, I argue that *Casino* specifically downplays the centrality of ethnicity in its representation of the Italian American mafia. While *Goodfellas* 'brings ethnicity to the fore,'[13] *Casino* places it on the surface of the image and leaves it there, precisely *as* a surface, a visual and narrative stereotype that lacks any depth.

The main surprise of the second part of *Casino* comes from the revelation, at a certain point, that Ace's voiceover is not that of a dead man speaking (as per the conventions of film noir from the 1940s), but that of a survivor. At the same time, we discover that Nicky's is not the voiceover of a survivor (in virtue of his familial connection to the Italian American mafia) but that of a dead man, who speaks until that moment and then suddenly desists talking. Indeed, after the assassination of Nicky as a character *within* the plot we no longer hear his voice as a vocal guide *of* the plot. A short time before his own murder, Nicky commented on the elimination of Andy Stone: 'As much as they liked him, I mean, he wasn't one of us. He wasn't Italian.' Yet soon after, Nicky is eliminated too, buried alive in a Midwestern cornfield. Ace, by contrast, sees his business transactions dramatically reduced, but he is spared, and he remains available on a market that still has some need of his services. In *Casino* the Italian is brutally slaughtered by other Italians; the 'ethnically marginal' Jewish man remains in his place.

As I mentioned earlier, there is something of a Rat Pack legacy in *Casino*. That something relates to the spectacular surface of Las Vegas, the way the city presents itself and the way a specific image of organized crime can become an object of fashion, male allure, humour, and exhibition. *Casino* does not show us the world of showbiz that is linked to gambling in Las Vegas. There is no sign of Wayne Newton, no Liberace, no Elvis, no Sinatra (who in the 1970s was at Caesar's Palace, no longer at the Sands). On the contrary, the Kansas City mafia is actually *against* Ace becoming a TV showman. The mafia is suspicious both of Nicky's excessive violence and of the TV broadcasting world that Ace wants to access, since both constitute risks, and both can attract public attention, distract people from gambling, and threaten their illegal profit-making activities. Ultimately, *Casino* is an invitation to look beyond the 'Rat Pack' style, beyond the image of a gangster that simply incorporates their ethnicity and their *mafiosità*. It shows how the appearances of these gangsters, too, are a part of Las Vegas's spectacular mythology.

Scorsese *pretends* to depict a process of ethnic exclusion and multiculturalist victimization. Yet in truth he shows that in decisive circumstances, ethnic differences are just like Ace's neckties: they are clichés, social conventions. They are form without substance. Scorsese depicts the mafia – in contrast to the folkloristic imagery that *Casino* exploits for spectacle and visual appeal – as an institution that readily abandons the defence of ethnic difference. Behind the spectacular façade of ethnicity, *Casino* is a materialistic film that repeatedly turns to the same point: all that counts, to quote Ace once again, 'the end result of all the bright lights and the comp trips, of all the champagne and free hotel suites and all the broads and all the booze,' is money. The 'desert of desire'[14] is not merely a land of success for small-time Jewish or Italian American criminals, nor is it a place of spectacle and excess. It is also and above all an economic machine. And the same can be said of the mafia. In essence, the way Scorsese represents the mafia in *Casino* is marked by the most radical simplicity: the mafia, at its essence and core, appears to be a pure and primitive force for capitalistic accrual.

NOTES

1 On the decline of mafia power in Las Vegas from the 1960s onwards, see Robert Casillo, *Gangster Priest: The Italian American Cinema of Martin Scorsese* (Toronto: University of Toronto Press, 2006), 379–82.

2 Scorsese's interest in films inspired by biographies of Martin and Sinatra is well documented. See Anita Singh, 'Martin Scorsese Portrayal of Frank Sinatra Angers Family,' *The Telegraph*, 18 August 2008, accessed 20 June 2017, http://www.telegraph.co.uk/culture/film/film-news/6043155/Martin-Scorsese-portrayal-of-Frank-Sinatra-angers-family.html.

3 This can be heard for example in *The Summit: In Concert by the Rat Pack*, Artanis Entertainment Group, 1999.

4 The only element that alludes to the mafia behind the scenes in the casinos is the character of Duke Santos ,who represents the interests of the robbed casinos and who has clear connections with the mafia underworld.

5 Critics read Ginger as a character through which Scorsese overthrows the stereotypical representation of the Irish woman, that is, the wife of a criminal who shares the same ethnic identity. Like many Irish American men on the big screen, Ginger is active and dynamic and ultimately dies. Interestingly, she is the only main character who does not have a voiceover in the film, and her actions are always rooted in the commentaries and perspectives of the two male protagonists. On Ginger, see Matt R. Lohr, ;Irish-American Identity in Martin Scorsese,;' in *A Companion to Martin Scorsese*, ed. Aaron Baker (Malden, MA: Wiley Blackwell, 2015), 195–213.

6 One sequence calls attention to such a hierarchy of gazes: while Ace states that '[i]n Vegas, everybody's gotta watch everybody else,' the dealers monitor the players, the boxmen monitor the dealers, the floormen monitor the boxmen, the pit bosses monitor the floormen, the shift bosses monitor the pit bosses, the casino manager monitors the shift bosses, Ace monitors the casino manager, and, finally, in Foucauldian style, the electronic eye of the surveillance cameras observes everyone.

7 See, for example, Casillo, *Gangster Priest*, 357–60; Robert Kolker, *A Cinema of Loneliness*, 4th ed. (Oxford and New York: Oxford University Press, 2011), 218–20.

8 Kolker, A Cinema of Loneliness, 209.

9 On the function of *Casino*'s soundtrack, see Giuliana Muscio, 'Martin Scorsese Rocks,' in *A Companion to Martin Scorsese*, ed. Baker, 259–76.

10 On the film's representation of ethnicity, see Casillo, *Gangster Priest*; Kolker, *A Cinema of Loneliness*; Vincent LoBrutto, *Martin Scorsese: A Biography* (Westport, CT, and London: Praeger, 2008); Jonathan J. Cavallero, *Hollywood's Italian American Filmmakers: Capra, Scorsese, Savoca, Coppola, and Tarantino* (Urbana. IL: University of Illinois Press, 2011).

11 Larissa M. Ennis, 'Off-White Masculinity in Martin Scorsese's Gangster Films,' in *A Companion to Martin Scorsese*, ed. Baker, 173–94.

12 Ibid., 190.

13 Ibid., 188.

14 I borrow this expression from William L. Fox, *In the Desert of Desire: Las Vegas and the Culture of Spectacle* (Reno: NV: University of Nevada Press, 2005).

17 'Nothing Romantic about It': Gender and the Legacy of Crime in Abel Ferrara's *The Funeral*

LARA SANTORO

In its conventional approach to plot, themes, and characters, Abel Ferrara's *The Funeral* (1996) is located well within the confines of the Hollywood mafia film genre. Set in 1930s New York, the film explores family, honour, and revenge by illustrating the events following the murder of Johnny Tempio, the youngest of three Italian American gangster brothers. As conventional as it appears on the surface, however, *The Funeral* distinguishes itself from tradition in its portrayal of female characters. In a genre in which female figures are typically absent or relegated to the background, in *The Funeral* Ferrara offers a representation of women that is vivid and forceful. Jean's character, in particular, stands out from the rest of the Tempio women because of her non-traditional behaviour. Despite playing what could be viewed as a conventional role as the boss's wife, Jean is by no means passive. On the contrary, she engages in a pervasive power struggle with her husband Ray about his plans to avenge Johnny's murder. Revenge, then, is necessary for Ray to maintain his position of power. With his authoritative role threatened, Ray sees no other alternative than to resort to violence in order to reassert his masculinity and neutralize female influence. However, Jean's confrontational message is neither diminished nor silenced. On the contrary, Ferrara uses the character as a vehicle to strongly condemn gangster life. Using her clear eye and harsh, practical rationale, the director unmasks the glamour of the mafia practices seen in films such as *The Godfather* and disavows any sympathetic reaction on the part of the viewer. Taking this approach, *The Funeral* demystifies the mafia genre and offers instead a significant example of what Rafter has called the modern 'critical crime film,' which is 'a critical alternative of alienated, angry movies that subject viewers to harsh realities and refuse to flatter either their character or their audiences.'[1]

The Funeral is structured around a night of mourning and begins when Johnny's coffin is delivered to Ray's house for the wake. Scenes of the private family ceremony held within the house alternate with flashbacks to the brothers' criminal activities outside of the household. From the outset, Ferrara presents an opposition between public and private domains, each with its own specific activities and duties pertaining to men and women. Outside the household is the male domain of business, where the men compete and conduct their illicit activities. For example, this is where two Tempio henchmen discuss the potential consequences of Johnny's death and where Ray arranges his violent reprisal. The women occupy a space apart – inside the house – where they perform 'womanly' duties such as praying for Johnny's soul, cooking traditional dishes (meatballs and cannoli are ready for the guests), and, as Ray reminds his wife, keeping the children quiet.

As the camera pans the room from one woman to another during the wake, they all look alike, with their black dresses and embroidered veils. Each woman holds a rosary and dutifully recites 'Ave Marias' next to Johnny's casket, participating intensely in the religious ritual. For the Tempio women, the wake is a private, intimate celebration to express their grief and pay homage to a departed family member, whereas the men use it as a public stage to give voice to their anger, reject enemies' favours, and publicly affirm their need to avenge their brother's death.

The outside world is clearly established as the domain of women with loose morals. In *The Funeral,* women who do not belong to the household are either prostitutes or adulterers, and they exist only as sexual objects to serve and satisfy male desires. With the figure of the mother relegated to the background,[2] the wife and the prostitute are the only two models of womanhood for male characters. This polarity – made graphically explicit by the contrast between dark-haired wives and fair- or red-haired mistresses – has two major implications. First, women who leave their 'domestic cocoon'[3] are bound to become contaminated, to succumb to all sorts of vices (they dance, drink alcohol, and smoke cigarettes). Second, in order to fulfil their wifely and motherly duties, these women are devoid of sexuality. As a consequence, they do not indulge in sexual practices with their husbands. Overt sexuality does not mix well with the virgin-like image of the gangster's wife or with the sanctity of his home. The fact that this sanctity should not be violated is evident in the scene where Johnny brings his lover to his brother Chez's home. Chez reacts violently, physically attacking Johnny while shouting repeatedly: 'This is *my* house! *My* house!' Ironically, Chez himself is not capable of maintaining the purity of his home, as we witness when he forces his wife Clara to have sex with him. Physical violence is a means for Chez to assert his dominance in the marriage, but it also occurs when he encounters other women. In one of the film's most graphic scenes, Chez sodomizes a young girl who offers herself to him for sex as the punishment for having 'sold her soul.' The scene is even more noteworthy because Chez's brutal act dissolves into a shot of the crucifix hanging above Clara's bed as she waits for him to come home. In this way, Chez's violent sexuality is shown as directly contrasting to the purity of his marital bed and the devout Catholicism of his wife. This characterization of Chez is in line with the macho image of the mafia man, to whom 'the relation to women appears unequivocal: they are to be dominated, used.'[4] Although otherwise portrayed as a good family man (he is a loving father and loyal brother), Chez is essentially the product of a distorted code of male authority that permits him to subjugate women to excess.

Although the dichotomy between the virgin-like wife and the prostitute is established early in the film, a closer look at the Tempio women reveals blurred boundaries between the two categories. With her docile, subservient disposition, Clara conforms to the model of a chaste wife. However, by treating her in the same way as he treats the young prostitute, Chez seems to be implying that there is no difference between the two: his marriage to Clara is less a product of love than a relationship of sexual exploitation. In contrast, Jean transcends the devoted spouse cliché by virtue of her strong personality and also because she shares some of the prostitutes' traits (she smokes cigarettes and drinks alcohol). Her husband Ray repeatedly attempts to inscribe her back onto a traditional role by giving her orders and instructions, but Jean resists being tamed. Clara and Jean are constructed as diametrically opposite characters, and significantly, they never interact with each other. Quiet and fearful, Clara has fully embraced her destiny of subjugation, and she passively absorbs Chez's tensions and ruthless violence as part of her wifely duties. No matter how insane or brutal Chez behaves, she stands behind him: her devotion is never shaken, her commitment never falters. As she watches Chez's mental state deteriorate after Johnny's murder, for example, she begs him to seek therapy in Italy. Clara is also a typical example of a woman who passively conforms to the mafia code that regulates silence and invisibility, as seen when she remains silent on the issue of revenge. In contrast, Jean is never depicted as a victim. An intelligent woman who has had two years of a college education, Jean has – by her own admission – 'ideas,' and she is not afraid to express them, even when they differ from those of her husband. Unlike Clara, Jean does not adhere to the mafia code of silence. She openly confronts Ray on issues concerning the business and states her opinion when it comes to his plans for revenge. For example, in an early scene Jean expresses concern for her children because of the repercussions of Johnny's killing and exhorts a promise from Ray that 'there won't be any trouble.' Subsequently, she confronts Ray on the effectiveness of revenge, claiming that 'killing somebody else is not gonna bring [Johnny] back.' Jean urges Ray to comprehend the moral consequences of his actions and strongly criticizes him when he refuses to accept responsibility for them.

Because she is so assertive and unafraid to speak her mind, Jean poses a threat to Ray's authoritative role in the relationship. As he loses control over his wife, Ray is deprived of the power he exerts over his family, and thus his masculinity is threatened. When Jean announces her intention to take the children and leave the home after Johnny's funeral, Ray's non-reaction illustrates his awareness and implicit acknowledgment of the New Woman's role in the relationship. With the prospect of his family collapsing before his eyes, he can only respond as his father had taught him many years before. As a child, Ray had been initiated into the culture of revenge by his father, who had forced him to execute a traitor in front of his brothers. He now must follow his father's lead again in defending the family's honour. The narrative thrust of the story is such that we feel Ray cannot do otherwise, because his destiny has already been planned for him ('Once you pull a trigger there's no going back,' he tells Johnny's killer). However, Ferrara draws attention to this character's troubles and uncertainties. Although determined to seek revenge, Ray does not act upon his first instinct to kill. On the contrary, he gives Johnny's murderer a chance to explain himself, and he is about to release him when he discovers that the young man lied about his motives for executing revenge. As he weighs the moral aspects of his actions, Ray questions himself and searches for an excuse to reach out and forgive. This hesitancy collides with the image of a heartless, self-controlled gangster persona alienated from any morality, which has shaped Ray's sense of identity since his childhood. In the mafia system of values, toughness is a sign of force and masculinity, whereas compassion and forgiveness imply weakness and are indicative of feminine conduct. In this sense, with the killing of Johnny's murderer, Ray reaffirms his masculine identity and rejects any temptation to yield to his feminine side.[5] Ray's decision to pursue revenge can also be viewed as his ultimate attempt to regain control over Jean and re-establish his dominant position in the marriage; this is confirmed when he faces Johnny's killer. Just before shooting him dead, Ray feels the need to explicitly mention Jean. In what is quite an unorthodox speech for a supposedly cold-blooded killer, he explains: 'My wife … has pleaded for your life. She asked me: let the law punish you, keep my hands clean.' Ray then engages in an ethical debate with his victim that clearly recalls the conversation that he had with Jean a few hours before. In a long and rambling monologue, he goes on to enumerate his own motivations for the killing, as if he were sanctioning his own authority against hers.

With revenge functioning as a symbolic act that nullifies female influence and reinstates male authority, Jean's rebellion against mafia code is contained. The woman is reinscribed onto the traditional value system, and the old regime of male power is symbolically, albeit only temporarily, restored. However, Ray's attempt to re-establish his authority fails for two reasons. Jean, as an emblem of female rebellion, creates solidarity among the women and provides a model for them to oppose male dominance and mafia values. As such, Jean's example will be passed on to the future generation of women, so that they will gain sufficient self-knowledge to reject subordinate roles and avoid involvement with the mafia. The second reason is exemplified in the film's ending. After having indulged in memories of happy times with his brothers, Chez goes back to Ray's house the morning of Johnny's funeral and succumbs to his madness. In a shockingly violent climatic scene, he kills two male family members, shoots Ray, and then turns the gun on himself. In what is by no means a coincidence, all adult male family members are killed in the final massacre, with only women and children remaining to continue the Tempio family. With the elimination of all adult male members, the old regime of male power is destroyed and a new order is created, where the women are now free to choose their own paths.

The new generation of women is represented in the film by Johnny's fiancée Helen, who, on account of her youth and inexperience, is an ideal recipient of Jean's example. The two characters are also complementary: Helen can be regarded as a younger version of Jean, while Jean mirrors Helen's future and is an example of what she would have become had she married Johnny. Invited by Jean to stay overnight after the wake, the two of them share the bedroom and even the marital bed. This forced intimacy creates the grounds for establishing a new female bond and sets the foundations for Helen's self-awareness. With her physical traits and demeanour, Helen is an obvious outsider to the Tempio family. Unlike the women of the family, she is blond, blue-eyed, and non-Italian: she is the only one praying in English by Johnny's casket and does not seem to belong to the mafia milieu. Her angelic appearance establishes her as a symbol of innocence and purity. Helen's naivety becomes especially apparent during her conversations with Jean, where she demonstrates limited knowledge of the family's involvement in organized crime. It is Jean who educates her about the realities of the mafia lifestyle and the risks women take when they try to oppose it. In their first scene together, Jean makes an unorthodox but effective use of religious imagery to convey to Helen the dangers of female rebellion. As she lights a candle before a statuette of Saint Agnes in her bedroom, she tells Helen the story of the saint, who was decapitated for refusing men's advances at the age of twelve. When Helen asks if she prays to her, Jean candidly admits she does not, and goes on to explain: 'She is just there to remind me what happens when you say no.' Far from being spiritual, Jean's use of the religious icon is material and practical. Saint Agnes is not venerated as a Christian martyr; on the contrary, her tragic death is significant only as an example of women's sacrifice. The startling image of the saint's slit throat suggests violent mob killings and foreshadows a gruesome ending for any woman who dares to oppose the mafia.

As the patron saint of purity, Saint Agnes is also symbolic of Helen's innocence. Because she has not married into the family, Helen has not yet become involved in or complicit with the family's criminal activities. Jean emphasizes the fortuitous circumstances that have allowed Helen to escape her destiny when she cynically invites her to celebrate Johnny's death and 'the fact that you're not gonna become one of their wives.' Jean makes a point of telling Helen that she went to college for two years before she married Ray. In college she had 'learned how to read books' and developed ideas. Now, as the boss's wife, she is tied to her husband's brutish destiny, trapped in an existence she can no longer control. Jean seems to identify education as the key to woman's self-fulfilment and emancipation. More importantly, however, she views education as an alternative option (and a possible antidote) to the mafia way of life. This is the important message that Jean passes onto Helen when she warns her not to be deceived by the brothers' glamorous facade. Although 'they pass themselves off as tough, rugged individualists,' they are, in fact, just criminals who keep perpetuating an illiterate way of life.

Jean's speech constitutes the most direct and critical rejection of the ignorance and violence that is transmitted from father to son in the mafia family. Ferrara wholly embraces Jean's standpoint by ending the film with a hypercritical message directed towards the Tempio men. By killing off all adult male members, the director suggests that their physical elimination is necessary in order for the family to progress. Only with the destruction of the men can the new generation be freed from the legacy of violence and embark on a new road to legitimacy. Although, as remarked by Johnstone, the early scene of Ray's sons playing with toy guns seems to suggest that they have already been contaminated and are therefore 'conditioned to continue their family's violent legacy,'[6] no male role model is left for them. Furthermore, the fact that Jean herself had been the one taking the guns away from her sons, while at the same time scolding Ray for buying them, is indicative of Jean's intention to provide a drastically different direction to their upbringing.

The decline of the Tempio gangster family had been to some extent anticipated by Johnny's character. The most feminine of the three brothers and something of an intellectual, Johnny was almost as much an outsider to the family as his blond, non-Italian fiancée Helen. Engaging and passionate, Johnny loved books, was infatuated with cinema, and had a strong social conscience, which compelled him to defend the working class even in front of his rival mobsters. As the youngest and therefore the least influenced by his father's legacy, Johnny had distanced himself from the family business and was drawn to break away from his destined life of crime. In the flashbacks, he emerges as an idealistic character who rises above his criminal trappings through a new sense of integrity. It is clearly not possible to foresee whether, had he not been killed, Johnny would have been an agent of change for his family. Perhaps he was too ambivalent a character to provoke true change. However, it cannot be argued that it is precisely his killing that begins the process of family disintegration and that allows the Tempio women and children an opportunity to start anew. Johnny's murder unleashes Ray's thirst for revenge and perturbs Chez's already unstable mind. Moreover, it disaggregates the family and ultimately brings about change, albeit in a very drastic way.

NOTES

1   Nicole Rafter, *Shoot in the Mirror: Crime Films and Society* (Oxford: Oxford University Press, 2006), 11.

2   Mama Tempio is present at the wake, but her character is marginal and at the limits of caricature. She fulfils the expected role of the Italian mother of a dead son: she assumes theatrical poses, alternates between silence and desperation, but for the most part is oblivious to what happened and why.

3   Stephen Farber, 'Coppola and the Godfather,' *Sight and Sound* 41, no. 4 (1972): 218.

4   Renate Siebert, *Secrets of Life and Death: Women and the Mafia,* trans. Liz Heron (London: Verso, 1996), 48.

5 As Siebert explains in *Secrets of Life and Death*: 'The mafia group represents a strengthened defense against all intrusion of the feminine. Externally, the group defends itself by admitting only men … Internally, at the subjective level, all are obliged to reject and excise the feminine sides of their own existence' (23).

6 Nick Johnstone, *Abel Ferrara: The King of New York* (London: Omnibus Press, 1999), 192.

18   Inside the Mafia: Mike Newell's *Donnie Brasco*

ROBERT CASILLO

Based on a bestselling memoir by former FBI undercover agent Joseph D. Pistone, Mike Newell's *Donnie Brasco* (1997) explores the lives of the rank and file of today's mafia. Between 1976 and 1981, Pistone penetrated the Bonanno crime family as Donnie Brasco. He expected that his undercover work would take about six months, but he proved so successful that the operation was prolonged to the point where his security could no longer be guaranteed.[1] While infiltrating the Bonannos' New York branch in the guise of a jewel thief, Pistone closely befriended Lefty 'Guns' Ruggiero, a made man who groomed Pistone for initiation into the mob. In those years the Bonannos were riddled with conflict, which led to the murder in 1979 of boss Carmine Galante, whose underlings resented his drug trade monopoly. Galante was succeeded by Rusty Rastelli, whereupon Ruggiero and Brasco were assigned to a crew led by the Brooklyn mob capo Sonny 'Black' Napolitano. Sonny Black subsequently appropriated Donnie as his protégé, a casually prepotent act that angered Ruggiero. When Black's illegal gambling operation in Florida was unexpectedly raided by local police, he realized there might be an informant among his subordinates. However, Pistone carried out his work so well that he was regarded even by law enforcement agencies as the criminal Donnie Brasco. But the demands of Pistone's job often prevented him from visiting his family, from which he grew estranged for several years. Thanks to Pistone's testimony, some two hundred criminals were indicted and one hundred of these were convicted between 1984 and 1992.

Newell's film takes some liberties with Pistone's memoir. Although the film shows that Pistone formed an intense friendship with Ruggiero, it ignores his increasing exasperation with his mentor, who dressed him down in public and expected him to carry his luggage. Nor was Ruggiero executed by Bonanno henchmen, as the film implies. Instead, he was sentenced to a long prison term as a result of Pistone's disclosures. Whereas in the film Sonny is a cold-blooded killer who abuses underlings and claims Pistone as his protégé, the real Sonny Black was a respected mafia capo whom Pistone preferred to Ruggiero. Moreover, it was not Ruggiero but rather Sonny whom the Bonannos executed for having failed to unmask Pistone.

A crucial difference between the book and film is that Pistone and his cinematic counterpart hold divergent attitudes towards both the FBI and the mafia. The memoir shows that Pistone's supervisors and colleagues not only applauded his undercover work but also worried over his safety. At one point, FBI director William Webster visited Pistone secretly in Florida in order to reiterate his high regard for his work as well as to pledge continuing commitment to his welfare.

Pistone was pleased by the visit, and following the completion of his mission was honoured in Washington at a ceremony held in the Great Hall of the Department of Justice.

During his six years of work, Pistone maintained a strong sense of his own identity and was never seduced by the criminal life he was immersed in. That he was an Italian American who had been raised in an ethnic neighbourhood was of no significance to him in working with the Bonannos, all fellow ethnics. Although he became deeply involved in mafia society, he always maintained a professional distance from his role, and he felt no guilt in betraying his mafiosi colleagues, since to him this was part of an essentially impersonal job. He gives the impression of an assimilated Italian American who has transcended the ethnic loyalties and biases of the group in favour of total allegiance to the national government.

In contrast to the memoir, the film portrays Pistone's relations with the FBI as impersonal and dissatisfying. In one scene, a supervisor from Washington shows little comprehension of Pistone's hazardous job and indeed, valuing only results, places unreasonable demands upon him. In another instance, FBI technicians monitor Pistone in a bugging operation when their tape recorder malfunctions. Regarding him as an expendable tool, the technicians respond heartlessly: 'We're getting what we want. Fuck him.' In the final scene, Donnie's award ceremony is rushed through perfunctorily by FBI bigwigs.

Unlike the author, Pistone in the film so prefers the mafia lifestyle that he ultimately has more in common with the Bonannos than with his FBI colleagues or even his family. It is as if, having escaped the Italian American neighbourhood, Pistone has been drawn back atavistically to the streets. Whereas in his memoir Pistone avoids being present at mafia murders and other brutal acts, in the film Donnie observes two major crimes. His deepening absorption in the criminal mentality is shown when, following a police raid on Sonny Black's gambling den, he keeps the $300,000 in winnings that has been presumed lost. Although the theft is motivated by Donnie's desire to buy a boat for Lefty, the transformation of his personality is apparent to his wife, who exclaims in horror on realizing that he has hidden the money in their suburban house: 'You're becoming like them, you know that?' Donnie answers her angry outburst with a slap, retrogressing into the stereotype of the wife-beating ghetto Italian.

Donnie Brasco surpasses most mafia films in portraying the details and codes of mob culture and the process of induction into the mafia. Whereas the classic gangster films of the early 1930s such as *Little Caesar* (Mervyn LeRoy, 1931) and *Scarface* (Howard Hawks, 1932) emphasize the gangster's Italian ethnicity, the depicted criminal organizations are based neither on blood kinship nor on fictitiously constructed familial ties. Their rituals and codes of behaviour receive very little attention; the focus is not on the group but on the gangster protagonist as an individual. In the syndicate films of the 1950s such as *The Big Heat* (Fritz Lang, 1953) and *The Big Combo* (Joseph H. Lewis, 1955), gangs are typically multi-ethnic and usually conduct themselves according to impersonal business standards. *Donnie Brasco*, by contrast, offers insights into the mafia code and culture. The basic requirement of an initiate or 'made man' is that he be what Lefty calls a 'stand-up guy,' that is, unwilling to inform on other criminals. Being embedded in a hierarchical structure, mafia underlings must respect their superiors, and indeed, Lefty behaves fawningly when introduced to Santo Trafficante. Nor can a mafia member refuse an order from above, even if it is for his own execution. But besides these unattractive features of mafia life, Lefty showcases for Donnie the privileged position of an inducted mafioso – or wiseguy – in the criminal world. 'A wiseguy is always right,' says Lefty, 'even when he's wrong.' A non-member of the mafia should never argue with a wiseguy, for in arbitrating such disputes a boss is likely to favour his own man. And though a non-member like Donnie is always vulnerable to intimidation by a mafioso, he should never 'touch a made guy', lest he pay with his life.

The mafioso must act the part, and Lefty therefore demands that Donnie always carry a money clip rather than a wallet. He is required to remove all facial hair as well, the mark of an old-fashioned mafioso, and to discard his cowboy-style pants, which are unworthy of the urban wiseguy. As one would expect, mafiosi judge one another on the basis of dress, as when Sonny Black, arriving at a nightclub, is told by a more stylish rival that he needs a new wardrobe. Yet despite Lefty's insistence that Donnie not dress like a 'cowboy' – mafia parlance for a reckless gunman – the mafiosi of *Donnie Brasco* find their masculine ideal in the heroic characters played by western film star John Wayne. They thus resemble the hoodlums of Martin Scorsese's *Who's That Knocking at My Door?* (1967) and *Mean Streets* (1973), who also regard Wayne as a role model. In one of the most memorable scenes in *Donnie Brasco*, the dumbstruck mafiosi, having imagined Wayne as indestructible, read a report of the actor's death. Like Scorsese's post-adolescents,[2] they make no distinction between Wayne and the cinematic characters he portrays, referring to the latter as John Wayne.

Donnie Brasco stands out for its depiction of male–female relations within the mafia and also for its depiction of intense male bonding, a behaviour that is deeply rooted in Italian America as well as in southern Italy. Italian American society has been characterized by a strict demarcation between the workplace and the domestic sphere as well as by a high degree of sex segregation and, in the more distant past, by father-absent households, with men spending much time outside the home either as migrant workers or in the company of male friends.[3] The latter practice exemplifies the homophilism of southern Italian society.

In *Donnie Brasco*, the mafia custom of excluding women from the male world of business affairs is evident when Lefty's girlfriend dutifully leaves the living room to allow Lefty and Donnie to discuss professional matters. Unavoidably, the film's mafiosi exemplify father-absent households, since their criminal careers carry them far from home for long periods of time. Ironically, Donnie's undercover work not only requires him to leave his family temporarily but also exposes him to fellow ethnics whose social code validates such behaviour. At the same time, these mafiosi congregating in all-male groups exemplify that southern Italian homophilism whose visible tokens consist of hugging, kissing, and other gestures of physical affection. Although Donnie's closeness with other males elicits unjustified accusations of homosexuality from his neglected wife, one cannot deny the intensity of affection among these mafiosi.

Building on the 'syndicate' films of the 1950s, many mafia films of the last several decades portray organized crime in terms of a highly questionable analogy with the modern business corporation. This mistaken view of the mafia, most thoroughly explored by Donald Cressey in his work, is prevalent in films from the 1950s onward.[4] Another predominant type of mafia film, best exemplified by Francis Ford Coppola's *The Godfather* (1972), defines the mafia as a 'family' business held together by blood loyalties and obligations. Family leadership is portrayed as hereditary, and furthermore, the chief positions within the organization are manned by blood relatives. However, a small number of films such as Martin Ritt's *The Brotherhood* (1968) and John Huston's *Prizzi's Honor* (1985) exhibit an at least intermittent or partial awareness that a mafia 'family' organization is usually based on artificially created or fictional relationships that supersede all considerations of blood kinship. Newell's film acknowledges as much when Lefty, informed by Donnie that he has no family, replies that henceforward his family will be the Bonannos.

In both text and film, *Donnie Brasco* lends support to Annelise Graebner Anderson's contention that mafia 'families' are most comparable to governments. Like governments, they invest authority in their leaders, spatially dissociate governors from the rank and file, afford privileges and protection to citizens or members, tax them in exchange for services, adjudicate disputes, and make treaties with other organizations. Although each mafioso has his place within a loose hierarchy, his superiors expect him to act as a largely independent entrepreneur reliant upon his own ingenuity and discretion. In no sense is he a paid employee, although a mob family usually guarantees certain benefits. His ability to operate, moreover, depends on the boss's permission. The mafioso is also required to turn over a percentage of his earnings to the boss and can expect severe punishment or even death in the event of non-payment. He must also be 'good earner', or risk being killed by a disgruntled boss.

This description of mafia operations is closely mirrored in *Donnie Brasco*. 'You never hear from the boss [until he dies or is assassinated],' remarks Lefty. Should the boss appear unexpectedly in public before his underlings, as in the scene in Manhattan's Little Italy, they must greet him with awed, respectful silence. In the film (as in Pistone's memoir), the typical mafioso is a hustling entrepreneur whose profits come from hijacking, loan-sharking, thieving, various scams, and the tacky illegality of breaking open parking metres. The film also shows that even a 'made man' must give to the boss a portion of his earnings as payment for the right to operate. Sonny Black and his associates are desperate to expand their criminal operations into the Sun Belt in order to meet the bosses' monthly tax of $50,000. 'We better start earnin' or somebody's gonna get clipped,' announces Sonny to his men – by no means an idle threat.

For many audiences, the appeal of *The Godfather* lay in its contrast between the mafia as the embodiment of personalistic and traditional values, including loyalty, friendship, and family solidarity, on the one hand, and the impersonality of state and business bureaucracies, on the other. Such an evaluation diverges markedly from gangster films of the 1950s, in which the criminal 'syndicate' sometimes seems indistinguishable from political and corporate organizations. That these conflicting viewpoints are relevant to *Donnie Brasco* is suggested in the film when Donnie observes that the mafia is 'kind of like the army' with its 'chain of command,' whereupon Lefty points out that the army 'sends you out to kill people you don't know.' Lefty's statement suggests that the difference between the mafia and a state or industrial–commercial bureaucracy lies in the cold impersonality of the latter, as shown in the film when the FBI treats Pistone instrumentally. Fortunately, however, Newell avoids a simplistic opposition between the mafia's warm personalistic loyalties and the calculating anonymity of bureaucratic organizations. Lefty must sit by helplessly as Sonny Black feels free (for business reasons) to intrude upon his friendship with Donnie. Lefty complains of isolation from the bosses; as he remarks of a fellow mafioso who had been killed merely on suspicion of betrayal, 'I'm a spoke in a wheel. So is he and so are you.'

The dramatic focus of *Donnie Brasco* is the character of Joseph Pistone, alias Donnie Brasco, and his deepening yet compromised friendship with Lefty Ruggiero. In its portrayal of Lefty, the film extends sympathy towards a criminal character without excusing his criminality. One never forgets that he is a seasoned mafioso boastful of twenty-six 'hits,' whose favourite television programs showcase ferocious beasts of the wild, and whose affinity for such predators is evident in the gift of a caged lion cub he receives from Sonny Black. Yet Lefty's brutality is offset by unintentionally comic touches. In the end, one sympathizes with the squalor and disappointment of his existence while acknowledging his loyalty, generosity, and friendship.

We first encounter Lefty in a Manhattan saloon, where he engages his fellow mafiosi in a banal conversation typical, as Pistone complains, of mafia society. Lefty's praise of the Fleetwood Cadillac, as having 'more acceleration, more power,' reflects indirectly on his stagnant and enfeebled career. Confined with his girlfriend Annette to a shabby apartment, Lefty owes major interest payments to Sonny Red, a Bonanno Family capo who is eventually murdered by Sonny Black's crew. His son, who lives with him and whom he supports, is a junkie, while his troublesome ex-wife lives in the same building. 'You don't know the worries I got,' he tells Donnie. Although Lefty had taken care of Sonny Black's family during a prison stint, he has not yet been compensated. His real future is implicit in the scene in which, as his associates cavort with their girlfriends on a Florida beach, he lies almost totally submerged in immobilizing sand, a portent of his future execution. In an attempt to counter these indignities, Lefty boasts of being 'known all over the world,' yet in reality his obscure forays are mainly confined to the Manhattan area. When Donnie is present for Christmas dinner, Lefty begins preparing coq au vin with the observation that 'wherever you go, the best cooks are men.' This statement, an implicit insult directed at Annette, is quickly ironized when Lefty nearly sets the kitchen afire and yields the cooking duties to his girlfriend. Yet whereas the typical mafioso feels obliged to keep a girlfriend on the side, Lefty praises Annette as a 'good woman … enough for any man,' and when faced with elimination by the mob, he arranges for her to receive his Cadillac, watch, jewellery, and other valuables.

Lefty's generosity to Donnie is motivated not only by his desire for a worthy son but also by sympathetic alignment with a person whose situation resembles that of Lefty himself. In claiming to be an orphan, Donnie masquerades as a social isolate, without protection and hence totally vulnerable – just the thing to awaken Lefty's sympathy. For despite his mafia membership, which should protect him, Lefty finds himself isolated and professionally vulnerable – an orphan of the mob, so to speak. Through Lefty, Donnie will receive protection both personally and in the form of the criminal family. Or, as Lefty tells Donnie in presenting him with a Christmas gift, now that he has Lefty as his patron, 'Nobody can touch you.' This statement, however, is immediately subverted by Lefty's request that Donnie 'spot' him money.

The dramatic counterweight to Lefty's friendship with Donnie is the latter's conflicted relationship with his patron. Although Donnie initially thinks of Lefty and his associates as only professional prey, his relationship to Lefty is more than simply predatory. Their friendship culminates when Donnie offers to buy him and Annette a seaworthy boat that will supposedly enable them to flee the mafia. Yet even if this offer expresses Donnie's sincere affection, it cannot assuage the guilt he carries for ultimately betraying his friend. His remorse is all the greater since, through his immersion in mafia society, he has reinternalized the old neighbourhood code against informing the police. The fact that Donnie sees himself as Lefty's murderer is shown in the transition from the scene in which Lefty is summoned to his execution for having admitted a traitor into the mafia to the one where Donnie, standing at a police firing range, mows down paper cut-outs of human targets. It is as if he has killed Lefty himself. The Joseph Pistone of the film thus emerges as a precariously assimilated Italian American torn between ethnic codes and loyalties on the one hand and, on the other, his allegiance to impersonal law and the state.

NOTES

1 For more on Pistone's involvement with the FBI and the mafia, see Joseph D. Pistone, *Donnie Brasco: My Undercover Life in the Mafia* (New York: New American Library, 1988); Annelise Graebner Anderson, *The Business of Organized Crime: A Cosa Nostra Family* (Stanford, CA: Hoover Institution Press, 1979); Herbert Gans, *The Urban Villagers: Group and Class in the Life of Italian-Americans* (New York: Free Press, 1965).

2 Robert Casillo, *Gangster Priest: The Italian American Cinema of Martin Scorsese* (Toronto: University of Toronto Press, 2006), 71–4, 232, 284.

3 See Joseph Lopreato, *Italian Americans* (New York: Random House, 1970), 81; Donna Gabaccia, *From Sicily to Elizabeth Street: Housing and Social Change among Italian Immigrants, 1880–1930* (Albany, NY: SUNY Press, 1984), 97; Casillo, *Gangster Priest*, 71–3.

4 Donald Cressey, *Theft of the Nation: The Structure and Operation of Organized Crime in America* (New York: Harper and Row, 1969).

19 Family Therapy: Harold Ramis's *Analyze This* and the Evolution of the Gangster Genre

LOUIS BAYMAN

Alongside the western, the gangster film furnishes textbooks with the classic example of a Hollywood genre. According to scholars such as McArthur and Schatz, the gangster film's brief heyday in the early 1930s established a series of traits, of an urban underworld that hosts immigrant kids who battle their way up a criminal hierarchy by employing of ingenuity and brutality.[1] These properties have been reworked, rejected, and ignored in the decades since, so that the gangster now inhabits an ever broadening range of works. The comedy of *Analyze This* (Harold Ramis, 1999) works precisely by spoofing the idea of the gangster as a classic figure who bears identifiable generic motifs. In doing so, it also confirms the changing position of the gangster amidst the sociocultural world of the 1990s. Appearing at the end of a decade that began with the acclaim awarded to *Goodfellas* (Martin Scorsese, 1990), the 5 March 1999 release of *Analyze This* coincided with the American premier of the first season of *The Sopranos*.[2] Again according to Schatz, a genre typically develops through various phases: convention turns to cliché and is then revised until familiarity eventually breeds the contempt of parody.[3] *Analyze This* served as a moment when the self-consciousness of pastiche indicated not exhaustion but rather new directions for the genre. For while *The Sopranos* affirmed the role of crime fiction in the revitalization of quality television, the series' appearance alongside *Analyze This* consolidated the transformation of the gangster into a domestic figure – an alteration that has had an important impact on almost all aspects of how he is represented on screen.

Analyze This restates a fundamental question: What kind of hero is the gangster? In the classical era he epitomized the bad guy as a larger-than-life figure, the captivating boss of a gang whose workplace ethics challenged the management philosophy that there is no 'I' in 'team.' The gangster was not another villain who served to prove the virtues of a vanquishing hero, but instead offered the pleasures of the *antihero*, and his glamorous lifestyle and gleeful flouting of authority carried the spectator along to the ultimate moral that crime does not pay. Writing in 1948, the American critic Robert Warshow argued for the definition of 'The Gangster as Tragic Hero.' Likening the gangster to the protagonists of ancient myth, Warshow reflected on the character's meteoric rise before a sudden, fatal fall.[4] In different circumstances, these qualities – in the gangster's case, those of energy, enterprise, and unflinching ambition – could be admirable. But the methods he had to employ to escape his lowly position meant he could only fleetingly realize the American Dream of wealth, as his irredeemable brutality could only lead to the final punishments of death or imprisonment.

Analyze This represents the gangster as a farcical rather than a tragic hero, testifying to the inadequacy of the rise-and-fall narrative in an epoch when conflicts are better understood as blockages to be worked through rather than violently terminated. Such motivation offers less space for heroes, whether anti- or tragic, than for human fallibility, and *Analyze This* privileges comic debasement over tragic aggrandizement. Its protagonists are deficient primarily in relation to the classic pantheon of gangster greats, and the film's retro atmosphere is established in the opening sequence, as Robert De Niro's recognizable drawl inaugurates mobster protagonist Vitti's reminiscence of the importance of the year 1956. Archival photos show the launch of Sputnik, The Dodgers lining up to 'say goodbye to Brooklyn' before their last game at Ebbets Field, and then a series of mob hits, while Louis Prima's swing version of 'When You're Smiling (The Whole World Smiles with You)' is heard on the soundtrack. The sequence then merges into live action with the last time the heads of the mob families met, as Vitti informs us that his father successfully evaded the cops by hijacking a tractor. The iconography of this opening is drawn as much from the decor of pizza restaurants as from journalistic record but nonetheless is a shared cultural memory. As a form of nostalgia the incipit is dynamic and enjoyable while placing the film immediately in the realms of 'affective memory', the term Jill Bennett has given to the contemporary cultural mode in which official record, family photographs, and retro artefacts combine to produce strongly emotional ties to the past.[5] Vitti's reminiscence interweaves family lore with New York social history, while the regretful tone establishes a complicity with the viewer over the end of the classic world of the gangster. The first-person voiceover was popularized by the more intimate picture of the gangster provided in *Goodfellas*, and De Niro performs a kind of impression of himself as Jimmy in that film (albeit his surname recalls one of his breakthrough roles, Vito Corleone in *The Godfather II*). The nostalgia inherent in the opening remarks therefore humanizes the previous film's unsympathetic character, which aids in reworking the gangster into a morally acceptable figure.

Analyze This pits Vitti's brutality against Billy Crystal's mild-mannered psychiatrist Dr Sobel. After the introduction to the competitive aggression of mob life, the film cuts to a woman crying in Dr Sobel's office. Sobel reassures her that acceptance of things ending is a fact of life – and that her husband's recourse to a restraining order 'is not a good sign' – but fantasizes shouting at her to 'stop whining … and get a fucking life!' Such boldness, however, is what this quiet family man lacks, distinct from Vitti and his henchmen. Their two worlds collide literally by accident: while arguing with his pubescent son, Sobel runs into the back of Vitti's henchmen's car. The comedy of mutual incomprehension commences as Sobel volunteers to exchange insurance details, oblivious that the trunk he busted open contains a gagged man. Vitti's first session begins when he bursts into Sobel's office and throws out a patient who suffers from a lack of assertiveness; at the end of it, Vitti, who deals with opponents by eliminating them, ensures his future appointments by the unique menace with which he tells Sobel how much he would enjoy the opportunity to 'clear your schedule for you.'

The film thus has great fun with the incongruity of a violent man being encouraged to work through his feelings. In so doing, it presents a mismatch between medical therapy and criminal destruction, which is performed by the two protagonists as an antagonism between Jewish intellectualism and obedience to authority on the one hand, and Italian brawn and impulsivity on the other. Even the ethnic stereotyping in the film contributes to a sense of loss; the New York of lore has disappeared amidst the impersonal forces of capitalist globalization, for example when Vitti's right-hand man states that they have to accept that times are being irreversibly changed by 'these Chinese, and crazy Russians' moving in. This scene ends abruptly in a restaurant shootout that constitutes a nod to *Scarface: The Shame of a Nation* (Howard Hawks, 1932). Thus, while the viewer is reminded of the days of the classic gangster film, the comic tone is underpinned by melancholy, which for Sobel means his inability to assert himself, while Vitti is melancholic for the loss of the energy of his father's generation. Indeed, the theme of male potency (or lack thereof) is made explicit when Vitti turns to Sobel, while flying direct to his hotel prior to the latter's wedding, because he is unable to maintain an erection with his mistress.

Comedy works in the film by revealing the underlying similarity beneath a surface opposition. While Crystal plays the schlemiel to De Niro's mobster, their relationship enables them both to get past their respective blockages: Sobel, like Vitti, stands in the professional shadow of his father, whose success as a doctor and published author Sobel has failed to emulate. Analysis meanwhile teaches Vitti to accept the bourgeois suburban reality of his middle-aged life and abandon a life of crime (what he earlier refers to as 'Schmuckville, where you listen to housewives piss and moan because their husbands don't fuck them anymore,' before bursting into tears). He is imprisoned in the end, but incarceration in a correctional facility is only the final conclusion to his acceptance of confinement, first to the psychiatrist's office and consequently to his domestic responsibilities. Sobel, for his part, stands in for an emotionally paralysed Vitti at the film's climax, ditching his wife at their second attempt at a wedding ceremony so as to successfully command the meeting of the family heads (employing his disarming emotional analysis to do so).

What the film does then is realize an essential comic structure that Jerry Palmer has termed 'the logic of the absurd': that is, a ridiculous or impossible incongruity that, even so, reveals a certain underlying rationality – just not the one that is conventionally supposed.[6] The film works by finding points in common between the therapeutic culture of Sobel and the mafia lifestyle of Vitti. Therapy is dubbed the talking cure, just as the wiseguy is reliant on verbal prowess. Sobel refuses to act as an informant as his medical obligation to client–patient confidentiality coincides with the Sicilian code of *omertà*. One could even suggest an analogy between the notion of healing provided by a session on the analyst's couch and that of absolution offered by the confessional booth. Furthermore, while there is ostensibly nothing more incongruous than a mob boss being encouraged to get in touch with his anger, the self-reflection that Sobel encourages in Vitti seems only a further development of De Niro's renowned performance style. In fact, the innovation of the first two *Godfather* films was to feature psychological complexity through the introspective technique of method acting. The Freudian associations of the gangster go at least as far back as Jimmy Cagney's performance in *White Heat* (1949), and *Analyze This* similarly articulates the forces of id, ego, and punishing superego as the motivating dynamics at work in the gangster hero's trajectory of rise and fall. For Freud, ancient myths offered proof of libidinal conflicts that are worked out in the domestic sphere, but as Dr Sobel remarks, 'When I got into family therapy, this was not the "family" I had in mind!'

The final, and in some ways insurmountable, incongruity remains that between tragedy and farce, between antihero and clown. The classical gangster film often takes a high moral tone that excuses the violence the films otherwise encourage, as testified by titles such as *Scarface: The Shame of a Nation* and the biblical or ancient allusions in *Angels with Dirty Faces* (Michael Curtiz, 1938) and *Little Caesar* (Mervin LeRoy, 1931), whose solemn opening citation is from Matthew 25:52, 'For all they that take the sword shall perish by the sword.' The tendency to aggrandize the gangster coincides with the gangster taking himself quite seriously, to the point of violently upholding his belief in himself. Perhaps for this reason, attempts at establishing the mob boss as a parodic figure have not always had a happy history, as Marlon Brando was to discover in 1990's ill-fated *The Freshman* (Andrew Bergman). In this film, Brando's theatrically heightened display of masculine potency simply replicates the exaggeration already present in the gangster as a generic type. In this regard, two of the more commercially successful spoofs in gangster history, *Some Like It Hot* (Billy Wilder, 1959) and *Bugsy Malone* (Alan Parker, 1976), recognize the play-acting that is central to the gangster persona, the former featuring two cross-dressing musicians and the latter populated by elegantly tailored, world-weary children.

Pastiche in *Analyze This* works in a similarly artistically self-conscious way, through incorporating the notion of dressing up in another's clothes. This in fact becomes its essential theme, as seen in the aforementioned awareness of failing to live up to past glories. For example, the iconic scene from *The Godfather* when Vito Corleone is shot on the street after buying oranges is re-created in Sobel's dream, where he is killed by hitmen as Vitti fumbles and drops his gun, then cradles him, screaming 'Papa!' (on hearing Sobel recount this dream, Vitti refuses to believe that he could have taken on Fredo's role). Patriarchal loss brings about a breakdown of authority that results in Vitti's psychological breakdown as he prepares for the first all-mafia meeting since when his father was in charge. Through psychoanalysis, Sobel learns that when he was twelve years old, Vitti witnessed, and still feels guilt over, the murder of his father. Thus the film's awareness of its generic history presents itself as a trope of a psychic inability to escape the past: Vitti is immobilized by his awareness of his own inadequacy in relation to his forefathers; 1950s New York of the film's opening has gone and, as the film implicitly tells us, they don't make movies like *The Godfather* anymore.

Hence, *Analyze This* points to underlying similarities it has with more classical gangster films while also producing genuine innovations. Unlike the western, that other exemplar of Hollywood genres – one, however, that mythologizes manly heroism – the gangster is often seen in relation to childhood: as the victim of an unfortunate upbringing and as still immature at heart (*Bugsy Malone* draws most fully on this facet). The gang in many mafia films becomes a surrogate family remade according to the hero's urge to dominate; the female is shut out of the homosocial milieu. In the men-only enclave, men can act out their aggressive energies in competition for city space, free from responsibility and family ties.[7] The radical departure presented by Martin Scorsese's *Goodfellas* lies in how it brings the domestic life of the gangster to the fore as a place where he fails to gain dominance and must contend with women who will not quietly retreat to their place – a factor that threatens to reveal the fragility compelling his drive to violence.

What was in the first era of the genre a tragic conflict played out among criminal competitors in the urban street thus becomes a conflict whose centre is the private sphere of the family home. While the earlier gangster films debuted during the reign of monopolistic and imperialist capitalist corporations in the interwar era and during the final crisis of laissez-faire capitalism, *Analyze This* speaks to a different phase, one of the rise of home-working and flexible labour, where the predominance of service industries and what is termed 'neoliberalism' encourages emotional articulacy and a greater emphasis on individual feeling. By the late 1990s the indulgences of an antihero had become less a source of moral anxiety for Hollywood, where anxiety itself, rather than innate badness, had become the master narrative explaining behaviour. Furthermore, while the tragic hero displays fatally misplaced values that society otherwise admires, wrongdoing was in this period seen as evidence of a malady in need of cure. This change in moral terms meant that on-screen bad guys were not repudiated as evil and ultimately brought down but instead were understood in terms of pathology and cure. Bad deeds (in Hollywood, but also perhaps in the world beyond) were seen as resulting from developmental complexes that needed to be talked through and remedied, because when all are victims, no one is wholly bad. As the teen good-guy vampires of *Twilight* (Catherine Hardwicke, 2008) suggest, the gangster film has not been alone in changing prevailing notions about evil – both monsters and villains can become domesticated and to some degree absolved.

Analyze This does not however get to grips with the challenge to gender roles that it suggests. It employs a stereotype of Italian American masculinity, which it then it undermines by satirizing its mobster characters' interest in nice clothes, occasional propensity to babble, lack of self-control, and tendency to hug and kiss. While these are lampooned as overcompensating pride, they betray anxiety on behalf of the film itself about the closeness of the male relationship at its heart. Vitti threatens Sobel in their first encounter that 'if I go fag, you die,' but this disavowal exists within a narrative that upholds the centrality of their relationship in the protagonists' realizations of themselves as full human beings. Lisa Kudrow's contribution as Sobel's wife-to-be is underdeveloped as she nags against Vitti's disruption to their wedding plans. Sobel abandons her twice at the altar for Vitti and in so doing successfully asserts himself as a man. Vitti's imprisonment at the end of the film resolves the otherwise intractable conflict between domestic and professional relationships, for it is the relationship between the two men that provides the narrative focus.

Thus, what is clearly a spoof also heralds the beginnings of an evolution of the gangster picture. Regarding the domestication of the gangster, *Analyze This* presages reality television shows such as *Growing Up Gotti* (2004–5) and *Mob Wives* (2011–16), where the daily tribulations of home life take precedence to inter-gang rivalries. Three years later, De Niro and Crystal were reunited in the sequel *Analyze That*, once again directed by Harold Ramis. As a sequel, it offers a different take on the genre; already in its first scene it combines references to both *The Godfather: Part II* and *The Sopranos* but also *Little Caesar* and *Scream 2*. Following Vitti's attempt to go straight, the mobster plot enters only intermittently amidst moments of prison drama, domestic comedy, farce, the buddy movie, and even, in its grand finale, the musical. While the first film presented the gangster as a classic type who only uneasily submits to change, the sequel indicates the potential for generic hybridity that the mobster milieu holds out. Taken together, the films nicely encapsulate a contrast within the gangster himself: a modern archetype whose appeal lies in his assertion of his own unbending will, and a cultural figure flexible enough to transform amidst a changing social landscape.

NOTES

1 See, for example, Colin McArthur, *Underworld USA* (London: Secker & Warburg, 1972), 23–59; Thomas Schatz, *Hollywood Genres: Formulas, Filmmaking and the Studio System* (New York: Random House, 1987), 81–111.

2 Although the basic premise seems to have first seen the light of day in the television movie *The Don's Analyst* (David Jabin, 1997).

3 Thomas Schatz, *Hollywood Genres: Formulas, Filmmaking and the Studio System* (New York: Random House, 1987), 36–45.

4 Robert Warshow, *Immediate Experience: Movies, Comics, Theatre, and Other Aspects of Popular Culture* (Garden City, NY: Doubleday, 1962), 85–8.

5 Jill Bennett, *Empathic Vision: Affect, Trauma, and Contemporary Art* (Stanford, CA: Stanford University Press, 2005), 22–46.

6 Jerry Palmer, *The Logic of the Absurd: On Film and Television Comedy* (London: BFI, 1987), 39–59.

7 An analysis employed by Fran Mason, *American Gangster Cinema from Little Caesar to Pulp Fiction* (Basingstoke: Palgrave Macmillan, 2002), 16–28.

20 Martin Scorsese's *The Departed*, or the Quest for a Departed (Ethnic) Identity

MARGHERITA HEYER-CAPUT

The theme of betrayal runs throughout Martin Scorsese's mafia films[1] and is at the very centre of *The Departed* (2006), not only as betrayal of (crime) friendships but also as unfaithfulness to one's ethnic identity. In this chapter I argue that, with *The Departed*, Scorsese exploits the brutality inherent in this film genre to express the violence that defines the loss of a relationship between signs and referents in the postmodern age of late capitalism. While visually extending Fredric Jameson's exploration of postmodernism to ethnic identities, *The Departed* indicates how ethnicity 'as "referent" finds itself gradually bracketed, and then effaced altogether.'[2] As Scorsese suggests, through the interweaving of multiple ethnicities in the film's texture, ethnic identities like 'Irish' or 'Italian' are reduced to simulacra, mere symbols of the real that replace the real itself. A univocal (ethnic) subjectivity can no longer exist when the realization of the American Dream coincides exclusively with materialistic values.

The hybrid dimension that distinguishes cultural representations of postmodernism also characterizes *The Departed*, a remake of the 2002 Hong Kong thriller *Infernal Affairs*. In particular, the ruthlessness of the film's protagonists expresses their violent reaction to the guilt attached to a fundamental betrayal of their ethnic identities. The loss of ethnic consistency is incarnated in the most powerful way by Frank Costello's character. A figure of ethnic contamination, *The Departed*'s Costello intertwines aspects of the filmic referent, the Chinese boss Hon Sam, his dual historical referent, the Irish American mobster James Bulger, and the Italian American gangster Frank Costello, born Francesco Castiglia.

Given the central role of religion in cultural identity in general, and of Catholicism for Italian Americans in particular, the sense of guilt that has accompanied Scorsese's protagonists has often been interpreted in religious terms.[3] Asked to define the strong legacy of his Catholic upbringing, Scorsese indicated it was '[g]uilt. A major helping of guilt, like a lot of garlic.'[4] However, in Scorsese's work, on a deeper and more universal level not limited to the Italian American culture, guilt derives from the acknowledgment of a betrayal of ethnic identity through the achievement of the American Dream. At the very centre of the violence in films such as *Mean Streets* (1973), *Goodfellas* (1990), *Casino* (1995), and *The Departed* is the difficulty of 'going on'[5] in the open-ended quest for an identity based upon the enduring conflict between two components that film scholar Lester Friedman has defined as '"descent" (relations determined for us by blood or nature) and "consent" (relations we choose to accept).'[6]

The establishing shots of *The Departed* introduce this theme through the voiceover narration of Francis 'Frank' Costello, which accompanies sepia-toned documentary footage of the social and racial unrest of the 1950s and 1960s. This was 'Boston Some Years Ago,' as the caption informs the viewer. Costello's credo values 'consent' over 'descent' at all costs, as the following line underscores: 'I don't want to be a product of my environment. I want my environment to be a product of me,' since 'no one gives it [power, recognition, success] to you. You have to take it.' At this point a jump cut takes us into a Catholic church through a close-up shot of an altar boy who is performing his part of the ritual during a funeral mass. The colour symbolism of the mise en scène, with a heavy predominance of red, and the off-screen voice of the officiating priest closely remind us of the first sequence of *Mean Streets*, in which Charlie explains through an interior monologue at the altar his moral philosophy of 'doing penance in the streets.'

In *The Departed*, a typically Scorsesean frantic intercutting intertwines Frank Costello's anti-deterministic vision of the world with the elliptical coming-of-age narrative of the parallel lives of two youngsters, Colin Sullivan and William 'Billy' Costigan. While both Colin and Billy descend from Irish families connected with local organized crime, both try to 'take it [their] own way' according to Frank Costello's principle. Thus, the film narrative follows Colin, 'adopted' by Costello, as he grows into an exemplary police officer in order to become the most effective informant for his 'dad.' Billy, in turn, is an equally commendable state trooper, who becomes an undercover agent in the Costello gang in order to be the most effective informant for his 'adoptive dad,' Captain Queenan.

During the fragmented account of these two parallel 'novels of formation,' camera angles reveal the essence of the ethnic identity's betrayal as perpetrated in different ways by Colin and Billy. For instance, the sequences centred on Colin's career are characterized by recurrent low-angle shots of the sparkling golden dome of the Boston State House against a terse blue sky, which also dominates the view from Colin's new upper-class apartment. These low-angle shots identify Colin's point of view and underscore his betrayal of his Irish community. Constantly pursuing social ascent at any price, Colin exploits a state police education to become a cop/ informant, thus climbing the ladder of success on the legal and the illegal sides at the same time.

By contrast, the sections devoted to Billy's career as an undercover agent who transforms into a young thug to infiltrate Costello's criminal network are dominated by high-angle shots, in particular during the decisive interview with Captain Queenan and Sergeant Dignam. Visually oppressed through the high-angle framing by the burden of his family ties with the underworld, something that his interviewers forcefully evoke, Billy is confronted with his split personality. Throughout childhood and adolescence, Billy has been divided between his north-shore, upper-middle-class upbringing with his mother and his South Boston identity embedded in the local organized crime hierarchy with his father's family. 'You're a double feature, kid, like different people,' Captain Queenan concludes. In more general terms, Billy, indeed, is torn between the obscure power of 'descent,' the legacy of violence epitomized by Costello to which his father succumbed, and the liberating energy of 'consent,' his conscious decision to serve the law even if this translates into becoming an informant in order to apprehend Costello.

During the interview with Captain Queenan and Sergeant Dignam, when Billy acknowledges, 'I don't have any family,' a flashback takes us to the deathbed of his mother. In a conversation he has with his hated maternal uncle, Billy declares: 'When my mother dies, we don't have any more connections.' The fragmented editing of this scene underscores the contrast between how Billy and Colin overcome their inherited life paths. For example, a sudden intercut portrays a very different exchange between Colin and his real estate agent, who gives him details on why the apartment's location under the visual (and moral) spell of the State House's golden dome is a status symbol.

At this point, another unexpected flashback confronts the viewers with the origin of the film's title. In a cemetery setting during the funeral for Billy's deceased mother, the off-screen voice of a priest recites, 'May her soul and the souls of all the departed through the mercy of God rest in peace.' The camera glides to a close-up of a sacred image of a female saint on her grave, and then zooms into a caption that reads 'Heaven holds the faithful departed.' The signature of Frank Costello at the bottom of the picture ties Billy once again to his Irish heritage, incarnated in the specific ideological context of Boston's South End by the legendary crime boss. The signature 'F. Costello' on the grave of 'the faithful departed' subtly alludes to the difficulty of 'going on' in search of an identity that strives to harmonize 'descent' and 'consent,' as Scorsese suggested when he commented on *Mean Streets'* disquieting finale. In addition, the proximity of 'the faithful departed' to Costello's handwritten name suggests an identification of 'the departed' in the film's title with Costello's character, as we shall see in the next pages.

Billy's flashback during his job interview ends abruptly with Captain Queenan's emotional appeal: 'Do it again for me.' Thus, Captain Queenan concludes Billy's reminiscence with a reference to his family ties with the underworld of South Boston, which Billy had rejected by choosing to become a police officer. Suddenly, a slow tracking shot follows a row of inmates behind bars in a state prison. Billy, who has honoured Captain Queenan's request, is one of them. Colin, by contrast, is shown while looking again from a low-angle perspective at the glittering dome of the State House. Only at this point does the image fade out and the title of the movie, *The Departed*, finally appear in white characters against a black background. Thus, editing, framing, and mise en scène cooperate to tie the theme of betrayal to the deception of an ethnic identity that has 'departed' in the quest for social and moral acceptance, in the case of Billy, or greater material power, in the case of Colin and, even more violently, of Frank Costello.

Therefore, it comes as no surprise that the first to succumb to the void left by the materialistic triumph of the American Dream is Frank Costello himself, the ultimate betrayer. After the final confrontation with the police at a drug deal, Costello is shot in medium close-up and occupies the centre of the frame. The point-of-view shot from Colin's perspective focuses on Costello's grey T-shirt. The magisterial mise en scène in the dark setting emphasizes the symbolic value of the only bright spot in the frame, Costello's T-shirt with IRISH written in capital letters on it. Costello admits to Colin that he is an informant as well, not for the Massachusetts State Police but for the FBI. Now aware that Colin, 'his boy,' has betrayed him just as he betrayed Colin, Costello shoots first and mumbles: 'All that murdering and f**ing and no sons ...' Colin, though, swiftly fires back and kills Costello, his betrayed and betraying 'Irish' paternal figure.

This symbolic death differentiates Costello's fictional character from its historical referent, the Irish American Boston mobster James 'Whitey' Bulger (1929–). This apparent separation between fictional and factual might surprise those who know Scorsese's predilection for the documentary genre, which he pointed out already in the mid-1970s: 'I read ... about how *Italianamerican* was the counterpart of *Mean Streets*. In many ways I think the documentary is far superior to the dramatic film. In the documentary there's more of a truth you can get at.'[7] Scorsese's faith in the realistic power of the film medium has accompanied his fascination with the expressionistic force of cinema throughout his career. Film scholar Maurizio Viano's apt definition of *Goodfellas* as a 'docudrama'[8] captures the duality of Scorsese's cinematic signature at work since his early productions, in films that came after *Mean Streets* and *Italianamerican* (1974). In an interview about *Goodfellas*, Scorsese elucidated his interpretation of realism as follows: 'I find that documentaries are so moving, especially if it is the old "cinéma vérité" style. It is something about the way people are captured. The sense of truth is what gets me … You re-create those moments and sometimes you do get that certain reality.'[9]

It is this tentative, precarious way of representing reality – and ethnic identities in particular – as a consciously chosen cinematic poetics that explains the link between Costello's character and his historical referent in *The Departed*. The real man is James Bulger, born in a working-class Boston suburb to a hard-working Roman Catholic family, who was the one-time leader of the Winter Hill Gang, an Irish American crime gang controlling narcotics traffic in the city's northeast end. A brother of a prominent Massachusetts Democratic politician, an alleged victim of sexual abuse in parochial school, and a former Air Force member, Bulger became an FBI informant in the mid-1970s.[10] For years he was a wanted fugitive – at one time placing second on the FBI's 'Ten Most Wanted Fugitives' list after Osama Bin Laden. In 2011 he was arrested and subsequently convicted before being murdered in prison in 2018.

The most striking feature of Bulger's biography is the constant presence of betrayal, actively chosen or passively endured. Suffice it to mention that it was only in 1999, thanks to the cooperation of his long-time friend and associate Kevin Weeks, that Bulger was conclusively linked to the Boston-based drug network by the DEA and placed on the FBI's list. Weeks was arrested in 1999 and decided to cooperate with federal prosecutors once he learned that Bulger had been passing along information on their own subordinates. 'You can't rat on a rat,' another inmate at Rhode Island's Wyatt Prison explained to Weeks.[11]

The historical reference to the 'most wanted' Irish American mobster James Bulger becomes more relevant in relation to the homonymy between Jack Nicholson's character and the Italian American New York underworld leader Frank Costello (1891–1973). *The Departed*'s Frank Costello, based on Bulger and the Chinese mobster Hon Sam from *Infernal Affairs*, epitomizes an inherently hybrid *persona*, the contamination of the Irish and the Italian, the West and the East, the real and the fictional. Thus Scorsese's remake of *Infernal Affairs* becomes a cinematic tale about the tangled quest for a (postmodern) 'departed' identity.

The first layer of this ontological pursuit is psychoanalytical in nature, as Scorsese underscores through the subplot centred on Madolyn, the state police psychologist who becomes involved with both Colin and Billy. The double, a perennial theme in the Western artistic imaginary since the Greek comic theatre with Plautus' *Amphitryon*, is rooted in the deepest psychological structure of the subject and has challenged the notion of the *individuum* itself, the undivided kernel of identity that constitutes the object of psychoanalytical investigation. Through artistic renditions of individual fragmentation and its relationship to madness, the double has thus developed into one of the most disconcerting ciphers of modernity, which the postmodern era has broadened through the hybridization of ethnicity. In *The Departed*, the theme of the double acquires the same ontological resonance that originates from the concept of the mask in the theatrical writing of Italian Nobel Prize–winning author Luigi Pirandello. In Scorsese's cinema, as in Pirandello's work, the theme of the double is inextricable from the philosophical idea of madness.[12]

For Billy and Colin, the menacing horizon of madness is closely tied to their respective double identities and hinges on a 'departed' ethnic identity. In *The Departed*, the second level of this identity quest emerges clearly through the apparent discrepancy between different elements of ethnic semiosis that characterize the representation of Costello. For example, Costello's voiceover narration of his anti-deterministic credo at the beginning of the film is accompanied by the fast-paced, disquieting song 'I'm Shipping Up to Boston,' performed by the Celtic punk band the Dropkick Murphys. Written by Woodie Guthrie, the lyrics of this piece hinge on an improbable quest for 'a wooden leg.' The rage that emanates from the music and lyrics of 'I'm Shipping Up to Boston' reminds us of Scorsese's gift for selecting musical motifs that enhance the narrative by contrast or analogy, thus making him 'a director of aural pleasure in narrative cinema.'[13] In addition, this Irish punk musical theme, with its tense, spiralling rhythm, clashes with other traditional Irish folk songs that impress an ineffaceable ethnic mark on the non-diegetic soundtrack of *The Departed*. A recurrent example is the theme for pipe and drums of 'Minstrel Boy,' the inspirational song written by the Irish poet and patriot Thomas Moore, who participated in the 1798 revolution of the United Irishmen. This musical emblem of the Irish heroic struggle for freedom is at odds with the rage of 'I'm Shipping Up to Boston,' which accompanies Costello's voiceover introduction. Even more blatantly, the Irish musical quotations collide with the Italian referent ingrained in the name of the protagonist in the same way that the referent was visually underscored through the capitalized IRISH label on Costello's T-shirt in his death scene.[14] For who was the historical Frank Costello?

Born Francesco Castiglia in the southern Italian region of Calabria in 1891, the later legendary 'Prime Minister of the Underworld' immigrated at the age of nine to the United States during the main migratory wave at the turn of the century. Appalled at the hardship of his parents' lives, Francesco left school in the fifth grade and completed his 'education' in the challenging New York neighbourhood of East Harlem.

While the earliest known instance of his first name being anglicized goes back to an Immigration and Naturalization Service record of Castiglia's enrolment in first grade, biographer Leonard Katz highlights young Frank's decision to change his last name from Castiglia to Costello a few years later by writing, 'What's interesting is that he gave himself an Irish name.'[15] More importantly, this choice to become Irish conveys a hidden anxiety about being accepted and integrated in an older and more established ethnic crime gang. The beginning of Prohibition in 1919 provided Costello with the opportunity to establish himself in the criminal underworld and 'to enlarge his world … with people in all walks of life: legitimate businessmen … killers, politicians.'[16] In particular, Costello became a close associate of the leading Jewish and Irish crime leaders of that time, including Arnold 'The Brain' Rothstein and William 'Big Bill' or 'Bill-O' Dwyer,[17] thus epitomizing the melting pot that the bootlegging trade forged among the Italian, Jewish, and Irish gangs in the 1920s. Later involved in the internal fights between the powerful Luciano and Genovese crime families, he became 'the most powerful political force in the nation's largest city,' who managed to die quietly from a heart attack in 1973. Always yearning most deeply for 'respectability,'[18] Costello would have been pleased to read his extended obituary on the front page of *The New York Times*.[19]

The coexistence of lawfulness and unlawfulness in the biography of the historical Frank Costello hints at the dual personality of *The Departed*'s main characters. In addition, the Italian/Irish twist in the morphing of Francesco Castiglia into the historical Frank Costello complicates the psychological loss of unity – as a result of the fragmentation of ethnic identity – that characterizes the violent nature of *The Departed*'s Costello.

By means of multiple ethnic contaminations in the fictional and factual planes of the film's narrative, Scorsese is insinuating that Irish, Italian, or any other ethnic signifier merely simulates a univocal ethnicity. Billy, who since the murder of Captain Queenan has understood who the mole is in the state police, asks Colin to give him his 'identity back.' Colin replies that he 'erased' Billy from the computer files once he understood that Billy knew about his double game. Thus the quest for a univocal (ethnic) identity is doomed to failure in the postmodern context of late capitalism. *The Non-Stop-Way,* as the literal translation of the original Cantonese title of *Infernal Affairs (Wu jian dao)* aptly suggests, refers to the lowest and worst of the eighteen hells according to Buddhism. As co-director Alan Mak explains, 'Once in Continuous Hell, you won't get out.'[20] In *The Departed,* the ultimate desperation that borders on madness derives from the acknowledgment of a seemingly unavoidable fragmented identity and ethnicity.

Both Billy and Colin, alter egos or Pirandellian masks of each other, die violently at the end of the film. The last intercutting between Billy's and Colin's plots, though, points out a revealing difference. Billy's burial ceremony is accompanied by the same ritual wish that resonated during his mother's funeral: 'May the souls of all the faithful departed rest in peace.' By contrast, Colin's murder is carried out in cold blood by his former colleague, Sergeant Dignam, and is followed by a non-diegetic musical score, Don Gibson's appropriately chosen 'Sweet Dreams,' which hints at the metaphorical significance of the film's title. 'Peace' is merely an ironic 'sweet dream' for the displaced subject of ethnicity that – like Billy, Colin, and, most violently, Frank Costello – has departed from a consistent ethnic identity to pursue solely materialistic values. In the concluding scene, the camera once again captures the enticing glamour of the State House's golden dome in a long shot while a rat crosses the frame from right to left and accompanies the viewer's gaze off screen in her/his own search for a 'departed' (ethnic) American identity.

NOTES

1 Vincent LoBrutto, 'Appendix F: Interview with Martin Scorsese,' in *Martin Scorsese: A Biography* (Westport, CT: Praeger, 2006), 395–6.

2 See Fredric Jameson, *Postmodernism or, the Cultural Logic of Late Capitalism* (Durham, NC: Duke University Press, 2005), 18.

3 The most recent example is Robert Casillo's *Gangster Priest: The Italian American Cinema of Martin Scorsese* (Toronto: University of Toronto Press, 2006).

4 Diane Jacobs, *Hollywood Renaissance* (New York: Delta, 1980), 129.

5 Scorsese in Mary Pat Kelly, *Martin Scorsese: The First Decade* (New York: Redgrave, 1980), 199.

6 Lester D. Friedman, 'Celluloid Palimpsests: An Overview of Ethnicity and the American Film,' in *Unspeakable Images,* ed. L. D. Friedman (Urbana, IL: University of Illinois Press, 1991), 19.

7 Kelly, *Martin Scorsese,* 200.

8 Maurizio Viano, 'Goodfellas,' *Film Quarterly* 44, no. 3 (1991): 43.

9 Peter Keough, 'Street Smarts,' *Boston Phoenix,* 21 September 1990, 6, cited in Viano, 'Goodfellas,' 49.

10 See Kevin Weeks, 'Author's Note,' in *Brutal: The Untold Story of My Life Inside Whitey Bulger's Irish Mob,* ed. Kevin Weeks and Phyllis Karas (New York: Regan Books, 2006), xv, 245–55.

11 Weeks and Karas, *Brutal,* 261.

12 Jerold J. Abrams, 'The Cinema of Madness: Friedrich Nietzsche and the Films of Martin Scorsese,' in *The Philosophy of Martin Scorsese*, ed. Mark T. Conrad (Lexington, KY: University Press of Kentucky, 2007), 75–6.

13 Viano, 'Goodfellas,' 46.

14 See also LoBrutto, *Martin Scorsese: A Biography*, 384.

15 Leonard Katz, *Uncle Frank: The Biography of Frank Costello* (New York: Drake, 1973), 39, 42; Jerre Mangione and Ben Morreale, *La Storia: Five Centuries of the Italian American Experience* (New York: Harper Perennial, 1992), 251–2.

16 Katz, *Uncle Frank*, 55.

17 See George Walsh, *Public Enemies: The Mayor, the Mob, and the Crime That Was* (New York: Norton, 1980). On Costello's testimonies during the Kefauver Committee hearings, see Salvatore J. LaGumina, Frank J. Cavaioli, Salvatore Primeggia, and Joseph A. Varacalli, eds., *The Italian American Experience: An Encyclopedia* (New York: Garland, 2000), 156–7.

18 Katz, *Uncle Frank*, 8.

19 Ibid., 259–60.

20 Alan Mak in 'The Making of *Infernal Affairs*,' in *Infernal Affairs*, dir. Wai Keung Lau and Alan Mak Siu-Fai, Miramax Home Entertainment, 2004, DVD.

1 *Little Caesar*: Little Caesar celebrates his abrupt and bloody ascent to power at the Palermo Club (Warner Bros./Photofest)

2 *The Godfather*: The Corleone gang rejects Sollozzo's offer to enter into the drug business, which provokes an attempt on Don Vito's life (Paramount Pictures/Photofest)

3 *The Godfather*: Don Vito Corleone shows his soft side while listening to undertaker Amerigo Bonasera's request for justice (Paramount Pictures/Photofest)

4 *Mean Streets*: Teresa attempts to break up a fight between cousin Johnny Boy and boyfriend Charlie (Warner Bros./Photofest)

5 *The Godfather: Part II*: Michael contemplates his solitary position as Don of a modernized and international mafia 'Family' (Paramount Pictures/Photofest)

6 *The Untouchables*: Eliot Ness multitasks during the climactic shootout with Capone's men (Paramount Pictures/Photofest)

7 *The Untouchables*: Oscar Wallace, Eliot Ness, Jim Malone, and George Stone/Giuseppe Petri (Paramount Pictures/Photofest)

8   *Goodfellas*: Henry Hill watches Tommy DeVito's temper flare in reaction to Billy Batts's put-down (Warner Bros./Photofest)

9   *The Godfather: Part III*: Mary, Kay, Michael, Vincent, Connie, et al. watch Anthony perform the lead in *Cavalleria rusticana* at the Teatro Massimo in Palermo (Paramount Pictures/Photofest)

10 *Casino*: Sam and Ginger find fulfilment in currency (Universal Pictures/Webphoto)

11   *Donnie Brasco*: Lefty passes on important lessons to 'Donnie' about mafia code and culture (Sony Pictures/Photofest)

12   *Analyze This*: Paul Vitti expresses the benefits of Family/family therapy (Village Roadshow Pictures/Webphoto)

13 *The Departed*: Double lives are revealed when Billy confronts Colin on the rooftop (Warner Bros./ Photofest)

14 *The Sopranos*: Tony addresses his 'Family' in Season Five (HBO/Photofest)

FRANCO RICCI

Language is a critical conditioning feature of *The Sopranos* (1999–2007). From Dr Melfi's opening salutation to Tony's rifling through song titles in the very last scene of the series, one of the latent motifs that drives the storyline can be placed at the foot of the conflict between the institutionalized discourses of word and image. It is a cultural struggle that traditionally pits fleeting female absence (speaking, nature, passivity) against male physical presence (writing, transcendence, action) as metaphors for sex, time, space, and power. Not until spoken language (Melfi's sessions, Tony's bravado) becomes written text (Melfi's journal article, Tony's song titles) and assumes important on-screen presence, thereby subverting orality, will Tony's existential dilemma be resolved and Dr Melfi have the professional fortitude to dismiss him as a patient, effectively ending the series. The final blackout is both a visual and an auditory testimony to the mafia of hereditary blindness and silence that is *The Sopranos'* legacy of *omertà*.

From a Platonic vantage, Tony Soprano lives in a state of metaphoric darkness. Our first impression of him completely ensconced between the thighs of the brazen green nude female statue in Dr Melfi's anteroom belies the notion that he is trapped within the vice of feminine power. Indeed, the statue displays an autonomous strength of character not usually associated with what, at least in Tony's world, is presumed to be the weaker sex. He appears uncomfortable with the unblushing virago. The initial visual image of Tony is of an emasculated, cowering, befuddled, indeed petrified male, stilled by the Medusa figure before him.[1]

This often-repeated scene marker sets up a traditional literary paradigm: the writer, Chase, has presented a spatial image (a description) of the main character of our story. This image is imprinted in memory. It becomes the indelible thumbprint that conditions the viewer's future responses to Tony and sets the stage for multi-coded relationships between what the viewer sees and what he will eventually hear.

As the viewer surveys the scene, his musings (and Tony's) are abruptly interrupted by a verbal utterance. The visual silence of the image is overtaken by temporality as the camera shifts to Dr Melfi entering the anteroom. It is important to note that not until Dr Melfi opens the series with language, with the active presence of speech, does description end and action commence. When Melfi peers into the scene and says 'Mr Soprano?,' she opens a series whose primary enterprise is spoken language: language properly used, misused, and abused, rarely sanitized, usually ethnicized; language that is often inappropriate, language that is misappropriated.

From the outset of the series, then, the spatial image of Tony is set in epistemological contrast to the words of Melfi. Where the image (Tony) appears weak and confused, words (Melfi) impart strength, power, certainty, and intelligence. And so they should. Communication is the vehicle of her practice. Her language offers metaphors of sight, wisdom, and revelation. It heals when it reactualizes deeply embedded memories, releasing the patient into an epiphany of sensations and subliminal images. Non-communication is Tony's realm. In his world, candour and clarity of speech are marks of betrayal, distortion and absence of language the hallmark of loyalty. His code of *omertà* is an assault on language. It begets a silence that demands tacit visual (spatial) collusion.

Language is power, its marshalling and persuasive potential a controlling social mechanism. The 'self' is constructed through language and is the vehicle of viable self-expression. Melfi and Tony are at opposing ends of the language–power spectrum. Both employ language to control their environment and are able to utilize their considerable persuasive skills to achieve precise objectives within their mutually exclusive realms. The ability of these two diametrically diverse characters to master their respective linguistic domains thus determines their status within their respective professions.

This linguistic determinism is apparent in the very first exchange between the doctor and her patient (1.1, or season one, episode one). Tony's world is a linguistic fallacy. It is grounded in misappropriated images and gestures from a limited cultural system. His signifiers float in a distorted realm of euphemisms (where a mob boss can become a 'waste management consultant') and inversions (a vicious beating becomes friendly banter while 'we had coffee') whose psychological processes are conditioned by a system of mafia values. Melfi's work consists of exposing this mimetic fallacy. By investigating the unconscious infrastructural patterns of her patient's language, she deciphers their content and eventually exposes their true meaning (for example, the symbolic order of the mother, or the blood imagery of capicollo).

Melfi is in the business of redeeming troubled souls, Tony in taking them. Melfi is empowered by language. Her professional success relies on her ability to translate embedded emotions and memories into spoken language. Tony, by contrast, is debilitated by language. His leadership relies upon the ability to translate media mob images and immigrant cultural memories into effective deception. Yet both willingly attempt a rapprochement of these distinct realities within the confines of psychiatry. The two are equally seduced by the confessional interplay of psychiatrist and analysand and are compelled to produce a coherent narrative despite being constricted, interestingly, by the professional and cultural imprimatur of *omertà*. Tony's 'singing' in a psychiatrist's office forebodes career-ending consequences. Melfi's professional restrictions of secrecy are no less impelling.

Melfi's reasons for studying psychiatry are never explored, yet it is intimated that she required control of personal, possibly ethnic, angst, and chose her profession to better control her being. As the reader of Tony's text, she must focus on a therapeutic interpretation of a story she knows too well. As she listens to her patient, however, she becomes aware of both his unreliability as a narrator and the malevolence of his character. She also becomes consumed by the seductiveness of his narrative and her own vulnerability to its prohibitive (male-charged) allure. She is enthralled enough by his mafia aura to peer out of Dr Cusumano's bathroom window one evening to view his home. She defends the image of her shared Italian heritage with pride, made evident in statements such as 'I like Murano glass' (1.10). But she rejects Tony's cheapening of their common Italian lineage. When he condescendingly asks her, 'What part of the Boot you from, Hon?' she coldly corrects him by asserting her linguistic marker, 'Dr Melfi' (1.1). Her rejection of his entreaties is curt and confident. Her definitive 'No!' to the albeit alluring prospect of siccing Tony on her rapist is chilling in its unequivocal moral resoluteness (3.4). By interpreting Tony's lies, Melfi is cognizant that she empowers her own ensuing enigma.

Tony's foray into therapy stems from loss of consciousness. He suffers panic attacks that stifle his speech and hence his control of reality. The series flows from his attempts to verbalize the root causes of this trauma. In essence, he must learn to use words to heal his image as a possibly vulnerable mob boss. Tony understands that orality is fleeting, occupies no physical space, and leaves no incriminating trace. The absence of speech subtends the shadowy semblances of his world, a place where secrecy and silence guarantee survival. Once language is written, appears in recorded format, or is corroborated by written testimony, it escapes the jungle of hearsay and becomes legal tender. Tony spends the better part of his life withdrawing from written language. He prefers furtive encounters steeped in mystery, business transactions executed in blood, coded messages deficient of traceable intention. Images are fleeting and therefore safer, which explains his attraction to The History Channel, classic westerns, and gangster films.

The written text introduces a fixed temporality otherwise absent from character dialogue and the timelessness of film. For example, book titles appear throughout the series – Carmela and other characters are often shot with a book in hand. If the viewer is already familiar with the book in question, he is engaged in new ways, which may include sympathetic bonding with the character.[2] Interestingly, pivotal moments of the series are usually corniced by words and become natural signs by implication. Street signs and storefronts blare ethnicity, book titles lend insight to both the character and plot of an episode, a shared secret, a verbal contract – even a poster can frame an encounter.[3]

By focusing on book titles, posters, epigraphs, store signage, and paintings, Chase gives the series a visual and temporal continuity that is usually lacking in TV programs. These recognizable cultural icons allow the viewer/reader to enter the series as performers, actively seeking/remembering the highlighted books, signs, posters, and paintings to better understand the characters and situations as they are presented. The mix of written and spoken text engages the viewer in ever-changing ways, keeping him constantly surprised, senses heightened to detect the abounding inferences. Chase privileges just this type of reading, for he has carefully included literary and artistic references to subtend his storylines. From Hawthorne to Burroughs, Machiavelli to Castenada, from Sun Tzu's *Art of War* to Arthur Miller's *Death of a Salesman*, book titles, references, citations, direct quotations (Yeats and 'The Second Coming') and specific works of art (Jusepe de Ribera's *Mystical Marriage of St Catherine*, Jacopo da Pontormo's *La Visitazione*) pepper the series and give it artistic corporeality. *The Sopranos* thus becomes a site where a fertile combination of words as dialogue and words as visual text live at the threshold of the word and image debate.

It is not surprising, then, that dramatic changes in the series are accompanied by major changes in the relationships characters have with either the visual imagery or the written text. Movies, pictures, and posters that display images of the mob, women, and violence are Tony's models. He usually misinterprets these images – a fact evident in his perception of Hannibal Lecter, for instance. He is therefore condemned to display an image of outward male bravado but is essentially an often inept, sometimes comical gangster figure. From this vantage, machismo is an empty construct ironically erected and simultaneously emasculated by the very images that promote its existence. Tony's weakness derives from his submission to temptation from his weaker 'feminine' side, by his need to use what, in his world of codified masculine behaviour, represents weakness. When he breaks the code of linguistic silence, when he uses words to construct a viable reality construct in Melfi's office, he no longer behaves the way a man 'should.' An old Sicilian proverb states that 'words are feminine,' the implication being that words are troublesome, the opposite of male action. But Tony wishes to understand his actions, perhaps in the hope of eventually changing them. Unfortunately, as the viewer is aware from the series' opening scene, he has been trapped between the statue's thighs all his life. Any attempt to move towards an understanding of self through words has been stilled by the petrifying stare of the Medusa female. This is his dilemma. When he is with Melfi, he feels himself slipping through the crevices of language, revealing and thus understanding too much of his own duplicitous image.

In opposition, Melfi's reality depends upon abstract linguistic signs. Her realm is an academy of written texts, professional literature, and corroborated facts that establish credentials and create the self. Her reasoning is linear, rational, and canonical. Her weakness during the series is submitting to the lure of the irrational gloss, to the bait of Tony and his attractive wickedness, to the temptation of the bad-boy image. She is seduced by his bacchanal sloth, his ultimately subversive cultural message. He is a warrior, a survivor; the prohibited fruit dangled before young women. Melfi knows she fits Tony's image of femininity. She is dark, Mediterranean, intelligent, and independent. But he married a fair-skinned Italian blond while Melfi chose to marry a traditional Italian American male. The struggles of Tony and Melfi with their respective contradictions motivate the series and carry them both into the heart of theoretical discourse itself: what, indeed, is the difference between the latent image of what they perceive and the concealed verbal content of what each knows? And what happens when each moves away from his/her respective opening stance and towards the other's realm? In other words, what happens when Melfi pursues the tantalizing imago-centric mania for her patient? Does Tony's desire to have the world captured within the word lead him to naive, logo-centric determinism? The mutual exclusivity of these domains ultimately determines the outcome of their respective fates. Since neither character exhibits a balanced centrist position towards the dominating male principle or the holistic female one, the establishment of a balance portends a realignment of priorities. But this linguistic shift will always come with a price. Its eventual resolution, given the series, must be violent.

When Tony exclaims 'I get it!' in the penultimate episode of the series, he has just awakened from a peyote-induced delirium. It is a sort of transcendental awareness, induced by drugs and consummated in the barren desert heat of Nevada, that springboards him to a new level of cognition, of anagnorisis. He exclaims to the universe that he has exited Plato's cave. The shadows and the simulacra of reality are gone. What remains is clarity, allowing him to see clearly. The word-riddled anomalies and image-laden memories that have heretofore battled for his soul have found respite in a newly conquered visual serenity. He clearly accepts the construct of himself as a mob image, as a killer. The repeated query 'Who am I? Where am I going?' that reverberated throughout the series and that found material expression during his prolonged coma (6.2–4) has now been answered. He will no longer be hampered by Melfi's words, nor will he accept notions of femininity (as expressed in Christopher's writing or in the latent homosexuality of his crew). These issues have been resolved.

The pain of finding a mimesis (in word or image) of his divided immigrant self, his delusions of becoming an American dream boy, the dilemma of facing his morally bereft choices, all have come to a head and been resolved. 'Plain truth,' he once confessed to Melfi, choosing words that expressed an unmistakable locution, 'I'm a fat f**in' crook from New Jersey' (6.1). He has survived multiple attempts on his life, murdered his closest friends, and revealed a well-spoken alter ego while in a coma. But only now is he able to transit to a new, differentiated space and wilfully acknowledge the beast that literally resides within.[4]

The words of the Hawthorne quotation sculpted into stone that we read on screen, 'No man can wear one face to himself and another to the multitude without finally getting bewildered as to which may be true' (1.5), and the many song lyrics that framed past actions, are now fulfilled. There will no longer be two Tonys. As he sloughs off his tiredness, he may live his moment of clarity. No longer fearful of the written word, he can search through song titles that resonate in his life and read them as epithets of his journey: 'Those Were the Days,' 'This Magic Moment,' 'I've Gotta Be Me,' 'Who Will You Run To?,' and 'Don't Stop Believin'.' His entire life has been spread out before him, and he, along with the viewer, reads the emblematic abstract all at once. Scrolling through the titles, one notes their melancholic conclusiveness but, more importantly, the resoluteness of the final song title that is never uttered by Tony but is read by both character and viewer: 'I've Gotta Be Me.' This title defines the man and empowers his self-validating visual myth.

A similarly complex change occurs with Melfi. Although she has not heeded the verbal warnings of her own psychiatrist regarding the empowerment of Tony's criminality through therapy, Melfi's stance regarding Tony changes once her visual fixation with his image is subordinated to the written word. The visual presence of words on the TV screen is the death knell of feminine values both metaphorically and literally in the series. In episode 6.2.8, 'The Blue Comet,' we find her reading in bed. The words scroll slowly across the screen. They are images of stalwart ink, pillars of canonic strength that offset any spatial imagery that might remain of Tony. Melfi and the viewer read the article's title: '*The Criminal Personality* by Samuel Yockelson and Stanton E. Samenov ... The criminal's sentimentality reveals itself in compassion for babies and pets.' [*Cut to Melfi turning page*] 'The criminal uses insight to justify heinous acts.' [*Cut to a worried Melfi*] 'Therapy has potential for non-criminals. [*cut to Melfi*]; for criminals, it becomes one more criminal operation.'

The written word, with all its intellectual and sociocultural baggage, now supersedes the spoken word and undermines her former interpretation of Tony. The written text reclaims special status, refutes any venturesome rhetoric. As Melfi replaces her trust in the text, we too, as readers, diminish the distance between our own feelings towards Tony and any potential emotional reaction we may still harbour. Reading thus becomes an assertive enactment. Not until she reads the written text and is set straight by its linear logic is she able to rationally and intellectually undo her imago-centric attraction to the likable bad-boy mobster. The left, analytical side of Melfi's brain now assumes control. Though she had been reproved on several occasions to reject Tony, the oral reprimand was not convincing. The same aggression that Tony imparts upon his foes subtends the cutting prose of Melfi's article. Both gestures are assertive acts. Tony's spoken words kill victims; Melfi's written text kills her relationship with Tony.

This gesture reinforces, ironically, the masculine principle. In essence, Tony is defeated not by the feminine, intuitive, right-brained side of his nature (the Medusa stare), as we have been led to expect by the series, but by Melfi's decision to abruptly declare a terminus. Interestingly, in their very last session, Melfi berates Tony for 'defacing my reading materials' by tearing pages from her anteroom magazines, literally accusing him of stealing *her words* for his own malevolent use. The significance of the utterance is lost on Tony, but not on the viewer, who is privy to the doctor's newfound resolve. She scolds him for his disregard for 'the body of work that's gone into building up this science.' Melfi wilfully relinquishes her linguistic primacy, or control, over Tony by allowing the written word to regain primacy in her intellectual life. No longer is she disabled by a subversive imago-centric interpretation of issues; the masculine logos legitimizes a newfound intellectual resolve to act like a man and kill her relationship with Tony. 'End of story,' she declares as she slams the door shut on her ex-patient in a gesture that mirrors her opening of the same door to commence the series. She has become and has ended temporal flow. From this point on, there is no more story to narrate.

The series, then, is not about killing Tony, as many expected and wished, but about making him whole. It is about addressing psychological issues that have rendered him a halved individual unable to act because he craves a spatial fix (a longing for his mother) while yearning for the freedom of his own temporal flow (the lack of a father). In essence, Chase has exposed Tony from a new angle by subverting any mundane referential remnant to mob movies. Instead, he has inserted a playful, elegant, and ultimately disruptive writing style that questions those very codes and conventions that subtend the mobster mystique. Importantly, Chase places words directly on screen. Thus the relationship of oral and written text is not only one of complementarity but also one of a struggle between two contesting modes of perception, the masculine and the feminine, one from which the written text emerges as victorious mafioso.

NOTES

1 The Medusa figure is a graphic symbol of female sexual energy and power. Able to still men with her stare, in Word and Image studies, she represents anticipated immobility and muteness, her stare cuts across space and disrupts action.
2 The list of books, posters, and artworks in the series is too long to cite here. Carmela, for example, reads or is attached to plenty of books. Among them are Arthur Golden's *Memoirs of a Geisha* (2.10), Fred Barnes's *Rebel-in-Chief* (5.5), Flaubert's *Madame Bovary* and *Abelard and Heloise* (5.6), and Sue Grafton's *C Is for Corpse* (6.2.2). Their themes and plots subtend the drama, peril, or personal issues she faces.
3 See Franco Ricci, 'Aesthetics and Ammunition: Art Imitating Life, Life Imitating Art in *The Sopranos*,' in *Reading the Sopranos: Hit TV from HBO*, ed. David Lavery (New York: I.B. Tauris, 2006), 139–59.
4 The song 'The Beast in Me,' lyrics by Nick Lowe, closes the pilot episode.

22 'Don't Stop Believin', Don't Stop … ': (De)Structuring Expectations in the Final Season of *The Sopranos*

GIANCARLO LOMBARDI

Volumes have been dedicated to the originality of *The Sopranos*, and although the creative freedom afforded by HBO was most clearly evidenced by the show's linguistic and visual transgression (foul language, brutality, and sex have often been noted as its defining traits),[1] it was at a different level that *The Sopranos* claimed its genuine uniqueness: at the level of generic structure. As its creator David Chase often reiterated, the show always tried 'to run away from what was done …] to run away from what people are doing.'[2] Unpredictability lay at the very core of a show that fostered unparalleled viewer expectations, mostly because it spun its narrative at an unsteady pace, marked by increasingly shorter seasons often separated by long hiatuses.

Adept at thwarting viewers' expectations (he once said in an interview, 'People hate that stuff. Doesn't matter, they're going to get it anyway. In fact, all that complaining makes me more determined'),[3] Chase perfected his auteurist independence with the final nine episodes of the show, which were eagerly anticipated by the world press.[4] As the opening credits to the first episode of that season began to roll, American viewers waited with baited breath, engaging in a game of predictions gloriously upset by the mastermind responsible for the architecture of the entire series. It is the structural unpredictability of the show that will be examined in this essay, at the intra-episodic and inter-episodic levels. This postmodern game of chess, during which Chase anticipated and thwarted each move of the audience, is what ultimately defined *The Sopranos* as quality television.

Recent studies on prime time drama have defined quality TV as programming that requires undivided attention from its viewers, who are virtually asked to turn off the lights, stop what they are doing, and pretend to be in a movie theatre. Held to consistently high standards, these shows are investigated for their unique take on society. It is in this light that I perceive the final season of *The Sopranos* to be structured around the very anticipation of an End. The entire season prepares viewers for an impending doom that cannot be averted, and like Tony's therapist, the audience is eventually asked to move on, and look away. Extraordinary expectations are thus reduced to a final gesture of dismissal and displacement: Dr Melfi ends Tony's therapy when she painfully learns that psychoanalysis enables instead of helping sociopaths, just as viewers are forced to break away from an addictive relationship with a family and a world that need to be frequented with critical caution.

At a macrostructural level, Season 6.2 (or season 6, part 2) can be divided into three parts: the first comprising episodes 6.2.1–6.2.4, the second covering the following two (6.2.5–6.2.6), and the third part consisting of the last three episodes (6.2.7–6.2.9). In the first part, viewers witness Tony's growing disenchantment with four key figures in his life: his brother-in-law, his nephew, his close friend and role model, and his financial adviser. Halfway through each episode, Tony clearly contemplates the possibility of murdering each of them, only to change his mind soon after. In each episode, viewers are invited to expect the occurrence of a pivotal bloody event, one that is eventually replaced by the fleeting portrayal of a death that appears to be insignificant within the economy of the individual episode. In the economy of the entire season, however, what appeared insignificant eventually assumes relevance: all of these initial 'little murders' prepare the ascent to power of Tony's nemesis, Phil Leotardo.

In the second part, just as viewers have adjusted to the anticlimactic character of Chase's narration, they are shocked by Tony's murder of his nephew Christopher. This event, occurring in 6.2.6, is preceded by an episode that diffuses the narrative tension by portraying the internal strivings of Tony's crewmen in highly comedic fashion. As a result, Christopher is killed when viewers least expect it, both because it happens in an unpredictable contingency and because it occurs at the beginning and not at the end of the episode.

The last group of episodes sees Tony dealing with two profound crises, one at home and the other at work. On both fronts he faces the potential extinction of his own lineage. His only son has attempted suicide at the same time as the head of *New York*,[5] Phil Leotardo, has attempted to decapitate *New Jersey* by having Tony's brother-in-law and his closest *consigliere* shot. When the former dies and the latter goes into a coma, despite the ambiguity of the closing sequence of the series, viewers are left witnessing the likely survival of only one family, Tony's nuclear family. In fact, the series ends leaving viewers with the certainty of Tony's impending indictment and the potential dismemberment of his organization. While viewers could anticipate the murder of several key figures, including the brutal death of Phil Leotardo, they could not have predicted that the show would end with an interrupted sequence that left wide segments of the audience shocked, frustrated, and angry.

On a macrostructural level, the empathetic performativity of the three different parts of the series is quite varied. While in the first part viewers still feel what Noël Carroll called 'sympathy for the devil',[6] mostly because the narrative appears to justify Tony's growing mistrust of his closest crewmen, in the second group of episodes the audience is confronted with Tony's brutality in a totally unforgiving fashion. His unforeseen murder of Christopher, previously portrayed in the show as Tony's putative son, should be read as his flawed and rather incomprehensible attempt to regain the control he has lost through a gambling addiction that has forced him to take a series of extremely selfish actions in 6.2.4. Once he kills Christopher, Tony is virtually dead in the eyes of the viewers, mostly because Christopher has suddenly come to represent, in the economy of the show, the possibility of salvation: a recovering addict with a new family, he has turned a new leaf through his film career.

Tony's reactions to Christopher's death only further viewers' disenchantment, and his final admission that Christopher's death ended his unlucky streak in gambling is the last straw: in the third section of the season, viewers, like his psychiatrist, are ready to let him go. In these last episodes, in fact, viewers are still inevitably *aligned* with Tony's perception of the events, since his field of vision continues to orient much of the visual narrative, yet their *allegiance* to him has began to falter: just as Dr Melfi, the other vantage point from which viewers filter the narration, has eventually come to face her inability to help Tony recover, the audience has lost all hopes for his moral salvation.[7]

Tony's only potential redeeming trait, in the eyes of the audience, is the turmoil he experiences upon witnessing his son's descent into depression. Soon after killing his putative son, Tony rescues his real son A.J. from an attempted suicide and bursts into tears as he holds him in a position reminiscent of Michelangelo's *Pietà*. A.J.'s depression acquires symbolic overtones not only because it is hereditary but also because it endows him with a clearer sense of vision that allows him to interpret the world around him in a deeper fashion. The war in Iraq, the Israel–Palestine conflict, racial tensions in the New Jersey towns of Newark and New Brunswick, and the fierce dispute between *New York* and *New Jersey* symbolically conflate in his eyes when A.J. utters Rodney King's famous words: 'Why can't we all get along?' Incidentally, territorial conflicts between neighbouring or invasive entities are repeated symbolically through the frequent sportscasts shown on screen.

Viewers' empathy for Tony is seriously tested once we witness his crew's careless disposal of asbestos. Garbage disposal here becomes more than just a business front for Tony and his crew: images of trucks loading and unloading asbestos, frequently shown at the start or at the very end of individual episodes, acquire symbolic relevance in the economy of the show. *Dumping* becomes a central metaphor for much of what happens during this entire sixth season: just as the illegal disposal of asbestos signifies the poisoning power of the sins of the fathers visited on future generations, depression is portrayed as a form of genetic pollution *dumped* by a father on his son. A.J.'s depression actually begins when his girlfriend *dumps* him. And Tony himself eventually feels *dumped* by his therapist. Much of therapy can indeed be perceived, by sceptics, as a form of *dumping*, and the disposal of the delicate information that Tony has handed to his therapist was once of great concern to his business associates, who came to see Dr Melfi as a potential threat to their organization.

In the first episodes, Chase plays with his audience by exploring and exploding the boundaries of genre: a few episodes exit the common framework of the gangster show to surprise viewers by borrowing from very different genres. The opening show, 'Soprano Home Movies', takes four of the leading characters away from their usual surroundings and brings them to a lake house in the Adirondacks. Viewers accustomed to episodes packed with violent action set in urban or suburban landscapes are faced with an intimate, theatrical piece set in an Arcadic world, where the unspoken rules of organized crime are powerfully rehashed through a game of Monopoly.

Chase indirectly responds to action-thirsty viewers by providing long shots of Tony staring across the lake, turned away from the camera. Although we are still seeing the world through his eyes, his actions increasingly become more cryptic as our access to his thought process gradually becomes less direct. Much of the episode is dedicated to the dinner and post-dinner conversation, during which old family anecdotes are merrily exchanged. A game of Monopoly turns particularly loud when Bobby, the brother-in-law, refuses to abide by Tony's added rules, which are presented as customary in the Sopranos' household. A clear reference to the nature of the rules of organized crime is subtly dropped: the family accepts them and lives off them without questioning, since they make the game 'more interesting', while the outsider is left doubting their necessity and legality. As drinking progresses, the family tales become racier, and Bobby proves his extraneousness by taking offence at a sexual remark against his wife, punching Tony and starting a dramatic fistfight. The explosion of violence is contained within the house, the family, and the peaceful lake resort, yet its power remains boundless. Always portrayed as a peaceful man, Bobby loses control when he cannot understand or accept a set of rules that suddenly exclude him. As competent viewers of the show, we know that Tony will not accept disrespect, and thus we inevitably fear for Bobby. Tony's revenge comes in a much subtler fashion, beginning our process of empathic disassociation from his character: instead of killing him, Tony asks Bobby to commit his first murder. By taking away his 'innocence', Tony is corrupting the only member of his crew with a clean (or more ambiguous) status.

All of the characters who were absent from the first episode return en masse in the following four episodes. *The Sopranos* opens its second instalment on a more conventional note, bringing back all the characters to their daily interactions, in their daily habitat. Revolving around the New York premiere of Christopher's film, this episode takes another unconventional road by turning its protagonists into viewers who are uncomfortably witnessing a fictional rendition of their own lives. Chase's postmodern take on prime time drama abandons generic experimentation in order to present a self-reflexive discussion on the (dis)pleasures of viewership. Once finally *projected* on the screen, Christopher's film unveils its creator's deep resentment against Tony, manifested as a form of psychoanalytic *projection*. In the movie, the character drawn after Christopher resembles the son of Frankenstein, portrayed in his final revenge against the man who created him. As later episodes reveal, Christopher's anger towards his relative does not drive him to murder, but rather towards a *legit* lifestyle, while his uncle, unsettled by his nephew's fantasies, eventually kills him.

Generic experimentation occurs again in the third and fifth episodes, the former redefining the tenets of the road movie and the latter evoking the world of cartoons. 'Remember When' (6.2.3) follows Tony and his associate Paulie on a trip to Florida and portrays Tony's growing disillusion with the man he once considered a role model. The physical journey becomes dangerous once it turns into a trip down memory lane – the man who once was an Italian Gary Cooper, 'the strong, silent type', has become an old *chiacchierone* who seriously jeopardizes Tony's safety. Viewers take a parallel journey as they revisit Tony's murder of another close friend, Pussy Buonpensiero. This memory further affects their empathic investment in the central character, setting the stage for Christopher's murder. 'Walk Like a Man' (6.2.5) portrays the explosive feud between Christopher and Paulie. The comedic traits implicit in the excessive acts of retaliation between the two minimize the dramatic implications of Christopher's lapse in sobriety. Likened to the action/reaction pattern of *Tom and Jerry*, whose fleeting images briefly appear on a TV screen, the vendetta between Christopher and Paulie paves the way for Christopher's demise: by the end of the episode, Christopher has submitted to peer pressure and re-entered his uncle's old world, forfeiting his sobriety in the process. Chase here turns the screws on Tony one more time, as the audience increasingly begrudges him, unaware that Christopher is about to be murdered.

The episode portraying the assassination (6.2.6, 'Kennedy and Heidi') is most striking for the occurrence of the murder a few minutes into the show. Although this is clearly cliffhanger material, Chase opts for a different path, demonstrating that in the economy of the show Tony's reaction is far more important than Christopher's death. A large part of the episode is dedicated to Tony's trip to Vegas, where he relives the life of his dead nephew, bedding his ex-girlfriend and taking peyote, in search of a final revelation that, once attained, is loudly welcomed yet never disclosed. By this time, the opacity of Tony's portrayal is such that viewers are virtually invited to stop caring for him.

The episodes comprising the coda of the series amplify the gulf between Tony and the viewers. Episode 6.2.7 finds its leitmotif in the opening lines of Yeats's 'The Second Coming,' from which it borrows its title. Often used in reference to the war in Iraq, this poem evokes the profound instability of the present ('Things fall apart; the centre cannot hold / Mere anarchy is loosed upon the world'), predicting an apocalyptic future that defies all hope. Tony's son A.J. hears this poem in class and is later seen reading it in bed, and eventually, at his uncle's funeral, he recites it to family and friends, who fail to appreciate its depth. A.J. encounters Yeats's poem before attempting suicide, and its bleak portrayal of the world throws him into further depression – the world that is falling apart, though, is not just A.J.'s, nor is it merely referring to the international conflict he now follows with such pathos. Tony's world is also about to shatter, and his failure to trust the members of his crew likens him to Yeats's falconer, who is no longer heard by his falcon. The apocalyptic Second Coming, initially announced by A.J.'s attempted suicide, thus refers also to *New York*'s blitzkrieg against *New Jersey*. The speed of the attack, evidenced by Phil's brutal assassination of Tony's brother-in-law and by the hit on Silvio, is evoked by the title of 6.2.8, 'The Blue Comet,' during which both actions are carried out. Fast like a comet, Bobby's assassination occurs while he is purchasing a collectible toy train ('The Blue Comet') for his older son. The most striking element of this sequence, masterfully arranged through complex frame composition, is the intra-diegetic portrayal of the viewers' reaction to an event that, while fully expected, retains a powerful dramatic quality. The ensuing astonishment, similar to that experienced with the anticipated passing of comets, is replicated in the show through the close-ups of the little figurines surrounding the tracks where the Blue Comet is running when Bobby suddenly collapses on the floor, crashing on the toys. The figurine of a woman with a hand on her mouth in surprise (or horror) replicates the reactions of intra- and extra-diegetic viewers: the customers in the toy store give loud screams, down on the same floor where Bobby's corpse and all the figurines eventually land. For us, actual viewers of the show, surprise and shock come not only as a result of the death of a pivotal character, but also in response to its masterful depiction.

Like the passing of comets, death occurs swiftly, as all fades to black, and in this (lack of) light we can read the lengthy black screen that closes the final episode, which could portray the assassination of Tony and his family through the eyes of one of the victims. Before I analyse it, however, I will turn to the character who, with Tony, has acted as the show's vantage point, Doctor Melfi. Episode 6.2.8 devotes large attention to Melfi's painful awareness that the work done with Tony has borne no fruit – as colleagues of hers have suggested, recent studies prove that therapy only strengthens sociopathic behaviour, so when Melfi is finally convinced of the truth of this argument, she is forced to terminate Tony's sessions. Often interpreted as the moral centre of the show, as the sole ethically viable vantage point offered to viewers, Melfi is shown reading the article that discusses these recent findings, and Chase adopts a Godardian mise en scène to remind us that Melfi is the intra-diegetic replica of the active viewer of the show. As she sits up on her bed, the camera zooms on the article, portraying one magnified word at a time: Melfi's eyes are ours, and like her we are about to abandon Tony forever. Much could be inferred about the symbolic reasons for such obvious conflation of internal and external gaze: why must we abandon Tony? Maybe because, like Melfi, by sticking with him, we would further glorify and glamorize his world, without reaching any valuable insight? This is a question that I believe needs to be raised at this point. Like Melfi, we have to let Tony and his family go: the final twists in their slow descent into hell are to be carried out in the darkness signified by the last black shot. Chase refuses to push his narrative further and in this way makes a very precise statement on the portrayal of mafia on television.

Further questions remain unanswered at the end of the much-debated final episode, 'Made in America,' where viewers are initially given their payoff through the murder of Phil Leotardo, yet are eventually left dangling when the series ends abruptly, on a black screen, just as the Sopranos are about to be reunited at the diner. My chapter ends with an analysis of this sequence, which proves the deep postmodernity of Chase's show. By the time this sequence begins, viewers' anticipation is predictably extremely high – the gradual arrival of Tony, Carmela, and A.J. at the diner is presented through shot/countershot editing that foretells a climax that, unfortunately for most viewers, never occurs. Mixing shots portraying the three characters in the diner with the image of Meadow struggling with parallel parking outside further enhances tension and a sense of foreboding. The show ends just as Meadow is about to enter, leaving these characters in a most conventional setting, but without a closure that would ensure their actual safety. The intra-diegetic notes of Journey's 'Don't Stop Believin'' run through most of the sequence, evoking a sense of hope further reinforced by the name of the band, a reminder of the journey that we, as viewers, have taken with these characters. What matters most, in the economy of this sequence, is the screen going to black halfway through the refrain, on the words 'Don't stop,' as if to superimpose viewers' desire to continue watching the show with the necessity, already voiced intra-diegetically by Melfi, to end it. At the same time, the musical imperative that closes *The Sopranos* is another potent reminder of its postmodernity: quality television is programming that demands viewers' undivided attention because it is essentially polysemic and therefore cannot allow simple decodings. At the end of the day – or better, at the end of *The Sopranos* – it is our process of interpretation that must not, cannot, and will not stop.

NOTES

1 See Janet McCabe and Kim Akass, 'Sex, Swearing and Respectability: Courting Controversy, HBO's Original Programming and Producing Quality TV,' in *Quality TV: Contemporary American Television and Beyond*, ed. Janet McCabe and K. Akass (London: I.B. Tauris, 2007).

2 Martha P. Nochimson, 'Interview with David Chase,' in *Dying to Belong: Gangster Movies in Hollywood and Hong Kong* (Oxford: Blackwell, 2007), 245.

3 Ibid., 244.

4 The last season was divided into two parts. I will refer to the two parts of the sixth season as 6.1 and 6.2.

5 When in italics, the words *New York* and *New Jersey* refer to the two rival families heading organized crime in those states.

6 Noël Carroll, 'Sympathy for the Devil,' in *The Sopranos and Philosophy: I Kill Therefore I Am* (Chicago: Open Court, 2004).

7 An opposite argument could be made, however, for the sympathetic overtones conveyed by James Gandolfini's nuanced portrayal of Tony Soprano in the very last episodes of the season. The quiet emotions manifested in his final encounters with his uncle and with his comatose *consigliere* could indeed be seen as genuinely redemptive.

23 'History Doesn't Repeat Itself, but It Does Rhyme'[1]: Fictionalizing History in *Boardwalk Empire*

PAOLO RUSSO

Most gangster tales follow a pattern: the rise to power and subsequent fall of the protagonist, who quite often is portrayed as an outsider as the story begins. HBO's *Boardwalk Empire* (five seasons, 2010–14) is essentially a gangster story. However, its protagonist Enoch (Nucky) Thompson – modelled after the real-life Enoch Johnson – is no outsider. In fact, he is already at the top of his game in the first episode of Season One and is planning to expand his illicit operations across the US Northeast through a network of alliances, both political and criminal. The FBI and enemies within and outside Nucky's own organization repeatedly threaten his dominant position, but for the first three seasons, Nucky retains it and indeed consolidates it. It is only in Seasons Four and Five, as he slowly loses his firm grip on that power, that the series shifts towards a looser structure and Nucky's role as the focus of dramatic attention is undermined.

To deviate from the generic pattern was a key choice made at the storylining stage – one that triggered the dramatic action, that plunged the protagonists *in media res* as concerns the gangster plotline, thus saving a substantial amount of screen time, and that utilized that time to establish and accommodate a broader focus on history rather than simply on plot development. While this general remark applies to the series as a whole, the main focus of this essay will be on Season One. For the most part, the narrative of that season weaves three main storylines that follow Nucky Thompson, Nucky's protégé Jimmy Darmody, and Nucky's love interest Margaret Schroeder respectively. Of course, a number of related subplots branch out – indeed, an incredibly high number of secondary characters are established in what becomes a very complex diegetic world.

Boardwalk Empire was inspired by chapter 5 of Nelson Johnson's bestselling book,[2] but the creators, led by Terence Winter, soon departed from that source, drawing from a complex canvas with deep roots in North American and international social and cultural history to mould their narrative material, very much based on the 'idea that the world was rapidly changing.'[3] A quantitative analysis sampling the first six episodes of Season One is quite indicative of the richness and complexity of this historical canvas; one can identify many different types of historical markers at play – that is, elements of the narrative that are used as vehicles for such markers. By taking into account both discrete markers (i.e., self-contained elements within scenes, usually as part of the dialogue or of the profilmic) and gradual or partial markers (i.e., those that play out over multiple scenes or even episodes), we can summarize the results of this analysis. Table 1 demonstrates how *Boardwalk Empire* taps into manifold issues – in terms of social, political, and cultural history – that made the 1920s an era of age-defining conflicts. After briefly contextualizing how the serial macrostructure works to define the time period at hand, I will provide a few paradigmatic examples – namely, the links among politics, organized crime, corruption, racism, activism, literacy, and the media.

Table 1. Quantitative analysis of history markers in Season One, Episodes 1–6

Marker category	173'	253'	351'	453'	553'	660'
Organized crime (people, facts, etc.)	6	1	1	2	1	1
Politics & corruption	3	2	1	4	2	0
Prohibition / bootlegging	7	1	0	1	1	0
Prostitution	1	2	0	0	0	0
WWI veterans	5	1	3	1	0	1
Immigration	5	0	0	3	2	1
Leagues (for decency, etc.)	3	0	0	0	1	0
Women's condition	4	1	0	2	1	2
Unions & labour	2	1	0	0	2	0
Industrializaton & technological advances	0	1	1	1	0	0
African Americans	2	3	2	2	0	0
Racism / Ku Klux Klan	0	1	1	4	0	0
Consumerism	4	1	1	0	0	1
Popular culture(movies, music, magazines, literature, press, fashion, sports, etc.)	5	2	3	3	3	3
Education	1	0	0	0	1	1
Self-made man myth	2	0	1	0	1	0
Disability	1	0	0	0	1	1
Drugs	1	0	0	0	2	0
Health issues (public and private)	0	0	3	1	0	6
Homosexuality	0	0	1	0	0	0
Totals	61	18	19	27	19	17

Table 2. Time frame spanning the *Boardwalk Empire*'s five seasons

SEASON	BEGINS	ENDS	SPANS
1	16 January 1920	November 1920	9 ½ months
Skips	2 months		
2	January 1921	August 1921	8 months
Skips	4 months		
3	31 December 1922	June 1923	5 ½ months
Skips	7 ½ months		
4	February 1924	January 1925	11 months
Skips	6 years, 3 months		
5	April 1931	October 1931	7 months
	+ Flashbacks to 1890s		

In an interesting essay on *Mad Men* (2007–1015), Dana Polan discusses the 'historicism' of the series as working on two levels. A general concern with large-scale punctual events – political, cultural, social – is accompanied by a systematic preoccupation with the small scale, with 'getting the surface details right.'[4] Both *Mad Men* and *Boardwalk Empire* provide distinct historical settings for their narrative: the 1960s in the former, the 1920s in the latter. Table 2 outlines in more specific detail the time frame of the narrative in each of the five seasons of *Boardwalk Empire*.

Season One covers most of 1920 and feeds almost seamlessly into Season Two, which is set in 1921. Season Three leaps forward to the first half of 1923. Season Four stretches through most of 1924 and into 1925. A gap of just a few months in the ideal chronology in between each of these seasons allows the writers to, at least partly, reboot their storylines. The exception to the rule is Season Five, which jumps forward more than six years to 1931, in the midst of the Great Depression, although with flashbacks all the way back to the 1890s providing insight into many of the protagonists' back stories from their youth – all experiences that would have defined these characters by the time we meet them for the first time in the pilot.

Where *Mad Men* and *Boardwalk Empire* differ is in how they make use of their respective historical references – which is also where I slightly disagree with Polan. In *Mad Men* large-scale events generally remain in the background, or, better, work *as* background: for instance, Nixon's first presidential run, JFK's assassination, the second US tour of the Beatles, the third US tour of the Rolling Stones, the man on the moon. All of these events have significant affective impact on the characters but rarely bear any immediate relation to their actions. In *Boardwalk Empire* the opposite is true: historical events become proper dramatic events, active story elements that propel the narrative – one reason for this being that most characters are fictionalized versions of real historical figures and therefore their actions do have a direct impact on those events and by such events are in turn influenced further on. The select examples below will illustrate how.

Politics and gangsters: The incipit of 1.1 (or season 1, episode 1) comes with a date stamp marked visually by the symbolic, if farcical, funeral of John Barleycorn: 16 January 1920, the day the Volstead Act is finally enforced nationwide, sanctioning the official start of Prohibition. As known, far from reaching its goal, Prohibition actually meant that organized crime was reborn virtually overnight after a rather long period when it had to keep a relatively low profile; in the series, this particular large-scale event obviously fuels the various gangster plotlines. Following on from this, in 1.1 and 1.2, Nucky Thompson and his former mentor, Commodore Louis Kaestner, mention both the ratification of the League of Nations (which occurred just a few days earlier, on 10 January, although President Wilson failed to have it pass the Senate vote) and, most importantly, the fact that 'this,' 1920, is an election year. Elections are a main narrative focus throughout Season One: in 1.4, Nucky spends his birthday party with Senator Walter Edge and Mayor Frank Hague; in 1.8, Nucky attends the Republican National Convention; and in 1.12, the last of the season, Election Day (2 November) ends with the victory of the Republican candidate Warren Harding, backed by Nucky.

Season One is thus strategically pegged to the election of 1920, which was a watershed year – politically, socially, and culturally – in that it brought an end to the two decades known as the Progressive Era. Although certain aspects remain controversial, under the presidencies of Theodore Roosevelt, Howard Taft (both Republicans), and Woodrow Wilson (a Democrat), the United States saw unprecedented reforms that tackled pressing issues related to women's conditions, immigration, labour, education, public health, and corruption. American intervention in the First World War brought all this to a sudden halt and plunged the country into a deep recession that would last into the early 1920s. The long-arc development of the electoral thread means that throughout Season One, much of Nucky's story plays out in tandem with the political machine he runs in Atlantic City. As we learn in 1.4, Nucky had managed to have Frank Hague appointed mayor a few years earlier: now he brokers a deal to have Hague support Walter Edge in his run for the Senate, where, as Big Elector, he will support Warren Harding. Despite being a dark horse, Harding wins the primary, in no small part thanks to Edge and Nucky's support, and becomes president by promising a return to normalcy, by which he does not mean a return to prewar progressive policies, but quite the opposite: a clampdown on unions and workers' rights, the endorsement of Prohibition and racial segregation, *de facto* toleration of the Ku Klux Klan, severe restrictions on immigration, and so forth. Eventually, Harding's administration would go down as the most corrupt in American history; when we factor in soaring unemployment and thousands of war veterans left in limbo, all of this paints a glum picture, still very far from that of the Roaring Twenties yet to come. It is this world, this new normal, that *Boardwalk Empire* engages with.

Corruption: The events in the political arena in both 1.8 and 1.12 run parallel to an apparently stand-alone subplot involving Arnold Rothstein, a professional gambler as well as one of New York City's most powerful mob bosses. When introduced for the very first time in 1.1 by Chicago crime boss Johnny Torrio, the first thing we are given to know about Rothstein is that he played a key role in fixing the 1919 World Series. This fleeting commentary is seemingly soon forgotten until 1.8, when Rothstein apprehends from the papers that legal troubles are looming over him. Rothstein is talking to his lawyer about the formal investigation that has been launched by the grand jury. In reality, the grand jury only convened on 20 September; in *Boardwalk Empire* the timing is altered to make it coincide with the Republican Convention attended by Nucky, which opens on 8 June. In 1.12, Rothstein learns that the investigation will lead to a federal indictment, which means he will stand trial. Historically, the grand jury's decision was handed down on 22 October, but in the series this is pushed forward by a few days, once again in order to make it run parallel to Nucky's final campaigning efforts and Election Day.

The reason for this obeys dramatic needs, even though we will have to wait to see the payoff. In Season One, Nucky and Rothstein are often at odds, pretending to be partners in business while actually trying to oust each other. The election of President Harding strengthens Nucky Thompson's economic and political power, which means Rothstein could use his help when in trouble. Much later, in Season Three, we are led to infer that thanks to his connections, Nucky managed to close down the prosecution of Rothstein, which makes him a new powerful ally.

Racism: At the beginning of 1.2, we catch a glimpse of a man handing out leaflets on the boardwalk publicizing the Ku Klux Klan. Although we notice him, this is a quick transition shot whose main focus is in fact on Jimmy Darmody, whose action we then follow. Because nothing happens throughout the remainder of the episode that can be linked to this momentary detail, we soon forget about it. However, at the end of 1.3 a young black man is killed and hanged by the Klan. In the subsequent 1.4, Nucky instructs his brother, Sheriff Eli Thompson, to storm the local KKK's church home, arrest their leader, and hand him over to Chalkie White, the leader of the African American community, who can and does take his revenge.

Nucky does not care for the Klan but he also cares little for justice. Surely he does not support the cause of black people per se. Most importantly, as he puts it to his brother once again, the last thing they need is a race war in an election year. This is not just some passing remark. The summer and autumn of 1919 were marked by race riots in several states that caused quite a media sensation at a time when there was a rising fear of socialist activism (the so-called Red Scare). In light of this, Nucky's comment is quite telling of a cynical attitude: his partner in business, Chalkie White, not only makes sure that black workers find jobs but also controls the vote of Atlantic City's African American population. Clearly, Nucky's action against the Klan is the result of political calculation.

Activism, literacy, and the media: One legacy of the Progressive Era was better education policies, which led to higher literacy rates. Around the same time, and not simply because of the war, the media truly became *mass* media. Also, advertising by then was playing a huge role in influencing people's tastes and choices in an era of mass-produced consumer goods, but also in health campaigns, which for the first time could reach a wider, more educated public. A striking element in *Boardwalk Empire* is that many characters seem to be reading all the time: newspapers, magazines, pamphlets, leaflets, even instruction booklets.

By 1.6, Margaret Schroeder has become Nucky's partner and is finally living her rags-to-riches fairy tale. However, she already has two children and only recently has had her second miscarriage, so the last thing she wants right now is another pregnancy. She seeks the advice of the president of the Women's Temperance League, whose meetings she attends mainly because they support women's right to vote. However, the league is deeply conservative on what they consider issues of public morality: for instance, they endorse Prohibition because they consider alcohol the cause of all depravity (as shown immediately in 1.1). It should come as no surprise, though, that far from being judgmental regarding Margaret's affair with Nucky, the president tells her that 'women may now have obtained the right to vote but they must look after themselves.' She also hands Margaret a copy of *Family Limitation* by Margaret Sanger, a how-to manual that educates women on how to avoid unwanted pregnancies using homemade contraceptive methods.[5] Sanger was a pioneer activist who was arrested and prosecuted several times in an era when contraception and abortion were illegal and when the dissemination of information on contraception was banned by anti-obscenity laws. Given historical references such as this one, it seems clear that Margaret Schroeder's character is not based on Nucky Johnson's real second wife; instead, she is deeply inspired by Sanger's activism and therefore becomes representative of the other America, the one that is fighting to improve its living conditions.[6] Margaret's role becomes more and more defined along this line in Season Two, when she uses Nucky's money to finance clinics specifically aimed at helping women.

The above shows how *Boardwalk Empire* is not an example of drama as mere illustration of historical events; instead, history and historical figures (and their fictionalizations) become integral components of the series narrative, with specific dramatic functions worked out at storylining stage thanks to painstakingly detailed research that reaches beyond general perceptions of the 1920s in today's public imaginary. Moreover, *Boardwalk Empire* shows how serial, multi-strand narrative lends itself to a clever representation of social and cultural changes in a way that rejects the deterministic linearity that is always questionable when we try to understand the complexities of historical eras. Nucky Thompson in particular, as the series' main narrative engine, is a fine example of a character who embodies and condenses that complexity and who transcends the typical gangster as 'a lonely, doomed, and tragic figure,'[7] torn as he is between the cynicism of the political and criminal world he inhabits – with all its positive and, most often, negative potential – and regret for the consequences of this at the much smaller yet all the more engaging personal level.

NOTES

1 Cited by Al Capone in season 5, episode 5.

2 'Chapter 5 – The Golden Age of Nucky', in *Boardwalk Empire: The Birth, High Times and Corruption of Atlantic City*, ed. Nelson Johnson (London: Ebury Press, 2011), 79–102.

3 'Conversation with Terence Winter', in *Inside the Writers' Room: Conversations with American TV Writers*, ed. Christina Kallas (Basingstoke: Palgrave Macmillan, 2014), 15.

4 See Dana Polan, 'Maddening Times: *Mad Men* and Its History', in *Mad Men, Mad World: Sex, Politics, Style & the 1960s*, ed. Lauren M. E. Goodlad, Lilya Kaganovsky, and Robert A. Rushing (Durham, NC: Duke University Press, 2013), 35–52; Caroline Levine, 'The Shock of the Banal: *Mad Men*'s Progressive Realism', in Goodlad, Kaganovsky, and Rushing, op. cit., 133–44.

5 The most easily available contraceptive method at the time was the Lysol douche, which is explained in *Family Limitation* as shown in 1.6.

6 It is fair to assume that the character's name itself is a telling conflation of Margaret Sanger's forename and Theodore Schroeder's surname. The latter, who was the founder of the Free Speech League, funded Sanger and helped her fight her legal battles.

7 Al Auster, 'HBO's Approach to Generic Transformation', in *Thinking Outside the Box: A Contemporary Television Genre Reader*, ed. Gary R. Edgerton and Brian Rose (Lexington, KY: University of Kentucky Press, 2005), 242.

24 *Mob Wives*: Exploitation or Empowerment?

JACQUELINE REICH AND FATIMA KARIM

The ubiquity of mafia representations in American visual culture sprang from big screen to small screen with *The Sopranos* in 1999. This self-conscious interrogation of our fascination with mafiosi in all their complexities was groundbreaking for (among many other reasons) its multi-layered representation of Carmela, Tony's long-suffering wife and matriarch of the family, as well as other female members of the family: his daughter Meadow, his sister Janice, and, for a brief time, Tony's mother Livia.[1] *Mob Wives* (2011–16), created by Jennifer Graziano, uses Carmela Soprano as a point of departure for a hybrid fusion of the *Real Housewives* franchise, which began in 2006, and the mafia movie. Graziano and her sister Renee, who stars in the show, are the daughters of Anthony Graziano, the former *consigliere* to the Bonanno crime family. *Jersey Shore* (2009–12) with its Guidos and Guidettes was the first foray of concentrated Italian American representation in reality television; *Mob Wives* turns its lens on the older crowd, women whose husbands, fathers, and assorted relatives are connected to the mob. The show borrows from popular representations of Italian Americans in gangster and mafia films in the context of the genre of reality TV. Throughout the show's six-year run, Graziano reappropriates these representations by culturally grounding the characters or 'wives' not in the previous docile and subservient silent mothers but rather in the male mafioso cinematic tropes of the *bella figura* (the public manifestation of the private self), *omertà* (the mafia code of silence), and violence. Marilyn Yaquinto observes how gangster films, while generally relegating female protagonists to the sidelines, 'provide glimpses into transgressive fantasies and illuminate portraits of women who often appear daring and rebellious.'[2] Our thesis is that *Mob Wives*, through empowerment rather than exploitation, allows the women of Staten Island to establish their own feminist narratives as strong matriarchs through the codes and conventions of reality television, albeit within the confines of capitalist and celebrity culture. A central question of our interrogation centres on the privileging of a masculinized auteur cinema over the more feminized genre of reality television, particularly 'docusoap': if we respect and revere Vito Corleone for being a mobster, can we also learn to appreciate and respect the *Mob Wives*?

Reality TV is a televisual genre that usually involves unscripted programming 'starring' everyday people. The content and format of these shows can vary widely, but like all genres, they have shared conventions: here, non-professional actors often filmed in real locations in both scripted and improvised situations. Reality TV can take on multiple, hybrid formats that borrow from other television genres: game shows, talent contests, dating shows, and, in the case of *Mob Wives*, soap operas.[3] In short, they are 'a hybrid form that plays with dramatic construction and social interaction,' with docusoaps highlighting the social interactions among the characters/actors/participants as well as 'off-camera' confessionals, which serve to construct the 'public' and the 'private.'[4]

Historically, these shows were developed for particular networks (MTV, Bravo, VH1) for both mass and niche audiences. Although 'pitched as spontaneous and real,' they were also 'tightly edited and carefully packaged with high doses of voyeurism, suspense, gossip, sensationalism, melodrama, affect and cruelty.'[5] They are connected to and examine 'the shifting dynamics of production and consumption, amateurism and professionalism, self-representation and branding, and democracy and citizenship.'[6] Many of these tensions are played out through the mechanisms at work in reality TV's celebrity culture, what Chris Rojek has termed reality 'celetoids,' in that they come cheaper than film star endorsements and can seamlessly integrate product placement with celebrity endorsement.[7]

According to Su Holmes and Deborah Jermyn, reality TV has recently 'witnessed a move away from an attempt to "capture" "a life lived" to the televisual arenas of formatted environments in which the more traditional observational rhetoric of documentary jostles for space with the discourses of display and performance.'[8] It interrogates the increasing role of commercialization and branding in everyday life as it not only promotes itself, its stars, and the network but also features multiple product placements and greater social interaction through two-way communication (via the Web and social media).[9] In *Mob Wives*, for instance, banner advertisements would appear to invite viewers to purchase music featured in the show.

Mob Wives is also selling a reappropriation of the Italian American mafiosa through performance, camp, and exaggeration. Clearly, as Graeme Turner argues, reality TV is invested in producing particular identities, or 'the performance of particular subjectivities,' that will attract the most viewers and attention off-screen: these identities are often the most exaggerated, colourful, and grotesque, thus tying reality TV to the aesthetics of camp.[10] In the case of *Jersey Shore* and *Mob Wives*, the performance of Italian American ethnicity centres on the excessiveness of codes and conventions related to Italian American screen representation that first arose in the silent film era – criminality, violence, working-class culture, and darkened skin (in this case through extreme tanning or make-up) – and that ultimately maintain and sustain traditional cultural hierarchies.[11] This amplification of constructed Italian Americanness is not limited to these shows: Jon Kraszewski argues that characters on shows like *Survivor* (2000–) such as 'Boston Rob' Mariano perform the gangster and the Machiavellian trickster in order to allow viewers 'to evaluate how historically situation, working-class, Italian American urban identities stack up against other versions of Americanness.'[12]

Mob Wives focuses on the women of Staten Island whose families are connected to the Italian American mafia. Season One featured four wives: Renee Graziano; Karen Gravano (daughter of Sammy 'the Bull' Gravano, the mafia underboss who famously cooperated with prosecutors to take down John Gotti and the Gambino crime family); Carla Facciolo (her ex-husband served six years for racketeering); and Drita D'Avanzo, who although not Italian (like Snookie of *Jersey Shore*) performs the tough ethnic through marriage to a mobster presently serving time. In Season Two they are joined by Ramona Rizzo (granddaughter of mobster Benjamin Ruggiero) and Angela Raiola (Big Ang), whose uncle was Salvatore Lombardi. From first survey what is evident is that while the main characters are indeed not all mob wives, all are 'married to the Mob' in one way or another. Despite it being known that it was their male counterparts who were the mobsters,

Graziano presents her 'wives' with similar traits and characteristics, putting forth the suggestion that the women are mobsters themselves and should be represented and/or respected just as much as the once patriarchs of their families. The representational mafia tropes on which they rely are the *bella figura*, the matriarchal mafiosa, violence, and *omertà*.

This female perspective had made significant screen appearances in Martin Scorsese's *Goodfellas* with Karen Hill's rare disembodied female narration (i.e., rare for that time period in American film history), and, for humour, in Jonathan Demme's *Married to the Mob* (1988). Karen, although she was not a police officer or soldier, embodied similar traits of bravery and dominance. When she points a gun at Henry's head, she establishes her dominant presence not only in the film but also in her marriage, as seen in the low-angle shot as she straddles her husband. Karen certainly becomes the icon for the *Mob Wives,* all of whom are tough women who speak their mind. Yet it was not until Edie Falco's multiple Emmy Award– and Golden Globe--winning performance as Carmela that the mob wife received an portrayal with more depth that those of the demeaning, subordinate, and acquiescent women of traditional mafia films.[13]

Typically in gangster films, the male characters are powerful, corrupt *bella figuras* who display their private selves through stylish suits, expensive cars, and lavish spending. Similarly, the women of *Mob Wives* are stylishly dressed even at the gym, from their perfectly styled hair and groomed nails to their expensive outfits. 'You have to have a mink if you're in the Mob, it's like, they go together. Someone who doesn't like furs, I would simply say you haven't arrived. Unlike me,' says Renee Graziano (1.3, or season 1, episode 3), explaining her love of furs. The promotional still for Season Five featured the protagonists in tailored suits that evoke the gangster aesthetic of films such as *Reservoir Dogs* and *Le Samurai*.

The gangster/mafia aesthetic also reveals itself in the aesthetics of surveillance that dominate the series' visual style. At the beginning of each episode each character appears through 'surveillance' mechanisms typical of the stake-out: blurred and then focused shots, as if appearing through a powerful distance lens; the iris shot, again evoking the camera lens; the sound of an automated camera clicking through multiple shots; and the freeze-frame with type giving their name and their relationship to the mob (ex-wife, daughter, etc.).

As this volume has clearly shown, 'traditional' Italian and American family values are very much apparent in mafia representation, from *The Godfather* up through *The Sopranos. The Godfather*'s use of pathos centres on the application of violence to establish order and on nostalgia for traditional family values, for the time white men were in control of their families and of society. The audience understands the motives of the mobster and sides with the don as he protects his family. Thus, although Italian American men are portrayed as criminals and aggressive, they still hold very important values of family and loyalty.

There is a very similar narrative in *Mob Wives*, especially that of Carla Facciolo. She, like the other women on the show, are strong, tough, aggressive, and dominant figures in their families. Carla is seen raising her twins by herself after her stockbroker husband has been jailed. Nonetheless, she continues to support and protect her family and is extremely adamant about making sure her kids have a better future than her own. After the first episode of *Mob Wives*, it is blatantly obvious that the 'wives' continue to support and defend their husband/father mobsters. 'Never rat on your family' and 'Don't talk to the Feds' are constant refrains; the women certainly value the same ethics of the mafia/mob: loyalty, family, *omertà*. 'I feel like the people you need to be loyal to in life is the family,' says Karen Gravano (1.1). Even though her father is a notorious 'rat,' Karen is highly defensive against any negative comments about her father, especially when it's from another woman in the series. Karen has even physically fought women who utter the word 'rat' with her father's name.

Nevertheless, the docusoap demands drama, and the confessional format brings out the tension between affect and allegiance. One feminized element in the series is the confessional, during which the characters directly address the camera and share their emotions, reactions, and thoughts on the action that is unfolding in the episode. It is in these moments that the psychological toll that multiple incarcerations have on a family are revealed from a female perspective. Here another television forerunner helps shape the discursive arc: *Sex and the City* (1998–2004). The quartet of New Yorkers, with their obsession with fashion and appearance and their frank talk of sexuality and plastic surgery, rewrite the Upper East Side educated whiteness of the HBO series for the Staten Island Italian American set.

Mafia films are commonly developed around the evil actions of criminals or gangsters, who utilize aggression and violence to assert their dominance. The mob wives are just as aggressive: they are rowdy, use vulgar language (the amount of bleeps per episode is astounding), and often resort to violence, particularly Drita D'Avanzo, who performs the hot-headed, unpredictably violent member of the tribe. D'Avanzo, whose family is Albanian, grew up on Staten Island. After marrying Lee D'Avanzo, a mobster of the Bonanno family, her family cut all ties with her: 'I'm sensitive, some people hurt my feelings and I punch them in the face,' she says in the first episode of Season One.

Much work has focused on the ways in which reality TV has raised 'fundamental questions about the wider contexts of social, political, and economic change in modern society, the political economy of television or the medium's contemporary address to its viewers.'[14] What does a show like *Mob Wives* say about contemporary American society? Certainly it is a commentary on celebrity and commodity culture. As performers, the protagonists are commodities that in turn sell commodities: the show itself, the products featured on the show (music, clothing, even plastic surgeons), and their own side ventures. In fact, all the women own successful businesses: Renee Graziano is the creator/founder of Jail Mail, a product that allows families to contact incarcerated relatives, is the author of two cookbooks and presently has a line of jewellery in her name. Carla Facciolo has her own line of soap and skincare products. Drita D'Avanzo works freelance as a make-up artist as she tries to support her family and has founded her own cosmetics company. And Karen Gravano, who returned to Staten Island to write her own memoir, has reportedly made millions from her book deal. Several of the stars have gone on to appear on other reality TV shows during and after the end of the series. If the traditional way of achieving the American Dream in the mafia film is through the back door or under the table, these women have become legitimate capitalists though the American Dream of reality TV fame construction and commodification of the public Italian American self.

The Italian American self these women express, however, is one of exaggeration, gaudiness, and camp: the flamboyance of the mafia lifestyle is on full display in their colourful characters, colourful behaviour, and colourful outfits. Yet we find it hard to condemn this series as one of patriarchal oppression. Clearly, as Turner argues, reality TV falls well short of the democratization of culture that it professes, for it perpetuates rather than challenges the status quo of class, race, and, in this case, ethnicity. It should be noted that none of the women are heads of or even remotely involved in a crime syndicate (that would make for an interesting but legally problematic spectacle). However, at the same time, it redefines a traditional trope in what P. David Marshall has called the new presentational media: *Mob Wives* challenges traditional and ubiquitous representations of mafia femininity.[15] We, the audience, come to see four empowered women who are proud to share their own narratives and success, which is not that of their male counterparts. This is perhaps why women everywhere have entered a frenzy, keeping up with every episode and of course every fight. And even if the fights are sometimes scripted, one thing is clear: mafia women are much more dynamic than the ubiquitous Madonna/whore dynamic would suggest, and moreover, with Carmela and the *Mob Wives*, they have entered into the cultural Zeitgeist. So much so, in fact, that a reboot of *Mob Wives* is being planned.

NOTES

1 Janet McCabe and Kim Akass, 'What Has Carmela Ever Done for Feminism? Carmela Soprano and the Post-Feminist Dilemma,' in *Reading the Sopranos: Hit TV from HBO*, ed. David Lavery (London and New York: I.B. Taurus, 2006), 39–55.

2 Marilyn Yaquinto, 'Tough Love: Mamas, Molls, and Mob Wives,' in *Action Chicks: New Images of Tough Women in Popular Culture*, ed. Sharon Innes (New York: Palgrave, 2004), 207–29.

3 Laurie Oullette, 'Introduction,' in *A Companion to Reality TV*, ed. Oullette (Oxford: Wiley Blackwell, 2014), 4–5; Jon Kraszewski, *Reality TV* (New York and London: Routledge, 2017), 15.

4 Annette Hill, 'Reality TV Experiences: Audience, Fact and Fiction,' in *A Companion to Reality TV*, ed. Laurie Oullette (Oxford: Wiley Blackwell, 2014), 117; Laura Grindstaff, 'DI(t)Y, Reality-Style: The Cultural Work of Ordinary Celebrity,' in *A Companion to Reality TV*, ed. Oullette, 326; Anita Biressi and Heather Nunn, *Reality TV: Realism and Revelation* (London: Wallflower Press, 2005), 7.

5 Oullette, 'Introduction,' 2.

6 Ibid., 4.

7 Chris Rojek, *Celebrity* (London: Reaktion Books, 2001), 20–3.

8 Su Holmes and Deborah Jermyn, 'Introduction: Understanding Reality TV,' in *Understanding Reality Television*, ed. Su Holmes and Deborah Jermyn (London and New York: Routledge, 2004), 5.

9 June Deery, 'Mapping Commercialization in Reality Television,' in Oullette, ed., *A Companion to Reality TV*, 13.

10 Graeme Turner, 'Reality TV and the Demotic Turn,' in *A Companion to Reality TV*, ed. Oullette, 321.

11 Grindstaff, 'DI(t)Y, Reality-Style: The Cultural Work of Ordinary Celebrity,' 333.

12 Kraszewski, *Reality TV*, 112–21.

13 Molly Haskell, 'The World of "The Godfather": No Place for Women,' *New York Times*, 22 March 1997.

14 Holmes and Jermyn, *Understanding Reality Television*, 16.

15 P. David Marshall, *Celebrity and Power: Fame in Contemporary Culture* (Minneapolis, MN: University of Minnesota Press), xxxiv.

PART THREE

Italian Mafia Movies and Television:
Resistance and Myth

25 Which Law Is the Father's? Gender and Generic Oscillation in Pietro Germi's *In the Name of the Law*

DANIELLE HIPKINS

In nome della legge (*In the Name of the Law*) was one of the most popular Italian films of 1949[1] and probably the first film made in Italy to represent the Sicilian mafia. Based on a novel by Giuseppe Guido Lo Schiavo called *The Small Town Magistrate*, it tells of a young magistrate, Guido Schiavi, who struggles to bring the mafia of a small Sicilian town under state jurisdiction. Apparently succeeding in a last-minute conversion of the mafia to state loyalty, Guido prompts an implausible but heart-warming ending in the tradition of popular film narrative. The film became one of the most controversial that year, leading to heated debate in the popular film journal *Cinema*, in which readers responded defensively to the journal's publication of a negative review by Carlo Doglio.[2] The film's director Pietro Germi was defined as the most 'American' director, and his use of the western genre to treat a distinctly Italian subject matter has been repeatedly underlined ever since.[3] As with any major Italian film released in that period, debates revolved around the film's relationship to the critically privileged mode of neorealism, launched by Rossellini and De Sica. Was Germi's populist approach, drawing on generic Hollywood traditions, another nail driven into the coffin of neorealism, considering the genre was already beset by poor box office returns and government censorship? Or was it, as Ennio Flaiano suggested, a 'middle way for Neorealism'[4] in which Germi fused gripping narrative with the movement's interest in the social? In other words, was the first Italian cinematic engagement with the Sicilian mafia anything more than a skilled exploitation of the latter's good storytelling potential?

The most obvious way in which to answer this question is to think about the film's generic categorization. As the 'new sheriff' (or magistrate) in town, Guido Schiavi finds himself attempting to apply the law to the mafia rebels. The use of the Sicilian landscape over which the outlaws canter towards and away from town, wrapping it firmly in the web of their own law, echoes the representation of Native Americans in the works of John Ford and Anthony Mann, as many western-oriented readings have observed. Germi's bold use of Hollywood-inspired conventions in the context of pertinent social issues went against the neorealist grain. Nonetheless, what is typical of analyses of this period is a perplexity on the part of critics as to the purpose of the female protagonist.[5] Cinema of the period rarely treated femininity in anything other than a melodramatic mode, and that treatment led to a situation in which the female characters appeared, as Guido Aristarco claimed in relation to Germi's film, 'too schematic.'[6] More importantly, however, Germi's inclusion of other generic references has gone undetected because the film has been read within a male-dominated critical and generic framework.[7] Dismissing the scenes between Guido and the baroness as lapses in judgment on Germi's part, no critic asks why such scenes might in fact be required in a film about the state and the mafia in 1949. Rather than berating Germi's incomplete realism or bemoaning his romantic representation of the mafia,[8] it is important to ask whether the apparently superfluous is really such. In fact, the 'feminine' subplot can shed more light upon Germi's depiction of the mafia and the state's struggle to know it. It also gives us insight into early cinematic processes of gendering the mafia as a symbolic entity: the logic of the film's framing of the mafia in relation to the state dictates Guido's gender oscillation, a role played by Massimo Girotti. This chapter asks which law is the father's, because that is the question the film asks. It is because the answer to that question is not immediately clear to Guido that femininity plays a particular role in the film. Articulated through elements of the gothic genre in the film, femininity is not only a confirmation of masculinity's dominance but also something to be passed through and discarded on the Oedipal trajectory of masculine development. The difficulty of this rite of passage, as depicted in Germi's film, delivers a political message about the relationship between the Italian state and the mafia.

The youth of the protagonist that Girotti plays is consistently emphasized in dialogue throughout the film. In his unformed state, Guido is thrown into a town riven by tensions between the local mafia and state law. He finds himself faced with a situation in which the paternal law he has inherited (that of the state) appears weak and an unfamiliar patriarchal law (that of the mafia) appears triumphant. Guido's initial failure to establish himself as a key link in the patriarchal line of this town inevitably aligns him with the feminine, which is presented as marginalized, standing in symbolically for what is outside of power. Implicitly accepting the status quo, as the film implies the state itself might be tempted to do, would annihilate his belonging to any paternal line, and with it, the idea of civilization to which the newborn postwar Italian state aspires. The necessity of establishing a paternal line in the face of an imperfect father was central to the concerns of Italian cinema of this period and tied up with discomfort over the disappearance of masculine honour during the fascist *ventennio* and the defeat of the Second World War. In the south, which lacked the symbolic salvation of the resistance, the mafia, cleared of the taint of fascism thanks to their apparent suppression under Mussolini, offered the opportunity for a new symbolic figuration of the honourable paternal law, more alluring than that of the state.

Primarily, however, I emphasize the paternal because these are the terms the film itself uses, in particular in the dynamic between Guido and the capo, Massaro Turi Passalacqua, whose very name carries echoes of the noble savage. He is represented in the old school 'man of honour' form of mafioso characterization, as someone who wishes to do the right thing because the state is 'far away.' His portrayal points forwards, as Umberto Mosca observes, to a tradition of 'the figure of the boss as possessing a charisma typical of tragic characters, indisputable patriarch and bearer of ethics that differentiate him from his young followers.'[9] It is those lesser men with whom Turi comes into contact that diminish him, the wayward mafioso who kills for lust, or the baron who only has his own interests at heart. The struggle between Turi and Guido is exquisitely Oedipal; the younger man must wrest power away from the worthy but aging father. In two separate exchanges with Guido, Turi refers to his own son, who is studying elsewhere: 'I have a son of your age, who will bring honour to his father.' On both occasions he then restrains his men from harming Guido, as if to drive home the notion of the good father who does not retaliate, and allows the son to identify with patriarchy. The second time, in the face of Guido's final showdown in the central town square, Turi tells him that he would be proud to hear his son talk that way, and that it was already his intention to hand over the delinquent mafioso to the state. This final act can be read as the wise move of a father who wants his son to be seen to succeed, in both senses of the word. In describing the positive resolution of the Oedipal complex, Fisher and Greenberg describe almost exactly what Turi offers Guido: 'He (the boy) gives up his acute competitive stance vis-à-vis the father because the father transmits friendly, positive messages inviting him to join up rather than fight … He invites his son to draw close, to form an alliance, to adopt his identity and accept his values.'[10] This inheritance of male power is unquestionably a homosocial matter that takes precedence over any incidental scenes between man and woman, which may be why scenes with Guido and Teresa appear to be distractions to some critics. However, at the same time the scenes act as a heterosexual alibi, all-important in a culture that is so clearly dependent on the homosocial, as Italy's is in this period.[11] His heterosexuality established, the vulnerability of the beautiful young townsman Paolino enables Guido to assume the mantle of the father, since Paolino's death at the end of the film triggers Guido's forceful entry into that role and his separation from the symbolic weakness of femininity. If we read Guido's experience as one of oscillation between the patriarchal (power) and maternal (powerlessness), in which the former ultimately takes precedence, Guido's bond with Paolino is a crucial part of that journey, cleared of homosexual suggestion by the affair with Teresa.

The scenes between Guido and the baroness cannot be explained away by a sexual voyeurism designed to appeal to a heterosexual male public. Teresa is dressed modestly and is not shot to exude a powerful sex appeal. The emphasis on romantic music in the soundtrack, both diegetic and extra-diegetic, situates her firmly in the pre-Oedipal maternal sphere of the aural and emotional, as opposed to the sexual and visual. It is the sound of her piano playing that initially attracts Guido, not the sight of her. Her interactions with Guido are rarely physical, but largely sentimentally loaded attempts to warn him away from the town. Teresa is Guido's neighbour, trapped in a loveless marriage of convenience to the baron, whose individualized brand of evil mitigates the mafia threat. Teresa's role is one of suffering (at one point her husband horsewhips her) and passive femininity. 'I no longer have a purpose, neither here nor anywhere else,' she tells Guido, her words conveying the redundancy of the maternal space. As such, she represents a mother figure who ought to be rescued, and union with her is both inviting and instinctive (as the shared passion for music suggests) but ultimately threatening to the self. Teresa exists in the realm of what Julia Kristeva describes as the 'semiotic' or, more specifically, in Elizabeth Wright's words, the *chora*, 'the site of the undifferentiated bodily space the mother and child share,'[12] something Kristeva claims must be repressed in order to achieve symbolic subjectivity.

Scenes with Teresa present a very different environment to that experienced by Guido elsewhere in the film. In these moments, his relationship with space casts him in a cinematic tradition, the gothic, which most often envisages this role for a potentially vulnerable female.[13] There is little doubt that Guido's story in the town echoes the trajectory of the gothic heroine, not only with its emphasis on the central investigative figure, but because 'the gothic narrative drive is more typically retrogressive than progressive, its complicated and unpredictable narration forces characters, protagonists, readers and viewers to move backwards as well as forwards, and to reprocess their present conditions and knowledge in relation to events or secrets in the past which were not known, or only partly known.'[14] From his arrival in the town, Guido is presented with a situation based upon secrets from the past (such as the history of his predecessor and why the sulphur mine was closed) and alliances that come to light (between the baron and government forces), which force him to reconsider his relationship to the law. One principal location for these discoveries, conforming to the classical gothic location, is the 'beast's castle,'[15] in this case, the house of the baron. In an early scene where he is making his first call at the palace, the hero appears dwarfed against the large wrought iron gate of his neighbour's residence, and the film thus spatially aligns him with the gothic heroine, who is overwhelmed by her encounter with the space of her new master (see Hitchcock's *Rebecca*, 1940). Guido then makes his way through its lavish, baroque interior, which is filled with mirrors and a mise en abîme of connecting rooms, accompanied by the baroness' passionate piano playing, which sublimates all her unspeakable repression. This is the stuff of melodrama to which critics object. The couple appear twice at night in the overgrown garden between their two properties, again displacing repressed emotion onto the lavish vegeta-tion, which is shot in what is described dismissively by Doglio as 'Turkish harem style.'[16] These internal or dark, claustrophobic spaces are cast in the classically Freudian reading of the maternal space as swamping, and contrast starkly with the arid, desert-like, open and challenging 'western' spaces of the daytime mafia confrontations.

It is not only the spaces of the film that mark out these two gendered and generic positions, which would appear crude if articulated only at this level. What gives them life blood is the filmic use of Massimo Girotti's fluidity as an actor. Girotti incarnates a typically masculine strength (drawn from his physique as former champion swimmer)[17] combined with a feminine grace and delicacy. The clarity of his light-eyed gaze and high forehead give him an openness that is able to connote vulnerability with a sideways glance. For most of his career this enabled him to cross between action and sentimental roles, appealing to audiences of all persuasions. His profile echoes Grecian ideals of male beauty, and at least one critic of the time observed the dangers of Girotti being beautiful as a man, suggesting that such ideals connote a weak and degenerate masculinity.[18] This aspect of Girotti's cultural context is fully exploited in this film, enabling us temporarily to read him as the gothic heroine who is venturing into Bluebeard's castle. He, *like* Teresa, runs the risk of remaining compromised, because of his resignation to his powerlessness, or because of his death or disappearance (like that of his predecessor).

Additionally, as Derek Duncan has suggested, Girotti's fluidity meant that in some films he could be screened as a 'tabula rasa'[19] upon which different characters could project their own desires. *In the Name of the Law* is one of those films: for Turi Passalacqua, Guido becomes the son he wants to inherit his own legacy; for Paolino, he becomes the protective father; for Teresa, he becomes the potential partner; and for his superior, he becomes the man who might toe the line and move on to a different job, quietly acquiescing to the state's incompetence.

Indeed, Teresa's ambitions to leave the town with Guido do coincide with his superior's advice to bow down in the face of this disorder and get out of town. Teresa and the superior appear in Guido's apartment together with the same message in different forms. Guido nearly does follow their suggestion when he joins Teresa with her bags packed on the road leading out of town. While he moves towards her and her car, he is interrupted by the appearance of his loyal *maresciallo* to be told something that will separate him from Teresa forever. As Guido moves towards and then away from the car, his oscillation between the feminine and the masculine is dramatized spatially once again. The news is that he has failed his surrogate son: Paolino has been shot by the mafia for attempting to marry his sweetheart, a girl wanted by a member of the mafia gang. It is at this point that Guido orders the ringing of the church bells to call the entire town to a 'trial' in the main square, where, witnessed by all, he assumes the guise of patriarch. In order to do so, the potentially 'feminine' state he represents must find a way to live by the law of the father. Ultimately it is the mafia father who allows this to happen by bringing Guido on side and allowing him to arrest the wayward mafioso. As Guido accepts this reconciliation, we see Teresa turn away and leave in tears, a 'mater dolorosa' sacrificing her 'son' to the salvation of mankind.

In conclusion, it is important to understand how the male hero fluctuates between the poles of a troubled 'western' sheriff and a persecuted 'gothic' heroine in his engagement with the mafia, between masculine and feminine, paternal and maternal identificatory trajectories. In this way we can see how the film uses gender and genre in a subtler fashion than hitherto assumed and shows how a resolution between the competing legal codes of state and mafia is as fragile as the resolution of gender identity itself. Alberto Crespi has defended the controversial ending of Germi's film as making sense generically, describing Turi's sudden 'conversion' as in keeping with a 'Western logic.'[20] However, when we acknowledge the role that gender, as well as the gothic genre, has to play in this – the hasty exclusion of the feminine underscoring the superficial nature of this shift in Guido's narrative from regressive to progressive – we can confirm that ultimately the ending does make a telling social commentary: which law is the father's? Mafia law.

NOTES

1 With box office takings of 401,000,000 lire, the film was ranked as the third highest grossing Italian film of the 1948–49 season.

2 Carlo Doglio, 'Personaggi equivoci e nuova decadenza,' *Cinema* 21 (1949): 96–7.

3 This was regarded as being in line with the Hollywood influence seen in his previous film *Gioventù perduta* (1947), associated with the film noir tradition. See Stefania Carpieci, 'Hollywood "all'italiana,"' in *Pietro Germi: Viaggio nel cinema italiano*, ed. Stefania Carpieci (Rome: Massenzio, 1995), 10–21.

4 Ennio Flaiano, *Il mondo* 9, 16 April 1949.

5 Doglio dismisses 'the abysmal relationship between the judge and the baronessa' in 'Personaggi equivoci e nuova decadenza,' 96; Guido Aristarco writes that 'perhaps the love interest is introduced more as a commercial compromise than a narrative necessity' in his review in *Cinema* 13 (1949): 412–13; Sandro Zambotti writes of 'the decidedly superfluous baroness and her affairs of the heart' in 'Pietro Germi,' *Cineforum* 35 (1964): 417; and see also the review of the film in *Bianco e nero* 5 (1949): 85–86.

6 Aristarco in *Cinema* 13, 412–13.

7 See Catherine O'Rawe, '"I padri e i maestri": Genre, Auteurs and Absences in Italian Film Studies,' *Italian Studies* 63, no. 2 (2008): 173–94.

8 Massimo Massara, 'Italiani di 2a categoria,' *Cinema sessanta* 32 (1963): 39–42.

9 Umberto Mosca, 'Cinema e Mafia,' *Panoramiche* 7 (1994): 11–12.

10 Seymour Fisher and Roger P. Greenberg, *The Scientific Credibility of Freud's Theories and Therapy* (New York: Basic Books, 1977), 222.

11 Sergio Rigoletto, 'The Normative Gender Rhetoric of *l'italiano medio*,' in *Italy on Screen: Inter-Disciplinary Perspectives on Italy and Cinema*, ed. Lucy Bolton and Christina Siggers (London: Peter Lang, 2010).

12 Elizabeth Wright, *Feminism and Psychoanalysis: A Critical Dictionary* (Oxford: Blackwell, 1992), 195.

13 See Helen Hanson, *Hollywood Heroines: Women in Film Noir and the Female Gothic Film* (London: I.B. Tauris, 2007), for a discussion of 'the female gothic cycle, one of the most popular, critically and commercially successful cycles of films in 1940s Hollywood' (33).

14 Ibid., 35.

15 Ibid., 68.

16 Doglio, 'Personaggi equivoci e nuova decadenza,' 96.

17 Girotti is referred to as a 'Weissmüller italiano' and 'nuovo Tarzan,' in F. Càllari, 'Massimo Girotti: dal pelago alla riva,' *Primi piani* (7–8 August 1942): 61.

18 Renzo Renzi, 'Massimo Girotti,' *Cinema* 13 (1949): 406.

19 Derek Duncan, 'Ossessione,' in *European Cinema and National Identity*, ed. Jill Forbes and Sarah Street (New York: Macmillan, 2000), 95–108.

20 Alberto Crespi, 'In nome della legge (del West),' in *Pietro Germi: Viaggio nel cinema italiano*, ed. Stefania Carpieci (Rome: Massenzio, 1995), 49.

26   The Visible, Unexposed: Francesco Rosi's *Salvatore Giuliano*

LAURA WITTMAN

What is most important in Francesco Rosi's 1961 *Salvatore Giuliano* is that which is not seen. The film takes its title from the name of the Sicilian separatist bandit who was beloved by the international media in the 1940s as a Robin Hood figure. It opens with his mysterious murder in 1950, moving on to explore the history and consequences of this event in a series of flashbacks and flashforwards. Yet Rosi and his commentators have insisted the film is not about Salvatore Giuliano or his murder: indeed, Giuliano is rarely present on screen, and the only close-ups are of his dead body.[1]

Rather, the film is about Sicily, and how more than two thousand years of external dominance have made the island's true identity almost impenetrable, like Giuliano's motives and features. As Rosi commented, '[W]e still don't know the truth after forty years.'[2] Thus Rosi's style uses the camera's claims to objective realism ironically, to question the truth of our perceptions and interpretations. As a result, the jumbled sequence of events we are presented with can be reassembled into more than one story, none of them entirely satisfactory. His film, then, is not only about Sicily but also about the power dynamics that underlie the political process.

This was Rosi's third film and is still considered his masterpiece, even though he went on to make quite a number of provocative films such as *Le mani sulla città* (*Hands over the City,* 1963), *Lucky Luciano* (1973), *Cadaveri eccellenti* (*Illustrious corpses,* 1976), and *Tre fratelli* (*Three Brothers,* 1981). Ultimately, these three elements – a 'hard clarity' that goes beyond neorealism,[3] an 'autobiographical'[4] focus on a specific cultural 'milieu,'[5] and an exploration of how violence always threatens political relations – make Rosi's film groundbreaking for directors from Gillo Pontecorvo to Martin Scorsese.

Salvatore Giuliano became an outlaw at the age of twenty-one, when he shot a policeman in order to escape arrest for transporting black market wheat. This was 2 September 1943, and the Americans had just landed in Sicily. Whatever Giuliano's motivations – anti-Fascist and/or Sicilian separatist sympathies, distrust of authorities, desire for power and money – he quickly became a charismatic figure. In 1945–46 he led guerrilla actions for the EVIS (Volunteer Army for Sicilian Independence) and became known as 'the king of Montelepre,' the small Sicilian town where he was born and continued to live, kept safe by silence, despite the authorities' increasingly desperate attempts to capture him. He was larger than life and infuriatingly elusive, resisting northern oppression in the name of the peasants whom both fascism and the postwar Christian Democrat government had disenfranchised.

On 1 May 1947, bandits attacked the peaceful Communist May Day celebration at Portella della Ginestra in Sicily, killing eleven and wounding fifty-six. Giuliano was implicated, and the world was shocked that he would attack his own people. This event remains the most mysterious in his life, and myriad books with different theories continue to fuel the Giuliano myth: he could have been recruited by anti-Communists, the Christian Democrats, the Americans, the mafia, or any combination thereof. When his body was found shot dead on 5 July 1950, in a court-yard in Castelvetrano, the official story was that the heroic forces of order had finally triumphed over an infamous, if seductive, criminal. In 1951, however, as the trial begins in Viterbo for the events at Portella della Ginestra, Giuliano's right-hand man, Gaspare Pisciotta, stuns the judge and the media by asserting that he killed Giuliano, 'having made a personal agreement with higher authorities' regarding Portella. When interrogated, a police inspector, a general, and a mafioso deny any knowledge of an agreement or of Giuliano's alleged diary, in which he identified those responsible for the massacre. Pisciotta is poisoned and dies in prison on 10 February 1954.[6]

I present this skeletal linear version of the events in order to help the viewer make sense of Rosi's film, as all these elements are in it, along with many other details that Rosi drew from his extensive research as well as his personal interviews with participants. More importantly, I give it in order to stress by way of contrast that Rosi's jumbled chronology is meant not only to provoke discomfort but also to induce scepticism towards any linear interpretation.[7]

The film's opening scene shows in a variety of ways Rosi's strategy of dislocation and suspicion.[8] The first view we have of Giuliano's body matches almost exactly with historic photographs, and as we move to see him from above, hearing the legal description, we develop an impression of quasi-scientific objectivity. It is only when we see the closed faces of the crowd staring down from the windows above that we begin to wonder why no one saw the crime. Then reporters arrive and are heard wondering why the blood is on the back of Giuliano's shirt, since he supposedly died here, face down. We begin to realize that we only thought the voiceover matched what we were seeing, when it reality it was masking it. This duplicity illustrates Rosi's claim that he 'continued' yet also 'leapt beyond' neorealism, because in his 'critical realism,' 'the image does not say everything, as it does in Neorealism'; instead, he said, it 'creates questions … for me and for the spectator.'[9] 'The only sure thing is that he's dead,' concludes a third reporter, on the phone to his newspaper.[10]

Rosi questions the iconic status of the image – its ability to convey a singular, mythological truth – throughout the film. For instance, about halfway through, after many flashbacks, we see the dead man's mother identify his body. As the ice is removed, the woman playing Giuliano's mother, who was not a professional actress but the mother of a man killed in similarly mysterious and violent circumstances, wails with grief, kisses the body, and then pulls away to reveal Giuliano in a Christ-like, foreshortened pose, typical of depositions. This creates a stark contrast with recent films that use the same iconic pose: Roberto Rossellini's *Open City* (1945), with the torture of Manfredi, and Pier Paolo Pasolini's *Accattone* (1961). *Open City* is unambiguously self-sacrificing, whereas Accattone, as evinced by his friend's crossing himself backwards, is a victim of the establishment, a Christ truer than that of the Church. When we see Giuliano as Christ, however, we cannot immediately interpret the reference. Does this mean he was also an innocent who was betrayed? Or is Rosi being ironic about those who wish to further his myth, including his mother? Furthermore, the mother herself also undercuts iconic interpretation. She is not the sombre yet serene Mary of the deposition or the *Pietà:* her wails are those of the archaic, pagan mourning of the Italian south, and her physical attachment to the body reflects Rosi's observation that in Sicily, 'it would appear that it is very difficult to let go of the dead.'[11] The power of the scene comes from her real mourning, and it effectively prevents us from seeing Giuliano or his mother as iconic figures; their stories, heroic or antiheroic as they may be, recede in favour of grief's continued reality in Sicily.

The official description of Giuliano's body and reporters' reactions to it are interrupted by flashbacks to 1945, when members of the EVIS are shown entering Giuliano's hideout. We do not see their actual meeting and can only infer from the scenes that follow, in which Giuliano's men stage guerrilla attacks against the authorities, that some agreement was reached between Giuliano and the separatists. This, in turn, makes us think back to the opening scene and wonder why the authorities seem to be covering up something about his death. This is a typical example of how Rosi's film is not so much *a* document as a suggestive *accumulation* of documents; each new element makes us revise our entire interpretation of events. However, unlike in neorealist films – such as Luchino Visconti's *La terra trema,* which Rosi worked on – the camera does not imaginatively fill in the empty space between documents for us; nor does it interpret for us. Instead, Rosi's jumbled chronology points us towards possible connections between events while simultaneously forcing us to see them as unverifiable. Even after we have watched the film more than once, we can never determine exactly what Giuliano's relationship with the separatists was. Thus Rosi creates a temporality that is fissured, not only by the tricks of memory and perception but also by awareness that history is mostly written by the victors and serves the needs of a shifting present. Franco Solinas, with whom Rosi crafted the screenplay (along with Suso Cecchi d'Amico and Enzo Provenzale), was important to the invention of this technique in which flashback and flashforward served as political critique. Solinas would go on to work on films such as Pontecrovo's *Battle of Algiers* (1966) and *Burn!* (1968), as well as on Costa-Gavras's *State of Siege* (1972). In this temporality created by Rosi and Solinas, there are no heroes and villains in an absolute sense, as there tend to be in some neorealist films; there is only the difficulty of partial, uncertain yet unavoidable ethical decisions.

Francesco Rosi was born and grew up in Naples, and the large majority of his films give fresh insights into Italy's long-standing 'southern question.' A contrast with Giuseppe Tomasi di Lampedusa's 1958 novel, *Il gattopardo* (*The Leopard*, made into a film by Visconti in 1963) is telling, for this work insists that in Sicily 'things must change in order to stay the same.' It is this widespread perception of Sicilian culture's impermeability to change that Rosi questions through the temporality of his film, and even more through his commitment to a subject matter that is at once documented and autobiographical. Thus Tullio Kezich, who helped substantially with research, comments that Rosi put 'nothing [in his film] that wasn't in the documents,' but Rosi adds that his 'method and structure were entirely personal.' Later, Rosi puts it more poetically when he says that he wanted to portray 'the truth of this milieu … the Sicilian sun.'[12] This milieu – which the sun metonymically evokes – is one in which the power and immobility described in *The Leopard* are real; but just as real, and more clearly autobiographical, is the individual's attempt to make sense of this world rather than merely to accept it. Thus, in the end, what is not in the documents but *is* in *Salvatore Giuliano* is the interaction between Rosi (and his film crew) and all the Sicilians who participated in the making of the film, many of whom were also part of the historical events it portrays. For them, the question is not whether 'Sicily' is impermeable to change, but *who* represents Sicily in this kind of statement.[13]

Two scenes in the film are particularly notable for their emphasis on the interaction between present-day individuals and their own history. This issue, however, is present throughout in Rosi's decision to use non-professional actors (the judge at the trial and Pisciotta being the only exceptions), in part at least because only they can convey the correct social class in their faces, accents, and body language. All of this is quite noticeable in the scene of the massacre at Portella della Ginestra, which was filmed on 2 and 3 May with participants who had come out for an actual May Day celebration. For many, this was not simply a re-creation but a reliving of the original events.[14] Their belief in the power of telling this story is quite remarkable.

An even more prescient scene with respect to Sicily and the question of change takes place a little earlier, when the women of Montelepre take to the streets because the government has been rounding up their men in an effort to find Giuliano. In an interview with Michel Ciment, Rosi explained that he wanted to film this scene with the actual women of Montelepre, but that as proper Sicilian women they didn't want to be on camera or be perceived as 'actresses.'[15] He thus hired a large number of women from nearby Palermo – prostitutes, the only ones willing to do the job – and had them bussed over to the location. Once he began filming however, the women of Montelepre also took to the streets, refusing to be represented by others. Thus Rosi concludes that this scene 'was written by the population.' What he means is not only that he based his film on eyewitness accounts but also that the contradictory and rebellious passions of both the Montelepre and Palermo women animate it. This is important cinematically and historically, for in the 1960s and much more noticeably in the 1970s and 1980s, the most effective and visible anti-mafia movements in Sicily were grassroots efforts organized by women.[16] These are prime examples of Rosi's conviction that cinema is a 'political instrument' and, even more, 'a social instrument,'[17] and can be a successful provocation to change.

'The Sicilian sun,' especially in its alternation with an oneiric, at times impenetrable, at times excessively lit darkness, is more than a representation of Sicily. Visually, the film juxtaposes extreme contrasts of light and dark (such as during separatist guerrilla shootings, but also during the night of Giuliano's murder), with longer shots in which actions, and the town itself, seem to fade into a distant haze (such as when the authorities seeking Giuliano are confronted with the silence of Montelepre). On the one hand, this is reminiscent of Resnais's 1955 *Night and Fog,* in which the horror of Nazi concentration camps is heightened by how much violence remains latent, shrouded in the darkness. On the other hand, it anticipates Antonioni's 1966 *Blow-Up,* in which violence is literally latent on film, until increasing blow-ups turn the play of light and dark into a murder scene, which nonetheless remains mysterious. Thus in *Salvatore Giuliano* actual violence is rarely seen (except at Portella, where nonetheless the general mayhem makes it hard to focus on a specific instance), but is a constant undercurrent in the cinematography itself. One gets the impression that indeed, 'the image does not say everything,' that at the same time it contains a hidden reality, a portion of film not yet exposed that, in later circumstances, might be.

The implication is not only that the nexus between power and violence in Sicily is impenetrable and might remain so but also that this nexus is essentially human yet deeply irrational, that it can be critiqued but never fully dominated. As we saw, the first scene showing Giuliano's body emphasizes all the ways in which Giuliano becomes an image upon which many parties can impose a story, all the more so in death. Further depictions of death in the film (the poisoning of Pisciotta, the killing of another man at the end who is meant to be understood as Benedetto Minasola) emphasize again the unknown, the impenetrable (we never see who or what kills either of them).

Thus for Rosi, death, which might be thought to make violence finally, fully visible as an image, is on the contrary the expression of the limits of human understanding. These limits are not only existential but also political for Rosi. A good way to grasp this is to consider, one last time, what Rosi does *not* do in *Salvatore Giuliano:* he does not make death dramatic, and he refuses to turn death scenes or shootouts into the objects of consumption that many Hollywood (and other) films reduce them to.

I believe this is why Scorsese insists repeatedly that Rosi is 'political and lyrical at the same time': his 'passion for justice' translates into a cinematography that evokes the emotional, the irrational, the spiritual, and the poetic, yet refuses them a clear-cut ideological packaging.[18] This is why *Salvatore Giuliano* has often been hailed as a precursor to Gillo Pontecorvo's *La battaglia di Algeri* (*The Battle of Algiers*, 1966) and should be allowed to stand alongside it as an example of truly contemporary political cinema.[19] As in *The Battle of Algiers,* music, the poetry of the landscape, the mystery of human faces whose motivations cannot be fully unpacked – all of these prevent us from either condemning or approving of violence via its political ends. As in *The Battle of Algiers,* what emerges is the violence of ideology itself, whatever it may be, which we cannot avoid but can become aware of.

In a recent interview, Rosi notes that the mafia is not simply (as has been often said) 'a state within the state,' but is 'a real political power,' because 'there is one state and then there is the other state.' In the same interview he expresses the immense gratitude we owe to anti-mafia magistrates, citing Giovanni Falcone (murdered in 1992 for his anti-mafia work).[20] It is therefore truly remarkable that he is able to see with so much compassion Giuliano's probable involvement with the mafia and, quite likely as well, with a deal made between the government and the mafia. Most importantly, his compassion does not take the form of attributing good sentiments or psychological struggles to Giuliano. Rather, we perceive it in how Rosi shows Giuliano to be at the mercy of forces greater than his own, those of ideology and its violence, made present in the pervasive shadow death casts on Rosi's Sicily. But as Rosi states at the end of his interview, 'death ... does not scare me ... [but] I don't like it ... I can't ask it any questions because there are no answers.'[21] For Rosi, then, to focus on death as an iconic, dramatic, consumable image is an evasion; in contrast, continuing to ask hard questions about the links between politics, violence, and culture is the stuff of life itself.

NOTES

1 'Giuliano, Mattei, Luciano are pretexts for the global analysis of a world.' Rosi, in Aldo Tassone, 'Le mani dentro la realtà,' in *La sfida della verità: il cinema di Francesco Rosi,* ed. Aldo Tassone, Gabriele Rizza, and Chiara Tognolotti (Florence: AIDA, 2005), 28.

2 In Roberto Andò, *Il cineasta e il labirinto*, 55-minute documentary, in Francesco Rosi, *Salvatore Giuliano,* The Criterion Collection, 2004, Double-Disc DVD.

3 Scorsese in Andò, *Il cineasta e il labirinto.*

4 'I consider my films absolutely autobiographical.' Rosi in Andò, *Il cineasta e il labirinto.*

5 '[I show] the truth of the milieu.' Rosi in *Witness to the Times,* a discussion with director Francesco Rosi and film critic Tullio Kezich, in Francesco Rosi, *Salvatore Giuliano,* The Criterion Collection, 2004, Double-Disc DVD.

6 See Ben Lawton, 'Salvatore Giuliano: Francesco Rosi's Revolutionary Postmodernism,' in Poet of Civic Courage: The Films of Francesco Rosi, ed. Carlo Testa (Westport, CT: Greenwood Press, 1996), 8, for Giuliano's popularity.

7 See ibid., 13, for a very useful scene-by-scene description of the film's chronology. Tonino Guerra gives the title to Laberinto when he comments in it that Rosi lives in a labyrinth, but 'this is a labyrinth that contains some truths.'

8 For Rosi as filmmaker for 'the age of suspicion,' see Callisto Cosulich, 'Il lungo viaggio di un napoletano di ceppo normanno,' in La sfida della verità, ed. Tassone, Rizza, and Tognolotti, 68.

9 Rosi in Witness to the Times.

10 See Ennio Mannucci, 'Di sicuro c'è solo che è morto,' in La sfida della verità, ed. Tassone, Rizza, and Tognolotti, 102, for a discussion of how this was the – very provocative and unusual – headline on Guiliano in L'Europeo in July 1950.

11 Rosi in Andò, Il cineasta e il laberinto.

12 Rosi in Witness to the Times.

13 For a description of interactions with Sicilians in 1960, see Tullio Kezich, Salvatore Giuliano (Rome: Edizioni FM, 1961).

14 See Witness to the Times in which participants commented, '[I]t's just like it was that day.'

15 Rosi in Andò, Il cineasta e il laberinto.

16 See Ann Cornelisen, Women of the Shadows: Wives and Mothers of Southern Italy, 2nd ed. (South Royalton, VT: Steerforth Italia, 2001).

17 Rosi in Andò, Il cineasta e il laberinto.

18 Martin Scorsese, 'Making a Film,' accessed 15 January 2009, www.independent.co.uk/opinion /commentators/martin-scorsese-making-a-film-is-for-me-a-journey-of-learning-and-reeducation -522586.html

19 See 'Testimonianze,' in La sfida della verità, ed. Tassone, Rizza, and Tognolotti, 141, for comments by (among others) Fellini, Coppola, Scorsese, Costa Gavras, and Tavernier.

20 Rosi in Andò, Il cineasta e il laberinto.

21 Ibid.

27 Modernity, Mafia Style: Alberto Lattuada's *Mafioso*

NELSON MOE

As we know, many movies about the mafia are not, in fact, about the mafia. Directors often use the figure of the mafia to talk about something else. This is certainly true of Francis Ford Coppola's *The Godfather* (1972), which the director stressed is not about the mafia but rather about the family and capitalism. And it is also true of Alberto Lattuada's *Mafioso* (1962). Lattuada's film mimics and deconstructs the stereotype of the Sicilian mafia in order to offer a dark commentary on the nature of modern capitalism. A key part of this critical and aesthetic project involves both dramatizing and dismantling stereotypes about the north and south of Italy. The stereotype of the Sicilian mafia is, if you will, embedded in the stereotype of Italy's south. Because received ideas about the mafia and the south are deeply interwoven, to deconstruct one entails deconstructing both.

Mafioso is relatively unknown today – a 'forgotten classic,' indeed – so it is worth taking a moment to rehearse its plot. The protagonist, played by the great Italian comic actor Alberto Sordi, is a Sicilian emigrant named Antonio Badalamenti (nicknamed Nino), who has made a successful career and life for himself in Milan. He has a good job as a floor supervisor in a factory, and he has married a beautiful, blond Milanese woman, with whom he has raised two beautiful, blond daughters. The film recounts the trip he takes back to Sicily with his family for a summer vacation. At the start, Antonio is overwhelmingly excited about taking his wife and daughters back to his homeland, but his wife is doubtful. During the course of their two-week visit, however, their feelings about Sicily are reversed. She (and her daughters) grows to love it there, and for him the sojourn becomes a nightmare. Antonio is unwillingly drafted by the mafia into committing a murder, for which he is sent all the way to New York, and by the end of the film he is desperate to return to Milan. The film closes with Antonio back on the factory floor, having returned to his successful and civilized life in the north.

One of Lattuada's chief aims in the film is to play with and deconstruct the traditional dichotomy between a modern, civilized north and a traditional, backwards south. Pictorial master that he is, Lattuada does this through images and sequences that are beautiful, dramatically compelling, and rich with conceptual content. As we will see later in the discussion, he employs both diegetic sounds and non-diegetic music for the same effect as well. As the credits roll at the start of the film, we see the interior of a factory in Milan, with close-ups of machinery performing highly precise operations. After a few minutes, Antonio appears in a white laboratory coat, pen and clipboard in hand. He wears a serious, focused expression on his face as he supervises the machinery on the factory floor. The overall function of this opening sequence is to establish the familiar image, the stereotype of the modern, industrial north, along with the associated characteristics of technology, efficiency, productivity, and precision.

However, in the following scene, Lattuada shows us that the north, while being as modern as the factory sequence suggests, also has close ties to Sicily, to the mafia, and to the United States. Before leaving the factory to pick up his family at home, Antonio hears his name being called out over the public address system. He is directed to report to the office of Dr Zanchi, the factory manager. When he enters the office, he finds Dr Zanchi's secretary on the phone, chattering in fluent German before switching to another phone to speak in equally fluent French. From the way she overplays her role, it is clear that Lattuada has constructed her as both a cipher for and a parody of Milan as modern, northern, and European. When Antonio walks into Dr Zanchi's office we see modernity on display here, too. The door, operated by remote control, slides open to let him in. Below Dr Zanchi's desk is a piece of state-of-the-art technology, evidently some sort of multi-system radio.

But why has Dr Zanchi called him to his office, Antonio wonders, just as he is about to set off on his vacation? Dr Zanchi gives him a direct answer. Looking through the personnel files, the doctor has discovered that Antonio is from a little village in Sicily called Calamo, where a notable named Don Vincenzo lives. He asks Antonio to do him a 'little favour' on his trip home, to bring Don Vincenzo a present from 'common friends.' In the course of the conversation, Antonio also learns that Dr Zanchi is from Trenton. 'Veneto?,' Antonio asks comically. 'No, New Jersey,' Zanchi responds.[1] And, as it happens, Dr Zanchi's family immigrated to Trenton from Calamo. The 'friends' they supposedly share are thus from the United States, all with ties to Calamo, and though Antonio does not understand that the word *amici* is a code word for *mafiosi* – thus exhibiting the cheerful cluelessness he maintains through much of the film – Lattuada leaves the spectator little doubt about their line of business.

What Lattuada has done at the beginning of the film, then, is to accentuate and even exaggerate the modern qualities of Milan and the north on the factory floor, in the boss's office, and subsequently in Antonio's home. As he and his wife Marta prepare to depart for the train station, Antonio spends much of his time using an electric shaver and an electric shoe polisher (at one point simultaneously, with one in each hand!) while his daughters experiment with a new electric blender. At the same time, however, the scene in Dr Zanchi's office indicates that the north is closely linked to cultural and economic realities far from and, in the case of Sicily, extremely different from it. It must be stressed here that linking the north to Sicily in this way would be surprising to an Italian audience in 1962. For many spectators, the familiar images of northern modernity at the start of a film called *Mafioso* would have called to mind instead the well-established notion of southern backwardness, of deep cultural and economic differences between the two parts of the country. Just consider Luchino Visconti's *Ròcco e i suoi fratelli* (*Rocco and His Brothers*, 1960), released two years earlier, in which north and south appear as profoundly alien realities. This, in fact, is the view of Antonio's father-in-law, who calls him from Bellagio not only to wish the family *buon viaggio* but also to express his concern about the trip his daughter is about to take. 'Don't worry,' Antonio tries to reassure him. 'What did you say? Vaccination? Papa, do you think we're going down to Africa? I'm taking them to my home!'

We will see that Lattuada aims to unsettle this view, to scramble the dichotomy between the two parts of the country, to show how much of the south is in the north and the north is in the south. But as he did with Milan, he must give us the stereotypical picture of Sicily first. And he does this with great cinematic gusto. The arrival of Antonio's family in Sicily highlights the stark contrast between Antonio's adoptive Milanese world and his native land by representing the latter through the two lenses that have been used to view the south and Sicily since the nineteenth century: that of the picturesque, on the one hand, and, on the other, that of backwardness, the stock image of a traditional, poor society lacking in civilization and modern economic development.[2] From the picturesque perspective, Lattuada shows us the sun-drenched Sicilian coastline, fishing boats on the beach, and splendid panoramic views from the hillsides down to the shining sea. 'Look at Sicily!,' Antonio cries out from the deck of the ferry carrying them across the Strait of Messina. 'Island of the sun and Cyclops! Praised by every poet in the world!' From the backwards perspective, we see their arrival in the ramshackle village consisting of small streets with donkeys passing by, while a traditional Sicilian funeral wake carries on around them. Hordes of family members cry out wildly upon their arrival, the women dressed in black from head to toe, Antonio's sister sporting a thick moustache. We also learn something significant through an exchange that Antonio has with a member of the family mourning the deceased. 'Friend, how did he die?,' Antonio asks. 'Two shotgun blasts,' the man responds.

This picture thus corresponds to the standard stereotype of Sicily, complete with the mafia. Nothing could be farther from Milan. Yet even here, as the stereotype of Sicily takes form before our very eyes, Lattuada suggests connections and similarities between the two places (and, we might add, the two moral worlds). On the bridge of the ferry crossing the Strait of Messina to Sicily, Antonio notices that his wife is looking glum. 'What's the matter, Marta?,' he asks. 'Nothing,' she replies, 'I'm just watching us move farther and farther away from Italy.' Antonio says cheerfully, 'Isn't this Italy, too? And we're not even separated anymore.' He points to the wires suspended between two huge electrical pylons on either side of the strait. 'The largest electrical grid in the world connects us to the continent!,' he exclaims with unbounded enthusiasm.

So how do we get from here to the Sicily that is radically different from the north, both backwards and picturesque? With a wipe (a cinematic wipe, that is). Upon their arrival in Messina, Antonio and his family set off by train towards Calamo. The first images of Sicily we see from the train are modern and industrial: a train yard, petroleum tanks, warehouses. There is no music, only the loud clickity-clacking of the train on the tracks. It would be hard to find a more industrial landscape than this (accompanied by thoroughly modern sounds). As the train proceeds, a thin strip of sea appears in the background, with a large promontory above it. This is a picturesque scene indeed, but throughout the sequence numerous electric wires – undoubtedly connected to the ones crossing the Strait of Messina – partly obstruct our view (just the kind of wires that many a tourist would say 'spoil the view'). And then the wipe: the train passes by a bunch of trees, blocking our view completely for a second; when it comes out on the other side, we have entered the realm of picturesque Sicily. A broad expanse of sea now fills most of the screen. The train passes by a beach filled with traditional Sicilian sailboats. We hear a few bars of music – some notes in a minor key, repeated without melodic development, suggesting a narrative transition and change of mood – which then resolve into a swelling pastoral theme in a major key. The music continues to crescendo as the camera, positioned on a height, offers a panoramic view of Antonio's family driving through terraced hillsides, with the beautiful Sicilian coastline spreading out far in the distance.

We have thus entered the realm of picturesque Sicily and, upon their arrival in Antonio's village, backwards Sicily as well. The economic and cultural realities here are light years away from

Milan and the north. But ever since Antonio's visit to Dr Zanchi's office, Lattuada has insinuated that these two worlds are not as separate from each other as they first appear. His aim in the rest of the film, in fact, is to show the links and similarities between them. And he does this through the figure of Antonio in the guise of the mafioso. About a week into their vacation, a shady character in the village befriends Antonio; he is a mafioso, though Antonio does not know this at the time. In the village square they go to try their luck in a shooting gallery. The mafioso shoots first, and misses most of the targets. 'I've lost my touch,' he says, with a dark comic effect. Antonio takes the gun and proceeds to hit every target with extraordinary precision and skill. 'You can always tell an old hunter, yeah?,' Antonio proudly asks the man of honour, who is deeply impressed by his skill and whose facial expression makes clear that Antonio would be the perfect man to commit a murder. The key point here is that Antonio developed the skill of precision in Sicily first, through the traditional, rural activity of hunting, and because of this skill he is useful to the mafia, which needs and values men with just such capacities. Precision, in other words, is native both to the south and to the north and plays a central role in two economic systems that are traditionally seen as distinct from, if not opposed to, each other: the criminal system of the Sicilian mafia and the capitalist industrial system of the north. The film thus breaks down the traditional dichotomy between north and south, along with the moral hierarchy intrinsic to it, and suggests both an analogy and an exchange between them.

The end of the film reinforces and consummates this connection. Soon after demonstrating his shooting skills to the mafioso, Antonio is blackmailed and tricked into committing a murder for the mafia, which for him involves a harrowing trip all the way to New York and back. New York and the United States serve as another marker of modernity here and offer another example of the interconnectedness between the modern world and a putatively backward and archaic Sicily. Here, too, the notion of precision is the key. When Antonio arrives in New York, the mafia boss greets him by saying, 'You're a precise fellow, aren't you? … What you need to do is easy, but you must be very precise.' After demonstrating his lethal precision by murdering his designated victim in a New York barbershop, Antonio returns to his village and family profoundly dismayed. Lying in bed next to his wife, a look of anguish crosses his face as he has a flashback of the murder, and we hear four loud pistol shots going off in his mind. Now Lattuada cuts directly and abruptly to the factory machinery we saw at the start of the movie (a cut, in other words, from Sicily to Milan). But this time he directs our attention to one machine in particular: a large mechanical hammer that repeatedly strikes the metal below it with great force. It makes a sound not unlike a gun, whose hammer also strikes metal – a bullet – to produce the desired effect; they both work using percussive impact (and, of course, precision). The metallic banging of the industrial machine here thus echoes the gunshots that rang out just moments before.

By matching a piece of factory machinery with the gun of a mafia assassin in this way, Lattuada clinches the link between northern industry and southern criminality, between modernity and backwardness, that he has been constructing over the course of the film. The final images of *Mafioso* provide a powerful representation of this as well. The film concludes with a reprise of the opening sequence of Antonio walking among the machines on the factory floor, dressed in his white coat, pen and clipboard in hand. But clearly this scene in its second iteration does not mean the same thing it did before: Antonio is here both a conscientious factory technician *and* the mafioso referred to in the film's title. The man who walks through the factory in the final frames is thus a sort of doubled figure, just as the northern industrialism and capitalism shown here are doubled with respect to the way they appeared at the beginning of the film. The productive, efficient north is not what it seemed at first; it is a sort of twin of the supposedly criminal south. The two have some crucial features in common.[3] The south is precise and efficient, just as the north is also criminal (the factory manager, Dr Zanchi, is of course a 'friend'). The familiar dichotomy between north and south has been scrambled.

Lattuada thus exploits and deconstructs the familiar stereotypes about both the mafia and the north and south in order to achieve what appears to be his primary polemical purpose in the film: to provide a dark commentary on the capitalist system (not only in Italy but also in Europe and North America) at the height of the economic miracle. Lattuada suggests that the idol of a legal, non-violent economic system at the base of the new Italy requires the symbolic projection of an other, which is the criminal mafia. As we have seen, however, Lattuada shows that this supposed other is in fact northern industrial Italy's dark twin. He replaces the familiar image of a polarity between north and south with an unfamiliar and unsettling vision of similarity and symbiosis. Ten years before *The Godfather*, Lattuada anticipated (and most likely influenced) Coppola's deconstruction of the time-honoured moral opposition between a 'good' (legal, legitimate, official) social and economic order and the 'bad' one of the mafia (criminal, illegitimate, violent). In this revisionism, both *Mafioso* and *The Godfather* are films of the 1960s and early 1970s, exploiting the mafia's negative conceptual and moral charge to wage powerful critiques of contemporary capitalism.

NOTES

1 The joke, obvious to an Italian audience, is that Antonio thinks Dr Zanchi said *Trento*, the city in the northern province of Veneto, instead of Trenton, New Jersey.

2 On the formation and development of these two perspectives on the south in the nineteenth century, see my book *The View from Vesuvius: Italian Culture and the Southern Question* (Berkeley, CA: University of California Press, 2002).

3 For perceptive observations on this and other aspects of the film, see Claudio Camerini, *Alberto Lattuada* (Florence: La Nuova Italia, 1982), 67–70.

28 Francesco Rosi's *Hands over the City*: A Contemporary Perspective on the Camorra

ANNA PAPARCONE

In his 2006 book *Gomorrah*, which has received worldwide acclaim, Roberto Saviano opens one of the most evocative and intense sections of his work (in chapter 3) with the remark that 'the clans' power remained the power of cement. It was at the construction sites that I could feel – physically, in my gut – all their might … Cement. The petroleum of the south. Cement gives birth to everything.'[1] Saviano's attack on the Camorra's real estate speculation is visualized in the very first scene of Francesco Rosi's *Le mani sulla città* (*Hands over the City*, 1963), which opens with a panning shot of Naples dominated by a dense row of imposing buildings – signs of an unstoppable, wild urbanization – looking down on a valley where the fertile agricultural land and a lonely pine tree still represent the fecundity of the city and its traditional Mediterranean beauty. The mass of threatening buildings is at first destined to proceed in another direction, but corrupt developer Edoardo Nottola wants to change the urban development plan, and build 'with no strife and no worries, at all profit and no risk,' in the farming zone surrounding the industrial city. He need only get the approval from the local administration, and in the second scene, Nottola achieves his goal.

This scene provides the film's first significant example of the collusion between political institutions and the economic world. Such collusion is the central topic of Rosi's work and is also in the foreground after a fatal accident in Vico Sant'Andrea, one of Naples' poorest neighbourhoods. An old building there has collapsed due to nearby construction, killing two people. Nottola, who is responsible for the accident, is also a member of the right-wing party in power at city hall. In exchange for economic favours from the municipal government (total control over bids, contracts, quarries, cement, and workers), he ensures that his party will have sufficient votes to win the upcoming elections. After the accident, Nottola's candidacy and the success of his party are at risk, since both De Vita, leader of the left-wing party, and the citizens of Naples hold him responsible for the casualties. Nottola refuses to withdraw his candidacy, and in order to continue his real estate speculation, he allies with the centrist Christian Democratic Party (DC). The DC wins the elections, and Nottola remains in power.

In *Hands over the City*, the parallels between Saviano's contemporary account of the Camorra and Rosi's analysis of the links between the economic world and the political administration multiply, thus confirming that as early as 1963, Rosi was able to provide a lucid analysis of what is today considered the true nature of the Camorra: it is a criminal organization that bases its power on an illegal alliance between economic forces and political institutions. Hence, Rosi's work can be considered a reliable forerunner of Saviano's book, and as such, its relevance is reaffirmed and reinforced in contemporary Italian cinema and society. But how did Rosi expose such profound connections between Camorra activities, the business world, and political power? Furthermore, why did Rosi not employ the word Camorra in his film?

Let us return to the second scene: it is set at city hall, where we find a reproduction of the Naples landscape – the buildings and the farming area we encountered in the first scene – in a miniature model that defines the urban plan. The mayor, representative of the right wing, employs a masterpiece of rhetoric to implicitly announce that Nottola's wish has come true. According to him, the city plan has been 'the subject of intense debate,' and a specially appointed committee of urban planners 'has chosen the area north of the city' to be developed, namely, the area in which Nottola is interested for his own speculation. Rosi's sarcasm is striking when we consider that the 'special committee' has been constituted to satisfy Nottola's demands. The 'intense debate' probably never occurred, and Nottola played a significant role in the council's decision. This becomes evident as the mayor speaks to the city council utilizing the same words with which Nottola had clearly manifested his intentions in the previous scene. Nottola's goal – summed up in his statement, 'We just need to convince the city to bring roads, sewers, water, gas, power, and telephone lines here' – is almost perfectly mirrored by the mayor's words: 'Where now there's only a squalid expanse, the city will bring roads, water, power, and gas.' The lexical correspondence between Nottola's list of the city's improvements and the mayor's speech is not the only formal element that defines Rosi's first example of the collusion between business and politics. In city hall, those buildings that appeared so threatening in the first scene are now presented on a small scale and paralleled by a row of politicians standing stiff and still next to the model of the city. Those men are truly in control of Naples, and the buildings are a manifestation and extension of their power. Rosi circumnavigates the model through three different camera angles, conveying that the suffocating buildings of Naples are only the direct expression of the asphyxiating presence of those politicians, who indeed have the city in their grasp, literally and metaphorically.

It is clear by now that no economic strategy can take off without the strong support of the political system. However, in this case, the commercial initiative is not a legal one, and it is perpetrated against the poor, 'the significant Other, the absent Other,'[2] victims who are absent from the scene but present in the viewer's mind as the objects of social discrimination. These people, in fact, die under their crumbling houses, or they are evicted and deceived with false promises of a better life.

Rosi's denunciation of illegal activities is delivered in the film by the engineer De Vita, who attacks corrupt politicians for distorting ethical values. He calls attention to the crucial problem of ethical responsibility, and his appeal to ethics is ironically echoed by the mayor of the city, who earlier asked the government for economic assistance and moral support: 'The support we request from the national government is not merely of a financial nature. It's also an ethical matter.' Later, the mayor will ask the inquiry board to investigate the accident since he intends 'to put forth ethical values [*moralizzare*] … relatively speaking, of course.'[3] But what kind of ethical initiative can ever come from politicians, for whom money is the essence of ethics? Rosi provides an example of distorted ethics when he shows the mayor giving money to the poor who come to city hall to ask for charity. The mayor's generosity, compassion, and sense of democracy towards the indigent are, in reality, a means to build consensus. 'Councilman De Vita, see how democracy works?,' the mayor jovially asks his companion after his munificent display. After all, Nottola, responding to attacks in a newspaper, had already candidly admitted that if city hall did not stop construction after the accident, it was because he (Nottola) held 'the purse strings.' Ethics also becomes an issue for Balsamo, a member of the DC, who wants to withdraw his candidacy because his ethical responsibility towards public opinion prevents him from being on the same electoral slate as Nottola. Professor De Angeli, leader of the DC, replies, 'In political life, moral indignation is a worthless commodity. You know what the only true sin is? Losing.' De Angelis's statement clarifies that the only possible logic is that of power. More than forty years later, Saviano points out that *camorristi* consider ethics to be 'the limit of the loser, the protection of the defeated, the moral justification for those who haven't managed to gamble everything and win it all.'[4] In other words, for *camorristi* in the past as in the present, ethics is a clear sign of psychological weakness and a limit to the achievement of political and economic power.

Though Rosi emphasizes the dishonesty and unlimited power of those who have money and who occupy political positions in the local administration, he also makes a plea for the common people – those on the screen and in the audience – to be more critical and active. A group of disenfranchised inhabitants of Vico Sant'Andrea are shown through theatrical and circular pans and medium close-ups as De Vita reminds them that they still have the power to vote. 'Did you give them your vote?,' he asks. 'And now here are the consequences. Can't you understand that you give them the power to do what they want? After all, what did they do for you?' Michel Ciment remarks that Rosi believes the spectator can perform an 'act of freedom' in choosing something different from the status quo. This act of freedom 'is however tied to the thought process of the director who involves the spectator in his inquiry, leads him to uncover and become aware of the hidden meaning of complex social relationships.'[5]

Throughout the film, Nottola and other politicians with whom he is affiliated can be regarded as the prototypes for the present-day Camorra bosses, especially in view of Saviano's contemporary insight into the Neapolitan criminal world. Nevertheless, in Rosi's film the words Camorra and *camorristi* are never pronounced, not even by De Vita, who unmasks the trade-off between politicians and businessmen. The latter are not delineated as typical Camorra leaders and henchmen: they do not violently and openly kill, they do not speak in dialect, and they seem to be well educated. They remind us of the (new) generations of bosses described by Saviano: 'New generations of bosses don't follow an exclusively criminal path; they don't spend their days on the streets with the local thugs, carry a knife, or have scars on their face, they watch TV, study, go to college, graduate, travel abroad, and are above all employed in the office of the mechanisms of power.'[6] Saviano underscores that contemporary bosses surround themselves with artworks, and they manipulate both their culture and their public image (often based on famous film characters) to express their power. In Rosi's film, De Angeli shows his knowledge of art and appreciation of beauty as he speaks with Balsamo about Luca Giordano's and Francesco Solimena's paintings, and Nottola comments harshly on his own picture chosen for public display during the elections. He is aware of the power of his appearance. In other words, the film offers an image of those in power that does not nourish the people's traditional perception of Camorra criminals. In this way, Rosi distances himself even from his previous mafia movie, *La sfida* (*The Challenge*, 1958), in which he offers a classic picture of *camorristi* who are mainly occupied with the illegal traffic of goods and the murder of those who do not respect the hierarchy established by Camorra bosses.

Let us return now to the questions posed at the beginning of this essay: What, then, is Camorra? Why doesn't Rosi employ the word 'Camorra' to identify the illicit activities represented on the screen? Why is Rosi's work considered a film on the Camorra? Rosi's *Hands over the City* has the merit of proposing and formalizing for the first time on the screen the true nature of the Camorra in its most dangerous aspect, namely, its alliance with political institutions. Rosi was certain that 'mechanisms leading to speculation would have originated political corruption, economic pressure without scruples and all sorts of compromises and alliances with the Camorra.'[7] According to the filmmaker, it was between 1958 (*The Challenge*) and 1963 (*Hands over the City*) that businessmen began their transformation into Camorra bosses.[8] If in 2006 Saviano contends that Camorra is an obsolete term that should be replaced with the word *Sistema* (a sophisticated system of illegal political and economic relations on a local, national, and international level), so Rosi in 1963 shows that the Camorra is not solely visible in serial murders, extortions, the smuggling of goods, or kickbacks; it is now encountered first and foremost in the illicit agreements between political representatives and businessmen often connected with Camorra clans. Today, according to Saviano, the *camorristi* are above all businessmen.

It could be argued that the absence of the word Camorra in the film is due to Rosi's adoption of a method of denouncement that was both conventional and safe. However, considering Rosi's previous films (*The Challenge* and *The Magliari*, 1959; *Salvatore Giuliano*, 1961) and especially the ones that followed *Hands over the City* – *Il caso Mattei* (*The Mattei Affair*), 1972; *Lucky Luciano*, 1973; *Cadaveri eccellenti* (*Illustrious Corpses*), 1976; *Cristo si è fermato ad Eboli* (*Christ Stopped at Eboli*), 1979; *Tre fratelli* (*Three Brothers*), 1981 – this explanation may be inaccurate and superficial. Let us go a bit further. According to Tom Behan, who studied the origins and the development of the Camorra,[9] the organization was already known in the 1960s for its illegal activities and especially for its links with local and national politicians. Therefore, when the film premiered in 1963, people were well aware of how the Camorra acquired power. Hence, spectators both then and today may connect the politicians in power in the film with the highest representatives of the Camorra, particularly if the context is the city of Naples. In commenting on his film, Rosi too takes for granted the connection between politics and the mafia: 'The developer Nottola ... in order to achieve his own goals involves the general political entourage of the various powers – political power, economic power with *the complicity of organized crime.*'[10]

Furthermore, one could argue that Rosi also omitted the word Camorra in order to expand its meaning so as to encompass all situations where power is manipulated to the disadvantage of those who are defenceless and subject to discrimination. The filmmaker hints that one can be a *camorrista* without necessarily being tied to the Camorra. Bribes, blackmail, secret and illicit agreements, corruption, dishonesty, venality, and lack of ethical values are features of the Camorra but also of individuals or groups that act illegally but cannot strictly be identified as affiliated with the Camorra. Manuela Gieri insightfully observes that the true story of the film 'deals with morality of power and its ethics, or lack thereof ... the true subject-matter is the inner logic of power.'[11] Finally, the absence of the word Camorra may also be ascribed to Rosi's personal poetics, his peculiar aesthetic creed that often makes litotes and understatements powerful and effective means of communication. In his films, understatements, along with music, lighting, and performance, increase the spectators' anxieties around absolute unchecked power.[12]

Numerous analogies between Rosi's film and Saviano's book strengthen the critical relevance of *Hands over the City* today. Another filmmaker, Marco Tullio Giordana, understood this importance when he inserted the very last shot of Rosi's film into his own film *I cento passi* (*The One Hundred Steps*, 2000), which is about the protagonist's fight against the mafia and its devious links to local political institutions. Giordana asserted that '*Hands over the City* in my film created an internal rhyme. It was a very explicit declaration.'[13]

In 1992, Rosi returned to Naples to shoot the documentary *Diario Napolitano* (*Neapolitan Diary*)[14] as a follow-up to *Hands over the City*. The documentary begins with the same wide-angle panoramic shot of Naples' sprawling periphery. The spectator is taken into a crowded tenement building that is strikingly similar to Le Vele, the housing project where Matteo Garrone sets part of the story of his film *Gomorra* (*Gomorrah*, 2008).[15] In *Diary*, juvenile delinquency is the film's initial focus. Then Rosi, both director and actor of the documentary, leads the viewer through the congested traffic of Naples to the University of Architecture, where a conference is taking place. In attendance are professors, architects, entrepreneurs, historians, students, and, most importantly, the director of the Camorra Observatory, the director of the Juvenile Justice Center, and a judge who attests to the film's connection to the Camorra. The purpose of the debate is to understand what has really changed in the thirty years since 1963. The screening of *Hands over the City* prompts comments that underscore a sense of stasis. If anything, problems have worsened. When the film ends, Rosi addresses the audience and establishes a direct parallel between Naples and Palermo. As Rosi speaks, the viewer sees images of the mafia's lethal attacks on Judges Giovanni Falcone and Paolo Borsellino (both killed in 1992). The Camorra that in *Hands over the City* is an obscure presence is openly denounced in the documentary as an organization that has increased its power over the last thirty years. The documentary proceeds with an homage to Naples through images of its beautiful coastline and of Mount Vesuvius, and of its artistic treasures, prestigious history, and culinary gems. However, several times Rosi disrupts the enticing harmony of these images with his troubled reflections on organized crime; we see an interview with a Camorra killer, as well as images from the films *Excellent Cadavers* (1976) and *Lucky Luciano* (1973), both of which expose the power of organized crime and its affiliations with political institutions.

Neapolitan Diary confirms and reinforces the relevance of *Hands over the City* today. It ends with Rosi meditating on the scene of the building collapse from his 1963 movie. As the spectator, too, watches the sequence, the images run slowly in reverse so that the building rises up and stands again. *Hands over the City*, then, is brought back together with Rosi's heartfelt hope in the rebirth of the city.

NOTES

1 Roberto Saviano, 'Cement,' in *Gomorrah: A Personal Journey into the Violent International Empire of Naples' Organized Crime System*, trans. Virginia Jewiss (New York: Farrar, Straus and Giroux, 2007), 210, 214.

2 Manuela Gieri, '*Hands over the City*: Cinema as Political Indictment and Social Commitment,' in *Poet of Civic Courage*, ed. Carlo Testa (Westport, CT: Praeger, 1996), 47.

3 Note that in Italian the adjective and noun 'morale' is also used in the political sphere. The direct translation, then, is 'ethical' or 'ethics.'

4 Saviano, 'Cement,' 112.

5 Michel Ciment, 'Dieci proposte per un elogio a Francesco Rosi,' in *Francesco Rosi*, ed. Vittorio Giacci (Rome: International S.p.A., 1995), 6.

6 Saviano, *Gomorrah*, 250.

7   Francesco Rosi cited in Enrico Costa, 'Francesco Rosi. *Le mani sulla città*. 1963–2003,' in *Cinemacittà: The International Journal of Architecture, Urban Studies, Cinema and Communication*, ed. Enrico Costa (Rome: Gangemi Editore, 2003), 25.

8   Francesco Rosi, interview with author, Rome, 31 July 2009.

9   Tom Behan, *The Camorra* (London: Routledge, 1996); *See Naples and Die* (London: Tauris, 2002).

10 Interview with Rosi in Manuela Gieri, '*Le mani sulla città*. Il cinema di Francesco Rosi,' *Corriere Canadese* (3 November 1994): 7.

11 Gieri, '*Hands over the City*: Cinema as Political Indictment and Social Commitment,' 50.

12 For instance, the tense soundtrack by Piero Piccioni that anxiously accompanies key moments in the film increases a sense of unease, particularly at the end of the film when the spectator reads on the screen that, although the film's characters are imaginary, the story reflects the social reality.

13 Marco Tullio Giordana in Costa, 'Francesco Rosi. *Le mani sulla città*. 1963–2003,' 42.

14 Initially created for Italian TV, this film (*Neapolitan Diary*) is featured in *Hands over the City*, The Criterion Collection, 2006, Double-Disc DVD.

15 Rosi wanted to shoot some scenes in Le Vele, but the neighbourhood committee did not approve the initiative. Rosi remarked, 'It is a matter of time. Today the Camorra is much more disclosed and Le Vele in Naples has become its representation.' Rosi, interview.

29   Prototypes of the Mafia: Luchino Visconti's *The Leopard*

ELIZABETH LEAKE

Many of the images used by Italian directors to depict the Sicilian mafia can be traced back to an unlikely source, a 1958 novel by Sicilian Giuseppe Tomasi di Lampedusa titled *Il gattopardo* (*The Leopard*). When the filmmaker Luchino Visconti adapted the novel for film in 1963, those images underwent the first of a series of transformations that would confirm them as shorthand for the mafia in the language of mafia movies, in spite of the fact that Tomasi's novel and Visconti's subsequent film only mention the mafia once,[1] while several other films had already depicted the mafia in great detail. This essay traces the path by which, starting with Visconti's cinematic adaptation, the Tomasi novel's early, powerful, fictional representations of Sicilians are mediated and transformed to provide an uncontested (and often unacknowledged) prototype for many of the subsequent films that deal with the Sicilian mafia. We are already familiar with the equation Sicilian *equals* mafioso as a result of Francis Ford Coppola's *The Godfather* (1972), which is arguably *The Leopard* translated into American vernacular.[2] Coppola's protagonists are not simply Italian and Italian American mafiosi; indeed, their very names (Corleone) declare their specifically Sicilian identities. This essay explores Tomasi's novel as a fundamental source of this equation. Specifically, I argue that images from *The Leopard*'s Sicily form a kind of unproblematic expedient that Italian directors take at face value, borrowing them but not necessarily correcting them for accuracy, so that what Tomasi presents as (potentially) merely Sicilian is collapsed later into representations of the mafia. Put differently, the mediatic apparatus around these images is so overdetermined that their origins *as fiction* have been largely forgotten.

I will support my argument by looking at three films that reference, with varying degrees of critical detachment, the Sicilians and Sicily of *The Leopard*, both through visual echoes and at the level of content. These are Francesco Rosi's *Salvatore Giuliano* (1961), Lina Wertmüller's *Mimì metallurgico, ferito nell'onore* (*The Seduction of Mimi*, 1972), and Pasquale Scimeca's *Placido Rizzotto* (2001). Of these three films, *Salvatore Giuliano* and *Placido Rizzotto* pay homage to Tomasi in their appropriation of the novel's description of Sicily. That passage, which forms the political centrepiece of the novel, creates a genealogical tie with the films that serves to complicate their aliquot of ideological critique. The second film, Wertmüller's *The Seduction of Mimi*, is similarly centred on the core assumptions of Tomasi's and Visconti's texts, but with the very different goal of deconstructing their status as literary myths.

How do these texts represent Sicily and the Sicilians? They disperse these mafioso-like figures across multiple characters and in various dimensions and to various degrees. Take, for example, the novel's description of the husband of Padre Pirrone's sister, whose hot-blooded character and overtly aggressive physical features effectively code mafioso stereotypes: '[W]ith his low forehead, ornamental quaffs of hair on the temples, lurching walk and perpetual swelling of the right trouser pocket where he kept a knife, it was obvious at once that Vincenzino was a "man of honour," one of those violent cretins capable of any havoc.'[3] Moreover, the Pirrone family conflict, mediated by the priest, evinces the overweening importance of 'family honour' and thus legitimates bloodshed and sexual violence. Beyond this specific instance, we encounter Tomasi's more general physical descriptions of thuggish Sicilians (Fabrizio and his family notwithstanding), the implication of which is that these men are dangerous by nature: 'Sinister-looking youths in wide trousers were quarrelling in the guttural grunts Sicilians use in anger.'[4] While this may be more symptomatic of Tomasi's class biases, the trajectory is clear: Sicilians are bestial (guttural grunts), and where there are Sicilians, there is dissent (quarrelling), which leads to wrongdoing (sinister).

To these physical descriptions, Tomasi (later, Visconti) adds broadly sweeping cultural ones. Prejudicial northern notions about the utter alterity of the south are strengthened in the scenes involving northern Italians, such as when Paolo terrifies the northerner Chevalley with stories about the true, hidden Sicily of violent vendettas and rotting corpses. In a lighter vein, the unfortunate northerner Caviraghi's courtship of Concetta is firmly rejected on cultural grounds – in effect, she refuses anything not Sicilian, evidence of a clan mentality humorously cloaked in a kind of culinary provincialism. Although humorously and self-consciously referenced by Sicilians themselves, depictions such as these of a violent, primitive, amoral, clannish society cement the impression that Sicilian culture lies in diametric opposition to northern culture. Hence, too, the themes of blindness and of *omertà* figure in the conversation between the Prince and Chevalley mentioned earlier as sociocultural characteristics: '[I]n this secret island, where houses are barred and peasants refuse to admit they even know the way to their own village in clear view on a hillock within a few minutes walk, here, in spite of the ostentatious show of mystery, reserve is a myth.'[5] These remarks find their visual correlatives in the Visconti film's obsessive contrasting of the brilliant, blinding light of the landscapes and the cool, dusty silence of the interiors. The fact that the character Fabrizio attributes much of Sicilian history and character to the island's climate naturalizes the feeling that Sicilian and mafioso characteristics are coextensive.

Another figure crucial to both the book and the film is Don Calogero Sedara, whose character traits incorporate the business side of the mafia. At once both a public figure and a private one, his real work happens behind the scenes; with his fingers in every pot, he buys up property and is on track to own more than the Prince. This is, fundamentally, a definition of the mafia – political and economic authority or sovereignty over a given district, over and above (or under and outside of) whatever legitimate governmental authorities are nominally in place. The character of Sedara supports the argument that both Tomasi and Visconti locate the roots of the modern mafia in the roots of the nation. The implication, by extension, is that the mafia is not 'another' state or a 'state within the state' so much as it is part and parcel of the state. Hence, after Sedara rigs the election results during the plebiscite, Tomasi's omniscient narrator remarks, 'Don Fabrizio could not know it then, but a great deal of slackness and acquiescence for which the people of the South were to be criticized during the next decade, was due to the stupid annulment of the first expression of liberty ever offered them.'[6] Again, this is Tomasi talking about Sicily – but applying this quote to the figure of Don Calogero strengthens the equation of the mafia with Sicily and implies a Sicilian political history that is inseparable from the mafia. Visconti's Don Calogero is also faithful to these questionable ideals. This is evident when he elaborates on his newly acquired status in the inordinately long (by conventional film standards) ball scene. Here, Don Calogero remarks several times on the cost of various aspects of the decor, the implication being that once he has acquired sufficient fiscal capital through illegitimate means, he will be ready to acquire legitimate cultural capital.

But legitimate Sicilian authority is also ambiguously coded. The transition from monarchy to republic is an opportunity to inscribe the properties of mafia culture on the traditional feudal structure of Sicilian society. This makes sense, insofar as the birth of the mafia is generally ascribed to the mid-1860s, and is evident in the fealty of Russo, one of the Prince's agents, to the Prince's possessions and person: 'There will be a day or two of shooting and trouble, but Villa Salina will be as safe as a rock; Your Excellency is our father, I have many friends here. The Piedmontese will come cap in hand to pay Your Excellency their respects.'[7] More importantly, Tancredi's political alliance-switching in the film culminates in his happy remark about how they can relax now that the rebels are being executed. This sign of his 'inner moral corruption'[8] ends the film but not the book, placing more emphasis on his political views than the book does and thus underscoring the image of Sicily as governed by the rules of political expediency. Things will have to change in order to stay the same – yes, and it is precisely the mafia that steps in to preserve the right *not* to participate in change.

There are many more examples, but I will leave them for the moment because I think we have seen enough to understand how novelistic and film images such as these seem to retroactively legitimate the Siciliano *equals* mafioso equation, providing identikits for cinematic mafiosi. Let us turn now to the deployment in other films of these and similar images. Films concerned with the theme of political transformation (the transition to new Italy, Sicilian independence after the war, agrarian reform, and so on) appropriate aspects of *The Leopard* and apply them explicitly to the question of the Sicilian mafia. Of the Italian films treated in this volume, two are of particular relevance to our discussion because of their acknowledgment of the precursor text: Francesco Rosi's *Salvatore Giuliano* (1961) and Pasquale Scimeca's *Placido Rizzotto*, 2000). Although Rosi precedes Visconti, his film resonates strongly with Visconti's source text, Tomasi's 1958 novel, by virtue of its appropriation of one of Fabrizio's declarations from *The Leopard*:

Sleep, my dear Chevalley, sleep, that is what Sicilians want, and they will always hate anyone who tries to wake them, even in order to bring them the most wonderful of gifts … All Sicilian self-expression, even the most violent, is really wish-fulfillment; our sensuality is a hankering for oblivion; our shooting and knifing a hankering for death; our languor, our exotic ices, a hankering for voluptuous immobility, that is for death again … [N]ovelties attract us only when they are dead, incapable of arousing vital currents; from that comes the extraordinary phenomenon of the constant formation of myths which would be venerable if they were really ancient, but which are really nothing but sinister attempts to plunge us back into a past that attracts us only because it is dead.[9]

These remarks anticipate analogous declarations by Don Pietro, the Sicilian separatist from *Salvatore Giuliano*, who urges the eponymous character and his band of outlaws to participate in the separatist movement:

Sicily, awaken! Your shameful slumber has lasted far too long. While you've slept, all has been lost, even your honor. Now the trumpets ring loud and you must no longer sleep because sleep would mean death. White roses of Sicily, you'll be stained red with our blood. But our sons and our sons' sons will live in a free land and will lift their gaze to the heavens and smile at the future.

The similarities are apparent. The visual representation of the Rosi film's landscape (hard, age-old, unchanging, silent) contradicts the scene's message about awakening (and thus changing), thus enforcing the film's connection with *The Leopard*. Similarly, the twin themes of sleep and death in these passages underscore relations between Sicily, history, and the law in such a way as to equate the Sicilian independence movement – the birth of Sicily, in a way – with the birth of Italy: two births that, by necessity, require mafia intervention in order to provide the right balance of movement and stasis. Moreover, Don Pietro's remarks are made on top of a hill overlooking the city, a visual reference to the moment earlier in the novel when Tomasi's narrator declared that the hilltop fires of revolution were being 'stoked by men who were themselves very like those living in the monasteries below, as fanatical, as self-absorbed, as avid for power or rather for the idleness which was, for them, the purpose of power.'[10] In Rosi's film as in Tomasi's novel, true power means being able to direct change *as well as* being able to prevent it; by the film's logic, Giuliano's band will be able to do both, according to the alliances it privileges and the forms of power it most covets. Of course it is not by chance that Francesco Rosi's exhortation to the would-be revolutionaries takes place from a hilltop overlooking the city. Though perhaps not inhibited by the presence of monasteries in the way that Tomasi's valley is, Rosi's 'svegliati, Sicilia' speech, placed as it is on a hilltop, and with its recollection of the Prince's articulation of a congenital Sicilian essence (in the second Tomasi passage quoted above), taints Giuliano's band with the stench of the dead and the threat of its enjoyment in the form of a kind of cultural necrophilia ('a past that attracts us only because it is dead').

Forty years later, Scimeca's *Placido Rizzotto* reverberates with analogous verbal and visual references. *The Leopard*'s description of the revolutionaries standing upon high and contemplating the valley below is echoed visually when Placido Rizzotto returns to Sicily from fighting in the Second World War. We see him first as he stands on a cliff, arms outstretched in the form of a cross, after which he devotes himself to fighting mafia corruption. This scene is another indication that if revolution means movement, as well as its opposite in its return to the starting point, then hillsides are the site of revolution par excellence.[11] In the novel, Fabrizio recounts the story of the time he gave a tour of his palace to some British naval officers: 'They were ecstatic about the view, the vehemence of the light; they confessed, though, that they had been horrified at the squalor, dirt, filth of the streets around. I didn't explain that the one thing was derived from the other.'[12] After the scene with Placido on the hilltop, we fast-forward to a scene at the same hilltop location, which offers a narrative closure in the film that the novel does not provide.

This visual echo is doubly inflected with *The Leopard*'s take on Sicilian perspectives, both psychological and historical. On the second visit, a real cross has been erected, in front of which Rizzotto's father Carmelo lectures to a group of rapt schoolchildren about Placido's life and violent death. At the film's close, we return to Carmelo, whose recitation of the events of his son's life, too, has come to an end. As the camera pulls back, we realize that the benches on which the children previously sat are all empty, and we wonder how much of his story has gone unheard. Nothing has changed, and the cycle remains unbroken in spite of Placido's efforts to combat the Sicilian need for 'sleep' to which the other texts referred, and which he seemed to invoke and reject during a speech made before the collective: 'battle your own transgressions, then turn to others.' The broader implications of this choice – regarding the deafness of the young generation, their indifference to the glories and the virtues (as well as the vices) of their forebears, the imbrication of space and place – echo the Prince's melancholy observation that he is the last of his kind. Put differently, Sicily's, or rather, Sicilians' relationship to their own personal and cultural histories is very much at the heart of both of these texts, and the haunting presence of the leopard behind the more modern narrative highlights the peculiarly local quality of this relationship. Tomasi does not lament the youth of today in general or universal terms; neither does Scimeca; rather, both refer to a specifically Sicilian incarnation of younger generations. It is interesting to note that that particularly local critique was mordant enough to require a disclaimer at the beginning of *Placido Rizzotto*, and the dislaimer seems to redefine the dimensions of the local and the historical as universal and fictional: 'In order to avoid errors or misunderstandings I declare that the Sicily that frames and accompanies this film is only Sicily by chance; only because the name Sicily sounds better than the name Persia, Venezuela, Brazil or Mexico. In any case, I imagine that all movies are shot with a movie camera and exposed on film.'

Yet that is a false disclaimer, a red herring that does *not*, in fact, discourage the spectator from identifying the film's depiction as specifically Sicilian. On the contrary, Scimeca's disclaimer achieves with a wink the opposite of what it claims, by virtue of the fact that it is a near-verbatim appropriation of yet another eminent, explicitly Sicilian text, Elio Vittorini's *Conversation in Sicily*, which contains the following postscript: 'In order to avoid errors or misunderstandings I declare that, just as the protagonist of this *Conversation* is not autobiographical, so the Sicily that frames and accompanies him is only Sicily by chance; only because the name Sicily sounds better than the name Persia or Venezuela. In any case, I imagine that all manuscripts are found in a bottle.'[13] Scimeca's reference to Vittorini puts a new spin on Tomasi; it creates a genealogical tie based on *sicilianità* that supercedes the many otherwise insurmountable differences between the two writers. This, in turn, evokes the end of Francesco Rosi's 1963 film *Le mani sulla città* (*Hands over the City*), which declares, 'The characters and events shown are imaginary. The social and environmental context is real.' The first part of the disclaimer closes the circle by which Tomasi's Sicilians are parsed as mafiosi (Sicilian *equals* mafioso *equals* Sicilian) at the same time as its second component ('In any case, I imagine …') reveals the *constructedness* of that equation: its status as novelistic and filmic fiction.

Finally, a third example is offered by Lina Wertmüller's *The Seduction of Mimi* (1972). Unlike previous films, whose references to *The Leopard* are simultaneously made and disavowed, Wertmüller's film is more straightforward in its relatively uncomplicated rejection of *The Leopard*'s apparent premises. *The Seduction of Mimi* tries to correct the assumptions made about clannishness and the family to which Tomasi's text has been subjected. Indeed, these do not become Wertmüller's point of departure towards other narrative shores; instead, they serve more as excavation sites. Questioning the connections and false identifications between the mafia and the Sicilian family that have endured for so long, Wertmüller dismantles the north versus south dichotomy at play in *The Leopard*. In Wertmüller, the north is equally prey to mafia power, and it is precisely in *Sicily* that Mimi thwarts their attempt to control him by voting against them in an election that he thought, mistakenly, was secret. Similarly, the cult of virginity and the oppression of female sexuality so typically invoked in relation to Sicilian culture are actually more appropriately applied to the north. Northerner Fiore is the virgin, then the faithful partner, and then the loving mother, while Sicilian Rosalia is the faithless home-wrecker whose narrative resonates with Tomasi's character 'Ncilina. And Mimi's return to Sicily is the paradoxical result of his having been so independent of mafia control – when he is spotted in Turin doing a good job, the mafia bosses offer him an even better position, but one that requires his return to Sicily, where he will, in fact, work for them. Overturning our expectations about a mafia-inflected Sicily (or a Sicily-inflected mafia), *The Seduction of Mimi* demonstrates that Tomasi's famous declaration is alive and that things really do change in order to remain the same – just not in ways we expect.

NOTES

1 During the novel's first encounter between Fabrizio and Tancredi, the Prince tells his nephew why he can't join the revolution: '[T]hey're all mafiosi and swindlers.' Giuseppe Tomasi di Lampedusa, *Il gattopardo*, trans. Archibald Colquhoun (New York: A.A. Knopf, Everyman's Library, 1998), 22.

2 George De Stefano makes a similar observation when he notes that for Americans, southern Italy is synonymous with the mafia. *An Offer We Can't Refuse: The Mafia in the Mind of America* (London: Faber and Faber, 2006).

3 Tomasi di Lampedusa, *The Leopard*, 148.

4 Ibid., 19.

5 Ibid., 26.

6 Ibid., 84.

7 Ibid., 27.

8 Millicent Marcus, *Filmmaking by the Book: Italian Cinema and Literary Adaptation* (Baltimore, MD: Johns Hopkins University Press, 1993), 47. It also supports my argument about the uses and misuses of Tomasi to make statements about Sicily and the mafia; whatever the intention, the effect of Visconti's edit is that it redimensions the text's ideological content.

9 Tomasi di Lampedusa, *The Leopard*, 131. The Visconti film contains a slightly abridged version of this exchange.

10 Ibid., 17–18.

11 Marcus makes a similar point in her discussion of *The Leopard*'s interest in astronomy in *Filmmaking by the Book*, 48.

12 Tomasi di Lampedusa, *The Leopard*, 135.

13 Elio Vittorini, *Conversazione in Sicilia* (Milan: Rizzoli, 1988), 341.

30 The Failure of the Intellectual: Elio Petri's Filming of Leonardo Sciascia's *To Each His Own*

DANIELA BINI

The film *A ciascuno il suo* (*To Each His Own*, Elio Petri, 1967) opens with a long shot of the island that slowly narrows down to a town, then a piazza, and finally the postman and the letter, as the camera becomes the investigating eye. The music accordingly changes from ample, melodic phrases on piano and strings to an ominous, syncopated beat of very low piano chords accompanying the steps of the postman. From now on, these same chords will alert the viewer to impending danger. The investigating role of the camera throughout the film, as it leads the viewer to the various clues, also creates an atmosphere of anxiety and suspense. This atmosphere is amplified by the fast-paced editing of the film, which seems to pull us by the hand from one scene to the next in search of more evidence as time runs short and the ominous end nears.

The novel of the same name, written by Leonardo Sciascia, begins with a letter that is delivered to the pharmacist Manno by the local postman. Manno immediately recognizes its anonymous character. It reads, 'For what you have done, you will die,' and becomes the topic of discussion among the various friends who gather in the evening at Manno's pharmacy. One of them, Paolo Laurana, becomes fascinated by the cut-out letters that were used to write the threatening message. He holds the letter close to a lamp, curious as to what can be read behind it, thus inviting the reader to do the same: not to stop at the surface appearance, but to look below. The letters behind reveal the identity of the newspaper used by the author of the anonymous letter: *Osservatore romano*, the Vatican daily. Manno is then shot to death at the opening of the hunting season together with his hunting partner, Dr Roscio. The hunters have been hunted. The search for the killer now begins. It will reveal that the real target was not the receiver of the anonymous letter, but Dr Roscio, whose wife Luisa is the niece of the powerful *arciprete* Rosello and the cousin and lover (probably discovered) of the *avvocato* Rosello, a 'potente who held the whole province in the palm of his hands.'[1]

Sciascia tells us that Professor Laurana, the protagonist of his novel, begins the investigation of the double murder of the pharmacist Manno and Dr Roscio out of 'intellectual curiosity,' thus setting the stage for a character who reasons, reflects, reads, and does not act. Laurana teaches literature at the high school, is reserved, and lives with his mother and in his world of books and fiction – he is painted as an inept man, cut off from reality. However, the professor is not simply an intellectual; he is a Sicilian, first and foremost. The product of centuries of various foreign occupations, and of exploitation by a variety of governments, he is imbued with an ancestral suspicion towards those who should administer justice. For Laurana, the murder is an intellectual challenge that will put his analytical abilities to the test. This 'obscure' mentality, the narrator explains, is the product of centuries of oppression, developed in the 'conviction that the highest right and truest justice … can only come from the barrels of a gun.'[2] Here we find the major difference between book and movie. The philosophical and Sicilian core of Sciascia's text is, in fact, taken over by the political commitment of Elio Petri's Laurana, who wants to go to the Palermo police and denounce the assassin: 'a murderer is a murderer that must be caught and punished.'

Elio Petri was the first director to adapt a mystery novel by Sciascia. It was 1967 and the book had just come out the year before. It was his third movie and inaugurated the popular genre that went by the name of *cinema politico* (political cinema). This type of politically committed film-making followed Gramsci's dictum that the intellectual must be committed to social causes and that cinema as a popular art form must speak to the masses, inspire action, and teach about social justice. Petri had been involved in the Communist Party and had written for the Communist daily *l'Unità*. Sciascia, too, was involved in social issues and connected with the Communist Party. However, the focus of his novel was the complexity of Sicilian history, and the mafia, but above all the act of writing and thus the centrality of the intellectual. Especially in the novel, writing is at the core of the plot, which originates in and develops from it. A self-referential work, *To Each His Own* presents us with a denunciation of the self-absorbed writer-intellectual, who with his literary culture is unable to understand the reality that surrounds him and that is obvious to everyone else. This inability to perceive reality will cause him to fall into the trap of the femme fatale and lead to his demise. The use of the femme fatale as a decoy to entrap Laurana carries in itself the Sicilian cultural implication of the erotic woman as evil. Luisa will become the architect of Laurana's demise. And Petri is faithful to the spirit of the text. In fact, he exploits it with great skill, using the camera to cut Luisa's body into segments under the gaze of Laurana, who is no longer in control of it, thus reversing Laura Mulvey's reading of the gaze as expressing male power over the woman as a mere object of desire. In both novel and film, Luisa is clearly presented as controlling the man's gaze by skilfully using her body.[3]

With this autobiographical novel, Sciascia tried to exorcise his own demons. The downfall of Laurana represents the failure of the bourgeois intellectual who lives in a Platonic world of ideas and is unable to step outside of them. Petri is faithful to the spirit of the novel precisely because his objective is to expose not only the corruption of the system but also the impotence of leftist intellectuals. He thus places the theme of writing at centre stage by adding to the story a mysterious notebook that the victim's father will give to Laurana, a non-existent diary that he pretends to keep at school in order to protect himself from Rosello's threats, and a few more anonymous letters sent to Laurana. All of this writing will prove not only ineffectual but also dangerous, thus underscoring once more the inability of the intellectual to change or understand the world in which he lives.

Petri politicizes his protagonist, making him much more concerned about issues of justice and social commitment. The encounter he has in Palermo (also present in the book) with an old school friend, now a Communist congressman, is, however, adapted to serve Petri's purpose. In the novel, the episode is nothing more than the recounting of the visit the congressman had received from the victim a few months before his death. During that encounter, Dr Roscio had asked the congressman about his willingness to expose an unmentioned person in power who held the entire province in his hands and against whom he could provide some documents. In the film, this encounter instead sparks a heated political exchange between the two friends, first about the absurdity of two communists going to the police to denounce a mafioso, and second about Laurana's disillusionment with the Communist Party. In opposition to this character, Sciascia's Laurana 'was by everyone considered a Communist, but he was not.'[4] He was only an impotent intellectual.

Petri's artistry in adapting Sciascia's novel consists of expanding the theme of the marginalized and thus ineffective bourgeois intellectual into a critique of the entire Italian Marxist intelligentsia, which is unable to affect society and bring about change. Whereas Sciascia remains attached to and dependent on the power of the written word and its inherent limitations, Petri uses the topic as a stepping stone for his social critique, thus suggesting and encouraging change. He had disclosed his objective in an interview when he rejected the label of *intellectual* attributed to him by critics. 'An intellectual is someone who grows in a greenhouse. Things are narrated to him, his subjectivity is never challenged.'[5] He then proceeded to accuse the so-called progressive intellectuals of essentially doing nothing to ameliorate the current political climate. Liborio Termine refers to this as 'bad faith transformed into ideology,' which becomes 'the supporting structure' of Sciascia's political novel.[6] Petri was intrigued by *To Each His Own* precisely because it embodies the bad faith of so many bourgeois intellectuals. He makes Laurana into a seemingly more committed intellectual in order to give more efficacy to his accusation. Laurana tries to reconstruct the anonymous letter by cutting letters from *Osservatore romano* – the episode is absent in the novel – in order to prove the innocence of the three illiterate farmers who have been wrongly accused and arrested.

In the novel, Sciascia is caught in the role of the ineffectual intellectual. Through Laurana he portrays his own ambiguities, his limitations, and his self-accusation. Literature is what rules his life, and the novel is filled with literary citations and evocations. His hope is that perhaps those who read him will learn how to take action, rather than close themselves up in their libraries, as the character Benito does.

Benito (after Juárez, not Mussolini – another example of Sciascia's warning for the reader not to stop at the surface) is the mature example of the disillusioned intellectual. He is a man locked up in his library, who reads and does not act, a character whom Petri understandably chooses to omit in his filmic adaptation. Yet, I would argue, it is precisely this character who provides him with the justification to make his movie more political than the book. Benito's observation, 'Ma il fatto è, mio caro amico, che l'Italia è un così felice paese che quando si cominciano a combattere le mafie vernacole, vuol dire che già se ne è stabilita una in lingua,'[7] extends Petri the right to address the issue of the Communist intellectual in general and his ineffectual relationship with the national situation. But it is the end of the chapter that sanctions Petri's right to adaptation. Benito, who considers books more real than people – to him, the latter are only puppets in a theatrical performance – gives a powerful monologue in which Sicily is metamorphosed into a beautiful but sinking pirate vessel. He concludes by pointing out how ridiculous it is at such a dramatic historical moment to worry about catching a small fish like Raganà (the paid killer). Laurana, perhaps with an urge for justice, replies that he does not agree. The chapter ends with Benito's comment, 'All in all, neither do I.'[8] Sciascia's own uncertainty closes the chapter, giving Petri the right to develop the hint that Benito himself drops for the reader at the end.

It is, however, with books and writers that Sciascia's major allegiance rests. In chapter 7, he explains to the reader the difference between a real investigation and a fictional one. If, in the mystery novel, he writes, the reader/investigator who knows how to interpret the clues is rewarded at the end by the discovery of the truth and the apprehension of the murderer, in real life, the truth is uncovered only with the help of informers, and above all by chance. The word *chance* is a clue, but of a different kind, one that Sciascia provides at this time to direct us towards a different discovery – not that of the murderer, but of his literary model. *Chance* comes to help Laurana twice: first, in Palermo when he accidentally meets his congressman friend, and second, on the steps of the tribunal, where he has gone to request a certificate to apply for a driver's licence. In the film, Laurana is instead lured to the place by an anonymous letter. At the tribunal, Laurana, who by now suspects Rosello, meets him in the company of a Christian Democrat congressman, the Honourable Abello, whom Rosello introduces to Laurana as a 'champion of morality and doctrine.'[9] The entire scene, which in the film is devoid of the literary implications, is a jewel of narrative artistry. As the Honourable Abello and Laurana engage in a brief discussion on poetry, the difference in their tastes is obvious. When the former hears of Laurana's love for Dino Campana and Salvatore Quasimodo, he is, the narrator comments ironically, 'stunned [*traffitto*] with disappointment.' Quasimodo's famous poem,

> Everyone stands alone in the heart of the world,
> Transfixed [*traffitto*] by a ray of sun,
> and it is suddenly evening

becomes emblematic of the desolate condition of our protagonist, whose 'ray of sun,' that is, the resolution of the murder case, will bring him shortly to his fatal 'evening.'

On the same steps, but somewhat distant, a strange character arouses Laurana's curiosity and fear; he is clearly a man from the country, but he is wearing an incongruous pair of fashionable sunglasses. It is the first time he appears in the novel, whereas Petri chooses to introduce him to us in the opening scene of the film, when the town is initially presented. We know nothing about him, just as the townspeople know nothing – in fact, they comment that he is not a local – and his appearance at the beginning of the film is immediately perceived as threatening. Dressed all in black, he gets out of a black car and moves about, observing everyone. Then he disappears, as the music that accompanies his movements reinforces the ominous feeling. When we see him again on the steps of the tribunal lighting a cigar, we know he is involved with Rosello and possibly with the murder. We have none of this certainty in the novel. Sciascia creates his climax and its resolution by allowing us to find the connecting link at the end of the chapter by means of the literary clue he has skilfully deposited throughout his story, which ultimately becomes more important than the discovery of the killer.

The only clues the police have about the case (since the letters cut from the daily *Osservatore romano* have been disregarded) are the various cigar butts of the Branca brand found at the scene of the murder. As the suspicious character takes a cigar out of its box, Laurana's eyes 'registered the colors red and yellow of the box.'[10] Twenty minutes later, he rushes into a tobacco store and requests a pack of Brancas. The long passage that follows is constructed with the dramatic suspense of a classic mystery. The reader knows we are close to a major revelation, and we can well anticipate what it will be. The real climax of the sequence, however, is not the identification of the killer but that of Sciascia's literary source, Luigi Pirandello's novel *The Late Mattia Pascal*.

Pirandello is a constant presence in this novel – sometimes hidden, sometimes hinted at, and in the end openly declared. But it is at this moment that his significance is revealed. Sciascia, in fact, chooses for his homage not only Pirandello's narrative masterpiece but also an image from within it that expresses the core of his philosophy: that of roulette, brought to mind by the red and yellow packaging of the cigars. Mattia Pascal wins in Monte Carlo, and this victory will change his life. It is, however, Pirandello's reflection on roulette as a metaphor for life that interests us. Players of roulette, he writes, 'want, in short, to extract a logic from chance, which is like saying, blood from stone; and they are convinced they'll succeed, today or at the latest, tomorrow.'[11] Human beings behave like roulette players. They think they can extract meaning out of life, find its significance, whereas life is a chaotic, irrational flux in the hands of chance. They deceive themselves into thinking they can discover some sense, just as the roulette players think they can find a system for winning. Laurana finds the killer by chance. His intelligent investigation would not have taken him anywhere had chance not come to his aid. And does it really come to his aid? This *raggio di sole* will turn against him and bring him to a dreadful end.

That Sciascia had contradictory feelings about the role of the intellectual and that he was also confessing his own ambiguities is confirmed in chapter 16, which takes place in the historical but seldom frequented Romeris Café. With the same technique of postponement that he had used in chapter 7 to create suspense, Sciascia does not reveal the name of the writer right away. He wants the reader to connect the clues he has placed throughout the novel and arrive at its discovery. Before the name appears – and it does only with his first name, as Don Luigi – another writer is mentioned and discussed, Pirandello's other, the highest representative of enlightened reason and civil commitment, Sciascia's esteemed model: the philosopher Voltaire. As Laurana waits at the café for Louisa, he takes out of his briefcase Voltaire's love letters, and this prompts a discussion among the customers and Signor Romeris. Looking at today's society, where corruption is rampant and power is abused, Judge Lumia states that it is clear nobody reads Voltaire anymore and that even our professor does not seem to understand him well. It is at this point that Don Luigi is mentioned for the first time, in a negative way, as someone who did not read Voltaire either. The two writers are immediately placed next to each other in a confrontation that embodies Sciascia's own contrasts and contradictions.

And now the real puzzle is uncovered, as Judge Lumia remarks: 'But the telegram to Mussolini, and the beret and tassel that he wore on occasion …'[12] Granting the greatness of Pirandello's writing, how do we then explain his swearing allegiance to the Fascist Party with a personal telegram addressed to Mussolini right after the murder of Giacomo Matteotti? Shouldn't an internationally renowned writer, following Gramsci's instruction, fight for civil liberties and even go to jail for them, as the great Voltaire had done? Can his ethical and social obligations be detached from his artistic contribution? These are the questions that Sciascia is directing to the reader, but first of all to himself. Should we agree with Signor Romeris when he exclaims, 'Don Luigi … has written books that the whole world admires, but here he's just the man who once sent a telegram to Mussolini and sometimes wore the fascist cap.'[13] In one simple sentence, Signor Romeris presents us with the dramatic question that is at the heart of the novel and that Petri will answer: the writer's responsibility to his readers, to society. There is no doubt that Sciascia felt this obligation, but there is also ample evidence that he realized how his love for the written text could isolate and insulate him from action. Petri understood this. If Sciascia finds himself torn between Pirandello and Voltaire, Petri decides for him, bringing him closer to the latter. Not only did he choose to delete the controversial Pirandello from his film (as he had done with Benito) but he also brings to it a more socially engaged Sciascia. In a scene that does not appear in the book, Laurana summarizes to a student during an exam the significance of the historical character, friar Diego La Matina from Racalmuto, who, during the Spanish Inquisition in Sicily, had been tried and executed for alleged heresy. *The Death of the Inquisitor* is the work where Sciascia reconstructs this trial, but Petri's Laurana uses it as a model in order 'to make us understand how these episodes repeat themselves uninterruptedly through the centuries.' Students reading them must therefore learn and apply what they read to today.

The 'battle with the contradictions between the positive ideal of the Enlightment … and a Pirandellian vision of life' that Claude Ambroise detected in Sciascia's investigation novels is present in his entire production.[14] He needed Voltaire to overcome Pirandello. By bringing *The Death of the Inquisitor* into his film, Petri takes the justified liberty of placing Sciascia in line with his beloved Voltaire and situates him in the social arena that his Pirandellian soul dreaded so much.

NOTES

1　Leonardo Sciascia, *To Each His Own*, trans. Adrienne Foulke (Manchester: Carcanet, 1989), 54. All other translations are mine, except where noted.

2　Ibid., 110.

3　Laura Mulvey, 'Visual Pleasure and Narrative Cinema,' *Screen* 16, no. 3 (1975): 6–18.

4　Sciascia, *To Each His Own*, 40.

5　Alfredo Rossi, *Elio Petri* (Florence: La Nuova Italia, 1979), 4, 5–6.

6　Liborio Termine, 'Il romanzo della malafede e il cinema in crisi,' *Cinema nuovo* 185 (1967): 46.

7　'Italy is country so blessed that for every weed you destroy, two spring up in its place.' What Sciascia is saying is that when you start defeating the local mafia, a national one has been born. Sciascia, *To Each His Own*, 120.

8　Ibid., 98.

9　Ibid., 84.

10　Ibid., 91.

11　Luigi Pirandello, *The Late Mattia Pascal*, trans. William Weaver (Hygiene, CO: Eridanos Press, 1987), 54.

12　Sciascia, *To Each His Own*, 128.

13　Ibid., 129.

14　Claude Ambroise, 'Verità e scrittura,' in Leonardo Sciascia, *Opere 1956–1971* (Milan: Bompiani, 1990), xxviii.

31　Damiano Damiani's *The Day of the Owl*: A Western Flirtation

PIERO GAROFALO

Adapted from Leonardo Sciascia's 1961 homonymous novella, *Il giorno della civetta* (*The Day of the Owl*, 1968) projects an image that conflates both the Sicilian territory with the Sonoran frontier and the mafia legend with the classic western to produce a hybrid genre that draws on these two narrative traditions. Sciascia's story offers a quasi-parallel montage between a criminal investigation in Sicily and political shenanigans in Rome, which the film eschews; instead, it limits the drama's geographic scope to an isolated town.[1] Privileging the story's dynamic elements, the film emphasizes an action-intensive narrative that is consonant with the Italian western. The film transposes the Wild West, with its heroes, villains, and innocent townsfolk, onto another fictive world, that of the indomitable isle, and grounds it in an ever-present violent reality. Extra-cinematic elements, narrative structure, and cinematographic strategies reinforce this nexus. Thus, *The Day of the Owl* defamiliarizes the mafia tale by making it both recognizable and strange. Such a tactic encourages audiences that might otherwise be dismissive of or complacent about organized crime to reconsider its presence in the Italian landscape.

The Day of the Owl was produced at a time when genre films dominated Italy's domestic screens and were commercially, if not always critically, successful. In the 1960s, Italian box office successes (such as the Sergio Leone–Clint Eastwood 'Man with No Name' trilogy) revitalized the western and provided Cinecittà, Italy's principal studio complex, with a steady stream of foreign actors whose names guaranteed cachet for film distribution. Drawing on this cinematic iconography, director Damiano Damiani, who had recently shot the political western *A Bullet for the General* (1966), cast actors whose screen *personae* spectators associated with the western genre. Top billing went to Claudia Cardinale, who had just completed *The Professionals* (Richard Brooks, 1966); she starred as Rosa Nicolosi, a woman caught between two competing systems of justice. Franco Nero, best known as the coffin-dragging gunslinger *Django* (Sergio Corbucci, 1966), appeared in the role of Captain Bellodi. Lee J. Cobb, familiar to audiences for both his westerns and his portrayal of Johnny Friendly, the corrupt union leader in *On the Waterfront* (Elia Kazan, 1954), played the local mafia boss Don Mariano Arena. These inter-filmic references reinforce a narrative structure (stranger rides into town, stranger rides out of town) and a spatial configuration (the showdown between hero and villain) that conform to the logic of the western. This generic imbrication elicits a sense of déjà vu – the film draws on cinematic conventions even while reformulating them.

This transposition of narrative systems was effected visually by Damiani's cinematographer, Antonio Delli Colli, who had just filmed Leone's seminal *Il buono, il brutto, il cattivo* (*The Good, the Bad and the Ugly*, 1966). Delli Colli applied the same techniques to *The Day of the Owl* that he had brought to Leone's film: long shots with full light to bring clarity to the details, close-ups with every feature defined, extreme close-ups of the eyes. In Damiani's film, the Sicilian sun replaces the Sonoran one, but its brilliance, imbued in blues and whites, is just as blinding and its shadows are just as deep and long. Delli Colli's effulgent skies belie the darkness that pervades the inimical territory. Set in the present in an unnamed town in western Sicily, the film's opening sequence establishes the inciting incident for the narrative: the murder of an honest building contractor, Salvatore Colasberna. Enter the handsome stranger – the investigating officer Captain Bellodi – who has come from afar to bring the rule of law to this wild frontier. Naively believing that right makes might, he refutes the 'crime of passion' subterfuge proffered by the 'peccantly' pristine mafia boss Don Mariano Arena. As the investigation progresses, Bellodi does indeed build a case against the men of honour, but the captain fails to appreciate the extent to which society, the institutions, and the state share a vested interest in sustaining the anonymity of the mafia. In the final show-down, Don Mariano emerges unscathed while Bellodi disappears into the sunset.

The nameless town at the film's epicentre is the arena in which the two men compete.[2] Within its oppressive confines the waging factions, reminiscent of Leone's feuding families in *Per un pugno di dollari* (*A Fistful of Dollars*, 1964), face off on opposite sides of the piazza. This spatial configuration fosters a stare-down between Captain Bellodi and Don Mariano, both of whom keep tabs on each other with binoculars. Extreme close-ups, characteristic of the Italian western, emphasize the competing controlling gazes. The two men engage in a surveillance game that is anything but surreptitious. The act of viewing becomes a means for both asserting control and projecting power. Theirs is a gentleman's *mano a mano* struggle for supremacy. What matters is not what the binoculars reveal but that the person observed is aware of the surveillance. Thus both parties engage in theatrical acts for the benefit of their audiences. When Bellodi orders the triggerman Zecchinetta to be arrested in the piazza, the action is merely a public performance to make manifest the power of the law. Similarly, Don Mariano's entrance into the local headquarters of the Christian Democrats is a clear statement to the police of how far his political reach extends. The public space is the arena over which the two sides battle and which, in the end, Don Mariano Arena controls. What lies outside the camera's frame is evanescent. Palermo, as a symbolic referent to political order, conveys an oppressive presence that weighs on the characters, but the city itself remains invisible. Everyone is metaphorically tied in the town. When people leave, they are either dead (e.g., Tano Nicolosi) or they simply disappear without a trace (e.g., Captain Bellodi). In the film's closing sequence, one set of binoculars remains: those of Don Mariano.

This Machiavellian 'might makes right' conclusion constitutes the defeat of reason. The cynical rule of the lawless that survives in Sicily is necessarily irrational and shifts according to the whims of those it serves. Audiences, however, had already been prepared for the triumph of power over principles through the Italian westerns' proliferation of ambivalent antiheroes and questionable 'happy endings' that had rewritten the conventions of the genre. While *The Day of the Owl* critiques the status quo, it remains subject to this realpolitik. Indeed, the investigation fails, but its failure is poignant.

This dénouement shares more with the western than with the crime genre. In traditional detective fiction, the investigation of a crime exposes the truth, which, once revealed, will restore the proper social order that the act of violence had threatened. In *The Day of the Owl*'s genre-bending exposé, by contrast, the crime is a coherent component of the social order, one that is threatened by none other than the truth. Thus, the murder investigation is supplanted in the narrative by the attempt to bring the rule of law to this Sicilian frontier. In a sense, the land itself must be tamed, which requires the cooperation of the townspeople; however, whether out of fear, ignorance, or self-incrimination, or because the outlaws' laws based on favours and friendship are all they know, the townspeople do not step forward. Without cover, as the film's title suggests, an owl by day is easy prey.

This imagery of death frames the narrative. Like Pietro Germi's 1949 feature *In nome della legge* (*In the Name of the Law*), Damiani's film opens with a bang. The title sequence is a two-minute panning shot in which the camera gravitates towards a series of objects (a rifle, cheese, bread, wine, a cigarette) while blatantly concealing the hired gun's face. In juxtaposition to the killer's calm and methodical actions, the commentative folkloric music accompanying his movements rises to a crescendo. Abruptly and synchronously, the music, the panning shot, and the title credits cut to an approaching truck. The murder sequence then explodes in an aural cacophony of diegetic sounds and in a visual pandemonium of saturated Technicolour. The laborious 120-second opening shot bursts into a rapid-fire thirty-two shots within which extreme close-ups and extreme long shots intermix (as they do in westerns), to emphasize the violence and spatial backdrop. These initial scenes establish the film's rhythm, which alternates unevenly between lengthy static situations and short-action sequences.

Specific shot selections reinforce the pace of the narrative. Like Italian westerns, *The Day of the Owl* extensively employs zooms. The zooms tend to be functional in that they are applied in lieu of editing and shots/countershots. A vivid example of this technique is Pizzuco's interrogation scene, in which the camera zooms out from a close-up of the clammy mafioso to a medium shot of the sergeant major in the foreground and the full figures of Pizzuco and a *carabiniere* framed by the doorway in the background. When the sergeant major points an accusing finger at Pizzuco, the camera zooms in for a telephoto close-up of Don Mariano's stooge. The camera is in constant motion and does not identify with any specific vantage point; in this way it emphasizes multiple perspectives and extends the shot's duration. By substituting montage with movement, the scene plays out longer in experiential terms for the spectator than it would using quick shot/reverse shot editing. This change in rhythm stylistically reinforces the investigative aspect of the narrative. The active camera scrutinizes from near and far but neither exposes nor reveals. It is a Diogenean lantern that illuminates Bellodi's search for truth, but the brighter it shines, the darker the shadows it projects.

This rhythm is not simply visual; it is underscored by the investigation, which stalls and surges. What obstructs the investigation is made immediately apparent: when the killer exits the scene, everyone ignores the bloody body. A truck stops, but then quickly moves on. A passing bus driver also feigns blindness to the grisly scene. The community's reticence to acknowledge the corpse reinforces visually the conspiracy of silence, *omertà*, which is a constant impediment to the investigation. This refusal to assist the police echoes the familiar western scene of cowering townsfolk who hide behind shutters rather than support the man who fights for them. Hence, the silence also underscores the lawman's physical and emotional isolation from the community he seeks to protect.

This sense of isolation is personified in Captain Bellodi, who disrupts the narrative rhythm both through his actions and through his didactic digressions. Similar to the requisite stranger riding into town, Bellodi is presented as an outsider. He pontificates variously on Sicilian honour, the meaning of cuckold, and anonymous letter-writing; the spectators perceive his observations as pedantic distractions, and the diegetic characters accept them with polite resignation. He is a stranger in a strange land; his accent, his physical features, his need for a 'translator', and indeed his world view mark him as different. Although he is a captain, he basically works alone. He is a solitary man who does not enjoy the undivided support of his colleagues. This tension is evident when the sergeant major notes that the murder victim, Colasberna, had been convicted during the fascist period for criticizing the head of state, Benito Mussolini. Bellodi's objection that such a conviction hardly constitutes a criminal record indicates the cultural abyss that separates him from the other *carabinieri* in the unit. In fact, Bellodi bonds more with his adversary than with his fellow officers: when Don Mariano articulates a fivefold division of humanity (real men, half-men, runts, panders, and honkers), both men congratulate each other on belonging to the first category. As in a western duel, the lawman and the outlaw face off as foils of each other. Being the sole representatives of celebratory virility, they have far more in common with each other than with their underlings or the general populace.

These finer distinctions between the characters, however, are relatively inconsequential. Rather than being individualized, the personalities tend to conform to stock types (e.g., the honest cop, the pusillanimous informer, the objectified woman, the unctuous middlemen, the stoic crime boss), which is a key component of genre fiction. These various types, given the necessary transposition, are the same as those stock characters that populate westerns. The personalities remain underdeveloped, reduced to their essences, so that they inform the narrative only to the extent that they perform specific functions. Leone's 'Man with No Name' trilogy promoted the anonymous protagonist – a filmic strategy that Damiani's film both adopts and adapts. Bellodi's personal life is absent from the drama (his first name is never revealed) so that his actions are all in the service of the investigation. He is the spectators' guide through the labyrinth of the Sicilian underworld. His failure is but a didactic metaphor for the defeat of reason by a relentless and immutable reality.

What is a viewer to make of this fractured exemplum in which good does not triumph? The film's title provides a possible interpretation. The source is Shakespeare's history, *Henry VI: Part III*, in which the absence of a central power leads to a struggle of ritualized anarchy. What appears as chaos is instead a manipulated struggle of might, in which truth is suppressed to advance individual positions of power. The title's referent, which also serves as the epigraph to Sciascia's novella, is the Duke of Somerset's exhortation of Prince Edward against the King:

> And he that will not fight for such a hope
> o home to bed, and, like the owl by day,
> If he arise, be mocked and wondered at.[3]

Although Prince Edward fails, the proverbial owl elicits an ambivalent imagery that inextricably binds the narrative's two social forces, which are perennially in conflict. Captain Bellodi, the investigating officer from northern Italy, is the presumptuous owl who, like Icarus, foolishly dares to spread his wings in the light of the Sicilian sun; Don Mariano, and the mafia in general, are like the mysterious owl, harbingers of death who reign in darkness. The allusion appears to speak to Bellodi's relentless pursuit of justice, yet the owl reappears in reference to the play's villain, Richard III ('The owl shrieked at thy birth – an evil sign'),[4] and underscores the insidiousness of deceit.

The film's title, however, also supports another allusion that is absent in the literary referent: the wordplay on *civetta*, which means both little owl and flirt. Whereas in Sciascia's story, Rosa Nicolosi's character is of secondary importance, in the film she is a central figure. Torn between two men and two worlds, she is, like Bellodi, an outsider. Standing between the man of honour and the honourable man, she flirts with both in an effort to locate her missing husband. Metaphorically, she is trapped between the law and the mafia. Unsure as to which way she should turn, she appeals to both. From the police station she crosses the piazza to enter Don Mariano's house. Although the mafia is able to provide more than mere words to sustain her, Rosa is continually drawn back to Bellodi. Reprising the western genre's conflated role of homesteader/prostitute, she is the nexus between the lawman and the land. Her position, however, is tenuous and unsustainable. Both parties vie for her; neither is able to win her over. When summoned by Don Mariano's henchmen, Rosa finds in their expressions the definitive proof that they have murdered her husband. When she then turns to Bellodi, her improbable evening visit exposes their mutual failure to achieve solidarity. Each of them will disappear from the film defeated and silent. She has flirted with both sides of the piazza, but in the end she rejects both. Ultimately, as in the western, the conflict can only be resolved by men.

The resolution comes in the form of a corpse. Bellodi's insistence that Parrinieddu testify in court seals the informant's fate and is the captain's undoing as well, because his case falls apart when Parrinieddu's corpse is recovered. The informant's death begets Bellodi's disappearance from both the town and the screen. In the final scene, Bellodi has been literally and figuratively cut from the narrative. With Don Mariano overseeing the piazza from his terrace once more, the town seems to come back to life again. In a series of long shots, Don Mariano and his lackeys assess the new police captain. Wearing a dark suit, as if in mourning for his worthy adversary, the provincial potentate pronounces, 'Bellodi was a man; this one looks like a honker.' His men laugh and begin to honk under a deforming wide-angle lens while the camera lingers on the one real man left standing, who, without a worthy opponent, is surrounded on all sides by honkers.

Perhaps predictably, such a conclusion ran afoul not of the mafia, but of the government. The film premiered with a motion picture rating that barred admission to minors. The review board cited the use of vulgar language as justification for this severe rating. Moreover, the head of the board further clarified that in addition to that objectionable language, the rating was justified by the film's story, which launched 'an extremely severe and corrosive criticism of society and of the institutions, with an ending that shows that even the one character who dares oppose or resist the mafia (the captain) is at the end overcome and defeated.'[5] In other words, the review board had recognized that *The Day of the Owl*'s western accoutrements accentuated rather than attenuated the film's salient political critique because its appropriation of generic conventions reinforced the Manichaean division between the man of honour and the honourable man. Although print reviews emphasized the absurdity of the rating (which was subsequently revoked), nevertheless, this political intervention fuelled the public perception that the mafia's sphere of influence extended well beyond Sicily.

Naturally, the ratings controversy that surrounded the film's release generated publicity, which, coupled with its all-star cast, certainly contributed to *The Day of the Owl*'s success: it was the highest-grossing Italian-language film of the 1967–68 box office season. The controversy notwithstanding, another factor that attracted audiences to the theatres was the dramatic portrayal of the eternal struggle of good versus evil in a distant but recognizable reality. The transposition of the epic western onto the contemporary epoch produced a conflated narrative that resonated with the moviegoing public.[6] By drawing on a successful and popular genre, the film both appealed to a broad spectrum of viewers and offered a coherent framework through which to view the sociopolitical drama that governed the Sicilian landscape. In *The Day of the Owl*, spectators found a film at once familiar and new.[7]

Although sharing many traits with *In the Name of the Law* (e.g., the lawman who comes to Sicily from the mainland), *The Day of the Owl*'s representation of the mafia is less idealized than that of Germi's film. While Don Mariano is granted a degree of respect, the mafia does not escape the damning critique of either its violent legacy or its political corruption. Nevertheless, what emerges from this struggle between the law and the mafia is a romanticized vision, rooted in frontier folklore, of both the mafia and the justice system: when two men face off, only one can survive. The stranger who rode into town has been ridden out of town, and everyone mourns his absence.

NOTES

1 Subsequently, in his short story 'Mafia Western,' in *The Wine Dark Sea* (New York: New York Review of Books, 2000), Sciascia alluded to the commonalities between the Sicily of the mafia and the west of the gunslingers.

2 *The Day of the Owl* was shot on location in Partinico, Sicily.

3 *The True Tragedy of Richard Duke of York and the Good King Henry the Sixth*, in William Shakespeare, *The Complete Works*, ed. Stanley Wells and Gary Taylor, 2nd ed. (Oxford: Clarendon Press, 2005), 121.

4 Ibid., 122.

5 From the censorship visa (n. 50887), which is quoted in Alberto Pezzotta, *Regia Damiano Damiani* (Pordenone: Cinemazero, 2004), 205. Rather than the vulgarity, the film's reviewers tended to identify the scene of Don Mariano entering the Christian Democrats' local headquarters as the smoking gun.

6 Upon its release, the critics Gregorio Napoli and Gian Luigi Rondi noted the 'western' influence on the film. See Gregorio Napoli, 'Il giorno della civetta,' *Il Domani*, 29 February 1968; Gian Luigi Rondi, 'Il giorno della civetta,' *Il tempo*, 23 February 1968.

7 Between 1964 and 1969, Italian westerns ranked either first or second (vying with the James Bond films for the top spot) in box office receipts.

32   Smaller and Larger Families: Lina Wertmüller's
The Seduction of Mimi

THOMAS HARRISON

The appeal of Lina Wertmüller's films derives from many sources – their visual opulence, their performative exuberance, their satirical and parodic charge – but all of these pleasures are anchored in the paradoxical structure of the narratives. In the case before us – *Mimì metallurgico ferito nell'onore* (*The Seduction of Mimi*, 1972) – our very likable main character begins as one of only a handful of people in a Sicilian town with the courage to defy the wishes of the mafia. He then goes on to capture the full extent of our sympathy in his efforts to become a self-made man. Yet all of it comes to naught when, for a series of very unfortunate reasons, he turns into the very mafia collaborator he inveighed against in the beginning. In the last scene, in an exact inversion of the film's opening, Mimi, his independence, hopes, and ideals all shattered, exhorts his fellow Sicilians to vote for the new mafia political candidate.

What Wertmüller stresses more strongly than any other Italian director with this kind of narrative reversal is not simply the ethical pressure that outside circumstances bring to bear on Italian males (this has been the recurrent theme of Italian comic cinema since the late 1950s). It is rather the *dependence* of such males on these circumstances and their abnormal subservience, which thoroughly compromises their morals. Wertmüller proposes an explanation, as it were, for why characters like Mimi, and Pasqualino in *Pasqualino settebellezze* (*Seven Beauties*, 1975), fail to be true to their better selves: their culture does not foster self-reliance. By no small irony, this makes them susceptible to the corruptive power of forces *that endow them with a semblance of self-reliance*, forces that ensure public respect for people who do not stand on their own two feet: forces like the mafia. At its most fundamental level, the mafia in this film is an allegory for group control over the individual, a syndrome that Wertmüller declares symptomatic of the entire country. The mafia is a synecdoche for Sicily – a part that stands for the whole, a whole that the film then equates with the Italian nation's body politic. By the close of the film, the mafia has turned into the 'true face' of Italy, denying its citizens any illusion of free choice, individuality, or subjective autonomy. This is the cynical and bitter comedy of Lina Wertmüller, achieved through paradoxical turns in the story.

Set in the years immediately preceding its release, *Mimi* pays particular attention to the travails of Italy during that stressful time – above all, to the ideological and political tensions that exploded in the 'hot autumn' of student and worker protests of 1969. Complicating the sociopolitical landscape further, the film's story straddles the geocultural divide between Torino and Sicily. It pits north against south, progressiveness against tradition, industrial against agrarian society, and the spirit of the metropolis against that of the province. These opposing elements in the peninsula's cultural infrastructure play crucial roles as Mimi migrates from one part of the country to another and falls into a conflict between two fundamentally incompatible ethical allegiances. One is to liberal individualism (which was taking root in the industrial north throughout the 1960s, much like the American model, and which was committed to the moral ideal of shaping one's own destiny); the other is to an ethics of communal, patriarchal honour (associated since time immemorial with southern Italy, the family, Sicily, and the subordination of the individual to the group). The narrative premise of this paradoxical story is that Mimi has the power to liberate himself from the second allegiance in the interests of the first one. In fact, the film seems to be the story of a successful emancipation, one that steadily grows until it finally comes undone. When Mimi's wife is unfaithful to him – liberating herself, ironically, from him – he devises an intricate scheme to defend his wounded honour. But it turns out that the master plan behind this and other events has already been laid by the mafia.

The film presents conflicting allegiances within one and the same man, yet the more we reflect on it, the more this struggle appears to amount merely to a secondary distinction within a single, unexamined allegiance of Mimi to the group that surrounds him and from which he tends to obtain his directives. When Mimi becomes a *picciotto*, or soldier, of the mafia – and *because* he becomes a *picciotto* – we begin to wonder whether even before, when he was acting as a liberal, proactive, politically responsible citizen in Torino, he was not simply adapting to the people around him, presenting another cinematic exhibit of the time-honoured Italian 'art of getting by.' In any event, public life determines Mimi's behaviour throughout the film by applying two forms of public pressure. The first is associated with a group of exploited leftist labourers in metropolitan Torino, the second with the close-minded community of the Sicilian town in which he was reared. Up north, our hero endorses the workers' communist ideology as willingly as he does the romantic anarchy of his girlfriend Fiore. This is the *new*, self-made Mimi, who proves so endearing to the film's viewers, now that he has left behind his home province's social constraints (grotesquely portrayed by his father, his whining wife Rosalia, and his aunts and widows, who dress like furies). When placed under pressure, however, his newfound northern persona proves no match for the power of his native Sicily, with its ideology of family honour and the fragility of the male reputation on which it stands.

This second power is given an unlikely face, that of the mafia. Mimi in no way chooses to bond with the mob; rather, he chooses to defend his honour, which just happens to be the mob's moral recruiting ground. By helping to restore his social standing, the mafia binds Mimi to them in such a way that he will never be able to shake them off. Although Mimi attempts to handle the disgrace of his wife's adultery in a modern and original way ('like a civilized man!'), Wertmüller implies that his very openness to this game of honour politics can only subject him to a coercive, male-centred system of power, whose symbol and perfected organ is the mafia. After condensing Mimi's second allegiance – the ideology of family honour, or southern group thought *tout court* – down to a mafia ethic, Wertmüller builds that ethic up to the level of a widely diffused, even nationally based, capitulation of the individual to a group. This becomes clear in the metaphor of worker–management relations. When Mimi acts as foreman for the mob's construction company in Sicily, he refuses to let his workers strike. In Torino, striking had been a means to rebel against systematically enforced conformity. (Even there he had stopped participating in strikes once his son was born, provoking the ire of his co-workers.) When striking is not allowed, mob thinking has won.

As the film progresses, the semantic associations of the smaller Sicilian family to which Mimi belongs get transferred to this larger Family.[1] It is as though Wertmüller intends to instantiate the belief that the very model for mob thinking lies in the patriarchal family structure – or more particularly, in the defensive, protective folds of that type of Sicilian family so intricately illustrated by the films of Pietro Germi, a family that is lorded over and coerced by a boss. This is not the aristocratic Sicilian family of Giuseppe Tomasi di Lampedusa's *Il gattopardo* (*The Leopard*, 1958), inheriting its power by birthright. It is rather a middle-class or lower-middle-class family that can gain its power only by force and that hones its instruments in the private domain (analogously, notes Siebert, the mafia family is 'a hybrid of peasant culture and petty-bourgeois culture').[2] Broadly speaking, this coercive family is the kind of patriarchal nuclear unit that the psychologist Wilhelm Reich locates at the base of fascist politics. Ordered by means of 'suppression and repression', it aims at 'the economic and authoritarian enslavement of women and children'.[3] When nuclear family identification is extended outwards (for instance, in a provincial town), it turns into clan identification. This broader clan, in turn, possesses its own patriarch. One complies with the will of the patriarch in both the smaller and the larger family, essentially to ensure protection, not least from the patriarch himself.

The 'genetic' tie between the nuclear family and the mafia one is drawn to great comic effect in the first sequence of the film, where Mimi's private household is conversing about the behaviour that an external, larger Family expects of them. Political elections are scheduled for the following day, and Mimi has already publicly declared what he thinks of the mafia candidate Cannamozza ('A son of a whore!'). Inside Mimi's house, he and his father are having their feet washed by four women (wives and relatives) and debating their political obligations. Over Mimi's very strong objections, his father declares that he plans to deliver the mob his promised six votes (his own, plus those of Mimi, his wife, and the other three women). The scene makes clear that the men of this family are expected to vote the way of the clan boss, and the women the way of their men. The subordination of the two males to a broader social order is of a piece with that of the women within this particular family. The ambiguous analogy between the two orders is ironically intimated by an outburst from Mimi's father in favour of the mob candidate Cannamozza: 'Shut up and vote for him! You're not going to marry him!'

The staging of this kind of discussion while the men's feet are being washed by the women reveals precisely the visual opulence, the performative exuberance, and the satirical charge that strengthens Wertmüller's paradoxical commentaries. The scene *illustrates* the family dynamics that underpin their external, communal allegiances and dramatizes the distributions of power that make such allegiances all but compulsory. The issue at stake is further elaborated in the film's next scene, where Mimi is attempting to make love to his wife. The young couple are sharing a room with the larger family and are thus compelled to whisper. Clearly, their behaviour is being subjugated by the patriarchal community, represented by the ancestral portraits looking down on them above the bed. Uncomfortable with the conditions of this interaction, Mimi's wife Rosalia has trouble experiencing erotic abandon. Mimi instead orders her to fulfil her wifely duties. Undone by her sniffling and squeaking voice, he ultimately gives up. But he does not let off before cursing her and insisting on his political privilege: 'Tomorrow I forbid you to vote for Cannamozza!' This injection of politics into the bedroom may be more than a way for Mimi to console himself for a loss. It suggests that the mafioso social structure to which he objects – governed by coercive interpersonal relations – is operative in his very own family.

The next day the pressure is on Mimi himself. He ends up defying more than one father with his anti-mafia vote, and finds to his surprise that he has no choice but to clear out of town. He picks up and heads to Torino, cursing the entire system of southern familism in an effort to embrace his freedom.[4] As mentioned, the sequence of events in the northern industrial city portrays a series of apparently successful adventures in self-making, as Mimi dictates the conditions of his work, establishes an original and personal relationship with Fiore, has a child out of love, and so on. But even so, the hoped-for emancipation fails. The main reason for the failure is to be founnd in Mimi's naive belief that the rule of this familism is restricted to his native Catania. In truth, that belief is challengèd the very instant Mimi applies for work in the city, where the entire workspace is revealed to be operating under the tutelage of the Sicilian mafia. Euphemistically labelled the 'Association of Sicilian Brothers,' they allocate migrant workers to illegal construction projects and exhort them to behave like brothers 'without breaking our balls.' One day, Mimi happens to witness the death of an undocumented worker and is threatened with murder. How does he save his skin? By invoking his family ties. He informs the boss of this Sicilian Association that Rosalia is the godchild of Don Calogero Liggio of the Corleone clan (or, more exactly, the godchild of the cousin of the boss). But still this matters, for the tentacles of the *piovra* reach that far. This genealogical tie is perfectly sufficient to make the Turinese boss Tricarico consider himself bound to Mimi in the folds of the larger Family. From such a parentage comes a proper job for Mimi at an auto plant, with state-backed benefits. Ironically, Mimi's entry into a national workers' union is enabled by precisely what it is designed to replace: the local family union.

The reach of familism into even the industrial north of Italy is the real reason for the failure of Mimi's self-making. No place in the country is outside of the Family. The grotesque mafia system gives the impression of grafting family structure onto vaster social networks, expanding family ethics and organization into the realm of politics proper, beginning with the *polis* and reaching out to the nation and eventually even beyond. Ideologically speaking, the mafia gains credit by invoking a sanctification *and* political apotheosis of certain principles of the patriarchal family, including the infrangible bonds of brotherhood, unconditional loyalty, and the ultimate power of a family head. Without a doubt, the mafia family is largely rhetorical – more of an idea than a sociological fact. It forges its bonds by vaunting a philosophy of brotherhood whose ideals are as strong as its basis is weak. The ritual, performative brotherhood of the mafia is an utterly relative phenomenon, subject at a moment's notice to revision.[5] What is more firm and less negotiable is the *filial* dimension of its obligation. Whether brother or father, the unquestioned issue is the lordship of the family over law. Where other societies grant God or the consensual agreements of men the prerogative of legislating justice, the mafia makes it a family matter.

The defence of masculine honour and the respectable standing of the family are no small part of the mafia's obligation and promise. Aiming at more than the material and political advantage of its members, the mob guarantees them a place in a stable ethical tradition. That tradition identifies public honour with private power, thus appealing especially to those whose place in the family has been offended. Prospective inductees into the mafia are socially 'rescued' at the expense of becoming permanently indebted to a larger and more powerful Family. They acquire a facsimile of self-reliance at the price of capitulation. The daily bread of mafia offerings – between its rarer and grander feasts – are honour crimes: restitutions through violence of an individual's standing within a family. This standing is judged, of course, by the standards of the broader Family.

Mimi's greatest illusions concern the reach of this larger Family. As the events of the film progress, it becomes clear that what appears to him at first to be merely a local, Sicilian institution is in fact geographically and culturally tentacular. The mafia controls the factories and corporate interests of the north, and it controls key figures in the federal government of Rome and in the Vatican. Considering how early the film was made, and the historical discoveries made soon after by the Italian press, this 'fictive' postulate proves to be nothing less than prescient. The mafioso Don Liggio in Catania explains how it works. He assures Mimi that his Sicilian organization needs no coup d'état to control the country; they achieve their ends through a nationwide strategy of tension, punctuated by well-placed bombs, kidnappings, and scattered acts of civil unrest. Roman politicians never forget to whom they owe the maintenance of public order. More than a decade would pass before the Italian judiciary and the media unearthed incontrovertible evidence of these bonds between the mafia and sectors of the national legislature and law enforcement – bonds running all the way up to prime ministers and symbolically condensed in an alleged kiss exchanged between Giulio Andreotti and Toto Riina, the reputed boss of all bosses of the Sicilian mafia.[6]

Wertmüller's *Mimi* brazenly inflates the mafia family to incorporate members of Italy's core political institutions. If most of the mafiosi are small-timers in Sicily, a considerably more important one turns up at the head of a homicide investigation in Torino. Others run for political office. And in this film's crescendo, another one appears in the guise of a Catholic cardinal at the scene of Mimi's botched honour killing. The result is that Wertmüller ultimately identifies the mafia with the very power structure of Italian politics. Never to be accused of excessive subtlety, Wertmüller gives them a special theme song in the soundtrack: the Italian national anthem. Each time a mafioso appears on the screen, the orchestra fires up the song 'Brothers of Italy,' written by Goffredo Mameli in 1847 and patriotically adopted as the unifying hymn of the nation. With these unusual visual referents on the screen, however, the words become profoundly ironic:

> Brothers of Italy, Italy has awoken, with Scipio's helmet binding its head.
> …
> Let us join in a cohort, We are ready for death. We are ready for death,
> Italy has called!
> …
> For centuries we were
> Downtrodden and derided, because we are not one people, because we are divided.
> …
> Let us unite and love one another …

Bathing the visuals of mafiosi in this sonorous hymn by Mameli is tantamount to equating Italian national unity with the brotherhood of the mob. The song's national brotherhood is nothing less than a family of the mafia, with no remainder. This opens the way for an endless series of explanations and alibis, including the very last one in the film, which offers its conclusive statement. Campaigning on behalf of the mafia, Mimi is abandoned by Fiore and his son, and cries out in desperate attempt to justify himself, 'But they are all cousins!!'

NOTES

1 The analogies and intimate connections between the nuclear family and the Family of the mob are elaborated by Renate Siebert in *Secrets of Life and Death: Women and the Mafia*, trans. Liz Heron (London: Verso, 1996). Exploiting the emotional charge of 'honour, shame and vendetta' (35), mafia leaders 'rule their own "Family" in the image and likeness of the blood family' (32). Wertmüller's own aversion to the nuclear family, which she blames in many ways for the broader ills of Italy, is eloquently stated in her interview with Gideon Bachman, 'Look Gideon …', *Film Quarterly* 30, no. 3 (1977): 2–11.

2 Siebert, *Secrets of Life and Death*, 32.

3 Wilhelm Reich, *The Sexual Revolution: Toward a Self-Governing Character Structure*, trans. Theodore P. Wolfe (New York: Orgone Institute Press, 1945), 10, 29.

4 This entire sequence – if not the entire film – is an oblique critique of the 'amoral familism' associated with southern Italian communities by Edward Banfield, where the governing ethical consideration is what profits the immediate nuclear family rather than the larger, concentric communities to which the family belongs. One's moral debts thus follow favours received, just as one builds up credit by bestowing such favours. See Edward C. Banfield with the assistance of Laura Fasano Banfield, *The Moral Basis of a Backward Society* (New York: The Free Press, 1958), esp. 83–102.

5 On the ritualistic dimensions of the mafia brotherhood, the characteristics of 'men of honour,' and the coalitions composing the unity they dub Family, see Anton Blok, *Honour and Violence* (Malden, MA: Blackwell, 2001), esp. 87–102.

6 For the historical discoveries this film adumbrates, see Alexander Stille, *Excellent Cadavers: The Mafia and the Death of the First Italian Republic* (New York: Pantheon, 1996). Giulio Andreotti, convicted of mob murder in 2002 but later acquitted of that charge, was the model for *The Godfather: Part III*'s Don Licio Lucchesi, a high-ranking Italian politician with ties to the mafia. More recently, Andreotti's mafia ties – and the kiss with Riina – were imaginatively dramatized in the film *Il divo* (2008) by Paolo Sorrentino.

33   Deconstructing the Enigma: Logical Investigations in Francesco Rosi's *Lucky Luciano*

GAETANA MARRONE

'In the future, when historians want to learn about Italy's postwar years,' the film critic Gian Piero Brunetta writes, 'Rosi's films will become vital sources of information, not less significant than many thousands of written pages compiled by the Anti-Mafia Commission or court proceedings, police reports, and state documents housed both in Italian and American archives ... Rosi's films most importantly will help understand the mafia's ascent to power, exposing its strategic control over the political, economic and social sphere.'[1]

Brunetta's assessment of Francesco Rosi's fascination with national history and politics confirms the director's reputation as an auteur who believes that the main function of cinema is to report and to witness reality.[2] What interests Rosi most is a method of inquiry grounded in factual interpretation and a strong sense of the director's responsibility to his audience. Rosi's films rely on an intricate, labyrinthine narrative structure in which the sense of an enigma replaces a unidirectional path that promises to lead one to a definitive truth. They bring to light the hidden threads that weave the fabric of what the director calls 'another possible truth,' one that challenges the official point of view.[3] Rosi is ultimately concerned neither with searching for the absolute truth nor with following a traditional story. The important thing for Rosi is to interpret reality and to look at facts differently, without attempting to solve the puzzle.

Francesco Rosi has tackled social and political subjects since the late 1950s. He has taken special care to examine the perspective from which criminal power groups will be investigated: from the Neapolitan Camorra (*La sfida* [*The Challenge*], 1958; *I magliari* [*The Swindlers*], 1959), to the Sicilian mafia and political conspiracy (*Salvatore Giuliano*, 1962; *Cadaveri eccellenti* [*Illustrious Corpses*], 1976; *Dimenticare Palermo* [*The Palermo Connection*], 1990), to the paradoxes of a criminal society in the portrait of mafia boss Lucky Luciano. His logical investigations are translated into a cinematic approach that presents the details of material reality through the perspective of a dispassionate observer. Over the years, Rosi has questioned the most notorious mysteries of the Italian Democratic Republic, from the murder of legendary bandit Salvatore Giuliano, to the death in a plane crash of oil tycoon Enrico Mattei, to the dark connections between American politicians and Italian mafiosi in *Lucky Luciano* (1973). 'One should be careful,' says the Neapolitan director, 'not to fall into a trap, which is almost inevitable for individuals in the performing arts, of mythologizing the mafia or of representing it in a romantic light ... One risks the danger of creating heroes, even negative ones, but they are still heroes.'[4]

Rosi chooses instead to make films based on real facts involving characters with real names in order to avoid inventive fiction. Indeed, filming and writing the mafia requires some preliminary reflections. In the late 1970s, Marcelle Padovani, a journalist with *Le Nouvel Observateur*, asked Leonardo Sciascia whether his view of the mafia had changed over the years. The Sicilian writer replied by recounting one exemplary episode: a funereal *carte-souvenir* printed by the family of Francesco Di Cristina (*capomafia* of the Sicilian town of Riesi) upon his passing in 1961. Besides the customary emblems, this document included an unusual eulogy:

> Realizing himself across the complete gamut of human possibilities, he showed the world how much a man could be. In him virtue and intelligence, wisdom and strength of soul, were happily joined for the good of the humble, for the defeat of the arrogant. He worked upon the earth, imposing on his fellow men respect for the eternal values of the human personality. The enemy of all injustice, he demonstrated in word and deed that *his Mafia was not criminal*, but respectful of the law of honor and the defender of every right.[5]

As Sciascia notes, the word "mafia" appears for the first time in a printed document used by the inner circle of the mafia milieu, in which a distinction is made between Di Cristina's mafia and other kinds, which can be merely criminal. In light of the battle that Italian society has begun to wage against the mafia, even more disquieting was the extent of the town's public display of mourning years later on 1 June 1978 at the funeral of Francesco's son, Giuseppe Di Cristina, who was killed while on bail from prison. For the citizens of Riesi, that ceremony was expressive of their lives, of a mode of being: 'it was a function of the one law they truly knew – a moral and practical law, ruling affections and effects, in both the interior and the social order.'[6] We are reminded of Luigi Barzini's historical introduction to the Sicilian *onorata società* in his book *The Italians* (1964). Indeed, more traditional mafiosi want to maintain the fiction that they are not ordinary criminals. The *società* is a rough version of the code of chivalry that the Normans brought to the island in 1070. This distinguishes the Sicilian mafia from strictly criminal organizations such as the American so-called mafia.[7]

In America, almost everything about the mafia appears mythical and monumental. This is true of its cinematic representations and of the stories of bloody survival that the very name of the mafia evokes. It is also true of the ordinary pursuits and passions that constitute the daily lives of mafiosi, men who can keep a secret and do favours and who enjoy unequivocal power and authority. Francis Ford Coppola's *The Godfather* (1972) elevates its story of an American mafia 'family' into an epic melodrama. Photographed by the great cinematographer Gordon Willis (who was famous for his low-key lighting), the film uses mainly top light, which creates suffocatingly heavy shadows . From the opening shot of Vito Corleone, the lighting effect is foreboding. In this shadowy world, a mythical figure is created, one that demands respect, *omertà* (a conspiracy of silence), and a code of honour. For Coppola, the film is not solely a story about gangsters; it represents a family chronicle as 'a metaphor for capitalism in America.'[8]

Mob violence is also an expression of larger social forces. Violence was a means of survival for Sicilian immigrants, who found themselves surrounded by a hostile society. In the *Godfather* trilogy, violence finds an almost perfect balance in the scene when a poor and helpless widow turns to a young Vito for protection in retaining her dwelling. This is a primordial and romantic expression of mafia power, with its blend of ruthless brutality and noble sentiments. It is modelled on the old Sicilian *società*, not on the more modern and lucrative mafia, which exacts tribute from all kinds of activities. But even in Martin Scorsese's *Goodfellas* (1990), which exemplifies the latter, the fluid camera moves create a lyrical atmosphere despite the abysmal breaking apart of the Cosa Nostra: at the end, the mafiosi betray one another for drugs. They commit what is the ultimate crime for all mafia men: *infamità*, or talking to the authorities.

There is no denying that the mafia in the American cinematic tradition expresses above all else a fascination with theatrical grandeur. In describing his own *Lucky Luciano* as a film about 'how' the mafia gains political influence and infiltrates the institutions of the state, Rosi warns us to be careful about how we interpret such stylized mafia films.[9] His investigation into the final years of the life of the notorious Italian American *capomafia* – who was handed a thirty- to fifty-year sentence by the State of New York in 1936, was parolled to the US Army during the Second World War, and was eventually deported to his native Sicily in 1946 – does not aim at establishing the incontestable facts. In the Luciano affair, the truth remains elusive: after years of thorough investigation, the confidential reports of the FBI and the Narcotics Bureau concluded that there was *no evidence* against him. Rosi's probing look at the dark connections between American politicians and (inter)national criminal practices provides a context, as Paul Taylor writes in *Time Out*, 'for the *Godfather* films which threatens to outdo their own cinematic forcefulness.'[10]

Rosi has a pessimistic view of corruption. For him, the 'spectacle' of corrupt power coexists with a close observation of daily life and behaviour. The story he tells is not meant to be entertainment but is represented as an ongoing drama, as something that affects people from all walks of life. Thus the mafia becomes a term of nuance and hidden meaning, not only in the cultural heritage of many Sicilians but also in the art of politics. In *Lucky Luciano*, Rosi seeks the real reasons why the so-called Boss of Bosses was sent back to Italy on 11 February 1946, at the intervention of New York governor Thomas E. Dewey, the same special prosecutor who had convicted him of racketeering on 19 June 1936. Is Luciano the greatest criminal genius of his generation, the founder of the new mafia, or is he a shallow and parasitic individual dominated by a craving for violent action, as the court documents attest?

While drafting the film's preliminary treatment, the director asked: 'Why invent when reality provides narrative possibilities which indeed are at the origin of every fiction? And most importantly when one can offer the audience the possibility of verification?'[11] Rosi's documentation of Salvatore Lucania (1897–1962), alias Charles 'Lucky' Luciano, aims at penetrating and remapping the maze of subterranean truths. Newspaper clippings, photographs, books, archival materials, interviews, witnesses, and television coverage of senate hearings become his interpretative tools for uncovering the facts.[12] The film keeps the audience at a distance, especially with its portrayal of Luciano himself, as is evident in the powerful, reserved performance of Gian Maria Volontè. Luciano appears to be a reclusive gentleman living a quiet life, and he has comparatively few lines of dialogue.

The basic plot of *Lucky Luciano* concerns the events that followed Luciano's repatriation to Italy in 1946. Rosi takes a raw journalistic approach, established by a typical newscast with voiceover and a documentary camera style. The main credits are shown over an inscription claiming that Luciano's mysterious release is due to special services provided to the armed forces during wartime. However, Rosi also alludes to his alleged contributions to Dewey's presidential campaign fund, and as the film unfolds, he makes it clear that the US Army bears some responsibility for the mafia's criminal activities.[13] The New York waterfront opening suggests that Rosi is conducting an audiovisual inquiry into the Luciano case and that he is attempting to go beyond the versions of the story conveyed by the printed word. For example, the audience witnesses Luciano leaving America from the point of view of a camera hidden inside the window of a disguised police van. Rosi also establishes a tie between Luciano and Charles Siragusa, a special agent of the Narcotics Bureau: both are Sicilians, though they represent the two opposing faces of Sicily.

Luciano, who was born in the small town of Lercara Friddi, became the 'Boss of Bosses' of the Italian American underworld on the night of 10–11 September 1931, when he climbed to power by eliminating some forty older and higher-ranking mafiosi (the so-called Sicilian Vespers). A few months earlier, on 15 April 1931, the mythical Joe the Boss (Giuseppe Masseria) had been executed inside Scarpato's restaurant on Coney Island while Luciano was washing his hands in the men's room. The film represents the massacre in a flashback sequence that is both operatic and highly graphic: the killings happen in smoky, dark alleys, parking garages, hospital rooms, and restaurants. Shot in slow motion, this bloody montage visualizes the appalling horror of organized crime. 'From that time onwards,' explains Giuseppe Prezzolini, 'the *gangster* has forged a path comparable to that of America, one that reflects her expansion, vitality, risks, and also political vicissitudes.'[14]

Rosi peers deep into the complexities of mafia life. When Luciano lands in Sicily, he first visits his hometown cemetery before moving on to Naples. In the cemetery, the camera pans from one tombstone to another, revealing that all the individuals had died violent deaths. Thus the past and the present are fused. But at no point does Rosi directly indict Luciano, who was suspected of controlling the flow of heroin from legal Italian pharmaceutical companies into the United States. In the scene when Eugene Giannini comes to visit him in 1952, we only get a tour of the ruins of Pompeii, with Luciano benignly uttering, 'My friends come to visit me like tourists.' Known to Interpol for drug trafficking, Giannini plays a dangerous double game between the Narcotics Bureau and the mafia and is eventually silenced by Joe Valachi (presumably on Luciano's orders). During a press conference in Naples, Luciano denounces the accusations made against him: 'Every time something happens, they point the finger at me … But my hands are clean. I regularly pay my taxes. They have no proof against me. They never will.'[15] Indeed, even Charles Siragusa, who plays himself in the film, is forced to admit to an Italian judge, 'What kind of crimes has he committed? He was arrested once, a long time ago, for a brawl. Then he was convicted once on prostitution charges. But is this a murder?'[16] For many years Siragusa had tried to gather evidence against Luciano, but he never succeeded in making a case against him, and he was eventually transferred off the case in 1958. During the production of the film, he continued to claim:

> Ten years after his death, I am convinced more than ever that Lucky Luciano was the real boss and genius behind the international drug smuggling operations. Had he not died, I would have arrested him, sooner or later. I must confess that I hated him. He was the exact opposite of a true Italian American like myself. This was not only a struggle between the law and organized crime, but also a personal fight man to man.[17]

But Barzini, among others, contradicts this theory about a worldwide conspiracy with headquarters in Italy:

There are Americans who believe that criminal groups in their country belong to the Sicilian Mafia … This myth is shared even by some naïve American criminals of Italian descent, who learned it by reading the newspapers. They sometimes land in Sicily believing not only that they belong to the *società* but they have a high rank in it … One of the gullible Americans was Lucky Luciano. When he arrived in Palermo, deported from the United States, the police official who had to watch his movements said: 'He believes he is a big shot in the Mafia, the poor innocent man.'[18]

To this day, the Luciano affair remains ambiguous. For Rosi, a character like Lucky Luciano is at once a criminal and an emblem of power relations.

Rosi is deliberately ambiguous in his treatment of these power relations. The film raises several unresolved questions about Luciano's release from prison, the nature of his Washington connections, and the needs of the American mafia. Near the end of the film, when he is brought in for questioning by the Italian police, in a rare speech, Luciano declares cynically that everyone, mafia and police alike, is used by politicians, who want to keep the people in the dark: 'They use us to cover up their muck. The politicians never had any trouble in manoeuvring with racketeering and mafiosi.' He also accuses Siragusa and the police chief of trying to build their careers by using him. Luciano becomes sick during the interrogation, and when he later goes to the Naples airport to meet a writer who has scripted his life story for a film, he suffers a fatal heart attack. The end credits run over a freeze-frame of the lifeless body of Luciano, while we hear in voiceover these concluding remarks:

SIRAGUSA: What do I do now?
ANSLINGER: Well, you keep on chasing Luciano, Dewey will keep on chasing us, Kefauver will keep on chasing Dewey, and when this running around is over, everybody will find himself back at the same goddamn place where he started.

From the beginning of his career, Rosi has disdained simplistic solutions to complex problems such as the mafia and political corruption. He has tried to capture the interplay of responsibility between legal and illegal power in order to shed light on why every attempt to eradicate the mafia has failed. *Lucky Luciano* remains enigmatic, particularly because Rosi deprives us of a reassuring ending. Instead, we are left on a macroscopic threshold above which we perceive a whole with one piece missing. The director acknowledges: 'I do not pretend to have made a useful film, but to have at least started a discussion, in historical and political terms, not fictional, about the so-called problem of the mafia in the cinema, beyond the picturesque and elusive image that so many films and literature have given and continue to do so.'[19]

Lucky Luciano may be, in Norman Mailer's words, 'the finest movie yet made about the Mafia, the most careful, the most thoughtful, the truest and most sensitive.'[20] And perhaps the only possible form of truth, as Sciascia puts it, is that of art.[21] Ultimately, we only expect films from Rosi that speak to our conscience, films that clear some but not all of the fog, films that in their unresolved endings encourage us to seek the solution for ourselves.[22] As for Lucky Luciano, who lived the legendary life of a boss of bosses and was forever tormented by his nostalgia for America, he died thinking of a film based on his life.

NOTES

1 'Rosi e il tempo del sud,' in *Francesco Rosi*, ed. Sebastiano Gesù (Acicatena, Catania: Incontri con il Cinema, 1991), 43. All translations are mine.

2 See 'Lezione di cinema a Cannes: Cinema ed educazione,' in *Francesco Rosi*, ed. Vittorio Giacci (Rome: Edizioni Cinecittà International, 1995), 49.

3 See 'Rosi parla di Rosi,' in Anton Giulio Mancino and Sandro Zambetti, *Francesco Rosi* (Milan: Editrice Il Castoro, 1995), 5.

4 Ibid., 6.

5 Leonardo Sciascia, *Sicily as Metaphor*, conversations presented by Marcelle Padovani, trans. James Marcus (Marlboro, VT: Marlboro Press, 1994), 36. Emphasis mine.

6 Ibid., 40.

7 See Luigi Barzini, *The Italians* (Toronto: Bantam Books, 1965), 267–8.

8 As cited in Robert Evans, *The Kid Stays in the Picture* (New York: Hyperion, 1994), 220.

9 See Francesco Rosi, 'Perché Luciano,' in Lino Jannuzzi and Francesco Rosi, *Lucky Luciano* (Milan: Bompiani, 1973), viii. This volume includes various excerpts from official documents on Luciano, among them testimonies by Meyer Lansky, Frank Costello, Joe Valachi, and FBI agent Charles Siragusa.

10 Cited in 'Illustrious Corpses,' *Pacific Cinémathèque Program Guide* (November–December 1994), 8.

11 I am quoting from Francesco Rosi, 'A proposito di Lucky Luciano,' October 1972, Francesco Rosi's personal archives.

12 Rosi's biographical and historical documentation relies primarily on Sid Feder and Joachim Joesten, *The Luciano Story* (New York: D. McKay, 1954); Frederick Sondern, *Brotherhood of Evil: The Mafia* (New York: Farrar, Straus and Giroux, 1958); Estes Kefauver's report on organized crime, *Crime in America* (New York: Didier, 1951); and the photographic services of *Life* magazine.

13 Army officers had installed known mafiosi in political positions and allowed them to control the black market (see, for example, the flashback that details the collaboration between an army officer and Vito Genovese).

14 Giuseppe Prezzolini, *I trapiantati* (Milan: Longanesi, 1963), 159.

15 From *Lucky Luciano*, promotional material from French Press Book, 1973, 6.

16 Ibid. Siragusa met Rosi in New York in 1972 during pre-production, and he was immediately asked to play his own role in the film.

17 Ibid., 20.

18 Barzini, *The Italians*, 282–3.

19 Rosi, 'Perché Luciano,' vi–vii, x.

20 Cited in 'Illustrious Corpses,' 8.

21 Sciascia, *Sicily as Metaphor*, 97.

22 See Lino Miccichè, 'Breve storia di un destino,' *L'espresso*, 11 February 1990, 71.

34 Power as Such: The Idea of the Mafia in Francesco Rosi's *Illustrious Corpses*

ALAN O'LEARY

Cadaveri eccellenti (*Illustrious Corpses*, Francesco Rosi, 1976) is a metaphysical detective story about state corruption and oppression in post–Second World War Italy. The film is adapted from the short novel *Il contesto* (*Equal Danger*) by the well-known Sicilian writer Leonardo Sciascia. The mafia appears in *Illustrious Corpses* in the form of two minor characters in the first section of the film, which takes place in a Sicilian setting, and it is shown to have close ties with the judiciary and so with the state.[1] I am not concerned in this chapter, however, with the film's portrayal of the literal mafia, but with its use of the mafia as a figure for arrogant, self-serving, homosocial structures of power. Peter Bondanella writes that *Illustrious Corpses* is 'a chilling parable of the intricate link between political power and corruption … in which the Sicilian mafia is transformed into a universally comprehensible metaphor for corrupt absolute power anywhere in the world.'[2] I follow Bondanella's interpretation of *Illustrious Corpses* to certain extent; however, I will place greater emphasis on the specific historical situation in Italy that generated the film, and also on the arguably perplexing (as distinct from the 'universally comprehensible') nature of the central metaphor it employs.

The story of *Illustrious Corpses* concerns the investigation of a series of murders of powerful judges, taking place first in a province identifiable as Sicily and then in the 'capital.'[3] The investigation is assigned to one inspector Rogas, a deliberately clichéd figure derived from any number of gruff literary and cinematic detectives. Rogas comes to believe the killings are the work of a man named Cres, who was wrongly accused of the attempted murder of his beautiful wife. The investigation becomes a political matter when the murders continue in the capital, and it seems to suit the powers that be to blame the youth protest movement for the assassinations. Rogas resigns, but continues his investigation and suspects that the murders are being exploited to facilitate a coup d'état, and indeed that the armed forces have been continuing the cycle of murders initiated by Cres. The detective decides to tell the leader of the Communist Party, Amar, about the conspiracy, but in the penultimate scene both men are shot and killed by an unseen assassin. Rather than tell the public the truth, and so risk violent confrontation between party supporters and the military, the Communist Party (represented in the film by the Revolutionary Party) adheres to the official line that Rogas murdered Amar.[4]

The fear of a coup d'état was very real in the first half of the 1970s in Italy. Indeed, there had been several attempted takeovers orchestrated by the military during the 1960s, the most recent having been the abortive coup attempt led by Prince Valerio Borghese in 1970. Successful coups d'état had, of course, taken place in Greece, Chile, and Portugal in 1967, 1973, and 1974, respectively, leading to dictatorial governments and the suppression of opposition. In response to this persistent menace, Enrico Berlinguer, the leader of the Italian Communist Party (the largest opposition party in Italy as well as the largest communist party in the Western world), offered a rapprochement with the Christian Democrats, the party that had been in government since the late 1940s, either alone or more often in a coalition. This arrangement, known as the 'Historic Compromise', would guarantee the qualified support of the Communists for the government in order to strengthen the democratic centre of Italian politics against any authoritarian threat. At the same time, the extreme right (facilitated by elements in the Italian secret services and armed forces) were engaged in a bombing campaign that targeted public spaces across the country and that came to be known as the Strategy of Tension.[5] The public was unaware that these acts of violence against innocent civilians were being perpetrated by state officials. This strategy was designed to foment widespread fear and lawlessness that would render a military or authoritarian takeover of the Italian government an attractive the idea to the public. It was also, to some extent at least, a reactionary response to the student and worker protests that had been a feature of Italian society in the late 1960s and that would continue for another decade.

This is the historical context in which *Illustrious Corpses* was made and in which it should be understood. At a fundamental level, the film is a fable about the Strategy of Tension as well as being a kind of polemic against the Historic Compromise, an agreement implicitly criticized in *Illustrious Corpses* as playing into the hands of the ruling Christian Democrat Party. The film shows the student movement as being well-intentioned but peripheral and as a convenient scapegoat useful for the renovation of the status quo – though such an interpretative choice may well have been a consequence of the focus on power as such that leads *Illustrious Corpses* into a kind of metaphysics. The film's metaphysics of power posit an all-male gerontocracy in the process of renewing itself, apparently through the facilitation of a military coup and the elimination of uncooperative figures in its own ranks. It is one of the film's two explicitly identified mafiosi who identifies the brutal procedure of renovation at work: accused by Rogas of the murder of Prosecutor Varga, this character pronounces what seems to be the real reason behind certain murders when he suggests that 'if this is a settling of scores … it's something between judges.' That a mafioso should identify the procedure at work is telling in that it points to the portrayal of the organization of power itself as a form of mafia in the film.

I do not intend to discuss here the degree of 'fidelity' of *Illustrious Corpses* to the novel from which this metaphor of the mafia derives, Leonardo Sciascia's *Equal Danger*.[6] However, it is worth recording a comment made by Sciascia in an afterword to his novel, because it offers an interpretative key to the film as well as to the source-text itself. Sciascia writes that his book is 'a fable about power anywhere in the world; power progressively deteriorating into an impenetrable type of association we can more or less call mafia-like.'[7] The mafia is by definition a heterotopic form of social organization – that is, it is an enclosed society with rules of behaviour at variance from the cultural norm, and entry into it is regulated by compulsion or ritual.[8] In the case of the mafia, this heterotopia is characterized by conspiratorial plotting and murderous tactics, just like the magistrature as portrayed in *Equal Danger* and in *Illustrious Corpses* (hence the aptness of the mafioso discerning in the murders an internecine settling of scores). However, Sciascia is not content to limit the application of his metaphor to a single, specific masculine heterotopia. As Joseph Farrell puts it, 'the mafia provided Sciascia with the fundamental metaphor he employed to describe first all crime, and later all power, everywhere.'[9] Thus it is not simply the magistrature, the various branches of the security forces, or even the higher echelons of government that are characterized by Sciascia as mafia-like; rather, it is power as such that is, for Sciascia, essentially mafia-like in structure.

The nature of the mafia is such that individuals (male mafiosi) or 'families' within the organization may manoeuvre to protect or enhance their positions, but ultimately the structure exists in order to perpetuate itself. The employment of the mafia as a metaphor to characterize the workings of power thus implies that Sciascia's vision, reprised by Rosi, is a mechanism served and operated by an obscure male elite that, however much its members might be motivated by self- or factional interest, essentially exists to perpetuate what I have called power as such. (Few women appear in either book or film. The latter includes brief portrayals of Cres's perfidious wife in fantasy flashback – she does not speak – as well as the resented spouse of a left-wing intellectual and a prostitute. No women are involved in the murders or in planning the coup d'état; power and politics are matters for men.) The vision of power as self-perpetuating, all-pervasive, and so impervious to political struggle is expressed in two main ways in *Illustrious Corpses*. One is through the employment of the conspiracy plot, an aspect I will return to below. First however, I wish to analyse an aspect of *Illustrious Corpses* that is arguably just as sinister as the portrayal of conspiracy in the form of the plans for a coup d'état discerned by Rogas.

This aspect is concerned with the extent to which Italian democracy is shown to have already been compromised by corruption (one of the murdered judges, Calamo, is implausibly wealthy), by state collusion with the mafia, and by the oppressive presence of surveillance. Such features of the state suggest that an authoritarian takeover of government would be less an overturning of Italian democracy than the realization of existing fault lines in the democratic structure.

The presence of surveillance, in particular, and the extent to which it might compromise the proper workings of democracy is indicated in several ways in the film. It is introduced in the macabre first scene, where the elderly prosecutor Varga consults the mummified remains of the Palermo rich arrayed in the niches of a crypt, supposedly gleaning the secrets of the still-living. Varga, an exaggerated incarnation of the gerontocratic Italian power elite, seems barely less ancient than the withered corpses that return his rheumy gaze, and he is murdered as he leaves the crypt. The symbolic valence of this sequence, beyond its linking of death with the mechanics of power, is clarified when Rogas recalls a conversation (replayed in black and white) about Varga with an army general who will later be linked to the planned coup d'état. The general remarks of the murdered prosecutor: 'Varga knew all the secrets of the city. He had a desk full of incriminating files. Some he took out at an opportune moment, others never … I liked him – he didn't do it for money; he lived only for power.' It is clear that Varga used his knowledge, however procured, to weaken, influence, or persecute others, to sustain his own power, and to perpetuate power as such.

If the opening sequence in the Palermo crypt seems as quaint and archaic as the architecture of much of the Sicilian episode (Baroque buildings – juxtaposed, however, with massive contemporary housing blocks), a perfectly contemporary version of the coercive employment of information for the ends of power is visualized in the film's panopticon scene, which takes place in a modern building in the capital.[10] Panopticon refers to a prison design whereby wings and cells are arranged around a central well so that inmates can be observed at all times. The term has come to be used in a metaphorical way to refer to the surveillance methods of modern societies, in which audio and audiovisual technologies are used to record the activities of the populace and the information so gained is monitored centrally by some arm of the security apparatus. Rogas witnesses this process at work in a room at the police headquarters, where white-coated operatives monitor innumerable phone conversations and screens show black-and-white images of people in the streets, including a clip of the Communist leader Amar emerging from a meeting.[11]

At moments during this sequence, the images on the monitors occupy the whole of the film frame, so that the content of the surveillance becomes identical with that of *Illustrious Corpses* itself. This points to a self-reflexive aspect of the film, one that encourages the viewer's awareness of film and photographic technology itself as a medium of surveillance. More importantly, it suggests how the perspective of *Illustrious Corpses* oscillates between the ethical, intellectual point of view of the detective and the ruthless and brutal eye of power. Indeed, the technological eye of the cinema is allied very explicitly with malign intent in the point-of-view shots that accompany the assassination of the third judge, Calamo, as he visits his bank, and the double shooting of Rogas and Amar as they converse in a room of the National Gallery. In both cases, the victims are observed from afar, from outside the windows of the buildings, using a long (telephoto) lens. The film retains this assassin's-eye view as the rifle is discharged, bullet holes appear in the glass, and the men fall dead. These and other scenes are accompanied by a peculiarly amplified quality in the recording of ambient sound in exterior spaces. It is as if these spaces are being recorded by audio surveillance equipment that does not distinguish between the different sounds in the environment – traffic, conversation, the wind, aircraft – or does not suppress (as the sound design of a feature film typically would) those sonic elements not germane to the narrative.

These and other sinister features – the folkloric origins of Varga's information about those in his jurisdiction, the panoptical surveillance of politicians and populace, the film's occupation of the perspective of the assassin and his controllers – cumulatively build to an ominous assertion: not 'democratic' in any but a formal sense, the Italian power structure is founded upon hidden intelligence dubiously accrued, and any threat to it is brutally extinguished. Seen in this light, the second aspect of the film that asserts a vision of power as self-perpetuating and irresistible is a reflection of the first. In other words, the conspiracy discovered by Rogas is seen not as an aberration in postwar Italian history or as an interruption of the democratic order, but as the logical expression of the essentially mafia-like character of the institutions and elites of Italian government.

This pessimistic vision has negative implications for those who aspire to reform Italian society and arguably signals a profound political ambivalence in *Illustrious Corpses*, discernable in the employment of the conspiracy mode. Certainly, the use of conspiracy theory in this and other Italian films (of the 1970s and since) gives expression to disquiet or dissatisfaction about the manner in which Italy has been governed, but it may also risk ascribing an exaggerated competence and potency to the conspirators, in this case the representatives of the Italian ruling order.[12] If the conspirators' will is irresistible, then resistance to it is pointless and political activism and reformist aspirations can only be in vain. Indeed, given that *Illustrious Corpses* was intended to denounce the masterminds of the Strategy of Tension, the use of the conspiracy mode may well have the paradoxical effect of confirming the extreme right's conception of society as ruled by violence, thereby validating the view that the effective exertion of authority and power is all that matters. Questions of ethics are certainly present in *Illustrious Corpses*, but these risk seeming unrealistic, in the sense that they are irrelevant to the real questions of political survival and national strength and of course to the perpetuation of power as such.

Mary P. Wood has written that 'conspiracy theories, and attempts [in Italian cinema] to visualize and put a face to those responsible for atrocities represent a failure in the hegemonic process because they foreground in whose interests society is ordered as it is.'[13] In Wood's positive assessment, the conspiracy mode expresses anxieties or exasperation about the mechanisms and distribution of power in Italy; but one might ask whether this expression functions as a critique of power or is ultimately a celebration of it. As we have seen, the figure for the secretive, violent, vindictive structure of power in Italy, borrowed from Sciascia, is that of the mafia. The perplexing and perhaps unanswerable question for the student of *Illustrious Corpses* is to what extent the film's creators may have been seduced by this metaphor: instead of being a denunciation of the anti-democratic workings of the Italian governing apparatus, might the film have become a paean to the ruthless effectiveness of the power-as-mafia it portrays?

NOTES

1 Both characters are associated with Prosecutor Varga, the first judge who is assassinated, and are shown attending his funeral in black-and-white still images that suggest journalistic or police surveillance photographs. One, referred to as an 'alleged mafioso' in the published script, seems in fact to be the mayor or some other high functionary of the town, and he delivers an address to Varga's funeral cortege. A group of young protesters shout that both he and Varga were 'mafiosi.' The second mafioso is visited in an island prison by the investigating detective and admits to having been friends with Varga when they were younger.

2 Peter Bondanella, *Italian Cinema*, 3rd ed. (New York: Continuum, 2004), 333.

3 Various recognizable locations are employed for both province and capital, including Naples and Lecce, as well as Agrigento, Palermo, and Rome. See interview with Francesco Rosi by Mary P. Wood, 'Francesco Rosi: Heightened Realism,' in *Projections*, vol. 8, ed. John Boorman and Walter Donohue (London: Faber and Faber, 1998), 272–95.

4 In Sciascia's book, unlike in the film, Rogas does actually kill Amar, presumably as a punishment for his party's acceptance and facilitation of the status quo.

5 For a short account of the Strategy of Tension, see Martin J. Bull and James L. Newell, *Italian Politics* (Cambridge: Polity Press, 2005), 101–4. For a more detailed analysis, see Anna Cento Bull, *Italian Neofascism: The Strategy of Tension and the Politics of Nonreconciliation* (Oxford: Berghahn Books, 2007).

6 For discussions of the process of adaptation, see Francesco Rosi's own short account, 'Il mio Sciascia,' in *Cadaveri eccellenti*, ed. Sebastiano Gesù (Catania: Giuseppe Maimone, 1992), 127–9; Linda Coremans' semiotic analysis, *La transformation filmique: du 'Contesto' à 'Cadaveri eccellenti'* (Paris: Peter Lang, 1990).

7 Leonardo Sciascia, *Il contesto* (Turin: Einaudi, 1971), 122. Translation mine.

8 See Mary P. Wood, 'Revealing the Hidden City: The Cinematic Conspiracy Thriller of the 1970s,' *The Italianist* 23 (2003): 158. My argument here and throughout is indebted to Wood, who in turn borrows the idea of heterotopic organization from Michel Foucault.

9 Joseph Farrell, *Leonardo Sciascia* (Edinburgh: Edinburgh University Press, 1995), 13. *The Day of the Owl* (London: Cape, 1963) and *To Each His Own* (Manchester: Carcanet, 1989) are examples of novels

by Sciascia that use the mafia as a metaphor for all crime, while *One Way or Another* (Manchester: Carcanet, 1987), like *Equal Danger*, makes the mafia a metaphor for power.

10 For an analysis of the use of architecture and mise en scène to communicate counter-hegemonic versions of the political and economic organization of Italian society in Italian thriller films of the 1970s, including *Illustrious Corpses*, see Wood, 'Revealing the Hidden City.'

11 The sequence is an elaboration of one in *Investigation of a Citizen Above Suspicion* (Elio Petri, 1970), with which *Illustrious Corpses* can very usefully be paired. See Mary P. Wood, *Italian Cinema* (Oxford: Berg, 2005), 190–1.

12 These films include *The Mattei Case* (1972) by Francesco Rosi himself, and many films of the Italian cop film genre, for example *Chopper Squad/Silent Action* (Sergio Martini, 1975). More recent films include *Strong Hands* (Franco Bernini, 1997) on the Brescia bombing of 1974, and *Five Moons Plaza* (Renzo Martinelli, 2003) on the Aldo Moro kidnapping. For a discussion of the latter two films, see Alan O'Leary, 'Moro, Brescia, Conspiracy: The Paranoid Style in Italian Cinema,' in *Imagining Terrorism: The Rhetoric and Representation of Political Violence in Italy 1969–2009*, ed. Pierpaolo Antonello and Alan O'Leary (Oxford: Legenda, 2009), 48–62.

13 Mary P. Wood, 'Navigating the Labyrinth: Cinematic Investigations of Right-Wing Terrorism,' in *Terrorism Italian Style: Representations of Terrorism and Political Violence in Contemporary Italian Cinema*, ed. Ruth Glynn, Giancarlo Lombardi, and Alan O'Leary (London: IGRS Books, 2012).

35 Marco Risi's *Forever Mary*: Desperate Lives Converge in Sicilia 'Non Bedda'

GEORGE DE STEFANO

In May 2008, the Italian media covered a particularly ugly hate crime: the stabbing of a gay teenager in the poor and mafia-dominated Brancaccio section of Palermo. The assailant was the boy's own father, who declared that it was a 'dishonour' to have a gay son. The fifty-three-year-old father, who had a criminal record, attacked his eighteen-year-old son while the young man was in the shower, inflicting several stab wounds. 'My father has never accepted me. He couldn't tolerate the fact that I'm gay,' said the boy, identified only as 'Paolo.'[1] The stabbing of Paolo by his father attests to the persistence of an archaic and oppressive culture of masculine 'honour,' whose pitiless values are embodied in the Sicilian mafia. It is a culture that valorizes male violence and that denigrates both femininity and homosexuality. Jane and Peter Schneider have described the intertwined nature of misogyny and homophobia in mafia culture. The Cosa Nostra's recruitment rituals and other traditions build solidarity among mafiosi, defining them by what they are not: women or homosexuals. The Schneiders cite the psychiatric transcript of an imprisoned mafioso who murdered two other gangsters and attempted to kill a third. He claimed he committed the murders to show to himself and to others that he was the equal of the other men, 'one of the boys,' capable of manhood, and not one of 'them' – the women. Indeed the killings had helped him deal with his growing concern that he might be inclined towards 'pederasty,' by which he meant being sexually attracted to young men.[2]

Twenty years before Paolo's father decided that upholding family honour required an attempted filicide, director Marco Risi indicted this culture and the social conditions that produced it in *Mery per sempre* (*Forever Mary*, 1989). Set in a Palermo boys' reformatory with the poetically apt name Rosaspina (rose thorn), the film depicts the efforts of a dedicated teacher to change the lives of his pupils wounded by poverty and violence. *Forever Mary* is groundbreaking in its treatment of homosexuality and gender nonconformity. Risi broke with the dominant tenor of 1980s Italian cinema by making a film indebted to neorealism, a style (and ideology) then out of favour. *Forever Mary* evinces a number of neorealism's defining elements: it uses 'contemporary, true-to-life subjects'; its plot is 'uncontrived, open-ended'; the protagonists are mainly working class; dialogue is mostly in the vernacular; and, finally, there is 'implied social criticism.'[3] The film also uses non-professional actors, another key neorealist practice, albeit mainly in secondary roles. Neorealist mise en scène relies on authentic locales, and *Forever Mary* was shot on location in Palermo – in an actual reformatory, in the streets of working-class neighbourhoods, and in the Vucciria marketplace. The Sicily depicted in Risi's film is not the 'bedda' ('eautiful) island celebrated in the cinema and in song as in 'Sicilian Bedda,' but the 'non-bedda.'[4] The ugliness of the urban environment couldn't be farther from the sun-kissed, seductive landscapes of Francis Ford Coppola's *Godfather* trilogy. The Sicily of *Forever Mary* is more reminiscent of the Naples of Francesco Rosi's *Le mani sulla città* (*Hands over the City*, 1963) and, more recently, Matteo Garrone's *Gomorra* (*Gomorrah,* 2008).

Based on the eponymous novel by Aurelio Grimaldi, *Forever Mary* stars Michele Placido as Marco Terzi, a teacher who leaves Milan to accept an assignment to Rosaspina. There is something inexplicable about Terzi's decision to take this lower-paying position for which he is overqualified. Terzi discovers that cynicism, mistrust, and violence prevail at Rosaspina. One of the teachers tells him that the institution 'is like a factory.' The time the boys spend in the reformatory is just one stage in a production process that ends in an adult prison. The guards regard their charges as worthless miscreants who must be kept in line using harsh discipline, including beatings. The young inmates seem to have accepted the institution's judgment and, by extension, society's as well. When Terzi urges Pietro to file a complaint against the guard who beat him, Pietro refuses, saying that if he were a guard he would do exactly the same. On his first day in the classroom, Terzi's sullen students greet him with mockery and open hostility. They know all too well that society considers them disposable, so anyone sent to teach them must be as inconsequential as they.

Though *Forever Mary* is set mostly within the grim walls of Rosaspina, we are introduced to the young inmates before their incarceration, while they are experiencing what passes for freedom in their world. Claudio, a shy fourteen-year-old, is arrested while he and an even younger boy are attempting to rob a store. Antonio is taken into custody as he is getting married to his pregnant fiancée. The eponymous Mery, né Mario, makes his living as a street prostitute. Glamorous, even beautiful in full drag and make-up, he earns his ticket to Rosaspina when he severely injures a john who tries to cheat him out of his fee. The police come for Mery while he is at home having dinner with his parents and siblings. He is wearing a cap, but his angry father isn't fooled. 'You still have that faggot hair,' he snaps, striking his son. Mery's mother comes to his defence as his father, brandishing a knife, threatens to stab him to death. The police step in, and his disgusted father is relieved that the boy's disruptive and, to him, disgraceful presence will be removed from the family home.

All of the boys, regardless of the circumstances that brought them to Rosaspina, have been shaped and damaged by the mafia's culture of masculine dominance and violence. Natale, the inmate who taunts Terzi as 'stupid,' has fully internalized the culture's values. He proudly calls himself *Minchia dura* (hard prick), because in his world, 'you're either a hard prick or a soft one.' Of all the boys, Natale challenges Terzi's authority the most. But the teacher meets and deflects these challenges. He responds to Natale's 'hard prick' rhetoric by reading a poem consisting of nothing but outrageous phallic references, one-upping Natale to the amusement of the other boys. Intrigued by his most difficult pupil, Terzi visits Natale's brother, who informs the teacher that as a boy Natale had seen his father, a mafioso, shot to death. At fifteen, Natale murdered his father's killer. Terzi asks Natale's brother why he never visits his imprisoned sibling. Natale, he replies, scorns him because he has rejected their father's heartless, predatory value system. He hates guns and violence, and that, in Natale's eyes, makes him less than a man and therefore worthless. In the classroom, Terzi directly confronts the issue of the mafia and the damage it has done to Sicily. When Natale responds by quoting his father, saying that the 'mafia is a good thing, mafia is always fair,' Terzi, indicating a wall map of Sicily, indignantly states, 'This is not only your country, it is mine, too.' He proceeds to name various Sicilian locales from the map, and, as he speaks, the coldly furious Natale picks up a pen and begins to write on the teacher's exposed arms. Terzi explains how Sicily once was a land of rivers, but now water has become scarce because it is controlled by the mafia. After gaining its private monopoly over what should be a public resource, the mafia murdered farmers and peasants, smothered the island in concrete, and built the oppressive slums where the boys, his students, all grew up.

The scene reveals significant and heretofore undisclosed aspects of Terzi's character. His passionate denunciation of the mafia provides a plausible reason for his return to his parents' homeland: moral and political outrage. We also see how far he is willing to go to demonstrate to his charges that he is an entirely different authority figure from the violent fathers and jailers they have known all their lives. All through Terzi's anti-mafia speech, Natale continues to write on his skin. The teacher permits this egregious breach of classroom protocol because he feels secure enough in his authority to allow Natale to test the limits of the permissible. Once he has made his point to the boys about the system that rules them and has deformed their lives, he reasserts his control. His unorthodox methods bear fruit when his pupils' initial hostility is gradually replaced by respect and, for some, something more.

Mery presents a different challenge to Terzi, and as with Natale, his response is startling in its unpredictability, yet entirely apt. Terzi is disturbed when he discovers that Mery has written 'I love you' to him on a homework assignment. When he confronts the boy, the latter candidly expresses his infatuation. Terzi insists that he is heterosexual, to which Mery replies that in his experience straight men 'avoid me like the plague during the day, but at night they all come for me.' Face to face with his teacher, Mery accuses him of cowardice. Terzi takes Mery's face in his hands and kisses him on the mouth. 'Who says I'm scared?' he says. He admits that 'this' – sex between men – 'can be beautiful.' 'But,' he adds, 'I'm not the one.' For Mery, being male is a source of profound anguish. He tells Terzi that when he was a boy, his gender nonconformity was encouraged by adults, who found it amusing. Now, as a cross-dressing young man, he is an outcast. Sought out for night-time assignations by men who otherwise avoid him 'like the plague,' he bears the brunt of his culture's sexual hypocrisy. He cannot be a man in the accepted sense, but he is not a woman either. 'I'm neither fish nor fowl,' he says to Terzi. 'I'm just Mery, forever Mery.'

Mery's sense of being trapped, doomed to a life in limbo with scant prospects for fulfilment and happiness, is shared by the other boys at Rosaspina. Pietro, the illiterate son of an ex-convict mother, tells Terzi that the remainder of his life will be spent in and out of institutions. 'I was born with this anger inside me,' he says. 'It's my destiny.' In a cruelly ironic turn of events, he does escape Rosaspina, only to be shot to death in a botched robbery. Claudio, the shy innocent, is shipped off to a prison in Naples after he violently fends off a sexual advance from Carmelo, an older boy. When Natale turns eighteen, he is sent to Ucciardone, a notorious adult prison that houses hardened mafiosi.

Terzi similarly feels frustrated, even immobilized, by the intransigence and brutality of the system at Rosaspina. The administrators and guards see him as a dangerous idealist, and they blame him for unleashing chaos when the boys protest Claudio's punishment. After Pietro's death, a distraught Terzi wakes the sleeping boys to tell them the news. 'Knives, guns … this is your language, and it was Pietro's, too,' he says. Before Pietro died, Terzi adds, 'he was crying like a kid.' Breaking down completely, the teacher cries, 'Don't let them do this to you!' Terzi, defeated and despairing, requests a transfer. But when he receives a letter informing him of his new posting, he tears it up, much to the delight of his pupils. He realizes that he has had more of an impact on the boys of Rosaspina than any of his predecessors, and he will not abandon them. The film's final shot is of a tree outside the classroom's grated window, a beckoning, if fragile image of life and beauty. And, perhaps, hope.

In *Forever Mary*, Marco Risi satisfyingly blends standard genre elements with some surprisingly original touches. The narrative of a dedicated teacher who struggles against societal and institutional barriers to 'reach' hard case youths is familiar from decades of Hollywood films and more recently in Lina Wertmüller's *Ciao, Professore* (1992), which depicts a northern Italian teacher's travails in a school of poor and unruly Neapolitan youths. Despite this, Risi brings to this oft-told tale a refreshing lack of sentimentality. The film's treatment of homosexuality and gender nonconformity is even more singular. Italian cinema pre-*Mary* represented these themes in disparate ways, both reflecting and at times challenging popular conceptions and prejudices. Gay men and lesbians generally have been rendered invisible on screen, and when they have appeared, they have often been reduced to comic stereotypes. What is more, homosexuality has even been deployed as a metaphor for fascist and/or bourgeois corruption, a tradition exemplified in Roberto Rossellini's *Roma, città aperta* (*Open City*, 1945) and the repressed protagonist of Bernardo Bertolucci's *Il conformista* (*The Conformist*, 1970).[5] Some Italian filmmakers have offered more nuanced and insightful treatments. But even in such films as Ettore Scola's *Una giornata particolare* (*A Special Day*, 1977) and Luchino Visconti's *La morte a Venezia* (*Death in Venice*, 1971), same-sex desire is either sublimated to other narrative threads (in the former, the persecuted gay protagonist makes love to an unhappy housewife) or is symbolic (Aschenbach's unconsummated lust for Tadzio is a metaphor for a doomed pursuit of youth and beauty).

Italy has a peculiar status among Western European societies when it comes to homosexuality. The persistence of conservative values rooted in family and faith (as well as the outsized presence of the Vatican in Italian cultural and political life) has impeded acceptance and even public discussion of homosexuality. Italy is the land of 'don't ask, don't tell,' where a kind of repressive tolerance prevails. As long as one's sexuality remains closeted, 'discreet,' it does not provoke much condemnation or stigma. But public gayness – homosexuality as constituent of individual and social identities – violates the repressive social contract premised on silence and invisibility. Although gay liberation as an ideology and an activist movement came to Italy during the 1970s, it has made fewer inroads there than in most other European societies. Italy, unlike France, Great Britain, and Germany, has not produced cutting-edge gay auteurs comparable to Andre Téchiné, Derek Jarman, or Rainer Fassbinder, all of whom have situated gay characters and themes within broader critiques of bourgeois society, religion, and heterosexuality. The films of the openly gay director Pier Paolo Pasolini are not lacking in homoeroticism, but he did not foreground same-sex themes or gay characters, and he was unsympathetic to Italy's gay movement, which was even more marginal in his lifetime than it is now. The only contemporary Italian filmmaker who is openly gay in his public and private life as well as his worklife is the Turkish-born Ferzan Ozpetek (*Hamam* [*The Turkish Baths*], 1997, and *Le fate ignoranti* [*His Secret Life*], 2001).

Forever Mary departs from Italian cinema's familiar representations of homosexuality, and not simply in its sympathetic portrayal of a transgendered gay prostitute. In Risi's film, same-sex desire both felt and acted upon is not exclusive to characters defined as gay or transgendered. Carmelo wants sex with Claudio, and he makes it clear that he will take what he wants if Claudio refuses. This is not, however, simply prison sex as an exercise of dominance, or a heterosexual turning to men for lack of a better alternative. Although he considers himself straight, Carmelo evidently enjoys sex with men. He tries to seduce Claudio with his idea of sweet talk, telling him that 'in [Rosaspina] everybody does it.' The film's non-judgmental stance, though, is exemplified by Marco Terzi's act of kissing Mery on the lips and acknowledging, 'This can be beautiful.' If gay sex can be *bello*, the film portrays the mafioso culture of honour and male violence as irredeemably *brutto*. The concept of *onore* (honour) is inextricable from gender and sexuality, or rather, oppressive social constructions of these categories. Honour as 'a system of stratification that marks off dominant and subordinate positions … reverberates through the life of every day and every night, through minute daily activities. This all-pervasiveness endows it with a terrible power and guarantees social control.'[6] In recent decades, scholars have questioned whether an honour/shame dualism characterizes Italian and other Mediterranean cultures. But in the subproletarian and mafia-dominated Sicilian milieu depicted in *Forever Mary*, honour and its flip side, shame, clearly shape attitudes and behaviours.[7] Women who defy convention in their sexual behaviour 'dishonour' their families, as do homosexuals by their very existence. The latter, especially if effeminate, are seen as gender traitors because they relinquish masculine dominance to become subordinate, like women. The plight of Mery illustrates where this all leads. The violent intolerance of honour-obsessed fathers depicted in *Forever Mary* remains a social fact in contemporary Sicily, as the stabbing of the young gay Palermitan 'Paolo' by his own father amply demonstrates.

Risi returned to the world of *Forever Mary* with his next film, *Ragazzi fuori* (*Boys on the Outside*, 1990), catching up with several of first film's characters after their release from Rosaspina. Though no longer incarcerated, they are trapped by unemployment and poverty and mired in illegality due to the notorious inability of the Sicilian system to provide opportunities that would improve their lot. And this time they have no sympathetic teacher to care about them. Natale, released from prison and unemployed, turns to robbery. Antonio becomes a drug dealer after the police shut down his unlicensed vegetable stand and seize his merchandise. Claudio, released from the Naples reformatory, has a girlfriend named Vita who wants to elope with him, but they have nowhere to go. Worse, a vindictive Carmelo, whom Claudio had blinded in one eye when he fended off his advances at Rosapina, finds Claudio in Palermo. Mery, still a street prostitute, lives in a squat that has no running water. His mother sometimes visits, but his social worker and parole officer have more of a presence in his life. Marco Risi's two films about desperate lives in Palermo, made twenty years ago, portray social conditions that persist today. International pop culture, feminism, and even gay liberation have undermined old attitudes and practices regarding gender and sexuality. Vigorous law enforcement and civil society movements have challenged the power of the mafia and the political and business figures complicit with it. But in the poor quarters of contemporary Palermo, good jobs remain scarce, the mafia continues to control territory and lives, and intolerant fathers still reject, with extreme prejudice, their gay sons.

NOTES

1 'Palermo, coltellate al figlio gay: "Era un disonore." Arrestato,' *La Repubblica*, 26 May 2008, accessed 10 September 2009, www.repubblica.it/2008/05/sezioni/cronaca/palermo-figlio-gay/palermo-figlio-gay /palermo-figlio-gay.html.

2 Jane C. Schneider and Peter T. Schneider, *Reversible Destiny: Mafia, Anti-Mafia, and the Struggle for Palermo* (Berkeley, CA: University of California Press, 2003), 92.

3 Millicent Marcus, *Italian Film in the Light of Neorealism* (Princeton, NJ: Princeton University Press, 1986), 22.

4 'Sicilia Bedda' ('Beautiful Sicily') is a popular folk song celebrating Sicily's beauty and people. I use *non bedda* to emphasize the opposite.

5 See Stuart Jeffries, 'Films Are a Way to Kill My Father,' *The Guardian*, 22 February 2008, accessed 22 September 2009, www.guardian.co.uk/film/2008/feb/22/1; Will Aitken, 'Leaving the Dance: Bertolucci's Gay Images,' *Jump Cut* 16 (1977): 23–6.

6 Renate Siebert, *Secrets of Life and Death: Women and the Mafia*, trans. Liz Heron (London: Verso, 1996), 36.

7 Letizia Paoli observes that honour, as identified with the mafia, 'lies in virility and strength, in the ability of every male to defend his person and his property rights,' with the women of his household included among the latter. *Mafia Brotherhoods* (Oxford: Oxford University Press, 2003), 74.

36 Threads of Political Violence in Italy's Spiderweb: Giorgio Ambrosoli's Murder in Michele Placido's *A Bourgeois Hero*

CARLO TESTA

This chapter elucidates how Michele Placido's 1995 film, *Un eroe borghese* (*A Bourgeois Hero*), recreates the brave life of Giorgio Ambrosoli and his tragic death, on 11 July 1979, at the hands of a mafia hitman. To achieve this goal, the first hurdle that needs to be cleared is the unusual complexity of the Italian politics of the time, which is fully reflected in the film – although, as I will point out in due course, not necessarily in the film's relatively unobtrusive style.

Most histories, national or otherwise, operate (or, for practical reasons, are presented) like the quintessential Aristotelian *linear* fiction: as in a yarn, they have a 'before,' a 'during,' and an 'after.' Italy's recent history, in contrast, functions – if that can be the word – more like a spiderweb; in it, there are a great number of radial threads, linked together by tangential connections, whose system of relations affects each of its constituent parts. In this chapter, Ambrosoli's death constitutes but one such strand, our first one. Many others are variously intertwined with it:

- The Banca d'Italia (BdI) – i.e., the Italian state's central bank, in charge of (a) managing the then national currency, the lira, and (b) supervising the activities of commercial and investment banks in the country. Guido Carli was BdI governor between 1960 and August 1975, and in this capacity appointed Ambrosoli, in September 1974, to his task as receiver, i.e., liquidator, of the collapsed Banca Privata Italiana (BPI), owned and run by the mafioso Michele Sindona (see below). Carli was succeeded by Paolo Baffi between August 1975 and September 1979, and thereafter by Carlo Azeglio Ciampi (who was later prime minister for a centre-left government, and subsequently president of the republic). In 1976 both Ciampi and Mario Sarcinelli were appointed deputy general managers of the BdI; in 1978, Ciampi became general manager.
- The Italo-American mafia and its then preferred banker, Michele Sindona. Sindona was an early mentor of Roberto Calvi (see below), and later a partner with him in shady offshore deals. When cornered by prosecutors for fraudulent bankruptcy of his US outfit, Franklin National Bank (FNB), Sindona blackmailed Calvi for return help; having been let down in this, he spilled the beans on his former protégé, conspiring in his eventual murder. In Italy, the drainage basin to collect the funds necessary for Sindona's illegal activities consisted of the two banks Banca Unione and Banca Privata Finanziaria, merged as of 1 August 1974 into the BPI already mentioned. Sindona commissioned Ambrosoli's murder in 1979 and later received a life sentence in Italy for this. He was eventually extradited to Italy and died in a maximum security penitentiary (Voghera, 22 March 1986), poisoned by a coffee laced with strychnine. (The mafia had already

killed in the same manner the well-known turncoat Gaspare Pisciotta in 1954.) Sindona was member of the secret Italian Freemason lodge P2, card #1612.

- The Italian magistrates, most of whom, at the time of the events, acted bona fide and spearheaded the attempt to hold accountable at least some of the many villains of this piece, whether or not the BdI was willing to follow their lead. Astonishingly, however, some of them were ill-advised enough to take the opposite tack and sabotage any such follow-up action by the BdI when it did finally come (see below).

- The politicians Aldo Moro and Giulio Andreotti and in general the *amici* (comrades) in their party, the Christian Democrats or DC, had been in near-absolute power since 1947. Surrounded by scandal and a reputation for putting competence, if any, below obedience to friends and friends-of-friends, at the time of the events the thirty-year-old DC regime nevertheless was regularly re-elected in Italy due to the Yalta-mandated partition of Europe. Although relentlessly competing with each other for power, Moro and Andreotti were, in the 1970s, eager to engage in dialogue with the Italian Communists. Unlike their less-intelligent *amici*, the two jointly and severally realized that despite the DC's weaknesses – indeed, because of them – it was vital for the political fortunes of their organization to cash in on the political strategy then called *compromesso storico* ('historical compromise,' see below), i.e., the Italian Communists' willingness to turn a blind eye to DC mismanagement. Moro was abducted by the Red Brigades while being driven to Parliament on 17 March 1978, and found murdered on 9 May.

- The legal *extra-parliamentarian* left-wing opposition (though, in fact, with a sliver of representation in Parliament), generally rejected the violence practised by the Red Brigades (see below), but nevertheless radically opposed the DC, and the historic compromise in particular.

- The Vatican, the American bishop Paul Marcinkus (chairman of the Vatican's state bank), and the banker Roberto Calvi. Calvi rose to prominence as chairman of the Milanese Banco Ambrosiano, owned by the Catholic Church and, *inter alia*, a conduit for the placement around the globe of Vatican money, along with money the Vatican was slipping into offshore trusts, out of sight of Italy's fiscal authorities on behalf of its favourite friends. Following a series of reckless investments and/or unauthorized embezzlements, Calvi lost the support of his powerful sponsors. Having threatened in vain to blackmail them by revealing details of their mutual accommodations, Calvi was eventually lured to London after much to and fro and killed (by the mafia? Sindona's hitmen? the Freemasons?). The murder was masqueraded as a suicide by hanging from the Blackfriars Bridge. He was a member of the secret Freemason lodge P2, card #1624.

- The Italian Communist Party or PCI. Under the moderate leadership of Enrico Berlinguer, in the mid-1970s the Communists were practising the strategy of the historic compromise, avoiding pressing home their opposition to the entrenched, thirty-year-old Christian Democrat regime. Mindful of the military coups carried out in Greece in 1968 and Chile in 1973, Berlinguer intended to avoid throwing, along with the dirty waters of the DC, the Italian baby into the abyss of a government crisis with a potentially tragic outcome for the entire country. While this strategy had responsible intentions, it also left Italy without any organized parliamentary opposition to speak of, with the undoubtedly unintended – and no doubt pathological – consequence of suspending the checks and balances necessary to the correct functioning of any democracy. In particular, the PCI's pro-government silence was consistently deafening in matters related to the Ambrosoli affair.

- Enrico Cuccia, the powerful, seemingly eternal (from 1946 to 1982!) managing director of Mediobanca, by far the largest investment bank in Italy.
- The Red Brigades and other extreme-left underground groups. These presented themselves as 'armed revolutionists,' but, by the long string of assassinations they carried out, Moro's first and foremost, in fact acted as a most powerful agent of conservation in Italian society. The reason is simple: the terrorists' threat to tear up the entire social contract virtually ensured that the PCI would rush, as it did, to prop up the crumbling DC out of fear of a worse alternative, be it from the extreme left or from the (quite literally) *reaction*ary extreme right.
- Paramilitary institutions of the Italian State: General Vito Miceli, head of the Secret Services (secret Freemason lodge P2 card #1605); General Raffaele Giudice (General Commander of the Financial Police or Finance Guards corps, P2 card #1634); General Donato Lo Prete, Major Chief of Staff – Capo di Stato Maggiore (P2 card #1600); and sundry extreme right-wing coup plotters and terrorists.
- The Italian Socialist Party or PSI and its secretary, Bettino Craxi. Craxi allied himself to the real estate developer Silvio Berlusconi (see below) and, in return for undying political support, kept changing the laws of the republic until they permitted Berlusconi's rise to tycoon of Italian TV and media. He became best known for his royal role in generalizing a system of 10 per cent kickbacks to be paid to PSI members by all private businesses seeking public contracts.
- Licio Gelli, Great Master of the secret Freemason lodge P2, and the true mastermind behind the authoritarian 'Plan of Democratic Rebirth' devised in the 1970s as an outline for any would-be Italian putschist to restrict, by hook or by crook, the liberties guaranteed by the anti-Fascist Constitution of 1947.
- The media I: the press. *Corriere della Sera*, the oldest and most recognized Italian daily, shaping the opinion of the Italian bourgeoisie from its headquarters in Milan to the remotest corners of the peninsula: director Franco Di Bella, P2 card #1887; and Rizzoli publishing house, the majority owner of said newspaper being director general (CEO) Bruno Tassan-Din, P2 card #1633.
- The media II: RAI TV (Radio Televisione Italiana, monopoly state radio and television corporation): politically under the watchful control of the Christian Democrats and the PSI. So many of its officials were P2 members that the list is too long to appear here.
- The media III: Silvio Berlusconi. In the 1970s, a came-from-nowhere real estate developer and businessman endowed with inexplicably abundant start-up capital. During the 1980s, Berlusconi became a tycoon of the press and a monopolist of private TV stations, thanks to laws passed by Craxi. When, in the 1990s, Craxi fell from grace in the wake of the Tangentopoli scandals,[1] fled to Tunisia, and eventually died there, Berlusconi let him drop. He founded – and richly funded – his own, privately managed political party, so as to be able to do in person what Craxi used to do for him. (Despite the strong personal and family bonds between themselves, Berlusconi has always glossed over the topic of Craxi.)
- Berlusconi – prime minister from 1994–95, 2001–6, and 2008–11 – has, among other things, (a) introduced strict limits on the Italian courts' ability to subpoena documents from abroad (e.g., Switzerland) in cases regarding the fraudulent export of capital; (b) retroactively decriminalized false bookkeeping and accounting (with which he had been charged by Italian courts); (c) offered evaders a raft of 'tomb-like amnesties' (i.e., plea-bargained extinctions of fiscal crimes at a nominal cost to the non-payer); (d) retroactively shortened time limits for statutes

of limitations (including for tax evasion); and (e) had his Parliament pass a bill exempting from prosecution the top four office-holders in the Italian Republic. P2 card #1816.

Placido's *A Bourgeois Hero* is shot in the matter-of-fact style of what could be called, in analogy to the best form of journalism, investigative cinema. Because of the powerful upswell of ethico-political indignation among the Italian public at the time it was made – the time of the 'Clean Hands' judicial investigations – Placido's film flees from any ambition to technicalize/aestheticize its own style of representation. Quite the contrary, the movie is saturated with a palpable effort by the director to be faithful, in respectful homage, to the ideal of understatement that inspired Ambrosoli until his last day. One clearly senses an authorial persuasion on Placido's part that if the camera did otherwise, and called attention to its own *virtuosismo*, such images would create a self-important discourse altogether dissonant with the sense of humility and 'bourgeois duty' that insistently and consistently guided Ambrosoli in his life. In that hypothetical case, the visual discourse *on the screen* would be at odds with the argument *in the plot* that celebrates Ambrosoli's conduct in deliberately unrhetorical detail.

In order to recount for the Italian movie theatres' mass public the truly heroic story of Ambrosoli's self-sacrifice, fifteen years in the past at the time of its release, the film weaves together many threads of the Italian politico-economic spiderweb of the 1970s. *A Bourgeois Hero* is composed of forty-one 'chapters' (narratively connected scenes) that cover the events leading to Ambrosoli's death, from 24 September 1974 – the day Ambrosoli was appointed receiver of Sindona's BPI – to the day of his murder on 11 July 1979. Some of these chapters amount to strictly factual *reports*, that is, they reflect events that actually occurred on a specific day. Others consist of *novelizations*, that is to say, condensed developments that may have occurred in a different sequence and/or in an iterative manner.[2]

A Bourgeois Hero opens with a prologue, based on newsreel footage, surveying the sleazy biography of Michele Sindona. The following scenes provide the information deemed by the director to be the essential minimum for spectators to know. FNB in the United States and BPI in Italy were mere fronts for Sindona's, and Sindona's mafia friends', recycling of money from drug dealing, real estate speculation, tax evasion, the illegal financing of anti-communist parties in the Italian government, and some reckless offshore financial operations. In the early 1970s, Sindona reached the peak of his influence: he was an admired power broker among anti-Communist Italo-American circles, and in Rome he had befriended the main DC politicians, who humoured his political requests in exchange for his liberal financial support. Then, in 1974, a series of failed gambles on the international currency markets spelled the beginning of the end for Sindona's empire. Despite Sindona's political connections, both FNB in the United States and BPI in Italy came under the scrutiny of the judiciary.

A Bourgeois Hero then flashes forward to a New York State prison in 1980 and shows us Sindona being questioned by a foreign visitor, Marshall Silvio Novembre of the Italian Finance Guards. Prologue and flashforward thus provide an important historical anchoring that is tantamount to a prerequisite of ethically committed cinema, at least in the Italian tradition.

The film now takes us to Milan, where we learn that Giorgio Ambrosoli, a Milanese accountant and lawyer of conservative (indeed, pro-monarchic) political views, specializing in bankruptcy litigation, has been put in charge of the liquidation of BPI by Guido Carli, the president of the Bank of Italy.

On one stressful day in early October 1974 – politically motivated street clashes are occurring nearby, and one of the demonstrators is killed by the police – Marshall Novembre shows up at BPI with a search warrant granted by the judiciary upon a request issued by the Finance Guards' top commander. Ambrosoli is suspicious of this intrusion, in which he (rightly) sees a naked attempt to intercept and derail his own investigation. Unafraid to speak his mind, Ambrosoli points out to Novembre in a heated scene that 'Sindona has very good friends among the top brass of the Finance Guards!' Novembre, an honest but – at first, anyway – naive servant of the state, takes umbrage at this suggestion; however, in the face of overwhelming evidence, he comes round to sharing Ambrosoli's opinion over time. He eventually becomes Ambrosoli's best collaborator, perhaps one of his few true friends.

As Ambrosoli, with Novembre's help, pores over BPI's books and deciphers their secrets, it becomes obvious to him that the activities engaged in by Sindona at BPI were inherently fraudulent, and that the only acceptable solution is to wind the bank down. This, we now realize with him, entails stepping on toes that are as powerful as they are dirty – and Ambrosoli begins to fear for his life. In a sequence all the more dramatic because it reflects unadorned actual facts, *A Bourgeois Hero* shows us Ambrosoli penning in his diary a comprehensive ethical testament addressed to his wife Annalori.[3] The document is not 'really' meant for her to read, but Giorgio somehow forgets the diary at home in a prominent location, so that Annalori eventually finds it and is forced to share her husband's anguish.

A Bourgeois Hero then shows us how Ambrosoli's prediction of a backlash comes exactly true. From his well-protected redoubt in New York City, a luxurious suite at the Hotel Pierre, Sindona begins to attempt blackmailing his way back to power. He calls his long-time acquaintance in Rome, Giulio Andreotti, threatening to reveal state secrets allegedly in his possession should he not receive satisfaction; he also hires a team of lawyers to put pressure on BdI officers, Ciampi first and foremost, for an emergency plan to rescue BPI. Ambrosoli flatly rejects the many versions of this proposal, wryly – and altogether correctly – commenting that the plan is 'an admirable … sophisticated system to make the community pay for [Sindona's] multi-billion[-dollar] debts.'

Meticulous to a fault, Sindona also entrusts an Italo-American mafioso (unidentified to date) to threaten Ambrosoli over the phone. Eight such phone calls occurred, of which five were recorded and later included as evidence in various court proceedings. Substantial excerpts from these truly chilling conversations are included in *A Bourgeois Hero*, the most terrifying of them featured in the soundtrack during the film's final credits. Nevertheless, Ambrosoli absolutely refuses to bend to Sindona's pressures. He testifies about his findings before the federal prosecutor in New York, and then again before the New York Federal Court judges when they take themselves to Milan in early July 1979 to collect his deposition.

By now Sindona has planned his next move, contracting out Ambrosoli's murder to a mafia killer, a certain Bill Arico. Having diligently researched his subject through a number of fact-finding trips to Milan, Arico flies to his lethal mission on the same day (indeed, the same plane) as do the US federal judges. *A Bourgeois Hero* shows us Arico shooting at close range and killing the unarmed, unescorted Ambrosoli on a sweltering summer night in a city deserted by most of its inhabitants, including Ambrosoli's own seaside-bound wife and children.

A Bourgeois Hero closes with a scene stressing the tragic loneliness that haunted poor Ambrosoli well into the afterlife. After framing, from street level, the few relatives and friends who are attending his funeral, the camera then gradually rises to the height of the roof of his apartment building and zooms out to encompass, to a striking effect, the entire, indifferent, empty city of Milan. This desolate conclusion to the film brings home the impression of just how quixotic Ambrosoli's self-sacrifice was at the time: no representative of the state was officially present at Ambrosoli's funeral – not from the central government or any central institution in Rome, and not from the Milanese political and financial centres of power, normally eager to bask in the rhetoric of Milan as the 'moral capital' of the country.

And this, of course, is the ethico-political essence of Placido's *A Bourgeois Hero*, which qualifies the film, made at the peak of the 'Clean Hands' investigations in the mid-1990s, as a landmark contribution to the history of ethically committed Italian cinema. The endurance, in Italian society, of a seemingly endlessly mutating spiderweb of corruption virtually guarantees that, alas, there will also be, for scholars of good will, no dearth of future occasions on which to analyse the art ready to coalesce aesthetic and ethical values, in movie theatres or outside them.

NOTES

1 Or the 'Bribesville scandals' of the early 1990s that unveiled pervasive corruption in Italy across the political spectrum.
2 Placido's film is based on Corrado Stajano's book by the same title, *Un eroe borghese* (Turin: Einaudi, 1995). Another good, though later, source is Renzo Agasso's *Il caso Ambrosoli: Mafia, affari, politica* (Milan: Edizioni San Paolo, 2005).
3 25 February 1975. See the full text in Stajano, *Un eroe borghese*, 102–4.

37 Sacrifice, Sacrament, and the Body in Ricky Tognazzi's *La scorta*

MYRIAM SWENNEN RUTHENBERG

'Pietro!' The name is cried out in despair by a father in response to loud gunshots outside his window. It is the name of his son, Marshall Pietro Virzì, the bodyguard of anti-mafia Judge Rizzo. Both men have just become the latest victims of mafia violence. The name contained in the scream is the first word pronounced in Ricky Tognazzi's 1993 film *La scorta* (*The Bodyguards*) and dramatically seals the movie's opening scene. Set against the backdrop of the northwestern Sicilian coastal city of Trapani, *La scorta* seems, at first sight, little more than a political thriller involving the slain judge's replacement, Michele De Francesco, and his four bodyguards. Indeed, the film was often dismissed as overly simplistic or insufficiently engaged. However, *La scorta* – inspired by an episode in the life of mafia hunter Judge Francesco Taurisano, sent to Trapani in 1989 to investigate government ties to the local mafia but removed from the case months later – is worthy of closer study: beneath the surface, Christian iconography and symbolism are cleverly and subtly exploited to foreground the role of sacrifice in Italy's battle against the mafia. In particular, Tognazzi examines father–son relationships in religious terms and rituals of consecration and communion that in Christian liturgy bring about transubstantiation manipulated to draw attention to the bodyguards' repeated sacrifice in an ongoing battle against an invisible enemy.

La scorta was filmed on the heels of the slayings of anti-mafia magistrates Giovanni Falcone and Paolo Borsellino in 1992 – whose story would find its cinematic repository in Tognazzi's *Excellent Cadavers* (1999) and Marco Turco's documentary *In un altro paese* (*Excellent Cadavers*, 2005), both inspired by Alexander Stille's eponymous book from 1995. Following more than a decade of intensified mafia violence and corruption, the Falcone and Borsellino tragedies became part of the collective conscious of an Italy that at the time found itself catapulted into a state of utter chaos. Tognazzi filmed *La scorta* in the tradition of the 'political cinema' of the late 1960s and 1970s, which espoused an ideology aimed at criticizing Italy's contemporary institutions of power.[1] Indeed, as Tognazzi notes, it is the sacrosanct duty of cinema to speak of reality and to interpret it and to act as a weapon against silence, against *omertà*.[2] In *La scorta,* however, he does more: he pays homage to those traditionally overlooked in the anti-mafia struggle by placing the emphasis on four bodyguards who are willing to sacrifice their lives to combat Cosa Nostra alongside the judge they have pledged to protect.[3] As such, *La scorta* can be thought of as an anti-mafia 'martyr film' alongside Marco Tullio Giordana's *I cento passi* (*The Hundred Steps,* 2000) and Pasquale Scimeca's *Placido Rizzotto* (2000), that is, as an 'epitaph' to mark the grave of 'unknown soldiers' of justice.[4] Whether or not the film had been conceived before the dramatic events of

1992, as Tognazzi contends, the timing of *La scorta* underscores the director's commitment to politically engaged filmmaking. In fact, according to Marcus, 'we would not be misled in identifying the Falcone/Borsellino tragedies as the unspoken signified of *La scorta*.'[5]

Despite winning five prizes in Italy, *La scorta* was initially given only a lukewarm reception on this side of the Atlantic by those who found that the film offered 'a simplistic view of honest and evil characters';[6] at Cannes it was criticized, among other things, for lacking the political impact that had characterized a previous golden age of a *cinéma engagé*.[7] The first criticism actually underscores the film's underlying mission: a careful reading of a few key episodes reveals that Tognazzi's intent was to stage a battle between good and evil. The second criticism ignores the director's uniqueness: *La scorta* denounces mafia violence and corruption and gives voice to those men who sacrificed their lives for justice. The first such man in *La scorta* is precisely Pietro Virzì. Let us therefore return to the opening scene, which is sealed with a scream that contains the name of a murdered son.

The assassination scene has interrupted the serenity of a dining room that, through the open window, looks out over a stretch of rocky beach. A greying, bearded man closes the window as an advancing storm darkens the sky and thunder rumbles in the distance. He quietly removes three glasses and three dishes from a cupboard and carefully places them on the table, which is covered with a crisp tablecloth. The old man subsequently lifts a spoonful of risotto to his mouth with the solemnity and delicate gestures that accompany the tasting of a precious, unusual dish. The solemn tone endures as he moves three bowls from the same cupboard to the table. A loud burst of gunshot then startles him; he knocks over a carafe of wine that stains the tablecloth. Calling out his son's name, he runs down a path and an exterior stairway to the street below, where a parked car contains the bloody bodies of the two victims. Bending over the young man and caressing his face, he sobs, 'Pietro, my son!' He then lifts his head and calls out a heart-wrenching 'Help me!'

The opening scene invites a reading in terms of sacrifice and Catholic ritual. What is more, the father–son relationship is recast as one between an archetypal father and an archetypal sacrificed son. In fact, the same way a priest readies the altar for the symbolic offering of the body and blood of Christ, so a father here solemnly moves between the tabernacle-cupboard and the table-altar to retrieve the receptacles for a symbolic meal. The simplicity of his gestures and the silence that engulfs them, combined with the crisp appearance of the surface readied for a dinner for three, add a quality of ritual to the scene through references to the Holy Trinity. Furthermore, the tasting of the risotto followed by the spilling of the wine functions as a culinary allusion to transubstantiation during the ritual of consecration. The symbolism of the moment is underscored by the coincidence of the off-frame diegetic sound of a gunshot, as if to signal that 'this is my blood.' The silent ritual of consecration together with that of a failed communion – the risotto will not be eaten – are evoked in the first scene and set the tone of the film.

Rituals of consecration and communion are visually echoed in subsequent scenes, starting in Angelo Mandolesi's mother's kitchen, which is decorated with family photographs (two are of a mother and child) and, less visibly displayed, a painting of a church interior. Images of family and church are the backdrop for the mother's frequent movements between cupboard and table, as she serves her son food and wine while discussing the recent double murder as the very reason for Angelo's return. Angelo states that he wishes 'to take the place of Virzì' while he gets up to open the window, and in bright sunlight mother and son share a conversation about the father's absence and the slain Virzì's place in Angelo's life. The kitchen scene follows Angelo's journey home on a night train from the mainland. His arrival in Trapani visually constitutes the film's brightest frame: as Angelo runs up the exterior stone steps, he moves from the shady alley below into a sunlit street, which opens up into a small square, where his arrival is announced by an old grandmother with a simple 'Angelo is here!', followed by his mother's embrace.

The arrival and kitchen scenes strike us as a positive replica of the tragic opening scene, the order of which is here reversed: Angelo's arrival is articulated upward towards the light, the opposite movement of the father's descent into the dark street in the first scene; instead of a father calling the name of his dead son, here an aging woman calls out that of a returning son with the joy of a triumphant Annunciation;[8] the mother's movements between the cupboard, refrigerator, and table replicate those of the previous episode; the window giving out over a threatening and darkening sky and rocky beach that was closed in the opening scene is here opened up to a brightly lit landscape; and the kitchen as a female space replaces that of an earlier male environment. Furthermore, the space filled with Christian iconography (Mother with child, the church) serves as the backdrop for the renewal of a father–son relationship that ended in the first scene. Indeed, Angelo takes the place of his slain friend, who previously had replaced his absent father ('Pietro taught me everything'). Allusions to transubstantiation are underscored by the pouring and drinking of wine and by the mother's recognition of her son's transfer as his replacement of Virzì. In fact, Angelo's 'transfer' from Rome to Trapani might well be interpreted quite literally as symbolic of one body to another, that is, as the 'rebirth' of a bodyguard. The act of transubstantiation left incomplete in a father's kitchen is completed in this maternal space.

A second re-enactment of the opening scene takes place in the apartment of the head bodyguard, Andrea Corsale, who is married with three young boys and continually negotiates his roles as head bodyguard and father. In discussing the ritualistic implications of the dinner attended by all four bodyguards and the judge in Andrea's second-floor apartment, Marcus points out the sacramental force of breaking bread as 'harking back to the biblical prototype of the meal of solidarity and self-sacrifice enacted in the ritual of Communion' whereby the 'holy wafer of the Sacrament is replaced by *cannoli* and the number of disciples is reduced to four.' As such, 'the ritual supper of De Francesco and his men is as solemn and binding as its scriptural antecedent.'[9] But there is more. The preceding scene explains the very reason for the communal gathering: Andrea had run up to Judge De Francesco's apartment in order to confess his ties to a representative of the Sicilian legal establishment, solicitor-general Salvatore Caruso, to whom he provided information that might best have been kept secret. Andrea catches the judge in his kitchen while he is preparing pasta with broccoli and listening to Beethoven's Seventh Symphony. He is welcomed with a glass of wine, which Andrea drinks while confessing his ties to Caruso and, for that reason, requesting his replacement by the more deserving Angelo Mandolesi. The judge's absolution and reconfirmation of Andrea as head bodyguard coincides with the burning of the broccoli and therefore the non-consumption of the pasta. In the next scene, the *scorta* is enjoying cannoli and breaking bread after having enjoyed the previously missed meal of pasta with broccoli, this time successfully prepared by Andrea's wife Lia, whose statement 'You were right, pine nuts work with pasta,' confirms that the dessert was preceded by the previously missed dish. The meal is consumed at Lia's table after her husband Andrea has been 'cleansed,' in the judge's kitchen, by confession, a ritual necessary before taking communion. The kitchen serves as the backdrop for the sealing of a pact between bodyguard and judge, as well as for the replacement of an 'unholy' alliance to Caruso (an alliance with potential benefits, as the couple was promised Caruso's help in finding a larger apartment); put another way, a 'corrupt' father–son relationship[10] is being replaced with a 'sacred' alliance with a judge that presupposes a willingness for sacrifice. In the opening scene, a father was preparing a meal for his son and a judge; here, the alternative father is involved in a similar activity with ultimately the same result: a never consumed meal, an incomplete ritual of sharing food. Andrea completes the ritual meal in his wife's kitchen in the same way Angelo had completed Virzì's meal in his mother's kitchen. Andrea becomes the symbolic son of Judge De Francesco and declares his readiness for sacrifice.

As in the first few scenes, in these two interiors highs and lows insinuate a good/bad dichotomy: De Francesco lives in a second-floor apartment, and the visitors' gaze is directed upwards. For instance, upon arrival from northern Italy, the judge's daughter and ex-wife look up at his window while he looks down on the street below. The dangers of descending into the street are accentuated when he is met by bodyguards for the first time: 'Never come down those stairs on your own,' Mandolesi warns. As for Andrea, he too is symbolically lifted from the ground floor to the second storey: We first meet him in a paternal role when his children welcome him from the second-floor balcony while he looks up to greet them. Once inside, he is questioned by his three boys about his work – and his vulnerability – 'below' in the streets: in the children's fantasy, the father's workspace conjures up images of car explosions, guns, bullets, armoured vehicles, and bulletproof vests – inadequate and available in insufficient amounts. Furthermore, Lia informs her husband that it is 'downstairs' at the neighbours' apartment that the children have learned about their father's vulnerability. Here too, the vertically upward and downward movements correspond with conventional 'good' versus 'bad' connotations and visually underscore the movie's moral structure.

A third ritual meal involves bodyguards Fabio Muzzi and Raffaele Frasca, who cannot be more different from each other. The former repeatedly emphasizes his desire to be reassigned to a safer environment – a cafeteria job would suit him just fine – while the latter keeps his engagement to a pastry shop salesgirl a secret for fear of being reassigned. This Last Supper of sorts is consumed at a seaside restaurant and includes the judge's daughter, Roberta. The judge, however, is absent due to a meeting scheduled with Caruso. In the absence of her father, the girl is escorted by Raffaele, who is seen playing ball on the beach with a group of children as if to underscore his innocence. During the meal and over a glass of wine, Fabio informs his friends of his imminent transfer. This is the third time that drinking wine coincides with a reference to a transfer, but here Tognazzi goes one step further. After Raffaele leaves the restaurant, as he unlocks his car, it explodes, throwing him to the pavement. Fabio kneels down next to his dying friend's bloody and sunlit body and, holding his hand, listens to him whisper his last words: 'They did not kill me. I'm not in pain. It is nothing. I don't feel anything.' For Fabio, Raffaele's violent death reinforces his commitment to refuse the transfer – instead he will take the place of his slain friend. Raffaele's words, 'They did not kill me,' take on an additional connotation: Raffaele will 'live on' in Fabio, who later refuses his much-awaited transfer and dedicates himself to the group.

The scene of Raffaele's death confirms the symbolic value of the high/low dichotomy. The restaurant is at street level, in the danger zone, although the nearby beach lends the illusion of safety. Unlike the family scenes in safe, 'high' interiors away from the street, this last family reunion takes place at ground level. In addition, a sense of surveillance is intrinsic to the scene via the high-angle camera both on Raffaele playing ball on the beach and on the party exiting the restaurant, and the viewer is left with the impression that the reunion 'below' is doomed. The camera's complicity is made clear through aerial shots of Trapani's chaotic geometry throughout the film and culminates in a night scene featuring an interview with a *pentito*. Here, the camera follows Angelo's car from above and then hovers over a brightly lit boulevard where, in effect, the screen is split into two dark areas. This symmetrical game contrasts with the dizzying geometry of the cityscape in other aerial shots, and strikes the viewer as a game of chiaroscuro that underscores the movie's division of 'good' and 'bad.'

La scorta's final scene is, therefore, not surprisingly vertically articulated as well: Tognazzi shoots it from a low angle as De Francesco departs for the mainland after having been removed from the investigation. De Francesco, addressing his bodyguards below, echoes the words pronounced by Raffaele: 'I will return.' He, too, is not dead. His pledge to return is not necessarily a promise for his own continued investigation, but a call to arms for a human collective willing to sacrifice and to fight for justice., *La scorta* takes viewers into 'obscure areas of our present'[11] but also into more brightly lit areas of the human condition. Ultimately, Tognazzi illuminates a dark and frenetically paced film with the lightness of ritual and responds to the cry for help of a father in the opening scene. To the desperate sound of 'Help me!' comes a movie that wants to be part of the solution to the diabolical workings of the mafia.

NOTES

1 See Millicent Marcus, 'In Memoriam: The Neorealist Legacy in the Contemporary Sicilian Anti-Mafia Film,' in *Italian Neorealism and Global Cinema*, ed. Laura Ruberto and Kristi Wilson (Detroit, MI: Wayne State University Press, 2007), 290–306.

2 Angelo Maccario, 'A Cannes, la Francia spara sulla "Scorta,"' *Corriere della Sera*, 15 May 1994, accessed 14 October 2009, http://archiviostorico.corriere.it.

3 Tognazzi says in a 1993 interview that there was an urgency to make bodyguards protagonists of a history that remembers them otherwise only in the moment of tragedy. See www.geocities.com /Hollywood/Location/2010/tognazzi.html?20095.

4 Marcus, 'In Memoriam.' See also the interview in note 5 of her essay where Tognazzi calls *La scorta* a 'war movie.'

5 Millicent Marcus, 'The Alternative Family of Ricky Tognazzi's "La Scorta,"' in *After Fellini: National Cinema in the Postmodern Age* (Baltimore, MD: Johns Hopkins University Press, 2002), 140.

6 Caryn James, 'Clinging to Justice in a Sicilian Town,' *New York Times*, 4 May 1994, accessed 20 October 2009, http://movies.nytimes.com/review.

7 Maccario, 'A Cannes, la Francia spara sulla "Scorta,"' 1.

8 Marcus, 'The Alternative Family of Ricky Tognazzi's "La Scorta,"' 147.

9 Ibid., 149.

10 For bodyguard–corruptive father relationships, see ibid., 147–8.

11 Gian Piero Brunetta, *Cent'anni di cinema italiano*, vol. 2: *Dal 1945 ai giorni nostri*, 4th ed. (Bari: Laterza, 2006), 397.

38 Pasquale Scimeca's *Placido Rizzotto*: A Different View of Corleone

AMY BOYLAN

Like many films set in Sicily, Pasquale Scimeca's *Placido Rizzotto* (2000) opens with an image of the bleak yet captivating Sicilian landscape, a type of image that often serves to evoke a whole series of associations about the rough, lawless, unforgiving agrarian existence of the exploited Sicilian people. Yet the casual viewer only knows this is Sicily because seconds earlier a message appears on screen stating that the film's setting is arbitrary. The epigraph reads: 'The Sicily that frames and accompanies this film is only by chance Sicily; only because the name Sicily sounds better than the name Persia, Venezuela, Brazil, or Mexico.' This prologue, as the director calls it, introduces several of the film's overarching themes. It foregrounds the intertwining of the local with the universal, which Scimeca achieves by mixing real historical people with characters from Sicilian folklore, traditional oral and non-linear modes of storytelling with documentary-like footage, poetic licence and epic tones with elements of Francesco Rosi's style of *film-inchiesta*. Scimeca himself explains that he tried to 'go beyond realism, intending the story to be a metaphor of the poor man who struggles against [the powerful], in Sicily, but also elsewhere.'[1]

The epitaph is not original – Scimeca has taken it from Elio Vittorini's 1941 novel *Conversazione in Sicilia*.[2] By quoting Vittorini, Scimeca draws a parallel between the neglect and suffering the Sicilians experienced under fascism (and before it) and their similar fate at the mercy of the mafia. For Vittorini, and seemingly Scimeca, this type of suffering – hunger, oppression, desperation – is the necessary experience that gives people their humanity. Thus the powerless are human, while the powerful do not enjoy the same moral high ground. Furthermore, just as Vittorini found the site of possible resistance to fascism at the traditional heart of Sicily,[3] Scimeca finds that same potential in figures like shepherds and wandering storytellers, all of whom, in his film, remain uncontaminated by the influence of the mafia.

In concentrating on the universal theme of the relationship between oppressors and oppressed, Scimeca, himself a Sicilian, has created a film that presents a different view of Corleone and its mafia than that represented in the most famous film associated with the town – *The Godfather* (Francis Ford Coppola, 1972).[4] He looks at the phenomenon from the perspective of the powerless and rejects the romanticized point of view of the powerful. Through his epic portrayal of Placido Rizzotto, hero of the subordinate and exploited classes, over and against Coppola's Don Vito and Michael Corleone, heroes of those struggling to be part of the dominant class, Scimeca creates a cinematic memorial to a previously forgotten young Sicilian man, offering his life story as a model of behaviour for future generations. Scimeca also gives Placido his rightful place among the many labour organizers and anti-mafia activists who had been martyred before him. Consequently, he provides Placido (and those who will eventually identify with the anti-mafia movement) with an ideological lineage and transforms the film into a collective memorial to all of the fallen in the war against the mafia. Moreover, in light of Scimeca's invocation of Vittorini, the fact that Placido himself represents a convergence of anti-fascist and anti-mafia activism reinforces his relevance to Italian collective identity and strengthens his position as a bridge between past and present.

Placido Rizzotto is based on the true story of the little-known union organizer and anti-mafia activist of the same name. It takes place in post–Second World War Sicily after Placido has returned to his hometown of Corleone from participating in the Partisan Resistance. Placido's return corresponds with what is often cited as a resurgence in mafia visibility in Sicily after the fascist years.[5] The film follows the story of Placido's growing political consciousness, which leads him to become secretary of the local Camera del lavoro (labour union headquarters) and heavily involved in trying to reoccupy land controlled and left fallow by the mafia. This activism eventually leads to his abduction and murder by Luciano Leggio and his accomplices on 10 March 1948. Placido dies halfway through the film; the remaining minutes deal with the labyrinthine investigation and devastating consequences that followed his disappearance. The film ends on a somewhat hopeful note after the responsible parties have been arrested and Placido's successor in Corleone has been chosen. It is only in the printed words that appear on screen before the credits that we learn the less rosy fate of the real-life characters.

Leggio, the man responsible for enacting Placido's assassination, and who later would become the head of the Corleonese mafia (the predominant mafia faction in Sicily), was arrested on suspicion of the murder, but the charges were dropped. To this day he has not been convicted due to 'insufficient evidence.' Although famous for his constant evasion of punishment, he was finally imprisoned for life in 1977. He remained behind bars until his death in 1993, while continuing to cultivate a strong influence.

The film also references the careers of two better-known anti-mafia activists who met violent ends at the hands of the Cosa Nostra. Pio La Torre, who replaced Placido as the secretary of the Camera del lavoro in Corleone and who is seen at the end of the film speaking to a crowd in the town square, went on to become a leader of the Communist Party in Sicily and a member of the Anti-Mafia Commission. He was assassinated in Palermo in 1982 by the Corleonese mafia. In the film, Pio La Torre interrupts his speech to chase after and introduce himself to Carlo Alberto Dalla Chiesa, the *carabiniere* captain who has been investigating Placido Rizzoto's death (and who discovered the assassins' identities). Their handshake never occurred in real life, but Scimeca claims it should represent 'the idea of lawfulness that unites a representative of the establishment [Dalla Chiesa] and a representative of the opposition [La Torre].'[6] The scene underscores the connection between the two men in that Dalla Chiesa too was gunned down by the mafia, in 1982, after he had become the prefect of Palermo. The fictional handshake by two real people (much criticized at its premiere by certain prominent socialist politicians as offensive to the memory of opposition leader La Torre, but much praised by other well-known anti-mafia activists, as well as by then-president Ciampi), is one example of the poetic licence Scimeca takes with his material. Yet leading up to this scene, he presents meticulously reconstructed accounts of the story of Placido's last hours from the point of view of three different possible witnesses/accomplices to the crime. Scimeca then shoots several black-and-white, news-footage-style scenes of Leggio and his two henchmen being arrested by Dalla Chiesa and the *carabineri*. The technique provides a stark contrast to the deep, painterly tones present in the rest of the film, and the sequence is clearly a reference to Rosi's 'documented' approach, which aims to present the facts of a situation as recounted in documents. It serves as well to intertwine the grit of the real with the nostalgic beauty of the mythical.

Scimeca's reliance on a true story lends the film its historical specificity. However, three characters locate this film *outside* of history, on the border between the specific and the universal. Placido's father, Carmelo, is the traditional Sicilian *pater familias*. He initially disapproves of his son's revolutionary tendencies, but after Placido's murder, he gains the courage to break the code of silence. He also serves as an iconic, folkloric figure. In his role as *cantastorie* (wandering storyteller) who opens and closes the main body of the film, he tells Placido's story in eleven episodes that correspond to naively painted pictures on his storyboard. He is a sort of timeless, otherworldly presence – an ancient man, but younger than he would have been had he aged in real time – who relays the simply narrated epic of his son's exemplary life in order to make sure Placido's memory stays alive. This frame situates the story among other folktales as expressions of collective memory and establishes it as one manifestation of the mythical hero's journey to transform himself and his community. The identification of Placido as hero and martyr becomes particularly evident in the Christ imagery Scimeca chooses to highlight Placido's quest – the monumental cross on the cliff above Corleone, the local passion play performed for an audience of farmers, union organizers, and mafiosi.

Likewise, the characters of Saro and his father the shepherd add a fable-like dimension to the film, even while they lament the disappearance of their own cultural relevance. In the film, the sole witness to Placido's murder is the red-headed Saro. He and his father live an insulated life on the periphery of the community – in fact, Saro, with his walking stick and long black cape, is often shown looking down on the town from the hills above, much like Placido does. But Saro's father, an impossibly huge man simply called 'Il Pecoraio' (the shepherd), has never allowed Saro to descend, literally or figuratively, into the belly of Corleone. (In the same way, it is Placido's ability to get outside of Corleone, to view it from the distant mountaintop, that aligns him with the shepherd outsiders.) While Saro's purity is not complete (we see him flagrantly disobeying his father's orders not to smoke), he represents the most innocent victims of mafia violence. After witnessing Placido's murder, the traumatized boy, who frantically and fruitlessly bangs on the townspeople's doors trying to get help, falls into a state of shock. Before he can relay what he saw, he is killed. In portraying the tragic demise of a young shepherd so far removed from the dealings of organized crime, Scimeca draws attention to the parallel between the disappearance of the traditional Sicilian lifestyle and the progressive suffocation of Corleone and its inhabitants by the mafia. Scimeca presents Saro's attempts to alert the residents of Corleone about Placido's murder, and his father's willingness to stand up with Carmelo Rizzotto in the face of mafia intimidation, as courageous and righteous behaviour that the 'more civilized' Corleonese lack. Furthermore, their resistance to mafia culture recalls Vittorini's rustic characters who reject fascist values.

While Saro, his father, and Placido display model behaviour, every hero needs a villain against whom to define himself. In Placido's case, there are two villains, one within the film and one who is intertextual. Theoretically, Placido was politically active in Corleone around the same time his fictional compatriot, Michael Corleone, was in hiding in Sicily after killing Sollozzo and Officer McCluskey in *The Godfather*. Michael's idyllic (until the car bomb) Sicilian world is populated by the likes of the benevolent Don Tommasino and the exotically beautiful Apollonia. He spends his time wandering through rustic towns, hiking scenic mountainsides, and living in a villa. Michael's lifestyle is often enviable. He is good-looking, tender with his wife, loyal to his family, and in the process of finding a sense of identity by absorbing his Sicilian and Corleonese roots. We are completely focused on Michael the budding mafioso and his journey of self-discovery, and despite his criminal tendencies, we are asked to identify with him and to support him. Sicily is romantically depicted as a place whose own identity is inextricably linked to the mafia, which in turn bestows added mystique onto Michael and his family's history. Regular inhabitants of the area other than stereotypical women dressed in black, bodyguards, and mafia bosses rarely make an appearance.

In *Placido Rizzotto*, however, the formula is reversed: we come to identify with the anti-mafia activist and the socialist union organizer and to abhor his criminal adversaries. Corleone is introduced to viewers by the *cantastorie*, who reminds his audience that when Placido returned from the war, the town was suffering from 'hunger, misery, and unemployment' and the unfair gap between 'people who owned all the land and others who had nothing to eat.' The storyteller's listing of the population's hardships carries over into a flashback onto the town's main piazza, where poor farmers come to look for work and where they commingle with young union organizers and mafiosi. In voiceover, the storyteller introduces some of the powerful local men who 'have everything,' as opposed to those who 'have nothing.' The heads of various mafia families are named, and all are clearly contrasted with the regular citizens they exploit in order to maintain power. While workers look for ways to 'feed their children,' these physically repugnant, prematurely wizened bosses look on with sinister expressions, intimidating the others. The naming culminates in the introduction of Michele Navarra, the head of the Corleonese mafia, with the disgusted storyteller saying, 'The useless thing over there … is Michele Navarra.' Scimeca orchestrates the scene to unequivocally communicate the inhumanity of the mafia. He divests it of its glamour by presenting bosses who are hard to distinguish from the other farmers; by publicly naming mafia members, who are used to operating under the shelter of *omertà*; and by giving specific examples of its ruthless and humiliating treatment of fellow Sicilians.

In *The Godfather*, mafiosi emphasize family loyalty and respect for (if not total exclusion of) women, whereas in *Placido Rizzotto*, the mafiosi in are all cowards out for personal gain. As if Luciano Leggio weren't repulsive enough, in order to dishonour Placido, cover up the real reason for his murder, and reconfirm his power all at once, Leggio rapes Placido's girlfriend, Lia, who is also Leggio's cousin. Adding to the sense of depravity is Lia's mother's complicity in her daughter's rape. She is so desperate to subdue Lia's rebellious tendencies, to silence her dissenting voice, that she betrays her in the vilest of ways. Lia's mother's actions can be read as an allegory of the self-destructive way in which many Sicilians have responded to the mafia's all-powerful grip on the island. Scimeca, though, gives us hope – Lia eventually rejects her mother and leaves Corleone entirely.[7] In doing so, she follows the path of many young Sicilians who have been forced to abandon their native land in order to lead a life free from the mafia. Except for a brief scene in which the *carabinieri* try to arrest one of Leggio's accomplices at his dreary dinner table, Lia's storyline constitutes our only look at interactions between mafia members and their families. Placido, by contrast, is portrayed as an eminently obedient son and caring brother, willing to work the fields with his father by day and entertain his sisters in the evening.

Millicent Marcus has identified a memorialist tendency in several recent anti-mafia films, such as *Placido Rizzotto* and *I cento passi* (*The Hundred Steps*, Marco Tullio Giordana, 2000), and has observed that through this film, Scimeca provides the lacking body and tomb of Placido

Rizzotto, in order to create a public memorial at which we can remember and learn from his life and deeds.[8] Through his exemplary portrayal of Placido, Scimeca resurrects a forgotten hero, inserts him into Italian historical memory, and ensures that, while his physical remains are scant, he will not be forgotten. I would suggest that Scimeca has also created the equivalent of a collective memorial for all those who have fought against injustice and perished for the greater good. This connection between 'War' with a capital 'W' and Placido's war against the mafia is evidenced by the second episode of the film's prologue, in which we see Placido during his partisan days trying in vain to save captured resistance fighters from their Nazi executioners. The clear parallel to be drawn is between the fight against the Nazi/fascist forces and the fight against the mafia's stranglehold on Placido's native Sicily. We watch as the nameless, voiceless prisoners are unceremoniously hanged, with no one to witness but Placido. In this sense, Placido's memory of their deaths gives them meaning, just as Scimeca's retelling of Placido's murder bestows meaning upon his death.

There are two scenes in the film where the listing of names of fallen heroes occurs, as if Scimeca is presenting us with the cinematic equivalent of the columns engraved on a war memorial. Early in the film, as Placido leads a union meeting, he recites the names, dates, and places of death of union organizers and anti-mafia activists to his collaborators, trying to incite them to action. Likewise, towards the end of the film, Pio La Torre re-recites Placido's list, this time to a larger crowd, after adding Placido's name to the top.

Jan Assman maintains that cultural memory – the set of commemorative practices that allows for the self-definition and survival of a given community and of which memorials are a part – is both formative and normative, educational and indoctrinating.[9] In the years after the Second World War, the memory of the resistance became representative of the way Italians wanted to think of themselves and present themselves to outsiders. It became integral to their identity as a nation. Can we, then, identify a new tendency in the new millennium? Is there, perhaps, a movement to construct a new national – or at least regional – identity based on anti-mafia activism by reviving the memory of fallen heroes like Peppino Impastato and Placido Rizzotto, and by evoking the comparison between anti-fascist and anti-mafia struggles? This nascent identity, then, would exist in opposition to the culture created by the mafia and the solidified values and behaviours that have allowed the mafia to operate unchallenged. The medium of commemoration is no longer necessarily the bronze of the state or the folktale of the countryside, but rather the cinema. The final scene of *Placido Rizzotto* depicts Carmelo the *cantastorie* sitting with head in hands after narrating the end of Placido's story to a group of empty benches. While the wandering storyteller may no longer have an audience, Scimeca suggests that the filmmaker might take his place as the agent of commemoration and thus the producer and keeper of memory.

NOTES

1 Maurizio Porro, 'Emoziona "Placido Rizzotto," sindacalista-eroe che sfidò i boss di Corleone,' *Corriere della sera*, 4 September 2000, accessed 22 September 2008, http://archiviostorico.corriere.it/2000 /settembre/04/Emoziona_Placido_Rizzotto_sindacalista_eroe_co_0_0009045926.shtml. Translation mine.

2 The work was first published episodically in the literary journal *Letteratura* between 1938 and 1939.

3 See Ruth Ben-Ghiat, *Fascist Modernities: Italy 1922–1945* (Berkeley, CA: University of California Press, 2001), 191–2.

4 In an interview that accompanies the 2001 DVD release of *Placido Rizzotto* (Istituto Luce, 2001), Scimeca expresses his admiration for *The Godfather* as a 'strong' and 'good' film, but is critical of the storytelling methods employed by Coppola.

5 While Mussolini's claims to have eradicated the mafia in Sicily have proved to be largely unfounded, there was a momentary decrease in mafia visibility.

6 Giovanni Bianconi, 'Divide il film sul sindacalista ammazzato dalla mafia. Lumia: Bellissimo. Del Turco: una manovra elettorale,' *Corriere della sera*, 15 October 2000, accessed 22 September 2008, http://archiviostorico.corriere.it/2000/ottobre/15/Divide_film_sul_sindacalista_ammazzato _co_0_0010153625.shtml. Translation mine.

7 The relationships that Placido and Leggio each had with Leoluchina Sorisi (on whom the character of Lia is loosely based) are still unclear. There are claims that she swore to take revenge on Leggio for Placido's death, yet when Leggio was finally captured in Corleone in 1964, he was discovered hiding in Leoluchina's home.

8 Millicent Marcus, 'In Memoriam: The Neorealist Legacy in the Contemporary Sicilian Anti-Mafia Film,' in *Italian Neorealism and Global Cinema*, ed. Laura E. Ruberto and Kristi M. Wilson (Detroit, MI: Wayne State University Press, 2007), 290.

9 Jan Assman, 'Collective Memory and Cultural Identity,' *New German Critique* 65 (1995): 132.

39 Marco Tullio Giordana's *The Hundred Steps*: The Biopic as Political Cinema

GEORGE DE STEFANO

During the 1980s, the political engagement that fuelled much of Italy's postwar realist cinema nearly vanished, a casualty of both the dominance of television and the decline of the political left. The generation of great postwar auteurs – Roberto Rossellini, Vittorio De Sica, Federico Fellini, and Pier Paolo Pasolini – had disappeared. Their departure, notes Millicent Marcus, was followed by 'the waning of the ideological and generic impulses that fueled the revolutionary achievement of their successors: Rosi, Petri, Bertolucci, Bellocchio, Ferreri, the Tavianis, Wertmüller, Cavani, and Scola.'[1] The decline of political cinema was tightly bound to the declining fortunes of the left following the violent extremism of the 1970s, the so-called leaden years, and, a decade later, the fall of communism. The waning of *engagé* cinema continued throughout the 1990s, with a few exceptions. But as the twentieth century drew to a close, the director Marco Tullio Giordana made a film that represented a return to the tradition of political commitment. *I cento passi* (*The Hundred Steps*, 2000) is Giordana's biopic about Giuseppe 'Peppino' Impastato, a leftist anti-mafia activist murdered in Sicily in 1978. The film was critically acclaimed, winning the best script award at the Venice Film Festival and acting awards for two of its stars. It was a box office success in Italy, with its popularity extending beyond the movie theatres. Giordana's film, screened in schools and civic associations throughout Sicily, became a consciousness-raising tool for anti-mafia forces as well as a memorial to a fallen leader of the anti-mafia struggle.

But how well does the film fulfil its civic and political commitments? Is *The Hundred Steps* 'a lesson in how to make a film from a historical subject,' as the historian Stanislao Pugliese has claimed?[2] And if so, how is it instructive? Millicent Marcus claims that the film presents 'unadorned, factually rigorous reportage.' She also maintains that *The Hundred Steps*, as well as *Placido Rizzotto*, another film about a martyred Sicilian anti-mafia activist released the same year, 'present themselves as epitaphic, as cinematic tomb inscriptions designed to transmit the legacy of moral engagement and social justice for which their protagonists died.'[3] Regarding *The Hundred Steps*, however, the latter assessment is considerably more accurate than the former, given questions raised regarding the film's factual accuracy by some of Impastato's friends and associates.

Giordana's 'mission,' according to Marcus, was to 'reinvent and transfigure the story of Peppino Impastato and to infuse it with meaning for a contemporary social context notoriously deficient in the kind of revolutionary fervor that animated the 1970s liberation movements and that drove this young man to martyrdom.'[4] *The Hundred Steps* presents Peppino Impastato as an exemplary figure, a model of idealism and political commitment worthy of emulation. It is an important film in that it brings to the screen the previously obscure story of a genuine hero who gave his life in the struggle against the Cosa Nostra. Peppino Impastato was murdered on 9 May 1978, the same day that Aldo Moro, the leader of the Christian Democrats, was murdered by the Red Brigades. With the nation focused on this trauma, the killing of a small-town Sicilian activist attracted little attention beyond the island. If not for the film *The Hundred Steps*, Peppino Impastato might have been remembered only by his family and former associates.

Impastato's story is all the more remarkable because he was born into the mafia. His father Luigi was an associate of Gaetano 'Tano' Badalamenti, a notorious boss who dominated the political and economic life of Cinisi, a town outside Palermo. His uncle, Cesare Manzella, also was a prominent mafioso. The film begins in the late 1950s, with Peppino, his brother Giovanni, and their parents driving to a banquet at Manzella's home in the countryside. There, Peppino reads a poem by Leopardi to the assembled mafiosi and their families, to the delight of his doting uncle. The mise en scène places Peppino 'in the midst of the environment into which he was born and was expected to meet its normative expectations,' that is, to become a mafioso himself.[5] The bucolic setting and familial conviviality notwithstanding, the evident hostility between Manzella and Tano Badalamenti, a guest at the dinner, foreshadows the violence that will erupt in a later scene, when Peppino's uncle is killed by a car bomb planted by a Badalamenti henchman.

The adolescent Peppino encounters the communist artist Stefano Venuti and under his tutelage begins to develop a political consciousness about the mafia and its ruinous impact on Sicily. But he is soon disillusioned by the Communist Party when it fails to support environmental and anti–organized crime protests over the expansion of the Punta Raisi airport. The young radical is disgusted by the party's timidity and insularity and by its refusal to back grassroots anti-mafia organizing. As he grows bolder and more outspoken, his clashes with his political father figure, Venuti, are mirrored by conflicts with his actual father.

Oedipal rebellion is, in fact, at the heart of *The Hundred Steps*. Luigi interprets Peppino's insistence on pursuing his anti-mafia activities as a refusal to 'honour his father,' that is, to honour Luigi by submitting to his authority. After a violent argument with his father, an enraged Peppino drags his brother Giovanni into the street and forces him to walk with him 'the one hundred steps' that mark the distance between the home of the Impastatos and that of Tano Badalamenti. The proximity of the two residences metaphorically represents the immanence of the Cosa Nostra, how deeply it is embedded in the social fabric of Cinisi.

Driven from the family home by his father, Peppino immerses himself in his revolt against the mafia. Over the airwaves of Radio Aut, a pirate station he founds with several comrades,[6] he broadcasts scathing satirical denunciations of the mafia and the local politicians who are complicit in organized crime. He mocks Tano Badalamenti as 'Tano seduto' – a play on 'Sitting Bull' – denouncing the 'chief' of Cinisi not only as a mafioso but also as a drug dealer with business in New York.[7] The scenes of Peppino's broadcasts, which establish 'an iconography of communicative power and revolutionary zeal,'[8] are some of the film's most gripping, in spite of their being set in the dark, narrow confines of a broadcast booth, where Peppino and his comrade Salvo Vitale are hunched over a microphone. That these scenes are so indelible is largely due to the superb performance of Luigi Lo Cascio as Impastato. Lo Cascio, a native of Palermo, registers Peppino's passion and bravado, his intelligence and iconoclasm, and his rage. In his bravura renditions of the Radio Aut routines, he also conveys Impastato's outrageous, transgressive sense of humour. The viewer laughs at Impastato's wit – and marvels at his audacity – yet the laughter is tinged with apprehension: the unamused, scowling men we see outside the studio listening to Impastato's scabrous broadsides include Tano Badalamenti.

When Impastato broke with the Communist Party, he became a leader of Cinisi's nascent New Left. As a Gramscian organic intellectual, he connected politics with aesthetics, demonstrating an extraordinary ability to 'penetrate the humus of popular culture to bring about its political awakening.'[9] In a scene from *The Hundred Steps* depicting a gathering at the Music and Culture Club (Circolo), he leads a group discussion of Francesco Rosi's celebrated film about Neapolitan organized crime, *Le mani sulla città* (*Hands over the City*, 1963). The scene, by referencing one of the canonical films of political cinema, situates *The Hundred Steps* within that genre. But here Giordana also acknowledges the challenges facing an organic intellectual: the youths at the Circolo, bored with Peppino's lecture on politically engaged cinema, would rather dance to rock'n'roll.

Historian Paul Ginsborg has characterized a particular tendency in Italian politics as 'the opposition of the martyrs.'[10] When the organized left is weak or embattled, exemplary heroes come forth to make personal sacrifices in defence of social justice and democracy. Peppino Impastato, according to Ginsborg, represented this tendency, which is imbued with 'Catholic symbolism.'[11] Peppino's *via dolorosa* through Cinisi is marked by stations of the cross that culminate in his inevitable martyrdom – expelled from the family home, scorned by the Communist Party, ousted from the pages of the newspaper *L'idea socialista*, banned from performing political street theatre by the local authorities, and, finally, when he decides to run for elective office, targeted by an anti-left backlash in the wake of the murder of Aldo Moro.[12]

Driving alone one evening, he is followed by a car. At a railway crossing, the car's occupants drag him from his vehicle and beat him to death. They strap his body with explosives, lay the corpse across the railway tracks, and blow it up. His killers stage the murder to make it appear that Peppino was plotting a terrorist attack and had accidentally detonated the explosives. The authorities are all too ready to collaborate in the cover-up, and, outraged over the Moro murder, the citizens of Cinisi are all too willing to believe it. But Peppino's loyal comrade Salvo Vitale memorializes his friend on Radio Aut and decries their enemies in the mafia and local politics.

In the film's final sequence, family members try to comfort Peppino's inconsolable mother, Felicia. A cousin bitterly wonders, 'Where are his comrades? Only we, his family, really care.' Then, through the closed shutters, a clamour is heard. The comrades, indeed, have come; they are marching through the streets of Cinisi carrying banners and angrily shouting slogans praising Peppino and denouncing the mafia. 'They have not forgotten him,' Felicia says, a line that 'endows Giordana's entire film with the double function of epitaph and call to arms.'[13] The screen goes to black, and a title card appears informing us that in 1997 – nearly twenty years after Peppino's murder – Gaetano Badalamenti was indicted for the crime.

Giordana presents Impastato's story efficiently and with considerable dramatic power; *The Hundred Steps* is engrossing from its opening sequences to its conclusion. Since no film biography can encompass an entire life, all necessarily are selective and interpretative. Yet the choices Giordana made in bringing Peppino Impastato's life to the screen can be questioned. Millicent Marcus praises the film's 'unadorned, factually rigorous reportage,' but the Sicilian journal, *Antimafia 2000,* cited twenty-seven inaccuracies, ranging from minor (Peppino is shown driving a car but he didn't know how to drive) to significant (Luigi Impastato didn't owe his livelihood to Badalamenti; in fact, the latter often sought help from Impastato, an established mafioso before he became an associate of Badalamenti).[14] Andrea Bartolotta, a comrade of Peppino's and one of the members of the Radio Aut group, criticizes *The Hundred Steps* for offering a 'heavily romanticized and distorted' version of Peppino's life. The film's protagonist is 'a half-Peppino' who is largely disconnected from the radical 1970s movement 'of which [he] was the "son" and the vanguard.' The film, says Bartolotta, fails to capture 'the substance of his revolutionary subjectivity, his profound capacity for analysis, that irrepressible capacity for communicating ...'

Bartolotta argues that Giordana was interested only in telling a powerful story that 'works on the emotions of the spectator, centred exclusively on the break between father and son, and the tragic end of Peppino.'[15] The family-centric focus of *The Hundred Steps* doesn't exactly violate biographical fact; Giordana's screenplay foregrounds the theme encapsulated in the title of an interview with Peppino's mother published in 1986: *The Mafia in My Home*. But Bartolotta's charge that the film overplays the family drama, and especially the Oedipal angle, does carry weight. Peppino, too, often seems driven less by political conviction than by an intra-psychic need to 'kill,' that is, rebel against, his own father, as well as the surrogate fathers Stefano Venuti and mafia patriarch Tano Badalamenti, to become his own man. His audacity at times comes across more as the recklessness of a youth with a grudge than as the boldness of a passionate but thoughtful revolutionary.

The other side of the Oedipal conflict is, of course, the son's relationship with the mother. Peppino was his mother's first-born, and he and Felicia were very intimate. In a scene of the Impastatos at the dinner table, Luigi bitterly remarks to his wife, 'Have you heard – the Communists have brought divorce to Italy. Now you can leave me and marry your son.' After Luigi has expelled Peppino from the home, Felicia visits him in the garage where he now lives. He opens a book to a poem by Pasolini and asks Felicia to read it aloud. In 'Prayer to my Mother,' Pasolini speaks of his mother as the first and most important love of his life, yet it is a love that he likens to slavery. With this scene, Giordana implies that Peppino, like Pasolini, was homosexual. Homosexuality as an 'unsuccessful' resolution of the Oedipal conflict and the mother-fixated homosexual are discredited Freudian clichés. But Giordana is on to something about his protagonist's sexuality.

Thus far, critics of the film have overlooked the representation of Peppino's sexuality. Even Millicent Marcus, who has otherwise astutely analysed the film's use of literature and literary culture, interprets the 'Supplica a mia madre' scene as 'expressing Peppino's Oedipal attachment' while also giving his mother, whom Peppino asks to read part of the poem with him, 'an active, culturally engaged role in the process.'[16] But the signs that Giordana's Peppino is a closeted homosexual, though subtle, are there to be read, certainly in the *Supplica* scene, and elsewhere as well. In *The Hundred Steps*, Peppino never speaks of, or is shown to have, a female love interest, and with the exception of his mother, all his closest attachments are with males. When a group of Italian and foreign hippies comes to Sicily, he mocks their concern with 'the liberation of the body,' but Peppino, whose life seems focused entirely on anti-mafia and socialist politics, plainly needs such liberation. *The Hundred Steps* could only have been suggestive, rather than definitive, in representing the sexuality of its hero; his family and former comrades didn't speak about it for the record. But Impastato did, in a journal entry that was included in a collection of writings by and about him, published in 2002. Impastato wrote: 'Right away I fell crazy in love with one of my young [male] comrades: I never expressed my desires, but I have constructed my political life to a large degree on this schizoid condition, tumultuously.' Impastato actually wrote 'my condition,' but then crossed out the possessive pronoun, which would have made the passage even more suggestive.[17]

Did he mean that repression of his homosexuality was fundamental to his life as a communist anti-mafia organizer? That seems a plausible interpretation. Given the pervasive homophobia not only in Sicilian society but also on the Marxist left during the 1960s and 1970s, it's hardly surprising that Impastato, were he gay, would be closeted. His inability to express a fundamental aspect of his humanity thus would add another dimension to his tragedy, as well as challenge Giovanni Impastato's assertion that his brother was 'a free man, but above all, a free Sicilian.'[18] Andrea Bartolotta, as well as other critics of *The Hundred Steps*' representation of Peppino Impastato's life, would have preferred a more rigorously analytical film, one more attuned to Peppino's ideological and political evolution and to his relationship with the movement of which he was both 'the son and the vanguard.' But such a film would not have had the same impact on the popular consciousness of average Sicilians and other Italians. At a 2008 conference in New York, I asked Antonio Ingroia, a Palermo prosecutor who was involved in bringing Tano Badalamenti to justice, about three Italian films about the mafia made in the past decade – *Le conseguenze dell'amore* (*The Consequences of Love*, Paolo Sorrentino, 2004), *L'uomo di vetro* (*The Man of Glass*, Stefano Incerti, 2007), and *The Hundred Steps*. Ingroia said that the first two were 'auteurist' works for a niche audience of cineastes. *The Hundred Steps*, he noted, was widely seen and discussed, and, as mentioned previously, has been used by anti-mafia forces to raise consciousness, particularly among Sicilian youth, about organized crime.

Three decades have passed since Peppino Impastato's death. Yet his memory lives on, providing inspiration for today's anti-mafia activists. Commemorations of his life were held in Sicily on 9 May 2008, the thirtieth anniversary of his assassination. The Sicilian singer-songwriter Carmen Consoli, one of Italy's leading popular musicians, recorded the song 'Flowers of the Field' with lyrics from a poem by Peppino. A double CD of *26 Canzoni per Peppino Impastato* (*26 Songs for Peppino Impastato*) by Sicilian and Italian folk, rock, and rap artists was released in 2008. In Palermo, the Centre of Giuseppe Impastato – Non-Profit Organization for Social Venues, continues its research, education, and anti-mafia advocacy.[19] But Marco Tullio Giordana's *The Hundred Steps*, its flaws notwithstanding, most likely will be the vehicle through which future generations will encounter that extraordinary rebel, Giuseppe 'Peppino' Impastato.

NOTES

1 Millicent Marcus, *After Fellini: National Cinema in the Postmodern Age* (Baltimore, MD: Johns Hopkins University Press, 2002), 4.

2 Stanislau Pugliese, 'I cento passi (*The Hundred Steps*)', *American Historical Review* 106, no. 3 (2001): 1109.

3 Millicent Marcus, 'In Memoriam: The Neorealist Legacy in the Contemporary Sicilian Anti-Mafia Film,' in *Italian Realism and Global Cinema*, ed. Laura E. Ruberto and Kristi M. Wilson (Detroit, MI: Wayne State University Press, 2007), 292.

4 Ibid., 303.

5 Pauline Small, 'Giordana's *I cento passi*: Renegotiating the Mafia Codes,' *New Cinemas: Journal of Contemporary Film* 3, no. 1 (2005): 41.

6 Radio Aut went on the air in 1977, one of many such 'radio libera' outlets established throughout Italy by young radicals of the extra-parliamentary left as media of agitation and political mobilization.

7   Badalamenti was one of the heads of the so-called Pizza Connection, the notorious drug trafficking ring that, from 1975 to 1984, used New York pizzerias to distribute heroin. In 1987 he was sentenced in the United States to forty-five years in federal prison. In 2002, an Italian court convicted him of the murder of Peppino Impastato and sentenced him to life imprisonment. Badalamenti died in 2004 in a Massachusetts federal prison.

8   Marcus, 'In Memoriam,' 298.

9   Ibid., 299.

10   From his keynote speech at Denuncia: Speaking Out in Modern Italy, a conference held at Casa Italia Zerilli Marimò, New York University, 27–8 March 2009.

11   According to Ginsborg, contemporary exemplars of this tendency include Roberto Saviano, the embattled author of *Gomorrah*, the political satirist Sabina Guzzanti, and the anti-Berlusconi journalist Marco Trevaglio. All three have faced serious consequences, including death threats and loss of employment, for their outspoken critiques of politicians, particularly Silvio Berlusconi, and, in Saviano's case, organized crime.

12   Aldo Moro, the former prime minister of Italy and then president of the Christian Democratic Party, was kidnapped by the left-wing terrorist group the Red Brigades on 16 March 1978. After spending fifty-four days in captivity hidden in an apartment in Rome, he was murdered by the BR on 9 May, the same day that Peppino was killed.

13   Marcus, 'In Memoriam,' 292.

14   'Antimafia 2000,' February 2002, 43, accessed 15 December 2009, www.peppinoimpastato.com/i_cento _passi.htm.

15   Andrea Bartolotta, 'Con Peppino, dalla scuola all'impegno politico,' in *Giuseppe Impastato: Lunga è la note*, ed. Umberto Santino (Palermo: Centro siciliano di documentazione Giuseppe Impastato, 2006), 187. Translation mine.

16   Marcus, 'In Memoriam,' 300.

17   Giuseppe Impastato, 'Due lettere e appunti per un'autobiografia,' in *Giuseppe Impastato*, ed. Santino, 28. Translation mine.

18   Giovanni Impastato, 'Appello per una Manifestazione nazionale contro la mafia in occasione del Forum sociale antimafia 2008 a 30 anni dall'assassinio di Peppino Impastato,' accessed 20 December 2009, www.genovaweb.org/doc/appello_impastato_30anni.pdf.

19   The centre was critical to bringing Tano Badalamenti to justice.

40   Roberta Torre's *Angela*: The Mafia and the 'Woman's Film'

CATHERINE O'RAWE

Roberta Torre's *Angela* (2002) is one of the few films to address the Sicilian mafia from a female perspective.[1] Based on a true story, the film follows the eponymous protagonist, wife of Saro, a Palermo mafioso and drug dealer, from her secure position at the film's beginning as go-between and co-organizer of the drug distribution network, to her downfall through her affair with her husband's subordinate, Masino. I will place the film in relation to the mafia film as a genre, which typically rehearses and questions ideas about masculinity, and attempt to gauge the film's mode of address. Can it be called a 'woman's film,' and does its positioning and its construction of its female character constitute an address to a female audience?

The gangster or mafia genre[2] has always revolved around questions of masculinity. Grieveson, Sonnet, and Stanfield describe gangster films as 'narratives that dramatize the boundaries of gender and sexuality'; Martha Nochimson calls them 'hypermasculine fare'; and Dawn Esposito talks of their 'self-absorption in the representation of masculinity.'[3] In a genre that traditionally foregrounds phallic masculinity (albeit haunted by a fear of effeminacy), the gangster's cultural resonance is as the archetypal tragic hero, a model of 'doomed individualism.'[4] In this model, women have, of course, traditionally been marginalized to the outer limits of the homosocial spaces these films investigate.[5] Although there has been much scholarship on the Italo-American gangster and masculinity, little critical attention has been devoted to the question in relation to Italian cinema.[6]

Torre's film marks a turning point in her own filmography as well as a rare attempt to bring to women centre stage in the mafia genre. After the grotesque and kitsch mafia musical, *Tano da morire* (*To Die for Tano*, 1997), with its use of a Greek chorus of local women as an integral part of the mafia pastiche, and her *Sud Side Stori* (2000), which used Nigerian prostitutes alongside locals in a similarly garish key, *Angela* is downbeat, almost subdued, certainly in terms of the film's colour palette, which I will discuss further later in the essay.[7] Torre's 'anthropological gaze,'[8] materialized in Daniele Ciprì's 'nervous, mobile' camerawork,[9] relentlessly investigates Angela's habitat: the camera constantly follows her down dark alleyways as she makes her deliveries, and a recurring shot captures her back as she walks away from the camera. This type of shot is normally associated with a woman-in-peril drama, but here the sense of menace is lacking, at least in the early part of the film. Rather, the camera adopts the conscious position of the voyeur, setting up the film's theme of surveillance. For example, when Angela makes the film's first transaction, handing over a parcel in an apartment block in return for money, the camera lurks behind a wall, aligning the spectator with this voyeuristic position. Similarly, when she goes to the market, the camera is positioned behind a wall, reinforcing a note of uneasiness, as we wonder who is watching her, apart from us. The camerawork thus makes us aware of a constant tension in the film: tension between Angela's invisibility (as a woman she can make deliveries, being 'above suspicion,' as one character says) and her visibility, in terms of the police surveillance that we realize later in the film is in operation against her, and the fact that as a mafia woman, she is taking a risk each time she steps outside the protective space of the backstreet shoe shop and its seemingly labyrinthine corridors and rooms.[10]

The repetition of shots of Angela walking to and from her drop-offs suggests the banality of her actions, even while they are never free from danger. In fact, many reviews of the film have noted the way in which the early part concentrates on the iterative, everyday quality of Angela's actions, 'the repeated gestures filmed always in close-up,' as she divides up drugs, delivers them, and takes phone calls.[11] As Michele Marangi notes, 'rarely has the everydayness of mafia behaviour been filmed with such simplicity and force.'[12] Angela is, therefore, presented in terms different from the usual representation of the bad or criminal woman, whose 'signification has to be overdetermined.'[13] Discourse on the criminal woman invariably asserts her exceptionality, as Dino points out: '[P]recisely by assuming this point of view – that crime committed by women is an exception – deviant women are required, almost as a complement, to have an "exceptional" nature, with all that term's many different shades, shifting from the mythical to the pathological.'[14] Instead, Angela lives the life of a busy shopkeeper, drug dealer, and housewife (although her domestic life is conjured up only fleetingly, in glimpses of her very bourgeois bathroom with its neoclassical bust, and in minimal encounters with her largely silent daughter, whose role in motivating Angela's behaviour is, significantly, downplayed).

Angela likes to walk the city streets (sometimes going out to make deliveries when she doesn't have to, such is her desire for escape), and her mobility on those noirish 'mean streets' is one of the key ways in which she asserts her limited agency. Pauline Small asserts that 'space in the Italian mafia is rigidly and hierarchically defined' and is particularly gendered in terms of representation.[15] Thus we can argue that Angela is permitted to make her repetitive journeys within the prescribed space of the Ballarò market and the familiar dark courtyards and *palazzi*, but when she transgresses the boundaries of that space, going with Masino to the open space of the port, and meeting him for assignations in an apartment block in the suburbs, both she and Masino are punished for the affair 'because it breaches the rigid boundaries allotted to them by mafia structures.'[16]

It is here that the film's visual scheme becomes very striking, as the noir tones of the shop interior and the crumbling *palazzi* are contrasted with the open space of the port, where Angela waits for Masino endlessly. Similarly, the film's use of red in the earlier sections to denote Angela's fatality to Masino (red lipstick, red blouse, red nail polish, red light in the phone box from which she rings him, red sheets on the bed they use, red packages of Marlboro cigarettes that are smoked afterwards) gradually gives way to a bare white palette: the white, hyper-real back projection when she and Masino return in the car from their first tryst, the blank walls of the prison where she is held, her white nails as she has to remove the nail polish, the light of the port area. Thus Angela is seemingly drained of her status as a femme fatale by the cinematography, which enacts her punishment both by the criminal justice system and by the mafia's patriarchal honour codes.

Angela's loss of her fatal status as mafia wife and her expulsion from the mafia world are also figured as a fantasy of escape by the film's visual scheme; the camerawork colludes in this, its manipulation of space and use of oblique angles giving a sense of oppression and exclusion in the earlier part of the film. Angela is shown several times excluded from the homosocial inner sanctum:[17] in one over-the-shoulder shot, the door to the office is closed on her face by Masino, as he says, 'We're talking about important stuff.' She is then framed in an excessively tight close-up against the dark wood of the door. This moment is clearly reminiscent of the memorable ending of *The Godfather*, yet while *The Godfather* scene was stylized and elegantly framed in an expansive, medium shot with Kay framed in well-lit profile and Michael and his subordinates beautifully positioned and fully visible in the office, the cramped spaces and hand-held camerawork of *Angela* give us only glimpses into these rooms and their secrets. In another scene, the camera pans from a shot into the dark and half-hidden room in which Saro is talking with his associates to Angela sitting outside, half-hidden and in semi-darkness, as she plays with a mule slipper and briefly looks directly into the camera, as if hoping for something, before turning her head and disappearing from the camera's mobile view. The idea that spaces are never fully revealed to us, that the camera is incapable of penetrating this darkness, is effectively maintained and supports the idea of partial vision that the film dramatizes. For example, when Masino first sees Angela, it is through bars on the window as she stands in the street oblivious to him; he follows her to the market and spies on her through a fence, which obscures part of her and our view of his face. Michele Marangi talks of Masino's gift to be able to see Angela in a different way, and describes these 'anxious, incomplete gazes' as characteristic of the early stages of the film.[18] They are also characteristic of the city as a whole, Torre implies: Masino's first gaze at Angela is accompanied by dialogue from his associate, who is unaware of what Masino is looking at, and who advises him to keep himself hidden for a while: 'Palermo isn't a safe city.' Rather, it is a city of constant observation, of quick, searching glances, of unnoticed observers.

The film addresses this notion of visual acuity directly, in the scene in which Angela and Masino first kiss, after he accompanies Saro to his optician's appointment. The point-of-view shot from Saro's blurry vision as he watches the two shapes move closer and embrace makes us, and him, question what happened. Angela and Masino rely on his inability to see. Their second kiss is also shot in almost total darkness, but with the camera positioned at a distance, as if they were being watched, either by Saro or by an unknown spectator.

At various points, the unusual sound design and mixing also work to promote the idea of surveillance and suspicion. When Angela and Masino return from their first encounter, their silent journey in the car is overlaid with their dialogue taped the previous day by police, and Masino's voice is then layered with that of the police sound recordist reading aloud the transcript, all against a musical background of the very Neapolitan Pino Daniele singing 'Appocundria.' Here, the audience is momentarily confused as to the chronology of events (Masino is heard planning their meeting after it has taken place), although we realize that even in the seemingly protected journey against this dreamlike backdrop, everything has already been noted and recorded.

Angela is a film that critics have struggled to categorize: several Italian critics note its melodramatic properties, perhaps referring more to its plotline of marital betrayal than to its stylistic qualities, as it lacks the elements of visual, emotional, and gestural excess normally associated with the melodrama.[19] The most interesting question is whether the presence of a strong female protagonist and a plotline centred on her romantic life permits the film to be characterized as a 'woman's film.' The 'woman's film' has never been theorized properly in the Italian context, as Danielle Hipkins points out;[20] however, the vast body of work on its Hollywood incarnation concentrates not only on its use of 'a female protagonist, female point of view, and its narrative which most often revolves around the traditional realism of women's experience: the familial, the domestic, the romantic,'[21] but also on its particularly gendered mode of address. Annette Kühn describes this address as constituted by 'narratives motivated by female desire and processes of spectatorial alignment governed by female point-of-view.'[22] As I mentioned, *Angela* deliberately plays with issues of point of view, vision, and looking, so that the spectator is never clearly aligned with Angela visually. A greater obstacle to female alignment, though, is surely the lack of affect displayed by the protagonist, and noted by commentators.[23] In fact, in the trial scene, when Angela is accused of lying to protect her husband, her defence lawyer describes her as someone 'totally incapable of understanding and desiring.' Her deliberate blankness and lack of motivation are enhanced by the understated performance of Donatella Finocchiaro. Finocchiaro's performance (in her first role) has led critics to liken her to the great Anna Magnani.[24] However, where Magnani's trademark performances were notable for their excess and gestural and vocal exuberance, by contrast, Finocchiaro has little dialogue in the film. Her movements are precise and neat, and her performance is about emotional restraint, as well as repression that rarely spills over. There is, however, a resemblance to Magnani at the film's end, in the montage of close-ups as Angela sits in her empty flat, hair unkempt, circles under her eyes. Interestingly, here again affect is limited, partly because of the use of an instrumental and slightly discordant jazz soundtrack ('El gato' by The Cool Elements), rather than a popular song with lyrics to evoke emotion; also, the oblique angles of the close-up and the movement from one to another is jarring, and disavows emotional proximity.

This performance style, and the laconic script and the near-elision of Angela's daughter, Minica, who works in the shop with her, all conspire to obscure Angela's motivations and choices. Mary Ann Doane discusses how, within the woman's film, 'it is important ... to know the woman as thoroughly as possible. Unlike the film noir, the "woman's film" does not situate its protagonist as mysterious, unknowable, enigmatic.'[25] The issue of knowability strikes me as a key one: Angela is neither the perverse, monstrous, overdetermined bad woman of popular fictions nor a character who can be understood through her placement in a familial or emotional context. The film distances us from her, just as it enacts the impossibility of emotional proximity, both between Angela and Saro (they press hands through the transparent screen in the prison) and between Angela and Masino (they each kiss the window when Angela is looking up at his flat from the phone booth); in fact, the film playfully dramatizes this impossibility of Masino and Angela 'knowing' each other, when they flirtatiously pretend to be strangers during a rendezvous. This emotional and visual distance and disjuncture endure until the film's final shot, a long shot as Angela gazes out to sea waiting for Masino's return, which is frozen as the explanatory credits inform us baldly that 'Masino has not returned' and that 'Angela Parlagreco works for a seamstress. She can often be seen in the bar at the port.'

What *Angela* demonstrates most strikingly and deliberately is the impossibility of the 'woman's film' in the mafia context, both in terms of the genre's conventions and in terms of the social reality that lies beyond it. As Valeria Pizzini-Gambetta notes, 'Women do not stand *per se* within the mafia organization. At most they are pale shadows of the power of their male relatives.'[26] Visibility and emancipation, she argues, are still at odds within the mafia. *Angela* refuses to allow us to 'know' its protagonist, and suspends her fate at the film's end (she is neither triumphant over her oppressive social environment nor clearly a victim of it, but rather seems resigned to it). Silent, exiled to the port area, and eternally waiting, as the non-diegetic score reaches a frenzy of dissonance, the figure of Angela denounces the fragility of any sense of female power or agency in this context. She is now visible in the light of the port, but unmoored from her surroundings, back to the camera and facing outward, totally devoid of affect in a move that leaves the spectator in a similarly unresolved and unquiet state.

NOTES

I would like to thank Danielle Hipkins and Alan O'Leary for their comments on this chapter, and Derek Duncan and Pauline Small for their generous help.

1 There have been several TV docudramas in Italy chronicling women involved with the mafia. The most high-profile of these is probably Giuseppe Ferrara's *Donne di mafia* (2001).
2 The two are not synonymous. See Steve Neale, *Genre and Hollywood* (New York: Routledge, 2000), 80–1.
3 Lee Grieveson, Esther Sonnet, and Peter Stanfield, Introduction to *Mob Culture: Hidden Histories of the American Gangster Film*, ed. Grieveson, Sonnet, and Stanfield (New Brunswick, NJ: Rutgers University Press, 2005), 4; Martha P. Nochimson, 'Waddya Lookin' at? Rereading the Gangster Film through *The Sopranos*,' in *Mob Culture*, ed. Grieveson, Sonnet, and Stanfield, 185; Dawn Esposito, 'Gloria, Maerose, Irene and Me: Mafia Women and Abject Spectatorship,' *MELUS* 28, no. 3 (2003): 95; Fred Gardaphé, *From Wiseguys to Wise Men: The Gangster and Italian American Masculinities* (London: Routledge, 2006), esp. 15–20.
4 Neale, *Genre and Hollywood*, 81.
5 See Luana Babini, 'The Mafia: New Cinematic Perspectives,' in *Italian Cinema: New Directions*, ed. William Hope (Bern: Peter Lang, 2005), 229–50. See Gardaphé's discussion of the representations of 'female masculinity' in Italian American gangster novels in 'Female Masculinity and the Gangster: Louisa Ermelino,' in Gardaphé, *From Wiseguys to Wise Men*, 109–28.
6 Studies of the representation of the mafia in Italian cinema are few and far between. Vittorio Albano's largely descriptive *La mafia nel cinema siciliano: da In nome della legge a Placido Rizzotto* (Manduria: Barbieri, 2003) gives a historical overview of the phenomenon.
7 The film's cinematographer is Daniele Ciprì, well known for his directorial collaborations with Franco Maresco, but also Torre's cinematographer on her two earlier films. Production design is by Enrico Serafini.
8 Roberto Escobar, 'Angela,' *Il Sole-24 Ore*, 10 November 2002, accessed 15 October 2010, www.mymovies .it/dizionario/critica.asp?id=9899.
9 Roberto Nepoti, 'Corri Angela, donna di mafia in un mondo regolato dal maschio,' *La Repubblica*, 5 November 2002, 45.
10 Alessandra Dino has discussed this tension between visibility and invisibility as a fundamental way of reading the social phenomenon of mafia women. See 'Symbolic Domination and Active Power: Female Roles in Criminal Organizations,' in *Women and the Mafia: Female Roles in Organized Crime Structures*, ed. Giovanni Fiandaca (New York: Springer, 2007), 67–86. Valeria Pizzini-Gambetta discusses the relation between visibility and emancipation for women in the mafia in 'Becoming Visible: Did the Emancipation of Women Reach the Sicilian Mafia?,' in *Speaking Out and Silencing: Culture, Society and Politics in Italy in the 1970s*, ed. A. Cento Bull and A. Giorgio (London: Legenda, 2006), 201–11.
11 Michele Marangi, 'Review of *Angela*,' *Cineforum* 421 (2003): 41.

12 Ibid.

13 Esposito, 'Gloria, Maerose, Irene and Me,' 96.

14 Dino, 'Symbolic Domination and Active Power,' 70.

15 Pauline Small, 'Closing the Door on Mafia Women,' paper presented at the SIS Interim Conference, London, 26 April 2008.

16 Ibid.

17 In an interview, Torre discusses the homosocial spaces of the mafia ('the dynamics of men in groups, who create spaces'). See Mary Cappello, Wallace Sillanpoa, and Jean Walton, 'Roberta Torre: Filmmaker of the Incoscienza,' *Quarterly Review of Film & Video* 17, no. 4 (2000): 321. Elizabeth Hart argues that *Angela* is 'weighted with stereotypes of performative Sicilian masculinity and male jealousy,' in 'Destabilising Paradise: Men, Women and Mafiosi: Sicilian Stereotypes,' *Journal of Intercultural Studies* 28, no. 2 (2007): 222.

18 Marangi, 'Review of *Angela*.'

19 *Positif* calls it 'a flamboyant melodrama … that awaits its Matarazzo to fill in all its contours.' J.A.G., 'Angela,' *Positif*, July–August 2002, 71. Alberto Crespi writes in his article 'Roberta Torre e Vanzina: viva l'Italia!' that it 'mixes the codes of crime reportage with those of melodrama.' " *L'Unità*, 1 November 2002, 25.

20 Danielle Hipkins, 'Why Italian Film Studies Needs a Second Take on Gender,' *Thinking Italian Film*, Special Issue of *Italian Studies* 63, no. 2 (2008): 213–34.

21 Maria LaPlace, 'Producing and Consuming the Woman's Film: Discursive Struggle in *Now Voyager*,' in *Home Is Where the Heart Is*, ed. C. Gledhill (London: BFI, 1987), 139.

22 Annette Kühn, 'Women's Genres,' in *Home Is Where the Heart Is*, ed. Gledhill, 339.

23 The *New York Times* review, for example, refers to her as a 'sleepwalker' and a 'walking zombie.' See Elvis Mitchell, 'A Sleepwalking Mafia Wife, Awakened by Some Irresistible Cheekbones,' *New York Times*, 4 April 2003, accessed 15 October 2010, www.nytimes.com/2003/04/04/movies/film-festival-review-sleepwalking-mafia-wife-awakened-some-irresistible.html?scp=1&sq=elvis+mitchell+angela&st=nyt.

24 Roberto Nepoti calls Finocchiaro 'an Anna Magnani for the new millennium' in 'Corri Angela ...'; *Positif* says that her performance is 'in perfect Anna Magnani style'; Leslie Blake describes her, somewhat improbably, as 'a cross between the buxom glamour of Sophia Loren and the earthy passion of Anna Magnani,' "The Godmother," www.offoffoff.com/film/2003/angela.php.

25 Mary Ann Doane, 'The Woman's Film: Possession and Address,' in *Home Is Where the Heart Is*, ed. Gledhill, 291.

26 Pizzini-Gambetta, 'Becoming Visible,' 208.

41 Organized Crime and Unfulfilled Promises in Gabriele Salvatores' *I'm Not Scared*

MICHAEL O'RILEY

In *Some Aspects of the Southern Question*, part of a larger attempt to define the economic and political separation of northern and southern Italy, Antonio Gramsci reaffirmed the redemptive nature of a political alliance and union between northern and southern Italy. The southern question, Gramsci argued, remained central to larger questions of Italian national liberation since the north was ultimately as dependent upon the south and its agrarian potential as the south was on the north for its industrial productivity.[1] Gramsci's reflections on the southern question inform the unfinished work, taken up again more recently in Italian politics, by one of the most important redemptive figures of mediation and union in Italy, Aldo Moro. Moro, leader of the Christian Democratic Party and architect of the notorious historical compromise with the Communist Party, has become a quasi-mythological figure haunting the Italian cultural landscape and has been immortalized in films such as Marco Bellocchio's *Buongiorno, notte* (*Good Morning, Night*, 2003).[2] Moro's kidnapping and assassination in March 1978 by the Brigate Rosse (Red Brigade) was a national trauma, the traces of which are clearly present in contemporary Italy, in that it signalled the end of the promise of national solidarity of a political and economic nature and amounted to a death knell for political reform. Gramsci and Moro were both politico-cultural exemplars of unfinished projects and past losses that are a part of Italy's legacy.[3] The unrealized potential of a past that would unite northern and southern Italy in a project of political and economic regeneration – one that has, however, been unable to find its narrative – manifests itself in Gabriele Salvatores' film *Io non ho paura* (*I'm Not Scared*, 2003).

In this essay I examine contemporary instances symbolically suggestive of an attachment to the unfinished projects of Gramsci and Moro in *I'm Not Scared*. Salvatores' award-winning feature film establishes resonances with the echoes that emerge from Gramsci's reflections on the so far unanswered southern question. The film also establishes a connection with the spectral figure and historical project of Moro. Although the film contains no overt references to Moro or Gramsci, it does evoke them in a symbolic register. Thus, my focus will not be on specificities and precise correlations between the film and its recall of the unfulfilled political projects of Moro and Gramsci, but rather on the symbolic evocations of a haunting and unfinished legacy that serve as a point of departure for the concepts of political and economic redemption with which the film engages. What is perhaps most compelling about Salvatores' film is how it projects the question of the unfinished projects of Moro and Gramsci onto a narrative about the southern question and its larger relationship to Italian culture. Although Salvatores' film does not directly treat the conventional conception of the mafia, it does address the concept of organized crime in the south. The theme of southern imprisonment and the cycle of victimization central to Salvatores' work play upon the wider theme of mafia corruption, and the film's focus on redemption represents one response to its dynamics. Moreover, the film offers a unique perspective to filmic treatments of the mafia in that it examines how the north and south of Italy and their failed union are implicated in the larger structural tenets of organized crime. Salvatores' film suggests the ways the north–south connection symbolically relates to larger patterns of national redemption. More importantly perhaps, the film, like the work of Gramsci and Moro, suggests broader correlations between the failed promises of capitalism, the failed union of northern and southern Italy, and the underlying ideology of organized crime.

An adaptation of Niccolò Amminiti's eponymous novel, Salvatores' film is set in a remote village in southern Italy in 1978, the year of Moro's death. No explicit mention of Moro's kidnapping or death is made anywhere in the film. The film's establishing shot presents southern Italy in 1978, with a wide view of the generic southern landscape. In the film, the themes of kidnapping and the corruption that links north and south, coupled with the prominent role that Moro occupies in the Italian psyche as a sort of *lieu de mémoire*, place Moro as the spectral figure of failed redemption, one that looms within the film's setting.[4] The film recounts the story of ten-year-old Michele Amitrano, who discovers another boy, Fillipo Carducci, held captive in a hole beneath the ruins of an abandoned house. The poverty and frustration of the adult villagers who, along with a Milanese collaborator, are holding the northern boy Filippo captive for a large ransom are evident throughout the film.

Throughout the film, the children, in ways reminiscent of René Clément's film *Forbidden Games* (1952), mimic the rituals of the village adults: they organize dangerous dare contests and dispense punishment, they establish gendered roles, and they share secrets, if only in innocuous ways. The children's world soon intersects with the adult sphere, however, when Michele discovers Filippo buried underground. Thereafter, Michele becomes a Christ-like figure, giving bread and water to the prisoner and beckoning Filippo,[5] who reiterates 'I'm dead,' to rise from the dead like Lazarus and come out of his cave. Indeed, it is Michele who rolls back the cover of Filippo's tomb-like prison. Moreover, throughout the film Michele makes great sacrifices for Filippo, unbeknownst to others, such as buying bread instead of candy with what little spare change he has, risking punishment by returning to the hiding place, and being beaten when it is discovered that he has found the prisoner.

Although the theme of potential redemption is omnipresent in the filmic diegesis, it is constantly in tension with the resolute and paralysed nature of the land and its inhabitants, a paralysis that aligns redemption with the systemic nature of victimization common to organized crime. The realism of the film, its widescreen shots of fallow fields and minute details of life and death in oppressive heat, have been lauded by spectators, but ironically these same spectacular cinematographic details underscore the ways the villagers remain metaphysical prisoners of their impoverished yet potentially fecund nature. The film underscores the myriad ways its adult characters remain stunted in fixed roles: Anna, Michele's mother, expresses her sadness briefly but powerfully to Michele when she avows in one very brief but potent scene that he must leave that place; Pino, Michele's father, remains confused and frustrated at times about the kidnapping and captivity, though he continues as an accomplice in the child's abuse; Felice Natale, a young accomplice from the village who checks on the prisoner and is part of the scheme, reveals a romantic, feminized side that can only be smothered by conformism to masculine-coded force and violence. The irony of his name reveals the dichotomy of his existence: the superficial and mimicked machismo of the exterior in contradistinction to the longing soul. Here, Michele comes to symbolically register a masculine-coded world of the mafia where conformity and the aura of masculine violence inhere. Nowhere in the adult world, it seems, might the victim transcend the role of victimizer. Even Michele's mother, victim as she is to the male dictates surrounding her, is unable to conceive how abuse of the northern child can only be ended through transformation from within the southern locale. The polarity of north versus south is implicit in her inability to see specifically the reflection of her own child Michele in Filippo. Michele imagines that the two boys are twins and initially fantasizes that his father is keeping Filippo in the hole to save him from the mother figure. Although Anna does tell Michele that he must one day flee the village, she ultimately remains excited about the potential payoff of the kidnapping, which is a coveted trip to the beach. Escape, distance, and removal remain the modus operandi rather than transformative acts, and ultimately distance the villagers from the landscape, which they only envision in terms of a prison from which to profit and escape.

However, it is clear that Salvatores is not simply casting the southern villagers as having crafted their own ill fate. The film cuts both ways, demonstrating at once a consciousness of exploitation and a simultaneous resignation, and ultimately illuminates the larger hidden dynamics that structure the villagers' lives. What remains more covert within the film is the larger structure of capitalist ideology that permeates it. For instance, Michele's sister plays with a Barbie doll that she holds submerged underwater. When Michele comments that this will kill Barbie, the sister responds that the doll is already 'broken.' Elsewhere, a toy van given to Michele's friend Salvatore as a gift from an uncle in America serves as a symbol of corruption. When Michele tells Salvatore about Filippo in exchange for the little blue van, Salvatore ultimately turns on Michele and reveals the secret in exchange for a chance to drive Felice Natale's car and thereby enter the adult world, a road that only delivers Felice's car to and from Filippo's prison. Felice subsequently discovers Michele at the site of Filippo's captivity. Here, the exchange commodity ultimately serves as a vehicle for entrance into the world of adult corruption, leading to disillusionment and the failed project of potential liberation undertaken by Michele. Elsewhere, a man sells shoes and goods from a truck to the villagers. Here, as elsewhere, the film focuses on material goods, images really, from somewhere else. Salvatores thus depicts a south deceived by the promises of an illusory capitalism, an exchange system where the promise of capital, like the ransom money the adult kidnappers so desperately desire, is ultimately located outside the south in a place impossible to reach. In *I'm Not Scared*, the lures of an impossible exchange system between north and south, and between the images of American-style capitalism and southern agrarian reality, ultimately remain deceptive. The children, and even the adults, play with the broken promises of a symbolically corrupt exchange system that is not fulfilling. The adults agonize over whether their ransom money will be tendered. It is within this larger structure that the village ultimately remains isolated. While this in no way exculpates the villagers for their acts (the film as we will see ultimately discloses the consequences of such ill will), it does provide the larger context for the commentary on north–south collaboration, particularly as that emerges through the sacrificial actions of Michele.

Moreover, by highlighting Filippo as a Lazarus figure, the film symbolically gestures to the opportunity for collaboration between an agriculturally rich south and an industrially salubrious north. The missed opportunities for economic transformation in the south, for example, are underscored by giant rolling combines in the fields. This scene points, in a larger sense, to the very question of opportunity by serving as a symbolic explanation of the historical trajectory of the southern peasantry and provides an explanation for the nefarious dependency on northern industrial capital that the film underscores. In many ways, the scene recalls the failure of the organized land occupation movements that swept across the south in 1949 and 1950 and involved hundreds and thousands of landless peasants, politicizing an entire generation. Of course, these failures were directly linked to the pervasive hold of organized crime. The consequences of the state's intervention – sometimes lethal – to end the occupations on behalf of powerful landowners and to side with a more capitalistic approach to landownership and development can be seen in the powerful machines that roll through the fields in the film, ultimately underscoring the lost opportunity for political and economic regeneration. This loss is further underscored by the fact that the peasant villagers can only view the land as a prison. Here, as elsewhere in the film, the wider consequences of the failure of state-inspired capitalism, and of a politicized opposition to it, are represented as missed opportunities with widespread national implications affecting both northern and southern groups. By gesturing to the question of the trajectory of the southern peasantry and its losses, which have wider consequences within the national topography, the film's critical perspective not only suggests loss but also gestures towards new directions for potential national, or at least north–south, collaboration.

Yet the potential opportunities for redemption highlighted by the film are ultimately only articulated in the dismal, melancholic light of ultimate sacrifice and wounding recognition. When Michele learns that Filippo is most likely going to be killed by the villagers in order to cover traces of their crime, he leaves the house that very night and helps Filippo escape. After carrying the feeble Filippo and pushing him over a high fence, Michele remains trapped and urges Filippo to run. We then hear a gunshot and discover that it is Michele's father who has shot his own son in place of Filippo. The film ends with Michele being carried by his father into the fields as police helicopters hover, their searchlights illuminating the scene. Filippo then emerges, and he and Michele reach out for each other's hand in the lights of the helicopter. The film ends with the boys reaching out to each other without achieving union. Ending this way, the film underscores the missed opportunities for redemption, both moral and economic, that the southern question raises. Michele's father, it would seem, recognizes in the end his tragic crime, albeit far too late. He cradles his injured son with Filippo looking on, a southern *pietà* embodying the villagers' failure to protect their own through their inability to see the northern reflection that is so intricately implicated in their own fate. The film's ending symbolically underscores how the union of north and south in liberation from the historical weight of corrupt exchange is a potential project of immense dimension.

Yet *I'm Not Scared* seems to suggest a larger problem with this type of national redemption, one that aligns redemption with the problems of capitalism underscored in Gramsci's larger conceptualization of the southern question and in Moro's conception of a new economic structure. This problem is made apparent through the transformation of symbolic liberation within the film. Throughout the film we see hawks soaring over the fields where Filippo is prisoner, symbols of the freedom that Filippo cannot have. In one scene Michele imitates the birds, running through the fields. The scene recurs as a variant as well when Michele rides his bike with arms outstretched and eyes closed. While the birds represent a sign of liberation, their substitution later in the film for *carabinieri* helicopters swooping in over the fields to liberate Filippo serves another purpose. The swooping helicopters recall scenes from *Apocalypse Now* (Francis Ford Coppola, 1979) and remind us of other promises of capitalist liberation. The symbolic substitution of a redeeming state force (in the form of the state whirlybirds) for natural forces in *I'm Not Scared* suggests a larger potential danger, a sense that the concept of the state might be viewed as a liberating ideal. Such an assertion neglects the potential of groups to harness their own revolutionary and transformative potential. The film demonstrates that the villagers' own inability to transform the cycle of corruption, despair, and longing through local mobilization is a part of this equation.

Here, the figure of Gramsci reappears. Gramsci's *Some Aspects of the Southern Question* paved the way for his later prison writings on the vicissitudes of political and economic transformation through state mediation. Such work developed the thesis that the sole focus of revolutionary potential should not be the state. As Marcus Green points out, in *Some Aspects of the Southern Question*, 'Gramsci moves away from the view that power is concentrated in the state and the view that the goal of revolutionary struggle is to capture state power.'[6] What Gramsci does, in shifting his focus from the state, is to ultimately empower the masses to envision their condition from within a nexus of collaborative and self-reflective vision. Gramsci's acknowledgment of the crucial union of north and south in a project of political and economic regeneration in *Some Aspects of the Southern Question* can only take place through critical reflection and a resultant solidarity.

I'm Not Scared concludes with the *pietà* as a figure of failure and potential redemption while the state-liberating forces hover above. In this way, Salvatores focuses on the reflection of the northern boy, Filippo, standing as a pale and ghostly figure and underscores how the reflection of the north in the south, and its relationship to the state, remains a national problem. Although no overt references to Gramsci and Aldo Moro appear in *I'm Not Scared*, we can see that the film's themes of kidnapping, the unrealized union between the north and south, and potential redemption through transformation – understood in the context of the film's appearance in 2003 and its political background of Berlusconi capitalism – return us to their unfinished work. *I'm Not Scared* remains, in its own way, an unfinished project, beckoning us as it does to return to that fated year of 1978 to contemplate the spectral figures of redemption and unfinished works it would like to return to the contemporary landscape. Such a movement would provide insight into the dynamics of organized crime and its larger relationship to capitalism and the nation-state.

NOTES

1 See Antonio Gramsci, *The Southern Question*, trans. Paul Verdicchio (West Lafayette, IN: Bordighera, 1995), 15–45. Gramsci's notes on *The Southern Question* are part of a larger tradition in Italy of attempting to define southern Italy's relationship to the north. This attempt has been central to the conception of Italian national identity.

2 For an in-depth discussion of the spectral aura of Moro in selected contemporary narratives, see Max Henning, 'Recurrence, Retrieval, Spectrality: History and the Promise of Justice in Adriano Sofri's *L'ombra di Moro*', *Italian Culture* 22 (2004): 115–36.

3 The spectres associated with these figures from Italy's political history evoke a melancholic remainder of the past, be they the invocation of unfulfilled promises represented by Gramsci's writings in *The Southern Question* or the ethereal outlines of Moro evoked in *Good Morning, Night* or by the very cover of Giampaolo Cassitta's popular novel *Il Giorno di Moro* (Rome: Frilli, 2006), which features a relief figure of Moro in white, conjuring a ghostly imprint.

4 Moreover, the film was released in 2003, the 25th anniversary of the kidnapping. The same year saw the release of two films based on Moro's life: *Good Morning, Night* and *Piazza delle cinque lune* (Renzo Martinelli).

5 Of course, Filippo, too, is positioned as a Christ figure in that he rises from the dead as a cover is rolled back from his prison.

6 Marcus Green, 'Gramsci Cannot Speak: Presentations and Interpretations of Gramsci's Concept of the Subaltern,' *Rethinking Marxism* 14, no. 3 (2002): 1–24.

42 Growing Up *Camorrista*: Antonio and Andrea Frazzi's *Certi bambini*

ALLISON COOPER

Antonio and Andrea Frazzi's *Certi bambini* (2004), based on Diego De Silva's eponymous novel, dramatizes the process by which the Neapolitan Camorra comes to supplant traditional Italian social institutions such as the Catholic Church and the family.[1] The film describes, through the story of its eleven-year-old protagonist, Rosario, the ways in which poverty, illiteracy, and unemployment in contemporary Naples force the city's youngest inhabitants into the street and into the arms of the Camorra. In highlighting the causal relationship between Naples' inadequate social structures and the social reproduction of violence perpetuated by the Camorra, the film aligns itself ideologically with such post–Second World War neorealist films as Vittorio De Sica's *Ladri di bicicletta* (*Bicycle Thieves*, 1948) and *Sciuscià* (*Shoeshine*, 1946), even as it makes a marked departure from those films' neorealist aesthetic in its employment of a distinctive cinematographic style best described as 'high-gloss neorealism.'[2] This essay examines *Certi bambini*'s treatment of organized crime in Naples within the film's broader cinematographic and cultural contexts, exploring in particular its relationship to Peter Brook's dystopian film *Lord of the Flies* (1963) and a Freudian world view that pits the aggressive individual, whose instinctual violence is exploited by the Camorra, against the processes of civilization.

Set in the early 2000s, *Certi bambini* depicts an unnamed yet clearly recognizable Naples and its surroundings in a period of pronounced mob violence.[3] By the time film was released in 2004, Campania, and indeed Italy as a whole, had become accustomed to the Camorra clans' internecine feuds, but the organization's increasing disregard for the lives of innocent bystanders and the minors it corrupts suggested that a troubling transformation of its criminal values was taking place. Scholars like Tom Behan, Felia Allum, and Percy Allum have linked this transformation to a fundamental change in the Camorra itself, which, from the post–Second World War period through to the early twenty-first century, has become less a social organization dedicated to personal advancement than a business enterprise devoted to making money.[4] The value of a human life, then, once discounted in a *camorrista* code of values privileging honour above all else, is depicted in *Certi bambini* and in more recent films such as Matteo Garrone's *Gomorra* (*Gomorrah*, 2008) as having decreased even further in the pursuit of increased profits.[5]

Certi bambini's subject is the failure of Italian society to protect its children against this corruption and the ease with which certain children adopt the Camorra's indifferent attitude towards human life. Perhaps the most troubling social consequence of this attitude has been the organization's increasingly successful exploitation of minors as drug runners and, in extreme cases, as child assassins.[6] This practice began in earnest in the mid-1990s in response to state crackdowns on organized crime, as bosses realized that the legally protected status of minors provided them and the Camorra immunity from prosecution. Between 1990 and 1992, for example, Campania saw a 93 per cent increase in the number of children under the age of fourteen who were charged with crimes.[7] This relatively new social reality in Naples is presented in *Certi bambini*, which recounts the adolescent Rosario's conversion by, and ultimate affiliation with, the Camorra.

The film locates Rosario at a crossroads where he must choose between the community of his local Catholic parish and the more seductive subculture of the Camorra. With only an aged, befuddled grandmother to act as his guardian, he forms tenuous relationships with the residents and volunteers at a local home for young women administered by the Church, but they are not enough to safeguard him from the attention of local *camorristi*. When events occur at the home that compel Rosario to defend his honour and avenge the death of a female friend who is also his precocious love interest, he is drawn to the Camorra and, in particular, to its recourse to violence as a means of resolving problems.

Adopting the conventions of the mafia movie as well as those of the coming-of-age film, *Certi bambini* presents Rosario's passage from child to *camorrista* through a series of flashbacks anchored in the film's narrative present. As Rosario journeys on a metro train towards a destination revealed only at the film's end, the events leading to the story's dénouement are disclosed one by one. This disjointed exposition underscores the lack of continuity in Rosario's upbringing, just as the premise of the film's opening sequence, in which Rosario and his friends dare one another to cross several lanes of traffic on a busy Italian highway, underscores the precarious nature of his existence. The prologue's suspenseful pace suggests that, like many mafia movies, *Certi bambini* will have a significant action component (and indeed, many of the film's sequences are equally suspenseful), yet an early visual allusion to Peter Brook's 1963 adaptation of *Lord of the Flies* alerts attentive viewers that the film has more to offer by way of social commentary than its action-packed prologue might otherwise suggest.

Brook's film, like the 1954 novel by William Golding upon which it is based, famously recounts the efforts of a group of British schoolboys to govern themselves after they are marooned on a deserted island, and the disastrous results that follow. As Rosario and his friends scramble up an embankment and through the brush in the opening frames of *Certi bambini*, graphic continuities between their journey and that of Ralph, Piggy, and the other boys in *Lord of the Flies* mark similarities between the films that are also thematic. In both works, adolescent boys are left to their own devices, and in the absence of adults, their social practices become increasingly brutal as violence supplants the rule of law. This visual allusion to *Lord of the Flies* in the opening frames of *Certi bambini* evokes the earlier film's setting of social isolation. The outskirts of modern-day Naples, it suggests, are just as isolated as *Lord of the Flies'* deserted island, at least for children like Rosario and his friends. As we soon discover, the Neapolitan children in the Frazzi brothers' film react to that isolation much like Ralph, Piggy, and Jack do in *Lord of the Flies*, forming gangs and adopting violent means to increase their chances of survival.

Unlike the spare mise en scène of *Lord of the Flies*, which facilitates the film's allegorical critique of modern society, *Certi bambini*'s mise en scène underscores the social realities of contemporary Naples. Youth gangs like the one formed by Rosario and his companions do indeed roam Naples' neglected neighbourhoods and waterfront, abandoning their schooling and tenuous family lives in search of alternative forms of social acceptance. As their members commit thefts and assaults, their actions bring them into contact with members of the Camorra, who then pressure them to commit increasingly violent criminal acts. Yet even as the graphic continuities that initially link *Certi bambini* to *Lord of the Flies* are succeeded by a more sweeping cinematographic vision of Naples' poverty and isolation, the earlier film remains a touchstone as it becomes clear that *Certi bambini* shares its thematic concern with the descent of the individual and the state into violence. The downward trajectory of the boys in both films implicitly criticizes the adults and the state that permit such a thing to occur: grown-ups are at fault in the diegetic world of the films due to their inability to safeguard society's youngest members, the representatives of its future and hope for a functioning society, as are the grown-ups in the non-diegetic world of the films' spectators. Both stories serve as an admonition that, without a return to civilization, the violence into which these children are raised will be socially reproduced through primitive, regressive rituals and rules intended to sanction and perpetuate it. This is what takes place in *Lord of the Flies*, when the murderous tribe formed by one of the boys to oppose the rule of another engages in ritualized slaughter, and in *Certi bambini* when Rosario confirms his participation in the Camorra with similarly ritualistic acts of slaughter. In both films, violence seems to offer surer prospects of survival than non-violence, the latter represented in *Lord of the Flies* by Ralph's attempt to civilize the island society and in *Certi bambini* by the efforts of Santino and Don Alfonso – figures associated with the Church's home for young women – to present Rosario with an alternative to the Camorra.

Freud's theory of the divided self is one interpretive key to the conflicts among the boys in *Lord of the Flies*, whose interactions are read in this light as an outward manifestation of the battle of will that takes place in the individual's psyche as the civilizing superego seeks to check the primal drives of the id.[8] The violence that increasingly characterizes Rosario's actions in *Certi bambini* issues from a related Freudian paradigm: that of the Oedipal complex. Characters and narrative in the film are organized neatly around a Freudian patriarchal structure in which male authority is predicated upon the Law of the Father – the paternal injunction that forbids the son from sleeping with his mother and, by extension, acts as an injunction against violence.[9] Rosario, for example, is a wayward filial figure who wishes to sleep with Caterina, the young woman who befriends him at the home. Caterina's pregnant state confirms her symbolic role as mother in the film, just as Santino's encouragement of Rosario casts Santino in a fatherly role. Rosario's decision to affiliate himself with the Camorra is conditioned by an Oedipal logic, as he discovers Santino and Caterina making love and, rather than repress his desire for Caterina, sets Santino up with a plan intended to publicly humiliate or even harm his rival.

The Camorra, with the mobster Damiano as its representative, presents itself to Rosario in the film as an alternative family: one that – unlike the one constituted by Santino, Caterina, and Don Alfonso – encourages him to express rather than repress his violent impulses. Damiano replaces Santino as a paternal figure, just as he replaces traditional Christian familial values of love and compassion with fear, indifference, and violence through a violent initiation ritual that has him ruthlessly shooting his own dog, 'Dottore,' and then demanding that Rosario finish the job. Damiano's cruel execution of a seemingly beloved pet, carried out to demonstrate his power and authority to Rosario, and Rosario's subsequent transformation into a *camorrista* as he is rapidly acculturated into the organization, is thus framed in the film as the violent consequence of the family's and the Church's failure to protect Italy's youngest generation. Moreover, the scene reveals the mechanism by which the Camorra, as an alternative to those institutions, ritualizes violence and guarantees its social reproduction through the induction of young recruits like Rosario.

If the Camorra is a substitute for Rosario's absent family in *Certi bambini*, it is a false one since one of the primary ways in which the Camorra distinguishes itself from (and has arguably gained primacy over) the Sicilian mafia is through its lack of insistence on blood ties for access to the organization.[10] Newcomers like Rosario may join with relative ease, as the film suggests, but they may just as easily be cast out of the group (as the dog Dottore's abrupt exit symbolically demonstrates). Yet the film does not, as some mafia films do, engage in a simplistic division of the world into good and evil, with family and Church in the former category and the Camorra in the latter. Beyond Rosario's own inadequate family (his grandmother's befuddlement is the result of the Rohypnol that she regularly takes), the other biological family we encounter in the film is composed of a mother who prostitutes her pre-adolescent daughter to Rosario's friends. This scene, like many others in the film, underscores the tenuous way in which children like Rosario survive, as well as the complicity of the failing family in their exploitation and delinquency. This scene also raises troubling questions about the highly gendered nature of female roles in the film – the depictions of Caterina and the young girl suggest an adherence to traditional conceptions of gender roles that we know, from sources like Roberto Saviano's *Gomorra* and the work of researchers like Felia Allum, no longer define the lives of women in Naples and in the Camorra.

As the failed efforts of Santino and Don Alfonso suggest, the Frazzi brothers' critique of the family extends to the spiritual family ostensibly formed by the Catholic Church, embodied in the film by Don Alfonso, the priest who administers the home – a sort of halfway house – for young women. Don Alfonso reveals the extent to which the Church has lost touch with modern reality when he reassures the young, unwed Caterina that her pregnancy is 'the most beautiful thing that could happen' to her. Yet that pregnancy, instead of being the most beautiful thing that could happen to her, kills her as she haemorrhages to death in a poorly staffed emergency room. Like Pope Benedict XVI, who recently observed that 'Naples obviously needs substantial political action, but first still, a profound spiritual renewal,'[11] Don Alfonso underestimates the devastating effects of the Camorra, and of Naples' related socio-economic decline, upon all of the city's inhabitants. Caterina and her unborn child are just two of the many human casualties of Naples' desperate lack of resources, a situation unlikely to change with its spiritual renewal.

Anti-mafia activists have condemned films like *The Godfather* for their commercialization of the criminal underworld,[12] but *Certi bambini* resists this kind of critique, as we have seen, through its refusal to elevate any social group in the film and in its commitment to depicting the everyday struggles of Naples' most marginalized, vulnerable inhabitants against a predatory Camorra. Indeed, the film's subject matter – the violent exploitation and corruption of youth in the harsh socio-economic conditions of an embattled Naples – suggests that its proper cinematographic context is as much Italian neorealism as it is the mafia movie genre. Like De Sica's *Shoeshine*, for example, *Certi bambini* utilizes child protagonists to underscore the enduring consequences of the failure of Italy's inadequate institutions. But both films' social critiques derive their power as much from their young protagonists' seemingly innate cruelty, as they do from their victimization. The young protagonists of *Shoeshine*, like Rosario and his companions in *Certi bambini*, become victimizers when confronted with society's indifference to their fate, capable of the same kind of violence as their adult role models. This uncomfortable reality – the Freudian notion that every individual is inherently violent, even (or especially) a child – is fully expressed in *Certi bambini*'s disturbing ending, when Rosario performs an execution at Damiano's behest and completes his assimilation into the Neapolitan criminal underworld. Once Rosario's hit has been carried out, he shrewdly conceals his actions by joining a group of children engaged in an innocent soccer game near the scene of the crime. Now a confirmed *camorrista* and killer, he hides in plain sight, and *Certi bambini*'s viewers are left to contemplate his bleak future and that of a society whose youngest, most vulnerable members are corrupt.

In conclusion, I'd like to reflect upon *Certi bambini*'s narrative structure, which might appear overly determined in relation to the neorealist mandate that cinema set aside artifice in the effort to depict reality. In the Frazzi brothers' film, a flashback structure ensures that we end up where we began, and underscores the impossibility of true progress in order to demonstrate contemporary society's regression to a less civilized state. It is worthwhile, however, to consider the extent to which Rosario's fate, and that of the young children upon which his character is based, is also overly determined, be it by Freud's death instinct or by a Camorra canny enough to exploit it. Ultimately, the hopeless, inexorable course of these children's lives *is* guided, if not by the hands of directors like the Frazzi brothers, then by those elusive hands over the city alluded to in Francesco Rosi's 1963 film *Hands over the City*. The latter have exerted their influence over Naples and its residents since the inception of the Camorra centuries ago and, judging by the bleak portrait of the city presented in *Certi bambini* and similar films, may well continue to do so for the foreseeable future.

NOTES

1 *Certi bambini* has been released in English-speaking countries under various titles, including *A Children's Story* (U.S.), *Certain Children* (Australia), and *Stolen Childhood* (Canada). For consistency's sake I will refer to it hereafter by its Italian title.

2 Stephen Holden, 'Film Festival Reviews: A Global View of Human Experience That Tells Some of the Stories behind the News,' *New York Times*, 26 March 2005, Arts Section (online edition), accessed 15 June 2009, http://query.nytimes.com/gst/fullpage.html?res=9400EFDD113FF935A15750C0A9639 C8B63.

3 For a recent description of the Camorra's activities in and around Naples, see Felia Allum and Percy Allum, 'Revisiting Naples: Clientelism and Organized Crime,' *Journal of Modern Italian Studies* 13, no. 3 (2008): 355.

4 See Allum and Allum, 'Revisiting Naples: Clientelism and Organized Crime,' *Journal of Modern Italian Studies* 13, no. 3 (2008); and Tom Behan, *See Naples and Die: The Camorra and Organized Crime* (London: I.B. Tauris, 2002).

5 For more on organized crime and the devaluation of human life, see Renate Siebert, *Secrets of Life and Death: Women and the Mafia*, trans. Liz Heron (London: Verso, 1996), 76–78.

6 See Felia Allum, "Becoming a Camorrista: Criminal Culture and Life Choices in Naples," *Journal of Modern Italian Studies* 6, no. 3 (2001): 343.

7 Behan, *See Naples and Die*, 160–63.

8 See Sigmund Freud, *Civilization and Its Discontents* (New York: W.W. Norton, 2005). Freud writes that 'the inclination to aggression is an original, self-subsisting instinctual disposition in man, and … it constitutes the greatest impediment to civilization' (118).

9 For a more thorough analysis of the function of the Law of the Father in the mafia film, see Danielle Hipkins's excellent analysis of Pietro Germi's *In the Name of the Law* in this volume.

10 For a detailed discussion of the symbolic significance of blood relationships among members of criminal organizations, see Anton Blok, *Honour and Violence* (Malden, MA: Blackwell, 2001), ch. 5.

11 Phil Stewart, 'Pope Condemns Camorra Violence on Naples Visit,' *Reuters*, 21 October 2007 (online edition), accessed 20 June 2009, www.reuters.com/article/idUSL2147706620071021.

12 See, for example, Luigi M. Satriani, 'Della mafia e degli immediati dintorni,' in *Mafia, 'Ndrangheta, Camorra. Nelle trame del potere parallel*, ed. Stefano Morabito (Rome: Gangemi Editore, 2005), 33–7.

43   Lipstick and Chocolate: Paolo Sorrentino's *The Consequences of Love*

MARY WOOD

What does a young Italian film director do when he/she wants to have a career in the film industry, combining many years of financial rewards with critical recognition? In this essay I examine *Le conseguenze dell'amore* (*The Consequences of Love*, 2004) as an example of a young man's bid to move his career forward coinciding neatly with the need to construct a comprehensible story world that is accessible to both Italian and international audiences. I explore the creative and intellectual choices made by Paolo Sorrentino in his depiction of the contemporary mafia.

For a young director there are dangers in becoming trapped in the low-budget/no-budget sectors, where a director is dependent on festival prizes that bring him/her to the attention of critics but where the films may be seen by only a handful of people. In Paolo Sorrentino's case, those 'handfuls' included critics who responded to the originality of his first film, *L'uomo in più* (*One Man Up*, 2001). Armed with critical recognition for his originality and visual style, Sorrentino then needed to make his name, while aiming at the mass audience in order to access a larger budget. These ambitions entailed a bid to enter the quality sector of the film industry. This is the top end of the authorial and art cinema market and is characterized by big budgets, stars, international distribution, and, visually, by spectacle.[1]

Sorrentino's directorial style had been recognized with his first film; but for his second film, he needed strong production values and a story with international appeal. He needed to be both global and local. In *Consequences*, Sorrentino would combine commercial and personal necessities with the demands of his chosen story. His track record meant that Indigo Film, a small company that had produced his earlier films, was in a position to achieve a partnership with Fandango, a large Italian company specializing in producing quality, authorial art films for international distribution. Fandango has a relationship with Medusa, a vertically integrated group of companies wholly owned by the Fininvest Group, which also 'owns a 35% share in the Mediaset group of television channels.'[2] Mediaset was founded by Silvio Berlusconi, sometime prime minister of Italy, and is a horizontally integrated empire that can ensure that any film with Medusa backing will not only receive wide exhibition in Italian cinemas but also be shown on terrestrial and satellite television and pay-TV channels in Italy, Europe, and South America. Thus, although this film is locally specific in terms of being in the Italian language and without prominent stars, its status as a mafia film meant that international audiences would have an understanding of the sorts of stories, characters, and iconography to expect. Although box office receipts for *Consequences* were predominantly earned in Italy, it achieved US distribution and has also succeeded along the long feeding chain of various television, satellite, and DVD opportunities. Sorrentino's negotiation with the contemporary media industries has a link to his story, which is an attempt to depict the face of the modern mafia.

As is the case with the film and media industries, mafia organizations have changed and mutated, becoming less like their 1930s stereotypes. In 1973, Francesco Rosi was set out to deglamorize the mafia in his film *Lucky Luciano*, showing, in Gian Maria Volonté's characterization, the banality of Luciano's views and existence, but also the parallels between legal and illegal power as exercised in the latter part of the twentieth century. When I interviewed Rosi in 1987,[3] I got him to talk about the problems of making contemporary political cinema and he pointed to the difficulties of falling into the trap of genre movies about the mafia, as well as the inappropriateness of the film format popular in the 1970s denouncing various abuses of power. Denouncing crimes was not enough. Times had changed, but some institutional relationships among political, economic, and illegal powers had not changed as much as Rosi had hoped, and whereas representatives of the mafia and the Camorra had been easily recognizable thirty years earlier, they were now hiding behind legal business opportunities. Also, changes in the film and media industries now required that a film have international appeal because an ambitious film was unlikely to cover its costs in Italy alone. References to a purely local, Italian situation created problems when it came to targeting audiences because they were less comprehensible and interesting to an international audience.

Seventeen years later, in the wake of the financial kickback scandals, trials of corrupt politicians, murderous mafia attacks on honest magistrates, and successive Berlusconi governments in which the prime minister attempted to put in place legislation that would make some corrupt business practices immune from prosecution, Paolo Sorrentino confronted the problem of representing the twenty-first-century mafia. Writers about the mafia, such as the Sicilian novelist Leonardo Sciascia,[4] have always stressed its long history and its early financial appeal to rural and provincial middle classes denied access to the circles of the upper class and/or rich political elite. The mafia has always functioned as a parallel and parasitic organization to the structures of legal power, occupying a zone between basic commodities and their potential consumers. For it to maintain this place, it needed to corrupt state functionaries and politicians needed to turn a blind eye to the diversion of monies from legitimate commercial organizations or from the state. Since the 1980s, mafia organizations have hidden their operations behind the facade of legitimate business in order to conceal the immense amounts of money generated through drug and human trafficking, gambling, and pandering to many human weaknesses. Money buys power, and money invested in legal industries and media empires enables illegal power networks to have a direct say in the decisions of contemporary states. As Eric Hobsbawm has pointed out, in a 'rapidly globalising world economy based on transnational private firms that are doing their best to live outside the range of state law and taxes,' even big governments find it difficult to control their national economies, let alone develop sufficient technical resources to police what flows in and out of national territory.[5] In a situation where everything becomes mafia, or where mafia dealings are deliberately concealed, it becomes difficult to represent the mafia convincingly. How did Sorrentino do it?

In *The Consequences of Love*, Sorrentino uses mainstream norms of characterization and mise en scène, and the conventions of Italian film noir, to make his ideas comprehensible. The protagonist, Titta Di Girolamo, is emblematic of how the mafia utilizes the panoply of professional business roles to achieve its financial objectives. Halfway through the film, Titta reveals that he had been a business consultant who invested for the mafia; as punishment for losing them $250 billion, he has been confined to a Swiss hotel, where he leads a restricted life, receiving mysterious suitcases full of money weekly, which he deposits in a Swiss bank. Titta's bleak life is disturbed by his love for Sofia, the hotel's young barmaid. For Sofia, he embezzles money from the suitcases, and eventually he is called to account by his bosses.

As I have explored elsewhere,[6] Italian noir uses the conventions of American noir but inflects them with disturbing asymmetry, chiaroscuro lighting, and imaginative uses of the cinematic spaces of Italian towns and cities through spectacular visuals and performative and visual excess. These draw attention to simple explanations that mask abuses of power and disturb the unquestioning acceptance of the status quo, strategies that have been characterized as neo-baroque and as a particularly Italian form of postmodernism. At the same time, Italian noir texts strive to persuade an audience that their interpretation is the right one through use of the realist mode, while emotionally signalling the importance of the mysteries explored. The effect of these visual, kinetic, and performative tensions is to destabilize the world of the film. In Sorrentino's *Consequences*, access to what is hidden (the nature of the mafia and how it operates) is achieved not only through the disruption of emotion into a sterile existence but also through visual and narrative tensions and excess. The film oscillates between cold tones and regular graphic patterns, and the warm tones and decorative richness characteristic of the neo-baroque. The film uses the cold colour tones and orderliness of modernist architecture, bland corridors, streets, and hotels to suggest order and regularity and the restricted nature of Titta's existence. However, within sequences composed predominantly in cold tones, Sorrentino uses several visual techniques to disturb the eye, preventing unquestioning acceptance of the story world. One of these is the diagonal composition, exemplified by the film's stupendous opening long shot of the moving walkway leading into the bank. The strongly diagonal orthogonal lines of the composition construct an asymmetrical composition within the frame and destroy 'the spontaneous and complete acceptance of illusion.'[7] Asymmetry is designed to disturb the eye, as are the cold, shiny reflective surfaces of the walls, the static camera, the slow movement of the bank functionary, and the slightly edgy music.

Early sequences also feature a number of disorienting shots through windows (as when the camera moves around Titta seated in front of the window of the hotel lounge, to catch the distorted reflection of a funeral carriage and horses in the street outside), or in mirrors and reflections. The effect, as Francesco Cattaneo has observed, is to underscore Titta's distance from the world around him and the fact that, although he looks at the outside world, he cannot be part of it.[8] However, the film provides clues that there is more to this pale, unsmiling, balding accountant. In a prescient early remark, he proclaims that 'it takes courage to die an extraordinary death.' His brother's visit on his way to the Maldives reveals that Titta has a best friend, Dino Giuffré, and it is at this point that Sofia demands that Titta acknowledge her existence. He plays cards with, and spies on the conversations of, the old couple who used to own the hotel, and gives himself a heroin injection at 10:30 every Wednesday morning. Titta's ordered and regular life is emblematic of how an illegal power system would exercise control, and its methods mirror modern management techniques in the use of order and repetition to maximize efficiency, and the use of coercion (the Sicilian hoods) to limit risk. However, the mafia, like the state, cannot dominate every area of existence.

What disturbs and thwarts the ultimate control of Titta's life is love. Emotion is associated with warm colours, the curlicues of the hotel's stairs, and the decorative clutter of the bar presided over by Sofia. Yellow tones also help here, deriving from the Italian use of the word *giallo* (yellow) for mystery stories of all kinds. Italian noir films all use yellow colours to indicate the presence of mysteries. In *Consequences,* we see yellow in lamps, furnishings, and reflections and in the target motifs in the hotel's decor. Sofia acts as the catalyst for the unravelling of Titta's secrets and for the eruption of emotion whose consequence is the revelation of the face of the contemporary mafia. Because Sofia forces Titta to acknowledge her as an individual, she represents a challenge to the cold appropriation of the methods of global business by illegal power systems: Sofia crashes the car that Titta had bought her; in a reversal of usual practice, the elderly couple whose gambling had lost them their hotel business receive unsolicited millions. Emotion escapes control, and chaos introduces questions.

If Titta embodies the exterior, business face of today's mafia, then the two Sicilian hoods who arrive from 1500 kilometres away to carry out a killing (and who it is later suggested were part of Pippo d'Antò's plot to steal one of Titta's suitcases) provide a more traditional face. Both men commandeer Titta's living space in an intimidating way, carrying out the killing in a cold, efficient manner and eliminating the only witness, a boy in a wheelchair. The younger hood, who never speaks, frets constantly over his appearance, concerned only to avoid getting blood on his immaculate shell suit. He embodies the 'slick elegance' and rigidly stylized behaviour identified by John Dickie when analysing the 'new' mafia.[9] Whereas the cynical, older hood looks rough and lower-class, the younger man indicates the importance of a clean, efficient exterior, even when carrying out a traditional assassination. The disappearance of the last suitcase, containing $9 million, introduces a large enough element of turbulence into the smooth organization of money laundering for the face of the boss to be revealed as Titta is called to account. Titta's journey from Switzerland to Italy to explain himself to Nitto Lo Riccio is a metaphor for the 'global reach' of late capitalist business strategies.

Titta's meeting with the boss takes place in the Hotel New Europe, whose bright red neon sign appears twice. At a deeper level, there is a suggestion that mafia ways are spreading to contaminate areas outside Italy. Thus, mafia business practices are coming to resemble to those of multinational corporations – a comment on the new realities of the European and globalized world economy. The film also suggests in an extremely subtle and humorous way that these controlling and ordered business practices, which impact in such deleterious ways on humankind, derive from a retrograde and excessive masculinist competitive culture. The headquarters of the mafia boss is in a typically anonymous, large hotel conference suite. As he is escorted along the obsessively red-patterned carpets of the hotel, a long tracking shot from Titta's point of view shows an inordinate number of men opening doors and turning to look at him. As Titta walks towards Nitto at the head table, the camera includes in its long shot the large conference screen announcing the subject of the meeting as 'Hypertrophy of the prostate. Refresher course.' Titta's character has functioned as an access point to the heterotopia of mafia operations, heterotopia being Michel Foucault's term for singular, social spaces with their own rules, such as the institutions of the police, prisons, and judiciary.[10] Titta's journey from Switzerland to the Neapolitan hotel makes visual the hierarchy of the mafia and shows how power is exercised by what Foucault typifies as 'the enclosed institution, established on the edge of society, turned inwards towards negative functions.'[11] The sheer number of men hanging around suggests the manpower necessary to enforce the discipline of acquiescence. There must be constant surveillance of everything that happens; specialized cohorts to deliver the punishments that will discipline other mafia members, or outsiders, into displaying the required behaviour (of compliance or silence); and specialized functionaries (such as accountants, investors), whose activities must be closely monitored. As Foucault suggests, disciplines are 'techniques for ensuring the ordering of human multiplicities', that is, of ensuring that human diversity does not escape the exercise of power and that power is exercised at the lowest possible cost, discretely and relatively invisibly, and with maximum intensity of effect.[12] Sorrentino illustrates all of this in his film.

At his meeting with Nitto, Titta admits that he found the suitcase that the hoods had attempted to steal, but his affirmation that he is stealing the suitcase because, without it, there's no life, is too great a challenge for the organization to ignore. Nitto closes Titta di Girolamo's account and has the last word in the contest: 'You're a good man. But we're more intelligent than you.' On the contrary, just how intelligent and active Titta has been is demonstrated in the bravura sequence in which he is driven to his death by Nitto's henchmen. The final mystery of Titta's personality is signalled as the car enters the underpass, which is vividly lit in yellow lights. At this point, the two henchmen start singing along to the words of Ornella Vanoni's song 'Lipstick and Chocolate', words that also explain the tensions in Titta's character, between patience and ability, recklessness and sensuality. As Titta looks out of the car window, a series of whip pans signal access to his memory of thwarting the Sicilian hoods' attempt to steal the suitcase. Displaying his knowledge of the hotel, he runs to cut the electrical current to the lift, forcing them to use the stairs, while he starts the lift again and arrives ahead of them in the basement car park, where he shoots them.

Titta's punishment – he is trussed up and dangled from a crane in a cold, grey quarry – makes reference to mafia control of the concrete industry and reiterates the survival of traditional mafia practices behind the modern business facade. The film ends enigmatically, as ever closer shots of Titta entering his concrete coffin alternate first with the stunned faces of the elderly couple opening their suitcase of money, then with shots of snow, electricity pylons, and a stocky, bearded man checking the cables aloft. At this point, Titta's voiceover claims, 'Dino Giuffré stops and starts to think that I, Titta di Girolamo, am his best friend.' Significantly, the final shot is of the enormous crosses of the pylon's struts, with a cold, freezing alpine panorama in the background. This is a fine example of homology, a rhetorical trope in which the same statement is made in different forms. Titta's voiceover is an affirmation of the warmth and humanity of friendship and the power of memory, while the crosses against the cold mountains indicate rejection of the cold, emotionless world to which acceptance of the mafia's reduction of every action to money or power would condemn us.

In *Gomorrah*, Roberto Saviano argues passionately that fighting the Camorra and realizing how the mafia works is crucial to understanding the functioning of global power relations:

> Resistence to the clans becomes a war for survival, as if existence itself, the food you eat, the lips you kiss, the music you listen to, the pages you read were not enough to give you a sense of living, only of surviving. Knowledge is therefore more than a moral obligation. Knowing, understanding, become essential. This is the only possible way to consider yourself worthy of living and breathing.[13]

After the success of *Consequences*, it is not surprising that Sorrentino chose Giulio Andreotti as the subject of *Il divo* (2008) – the former prime minister was investigated for corruption and complicity with the mafia in 1993 – nor that *Il divo* won the Special Jury Prize at the 2008 Cannes Film Festival. *Consequences* had won five David di Donatello prizes, Italy's equivalent of the Oscars. Unlike many Italian films, it had effective international distribution, reflecting the popularity of film noir as a strategy to understand social and political realities. Sorrentino's career bid had a favourable outcome in terms of personal recognition and identification of a fruitful subject area. Sorrentino's visual flair – the subtle and multi-layered ways in which he communicates complex ideas about power, legality, and the ordering of social and business life in the contemporary world – signalled that he was an exceptional talent and that this was a serious work. This immensely stylish film uses a spectacular mise en scène, visual, and narrative complexity to indicate that behind order, regularity, and cold luxury lies quite a different reality. In doing so, it shows the mutated form of today's mafia.

NOTES

1 Mary P. Wood, *Contemporary European Cinema* (London: Arnold, 2007), 43–5.
2 André Lange and Susan Newman-Baudais, *Film Distribution Companies in Europe* (Strasbourg: European Audiovisual Observatory, 2007), 182.
3 Francesco Rosi, interview with author, Cambridge, UK, 1 June 1987.
4 Leonardo Sciascia, *La corda pazza: scrittori e cose della Sicilia* (Turin: Giulio Einaudi, 1970).
5 Eric Hobsbawm, *Globalisation, Democracy and Terrorism* (London: Abacus, 2007), 37, 145.
6 Mary P. Wood, 'Italian Film Noir,' in *European Film Noir*, ed. Andrew Spicer (Manchester: Manchester University Press, 2007), 23–72.
7 John White, *The Birth and Rebirth of Pictorial Space*, 3rd ed. (London: Faber and Faber, 1987), 158.
8 Francesco Cattaneo, 'L'amore disegnato nel calcestruzzo,' *Cineforum* 439 (2004): 25.
9 John Dickie, *Cosa Nostra: A History of the Sicilian Mafia* (New York: Palgrave Macmillan, 2004), 310.
10 Michel Foucault, *The Foucault Reader: An Introduction to Foucault's Thought*, ed. Paul Rabinow (London: Penguin Books, 1991), 252.
11 Michel Foucault, *Discipline and Punish: The Rebirth of the Prison*, trans. Alan Sheridan (London: Penguin Books, 1991), 209.
12 Ibid., 218.
13 Roberto Saviano, *Gomorra: Viaggio nell'impero economico e nel sogno di dominio della camorra* (Milan: Mondadori, 2006), 330–1.

44 The In(di)visibility of the Mafia, Politics, and Ethics in Bianchi and Nerazzini's *The Mafia Is White*

ROBIN PICKERING-IAZZI

In Sicily they say the doctors' coats are white, the clinics are white and the workers are white collar. And if the Mafia is also white, how can I see it?

The Mafia Is White (2005)

In recent years, Italian documentary filmmakers have increasingly trained the camera's eye on the social, economic, and political realities of daily life as produced by both the mafia and individuals who have combated it. For instance, Marco Amenta's *Il fantasma di Corleone* (*The Ghost of Corleone*, 2006) takes viewers on a suspenseful manhunt for Bernardo Provenzano, the super-boss of the Cosa Nostra and a fugitive for some forty years until his capture in April 2006; Matteo Scanni and Ruben H. Oliva's *The System: An Uncensored Investigation of the Camorra* (2006) catches graphic scenes of prostitution rings, heroine traffic, racketeering, and clan warfare orchestrated by the Neapolitan Camorra. Several films have focused instead on the lives of women and men who have become symbols of anti-mafia practices and values. Amenta's *Diario di una siciliana ribelle* (*One Girl against the Mafia*, 1997) reconstructs the life story of Rita Atria from her upbringing in a mafia family to her invaluable role as a collaborator with justice;[1] Marco Turco's *In un altro paese* (*Excellent Cadavers*, 2005) recalls the exceptional accomplishments that anti-mafia prosecutors Giovanni Falcone and Paolo Borsellino achieved in the face of the mafia wars of the 1980s; and Alberto Coletta's *Oltre la paura: Bruno contro la mafia* (*Beyond Fear: Bruno against the Mafia*, 2007) follows in the footsteps of a common working man who took extraordinary action and filed official complaints against the mafia, only to see his pub bombed three times and to become the target of death threats.

In the frame of these internationally acclaimed non-fiction films, *La mafia è bianca* (*The Mafia Is White*, 2005)[2] by Stefano Maria Bianchi and Alberto Nerazzini makes a particularly unique contribution as it captures on tape the post-1993 history of the 'invisible' mafia, headed by Provenzano, and its collusion with elected officials of national stature, and scrutinizes bodies of evidence charting that collusion. Specifically, by means of audio and video recordings of intercepted mafia communications destined for politicians' ears, testimonies from *pentiti*, and interviews, the documentarists put before our very eyes a visible chain of evidence that indicts such figures as the millionaire Michele Aiello, an engineer and front man for Provenzano; Giuseppe Guttadauro, a surgeon and powerful mafia boss in the Brancaccio district in Palermo; and Salvatore Cuffaro, a doctor and vice-secretary of the political party UDC (Union of Christian and Center Democrats) for their collaborative financial exploitation of the health care system. The majority of government funding bankrolls expensive, specialized private clinics whose chief administrators are virtually hand-picked by the mafia and politically appointed; meanwhile, public hospitals are bled dry. This gripping case has far-reaching significance, for it functions in metonymic fashion for the entrepreneurial politics cultivated by members of the government and the mafia, who for their own illicit profit capitalize on the diversified market of government contracts for an array of public works and services in such fields as building and road construction, transportation, and waste disposal.

Released in bookstores in 2005 as a boxed set that includes the documentary in DVD and a book, the phenomenal bestseller *The Mafia Is White* warrants attention for what it shows about the history of both the mafia and non-fiction film being made today. As Falcone argues, the Cosa Nostra masterfully adapts to changing social, political, economic, and cultural conditions. Thus, amidst the public outrage voiced against the mafia in 1992, followed by the 1993 arrest of the infamous boss Salvatore Riina, the criminal organization opted to fade from public view and to let the trail of excellent cadavers marking its presence run cold. No more thunderous rounds of machine-gun fire targeting prominent individuals. No more catastrophic bombings. Instead, the mafia launched a period of quiet cooperation with the state, crafting new business relations with certain politicians representing it. The meticulous investigation that Bianchi and Nerazzini conduct in their documentary, likened to Francesco Rosi's investigative fiction films of the 1970s, amply documents the infiltration of both political and business sectors by members of the mafia, who increasingly work in the professions as doctors, lawyers, engineers, and so forth. It thus breaks the silence on the relations between the Cosa Nostra and politics – relations that, according to some social commentators and filmmakers, have become a taboo subject in Italian media. The collusion between political and criminal elements and the freezing effects that Silvio Berlusconi's 2002 'Bulgarian edict' had on news reporting have contributed to the reconceptualization of documentary as the medium par excellence for telling politically sensitive stories that might otherwise be suppressed or censored.[3] In other words, documentary filmmaking has emerged as a 'voice' that serves the ideals of democracy.

As with many documentaries, credibility and verisimilitude are especially consequential factors in *The Mafia Is White*'s exposé. They determine the efficacy of the truth-claims about both the specific case of criminal activities in the health care system and the broader socio-economic and ethical problems of entrepreneurial politics for which this example stands. Several elements in the documentary serve to foster believability, including the roles the filmmakers perform on camera, the evidentiary editing, and the forms of evidence. For many Italian viewers, Bianchi and Nerazzini are familiar faces, recognized as investigative journalists whose groundbreaking reports broadcast on the news show *Sciuscià* (2000–2) exposed controversial social and political realities.[4] As news reporters filming on location in Sicily, they enjoy a certain credibility, strengthened by their on-camera demeanour, which is consistently polite, calm, and mindful of the facts. They thus come to embody reason and knowledge, in contrast to some of the subjects they interview, who, through artful camerawork and editing, are shown as nervous and evasive. For example, when questioned about mafia dealings in the health care sector or their own potential involvement, Dr Angelo Giammaresi and Salvatore Cintola (chairperson of the budget for the regional Sicilian government) appear visibly rattled and given to outbursts. In support of the case the filmmakers build against Cuffaro, the documentary includes several sequences in which he dodges the film-makers' requests for an interview with the comment 'later, later,' casting him in a dubious light.

The frequent scenes picturing Bianchi and/or Nerazzini shot with a hand-held, roving camera as they pursue each step of their inquiry create suspense and the sense that viewers are eye-witnesses to the very discovery of factual information. These effects are enhanced by the skilful selection and sequencing of material evidence. While the opening frames of the documentary narrative vividly encode poverty through the night-time shots of dirty streets and buildings in disrepair, the voiceover informs us that the story is about the mafia operating not in crime-ridden, poor neighbourhoods, but in reputable places of residence and work. The film immediately intro-duces the first clue to tracking the mafia's presence: one of the now famous *pizzini*, little pieces of paper that mafiosi use for notations about their business activities, discovered in Salvatore Riina's pants pocket upon his arrest. The note links him directly to Aiello and his road construction com-pany, the initial source of Aiello's vast fortune. From this point on, a series of evidentiary materials link one person of interest to another, thus structuring the documentary as if it were a police flow chart. The representation of an intercepted phone conversation then connects speakers Aiello and Cuffaro as they make an appointment for one of their many meetings. Indeed, Cuffaro's name recurs in riveting information reaped from multiple bugging devices planted by law enforcement in the home of the mafia boss Guttadauro. Taking us on location in several sequences, the camera shifts from middle-range night-time shots of the apartment building where he lives to focus on a large window, light seeping through the blinds, as the taped conversations unfold. We hear with our own ears the words of the powerful mafioso and his friends, and we discover inside informa-tion about their connections and plans. The first such audiovisual sequence deserves special com-ment because it enables us to learn about the invisible mafia and its interest in politics and health care. Intercepted on the evening of 1 February 2001, the conversation takes place between Gut-tadauro and Domenico Miceli, a doctor of respect, aspiring politician, and close friend of Cuffaro. First the boss asks how they are doing on the political front. Miceli assures him things look good; he saw Totò (Cuffaro) the night before and the UDC may ask him to be a candidate for president of the region. The boss's response is suggestive, and worth quoting as an example of his charac-teristic mixture of Italian and Sicilian dialect. He states, 'I know it will be him. At the last moment Miccichè will withdraw and he ...' Implying that he already knows how political manoeuvres will play out, he concludes, 'The only one who can screw Orlando out of the presidency of the region is Totò Cuffaro.'[5] Cuffaro, in fact, wins. Here, as in subsequent intercepted talks, Guttadauro con-firms Miceli's role as his go-between with Cuffaro. Furthermore, they discuss which men among their own people must either be put up as candidates for certain political offices in elections or be appointed to positions as directors of hospitals or medical departments.

For anyone unfamiliar with the health care system in Italy, the importance the mafiosi place on the coupling of politics and medical positions may seem puzzling. However, as the voiceover explains in measured tones, when patients receive medical care at accredited private clinics, the services are billed directly to the regional government. As the data illustrate, of the entire budget for Sicily of 20 million euros, nearly 50 per cent is spent on funding private and public health care. The profitability of private clinics such as the Villa Santa Teresa, a cutting-edge diagnostic and cancer treatment centre owned by Aiello, depends entirely upon accreditation and the inclusion of medical procedures and prices on the list of billable services, both of which are in the hands of politically appointed and elected officials. The high stakes the mafia has in both political and medical affairs appear self-evident yet have unforeseeably complex repercussions. Thus Bianchi and Nerazzini incorporate videotaped testimonies from trial proceedings given by *pentiti* such as Nino Giuffrè and Angelo Siino, who wielded substantial power in the Cosa Nostra hierarchy and provide incontrovertible evidence of diverse illegal activities committed by an ever-expanding network linking mafiosi, doctors, government workers, and even members of law enforcement. Such sequences and the audio and visual reframing of conversations and meetings, intended to be secret yet captured on tape through tools employed by the law, ground the film's claims to truth while introducing various aspects of the problem.

Leaving few if any visible signs of violence and bloodshed, the mafia's lucrative infiltration of health care and politics may seem to be a victimless, white-collar crime. This guise promotes complacency and, in some instances, complicity, as demonstrated by comments voiced by passers-by on the streets of Bagheria. In response to the documentarists' questions about the mafia, some reply that the mafiosi are 'saints.' 'They'll do everything in their power to do you a favour,' says one man. Penetrating this cloak of respectability and benign generosity, Nerazzini and Bianchi put before our eyes the victims of mafia crimes, present and past. First of all are the public doctors and medical facilities and the patients who must use them. In contrast to the lush images of Aiello's private Villa Santa Teresa, where no expense was spared on lavish interior design and equipment, the tour of the public Villa Santa Sofia Hospital documents deplorable conditions. Here, leaking ceilings, dirty, peeling plaster, and mould taint exam rooms; broken floors expose patients to hazardous cables and wires. Some essential equipment does not work; other machines for diagnosis and treatment function perfectly, but the hospital lacks technicians to operate them. The most compelling evidence, however, is conveyed by the patients. The combination of close-up shots and tragic stories told in the patients' own words enables viewers to empathize with the speakers as victims of injustice. Part of the taxes they pay funds health care, yet they have no access to reasonable medical services.

Recalling to public memory some of the victims who have died at the mafia's hands, Bianchi and Nerazzini employ a range of documentary conventions that revisualize the vicious face of the criminal associates and their business. For example, a black-and-white crime scene photograph of the site where medical examiner Dr Paolo Giaccone was gunned down in a 1982 mafia hit introduces this 'incorruptible man.' His daughter then shares her personal memories of her father, who refused to alter an evidence report placing mafioso Filippo Marchese's nephew at the scene of the Christmas Massacre in Bagheria. The filmmakers take viewers inside the country home where Giovanni Brusca, reported friend of Cintola, strangled eleven-year-old Giuseppe Di Matteo and then dissolved the boy's body in acid. Touching archival footage from a 1991 episode of the Maurizio Costanzo show, devoted to the problem of the mafia, pictures Judge Falcone in dismay as Cuffaro rants about this kind of 'mafioso journalism,' which he claims is a 'vulgar, aggressive attack on the Christian Democrat Party.' The narrative then cuts to black-and-white footage of the 1992 Capaci bombing, detonated by Brusca, which claimed the lives of Judge Falcone, his wife Judge Francesca Morvilla, and three of their bodyguards. Last, as taped testimony provided by Siino describes a mafia-sponsored dinner given for Cuffaro during his 1991 campaign, he names three known mafiosi in attendance: Santino Pullarà, boss of Santa Maria di Gesù; Santino Di Matteo, who placed the explosives for the Capaci massacre; and the killer Nino Gioè. Their black-and-white mugshots appear beside one another on screen as the voiceover highlights the major crimes each one has to his name. Such sequences make manifest the inseparability of the 'respectable' and murderous sides of the Janus-faced mafia while also calling for a judgment on the innocence or guilt of Cuffaro and fellow politicians who have dealings with members of the criminal organization.

In the process of spotlighting the web of relations between individuals holding public office and the mafia, *The Mafia Is White* implicitly and explicitly raises the question of ethics in the Cuffaro case, and in Italian political life in general. The first hint of the regional president's breach of ethical conduct is evoked through images appearing prior to the documentary narrative proper, as a close-up of Provenzano's face looms on the left side of the screen and on the right side shots show Cuffaro shaking hands and kissing the faces of people alongside him. The film thus creates a visual linkage between the two figures and introduces a line of inquiry that gains credibility by virtue of material pieces of evidence and logical arguments. Court documents and testimony provide proof that in addition to enlisting mafia support for his political campaign with votes from Siino and funding from Aragona, Cuffaro essentially rubber-stamped the billable services offered at the Villa Santa Teresa and price tables set by Aiello himself, who was the front for Provenzano. Cuffaro's clear betrayals of the moral principles and duties incumbent upon both public officials and, ideally, the citizens electing them are represented as a symptomatic problem in Italian politics. This point is exemplified by two brilliantly edited sequences placed near the film's conclusion. First, footage from the 2005 National Congress of the UDC takes the viewer inside the meeting, over which Cuffaro presides. Focusing on the speech delivered by the president of the Italian Chamber of Deputies (or lower house of the Italian Parliament), Pier Ferdinando Casini, the clip catches the moment when he gazes over at Cuffaro and passionately declares, 'We aren't leaving the question of ethics and the fight against the mafia to the Left.' The irony can hardly be lost when the camera pans over several politicians connected with the mafia as they applaud the words. The documentary then shifts to a police surveillance tape recording Cuffaro's movements just three weeks after he became president of the region of Sicily four years earlier, in 2001. In the scene, Cuffaro arrives for a meeting with Miceli and Vincenzo Greco, both mafiosi and doctors; then the three professionals disappear from view behind some bushes. They thus give performative evidence of the invisible mafia in action and the entrepreneurial politics enabling it to flourish.

Recalling such films by Rosi as *Salvatore Giuliano* (1961) and *Le mani sulla città* (*Hands over the City*, 1963), the end of the documentary narrative provides no comforting solution. Rather, it turns upon a provocative question that invites spectators to draw their own conclusions. As the screen is filled with images of the poor, some raising their sick children up towards a statue of Christ and, in the absence of social justice, seeking divine mercy so they may be healed, the voiceover speaks the final words of the film, cited here in the epigraph and concluding: 'If the Mafia is also white, how can I see it?' The question is in part rhetorical, and begs a response. Thus viewers may reflect upon the various pieces of visual evidence that record for all to see the mafia's activities in politics and the white-collar business sector. Engaging in this process of decipherment involves making judgments on what constitutes unlawful conduct, guilt, and innocence. In this sense, the film forces the question of ethics, ideally generating debates in the spheres of Italian life, society, and politics. Moreover, if the mafia's aim is to fade from sight and memory, then such documentary films as *The Mafia Is White* and *Excellent Cadavers* perform an invaluable ethical function. They force us to see the mafia along with its victims and to remember, thereby creating the opportunity to bear the responsibility of witnessing the visible testimony, which calls for justice.

NOTES

1 For an analysis of Amenta's *One Girl against the Mafia*, see my 'Re-Membering Rita Atria: Gender, Testimony, and Witnessing in the Documentary *Diario di una siciliana ribelle*,' *Italica* 84, nos. 2–3 (2007): 438–60.

2 I wish to thank Suzanne M. Ribish for drawing *The Mafia Is White* to my attention and for providing me with the DVD and book. All translations from Italian to English are mine.

3 The Bulgarian edict refers to the statement made by Berlusconi in 2002 when he was prime minister of Italy. Speaking at a press conference with the prime minister of Bulgaria, Berlusconi declared that Enzo Biagi, Michele Santoro, and Daniele Luttazzi made 'criminal use' of public television and that the new leadership should not allow it. The new management of the state-owned RAI television station then essentially banned the three from working there.

4 The positions Italian viewers adopt in relation to Bianchi and Nerazzini as social actors in *The Mafia Is White* would also be contingent on their socio-economic class and political orientations, among other factors.

5 'Io 'u saccio che sarà lui. All'ultimo Miccichè si tirerà fuori e iddu [...] L'unico che può fottere Orlando alla presidenza della regione è Totò Cuffaro.'

45 Marco Turco's *Excellent Cadavers*: An Italian Tragedy

MADDALENA SPAZZINI

In un altro paese (*Excellent Cadavers*), released in 2005, is based on Alexander Stille's 1995 exposé *Excellent Cadavers: The Mafia and the Death of the First Italian Republic*.[1] The film focuses on the heroic activities of two judges, Giovanni Falcone and Paolo Borsellino, whose lives, careers, and, ultimately, deaths are described in a journalistic yet emotional tone. The film was released during a delicate moment in Italian politics, when Silvio Berlusconi's centre-right coalition, the longest-lasting government in the history of the republic, was about to finish its mandate. *Excellent Cadavers* contends that Berlusconi's Forza Italia party had tolerated the presence of the Cosa Nostra on the peninsula and had never taken it to task. Turco's film attempts to make a case against the future re-election of Berlusconi. *Excellent Cadavers* is structured like a journey, and the narrative style is akin to that of a classic tragedy and concludes by reminding the viewer that past catastrophes might indeed repeat themselves. Like other Italian contemporary documentaries I will discuss later, *Excellent Cadavers* works as a *memento* for the public by turning attention to a national trauma.

Excellent Cadavers returns to the famous maxi-trial of the 1980s. Judge Alfonso Giordano, as narrated in the film, 'inflicted guilty verdicts on 344 defendants, for a total of 2,665 years ... In another country the architects of such victory would have been considered national treasures ... but not in Italy.' The documentary recounts Judge Giovanni Falcone's investigation into the financial operations of alleged mafiosi and narrates the events that led Tommaso Buscetta to become the infamous *pentito* at the maxi-trial. The story ends with the tragic deaths of the two judges in 1992 and the bitter declaration of both Stille and Turco that in another country these men would have been considered heroes, but in Italy their lives were not adequately protected.

This story is narrated in several different ways: through Stille's voiceover, and interviews with Falcone's and Borsellino's ex-colleagues and friends, but also through the inclusion of powerful photographs taken by journalist and anti-mafia activist Letizia Battaglia. The most immediate method is Stille's expository voiceover.[2] Images of Stille walking through Palermo while he connects mafia-related events to geographical spaces (the shop owned by the Buscetta family, and the Ucciardone prison, for example) liken the film to the *giallo*, or Italian thriller. Footage of newsreel images of the massacre at Capaci (where Falcone was killed) and Via D'Amelio (where Borsellino died), however, ground the film in a decisive historical moment and remind the viewer that the events are far from fictional. Archival material of the maxi-trial that shows mafia bosses behind bars in the Ucciardone prison in Palermo creates the effect of déjà vu and at the same time demythologizes the image of the mafioso. Many Italian viewers surely remember the hyper-televised moment when Tommaso Buscetta entered the courtroom during the maxi-trial. Similarly familiar are sequences showing several mafiosi in stressed and uncomfortable situations, either complaining to the judge about the imposing presence of the police in front of their cells or screaming out of frustration. In these cases, these mafiosi are presented as far from charismatic and powerful.

Furthermore, the documentary includes a series of direct interviews with magistrates Leonardo Guarnotta, Giuseppe Di Lello, Giuseppe Ayala, Ignazio De Francisci, and Antonio Ingroia and journalist Francesco La Licata. The presence of Falcone's and Borsellino's colleagues – the survivors – gives credibility to the film and allows the director to distance himself from the topic. This technique, known as the interactive mode, is used broadly in interviews with Holocaust survivors.[3] It does not, however, guarantee objectivity. For example, in concluding interviews, Guarnotta and De Francisci are decidedly more emotional, intense, and distraught than in earlier interviews; De Francisci, in fact, even sheds a tear. Turco's technique recalls that used by Claude Lanzmann in *Shoah* (1985),[4] where the director prompts Holocaust survivors to relive their trauma in the present. During one such notorious re-enactment, Abraham Bomba, who cut female inmates' hair just before they entered the gas chamber, bursts into tears as he recounts his experiences in the camp while simultaneously cutting hair in a present-day barbershop. Similarly, *Excellent Cadavers* is at its most lyrical when De Francisci breaks down while remembering the day when Falcone was killed and he went to the emergency room to see his body. In this way, Turco links personal experience with collective trauma. Falcone was a friend and colleague to De Francisci, but Falcone's death affected the entire nation. In addition, these interviews contribute to the documentary's critical tone. Ayala and Ingroia, among others, remember how the anti-mafia movement lost its powers after the maxi-trial's sentences in 1987 and then with the arrival of Antonio Meli as successor to Antonino Caponnetto (chief of the court of Palermo since 1983). Meli, in fact, was elected instead of Falcone, and his earlier actions are described as deeply negative for the anti-mafia investigations in general and as oriented against Falcone's activities in particular. To underscore the negative situation created in the post-Caponnetto era, Turco includes images of the boss of bosses Totò Riina smiling and of lawyer Giulia Buongiorno screaming with joy when defendant Giulio Andreotti is acquitted. Subsequently, Stille explains that all of the victories of the anti-mafia pool (such as the witness protection program) were recently nullified under Berlusconi's watch.

Both the book and the film underscore how the end of the maxi-trial also implied the end of an era. The documentary, however, insists on a sense of imminent tragedy. Falcone is described as a 'dead man walking,' and the interviews given by his friends emphasize his awareness that his death was about to happen. Furthermore, recurrent images of a stressed Falcone and a nervous Borsellino reflect a sense of national tension. It is clear that the director is suggesting that the nation needs to re-experience these deaths in order to not to let such a tragedy reoccur. Living witnesses in the film describe the murder of the anti-mafia judges in intricate detail and then question whether their sacrifices were useless, given the unchanged political situation in contemporary Italy. Hence, the presence of heroic, fallen figures, a chorus composed of their friends who comment on their dreadful destiny, and a general sense of catastrophe unleashed by mysterious, unseen gods make the film resemble a Greek tragedy. It appears that the battle is useless, and in this regard, Turco suggests that change must begin at the level of politics. As De Francisci explains in the film, 'The battle against the mafia is fought in Palermo but can be won only in Rome.'

The structure of both the book and the film is that of a journey into the past in order to better analyse the present and propose that in another country such tragedies would never have occurred. Indeed, the Italian title of the film is *In un altro paese*, or *In Another Country*. Stille journeys from the United States to Italy while photojournalist Letizia Battaglia journeys into the past through her discussion of her memories and photos. The journey motif is highlighted by the analogy created between the two friends – Stille and Battaglia – and the literary figures of Dante and Virgil. Turco himself declared that 'like Virgil with Dante, [Stille] is always accompanied by Letizia Battaglia.'[5]

The documentary opens with an image of the writer sitting in his Manhattan office and recounting his experiences with the Italian mafia as a journalist and correspondent. Stille then meets up with Battaglia at the Palermo airport, aptly dubbed 'the Falcone-Borsellino Airport.' From this point on, Turco juxtaposes images of Stille and Battaglia in the present with Battaglia's photographs of mafia-related victims and other archival materials, such as the announcement of the killing of Borsellino on the Italian news and a sequence showing the motorway and the police presence after the explosion of the bomb that killed Falcone, his wife, and their escort. The book and the film share the same thesis: the mafia is not invincible. They both support the notion that, if seriously attacked, the mafia could be defeated. Stille is the living link between the two works. He addresses the audience directly and also is cast as a participant in the national trauma, as someone who is trying to understand Italy's past.[6]

As an eyewitness, Battaglia represents the living memory of mafia violence. As a professional photographer she sets her eyes – and her camera – on many of those fallen to the mafia over the last thirty years in Palermo. While she narrates, we see cadavers, streets covered with blood, weeping women, and curious children. In the book, Battaglia has a minimal presence; the author mentions her name only in relation to certain photographs. In the film, however, she is memory incarnate[7] and renders the film tragic. Akin to Lanzmann's survivors who return to the scene of the crime, Battaglia is not trying to understand – she barely asks herself why. Having accepted that something dramatic happened (the general sense of hope after the maxi-trial has dissipated after the killing of the judges), towards the end of the film, she declares that she left Sicily because living in a damned land had become unbearable. Ultimately, the film presents an infernal journey, which the public must undergo in order to 'to see once more the stars.'[8]

Excellent Cadavers was released when the subject of the mafia was less in vogue with the Italian media and, therefore, when the organization appeared less dangerous. Turco chose a meaningful moment to release his film: Silvio Berlusconi became prime minister in 2001, after his short-lived experience in 1994. In 2005, the businessman-turned-politician was about to end his second mandate and Italy was on the eve of national elections. The Second Republic, born out of the collapse of the first as a consequence of the *tangentopoli*, or bribesville, investigations in 1992, was being put to the test. After the 1994 national elections, the newly founded party Forza Italia had become the most popular political force in the country, and the mafia was able to move a substantial quota of votes in Sicily. Thus it appeared that Berlusconi's party was the political force that the Cosa Nostra had decided to support. As Giuseppe Ayala explains, the mafia has no specific ideology, yet it always backs the winning faction. Berlusconi's friend and colleague Marcello Dell'Utri was found guilty of collusion with the mafia and received a nine-year sentence, which he appealed. At this point, Stille's underlying query – 'The question is whether the new political parties that have grown up from the ruins of the old will have the strength to reject the "help" offered by organized crime figures' – acquires a new, dramatic dimension.[9] The conclusion of this film, in fact, seems to assert that the state has not yet been able to reject such help.

The mafia in general disappeared from national news headlines but has recently reappeared in several documentaries released over the last four years, such as Stefano Maria Bianchi and Stefano Nerazzini's *La mafia è bianca* (*The Mafia Is White*, 2005), Marco Amenta's *Il fantasma di Corleone* (*The Ghost of Corleone*, 2006), and Alberto Coletta's *Oltre la paura: Bruno contro la mafia* (*Already Dead: Bruno against the Mafia* 2007). All of these films underscore how the mafia is connected to politics. The first film offers an investigation into the corruption that links private health care and the mob, whose central figure is the ex-president of Sicily, Salvatore Cuffaro. Particularly striking are the opening declarations conveying that this new mafia of the 2000s no longer produces 'excellent cadavers' but instead has become part of the community's everyday life. In this way, the actions of the Cosa Nostra are less manifest but equally or even more catastrophic, because they are interrelated with quotidian political life. A similarly accusatory tone is present in *The Ghost of Corleone*, which recounts the odd circumstances that allowed the boss of bosses Bernardo Provenzano to evade arrest for more than forty years. The film suggests that the state protected him and, as such, any intervention on the part of the police force would have been useless (he was, however, finally arrested in 2006). *Already Dead* also connects a mafia event (the constant threats Bruno Piazzese received after he refused to pay the 'protection fee' or *pizzo* to the mob) to the political climate of contemporary Italy. Piazzese's entire narrative is recounted in parallel with the imminent regional elections, whose candidates, as opposed to Piazzese's personal rebellion, will end up doing very little to combat the mafia.

Similarly, Marco Turco's film insists on a generalized national lack of governmental support in the struggle against the Sicilian mafia. The title of the documentary, quoted from Stille's book, suggests that in Italy organized crime wins out over those who combat it. Both novel and film represent clear denouncements of a corrupt political and judicial system and its ties to the Cosa Nostra. *Excellent Cadavers* affirms that today's mafia is silent but far from dead and that its existence is guaranteed by a system of quid pro quo. Ultimately, both the film and the novel propose that the Italian state has no real interest in defeating the mafia. In such a context, the state – here embodied by Berlusconi's ruling party – plays the role of ineluctable fate, the excellent cadavers are the heroes sacrificed by the gods, and the audience is the chorus, the weeping witness of an Italian tragedy.

NOTES

1 Alexander Stille, *Excellent Cadavers: The Mafia and the Death of the First Italian Republic* (New York: Pantheon, 1995).

2 Turco used this term to describe his style in Miriam Tola, 'Locarno Against the Mob,' accessed 14 September 2009, http://news.cinecittà.com/people/archivio.

3 Joshua Hirsch, *Afterimage: Film, Trauma, and the Holocaust* (Philadelphia, PA: Temple University Press, 2004).

4 For a detailed description of Lanzmann's approach, see ibid.

5 Tola, 'Locarno Against the Mob.'

6 For some critics, however, Stille's narration and constant screen presence is out of place. See Martha Fischer, 'Excellent Cadavers,' 11 July 2006, accessed 30 September 2008, www.cinematical.com.

7 Battaglia was called 'survivor and eyewitness' in A.O. Scott, 'Excellent Cadavers, an Italian Documentary Dissects the Mafia,' *New York Times*, 12 July 2006, accessed 10 September 2008, http://movies.nytimes.com/2006/07/12/movies/12cada.html.

8 Dante Alighieri, *The Divine Comedy: Inferno* (New York: Penguin Classics, 1984), 383.

9 Stille, *Excellent Cadavers*, 412.

PIERPAOLO ANTONELLO

Gomorra (*Gomorrah*, 2008) is the sixth feature film by Matteo Garrone, one of the most interesting and promising Italian directors of his generation, creator of the much-praised *L'imbalsamatore* (*The Taxidermist*, 2002). *Gomorrah* is based on the highly successful book by Roberto Saviano, *Gomorrah: A Personal Journey into the Violent International Empire of Naples' Organized Crime System* (2006), a semi-fictional account of the economic and military power of the Camorra. This Campania-based crime organization has been ruling the Caserta and Neapolitan hinterland for decades, killing more people than any other criminal organization in Europe and extending its interests and 'tentacles' well beyond regional and national borders.[1] Saviano's book, which sold more than one million copies in Italy, is an overt denunciation of the forgotten war that has been devastating and poisoning an entire Italian region but that has achieved little resonance in the collective national consciousness: '[I]n 30 years the *Camorra* murdered more than 10 thousand people, more than the people killed in the Gaza strip; its empire has an economic turnover that is more than three times FIAT's worldwide.'[2] Despite being more ferocious and brutal than the Sicilian mafia, and more ruthless in the open display of its criminal actions, the 'System,' as it is called locally, has been given much less attention in the Italian media (and in international mythology), perhaps being considered just one more endemic or chronic social disease of the south (no different from the mafia in this). Saviano's book was so hard-hitting and so effective in opening up the phenomenon to national attention that an inevitable death threat from the Camorra has forced him into hiding, making the author a sort of 'Italian Salman Rushdie.' The media attention and public and critical praise inevitably prompted various adaptations of the book, in particular a theatrical version by Mario Gelardi (2007) and Matteo Garrone's movie.[3] Because the film was produced in the midst of the public plaudits for Saviano's work, and because the writer co-authored the screenplay,[4] a contextual discussion of both the novel and the film is needed, as they could be considered two complementary parts of a similar artistic and political project.

The title of both book and film is obviously a biblical reference; the play draws a parallel between the Naples crime system and the ancient Palestinian city of Gomorrah, which according to Genesis 19:24 was destroyed (along with Sodom) by fire from heaven because of the wickedness of its inhabitants. However, although an underlying moral tension inspired both the book and the movie, in Garrone's film the diegetic narrator is ostensibly omitted. The testimonial nature and moral indignation at the core of Saviano's social denunciation, which forms the general rhetoric of the book,[5] is totally bracketed off in the film, where the camera is the only witness to events that are explored in a raw, hyper-realistic manner, without further comment or judgment. In fact, the crudeness and the brutal aspects of the movie are arguably more effective in showing a reality that evinces apocalyptic features, and in which no redemption or hope is in sight either for the protagonists or for society as a whole. In that sense, the title is more apt to describe the film than Saviano's book, for it vividly depicts in a stunning, unsettling manner the Camorra underworld as sort of modern Dante's *Inferno*: the claustrophobic *univers concentrationnaire* of failed modernization represented by the Vele housing project with its cramped flats, dirty grey walls, and dark, ominous corners and walkways, where drug dealing, guns, and killing are the daily bread; the raping of a countryside once dubbed *Campania felix* for its fertility, now polluted and poisoned by tons of chemicals and trash; the heavy, grey sky that hangs over sleazy landscapes, as if the sunshine and conventional postcard beauty normally associated with this part of Italy has disappeared and a moral darkness has taken its place.

Just as the book is a narrative reportage structured in different episodes, the film is organized around five intertwined stories presented chronologically without flashback. The first story is that of Don Ciro, the 'submarine,' whose job is to discreetly distribute a monthly salary to families who have a relative in prison because of service to the local bosses. In one case (the second story), Maria is the mother of a 'Scissionista,' a young man who has recently defected from the criminal group Don Ciro to work for a rival one. For this reason she will be killed mercilessly, and her murderers will use a young local delivery boy, Totò, as a decoy to lure her to her death. The third narrative strand is the story of Franco, a 'stakeholder' who helps dispose of the toxic waste produced by the chemical industries of northern Italy, illegally filling up old mines and poisoning a vast part of the Neapolitan region in the process. This episode highlights the complicity of the rest of Italy in feeding the Camorra's illegal activities, one of the main tenets of Saviano's book. Central to the episode is the presence of Roberto, Franco's young assistant, who eventually decides to quit his job as an act of revolt against his supposedly 'clean' but, in actuality, morally rotten trade. His first name clearly refers to Saviano himself, for the character seems designed not only to showcase Saviano's political and ethical stand but also his status as an insider who has seen the 'System' first hand. The insertion of Roberto perhaps signals a felt need for at least an instance of moral critique in the film but is, in fact, a rather watered-down version of Saviano's moral indignation and the strong diegetic voice presented in the book. The character of Roberto might easily have been removed from the film without causing damage to it; his presence arguably has only a weak resonance with the spectator and possibly produces an opposite effect to that intended. The solitary and individual act of revolt is far too feeble within the overall ethos of the society described in the film, and it appears only as a hopeless, romantic, quixotic gesture.

One of the most memorable of Saviano's chapters, which has been retained for the screen with good reason, is the story of Pasquale, an exploited master tailor who crafts expensive dresses for major northern Italian fashion brands, whose wages are very low. Persuaded by a need for money and respect to teach his craft to workers in a Chinese-run factory, he barely escapes being assaulted by armed men, an act intended as a warning from the local bosses; he decides to leave his trade thereafter and becomes a truck driver. In the final scene of his story, he watches on the bar television at a gas station as one of his dresses is worn by Scarlett Johansson at the premiere of the Venice Film Festival. Finally, the closing episode – possibly the most brutal and vivid – is the story of two young 'stray dogs' named Marco and Ciro who try to live up to the myth of the self-made gangster, epitomized in their imagination by Tony Montana, the protagonist of Brian

De Palma's film *Scarface* (1983). Attempting to break into the criminal underworld with adolescent audacity and recklessness, they defy the control of the local boss and come to an inevitable violent end. They are ambushed and unceremoniously killed, treated as a simple inconvenience by the gangsters in control of the area, and their bodies are disposed of with a bulldozer as though they are useless waste.

Despite the apparent narrative complexity, the storylines are never heavily plotted and there is no real psychological investigation of the characters. The daily reality of thousands of Italians who live outside of any legal boundaries is explored with obsessive camerawork that is mostly carried out by the director himself, making this film almost a work of social anthropology. On this score, both Garrone's movie and Saviano's book have been seen as signalling the exhaustion of the postmodern aesthetic dominant in Italy as it was elsewhere in the 1980s and 1990s; book and film have been emphatically celebrated as a 'return to reality' and as a call for new forms of social and political engagement.[6] However, as in any art form, there are formal and representational elements that cannot be neglected and that are clearly present in both works. Although documentary-like in nature, Saviano's book is actually a 'docu-fiction,' and it adopts imaginative twists and explicit stylistic and rhetorical modalities to engage the reader. Garrone's movie, notwithstanding its hyper-realistic charge, is never presented as a documentary (although the cinematographic style was, according to Garrone, borrowed from war reportage) and is deliberately structured as a work of fiction, of imagination. 'If there is any political value in the film,' Garrone has noted, 'it is because of the language it adopts rather than the theme it presents.'[7]

On this score, the director seems to borrow, more or less consciously, the critically celebrated Dogma 95 cinematic style.[8] Filming was done on location, mostly at the Vele housing project in Scampia, a neighbourhood north of Naples. Apart from the pulsing, hypnotic tune of the closing titles ('Herculaneum' by Massive Attack), and a few seconds during the title sequence, all of the music in the film is diegetic – heard on jukeboxes, CD players, or car radios. Hand-held cameras are extensively used to follow the action closely. Special and artificial lighting and optical filters are never employed. There is no temporal or geographical alienation (the film takes place 'here and now'). The aspect ratio of 4:3 is maintained, and the spectacular widescreen that Garrone used in *The Taxidermist* to shoot the Campania coast is avoided.[9] Finally – and most importantly for a film that deals with organized crime – it cannot be straightforwardly defined as a 'genre' movie (although it can surely be analysed as such), nor can it be easily pigeonholed as a return to neorealism (a label that has been greatly overused in Italian cinema). Garrone seems to explicitly resort, at least in part, to the acting approach made famous by neorealist masters like Vittorio De Sica and by later practitioners of realist filmmaking such as Pier Paolo Pasolini. In fact, he spent several months on location at the Vele housing complex, familiarizing himself with the neighbourhood, the local people, and their ethos. Some of the locals perform in the movie, both as protagonists and as extras. This is undoubtedly one of the strengths of Garrone's film, and the performances elicited from the non-professional actors represent a brilliant accomplishment by the young director. 'The population was very available,' Garrone commented on this score. 'They participated wholeheartedly, and they were the first spectators of the film. When we shot these scenes, they were always looking on, providing advice, and participating actively.'[10] However, the reality he depicts is never 'innocent' or 'authentic' in Pasolinian terms, because it is already imbued with spectacular and cinematic elements: 'Often, it's the cinema that helps to shape these people's taste, and not the opposite … Even if the film denounces a given "reality," it moves in a different direction. It's not designed to be a kind of an inquiry.'[11]

The mark of this awareness is present in the very first scene, which takes place even before the opening titles. The scene is set in a beauty salon, where three gang members are gunned down while they are tanning themselves and having their nails buffed. The estrangement and the grotesque oddness produced by the juxtaposition of the violent act, the inanimate bodies clumsily trapped within the sun booths, the artificial, almost science fiction-like blue hue of the fluorescent lamps, and the incongruous (but typically Neapolitan) 'neomelodic' tune that is playing in the background make the opening scene a 'spectacular,' almost Tarantinosque exercise that is both real and performative, as it obviously plays with the variation on the barbershop murder scene made famous by a number of genre movies.

There are also various inter-cinematic references in *Gomorrah* – for instance, in the scene where a large statue of Padre Pio is dropped down by rope from a balcony in the Vele housing project, possibly a reference to the statue of Christ hanging from a helicopter in the opening scene of Federico Fellini's *La dolce vita*, an allusion that adds a bittersweet ironic twist to the setting. This sense of incongruity is reinforced by a wide panning shot over a group of boys who are playing in a shallow plastic swimming pool on one of the highest terraces of Le Vele, as if it were an unlikely Hollywood setting (also a reference to the initial scene of *La dolce vita*). The powerful scene in which Ciro and Marco unload their stolen rifles and Kalashnikovs into the empty swamp under a gloomy sky, yelling and singing, is vaguely reminiscent of *Apocalypse Now*, while the lap dance parlour they venture into at one point was made paradigmatic by the famous Bada Bing strip club in *The Sopranos* (itself a *Godfather* reference). Finally, the disposal of Ciro and Marco's bodies with a bulldozer after they are killed reflects a similar sequence in *Il camorrista* by Giuseppe Tornatore (1986).[12] However, the most revealing scene is Marco and Ciro's aping of Tony 'Scarface' Montana's gestures and way of speaking. This scene was actually filmed in the house (later confiscated and burned to the ground) belonging to a real Camorra boss, Walter Schiavone, who had had his villa (locally dubbed 'Hollywood') planned and constructed as a perfect replica of Montana's house in *Scarface*.

By making all these inter-filmic, inter-cinematic references, Garrone is not trying to play a clever postmodern game with the audience. Instead, he is attempting to convey the particular short circuit between reality and fiction that was highlighted by Saviano in his book (and that had already been parodically explored in *The Sopranos*). The gangsters have such a deep desire to be represented and glamourized by the movie industry that they borrow their mannerisms and general attitude from what they see on the screen. Commenting on Saviano's book, Antonio Tricomi writes that '[the bosses] know that in our contemporary society one has to be constantly "on stage," and that the media representation is more important than reality, to the point that the former replaces the latter. Therefore, they do aesthetize their power, which will run short if not transformed in a ritualistic spectacle.'[13] This is why they constantly try 'to impersonate the most famous cinematographic models of killers, cleverly exploiting the media, aping those film characters in front of TV crews and cameras.'[14]

This appears to be something of a central concern for Garrone. He makes explicit his awareness that every film is artificially constructed and that most mafia films are inherently conventional (as the present book testifies). However, as a political gesture, he deliberately works against the common expectations attached to the genre. He opts for a radically realistic, almost documentary-like approach in order to deny the mobsters any potentially enthusiastic or self-congratulatory response to the film. He offers an unglamorized image of their lives and their business: they are sweaty, dirty, badly dressed, overweight, unhealthy (one of them suffers from throat cancer and speaks with an artificial voice aid in a way that is grotesque and ominous). The crudeness of the photography, the roughness of the settings, the fact that some of the actors are non-professionals – all of these things provide a direct antidote to the glossy outlook of much of the film production on the subject of organized crime. The gunfight and execution scenes are brutal but unspectacular; guns are never displayed as they are in westerns or mob movies but are instead effectively and sparingly used by killers, as in real life. Sound seems realistic and is not lent emphasis by special effects. Suspense is kept to a minimum, to the point that spectators are surprised by the murderous actions of the mobsters in much the same way as their victims. In this sense, Garrone seems to be more radical than Saviano in peeling away any form of allure and glitz from the lives of the gangsters. Indeed, Saviano's book may risk glamorizing the Camorra phenomenon. On the one hand, by emphasizing the capacity of the new generations of *camorristi* to navigate the economic complexities of a globalized society, their ability to defy the law and institutional control, and their sophisticated and self-aware use of mass media, the Neapolitan writer appears to endorse the idea that the mafia system is the most appropriate and successful model available for navigating and flourishing in our globalized, post-democratic society.[15] On the other hand, he indirectly flirts with the darker side of the alluring evil by presenting in a vivid and effective manner the jaw-droppingly brutal deeds of these gangsters. Conversely, Garrone's film has a political and ethical relevance without seeming to signal it as a deliberate and programmatic gesture. It proffers a new gaze into the Camorra underworld, stripping away its mythology, magnifying the incongruous mannerisms of the *camorristi*, surveying with an almost anthropological gaze the total desolation of their lives, their confinement in a world without hope, without a single moment of truce or reprieve. *Gomorrah* is a sort of 'degree zero' representation of the mafia, in a manner that is highly effective from a cinematic standpoint and well as an ethical one.

NOTES

1 Roberto Saviano, *Gomorra. Viaggio nell'impero economico e nel sogno di dominio della camorra* (Milan: Mondadori, 2006). English translations: *Gomorrah: A Personal Journey into the Violent International Empire of Naples' Organized Crime System*, trans. Virginia Jewiss (New York: Farrar, Straus and Giroux, 2007); *Gomorrah: Italy's Other Mafia*, trans. Virginia Jewiss (London: Macmillan, 2008).

2 Giuseppina Manin, 'Ma il vero eroe si chiama Saviano,' *Corriere della Sera* 19 (May 2008), accessed 19 September 2008, www.corriere.it/Cinema/2008/Cannes/saviano_eroe_45d8ce46-2564-11dd-9a1d-00144f486ba6.shtml.

3 See Roberto Saviano's website, www.robertosaviano.it.

4 The others are Maurizio Braucci, Ugo Chiti, Gianni Di Gregorio, Matteo Garrone, and Massimo Gaudioso.

5 On the unresolved and ambiguous tension between the testimonial and rhetorical aspects of Saviano's book, see Gilda Policastro's review, 'Gomora,' *Allegoria* 57 (2008): 185–90.

6 See, for instance, Raffaele Donnarumma, Gilda Policastro, and Giovanna Taviani, eds., 'Ritorno alla realtà? Narrativa e cinema alla fine del postmoderno,' *Allegoria* 57 (2008): 7–93.

7 Garrone quoted in 'Gomorra. Intervista al regista Matteo Garrone,' accessed 17 September 2008, http://it.youtube.com/watch?v=X1V4l-PIT8E.

8 Dogma 95 was an avant-garde filmmaking movement started in 1995 by the Danish directors Lars von Trier and Thomas Vinterberg with the signing of the Dogma 95 Manifesto and the 'Vow of Chastity,' which included ten rules to which any Dogma film must conform. The goal of the Dogma collective is to purify filmmaking by refusing expensive and spectacular special effects, post-production modifications, and other 'gimmicks.' The emphasis on purity forces the filmmakers to focus on the actual story and the actors' performances.

9 See Gianni Valentino, 'Garrone: "In due mesi a Scampia ho capito la lotta per sopravvivere,"' *La Repubblica*, 25 April 2008, accessed 10 September 2008, http://napoli.repubblica.it/dettaglio/Garrone:-In-due-mesi-a-Scampia-ho-capito-la-lotta-per-sopravvivere/1450076.

10 Garrone quoted in *Gomorrah*, Cannes Festival Press Release, accessed 12 September 2008, http://www.festival-cannes.fr/en/article/56095.html.

11 Ibid.

12 The scene where Franco and Roberto exit a container filled with toxic waste wearing astronaut-like gas masks and suits, with the only sound that of their diegetic breathing, is reminiscent of outer space sequences in Stanley Kubrick's *2001: A Space Odyssey* (1968).

13 Antonio Tricomi, 'Roberto Saviano, *Gomorra*,' *Allegoria* 57 (2008): 192.

14 Ibid.

15 See, for instance, Charles Tilly, 'War Making and State Making as a Organized Crime,' in *Bringing the State Back In*, ed. Peter B. Evans, Dietrich Rueschemeyer, and Theda Skocpol (Cambridge: Cambridge University Press, 1985); Luigi Cavallaro, *Il modello mafioso e la società globale* (Rome: Manifestolibri, 2004).

47 From Comedy to Commemoration: Pierfrancesco Diliberto's *La mafia uccide solo d'estate*

MILLICENT MARCUS

In the years during and after the Cosa Nostra's most intense violence against the Italian state, a mini-genre of films emerged involving biographical re-creations of historic figures who died in their service to the anti-mafia cause. The portrait gallery of activists included in this body of work features most obviously the renowned magistrates Giovanni Falcone and Paolo Borsellino. The former was the subject of two films: *Giovanni Falcone* by Giuseppe Ferrara (1993), and *L'uomo che sfidò Cosa Nostra* (*The Man Who Challenged Cosa Nostra*, Andrea and Antonio Frazzi, 2006); the latter was the subject of the eponymous television film *Paolo Borsellino* (Gianluca Tavarelli, 2004). The portraits of anti-mafia crusaders memorialized in this mini-genre include an array of other figures: Carabiniere General Carlo Alberto Dalla Chiesa (*I cento giorni a Palermo* [*A Hundred Days in Palermo*], Giuseppe Ferrara, 1984), the little-known judge Rosario Livatino (*Il giudice ragazzino* [*Law of Courage*], Alessandro di Robilant, 1994), the cultural and political activist Peppino Impastato (*I cento passi*), the labour organizer Placido Rizzotto (*Placido Rizzotto*), the anti-mafia clergyman Don Pino Puglisi (*Alla luce del sole* [*By the Light of Day*], Roberto Faenza, 2005), and Rita Atria, the daughter of a mafia family who turned state's evidence (*La siciliana ribelle* [*The Sicilian Girl*], Marco Amenta, 2008). Though outside the Sicilian context, another film that claims a rightful place in this genre is the searing portrait of the anti-Camorra journalist Giancarlo Siani (*Fortapàsc*, Marco Risi, 2009).

While the Hollywood term 'biopic' would seem best to describe these films, I prefer to characterize them less by narrative structure than by their debt to a venerable Italian cinematic tradition. I am speaking of *cinema d'impegno* (engaged cinema), which harks back to neorealism and to its offshoot in the *cinema politico* genre of the 1960s and 1970s. Of utmost importance in linking the anti-mafia martyr films to their neorealist origins is a strong commemorative impulse – an insistence on cinema's role in the construction of a monumental history to celebrate heroic activism and to instil the desire for it in new generations of viewers. This memorialist undercurrent is palpable in the 'founding' films of neorealism: *Roma città aperta* (*Rome, Open City*, Roberto Rossellini, 1945), which eulogizes the populist heroics of the historically based characters Pina, Manfredi, and Don Pietro; followed by three of the episodes of *Paisà* (*Paisan*, Roberto Rossellini, 1946), which commemorate fictional characters whose martyrdoms stand as emblems of the resistance activities of unassuming civilians (Carmela in the Sicilian sequence), untutored partisans (the anonymous fighter who dies in Harriet's arms in the Florentine sequence), and the OSS combatants in league with Italian resistance members (Dale, Cigolani, etc. in the Po River sequence).

Pierfrancesco Diliberto's *La mafia uccide solo d'estate* (*The Mafia Only Kills in Summer*, 2013) may appear to be an unlikely candidate for inclusion in this venerable genealogy of films. Its narrative focuses on an ordinary citizen, Arturo Giammarresi, who undertakes no heroic action and who remains a spectator as the painful history of the anti-mafia struggle unfolds. More importantly, the film belongs to the genre of romantic comedy, foregrounding the love story between the protagonist and Flora Guarnieri, whose relationship begins in childhood and culminates in marital union. And finally, the film's director, who also plays the role of the adult protagonist, hails from the world of Italian television. Exploiting his prefabricated celebrity, he both imports into the film his televisual persona (known as Pif, a pseudo-acronym for his given name) and stages a highly charged encounter between the languages of the small and large screen.

It is the very deviations from the norms of the anti-mafia martyr tradition – the movement away from the heroic to the ordinary, the foray into romantic comedy, the intrusion of a TV aesthetic – that make *La mafia uccide* such a striking effort to update and reactivate the monumental history of the struggle against the Sicilian crime syndicate. Indeed, I would argue that the film enacts, in very explicit terms, the tension between a pull towards entertainment and a solemn testimonial imperative. The framing of *La mafia uccide* – its written dedication 'to the officers of the Palermo police squad, to the members of the Quarto Savona 15 (Giovanni Falcone's escort), to all of the police escorts fallen in the line of duty' – gives way to Diliberto's narration in voiceover: 'See that girl … I have been in love with her since we were kids.' The clash of registers between the solemnity of the paratext and the frothy lightness of the narration could not be more evident, leaving the spectator in a state of generic uncertainty.

The interplay between mafia chronicle and the course of love is explicitly announced in the protagonist's next quip. 'I never had the courage or the chance to declare my love because … we are in Palermo. And here the mafia always influenced everyone's lives, particularly mine.' These opening frames function as a kind of overture, sounding the themes and forecasting the generic mechanisms that will govern the film as a whole: its commemorative thrust, its characterization of Palermo as both physical setting and social organism in thrall to organized crime, and its storyline of mafia-thwarted romance.

The bulk of the film is characterized by its upbeat tenor, the product of the witty voiceover narration, the bouncy musical score, the good-natured relationships between adults and children, and the ingenuity of the plot's mafia-based impediments to Arturo's pursuit of Flora. But in its final moments, the register changes drastically as breeziness and irony give way to urgency tinged with anger. Here the story leaps forward to the birth of a baby boy, followed by an intense montage of father–son visits to commemorative sites around the city. The visits are presented as a series of vignettes in which Arturo explains to his son, at successive ages (from infancy to young boyhood), some aspect of a fallen hero's role in the anti-mafia campaign. These exercises in pedagogy, especially when addressed to an infant, could well strike us as laughable were it not for the utter seriousness and urgency of the father's delivery. Like the ending of the Taviani brothers' *La notte di San Lorenzo* (*The Night of the Shooting Stars*, 1982), in which the audience of the narrator's account is revealed to be a sleeping baby, we understand that Arturo's speech to his infant son is not an exercise in futility but rather an affirmation of the necessity to bear witness, to transmit to future generations the need for historical knowledge and the imperative to act upon it.

From the perspective of this ending, the film becomes a means for reviving collective memory, bringing life and movement to the static newspaper obituaries that languish in state archives and to the frozen plaques that adorn the city walls. This process of reanimation does not take the form of heroic biography; rather, it emerges from the testimony of an ordinary citizen-witness whose own life story features cameo encounters with these historical figures. The genius of the film's narrative structure is thus twofold – it devotes most of its account to Arturo's childhood, thereby exploiting the critical/ironic possibilities inherent in the young boy's naive perspective, and it organizes the love story around intersections with mafia history from the 1970s to 1992. The plot thus serves as satiric enactment of the truth announced in the film's opening voiceover about how the mafia saturates everyday life.

Pivotal events in the protagonist's own life coincide with landmarks in Palermo's collective ordeal under mafia rule. In a characteristically destabilizing move, Diliberto uses broad humour and hybrid visual techniques to link the physiology of Arturo's own conception with the rise to power of Totò Riina. Employing parallel montage to great comic effect, the narrator recounts how his parents conceived him in the same building and at the same time that Riina's men staged the assault on his rival, Michele Cavataio. The scene of fertilization is represented as a cartoon encounter between an egg and a flotilla of sperm that withdraw in fear as the building trembles under the impact of the mafia assault below. A single sperm cell, oblivious to the mayhem, arrives belatedly to pierce the egg. 'That sperm cell,' the voiceover explains, 'was me.'

The coincidence of Arturo's conception and Riina's rise to power will have a profound impact on the boy, making him preternaturally attuned to the mafia presence despite his parents' strenuous efforts at denial. Concerned that their toddler has not yet begun to talk, they try desperately to extract at least a 'mamma' from the reticent child, whose first word, instead, is 'mafia,' uttered in the wake of a visit by the parish priest, who is known to have underworld ties. But the child's hyperawareness of the mafia threat is short-lived. In the light of his society's penchant for denial, the boy falls prey to the euphemisms required by the pact of *omertà*, taking literally the reassuring explanations for a spate of killings, explained away as crimes of passion: 'issues about women,' claims the butcher; 'a problem with another woman,' echoes the barber; 'he was too fond of skirts,' opines the barber.

The most dangerous and consequential discourse of denial is the one issuing from Giulio Andreotti, who claims that 'emerging criminality is in Campania and Calabria.' Because the young boy has developed a reverence for Andreotti bordering on cult worship, climaxing in his impersonation of the Christian Democratic leader for Carnevale, Arturo is particularly vulnerable to his idol's strategy for explaining away the mafia threat. The incongruity of a child's veneration for this dry, austere, aloof public figure – a figure who lends himself easily to the grotesque, as Sorrentino's *Il Divo* (2008) so brilliantly demonstrates – is not a mere pretext for humour, however. There is a pointed social commentary in Arturo's childish fandom, which casts the Italian public itself in the role of credulous followers, naive consumers of the DC leader's piously deceptive persona.

The assassination of Generale Dalla Chiesa, the *carabiniere* chief sent to Palermo to lead the government's anti-mafia campaign, marks a radical turning point in Arturo's formation. During the scene of Dalla Chiesa's funeral, Arturo's voiceover account grows increasingly bitter as he asks why Andreotti would downplay the mafia threat and why he had not joined the ranks of mourners, which included all other top government officials. Of utmost significance is the fact that this turning point in Arturo's development coincides with a jarring technological effect within the language of *La mafia uccide*. The scene of Dalla Chiesa's funeral is composed of archival footage – its imagery is blurred and the colours are garish, in striking contrast to the sharp resolution and chromatic sobriety of the rest of the film. The eye experiences the shift from the fictional footage to this documentary clip as a radical change in texture, as if vision had given way to touch. At this point, the film gains a degree of thickness and layeredness that draws the spectator into an ethically charged relationship to the action portrayed. Most obviously, the documentary footage anchors the entire film, no matter how unabashedly fictional, to a verifiable referent in the realm of historical experience. The newsreel clip releases the full indexical power of the image to commandeer belief in the mind of the viewer. To borrow the terminology of Marco Dinoi, it is a 'specimen – a document from the past, an archaeological trace or residue that engages the text in an historical situation.'[1]

The archival footage serves to authenticate and validate the referential thrust of the film – it is the gold standard of representational truth. At the same time, it calls attention to the constructedness of the fiction film within which the clip is embedded. The aesthetic shock of encountering the documentary image – a 'foreign body' in Christian Uva's terms[2] – within the fiction film triggers a metalinguistic awareness on the part of the viewers, prompting them to actively engage with the history to which it points. In other words, the use of the archival image as a springboard for artifice announces to the viewers that the film is exhibiting 'a way to reason about facts that emerges from the exegesis and from the interpretation of a rich documentary research.'[3] It serves as an impetus not only for the viewers to judge the validity of the filmmaker's interpretive 'take' on historical events but also as a stimulus for them to elaborate their own acts of historical re-creation, to embark on imaginative and personal recastings of the factual record as a form of liberation from the received, officially sanctioned readings of history.

The ethical nature of the viewer's relationship to the 'specimen' hinges importantly on the issue of time. It is impossible to ignore the temporal journey along which older technologies lead us. Just as sepia-toned photography immediately catapults us back to the dawn of the 1900s and Super 8 home movies to the 1950s, the newsreel clips of Dalla Chiesa's funeral have the power to transport us to the moment of their filming in 1982. This documentary insert replicates how Italians experienced public events in the immediacy of their reportage, sitting in living rooms or watching collectively in bars or other televisually equipped spaces. Because mass media imagery serves to reveal how an era represented itself to itself, we are temporarily invited to occupy a 1980s Italian subject position not only in the immediate processing of a given news item but also in the total cultural immersion that this older technology makes available. As spectators of *La mafia uccide* we are invited to take responsibility for the course of historical injustice and to acknowledge its traces in the contemporary status quo.

To complicate our reading of this richly stratified moment in the film, Diliberto executes a technological sleight of hand that crosses the border between fiction and documentary, between outer film and embedded video clip. At a certain point in the funeral footage, Francesco, Arturo's journalist friend and mentor, makes his way through the crowd, his figure blurred and chromatically coordinated with that of the individuals who surround him. Soon after, Arturo himself makes an appearance amidst the documentary throng, desperately searching for the absent Andreotti. At the end of this archival clip, a grim-faced Chinnici materializes, looking into the camera, as if contemplating the similar doom that awaits him in his anti-mafia crusade.

This insertion of fictional characters into documentary footage, using the technique known as 'compositing,' heightens our awareness of the artifice and gimmickry of the film while at the same time raising the scene's ethical stakes. Through compositing, Arturo has been able to 'enter' the historical arena – he becomes a witness, via video simulation, of the communal grieving that will serve as a preliminary step in mobilizing the anti-mafia movement of Palermo. His simulated presence within this documentary space prefigures his adult debut as an anti-mafia activist in the rally that will follow the funeral of Borsellino's escort towards the end of the film. Not coincidentally, this later scene marks the moment when Arturo can finally declare himself to Flora, who is also at the rally and who is more than willing to reciprocate the young man's passion for her.

It is of the utmost significance that the ritual of mourning stands at the centre of the film's 'happy' ending, both at the level of the love plot and at that of the political awakening experienced by the populace of Palermo. If mourning is the appropriate therapeutic response to traumatic shock,[4] and if, as Dana Renga has argued,[5] mafia violence is experienced as trauma in the collective Italian psyche, then Diliberto's scene of Borsellino's funeral-turned-protest rally enacts that therapeutic function. The cathartic release of repressed energy in this mass gathering enables Arturo to overcome his inhibitions with regard to Flora, just as Palermo is able to emerge from its fatalism, fear, and paralysis and publicly denounce mafia rule. For both our protagonists and the Palermitani, the result is the birth of a new order: a burgeoning family unit for the young couple, and 'an idea [born from a group in mourning] of a civil society capable of elaborating a collective commitment and strategy where young generations still too uninformed and disillusioned, carry out a role in the foreground as an antidote'[6] for the public at large.

La mafia uccide is not Diliberto's first cinematic effort devoted to memorializing the martyrs of the struggle against organized crime. Significantly, he served as apprentice to Marco Tullio Giordana in the making of *I cento passi*, an experience that surely contributed to his technical mastery of the cinematic art[7] as well as to his determination to use the medium to revive historical memory and instil activist fervour in a public notoriously deficient in it. The most explicit homage to Giordana's film emerges in the climactic scene of the funeral-turned-rally, echoing the analogous moment at the end of *I cento passi* when Peppino's mourners erupt into a spontaneous chant, raise their fists in defiance, and manifest their will to resist mafia rule. Giordana's film does not resort to archival footage in this scene – it contents itself with a fictional re-creation, making recourse to documentary images only at the end, with a series of still photographs of the historical Peppino Impastato. Diliberto's frequent recourse to newsreel clips, instead, testifies to his abiding interest in transmediality, with a particular focus on the conflictive montage effects produced by the inclusion of TV footage within the body of the fiction film, as analysed in the scene of Dalla Chiesa's funeral. This technical interest in televisiual versus cinematic imagery speaks to the larger issue of Diliberto's awareness that he is importing his small-screen celebrity into the large-screen medium, with all of the cultural implications of such a move. Aware of the venerable film history into which he is entering, thanks to his experience with Giordana, Diliberto stages the transformation of his TV persona, from the *leggerezza* of his 'candid camera' character in the show '*Le iene*' (*Hyenas*), to his MTV reportages in *Il testimone*, (*The Witness*), to the eventual *gravità* of the father who transmits anti-mafia history to his son at the end of *La mafia uccide*. In other words, Diliberto has opted to exploit his celebrity status as a TV star with particular appeal to a young demographic, in the service of civic engagement. Leveraging his popular allure, Diliberto entices a new generation of viewers to *La mafia uccide* with the promise of hip entertainment, but in the process he manages to transform 'comedy into tragedy, reminding us that it is possible to rebel.'[8] It may be pure coincidence, but I cannot help but connect the title of his MTV series, *Il testimone*, which features Pif as interviewer of pop-cultural figures, to the testimonial function of *La mafia uccide*, where the true meaning of bearing witness – the forging of an ethically charged relationship between a representation and its audience – becomes a call to judgment and a summons to act.

NOTES

1 Marco Dinoi, *Lo sguardo e l'evento. I media, la memoria, il cinema*, cited in *Strane storie: Il cinema e i misteri d'Italia*, ed. Christian Uva (Soveria Mannelli: Rubbettino, 2011), 14, my translation here and throughout.

2 This is Christian Uva's term. See 'I misteri d'Italia nel cinema. Strategie narrative e trame estetiche tra documento e finzione,' in ibid., 16.

3 Vittorio Fantuzzi, *Intervista a Paolo Benvenuti*, cited in Uva, ed., *Strane storie*, 13.

4 This is Eric Santner's argument in 'History Beyond the Pleasure Principle: Some Thoughts on the Representation of Trauma," in *Probing the Limits of Representation: Nazism and the Final Solution*, ed. Saul Friedlander (Cambridge, MA: Harvard University Press, 1992), 144.

5 See Dana Renga, *Unfinished Business: Screening the Italian Mafia in the New Millennium* (Toronto: University of Toronto Press, 2013), especially 6–16.

6 Uva, 'I misteri d'Italia nel cinema,' 27.

7 Antonio Pettierre finds much to admire, from a technical point of view, in Diliberto's filmmaking debut. See, www.ondacinema.it/film/recensione/Mafia_uccide_solo_estate.html.

8 See Marzia Gandolfi's review of the film at www.mymovies.it/film/2013/solodeste.

48   Fabio Grassadonia and Antonio Piazza's *Salvo*: The Sound of Redemption in an Infernal Landscape

AMY BOYLAN

Salvo (2013), the first feature film for both Fabio Grassadonia and Antonio Piazza, is inspired by their collaborative short film titled *Rita* (2009). In *Rita* a ten-year-old girl, blind since birth, encounters a mysterious teenage boy who materializes out of nowhere and leads her to the beach, then into the sea, at which point she finds herself completely alone. The film ends with an extreme close-up of Rita's face, wearing an ambiguous expression, accompanied by the lapping sound of waves. While sharing some stylistic (extreme close-ups, heightened attention to sound) and narrative (a mysterious male character arriving unannounced in Rita's life, Rita's blindness, an open ending at the seaside) elements with the earlier film, in *Salvo* the focus shifts from Rita's character to that of the eponymous stoic mafia hitman. Through a mystical love connection with Rita, now a young woman, Salvo is transformed from a superhuman killer into a vulnerable protector. The directors' choice to focus on a narrative of love and redemption played well with many critics – the film won the Critic's Week Grand Prize at Cannes in 2013 and garnered a number of Nastro d'Argento nominations, including a win for Best Cinematography for Daniele Ciprì – even though box office returns in Italy were quite modest. Particularly noteworthy for these critics is the film's haunting use of sound – grinding metal, relentless hammering, broken air conditioners, howling wind, and Rita's piercing screams – which I discuss below.

The love story begins when Salvo, already established as a macho man of few words, shows up at Rita's house and kills her brother. He tries to kill Rita too, but upon touching her face a moral awakening overwhelms him. Interestingly, this is a reversal of the scene in *Rita* when the boy first appears to her and she explores his face with her hands. Here, instead, Rita puts her hands on Salvo's face and he knocks them away, aggressively covering her eyes and forehead with his hand. These violent actions deny Rita the dignity afforded her in the earlier film. Yet in his bewildered state, instead of murdering Rita, Salvo hides her in an abandoned factory that his boss uses for torture and executions. Salvo's failure to kill Rita initiates his inevitable spiral towards death, but the pseudo-romantic relationship they develop is also his path to redemption. Unfortunately, since much of Salvo's masculine identity in the film depends on his ability to suppress emotions like fear and grief, its preservation depends on his self-annihilation.[1] The relationship transforms Rita as well. When Salvo touches her for the first time, she begins to see light, and by the end of the film she is fully sighted.

Salvo is unusual in the context of other Italian mafia movies released in the first decade of the 2000s, which tend to commemorate the courage of anti-mafia figures such as Peppino

Impastato, Placido Rizzotto, and Rita Atria. Salvo, on the contrary, is a criminal antihero. Viewers are prompted to sympathize with him in a number of ways: he is movie-star handsome, conflicted, and lonely; he offers comfort to his landlords' neglected dog and, eventually, rejects his boss's order to kill Rita. Yet while *Salvo* departs from the anti-mafia themes of films like *The Hundred Steps*, *The Sicilian Girl*, and *Placido Rizzotto*, it does align with a new trend in recent films identified by Dana Renga as the 'mob weepie,' a subgenre of the male melodrama. Writing about Davide Barletti and Lorenzo Conte's *Fine pena mai: Paradiso perduto* (2008), Renga comments that while '[d]epicting a criminal in a sentimental light in the cinema is nothing new, especially in the Hollywood gangster tradition, [s]uch a poignant representation of mafia perpetrators, however, is anomalous in the Italian tradition … in which compassion is usually aligned with those fallen in the battle against the mafia.'[2] Renga goes on to explore the ways in which *Fine pena mai* privileges the male protagonist's melancholia over the development of the main female character and posits that she, like many female characters in narratives of male self-realization, functions as a 'salvific' presence at the service of the male protagonist.[3] Likewise, in *Salvo* the martyr narrative is centred around the mafioso. Although it is ultimately Rita who survives and Salvo who dies, the dynamic described by Renga can be seen in the way Salvo's redemption requires Rita's imprisonment and suffering. Her display of extreme emotions is the catalyst for his self-realization, but when he dies her story ends too. Thus the ambiguity of the film's title: Who is really saving whom?

Besides narratively foregrounding Salvo's self-realization, the filmmakers rely on Rita's character for the realization of their creative interests. They employ the literal and metaphoric possibilities of Rita's blindness in order to experiment with disorienting cinematic techniques such as out-of-focus shots, obstructed views, action that frequently takes place off-screen but that can be heard by viewers, long periods of darkness or semi-darkness, and the exclusive use of diegetic sound. In this way, Rita becomes an instrument both of Salvo's salvation and of the directors' creative self-realization.

The emphasis on redemptive love, the driving force behind the film's mob weepie status, is further amplified by the directors' use of the song 'Arriverà' by Modà (featuring Emma). The directors stated that they used the song because 'it is very popular, melodic, and catchy with a distinctly sentimental quality.'[4] Its lyrics narrate a reconciliation between two lovers. The verses 'Poi di colpo il buio intorno a noi / Ma si sveglierà / il tuo cuore in un giorno d'estate rovente in cui / il sole sarà' (Then all of a sudden darkness around us / But your heart will awake / on a scorching summer day when / there will be sun) work well with the infernally hot, dark, and claustrophobic mood of the film. The transition between dark and light, facilitated by an awakening of the heart, also speaks to the spiritual and physical awakenings of Salvo and Rita. Additionally, the song's title, with its potentially religious connotations of a saviour's arrival, captures Salvo's mystical presence and Rita's fantastical longing for a knight in shining armour. It also anticipates Salvo's self-sacrifice (which is later explicitly compared to that of Christ, through Salvo's deposition-like pose in the film's final scene).

Before Salvo sees Rita for the first time, he hears what viewers will learn is her personal theme song. Early in the film, as he peeks over walls and through blinds, searching for Rita's brother Renato, 'Arriverà' fades into the diegetic world. Salvo descends into a cave-like basement and discovers Rita counting money (presumably for her brother's criminal endeavours) while repeatedly playing the song on her CD player. Viewers then follow Salvo through the house as he continues to look for Renato. While we watch Salvo, we hear Rita's activities – she talks on the phone and receives a grocery delivery (during which the delivery boy comments that she is always listening to the same song). As she becomes more suspicious, Rita walks through the house nervously humming the song's words to soothe herself. She appears in an extended medium close-up shot showing her distressed face, while Salvo, out of focus, looms behind her. This tense situation continues until Renato returns. Salvo then throws Rita down the stairs, and she listens to Renato's murder as it takes place off screen.

Yet, as discussed above, when it comes time to kill Rita, Salvo cannot. The unironic use of a sentimental song such as 'Arriverà' in this extremely violent sequence, which includes Rita's physical assault, helps privilege Salvo's internal conflict. While the song is associated with Rita, and the camera at certain points shows her point of view as she begins to see light, it becomes clear that Salvo's existential anguish both relies on and becomes more important than Rita's ordeal. Her terrified expressions create the emotionally charged situation in which Salvo experiences his transformation. Furthermore, the song's repetition first in its CD form and then as sung by Rita becomes the frame within which Rita's attachment to Salvo develops.

'Arriverà' returns in two other scenes. Rita sings it to herself during her captivity at the abandoned factory. She has endured the double nightmare of imprisonment and having to adapt to suddenly being able to see her surroundings. She lies on a dirty mattress staring at her hand from various angles and sings the song's first verses: 'Piangerai / come pioggia tu piangerai / e te ne andrai / Come le foglie col vento d'autunno triste / tu te ne andrai' (You will cry / you will cry like the rain / and you will leave / Like leaves with the autumn wind, sad / you will leave). Unlike in the earlier scene, here Rita sounds bitter. She repeats the words without continuing to the subsequent verses in which the lovers are reunited. It would seem that she is both lamenting and anticipating a loss, but she is still portrayed as unable to process her situation outside of the emotional possibilities offered by the song.

In a later scene, after days of imprisonment and consequent self-harm, Rita emerges from her room into the daylight. She attempts to escape on foot but soon hears the song's verses echoing from the factory's tower, which protrudes from the landscape above her (recall that Salvo took the CD when he kidnapped Rita.) She returns to the factory wielding a knife but quickly drops it when Salvo, without a word, looks apologetically at the ground. She slaps him, asking 'What do you want from me?' He initially accepts the punishment with a bowed head but then forcibly embraces her until she stops struggling. It is settled: she can't leave and he can't kill her. The song's prophecy has been fulfilled. The use of the song in this scene allows Salvo to communicate his feelings to Rita while still preserving his stoic masculinity. He never cries, in fact he never says a word, and still physically dominates Rita. Yet viewers (and Rita) are meant to understand his heart. The song and Rita's reaction to it do his emotional work for him.

While 'Arriverà' serves to aurally sentimentalize what is in fact a disturbing relationship between captor and captive, the film's scenery precludes any visual romanticization of Rita and Salvo's surroundings. Indeed, while many films about the dire social and economic conditions in southern Italy tend to offer a sense of perspective, or even heightened tragedy, through the occasional view of spectacular mountains or seaside villages, *Salvo* presents an unrelentingly bleak view of its sordid world.

The first appearance in the film of what might be called a landscape (an urban landscape) is from Salvo's point of view as he drives along the labyrinthine, graffiti-ridden streets of Palermo's Arenella neighbourhood. As he drives, we see extreme close-ups of his eyes reflected in the rearview mirror alternating with fragments of the passing buildings and streets. Each one is seemingly a dead end, blocked by high walls. As the film continues, the landscapes – urban and otherwise – become increasingly generic and unappealing, dominated by abandoned construction sites, neglected farmlands, and congested ports. In keeping with the filmmakers' commitment to featuring sound, viewers also 'hear' the scenery (metal being crushed at junkyards, gunshots, neglected dogs barking, motorcycles revving) and sometimes also hear *about* the landscape. The first words spoken in the film are heard as Salvo drives through Palermo. An announcer on the car radio laments, 'There's no end to this hell in Palermo. Scorching hot 100-degree temperatures, and like every summer, a rash of arson fires.' Even the hillsides, literally on fire, offer no relief from the squalor.

The Sicilian landscape has a long history in cinema and other media. Depictions of Sicily's terrain often alternate between idyllic, nostalgic, and unrelentingly harsh. In Italian films about the mafia, expansive views have been employed to evoke fear of the unknown, the beautiful setting in which violent acts take place, or feelings of optimism and emancipation from mafia oppression, which are often expressed by anti-mafia characters (such as in *Placido Rizzotto* and *The Hundred Steps*). In her essay in this volume, Elizabeth Leake notes that in a number of Italian mafia movies views of hillsides are part of an intertextual network in which they signify 'a site of revolution par excellence' (197). In *Salvo*, though, even hillsides have been beaten into submission – ruined by fire, mining, discarded industrial metal parts, and intimidating structures, and divested of their revolutionary potential.

Millicent Marcus uses the term 'antipicturesque' to describe Ricky Tognazzi's 1993 film *La scorta*. Marcus maintains that the film has an 'austere, essential – indeed, antipicturesque' visual quality in which '[a]rchitecture is invariably functional/modern, office interiors are washed out and flat, lighting is undistinguished. Even when landscapes are breathtakingly lush or dramatic, the cinema-politico camera cannot linger on them.'[5] Marcus further posits that the film's famous car chase through Trapani is a distorted version of the traditional Sicilian religious procession and thus challenges the notion of Sicily as 'archaic and unchanging,' instead asserting the possibility that there is no longer a place for nostalgia during such a crisis.[6] Matteo Garrone takes a related approach in *Gomorra* (2008), creating what Pierpaolo Antonello terms in his essay in this volume a claustrophobic Dante's Inferno, complete with 'cramped flats, dirty grey walls, dark ominous corners' and 'the digging and raping of a countryside once dubbed *Campania felix* for its fertility' (295). *Salvo* aligns with these two films in its anti-picturesque and anti-nostalgic qualities. Rural and country settings offer no relief from the claustrophobic city streets, no glimpses of freedom or ennobling potential.

A complete dehumanization of the characters takes place within these landscapes as well. A sequence in a scrap metal yard shows a crane hoisting a car into a compacter and then swinging menacingly towards Salvo. As he walks away we see him in a long shot from the back while in the foreground a car is being ruthlessly crushed. Then there is a cut to Salvo walking down a quiet street, a giant crane from the seaport looming in back of him, and government buildings obstructing what is clearly a view of the sea. The alienation of the human form in front of the government building and the giant crane allude to the widely acknowledged (by anti-mafia activists at least) and mutually beneficial relationship between government and organized crime and point towards another element of the landscape that we rarely see in the film: the mafia, represented in the film by a nameless 'boss' who wields power from his secret lair. His dimly lit subterranean residence can apparently only be reached by an also very dimly lit freight elevator that seems to descend into Middle Earth. His demonic qualities manifest themselves physically and through the words he speaks, and his hellish domain extends to the anti-picturesque landscape.

One seemingly self-conscious example of the anti-picturesque attributable to the boss's total dominance of the landscape comes almost exactly halfway through the film when Salvo looks out at the hillside wondering what to do with Rita. The unusually expansive view should hold the potential for escape, but instead of a lingering panorama shot, there is a jump cut to Salvo's chair, now abandoned, and then another cut to the factory tower, back-lit and shot from a low angle, enhancing its ominous and overwhelming qualities and squashing any hope that the open landscape might have offered. The imposing tower marks the hillsides and reminds us that only in death can one escape this tyranny.

In conclusion, even the beach becomes a problematic location that cannot succeed in tempering the decrepitude of daily life as it often does in Italian cinema.[7] In the film's final scene, Rita and the mortally wounded Salvo return to her home. Filmed from behind and at a slightly elevated angle, they sit next to each other facing a patio wall. A sliver of blue water is barely visible above the wall, but it is unclear whether they can see it from their lower angle. One can, however, hear the waves lapping, and this is the first time in the film that the rhythms of nature can be heard without interference from thumping construction noises or revving engines. The film's final minute shows Rita walking out of the frame, leaving the dead Salvo behind. We hear the door open and close behind her while the camera stays trained on the horizon. The filmmakers describe this story as depicting how a chance encounter can impact the course of people's lives.[8] But while the open ending leaves space for viewers to feel a glimmer of hope (after all, it does not replicate the numb finality of the cadavers of Marco and Ciro being dumped on the beach at the end of *Gomorrah*), it also reminds us that this hope is precarious and that the tyrannical boss still controls the world in which Rita must live. Salvo spared Rita's life and gave her someone to love, and Rita saved Salvo's soul; but when she walks out into the unchanged apocalyptic landscape where she remains a target of mafia vendetta, viewers may find themselves asking, 'What's the point?'

NOTES

1 On death, resurrection, loss of masculinity, and melodrama, see Tania Modleski, 'Clint Eastwood and Male Weepies,' *America Literary History* 22, no. 1 (2010): 150.

2 Dana Renga, *Unfinished Business: Screening the Italian Mafia in the New Millennium* (Toronto: University of Toronto Press, 2013), 131.

3 Ibid., 119.

4 '"Arriverà" di Emma e dei Modà nel film "Salvo,"' accessed 14 May 2017, https://goo.gl/uRWS1q.

5 Millicent Marcus, *After Fellini: National Cinema in the Postmodern Age* (Baltimore, MD: Johns Hopkins University Press, 2002), 138.
6 Ibid., 139.
7 Renga, *Unfinished Business*, 147.
8 David Gregory Lawson, 'Interview: Fabio Grassadonia & Antonio Piazza,' accessed 14 May 2017, https://www.filmcomment.com/blog/interview-fabio-grassadonia-antonio-piazza.

49 Of Renegades and Game Players: Shifting Sympathies in *Gomorra: la serie*

GIANCARLO LOMBARDI

Through its title, *Gomorra: la serie* (2014–) claims a double connection to texts that preceded it. It is tied to *Gomorra*, Roberto Saviano's 2006 exposé on the Camorra, and to Matteo Garrone's eponymous film (2008); it is also linked to *Romanzo criminale: la serie* (2008–2010), another drama, this one based on *Romanzo criminale* (2002), Giancarlo De Cataldo's novelized history of the Banda della Magliana, adapted for the big screen in 2005 by Michele Placido. Broadcast by Sky, both series represented the coming of age of Italian television drama, until then virtually unexportable. The generic marker *la serie*, included in the title, is now integral to the Sky Italia brand.

Much can be said about the two series' stylistic and structural similarities. Heavily indebted to the auteurial vision of Stefano Sollima, who directed *Romanzo criminale: la serie* and who served as artistic director of *Gomorra: la serie*, filming most of its episodes, both adopted a distinct use of filters that re-created periods and environments through coded reliance on warm or cold colours. At the same time, both series posited viewer sympathy within the confines of deeply flawed protagonists whose narrative development is foregrounded in a way that compels spectatorial alignment.

Gomorra: la serie departs from *Romanzo criminale: la serie* in its reinvention of the source-text. While the latter remained faithful to De Cataldo's novel, finding its serialized nature optimal for narrative twists of the sort that had been compressed in Placido's film, *Gomorra: la serie* chose a different path in its adaptation of a journalistic exposé, whose generic constraints resist conventional forms of dramatic storytelling. Unlike Garrone's film, which maintained the narrative distance of the source-text through its quasi-documentary style, the series reorients Saviano's book by placing particular emphasis on compelling characterization.

In its two seasons, instead of depicting the Camorra through synchronic snapshots of its activities, *Gomorra* traces generational struggles internal to a single clan, headed by Pietro Savastano. The focus of the twelve episodes comprising the first season is divided among three members of the Savastano family: incarcerated at the end of the second episode, Pietro controls the clan for two more instalments and then is replaced by his wife Imma from 1.5 (or season 1, episode 5) to 1.7, in which she relinquishes control to their son Genny, who is in charge until 1.12. As a helper soon turned antagonist, Ciro Di Marzio threatens the established order from the inside, questioning Pietro's and then Imma's leadership while acting as Genny's mentor. When Genny ascends to power, forfeiting loyalty to his elders, Ciro jumps ship and destroys the clan, murdering Imma and leaving Genny for dead as 1.12 ends.

Despite the centrality of the Savastanos, viewer engagement throughout the first season is mainly aligned with Ciro, the Camorra soldier whose long exchange with his trusted friend Attilio opens the series. Their conversation, as noted elsewhere,[1] draws younger viewers with a humorous discussion of social networks: privacy is sacred to a society regulated by *omertà*, and its infringement by social media is perceived as threatening to older generations, who thus resist these forms of communication. Partly drowned out by the notes of Neapolitan rap, which mixes tradition (dialect) with innovation (rap music), their conversation shifts to a discussion of their clan leadership. The age difference between Ciro and Attilio, evidenced by their different views and tastes, reappears through their degree of engagement with the organization; this speaks directly to a desired target viewership, possibly aligned in age and preferences with Ciro. Like his peers, Attilio is fiercely loyal to Pietro's leadership, and he finds Ciro's questioning of his decisions inappropriate. By the end of the first episode, those decisions have led to Attilio's death, leaving Ciro, already christened as *Immortale*, alone and firm in his convictions. Close spectatorial engagement with Ciro is reinforced by the fact that viewers enter the Savastano mansion with him, meeting the entire family as he and Attilio report to Pietro on their latest action. Later, witnessing the arrival of the police and the disposal of Attilio's body from afar, viewers come to share more with Ciro than a physical vantage point: having seen the consequences of Pietro's orders, viewers inevitably embrace Ciro's positions. Such allegiance, to employ Murray Smith's terminology,[2] is complicated by the ensuing discovery that Ciro may be collaborating with the police to neutralize the clan. By then, viewers have witnessed Ciro's painful humiliation as Pietro orders him to prove his submission by drinking his urine. Having shared his indignation, after Pietro's imprisonment they also share Ciro's hope for a better future through his partnership with Genny.[3] This hope for the future, reinforced by the lyrics of the song that closes each episode, sutures viewer engagement throughout the series, becoming abstract when allegiance with any given character falters because of the unpalatability of their actions.

The first four episodes of the series place Ciro safely at Genny's side and closely align the viewer with a character likely to influence a new course for the clan. Such is Ciro's *hope*, should control follow the dynastic rules of succession. However, Genny is too immature to replace his father, and according to Imma, he is too susceptible to Ciro's influence. The fifth and sixth episodes mark a significant shift in narrative continuity. Troubling the assumption that the Camorra is a southern affair, the action moves north: 1.5 takes place almost entirely in Milan, where a corrupt businessman has long been tasked with laundering the Savastanos' earnings, while 1.6 is filmed in Barcelona, to which the Savastanos' nemesis Salvatore Conte has repaired. The location change in 1.5 is paralleled by a change in intra-diegetic and extra-diegetic direction. At the intra-diegetic level, the first four episodes were dominated by the male protagonists, whereas the fifth marks the temporary takeover of Imma, who demonstrates brutal leadership skills in disposing of the men who surround her: a son who is more concerned about his girlfriend than about the current upheaval; a financial consultant who puts his own interests before those of his clients; and an ambitious crew member who threatens to gain from the current crisis by taking control of the organization through her immature son. At the extra-diegetic level, the portrayal of Imma's all-seeing gaze on the city, her family, and her crew is entrusted to a female director, Francesca Comencini, who returns in episode 1.7, during which Imma's 'regency' suddenly ends. Comencini's first episode begins to threaten the viewers' engagement with Ciro, whose marginal presence is limited to brief conversations with Genny and Imma. It is when the latter orders him to go to Spain to make peace with Conte, and to resume collaboration in drug trafficking, that viewer engagement is literally bisected: Imma's final comment, unheard by Ciro, 'And this one is done,' continues to align the spectator with her, yet by assigning Ciro a virtually impossible task, it renews viewer allegiance with the mistreated 'underdog.' Ciro is reinstated at the centre of the structure of spectatorial sympathy in the following episode, which focuses on his trip to Barcelona, where he survives an attempted drowning at the hands of Conte's goons and, later, a game of Russian roulette ordered by one of Conte's rivals. His humiliating treatment as a disposable pawn by Pietro, Imma, and later Conte serves to reinforce his image as renegade, already presented iconically since the first episode, when, after Attilio's death, upon burning the car in which he began the episode singing, Ciro sheds his skin, puts on a new hoodie, and bends his long neck like a skilled boxer who has been only temporarily defeated.

Because of the general absence of any law-abiding characters, viewer engagement in the series is not as steady and unidirectional as my discussion of the first six episodes might seem to suggest. Notwithstanding the centrality of Ciro, the presence of a large cast of principals encourages multiple vantage points of spectatorial sympathy. In this regard, Ciro's killing of four female characters (the teenage girlfriend of a young associate, Imma, her bodyguard, and lastly his own wife) within the space of five episodes (1.9–2.1) troubles what could have been perceived, until then, as a stable spectatorial allegiance. Violence against women exacerbates the graphic nature of the final episodes of the first season, and the narrative uncomfortably suggests that the inception of that violence might be located in the actual brutality of Imma's brief regency, which began with her impassive call for the corrupt businessman's suicide (1.5) and ended with the assassination of Marta/Luca (1.7), Imma's young transgender protégée, who, as Pierpaolo Antonello notes, serves as a 'metonymy or synecdoche for Imma, for he embodies in flesh the transitional gender position Imma is trying to hold within the hierarchical power structure of the camorra.'[4] Shot to death in a white bridal gown while running across a desolate Neapolitan street, Luca meets the same destiny Imma will later encounter: both characters are similarly killed, and their deaths are filmed through long shots from a vantage point that, although suggesting physical detachment from the events, actually reinforces the viewer's ensuing alienation from sympathetic engagement with the perpetrators.

Genny's return from Honduras, where Imma dispatched him on a journey of initiation disguised as a business trip, leads to further unrest in the Savastano clan, which has been shaken to its core by a generational slaughter instigated by Ciro, who is miffed by Genny's newly acquired independence. Aware that neither Genny's nor Imma's leadership will protect his interests, Ciro sows chaos (as Pietro will in the second season), thus fuelling the rebellion of Genny and his men against their elders. Viewers are asked to bear witness to Ciro's calculated estrangement from both sides, which is reinforced by his age, which falls between that of the two opposing factions. Along the way, their allegiance to Ciro will be tested – and possibly forfeited, when they watch him torture and kill an adolescent and hear him declare his hatred of Imma shortly before she is murdered by his men. The events leading to Imma's demise may shift viewer allegiance again to her side, if only because of the sense of understated justice with which she confronts her enemies and her destiny. After her death, in 1.12, viewer allegiance goes adrift as the two remaining rivals, Ciro and Genny, endanger children in their final duel, which leaves the latter apparently dead on the stage of a school play. At season end, the contempt and disbelief of Ciro's wife Deborah resonates with viewers, who partake extra-diegetically of her hinted abandonment: the two brief final sequences are meant to suture spectatorial engagement through the emotional charge promised by Pietro's prison break and Genny's unexpected survival. Once again, hope for the future sutures viewer engagement when actual allegiance becomes unthinkable.

It should come as no surprise, then, that Deborah plays a pivotal role in 2.1; although her demise at the end of the episode may appear rushed, it resounds with the different structure of the second season, which favours episodic closure over long narrative arcs. Important characters such as Deborah, Salvatore Conte, and Il Principe are quickly eliminated at the end of the episodes of which they were protagonists. In this respect, Deborah's justifiable paranoia, which drives most of her actions in 2.1, alienating her from Ciro and her surroundings, announces the mood that will dominate the entire season. Hers is the paranoia of the surviving protagonists and of their collaborators, informed by the unpredictability of past events and their fatal consequences. Re-encountered by viewers two years after Season One aired, Ciro, Genny, and Pietro must be re-established as characters worthy of sympathetic engagement, if only for their new placement on the chessboard on which they design new strategies of attack.

The rigorous structural order of the first season, which parallels the equally rigorous 'natural order' that mandates succession from Pietro to Imma to Genny, disappears in the following twelve episodes, which open with Ciro's ascent to power, his alliance with Conte, and the creation of a new organization. In the second season, viewers follow a more chaotic narrative that alternates three interweaving threads connected to its protagonists: Ciro, Genny, and Pietro. And while 2.1 shows Ciro's increasing isolation, epitomized by the assassination of Deborah driven by his impulse for self-preservation, the following episode is dedicated to Genny's recovery and his encounter with Pietro in Germany. The solitude of father and son is reinforced by their brief reunion, which is shortened by Pietro's decision to regain control of Secondigliano without any help from Genny.

Pietro's prison break in 1.12 places him in the outsider position previously occupied by Ciro. Just as Ciro disseminated chaos and paranoia within the Savastano clan in the final episodes of Season One, Pietro threatens Ciro's new leadership role by poisoning the relationships among his crew. Indeed, the two metaphors he adopts for his revenge plan are those of 'dogs against dogs' and of the 'slow descent of poison into the heart,' that of the organization, and of the two men who will bring about his death: Genny, who will disclose his father's whereabouts, and Ciro, who will shoot him beside Imma's grave in 2.12. Pietro and Genny's estrangement, motivated by Pietro's lack of trust in his son, is likely to greatly disturb viewers. Throughout the season, they witness Genny's growing disillusionment with his father, coupled with his attempt to put down roots in Rome. The same young man who, like pious Aeneas, carried his ailing father on his shoulders as they ran from the German police in 2.2, eventually accepts the necessity of his death as he welcomes the birth of his new child, in the final scene of 2.12, naming him Pietro. Incidentally, Aeneas and Genny share a destination: Rome. And while the first season ended with Genny's near-death experience and with a metaphorical rebirth of his father, the second season closes on the simultaneous death of his father and birth of his son.

Season Two unquestionably calls for a different form of viewer engagement, in part because its three male protagonists alternate as the focus of the narrative, occasionally disappearing from the screen for long stretches of time. Episodic closure facilitates temporary alignment and allegiance with secondary characters, who disappear too soon to be established as pivots of spectatorial investment: this is true particularly of Ciro's wife and of two male characters who are granted unexpected narrative depth, Conte and Il Principe. The greater narrative range of these episodes, due to a wider cast of principals, who offer multiple and shifting options for spectatorial engagement, undercuts the stability of such engagement. The metaphor of game playing dominates a pivotal sequence in 2.7, to echo a structural specificity of the entire season that speaks to this issue. In a last appeal to Pietro's clemency, Il Principe confesses that he has been playing both sides and that his role in Ciro's organization hides that he is 'on Genny's side': to this, Pietro responds, shortly before murdering him, 'you work better for my game.' In the new narrative environment established in the second season, characters become actual cards in a game that now has three sides: as cards, despite their narrative depth, these characters become dispensable, and any form of spectatorial allegiance thus appears volatile. Too compromised to act as an effective pole of allegiance, Ciro temporarily reclaims this function only once he acknowledges, in 2.5 and 2.10, his inability to do any more killing. The dramatic event leading to the parallel closing sequences of 2.12, portraying Pietro's death and the birth of Genny's son, places Ciro steadfastly at the centre of the structure of sympathy: the same man who had declared his inability to kill becomes a murderer again in order to avenge the death of his young daughter. The same hope for the future (represented by the birth of little Pietro) that sutures viewer engagement when it is endangered by extreme acts of violence is cut short intra-diegetically for Ciro upon the death of his own child. At season end the renegade is turned – to return to Pietro's animalistic metaphor – into a *cane sciolto*.

One last card remains unplayed – that of the only new character likely to claim hegemony, in retrospect, over the structure of sympathy of the entire season: Patrizia, the niece of Pietro's closest collaborator, who is charged with his custody and acts as his surrogate and courier throughout the season before becoming, eventually, his lover. Alien to the organization, for which she works in order to ensure the well-being of her younger siblings, Patrizia fills the gap left in the narrative by Imma's death through her assertive presence, her ability to speak to power, her courage, and her selflessness. Like Imma, Patrizia is portrayed as the voice of reason, as the only *consigliere* who attempts to diffuse the growing tension between Pietro and his son: prey to the Freudian family romance, however, Genny antagonizes Patrizia long before her collaboration with Pietro takes a romantic turn. And Genny's jealousy, expressed by his destruction of an old family portrait, possibly plays a role in his decision to arm Ciro against his father. Patrizia remains a viable alternative to Ciro for spectatorial allegiance because, unlike Imma, she remains an outsider and never assumes responsibility for Pietro's atrocities. Having accepted Pietro's ring shortly before his death, Patrizia is destined to play, in future episodes, a prominent role in his organization: the possibility of her entrance into the game as an antagonist to Ciro and Genny is the anticipated plot twist suturing viewers, once again through spectatorial hope and speculation, to a narrative surprising for its uncanny ability to reinvent the game in each new instalment.

Thirty-Six and Counting: Afterthoughts on Season Three

Gomorra: la serie returns with a third season after an eighteen-month hiatus: nothing seems to have changed, yet everything has. The discovery of Pietro's body, his funeral, and Genny's apparent search for his killer lead to the demise of Malammore, the last player associated with the old generation. Following his death, which symbolically closes a cycle, the narrative zooms out to encompass the 'System' in its wider control of the Neapolitan territory. In doing so, it renews itself, introducing new characters, fields of action, and overarching metaphors.

Spectatorial sympathy with established characters continues despite their brutality: Patrizia plays a limited role in the early episodes, leaving the viewer to side either with Genny or with Ciro, both hitting rock bottom by 3.4. While Ciro's self-imposed exile in Bulgaria is a journey through hell that re-establishes the character's empathic viability, Genny's complete dispossession (of family, power, and material goods) at the hands of his father-in-law hardly facilitates spectatorial sympathy because of emphasis placed on the character's manipulative behaviour.

Dispossession is a core element connecting several protagonists throughout the season. Ciro's austere hotel room replaces the mansions of the first season, while Genny's new shelter faces Le Vele as Pietro's hiding place once did. Unlike Ciro, Genny shares dynastic dispossession with another character, Enzo Sangue Blu, introduced in 3.3 and soon established as pivotal to the entire narrative. The leader of a gang of drug-dealing bikers whose long beards warrant their street name of Talebani, Enzo descends from the disowned ruling family of Forcella, the area that replaces Secondigliano as centre stage for much of Season Three. Genny and Enzo are 'kings' children', out to claim rights that exclude Ciro, whose 'immortality' (1) descends from his survival of an earthquake that killed his entire family, and (2) is proven, by season end, to be untrue.

Metaphors abound throughout the season, mostly belonging to the semantic fields of the epic and the fairy tale, granting new connotations to the narrative and its players. The title of 3.1, 'Long Live the King', re-establishes the importance of the dynastic component, which is significantly reinforced by episode end with the introduction of the fairy tale motif through the presentation of Genny and Azzurra's new house as a 'fairy tale home'. Legend is invoked from the beginning, as Genny's behaviour at his father's funeral reminds bystanders that 'at the king's funeral, the only one who doesn't cry is the son'. Pietro's coffin traverses Secondigliano's adoring crowd on a golden carriage, and on that same coffin, resting in the Savastanos' private chapel, Patrizia symbolically places her engagement ring. Soon afterwards the action moves, for the very first time, to the centre of Naples, to a courtyard surrounded by haunting arched windows, whose darkness serves as the prelude to a new indoor setting, a room dominated by a roundtable around which the heads of the Neapolitan families administer the 'System'. Fairy tale and epic elements, already evoked by this setting, return through the street names of two bosses, Stregone and Charmant, and by that of Enzo's late grandfather, Il Santo.

Throughout the third season, Ciro, Genny, and Enzo are in open opposition to the rulers of the System and, most importantly, often plotting against one another. Initially encountered during his stay in Bulgaria, Ciro enlists Enzo once he realizes that, like a medieval knight, Enzo is fiercely loyal to his own people and is eager to join forces with the man known to all as The Immortal. Enzo's admiration for Ciro stems from a shared sense of revenge against past injustices. 'Children of Ghosts' is what Enzo calls his army, whose motorbikes replace the horses ridden by legendary knights.

Impatient to be reunited with his wife and child, Genny sows discord between Ciro and Enzo as declarations of brotherly loyalty are made and broken on multiple sides. Ultimately, this discord leads to a dramatic resolution that stages the unthinkable: legends exist to be proven false, as Ciro the Immortal pays the ultimate price for Genny's betrayal, dying at his hand upon Enzo's firm request. Season Three ends with a sequence meant to dismay its viewers, who are left fatally unsutured from the character with whom they had most stably aligned throughout thirty-six episodes. Ciro's death is the result of the same *doppio* and *triplo gioco* that led to the murders of Salvatore Conte, Il Principe, and Pietro.

Similarly, 3.11 and 3.12 see Patrizia taking ownership of her own game through repeated murders. The game play metaphor returns to the centre of the series once she is introduced to the bosses of the roundtable as *il jolly*, an unpredictable wild card that repositions itself endlessly. No longer hopeful for the future, Patrizia is eventually absorbed by the 'System,' leaving viewers with the bleakest horizon of expectations ever experienced since the inception of the series.

NOTES

1   Giancarlo Lombardi, 'I.I: Of Generational Clash and Sympathy for the Renegade (Il Clan Dei Savastano, Stefano Sollima),' *The Italianist* 36, no. 2 (2016): 293–8.

2   Murray Smith, *Engaging Characters: Fiction, Emotion, and the Cinema* (Oxford: Oxford University Press, 1995).

3   Dana Renga maintains that sympathy for Ciro also derives from his rich backstory: 'Making Men in *Gomorra la serie*,' *L'avventura* 1 (2015): 115.

4   Pierpaolo Antonello, 'I.7: A' Storia E' Maria: Gender Power Dynamics and Genre Normalization (Imma Contro Tutti, Francesca Comencini),' *The Italianist* 36, no. 2 (2016): 323.

PART FOUR

Italy's Other Mafias in Film and on Television: A Roundtable

Introduction – The Banda della Magliana, the Camorra, the 'Ndrangheta, and the Sacra Corona Unita: The Mafia On Screen beyond the Cosa Nostra

DANA RENGA

With its late spring release in 2008, the acclaimed hit *Gomorra* (*Gomorrah*, Matteo Garrone, 2008) secured a stronghold for the Camorra in the international imaginary and provided a visual counterpoint to Roberto Saviano's eponymous book from 2006, which was already a national best-seller.[1] In 2008 the mafia of Campania was in the media spotlight both within and outside of Italy: newspaper headlines spoke of the rubbish disposal crisis, the Ecomafia, toxic dumping, and the resulting dioxin scare affecting the production of local mozzarella that was being exported internationally. Later that year, Campania was again the focus of public attention following the mafia-related attacks on a group of Africans in Castelvolturno and ensuing rioting, events that led to the government's decision to send five hundred troops to the region to help battle organized crime. For the second time in twenty years, the army had been enlisted to combat the mafia; the first had been dubbed 'Operation Sicilian Vespers' and involved the deployment of 150,000 soldiers to Sicily over a six-year period beginning in 1992 in the wake of the assassinations of Giovanni Falcone and Paolo Borsellino.

The Camorra had become, in the words of one reviewer, Italy's 'new mafia' in that it had replaced the Cosa Nostra in public scrutiny, now more so than ever with the international success of *Gomorra: la serie* (2014–).[2] And similar language is now being used to describe other Italian mafias: the Sacra Corona Unita of Puglia is being referred to as Italy's 'fourth mafia', after the Cosa Nostra, the Camorra, and the 'ndrangheta, and the Roman Banda della Magliana is now being referred to as the 'fifth mafia',[3] while a book on the 'ndrangheta, the mafia of Calabria, has labelled that organization 'Italy's new mafia.'[4] Historically, Italy's other mafias have received less critical attention than the mafia of Sicily, even though the Camorra predates the Cosa Nostra and the 'ndrangheta is considered Italy's most powerful mafia. At the same time, the 'ndrangheta was Italy's least visible mafia until its entrance onto the international scene following the Duisburg massacre in 2007, when members of the organization murdered six men from a rival clan outside an Italian restaurant in that German city. More than one hundred Italian feature films, documentaries, television shows, series, and soap operas have been produced that foreground Italy's other mafias, most of them released over the past twenty-five years. Moreover, although some scholarly attention has been paid to representations of Italy's other mafias – especially the Camorra, in the wake of the hit series *Gomorra: la serie* – most scholarship on on-screen depictions of organized crime has focused on the Cosa Nostra or the Italian American mafia.

This roundtable aims to fill this lacuna in mafia screen studies. Begun as a roundtable discussion at the May 2012 meeting of the American Association for Italian Studies at the College of Charleston, this part of the present volume has ten contributors. The roundtable's clear focus is on mafias other than the Cosa Nostra, and the contributions treat more than fifty feature films, documentaries, made-for-television movies, and series that centre on the Banda della Magliana, the Camorra, the 'ndrangheta, and the Sacra Corona Unita. Yet perhaps inevitably, at times films about the Cosa Nostra, the mafia that has secured a stronghold in the public imagination, creep back into discussions of these other mafias.[5]

Cinema Camorra

In February 2012, Paolo and Vittorio Taviani's *Cesare deve morire* (*Caesar Must Die*, 2012) won the Golden Bear at the Berlin International Film Festival. Shot on location in the Rebibbia prison, the film is a docudrama about a group of inmates who stage a production of *Julius Caesar*. Early on, viewers learn that two prisoners with key roles in the play have been incarcerated for Camorra-related activities: Cosimo Rega (Cassius) is serving a life sentence for murder, and Sasà Striano (Brutus) has been imprisoned for fourteen years for undisclosed crimes. Not until the end of the film, however, is it revealed that Striano was released in 2006 and enjoys a lively acting career. He played a *scissionista* (someone who defects from one Camorra clan to another) in *Gomorra* and also appeared in Marco Risi's *Fortapàsc* (*Fort Apache Napoli*, 2009), a biopic that tells the story of idealistic reporter Giancarlo Siani, who stands up to the Camorra and pays with his life.

   Cesare deve morire raises compelling questions regarding the performative aspects of criminality, in particular when we keep in mind that Striano is an ex-*camorrista* playing a *camorrista* on screen. While in the Tavianis' film it is suggested that acting is cathartic and potentially liberating, Garrone's film depicts mobsters whose lives are mirrored in the characters they emulate. This is the case with Marco and Cirò, who model their behaviour on Tony Montana or Raffaele Cutolo, the now imprisoned boss of the Nuova Camorra Organizzata and protagonist of Giuseppe Tornatore's *Il camorrista* (*The Professor*, 1986), a highly stylized film that focuses on a self-made and charismatic gangster.

   The Tavianis' film also makes plain that there exist no specific generic attributes to the Italian mafia movie. Italian films that represent the country's various mafias resist being uniformly characterized and instead represent a compilation of various genres. For example, although mafiacinema from the 1960s and 1970s by Francesco Rosi, Elio Petri, and Damiano Damiani is commonly placed under the rubric of engaged or political cinema, several films by these directors share affinities with the western, the gothic film, and film noir. As many of the pieces in this roundtable suggest, recent mafia cinema is also far from homogeneous and is indebted to traditional film models such as melodrama, male melodrama, film noir, the political thriller, the coming-of-age film, the prison film, the road movie, the woman's film, and the biopic. Rethought in this way, the mafia in film might be best labelled a motif rather than classified as a genre.

   Of the more than one hundred films and television shows on Italy's other mafias, close to half are feature films about the Camorra. Although some of these, such as Francesco Rosi's seminal *Le mani sulla città* (*Hands over the City*, 1963) and (in part) his earlier *La sfida* (*The Challenge*, 1958), can be considered forerunners to the engaged and political cinema of the 1960s and 1970s, most feature films on the Camorra fall into different, and disparate, categories such as the *poliziesco*, the comedy, the musical, and, in the case of Antonio Capuano's *Luna rossa* (*Red Moon*, 2001), the (Greek) tragedy. During the 1970s, some of Italy's best-known genre directors such as Pasquale Squitieri, Umberto Lenzi, and Alfonso Brescia set popular *polizieschi* in Naples, the narratives of which focus on a battle of wills between the powerful Camorra and the authorities struggling to maintain order in the city, many of whom have been sent to Naples from northern Italy. Titles such as *La legge della camorra* (*The Godfather's Advisor*, Demofilo Fidani, 1973), *Napoli violenta* (*Violent Naples*, Lenzi, 1976), *Napoli si ribella* (*A Man Called Magnum*, Michele Massimo Tarantini, 1977) and *Napoli... la camorra sfida, la città risponde* (*Naples ... the Camorra Challenges, the City Responds*, Brescia, 1979) conjure up images of a city under siege, and although *Napoli si ribella* ends with the death of the local gangster, the film implies that the Camorra's threat to the city is by no means contained.

Although typically discussed as an example of Holocaust cinema, Lina Wertmüller's *Pasqualino Settebellezze* (*Seven Beauties*, 1975) is also a Camorra comedy, a classification that includes her later *Ciao, Professore!* (1992), Nanni Loy's *Mi manda Picone* (*Where's Picone?* 1983), and Giancarlo Giannini's *Ternosecco* (*The Numbers Game*, 1985). Wertmüller's film juxtaposes the worlds of Neapolitan organized crime and the concentration camp and performs a critique of gangsteresque masculinity while problematizing notions of honour, victimhood, and survivorship. Several films made about the Camorra during the 1990s and 2000s focus on children in and around organized crime. While Nanni Loy's *Scugnizzi* (*Street Kids*, 1989) is a dramatic musical depicting a group of young boys who stage a production in a reformatory, other films such as *Vito e gli altri* (*Vito and the Others*, Antonio Capuano, 1991), *Baby Gang* (Salvatore Piscicelli, 1992), and *Certi bambini* (*A Children's Story*, Antonio and Andrea Frazzi, 2004) take place in the streets and depict characters, such as the young eponymous protagonist of Capuano's film, who become increasingly involved in the violent world of the mafia. Together with *Gomorra*, these films depict the harrowing conditions of daily life in territories dominated by the Camorra and thematize the pull of a life of crime for an ever-growing group of preadolescents with few if any alternatives.

The Camorra and the Ecomafia: 'They Are Killing Us Lawfully'

Campania's *emergenza rifiuti* or 'waste emergency' (1994–) has brought the problem of the Ecomafia to international attention and has spawned several documentaries that examine the Camorra's role in waste management, toxic dumping, and political corruption and that chronicle various efforts at civil resistance across the region.[6] Films such as *Biùtiful cauntri* (*Beautiful Country*, Esmeralda Calabria and Andrea D'Ambrosio, 2007) and *Toxic: Napoli* (*Toxic: Naples*, Santiago Stelley, 2009) present harrowing images that include monstrous animals deformed by pollutants found in their grazing pastures, a woman named Lucia de Cicco who is set on fire after she covers herself in gasoline and chains herself to a fence in order to protest an illegal dumping site, heaps of decomposing and burning garbage lining city streets, riot police who beat and shoot at activists marching against the illegal disposal of deadly toxins in their region, and mountains of *balle* (bales) of waste that sit for years in areas that were once naturally beautiful but that now resemble post-apocalyptic landscapes.[7]

La bambina deve prendere aria (*The Baby Needs Some Fresh Air*, Barbara Rossi Prudente, 2009), *Una montagna di balle* (*A Mountain of Bales*, Nicola Agrisano, 2009), *Campania In-Felix* (Ivana Corsale, 2011), Calabria and D'Ambrosio, and Stelley's films underscore the precarious nature of human life in a geography that often seems a war zone. No longer the lush and fecund 'Campania Felix' of the Romans, the region appears in a state of decomposition. Residents compare Campania to Chernobyl, complain that they are being poisoned, and talk of the dramatic increase in cancer rates in the area. Many insist that the government is protecting both big business and the mafia and point out that they are being killed 'slowly' (*Biùtiful cauntri*) and 'lawfully' (*Toxic: Napoli*). Several of these films pay particular attention to the flocks of thousands of sheep that have had to be destroyed due to dangerous levels of toxins in their blood, and one man affirms, 'se hanno distrutto un gregge di 2500 pecore, noi che fine stiamo facendo? Stiamo facendo la fine delle pecore' (If they destroyed a flock of 2,500 sheep, what will happen to us? We will end up like the sheep). While at times we are shown images of mobilized protests, more frequently these films emphasize a general sense of fatalism with regard to the crisis. Many interviewees feel that opposition is pointless as organized crime has successfully infiltrated legitimate business; one person points out that the Camorra operates with 'mani bianche' (clean hands).

A sense of bitter irony, clear in their titles, pervades many of these films. For example, *La bambina deve prendere aria* turns from fairy tale to urban nightmare as the reassuring voice of the narrator (an actor who stands in for the director) describes to her baby daughter the items that make up her 'emergency kit: a set of objects to protect and aid within the limits of their own capacity.' The light-hearted tone of the animated introduction turns macabre when we realize that the fresh 'air' the mother is instructed to provide for her healthy newborn on daily walks is heavy with the odour of putrid waste. On a more sinister note, we learn that the breast milk of several women in the area is contaminated with detectable levels of dioxin. Rossi Prudente's film highlights that in such a polluted and corrupt society, survival is tenuous. In the film's concluding moments, the narrator notes that garbage has completely disappeared from the urban centre. This finale is far from comforting, however, and her rhetorical 'But where has it gone? No one knows' reminds us of the Camorra's tentacular reach and ability to turn social crises to economic gain.

The 'Ndrangheta: 'The Most Terrifying Mafia'

According to the directors of the documentary *La santa, il viaggio nella 'ndrangheta sconosciuta* (*The Saint: The Journey of the Unknown 'Ndrangheta*, 2007), the 'Santa,' as the mafia of Calabria is also called, is 'the most terrifying mafia.' The organization is the most terrifying, Ruben H. Oliva and Enrico Fierro explain, because it is the most 'powerful, rich, violent, and protected' and also the oldest, 'the least battled against, the most undervalued, the most bloody and cruel.'[8] Paradoxically, it is Italy's strongest yet most hidden, least understood, and, until recently, least studied mafia. *La santa* includes interviews with the mothers of two of the many victims of *lupara bianca*, or 'killing without leaving a trace,' in Filadelfia, the land of the *desaparecidos della Calabria* (missing persons of Calabria). This mode of killing ensures that bodies disappear and helps the organization keep its low media profile.

After the 2007 Duisburg massacre, the organization was a frequent topic of television talk shows. It was also the subject of Francesco Sbano's *Uomini d'onore* (*Men of Honour*, 2009), a documentary that looks at the organization from within and includes haunting interviews with *'ndranghetisti* both in Calabria and abroad in Germany, one of whom explains that the Honoured Society is the mother of all Calabrians. The documentary unveils how the 'ndrangheta has stood in for an absent state and depicts men of honour who swear to live and die by the laws of the organization. Mafiosi in Sbano's film attest that they are good businessmen, are honourable and idealistic, respect their wives and mothers, and help those in need.

Feature-length films have been made on the 'ndrangheta, including *Il brigante Musolino* (*Outlaw Girl*, Mario Camerini, 1950), *Il coraggio di parlare* (*The Courage to Speak*, Leandro Castellani, 1987), and *Anime nere* (*Black Souls*, Francesco Munzi, 2014). Also, several popular television serial dramas and mini-series focus on the organization, such as *Un bambino in fuga* (*A Boy on the Run*, Mario Caiano, 1990), *Un bambino in fuga – tre anni dopo* (*A Boy on the Run – Three Years Later*, Mario Caiano, 1991), *Gente di mare* (*People of the Sea*, 2005–7), and *Era mio fratello* (*He Was My Brother*, Claudio Bonivento, 2007). The entanglement of blood and mafia families and vendetta are common themes to these series and mini-series, and *Un bambino in fuga* and *Era mio fratello* both begin with the death of a parent or parents during a clan war. The resulting narratives focus on the surviving children (in both cases, two sons), who ultimately stand on opposite sides of the law. In *Era mio fratello*, brothers Sante and Luca are separated when their parents are murdered, and while Sante is taken in by the mafioso whom we later learn is responsible for the double homicide, Luca is adopted by Vincenzo, a police captain dedicated to the anti-mafia struggle. Paternal abandonment fuels the narrative of *Era mio fratello* as the brothers attempt to come to terms with their pasts. In the end, the 'good' brother Luca avenges a series of murders, including his adoptive father's, with the law on his side, and seemingly defeats the local clan. He also wins the girl (his brother's beautiful wife, after his brother is gunned down in front of him) and inherits a new adoptive son in his nephew Nicola. Hence, the series concludes on a hopeful yet unrealistic note with the creation of a new (anti-mafia) nuclear family that, the series implies, is capable of defeating the 'ndrangheta.

The Sacra Corona Unita: 'A Postmodern Mafia'

As Italy's newest mafia, the Sacra Corona Unita was founded in the Italian prison system in Puglia in 1983. Contrary to reports in the media and in public discourse, the ever-expanding organization is quite active and powerful.[9] Most feature films on 'Italy's fourth mafia' are set during its most violent and hostile years, the 1980s and the early 1990s, although Gabriele Salvatores' *Io non ho paura* (*I'm Not Scared*, 2003), focusing on a group of villagers vaguely connected to a larger and unnamed organized crime syndicate, takes place in a small community in Puglia during the historically hot summer of 1978. In films such as *Fine pena mai: paradiso perduto* (*Life Sentence*, Davide Barletti and Lorenzo Conte, 2007) and *Galantuomini* (*Brave Men*, Edoardo Winspeare, 2008), the mafia of Puglia is represented as belonging to the past. This post-mafia mentality is challenged in Aldo Zappalà's recent *Sacra corona unita e il pericolo che viene dall'est* (*Sacra Corona Unita and the Danger Coming from the East*, 2012), a documentary that explains the organization's history, structure, financial endeavours, and ties to international markets. The film looks closely at connections between the Sacra Corona Unita and the 'Eastern mafias' (The Balkans, Russia) and concludes on a sombre note by insinuating that these organizations are already firmly established in Italian economic and social life. A less serious take on the mafia diaspora is found in the popular low-budget 'postmodern indie crime comedy' *La capa gira* (*The Boss Turns*, Alessandro

Piva, 1999) shot on location in Bari almost entirely in the Barese dialect.[10] This fast-paced and upbeat film follows a group of criminals who attempt to track down a missing cocaine shipment from the Balkans before having to explain themselves to the local mob boss.

The Sacra Corona Unita has been defined as a 'post-modern mafia' as it is a hybrid organization that has borrowed rituals and structures from other Italian mafias, in particular the Camorra and the 'ndrangheta. The organization's peculiar birth in the prison system meant that women would by necessity occupy powerful, active, and formal positions throughout the hierarchy while their husbands and family members were behind bars, and work as messengers, administrators, money collectors, and advisers.[11] Such a structure might suggest that women in the Sacra Corona Unita have achieved a certain level of emancipation, keeping in mind the organization's genesis after the feminist movement of the 1970s. *Galantuomini* is a melodramatic woman's film that focuses on Lucia Rizzo, a powerful and decisive clan boss who commands a group of men during the 1990s. However, the various men in her life persistently challenge her power position. She is the target of graphic sexual innuendo, men insinuate that she has slept her way to the top, and a member of a rival clan rapes her in front of her young son. Such a traumatic event demands a narrative response, and after avenging her attacker, Lucia engages in a passionate and short-lived romance with anti-mafia prosecutor Ignazio De Raho. Lucia is far from empowered: she is punished through rape and tamed through romance, a plot twist in line with the rape revenge narrative.

The documentary *Diario di uno scuro* (*The Diary of an Affiliate*, Davide Barletti, Edoardo Cicchetti, and Lorenzo Conte, 2008) also centres on a woman who experienced the Sacra Corona Unita from within. Both the documentary and the film *Fine pena mai: paradiso perduto* are based on a memoir by Antonio Perrone, who was condemned to the harsh prison regime 41bis for mafia-related crimes.[12] The feature film, which is a male melodrama, unfolds from Antonio's perspective as a series of memories post-incarceration and comes across as an apologia for his life of crime. His wife Lela features in the film and takes centre stage in the documentary; we see footage of her as she recounts her history with her husband and their two children, details the couple's heavy drug use, and explains his life of crime, involvement with the mafia, and eventual arrests and periods of incarceration (Perrone was released from prison in 2018). The documentary includes interviews with journalists, Perrone's lawyer, and anti-mafia activists, including Nichi Vendola, former president of Puglia, who all speak of the Sacra Corona Unita's history, structure, and criminal activity. Overall, however, like the film, the documentary presents Perrone and many of his criminal associates as sympathetic, an approach also at work in *Cesare deve morire*. The final scene of the family visiting Perrone at the Rebibbia prison is followed by several happy and, for the most part, smiling photos of Perrone, Perrone and Lella, and Lella and one of her sons. In the tradition of the mafia film in Italy, such a consolatory finale is generally reserved for biopics focusing on anti-mafia martyrs (such as *I cento passi* [*One Hundred Steps*], Marco Tullio Giordana, 2000; *Placido Rizzotto*, Pasquale Scimeca, 2000; *L'uomo di vetro* [*Man of Glass*], Stefano Incerti, 2007; *Fortapàsc*; *La siciliana ribelle* [*The Sicilian Girl*], Marco Amenta, 2009) and thus raises compelling questions regarding the representation of mafia perpetrators in recent Italian cinema. Media representations of Italy's other mafias are ethically ambivalent, and their generic diversity reflects the nature of the organizations themselves.

NOTES

1 Roberto Saviano, *Gomorra: Viaggio nell'impero economico e nel sogno di dominio della camorra* (Milan: Mondadori, 2006).

2 Cosmo Landesman, 'Gomorra,' *Times Online*, 10 October 2008, accessed 12 September 2013, http://entertainment.timesonline.co.uk/tol/arts_and_entertainment/film/film_reviews/article4907928.ece. For more on the Camorra's greater visibility in the press, see the introduction to Dana Renga, *Unfinished Business: Screening the Italian Mafia in the New Millennium* (Toronto: The University of Toronto Press, 2013).

3 The Banda della Magliana is frequently labelled Italy's 'fifth mafia' and is structured similarly to other mafias in Italy. See, for example, 'La quinta mafia a Roma e nel Lazio dalla Banda della Magliana a oggi,' *La Repubblica*, 15 December 2009, accessed 15 July 2014, http://roma.repubblica.it/dettaglio/la-quinta-mafia-a-roma-e-nel-lazio-dalla-banda-della-magliana-a-oggi/1805078. For more on the history of the Magliana gang, see Angela Camuso, *Mi ci fu pietà: la vera storia della banda della Magliana dal 1977 fino ai giorni nostri* (Rome: Castelvecchi, 2012); Otello Lupacchini, *Banda della Magliana: alleanza tra mafiosi, terroristi, spioni, politici, prelati* (Rome: Koinè, 2004).

4 Gianluigi Nuzzi and Claudio Antonelli, *Blood Ties 'Ndrangheta: Italy's New Mafia*, trans. Jonathan Hunt (Basingstoke and Oxford: Pan Books, 2012).

5 This is also the case for the television series *The Sopranos* (David Chase, 1999–2007), which was the topic of much discussion during the question-and-answer portion of the Charleston roundtable, and whose characters were, after all, not of Sicilian but of Neapolitan origin.

6 Serenella Iovino maintains that the Ecomafia is involved in the following illegal endeavours: 'Traffic in toxic waste, in protected animal and plant species, illegal gambling on exploited animals, systematic devastation of "local" territory for abusive building developments that cause severe ecological damage.' 'Ecocriticism and a Non-Anthropocentric Humanism,' in *Local Natures, Global Responsibilities: Ecocritical Perspectives on the New English Literatures*, ed. Laurenz Volkmann et al. (Amsterdam and New York: Rodopi, 2010), 29–53, 31.

7 For two excellent analyses of films on the Ecomafia, see Anita Angelone, 'Talking Trash: Documentaries and Italy's "Garbage Emergency,"' *Studies in Documentary Film* 5, nos. 2–3 (2011): 145–65; Elena Past, '"Trash Is Gold": Documenting the Ecomafia and Campania's Waste Crisis,' *ISLE: Interdisciplinary Studies in Literature and the Environment* 20, no. 3 (2013): 597–621.

8 Iacopo Gori, 'La "Santa" che comanda è calabrese,' *Corriere dell sera*, 4 October 2007, accessed 14 June 2013, http://www.corriere.it/cronache/07_ottobre_04/santa_ndrangheta_oliva_Fierro.shtml.

9 References to the SCU as 'defeated' abound. The directors of *Fine pena mai: paradiso perduto* maintain that the 'SCU degli anni 80 non esiste più, sconfitta dall'azione della magistratura e dai maxi-processi degli anni 90.' *Fine pena mai*: Press Book,' accessed 15 July 2013, http://www.mymovies.it/filmclub/2008/02/047/mymovies.pdf. Giacamo Panizza writes: 'The Sacra Corona Unita Was Defeated in Only a Few Years,' in *Qui ho conosciuto purgatorio, inferno e paradiso* (Milano: Giangiacomo Feltrinelli Editore, 2010), 130. Cataldo Motta is described as 'The judge who defeated the Sacra Corona Unita.' 'Procuratore Motta: miei cari ragazza ci avete dato una lezione,' *La gazzetta del mezzogiorno*, 24 May 2012, accessed 16 June 2013, http://www.lagazzettadelmezzogiorno.it/notizia.php?IDCategoria=2699&IDNotizia=521632. A book by Giuseppe Mariano is titled *La sconfitta della SCU e il pericolo Albania: attività criminali nel Meridione: legami, differenze e analogie fra mafia, camorra, 'ndrangheta e SCU* (Melendugno: Zane, 2002).

10 Jonathan Crow, 'LaCapaGira,' *New York Times*, accessed 13 June 2013, http://movies.nytimes.com /movie/187037/LaCapaGira/overview.

11 For more on women in the Sacra Corona Unita, see Monica Massari and Cataldo Motta, 'Women in the Sacra Corona Unita,' in *Women and the Mafia: Female Roles in Organized Crime Structures*, ed. Giovanni Fiandanca (New York: Springer, 2007), 53–66.

12 Antonio Perrone, *Vista d'interni. Diario di carcere, di 'scuri' e seghe, di trip e di sventure* (Lecce: Manni, 2003).

51 Historicizing Italy's Other Mafias: Some Considerations

JOHN DICKIE

The Visibility of the 'Ndrangheta and the Camorra

The public debate about the mafias, the ways they are imagined in broader culture, the tradition of academic analysis of them, and the movies made about them, are all an integral dimension of the history of the mafias themselves. One thing that distinguishes the mafias from ordinary organized crime is their ability to win consent among at least a part of the population. And one of the ways they win consent, directly and indirectly, is by shaping how they are represented.

A book by Salvatore Lupo does a very good job of playing back the history of the mafia in the United States and Sicily against the background of its alternating periods of fame and invisibility. He shows, for example, how the mafia debate in the United States got confused with worries about immigration at the start of the century, and about capitalist corporations after the Second World War, and about Italian American identity from the 1970s.[1] Here I offer a very brief sketch, along the same lines, of how the 'ndrangheta and the Camorra have been perceived or ignored over time, both in Italy and internationally.

Only since the Duisburg massacre in Germany in 2007 has there been much discussion about the 'ndrangheta outside of Italy. Only in its wake did journalists begin to write about the organization since they now had a 'mafia expands beyond Italy' narrative to write up, as well as an 'exotic', 'new' mafia that few had heard of before. Let us hope that Duisburg marks the end of the history of the 'ndrangheta's invisibility, which dates back to its emergence from the prison system in the 1880s. I should stress that the 'drangheta's invisibility is primarily a political and cultural phenomenon. The police, by contrast, have always known a great deal about the 'ndrangheta – not least because, *omertà* or silence before the law notwithstanding, a great many Calabrian mafiosi have been police informers and witnesses. However, the police's knowledge failed to make much of an impact on public opinion. The 'ndrangheta's invisibility, in this sense, is explained by the simple fact that Calabria is not a key political region. One cannot rule Italy without ruling Palermo and Naples: both are politically central. In that Palermo and Naples are so important within Italy, the Camorra and the Sicilian mafia have much greater visibility and face much higher political stakes. Historically, southern Calabria has been a supplier of tame Members of Parliament for whichever majority (the Historic Left, Giolitti, or the Christian Democrats) was in power. For this reason the 'nrangheta has also been safely ignored outside of Italy.

However, the 'ndrangheta experienced moments of visibility earlier in its history. In 1955 the 'Marzano operation,' a brief and ineffective crackdown on organized crime in Calabria, was launched and generated a short-lived debate in the press that left one lasting legacy: the name 'ndrangheta acquired its place in the public domain, particularly as a result of the novelist Corrado Alvaro's use of the word in his *Corriere della Sera* column. (Before then, the organization was referred to by a series of different names, the most frequent of which was Picciotteria.) In the 1970s and 1980s Calabria experienced a long and horrific period of kidnappings, with many victims held for months on end on the Aspromonte massif. The most high-profile cases were the Getty kidnapping in 1973 and that of Cesare Casella in the late 1980s. (Casella's mother earned the name 'courageous mother' through her protests.) But here the public focus was less on the 'ndrangheta *qua* organization and more on the kidnapping system.

We see one particularly instructive case of the 'ndrangheta's invisibility in the film *Il brigante Musolino* (*Outlaw Girl*, Mario Camerini, 1950), starring Amedeo Nazzari and Silvana Mangano. Not an 'ndrangheta movie per se, it focuses on Giuseppe Musolino, who was a famous renegade – an escaped convict who evaded the law for years on Aspromonte. The film tells his story as that of a man who is the victim of the local Honoured Society and who goes on the run and takes his vengeance against them. This is a quite extraordinary inversion of the reality. I have seen the police papers from the Musolino case at the turn of the century, and he was certainly an *'ndranghetista*, an oathed member from Santo Stefano, and his father was the founder of the local chapter of the Picciotteria.[2] Everything he did was derived from his status as a *picciotto*, or someone at the bottom of the mafia hierarchy. He was finally captured and put on trial in Lucca in 1902; the event was well covered, both nationally and internationally. At the same time, the police were trying to mount a trial using the criminal association laws against the Picciotteria in Santo Stefano. But this second trial fell apart as the witnesses retracted their statements. And Musolino – despite having killed seven people – managed to present himself in Lucca as a sort of noble bandit. He received a life sentence, yet the script of him as the noble, lone renegade won out. Musolino rewrote his own history, essentially erasing his 'ndrangheta background. This is the core of the story that comes across in Camerini's film.

The Camorra had two moments of international celebrity early in its history. The first was during the Risorgimento. In 1854, Gladstone visited Neapolitan prisons and denounced what he called the *Gamorra*, with a 'g,' that ran the prison system then.[3] In 1860, at the moment of Unification, *camorristi* were recruited as a police force during the summer interregnum between the collapse of the Bourbon state and the arrival of Garibaldi. Some newspapers celebrated the *camorristi* as patriotic heroes, redeemed by the cause of Italy.

The second moment of celebrity was the Cuocolo trial of 1911–12, which is actually the trial that destroyed the Camorra as an Honoured Society, or a freemasonry of crime on the same model as the Cosa Nostra and the 'ndrangheta. The Camorra in that period was much better known, and much more on everyone's lips internationally, than was the Sicilian mafia. Pathé News covered this trial, and several American journalists crossed the ocean to cover it. The trial could be followed from as far away as Australia and what is now Zimbabwe. In the postwar period, the Cuocolo trial was the focus of a film *Processo alla città* (*The City Stands Trial*, Luigi Zampa, 1952), once again starring Nazzari.[4]

Between those dates – 1860 and 1912 – the Camorra was also much more visible within Italy; it was a secret society with very few secrets. For example, the Neapolitan press covered Camorra funerals, and positivist criminologists wrote about the organization's tattoos and rules. Unlike the Sicilian mafia, which had managed to disguise its very existence, the Honoured Society of Naples was public knowledge; however, it also was viewed (rather simplistically) as alien to the bourgeois city in that it seemed to belong to the world of the subproletariat of the slums.

After the Cuocolo trial, this moment of national and international press came to an end and the debate around the Camorra ceased completely, for the simple reason that the Camorra did not exist anymore, at least in the city. Then the Camorra experienced one more moment of visibility before the Second World War, when Mussolini launched a campaign to repress it in the so-called 'Mazzoni' in 1926 and then proclaimed the campaign's triumphs in his Ascension Day speech in 1927.

Inventing Pupetta Maresca

Francesco Rosi's *La sfida* (*The Challenge*, 1958) tells the story of Pupetta Maresca.[5] Essentially – and naively for a filmmaker as good and careful as Rosi – the film presents a version of the script that Pupetta Maresca herself recited in court. The real events that inspired the film took place in 1955. What's more, this episode restarted public debate about the Camorra, the 'new Camorra' as it was called then, after decades of silence. Pupetta's husband, Pasquale Simonetti, known as Pasqualone 'e Nola, a fruit market extortionist also called the 'president of potato prices,' was shot dead in the Vasto quarter of Naples next to the market. Pupetta was pregnant at the time and was only twenty-one. A few weeks later, she and her younger brother and possibly also a bigger firing party hunted down the man who had shot her husband and killed him in front of a crowd. The murder caused a huge sensation, there was a big trial, and many photos of Pupetta in various glamorous poses were released. She had been a beauty queen in a local contest, and the murder made her into a lasting celebrity. The script she recited in her own defence at her trial was a sort of crime-of-passion narrative: a classic script, one that seems to have worked to some extent. She ended up spending eight or nine years in prison, and essentially covered up her precise role in the configuration of Camorra power at the time. In a way, Rosi's film presents Maresca as a Madame Bovary of the underworld, as a naive girl influenced by melodrama and trying to live according to its myths, which is similar to how Pupetta tried to portray herself in her own trial.

Maresca's story retained its appeal. Two years after her release, she starred in *Delitto a Posillipo* (*Murder in Posillipo*, Renato Parravicini, 1967), a film based loosely on her own life. In 1982, Maresca successfully stopped a TV movie called *Il caso Pupetta Maresca* (*The Case of Pupetta Maresca*, Marisa Malfatti and Riccardo Tortora, 1982) from going to air; it starred Alessandra Mussolini. (The program did finally air in 1994.)

The Mafias and Representation

Throughout their histories, these organizations have been both producers of representations about themselves in the public domain – this is particularly true of the Sicilian mafia – and also avid consumers of representations of organized crime in the culture. We see a strange feedback loop that is as old as the organizations themselves. There are good reasons for this. Mostly importantly, the mafias need an ideological glue to hold them together, and we shouldn't be surprised if they steal it from the legal world around them.

For example, when the Camorra was an Honoured Society, it used to believe that it was founded on the basis of a Spanish secret society called the Garduña, which supposedly dated back to fifteenth-century Spain, but which actually made its first appearance in a historical novel in 1847, when the Camorra was emerging from the prison system. So that story has clearly been taken in and used by an organization that wants to pretend it has ancient roots. The same is true of the Sicilian mafia, with the Beati Paoli, the sect of medieval avengers to which mafiosi like Totò Riina and Tommaso Buscetta traced back the Cosa Nostra's origins.

Moreover, there existed a huge fashion in 1890s Naples for plays about the Camorra in the Teatro San Ferdinando, right in the heart of what is now Forcella, the most notorious quarter in the city for Camorra influence. The police reports of the time say that the audience was absolutely full of *camorristi*. So, they watched themselves on stage. Obviously, another famous case is *The Godfather*. We know that the film was partly funded by the Franklin Bank, which was laundering mafia drug money. Also, famously, the mafia prevented Coppola from using the word 'mafia' in the film. As this roundtable on Italy's other mafias attests, we see a similar pattern at work in mafia cinema at large: life imitating art, imitating life.

NOTES

These observations are drawn partly from my book, *Mafia Brotherhoods. Camorra, Mafia, 'Ndrangheta: The Rise of the Honoured Societies* (London: Hodder & Stoughton, 2012), which is a parallel history of the three major mafias from their origins to the end of the Second World War, and partly from the sequel to that volume, *Mafia Republic: Italy's Criminal Case. Cosa Nostra, 'Ndrangheta, and Camorra from 1946 to the Present* (London: Sceptre, 2013).

1 Salvatore Lupo, *Quando la mafia trovò l'America: storia di un intreccio intercontinentale, 1888–2008* (Turin: Einaudi, 2008).

2 The key archival material on Musolino is in the Archivio di Stato di Reggio Calabria: Gabinetto di Prefettura, n. 1089, Associazione a delinquere in S. Stefano, b. 27, inv. 34; and Gabinetto di Prefettura, Serie prima, affari riservati. Bandito Musolino. The fundamental study of the Musolino case remains Gaetano Cingari, 'Tra brigantaggio e "picciotteri": Giuseppe Musolino,' in *Brigantaggio, proprietari e contadini nel Sud (1799–1900)*, ed. Gaetano Cingari (Reggio Calabria: Editori Meridionali Riuniti, 1976), 205–66.

3 W.E. Gladstone, *First Letter to the Earl of Aberdeen, on the State Prosecutions of the Neapolitan Government* (London: John Murray, 1851).

4 Marcella Marmo has written several perceptive articles on the Cuocolo trial, such as: Marcella Marmo, '"Processi indiziari non se ne dovrebbero mai fare." Le manipolazioni del processo Cuocolo

(1906–1930),' in *La costruzione della verita` giudiziaria*, ed. Marcella Marmo and Luigi Musella (Naples: Cliopress, 2003), 101–70.

5 On Pupetta Maresca see, first and foremost, Marcella Marmo's 'La rima amore/onore di Pupetta Maresca: Una primadonna nella camorra degli anni cinquanta,' *Meridiana* 67 (2010): 113–43.

ALLISON COOPER

Traditionally, mafia movies have been set in the South, the territory of well-known criminal organizations like the Cosa Nostra, the Camorra, and the 'ndrangheta. This has changed with films such as Paolo Sorrentino's *Le conseguenze dell'amore* (*The Consequences of Love*, 2004) and Cupellini's *Una vita tranquilla* (*A Quiet Life*, 2010), which have emphasized the global reach of criminal organizations through their settings in northern Italy and beyond.[1] Placido's *Romanzo criminale* (2005) recounts the story of Rome's Banda della Magliana, combining aspects of two popular film genres, the mafia movie and terrorist film, to explore the collusion of organized crime and the state in the leaden years, that is, the period of intense terrorism in Italy between 1968 and the early 1980s. The film's hybridization of genres underscores the violent historical union in Italy between mafia families and state, which together formed a redoubled hegemonic system that, when expedient, eliminated its subjects. In this presentation I examine the symbolic uses of Rome in *Romanzo criminale*, in particular allusions to the city's imperial past, and demonstrate how they function to expose a modern authoritarian state that absorbs all who would harm it, the mafia included.[2]

Historical events dictate *Romanzo criminale*'s uncommon Roman setting (the city was, after all, the territory of the Banda), but *Romanzo criminale* may also be understood as an attempt to reanimate Rome and imbue it with political and social relevance for twenty-first-century filmgoers. Emphasizing the marketability of Italy's tainted heritage, Alan O'Leary observes in his analysis of 1970s *poliziotteschi* 'crime dramas' that 'the metropolis envy which identifies the Italian urbs with the very exemplum of modernity, the American city, presents the degradation, criminality and political terrorism of contemporary Italy as essential to its vitality.'[3] As Catherine O'Rawe notes in her contribution to this roundtable on the *Romanzo criminale* series for television, the Roman setting may also be understood as an idealized re-evocation of a place and time associated (however erroneously) with ideological certainties and unambiguous social and political stances missed by many twenty-first-century Italians.

As capital of the Italian state and, traditionally, *caput mundi*, Rome's violence and corruption metonymically stand for the corruption of the country as a whole. *Romanzo criminale* transforms Rome from *caput mundi* into *caput violandi*, a modern capital of violence, by making provocative connections between the city's imperial past and its narrative present. An early example of this occurs in the opening title sequence, which identifies the Banda with a long line of Rome's would-be conquerors: 'In the mid-1970s a band of delinquents left the suburbs to conquer Rome.' This language of conquest is made more explicit later in the film, when the liberation of Libano, the gang's leader, from prison causes his fellow gang member Dandi to declare enthusiastically, 'Rome!, We will break her!' There is an ironic gap between the gang members' audacious vision of themselves as successors to a long line of Rome's conquerors and their subsumption by the state as they become instruments of its strategy to consolidate its own power. This irony is made clear when Libano is betrayed and stabbed to death by a fellow gang member, Gemito, in a *vespasiano* or public urinal in Piazza Santa Maria in Trastevere.[4] Gemito's betrayal of Libano recalls, of course, one of Rome's most famous betrayals, that of the Senate against Caesar, but Placido's setting of the gang leader's murder in a considerably less exalted setting than the Theatre of Pompey ironizes Libano's ambitions to rule Rome, calling attention to the ignoble, transitory nature of his power and to the instrumental relationship between the mafia and the state.[5]

In contrast, Placido highlights the enduring power of Italy's elite ruling class through the film's frequent establishing shots of the city's skyline, which focus on the complex of Trajan's Market and the Torre delle Milizie. These shots introduce scenes with the film's nameless agent of the state, visually linking him to the imperious and callous rulers historically associated with the imposing monolith.[6] Similarly, Placido uses the Vittoriano, a monument that looms large on the Roman skyline and in popular imagination, to suggest the monolithic and panoptic nature of the state. Commissioned in the late nineteenth century to honour Italy's founding father, Vittorio Emanuele II, the monument also served to confirm the legitimacy of the modern Italian state and of Rome as its new capital. The aforementioned agent of the state, who indirectly involves the Banda in the kidnapping of Aldo Moro, commands his subordinate, Carenza, to abandon the search for the hideaway in which Moro is being held in a scene that takes place just before the Brigate Rosse's announcement of his death. The shot following this scene is of the Vittoriano, with a sound bridge to the historical audio clip of the Brigate Rosse proclaiming Moro's death. The agent of the state appears to know Moro's fate, then, before it has been formally made public by his captors, and his seeming omniscience, combined with the imposing image of the Vittoriano, with its all-encompassing perspective of the city, implies that the city and its citizens are under constant surveillance.

Via his proxy Carenza, the shadowy agent of the state colludes with the Banda to perpetuate and increase violence in Rome, and this relationship exemplifies the ways in which those in power use their enemies to destabilize opposition and strengthen their own position. *Romanzo criminale* performs this co-dependency of state and organized crime structurally, through its hybridization of the terrorist film and the mafia movie. The figure of Freddo, perhaps the film's most sympathetic character, is positioned at the nexus of this co-dependency and thus provides an interesting and unexpected commentary on its implications for the individual. The object of intense scrutiny in the film, Freddo is the subject of a panoptic state. His adult character is introduced by means of a high-angle shot that paradoxically suggests surveillance at the very moment of his liberation from prison. Editing in this scene suggests that the shot represents the point of view of Libano, who awaits his friend. Freddo's liberation from prison, then, is false in that he steps directly from an existence rigidly observed and controlled by the state into one that will be similarly controlled and observed by his mafia family, as several later instances of him being observed by his fellow gang members demonstrate. The camera, like Libano, is complicit with the state. Placido's camerawork makes us complicit with the state as well, as the voyeuristic pleasure that we take in the presentation of Freddo, played by the attractive Kim Rossi Stuart, distracts us from the violence that his character and the Banda commit.

Freddo's lack of freedom as a subject of the state is impressed upon viewers when he is liberated from prison again in a parallel scene near the end of the film. This time, Freddo escapes confinement through an elaborate ruse that involves injecting himself with tainted blood that he knows will eventually kill him. The state builds immunity against those who would harm it – in this case, the mafia – by incorporating them into its own body: Freddo's false 'immunization' symbolically mimics this process of control even as he attempts to resist it himself by choosing his own death.[7] Placido highlights the futility of his protagonist's attempt to escape late-twentieth-century biopolitics when, at the film's conclusion, Freddo is denied even this act of resistance and is killed instead by a sniper, hired by the nameless agent of the state to protect himself and Italy's future leaders from the gang member's dangerous knowledge.

Romanzo criminale is marked by a combined repulsion for and attraction to state power. Through Freddo's narrative, Placido presents a critique of the state's repression of the individual, yet the state's control of an equivocal figure like Freddo is essential to the film's nostalgic evocation of the 1970s-style conspiracy thriller, a genre that Mary P. Wood has argued can 'be considered an attempt to impose order on a world which is perceived as difficult to understand, complex, mysterious, controlled by people who mask their control behind commonsense assumptions, coercion and ritual.'[8] Placido's recourse to Rome as a symbol of power and of those who abuse it reveals the film's inner tension, as well as the continuing relevance of social anxieties about living in a totalitarian state for twenty-first-century filmmakers and their audiences.

NOTES

1 Dana Renga, 'The Corleones at Home and Abroad,' in *Mafia Movies: A Reader*, ed. Dana Renga (Toronto: University of Toronto Press, 2011), 27–8.

2 For more on the relationship between the political film and the city in Italian cinema, see Mary P. Wood, 'Revealing the Hidden City: The Cinematic Conspiracy Thriller of the 1970s,' *The Italianist* 23 (2003): 150–62.

3 Alan O'Leary, 'Italian Cinema and the "Anni di piombo,"' *Journal of European Cinema Studies* 40, no. 3 (2010): 243–75, 246.

4 For more on *Romanzo criminale*'s gangster emperors, see Danela Turco, 'The Unforgiven,' *Filmcritica* 560 (2005): 547–51.

5 I am grateful to Giancarlo Lombardi for his observations about the *vespasiano* in our roundtable discussion.

6 Nero is anecdotally said to have watched Rome burn from the *torre*, and it is worth noting that the assassin Nero, the character in the film least interested in the welfare of others (as he declares, 'A me la colletività fa schifo') shares a name with one of the Roman empire's cruellest emperors.

7 On the concept of immunity in biopolitics see Roberto Esposito, *Immunitas: protezione e negazione della vita* (Torino: Einaudi, 2002). For more on the relationship between De Cataldo's *Romanzo criminale* and biopolitics see Lorenzo Fabbri, 'Italy: A Post-Biopolitical Laboratory. From Pasolini's "Il romanzo delle stragi" to De Cataldo's *Romanzo criminale*,' *California Italian Studies* 2, no. 1 (2011), http://escholarship.org/uc/item/2bk6p867.

8 Wood, 'Revealing,' 153.

CATHERINE O'RAWE

Romanzo criminale: la serie, which ran for two seasons on Sky Italia (2008 and 2010), co-produced by Cattleya and directed by Stefano Sollima, achieved huge cult success. It has as yet attracted little critical attention, but its portrayal of the real-life criminal gang the Banda della Magliana in the Rome of the 1970s and 1980s, based on Giancarlo De Cataldo's 2002 novel, is striking: it foregrounds ideas of masculinity and nostalgia, ideas that are heavily present elsewhere in Italian cinema and cultural production.

The series tracks, in fictionalized form, the rise and fall of the gang from its origins on the streets of the Magliana district to its ascent to take control of the drug trade in Rome. The greater scope of the series (twenty-two fifty-minute episodes) allows it to develop in more detail than could the 2005 film directed by Michele Placido the gang's dealings with the Cosa Nostra and the Camorra, and their links to the Secret Services. After the death of gang leader Libanese at the end of Season One, much of the second season is taken up with new leader Dandi's deals with the Sicilian mafia in particular, and the triangular relationship between the shadowy forces of the state, the mafia, and the gang in the darkest days of the leaden years.

One reason behind the success of the series is its re-creation of the period of the *anni di piombo* in a popular key,[1] through retro fashion and soundtrack, the use of phrases in demotic Roman slang that have become cult, the creation of new stars, and its emphasis on certain well-known historical events: from the kidnapping of Aldo Moro in 1978 and the Bologna bombing in 1980 to the murder of General Dalla Chiesa in 1982 and the Banco Ambrosiano/P2 scandal. The series, like the book and the film, is marked by nostalgia from the start: it opens with the only surviving gang member, Bufalo, being viciously attacked by some young thugs in the Magliana who have no idea who he is, before he exacts bloody revenge. The series, even more than the film, is marked by extensive scenes of physical violence, mainly bloody beatings inflicted on or by the Banda, and it is this ostentatious display of violence inflicted on the male body that interests me here, partly because the excessive violence and the nostalgia for the recent past are, I think, connected: I have written elsewhere of the strongly homosocial nature of current Italian cinema and its representations of post-'68 history, and the homosocial display inherent in the scenes of wounded bodies as spectacle is striking.[2] It recalls Steve Neale's description of the violence in Anthony Mann's films:

> [I]n a heterosexual and patriarchal society, the male body cannot be marked explicitly as the erotic object of another male look: that look must be motivated in some other way, its erotic component

repressed. The mutilation and sadism so often involved in Mann's films are marks both of the repression involved and of a means by which the male body may be disqualified, so to speak, as an object of erotic contemplation and desire.[3]

I would further argue that the series' representation of masculinity, often centred on this corporeal vulnerability, can be situated not just in relation to anxiety about homosocial desire, but in relation to contemporary discourses in Italy that focus on the crisis of masculinity, which is often linked to anxieties about the 'feminization' of men that are supposedly embodied by Berlusconi. Sandro Bellassai says of Berlusconi that 'he is none other than the sexual autobiography of the masculine nation';[4] however, essays on Berlusconi have talked of how the supposedly uneasy fit between his excessive and compulsive sexual activity and what they speak of as his 'feminization' – his love of plastic surgery and make-up, his penchant for bodily self-care, his hair transplant, his tendency to rely on narratives of emotional intimacy – all render him, according to some theorists, 'feminized.' A key reference here in the anglophone context is Stephen Gundle's 1995 description of Berlusconi as 'a feminized, powdered man.'[5] Marco Belpoliti in his book *Il corpo del Capo* goes even further, at various points calling Berlusconi both a transvestite and a transsexual.[6] Leaving aside some of the implications of this – it is clearly not a positive thing to be compared to a woman or a transsexual in this context – it is apparent that anxieties about male feminization are circulating in public discourse.

In De Cataldo's novel these anxieties about the decline of Italian masculinity are explicit, with the character of Il Vecchio, the Secret Service puppet master, saying to the detective Scialoja, who takes his place at the series' end: 'You will all long for these times that you now consider dark. You are fortunate to live in close contact with the last real men. Men that have passion and identity.'[7] This nostalgia for a lost masculinity fits in with what Emiliano Morreale has discussed as the 'nostalgia for History' exhibited by many contemporary Italian films about the 1970s.[8] We might, for example, question the series' return to the 1970s and 1980s, decades that are, notably, depicted with barely any reference to one of the key elements of social change of the period, feminism. Female characters in the series are either girlfriends, mothers, or prostitutes, and in Season Two it is the decision by Freddo to promote Donatella, the girlfriend of one of the Banda's associates, Nembo Kid, to 'zone leader,' that causes conflict within the band and anxiety about Freddo's decreasing authority. The threat represented by female power is made glaringly literal in Season Two's ninth episode, when Donatella manages to kill two enemies of the Banda by hiding a gun in her underwear and whipping it out to shoot them. Here the threat of the castrating woman, along with Donatella's 'look' (she is very obviously of the 1980s with her Brigitte Nielsen-style short blonde hair) is developed until Donatella becomes the figure who, unlike in the novel, kills Freddo and finally dissolves the Banda.

Just as the series (and the film) depicts a return to a 1970s without feminism, so Rome is depicted as a pre-multicultural city, where the only people of colour are prostitutes, with a few Chinese and South American drug dealers thrown in. The nostalgia for a white male past is made obvious in the opening of the novel, when Bufalo is attacked by the young pretenders who control the Magliana: 'He thought that they could be his sons. Besides the black one, obviously. He thought that some years earlier, upon only hearing his name, they would have shot themselves on their own, rather than facing vendetta. Some years earlier. When times had not yet changed.'[9] The series elides this, as the three boys who attack Bufalo are clearly white. Nevertheless, the series adopts multiple strategies – including, interestingly, the pop soundtrack – to demonstrate an uneasy relationship between the Banda and non-white masculinities: one could think of the scene in Season One's third episode when Dandi is teased by Freddo and Libano for listening to the camp disco classic 'You Make Me Feel (Mighty Real),' by Sylvester (released in 1978), and Freddo mocks Sylvester's falsetto, announcing his own preference for the Roman singer Claudio Baglioni.

The idea of an 'authentic' masculinity in crisis is explicitly linked by Il Vecchio to Berlusconismo: in the novel, when he laments the decline of 'real men,' he continues: 'today dies and tomorrow will be the exclusive domain of capitalists and technocrats. Ah, and obviously of the young kids made stupid by television!'[10] The series adds a scene (in Season One's twelfth episode) in which Il Vecchio turns on the TV to see the first national broadcast of Mediaset's Canale 5 in 1980 and denounces the changing times (and as Giancarlo Lombardi has pointed out, this scene is clearly directed at today's extra-diegetic viewers);[11] thus Berlusconi and the crisis of authentic masculinity are neatly linked in *Romanzo criminale*'s textual universe.

As I discussed, the physical wounding of the men of the series, and often their bodily abjection (there are many scenes of weeping, vomiting, pissing, and hysterical shouting, and Scialoja is physically dumped into a skip and covered with rubbish in Season Two's ninth episode) seem to speak to such a crisis. As Sally Robinson points out in her book *Marked Men*, 'representations of a hysterical, masochistic, or wounded white male body testify to the real, material effects of a perceived displacement of white masculinity away from the centre, from the normative, from the mainstream.'[12] The ways in which the series makes visible the wounded and anguished bodies of the gang seem to speak to such a contemporary perception of displacement or crisis. Yet the series' ending can complicate this reading further: the aged Bufalo walks into Bar Franco and moves from seeing it in its present state to watching the old (dead) Banda members as they interact cheerfully, before the collapse of the gang. He chooses to die with them rather than keep living in the degraded present, as his outraged cry to his attackers had made clear: 'I was with Libanese!' The heartfelt nostalgia, accentuated by the use of the Vasco Rossi song 'Liberi… liberi,' is complicated by the fact that the series (like the film and book) is imbued with nostalgia from the very start. The gang are already lost in the series prologue, and as early as episode two of Season One Freddo and Libanese are discussing how the Banda is no longer what it was; furthermore, in Season Two the ghost of Libanese appears regularly to Dandi to utter guidance on how to behave like a man. To that extent mourning and nostalgia are already inscribed onto the Banda's representation: thus rather than simple nostalgia for a period before a putative crisis of masculinity, loss is a condition of representation in the series. The gang's homosocial attachment is figured as impossible to sustain, and their uncertain fraternal affection as doomed to violent rupture and disavowal.

NOTES

1 See Monica Parissi, 'La peggio gioventù di Romanzo criminale,' *Ol3Media* 2, no. 5 (2009), http://host .uniroma3.it/riviste/Ol3Media/Archivio_files/Ol3Media%2005.pdf.
2 See Catherine O'Rawe, 'Brothers in Arms: Middlebrow *Impegno* and Homosocial Relations in the Cinema of Petraglia and Rulli,' in *Intellectual Communities and Partnerships in Italy and Europe*, ed. Danielle Hipkins (Oxford and New York: Peter Lang, 2012), 149–67.

3 Steve Neale, 'Masculinity as Spectacle: Reflections on Men and Mainstream Cinema,' *Screen* 24 (1983): 2–17, 8. Neale is paraphrasing Paul Willemen's argument about Mann.

4 Sandro Bellassai, 'Il nocciolo politico del desiderio maschile,' *Il Manifesto*, 8 February 2011.

5 Stephen Gundle, 'Il sorriso di Berlusconi,' *Altrochemestre* 3 (1995): 14–17.

6 Marco Belpoliti, *Il corpo del Capo* (Parma: Guanda, 2009), 71.

7 Giancarlo De Cataldo, *Romanzo criminale* (Turin: Einaudi, [2002]2011), 371.

8 Emiliano Morreale, *L'invenzione della nostalgia* (Rome: Donzelli, 2009), 220.

9 De Cataldo, *Romanzo criminale*, 5.

10 Ibid., 5.

11 Giancarlo Lombardi, 'Enigmi a puntate,' in *Strane storie*, ed. Christian Uva (Soveria Mannelli: Rubbettino, 2011), 173–87.

12 Sally Robinson, *Marked Men: White Masculinity in Crisis* (New York: Columbia University Press: 2000), 190.

54   Toxic Tables: The Representation of Food in Camorra Films

AMY BOYLAN

Towards the end of Antonio Capuano's *Pianese Nunzio, 14 anni a maggio* (*Pianese Nunzio, Fourteen in May*, 1996) the protagonist, Nunzio, and his brother, Giovanni, dine together in a traditional Neapolitan pizzeria. Giovanni attempts to teach Nunzio a lesson: 'Without the Camorra we'd all die of hunger …Who do you think is paying for the pizzas?' Giovanni's words foreground the importance of the relationship between the Camorra and sustenance and reinforce the reality that the Camorra controls the production, distribution, acquisition, and consumption of food, and thus, as Roberto Saviano's editorial in *La Repubblica* asserts, intrudes into one of the most important rituals of human society: mealtime.[1]

Over the last two decades, Italian films about the Camorra, including *Pianese Nunzio, 14 anni a maggio*, *Certi bambini* (*A Children's Story*, Andrea Frazzi and Antonio Frazzi, 2004), *Vedi Napoli e poi muori* (*See Naples and Die*, Enrico Caria, 2006), *Gomorra* (*Gomorrah*, Matteo Garone, 2008), and *Mozzarella stories* (Edoardo DeAngelis, 2011), have used food to convey the absence of and longing for familial and social bonds, symbolized by the dining table, as a refuge from the Camorra's dehumanizing forces. This cinematic concern with the absence of nutritive environments also reflects the larger issue of Camorra-dominated food distribution networks and Camorra-induced food crises such as tainted produce and toxic mozzarella.

My thinking about food in these films has been informed by film studies as well as by food scholars who maintain that food and foodways (a term that refers to the social meanings surrounding the acquisition, preparation, and consumption of food) function symbolically as a marker of crisis, a symbol of life and death, and an expression of power relationships and gender roles.[2] Rebecca Epstein's work on American gangster movies, which examines how food functions in specifically non-foodie films – that is, how food and its consumption, preparation, or absence 'lend[] depth to characters, advances the narrative, and, ultimately intensif[y] the brutal displays of violence' – has also been very helpful.[3] The way in which food is treated in these Camorra films provides a strong contrast to the way food appears in the kinds of European art house 'foodie' films that appeal to international and especially American audiences. For instance, Hoecherl-Alden and Lindenfeld assert that the latter allow foreign audiences 'to position themselves as cinephiles appreciating exotic images and "authentic" scenes of foreign cultures.'[4] Thus, while films like *Pranzo di Ferragosto* (*Mid-August Lunch*, Gianni DiGregorio, 2010), *Pane e tulipani* (*Bread and Tulips*, Silvio Soldini, 2000), and *Le fate ignoranti* (*His Secret Life*, Ferzan Ozpetek, 2001) incorporate food in ways that challenge societal norms regarding personal and national identity but that also ultimately consolidate communities and offer comfort, the Camorra films defy audiences to find pleasure, beauty, or a sense of pride in Italian cuisine.

In many of these films the instability wrought by the Camorra's grip on certain neighbourhoods is reinforced by the striking absence of a most basic act of human solidarity: eating together. In *Certi bambini* and *Gomorra*, for example, the directors present viewers with decidedly non-nutritive environments where drugs, semen, and blood – substances that constitute sustenance in the distorted world of the Camorra – get consumed instead of food, and the refuge provided by the family home, so often solidified by communal dining, no longer exists. In *Gomorra*, kitchen tables, appliances, and utensils like blenders and silverware serve as tools for the preparation, packaging, and inventorying of drugs. To further underscore the comparison between the circulation of drugs and that of food, in one sequence Garrone uses parallel montage to cut back and forth between the young Totò delivering groceries and anonymous hands exchanging drugs for money through iron grating. Correspondingly, in the warped universe of *Certi bambini*, young boys receive protection and a sense of belonging by consuming potentially dangerous bodily fluids (by performing oral sex on older men or licking murder victims' blood off their own hands) as a substitute for both sustenance and nurturing family relationships.

On the rare occasions when characters do share meals in these films, the act becomes intensely problematic and these scenes often undermine audience expectations. For instance, in *Pianese Nunzio* and *Certi bambini*, scenes of shared meals between the young protagonists and clergy members in religious institutions initially convey a sense of nurturing and respite from the troubles of the larger community. Furthermore, the procurement and preparation of these meals seems to resist the network of food distribution controlled by the Camorra – in both *Certi bambini* and *Pianese Nunzio*, food donated by honest community members is prepared in communal settings by people donating their time. However, these seemingly nurturing spaces reveal themselves to be less than ideal as alternatives to collaboration with the Camorra. In *Pianese Nunzio*, for example, the warmth and bonding portrayed in a scene where Nunzio and Father Lorenzo dine together turns sinister as a cut moves us from thirteen-year-old Nunzio's smiling face and clothed torso in the church dining room to a panning shot that reveals his pensive expression and naked torso lying next to Father Lorenzo in bed. In *Certi bambini*, communal meals at a Catholic halfway house routinely dissolve into chaos and tragedy.

Likewise, in *Gomorra*, characters who are associated with the sharing of food tend to be sympathetic but doomed. When Totò delivers groceries to Maria as she prepares a large bowl of pasta in her kitchen, Maria offers Totò a gratuity – the only nurturing act directed to him in the entire film. Later, Totò is forced to lure Maria out of her apartment to be assassinated. In another scene, Totò sees his friend who has joined a rival group and asks if they can still have a pizza together once in a while. The boy responds that since they are now enemies that will no longer be possible. Here, Garrone uses the cessation of dining altogether as a way to underscore the inhumanity of Camorra-generated divisions between community members.

Another character in *Gomorra*, the tailor Pasquale, forges a strong bond, initiated by sharing food, with his Chinese collaborators. When he enters their kitchen, they immediately offer him what he later claims is a delicious fish dish. Significantly, after Pasquale has secretly begun his collaboration with the Chinese, at the very moment in which he is asking Xian when he will get to taste potstickers, their car gets ambushed. In these films – *Gomorra*, *Certi bambini*, *Pianese Nunzio* – the violence and betrayal associated with food imagery serve to unravel the myth of

Camorra (and mafia) 'family values,' especially in relation to children, as those values are often portrayed both within the organization itself and by the film industry.[5] These filmmakers expose the real-life Camorra's distortion of social connections and rituals by focusing on the absence of conviviality and nourishment, while also challenging the cinematic cliché of mob bosses and their families (both biological and professional) solidifying their bonds and reaffirming their hierarchical relationships at the dinner table.

It should be mentioned that Caria's 2006 'docu-fiction' *Vedi Napoli e poi muori*, unlike the films mentioned above, does overtly portray the act of communal dining as a civilizing, problem-solving, solidarity-building tactic. Scenes of the director and his friends recounting terrifying experiences and discussing the troubles of Naples while gathered around the dinner table are interspersed with interviews in which lone interviewees – most notably Roberto Saviano – speak despairingly into the camera, and with footage (real and fictional) of daily life in Camorra-controlled neighbourhoods. These lighter moments, where the focus is not on what the group eats but on the communication and solidarity elicited by the mealtime setting, seem to suggest a creative and productive way to deal with the apocalyptic nature of the surrounding city.

In the first minutes of *Pianese Nunzio*, Father Lorenzo emerges from the darkness of his church to encounter two boys on a scooter, one of whom dangles a bunch of grapes in his face. Lorenzo asks how they acquired the grapes, as the fruit is out of season. The boys respond that if you know the right people in Naples you can get anything. The specific use of an agricultural product in this scene in order to highlight the Camorra's damaging influence on young people reflects a concern not only with social issues but also with the connection between nefarious environmental practices and health.

On the whole, the films discussed here identify the Camorra as the source of a number of food safety crises, both large and small in scale. *Mozzarella stories* responds to the toxic mozzarella incidents of 2008 in that DeAngelis employs dark comedy to reveal the extent to which this typically Campanian cheese has become the object of countless shady business practices involving the Camorra, Chinese entrepreneurs, and local businessmen. The film's resolution can be read as an attempt to reconcile social and cultural conflict through the collaborative function of mozzarella production. The Chinese and the non-Camorra family, while initially rivals, end up collaborating to avoid mob extortion.

In one of his frenetic voiceovers in *Vedi Napoli e poi muori*, Caria mentions that his film was originally intended to be about the Annurca apples typical of Campania, but, he says mysteriously, he and his companion were told that they had all disappeared. The reality is that these apples, like so many other agricultural products, have been gravely affected by toxic waste dumping. Similarly, *Gomorra* features a storyline about toxic peaches. Roberto, a recent university graduate working in his first job in waste management, and his boss Franco, visit a family that has been leasing its property as sites for dumping. As they leave, an old woman gives Roberto a crate of peaches – a striking gesture in its generosity, particularly as opposed to the obsessive exchange of money that pervades the rest of the film. While most food consumption in the film up to this point has been represented by discarded bottles, pre-packaged convenience store items, and McDonald's containers in the background of many scenes, Garrone shoots these peaches in bright, appealing colour, centred in the frame. Significantly, when Franco reveals to Roberto that he must not eat them because they are toxic, Roberto finally takes a stand against the business.

Since Italian cinema has long been focused on the vicissitudes of family life, it seems logical that one approach to telling the story of Camorra power would be to narrate its corrosive effects on the dining habits of the family unit as a metonym of civilization. The films discussed above address two intertwining issues pertaining to food and the Camorra, both of which can be considered 'food crises': first, the effect of Camorra control on food distribution and safety, and second, the way the Camorra alters affective relationships, so many of which are solidified through communal dining.

NOTES

1 Roberto Saviano, 'Dalla carne alla mozzarella: Camorra Food Spa serve a tavola,' *La Repubblica*, 23 July 2012, http://www.repubblica.it/cronaca/2012/07/23/news/camorra_cibi-39529644/.
2 See Mervyn Nicholson, 'My Dinner with Stanley: Kubrick, Food, and the Logic of Images,' *Literature Film Quarterly* 29 (2001): 279–90, 280; Helene Shugart, 'Sumptuous Texts: Consuming "Otherness" in Food Film Genre' *Critical Studies in Media Communication* 25, no. 1 (2008): 68–90, 71.
3 Rebecca Epstein, 'Crime and Nourishment: The Food and Foodways of the Hollywood Gangster Film' (PhD diss., University of California, 2006), 195.
4 Gisela Hoecherl-Alden and Laura Lindenfeld, 'Thawing the North: Mostly Martha as a German-Italian Eatopia,' *Journal of International and Intercultural Communication* 3, no. 2 (2010): 114–35, 120.
5 For a discussion of the Camorra values of 'honour, family and friendship' see Felia Allum, 'Becoming a Camorrista: Criminal Culture and Life Choices in Naples,' *Journal of Modern Italian Studies* 6, no. 3 (2001): 324–47, 329–35. Particularly relevant to the films under discussion is Allum's assertion that the core Camorra values of honour, family, and friendship 'were more apparent values than true, solid ones, and masked double-dealing and conniving,' 334.

55   The New Mafia in *Una vita tranquilla*

'The son shall not bear the iniquity of the father, neither shall the father bear the iniquity of the son: the righteousness of the righteous shall be upon him, and the wickedness of the wicked shall be upon him.'

(Ezekiel 18:19–20)

Cupellini's *Una vita tranquilla* (*A Quiet Life*, 2010) tells the story of a man who has made a new life for himself in Germany after his past as a hitman in the Camorra. It contradicts the biblical statement in Ezekiel whereby the son does not pay for the sins of the father; it also underscores one of the strongest rules of organized crime: those who commit a *sgarro* (mistake) must pay with a life, either their own or that of someone they love.

In the film, the protagonist Rosario owns an inn in Germany and seems fully integrated into the community. We learn that it took him fifteen years to establish his quiet life, which is suddenly shaken by the arrival of Diego and Edoardo, *camorristi* sent to kill a German waste disposal manager who is threatening the Camorra's monopoly on the waste industry. Diego is the son that Rosario abandoned in Naples. In setting his film in Germany, Cupellini underlines how the Camorra has extended its power beyond the boundaries of Campania and has morphed into a complex organization that employs both traditional practices and new modes of operation.[1]

Una vita tranquilla was released three years after the killings in Germany of six members of the Pelle–Romeo clan of the Calabrian 'ndrangheta. An international targeted killing of that magnitude had been unprecedented in the history of the 'ndrangheta and brought the organization into the international spotlight. Until then, many assumed that mafia-related crime was generally confined within Italy's borders. This episode demonstrated how much the 'ndrangheta had evolved and grown and how far afield criminal networks had travelled.

Roberto Saviano has discussed the effect of the Duisburg massacre on European psychology:

In reality nothing more international exists than criminal organizations. Calabrian and Neapolitan above all. For one simple reason: they are at the economic-financial avant-garde. I regret only that Europe becomes aware of this only when there are massacres. Duisburg opened the mind towards Germany and glances towards Europe. What has this entailed? That organized crime perhaps after Duisburg can be defined as a European problem and not just an Italian one.[2]

Cupellini's film is an expression of this borderless state of the mafia. Deleuze and Guattari's concept of 'deterritorialization-territorialization,'³ and the idea of 'gattopardesimo' discussed by Raffaele Cantone and Luca di Feo, can help us understand how local organized crime has transformed and expanded.⁴

Deleuze and Guattari use the term 'deterritorialization' to describe a process that decontextualizes a set of relations and renders them virtual and harder to be realized in a practical manner. The term is also employed in reference to a weakening of ties between culture and place when cultural subjects and objects are removed from a certain location in space and time. This operation implies a continuous movement whereby elements that are removed from specific places then 'reterritorialize' somewhere else and achieve a different meaning and cultural function without losing their original characteristics. These concepts help us explain the movement of Italian organized crime abroad where the criminal becomes integrated into a new culture and assumes a legitimate role within it, much like the leopard that changes its spots yet remains the same.

Cantone and di Feo apply Lampedusa's concept of *gattopardesimo* to the mafia. They tell us that after the destruction of the Corleonesi clan, which culminated in the arrest of Bernardo Provenzano in 2006, criminal behaviour migrated to white-collar workers and professionals (architects, doctors, lawyers). Many citizens distrusted institutions and regular legal practices and preferred to do business with those involved in the mafia. Nowadays, mafiosi, like the leopards at the time of Italian unification, have adjusted their business practices without changing their criminal spirit.

We see such a transformation at work in Cupellini's film. Diego and Edoardo make contact with Enzino, a factory worker also from Caserta, who provides the men with the weapon and the logistical information to kill the German manager. Enzino's character is emblematic of the transformation of the Camorra. He seems integrated into German working life. Nevertheless, he leads a duplicitous existence: he is the Camorra's informant as well as the provider of the weapon that will kill the German manager. The film's assassination sequence hints at a general sense of ignorance abroad regarding the power and reach of Italian organized crime: the manager leaves work on his bicycle, unaware that signing a contract for garbage processing will provoke his murder.

After the assassination, it is suggested that Diego is considering a crime-free lifestyle, but in the end the Camorra proves inescapable. A sensitive, educated young man who is wounded by his father's abandonment, Diego at first remains loyal to the Camorra, which had become a surrogate family in the absence of his father. But he betrays the Camorra by choosing to save his father (and so repeats his father's betrayal), an act that leads to his death at the hands of the organization.

Rosario betrays the Camorra so as to maintain a position of power. He is the chef and authoritarian owner of a restaurant where he can serve whatever he wants because 'they are German – they eat everything.' He also betrays his new German wife and minimizes her worries. Because he wants control over the kitchen, he often forgets to pick up his young son Mathias from school and tries to bribe the boy's teacher so that she will not complain. In order to expand his restaurant, he is willing to destroy old trees protected by law. His assassination of Edoardo raises an important question: Did Rosario kill the young man because he was a threat or because he challenged the chef's return to a semblance of authority? Perhaps he simply despised the arrogance of the younger *camorrista*. Despite changes in his identity, Rosario remains a killer who twice abandons his family.

Ultimately, it is Rosario who most embodies the idea of *gattopardesimo*. When he learns earlier in the film that Edoardo has discovered his secret, Rosario reverts to his former *modus operandi* and *modus sentiendi.* He kills Edoardo to regain equilibrium and maintain the new status quo that he has worked so hard to achieve. Thus the veteran assassin re-emerges, falling victim to an unalterable identity.

NOTES

1 Italian organized crime today is by no means confined to the country's borders.due to the creation of the European Union, globalization, and large-scale immigration that links Africa and Eastern Europe to Western Europe. Italy's new mafias have a bourgeois outlook; they are global and modernized, with outposts throughout Europe. The days of mere protection rackets are long gone. Instead, revenue is derived from intricate networks of black market operators that trade in illicit drugs, textiles, arms, and illegal waste. Seemingly legitimate businesses, in Italy and abroad, serve to launder mafia money.

2 Adriana Farano, 'Roberto Saviano: La camorra? Un problema europeo,' *Café Babel*, 8 October 2007, http://www.cafebabel.it/article/2782/roberto-saviano-la-camorra-un-problema-europeo.html.

3 Gilles Deleuze and Felix Guattari, *Anti-Oedipus: Capitalism and Schizofrenia*, trans. Robert Hurley et al. (Minneapolis, MN: Minnesota University Press, 1983).

4 Raffaele Cantone and Gianluca Di Feo, *I gattopardi* (Milano: Mondadori, 2010).

GIANCARLO LOMBARDI

Italian serial drama has long nurtured an approach to the portrayal of organized crime that is strikingly different from that offered by its American counterpart. Widely exported American series and serials have not shied away from centring their narratives on the life and torments of mobsters and their families, if only to portray, as David Chase does, the slow descent into hell experienced by those who choose to embrace such a way of life. Italy, however, has yet to produce the equivalent of *The Sopranos*, *Boardwalk Empire* (2010–), *Brotherhood* (2006–8), or the French competitor *Mafiosa* (2006–).

Instead, Italy has portrayed organized crime through the eyes of those on the other side of the law: either the detectives who seek to dismantle it, or Italian citizens who refuse to be involved in it. In the first category, we should remember the ten seasons of *La piovra* (*The Octopus*, 1984–2001), which portrayed the demise of several investigators at the hands of an 'octopus' that could suffer amputation but never decapitation; the three instalments of *Ultimo* (*The End*, 1998–2004), a biopic focusing on the courageous Italian police who brought to justice Totò Riina and Bernardo Provenzano, the most powerful mobsters of recent years; the seasons of *La squadra* (*The Squad*, 2000–7) and *La nuova squadra* (*The New Squad*, 2007–2009), centred on the activities of a Neapolitan police squad that engages in an endless struggle against the Camorra; and Mediaset's attempt to recreate *La piovra* through the four seasons of *Squadra antimafia: Palermo oggi* (*Antimafia Squad: Palermo Today*, 2009–), where uncharacteristically the lead investigators are women.

In the second category, we should include those serial dramas whose wider narrative focus leads to a more incidental treatment of organized crime: this is particularly true of soap operas such as *Un posto al sole* (*A Place in the Sun*, 1996–) and *Agrodolce* (*Bittersweet*, 2008–9), as well as serials such as *Vento di ponente* (*West Wind*, 2002–4), *Capri* (2006–10), and *Incantesimo* (*Enchantment*, 1998–2008). The focus of my remarks here will be limited to this second case, and in particular to the portrayal of the Camorra in Italy's longest-running serial drama, *Un posto al sole*. Indeed, it is thanks to the uncommon longevity of this program, at least in Italian terms, that organized crime has enjoyed a complex and multifaceted treatment that deserves to be unpacked.

The very title of the soap evokes a central ambiguity in the treatment of its diegetic universe: the urban environment that acts as the backdrop to the entire narrative is defined by the title as 'a place in the sun.' It is in this light, as I have explained elsewhere, that we should interpret the choice to bring together, in a Neapolitan palazzo, a cast of characters born all over Italy.[1] Their trajectory is thus portrayed as counter to common migration patterns, which have rarely evidenced the trend of northern Italians moving south, and their journey appears to be motivated by a quest for a place in the sun that so rarely shines in the foggy Po Valley. The very naming of this soap, 'a place in the sun,' evokes, however, the complementary (and adjacent) presence of the darkness surrounding such a locus, or a shadow that cannot solely be assigned to geographical areas north of Naples. Because *Un posto al sole* downplays the melodramatic overtures common to daytime drama in favour of the social realism that is perceived to inform British 'real' drama,[2] it does not portray Naples in a solely picturesque and romanticized fashion. Those familiar with the city's urban landscape will recognize that the Naples portrayed in the series is split between Posillipo, a real 'place in the sun,' and its underbelly, the Quartieri Spagnoli, which is dominated by the hegemonic presence of organized crime.[3] *Un posto al sole* rests firmly on the side of those who fight or resist organized crime, and forays into the Quartieri Spagnoli are presented through the eyes of Neapolitans who suffer the presence of the Camorra. Unlike *The Sopranos*, whose Neapolitan antecedents mark its central protagonists as *camorristi* and not as mafiosi as is often believed, the soap opera never celebrates the power of the criminal organization.

Un posto al sole replaces the horizontal spatial structure of *Neighbours* (1985–), the Australian soap that served as its prototype, with a vertical structure that better represents the class-bound system of the society it portrays. Thus, the soap depicts neighbourly relationships that evolve not in a street inhabited by the characters (as in *Neighbours*) but rather in a noble palace converted into condominiums populated by families from different walks of life.[4] Entrepreneurs, freelance journalists, private detectives, civil servants, and social workers share the same roof and occupy apartments whose varying sizes and positions appropriately signify different redefinitions of their 'place in the sun.' The Camorra touches the lives of the soap's protagonists in different ways and remains a dark presence looming outside their sunny abode. The open, protracted structure of the serial narrative lends itself well to a realistic portrayal of a phenomenon that unfortunately can never truly be defeated. Thus, the Camorra enters and exits the lives of the protagonists of the show, yet even when the threat of the organization is temporarily removed, it never truly disappears from the scenario.

In a constant attempt to remain socially relevant and informative, *Un posto al sole* launches storylines informed by events borrowed from the newsroom. The long-standing character of freelance journalist Michele Saviani was rewritten in terms that clearly define him as a fictional alter ego of Roberto Saviano, the author of *Gomorra*. Viewers watch him investigate the darkest recesses of the Camorra and its collusion with the worlds of business and industry, and witness how the organization affects him and his family after he decides to expose local *camorristi*. The show's treatment of nuclear waste disposal raises the issue of the shared responsibility of two local industrialist families, the Ferris and the Palladinis, both central to the show. The moral and ethical implications of involvement with the Ecomafia are placed centre stage when the younger industrialist Filippo learns that the Camorra expects him to allow the disposal of nuclear waste under the foundations of an elementary school that his firm is about to build. The symbolic implications of such a gesture, powerfully raised in *The Sopranos* during its last season, bear particular relevance when we consider that Filippo is the illegitimate son of the ruthless entrepreneur Roberto Ferri and is later made to pay for the reckless business deals of his father and his other predecessors.[5]

The target viewership of *Un posto al sole*, as discussed elsewhere,[6] is clearly wider than that of most serial dramas, and the soap has centred its most powerful treatment of Camorra-related storylines on its female characters. In many cases, it has used pivotal characters to narrate tales of redemption. The necessity to telescope narratives centred on the possibility of rehabilitating (un)willing participants in organized crime speaks to the very mission of a serial drama committed to social realism, although redemption itself could easily be viewed as a lynchpin of melodrama. *Un posto al sole* has long depicted women as agents or subjects of redemption, which is contrary to common understanding of gender roles in organized crime. Through the pivotal figure of Giulia Poggi, a social worker committed to establishing, in the heart of the Quartieri Spagnoli, a *centro d'ascolto* or community centre that would serve as a counter-agent to local recruitment by the Camorra, the soap has effectively gendered a form of civil resistance. In the episodes aired in Spring 2012, viewers see Giulia facilitating the ultimate act of redemption, the rehabilitation of a Camorra leader whose 'conversion' is later made into a public example through social networks. In *Un posto al sole*, much like in the films from which the soap takes inspiration such as *Amici miei* (*My Friends*, Mario Monicelli, 1975) and *Totò, Peppino e la malafemmina* (*Toto, Peppino, and the Hussy*, Camillo Mastrocinque, 1956), women are actively involved in organized crime, yet their illegal activities are portrayed as a necessity and not as a personal choice. Such fated conditions ultimately lead to these characters' eventual redemption and facilitate viewer empathy when they, initially presented in guest roles, are later granted protagonist status. Only after being redeemed can they begin to find their 'place in the sun.'

Interestingly, the open-ended structure of the soap opera aligns itself with *Un posto al sole*'s commitment to social realism, as it would be unrealistic to portray a complete demise of the Camorra. Serial drama rests firmly on the staging of cyclical behaviours, which are often repeated in compulsive fashion and thus defy closure. Yet the ethical mission of the public broadcaster requires the portrayal of inspirational storylines, served up as *exempla*. For example, the character of Franco Boschi has long played a pivotal role in such inspirational storylines: initially portrayed as the young man from the 'wrong side of the tracks,' if only because of his humble origins, Franco has long acted as the agent of redemption for many characters. His decision to open a gym in the heart of the Quartieri Spagnoli to encourage local youth to channel energy in a positive direction is central to the soap's ethical mission. The boxing tournaments organized at his gym are a metaphor for the struggle against organized crime. The Camorra may never be fully defeated, but *Un posto al sole* suggests that it can be weakened through partial victories, such as the redemption of one ex-member at a time. The need to continue to develop the storylines of a wide cast of characters mirrors such structural ambiguity and makes each tale of redemption potentially fallible and volatile.

NOTES

1 Giancarlo Lombardi, 'Days of Italian Lives: Charting the Contemporary Soapscape on Italian Public Television,' *The Italianist* 28, no. 2 (2009): 227–48.

2 For a discussion of the melodramatic qualities of soap operas, see Tania Modleski, *Love with a Vengeance: Mass Produced Fantasies for Women* (London: Routledge, 1984); Robert C. Allen, *Speaking of Soap Operas* (Chapel Hill, NC: University of North Carolina Press, 1985); Martha Nochimson, *No End to Her: Soap Opera and the Female Subject* (Berkeley, CA: University of California Press, 1993). For a discussion of social realism in British 'real drama' see Christine Geraghty, *Women and Soap Opera: A Study of Prime Time Soaps* (Oxford: Polity, 1990), 32–5. Geraghty claims that serial dramas such

as *Coronation Street*, *Eastenders*, and *Brookside* demonstrated their commitment to social realism by attempting to portray issues that are 'contemporary and important,' 95. Similarly, as I demonstrated in 'Days of Italian Lives,' *Un posto al sole*, and its Sicilian counterpart *Agrodolce*, have strived to remain true to one of the most famous slogans of their public broadcaster: *Rai per il sociale*.

3   Milly Buonanno and Marcia Gomes discuss the symbolic importance of the Neapolitan setting of *Un posto al sole* in 'Il programma dell'anno: *Un posto al sole*. Una duplice lettura della prima *soap opera italiana*,' in *Provando e riprovando: la fiction italiana, l'Italia nella fiction*, ed. Milly Buonanno (Rome: Rai-ERI, 1999), 91–8. Jean Mottet juxtaposes the Italian soap's domestic and urban spaces in *Série télévisée et éspace domestique: la télévision, la maison, le monde* (Paris: L'Harmattan, 2005), 103–19. Anna Lucia Natale provides a detailed comparison of the importance of geographical settings in all Italian soap operas in 'Comunità imperfette: il mondo delle soap,' in *Realtà multiple: concetti, generi e audience della fiction TV*, ed. Milly Buonanno (Naples: Liguori, 2004), 120–9.

4   For a discussion of the worldwide success of *Neighbours*, see Stephen Crofts, 'Global Neighbours?,' in *To Be Continued …: Soap Operas Around the World*, ed. Robert C. Allen (London: Routledge, 1995), 98–121. For a discussion of the hybridization of the Australian soap in Italy, see Milly Buonanno, *Indigeni si diventa: locale e globale nella serialità televisiva* (Milan: Sansoni, 1999), 144–50.

5   This storyline seems to echo quite directly the events narrated in *The Sopranos*, where the disposal of asbestos in elementary schools is at the centre of the dispute between mobsters from New York and New Jersey. When juxtaposed with the parallel descent of Tony Soprano's son into the same form of depression that has long plagued his father, the presence of asbestos in buildings populated by children is perceived as a different form of hereditary pollution that mandates that the sins of the fathers shall be visited upon their children. For a discussion of the symbolic relevance of waste disposal in the last season of *The Sopranos*, see Giancarlo Lombardi, 'Don't Stop …: (De)Structuring Expectations in the Final Season of *The Sopranos*,' in *Mafia Movies: A Reader*, ed. Dana Renga (Toronto: University of Toronto Press, 2011), 192–200.

6   See Lombardi, 'Days of Italian Lives.'

57 Response #1

ROBERT GORDON

Reading the varied and stimulating contributions to this roundtable on 'Italy's Other mafias' as a non-specialist – that is, as someone who works on the cultural history of modern Italy, but not specifically on the mafias or on their movie or other media representations – I'm struck most of all by the eclectic range of material and method on display and by the underlying challenges this collation of approaches poses for scholarship. It is hard indeed to see how scholarly work might map out a coherent terrain that includes (1) the complex historical phenomenon of organized crime itself in its distinct forms, born in several different regions of Italy at different times, each with its own particular genesis, history, and social and geographical evolution, but also each running in resonant parallel with others, suggesting patterns of anthropological affinity and continuity (all of them kill, as Anthony Fragola points out, and all of them have variously poisoned the nation-state of Italy over a century and more, as John Dickie's work has shown so vividly); (2) the fluid field of perceptions of these phenomena in wider contexts, in and beyond Italy, in which context the distinct mafias often merge and blend indifferently, however specific and localized the evocation; (3) the causes and effects of these perceptions and blurrings as they work their way through bodies of work in film, television, and other media, out into broader fields of cultural transmission of knowledge; (4) the different tools and categories we use to analyse single works or threads within those corpora of representational material, from studies of single motifs to structural analyses of patterns of genre in possibly hundreds of films or TV episodes; and, finally, (5) the self-conscious feedback loops that connect the layers of this terrain, whereby the histories influence the perceptions that influence the works of representation in turn, as we might commonsensically expect, but also and as much vice versa and all other orderings in between (much like Umberto Eco's hypothesis in *Il cimitero di Praga* that a kitsch but tragic causal chain led from bad nineteenth-century fiction to *The Protocols of the Elders of Zion* to the Holocaust). And all of this comes before we acknowledge that each strand in this weave, each coordinate of the map, also intersects with other terrains and histories: of the Italian south and its migrations to the north, of national or 'post-national' film history, of Hollywood genre, of the modalities of TV soaps, and so on potentially ad infinitum.

The complexity of this field of historical and cultural processing is precisely the point, however. If the phenomena within it are to enter into sustained and useful contact with one another, there is essential groundwork to be done, work of thick and broad description of the terrain. The capacity to navigate between so many sites within it is perhaps one of the many reasons why

Roberto Saviano has had such success and resonance, in this field and in the field of contemporary Italian media and culture more broadly: because of his uncanny ability to traverse so many of the intersecting spheres and sites of cultural activity touching on Italy's mafias, from on-the-ground experience in Campania, to the idiolects of committed literature and reportage (*Gomorra*), to the voice of the public intellectual and political polemicist, in print and virtual forms (*La Repubblica*; www.robertosaviano.it), to the transposition of his writings into genre- and politically inflected cinema (Garrone), to the glamour of international literary circuits and festivals (Saviano as the Italian Rushdie), to a series of carefully staged, charismatic performances as a pop figure of moral conscience on peaktime television (with Fazio, *Come Away with Me*, RAI 3; and now on La7 and YouTube). The roundtable collectively suggests the sheer cartographic effort required to keep up with this form of dynamic mobility, to trace and interpret the vectors that, among many other agents and phenomena, Saviano so knowingly embodies and manipulates, across this multiple cultural field.

DANIELLE HIPKINS

The waves of visibility and invisibility that characterize media representations of Italy's other mafias, explored so engagingly in this roundtable, are thrown into particular relief by the synecdoche of toxicity, examined here by Amy Boylan. The narrative potential of Camorra activity as it seeps into widely consumed foodstuffs of everyday life is significant, for it conveys the uneasy relationship between Italian culture and its other mafias. We might presume that these mafia forms are more or less constantly present in Italian daily life, but it is only in particular generic forms and historical moments that they are articulated in its media culture. In this light, and following the productive discussion established here, we might be led to interrogate further areas of apparent silence in such representations. While I agree that the films set in northern Europe speak to a transnational quality of the mafia, might it not also be possible to read this insistence on northern *Europe* as a symptom of an apparently peculiar absence of northern *Italy* in recent cinematic mafia narratives? Several contributors speak of the links between north and south, but it seems that the films and television programs examined here rarely move farther north than Rome (with the odd exception, such as the scene set in Venice in *Gomorra*), as if the issue of the infection of the entire Italian body politic might still be too painful to contemplate. In Sorrentino's *Le conseguenze dell'amore*, for example, most of the action takes place in a faux 'national' space, the Ticino, before swiftly moving south for its mafia-saturated dénouement. That said, in very recent years there has been a turn of attention to mafia-related narratives set in northern parts of Italy, such as the television mini-series *Faccia d'angelo* (*Angel Face*, Andrea Porporati, 2012) and *Vallanzasca: gli angeli del male* (*Angel of Evil*, Michele Placido, 2010), so further investigation of this theme and its film history would be worth undertaking. Such connections are evident in earlier films, such as those of Lina Wertmüller and Alberto Lattuada, but these relate to the Sicilian mafia. If the widespread influence of the Sicilian mafia is acknowledged, perhaps representations of Italy's other mafias are a new way of holding the south out as a separate space?

Anthony Fragola is troubled by the 'lack of any serious acknowledgment of the actual deaths for which the mafia is responsible.' But in this regard, perhaps we should be questioning the media forms themselves, and all of the contributions in this article do in fact highlight sensitively how different genres and forms dramatize the deadly incursion the other mafias may make into individual lives. The frequent appearance of children in these narratives – discussed by Amy Boylan, for example – connotes with particular force the sense of vulnerability the mafia conveys. In this respect I would agree with Claudia Karagoz that Italian photography could also be engaged usefully in this debate. For example, does *Gomorrah Girl*, the recent collection of photographs by Valerio Spada, sharpen our perceptions of damage caused by the Camorra because it engages that most effective symbol of cultural and social collateral damage in contemporary Italy: the teenage girl?[1] If, by the very nature of popular fictional narrative and its focus on the individual, we may lose some sense of the scale of damage and loss the other mafias cause (although not always), the potential to draw the viewer into an ambivalent position of sympathy that blurs the line between perpetrator and victim is surely visual fiction's sharpest instrument. The process of 'othering' Italy's other mafias will only increase fear and repel attempts at further understanding; the narratives that show how many become entangled in their grasp give all viewers, both inside and outside Italy, reason to care about finding real ways to deal with Italy's other mafias and to acknowledge their pertinence to Italy as a whole.

NOTE

1 Valerio Spada, *Gomorra Girl*, 2nd ed. (Paris: Cross Editions, 2011).

ROBIN PICKERING-IAZZI

'The Camorra, I don't even want to speak of it, as I don't bother myself with buffoons even capable of enlisting municipal guards. But regarding the 'Ndrangheta, your Honour, is it certain that it even exists?'

Tommaso Buscetta, *Cose di cosa nostra*[1]

Ever since the mafia informer Buscetta voiced his own provocative, cryptic images of the Camorra and 'ndrangheta to Giovanni Falcone, perceptions of Italian criminal organizations, practices, and geographies of illegality have changed in subtle and spectacular ways. Indeed, by drawing together diverse lines of inquiry related to multimedia representations of the different criminal clans operating on the Italian peninsula and beyond – clans largely eclipsed by discourses devoted to the Cosa Nostra – this roundtable offers a diachronic frame for scrutinizing the ways in which the Camorra, the Banda della Magliana, and the Sacra Corona Unita, for example, are delineated in relation to various spaces, temporal contexts, and genres. The resultant vantage point enables readers to see how certain issues recur in images of the distinct organizations produced in a variety of fiction and non-fiction works and sociohistorical contexts, ranging from the 1800s to today. Among these are female and male gender roles, generational bonds and conflicts, class relations, and performance. But what particularly interests me are the insights regarding the various models of identity underpinning the 'other mafias' as fashioned respectively in the stories told by the criminal members and in sociocultural narratives produced in print media, theatre, film, and soap operas, for instance.

By mapping relatively unexplored territories surrounding less infamous criminal organizations, the ensemble of studies highlights points of intersection and divergence exhibited by the particular myths and features making up the models of identity crafted for public consumption by the Camorra, the 'ndrangheta, and, more recently, the Sacra Corona Unita. For example, Dickie's discussion of the origins claimed by the Camorra and the forms of self-performance enacted respectively by *camorrista* Pupetta Maresca and *'ndranghetista* Giuseppe Musolino provide salient examples for illustrating the diverse roles played by myths of origin as guarantors of long-standing lineage and nobility, and by such elements as honour, loyalty, hypermasculinity, and vendetta. Offering fascinating points of contrast and comparison are the testimonies by members of the 'ndrangheta featured, as Renga tells us, in the documentary *Uomini d'onore* as well as the insights about the postmodern mafia revealed by Zappalà's non-fiction film *Sacra corona unita e il pericolo che viene dall'est.* These works also invite analysis regarding how the elements of the criminal associations' particular identities may change, adapting to different social, economic, political, and geographic realities, both national and transnational. In this respect, the notion of criminal identity as subject of redemption is especially important. As discussed in various essays, this issue is articulated in such diverse works as the films *Fine pena mai* and *Cesare deve morire*, as well as the socially engaged soap opera *Un posto al sole*, which present the possibility of interrogating the roles and meanings of redemption in both criminal and civil cultures. Such contemporary images delineating the 'reformation' of criminal identity, like those of the heroic *camorristi* described in the newspapers of the 1800s and cited by Dickie, also tell us much about the particular hopes, fantasies, and fears of the sociocultural forces producing them. By foregrounding cultural constructions of the often overlooked Italian criminal associations, this roundtable brings into high definition a variety of texts and critical directions of inquiry. Moreover, it amply testifies to why stories about the 'other mafias' warrant continued attention as the subject of serious discussion.

NOTE

1 Giovanni Falcone in collaboration with Marcelle Padovani, *Cose di cosa nostra* (Milano: Rizzoli, 1999), 109.

ALLISON COOPER

John Dickie writes of a 'strange feedback loop' between Italy's other mafias and the media that represent them and demonstrates how mafiosi are both the producers and consumers of cultural representations of organized crime. Many of the contributors to this roundtable similarly note the ways in which images of mafia violence circulate among criminals and the televisual, filmic, and newspaper accounts of their activities. We see this in particular in Renga's account of Sasà Striano's double career as *camorrista* and actor specializing in the representation of *camorristi*, as well as in her reference to *Gomorra*'s Marco and Ciro, who model their identities after *Scarface*'s Tony Montana; and in Dickie's own account of nineteenth-century *camorristi* and their penchant for theatrical representations of themselves. We see a circularity of violent images at work as well in recent on-screen and real-life reclamations of the Banda della Magliana, which O'Rawe and Karagoz link to Italy's contemporary crisis of masculinity. Reading these essays, it almost seems that the feedback loop to which Dickie and others refer is a constitutive component of organized crime.

To what might we attribute this interdependence between Italy's mafias and its diverse medias? Dickie suggests that media representations of criminal organizations can provide them with history and coherence, the 'ideological glue' they otherwise lack. Conversely, the Camorra and other groups such as the 'ndrangheta, the Sacra Corona Unita, and the Banda della Magliana furnish medias in Italy and abroad with dramatic narratives that make good copy and sell tickets at the box office. In her introduction, Renga highlights the performative aspects of criminality in Italy, observing the ways in which it is cathartic for mafiosi to act out their violent tendencies on screen even as clan members model their actions after media representations of other mafiosi. The relationships between Italy's other mafias and the medias that depict them reveal, to echo Pickering-Iazzi, the degree to which mafia identity is a cultural construct.

Robert Gordon draws attention to the wide array of texts and methodologies presented in this roundtable, noting 'the sheer cartographic effort' employed to interpret this 'multiple field.' His allusion to maps is fitting: this collection of essays represents a first attempt to explore previously uncharted territory. Dickie's 'strange feedback loop' conjures yet another kind of map, however – the one invoked at the beginning of Baudrillard's *Simulacra and Simulation*.[1] Baudrillard's map, which comes to precede the territory it represents, describes the postmodern rupture between the signifier and the signified. The circularity of violent images explored in many of these brief essays and their proliferation in fraught genres such as the docudrama suggest that we are enmeshed in

Baudrillard's precession of simulacra, a disorienting territory indeed. Do our attempts to chart its virtual contours align us with his cartographers, whose very efforts obscure – or even contribute to – an increasingly eroding sense of reality?

NOTE

1 Jean Baudrillard, *Simulacra and Simulation*, trans. Sheila Faria Glaser (Ann Arbor, MI: University of Michigan Press, 1995).

PART FIVE

Double Takes

DOM HOLDAWAY

Marlon Brando's performance as Don Vito Corleone is without doubt among the most universally lauded roles in the history of Hollywood. The conception of the part is the stuff of legends. Coppola and Fred Roos, the film's casting director, had considered many acting greats as possibilities for the role, including Brando, Lawrence Olivier, Orson Welles, George C. Scott, and even Carlo Ponti, though the latter had never acted.[1] Though their preference for Brando was universal, the actor's reputation as a troublemaking contrarian led Paramount to reject him point-blank initially. Coppola has recounted how they came around to the idea only under certain conditions: zero salary, a million-dollar bond, and a screen test. Ultimately it was the latter, and Brando's experiments with make-up, dyed hair, and cotton balls stuffed in his mouth to accentuate Don Vito's trademark drawl, that led the studio to accept his casting. And though his fellow actors have spoken only positively of Brando, the scandals were to continue beyond the film: the performance was honoured with an Academy Award that the actor infamously refused, in protest of the mistreatment of Native Americans in Hollywood.

Infamy and scandal aside, the brilliance of Brando's interpretation is clear to see. He epitomizes the antiheroic gangster: formal and stoic, and fiercely loyal to his family, his community, and his code of honour, while constantly incorporating a silent threat and the potential for violence against those who contravene that code. Like many great fictional antiheroes, he thus represents a set of values while simultaneously debasing them through excess and violence; he engages our empathy even while challenging and undermining it. The values we see in the film overlap with key elements of American/Italian society, between family and business, and thus Brando's character embodies and extends the cultural symbolism of the gangster as the corrupted vision of the American Dream, as Warshow wrote in his canonical reading of the genre (twenty years earlier).[2]

All of these aspects and the legacy of the role owe much to Brando's star persona. He emerged in the 1950s in a series of plays and films – among which perhaps the most symbolic was his first film collaboration with Elia Kazan, in *A Streetcar Named Desire* (1951) – that established three key characteristics of his image: an anti-establishment ethic, the hidden essence of danger in his characters, and the seriousness of his 'method' approach. By lending these elements to the characterization of Vito Corleone, Brando would redefine the cultural legitimacy of the mafia movie. And more than this, he handed down his ethics and approach to the next generation of those serious, new Hollywood actors who went on to establish their own *personae* in this film, including Al Pacino, Robert Duvall, and James Caan.

NOTES

1 Stefan Kanfer, *Somebody: The Reckless Life and Remarkable Career of Marlon Brando* (London: Faber and Faber, 2008), 236.
2 Cf. Robert Warshow, *The Immediate Experience: Movies, Comics, Theatre, and Other Aspects of Popular Culture* (Cambridge, MA: Harvard University Press, 2001), 97–103.

ALBERTO ZAMBENEDETTI

As *The Godfather Notebook* has revealed, Francis Ford Coppola approached the task of adapting Mario Puzo's bestselling novel for the screen with scepticism: 'My initial reaction [to the book] was surprise and dismay,'[1] he confesses. Yet Coppola was able to identify at the heart of this pot-boiler 'a story that was a metaphor for American capitalism in the tale of a great *king* with three sons'[2] – aristocratic lineage being a European way of understanding the dynastic transmission of privilege. Coppola's *Italian* American-ness is what allowed him to recognize the novel's potential both as crime fiction and as a vehicle for ethnic revival: 'Whenever I saw the opportunity to include the fact that Italian Americans behave a certain way, I made note of it.'[3] The result is an epic journey through space and time: Kael remarked that Coppola gifted this tale 'with the spaciousness and strength that popular novels such as Dickens' used to have.'[4] For the first time in American fiction, the gangster genre elevated rather than disparaged an immigrant family. 'Genre for Coppola is like the rituals of religion';[5] genre films honour past traditions while moving society into the future. Despite the problematic conflation of ethnicity with organized crime, 'The Godfather has done more to create a national consciousness of the Italian American experience than any work of fiction or nonfiction prior to or since its publication.'[6] In Bakhtinian terms, the discourse of both the novel and the film trilogy is a double-voiced one: 'it represents the moment when Italian American artists ... come to occupy the position of language (novelistic and cinematic) in mainstream culture and thus to control, to a certain degree, their self-representation.'[7] By rewriting the gangster genre from the point of view of the same ethnic group whose reputation it had actively tarnished, *The Godfather* 'introduces into a pre-existing discourse a semantic intention directly opposite to the first voice.'[8] In essence, Coppola's adaptation is not an antagonistic exercise between competing signifying systems, but a site for the enactment of a series of transformatory operations[9] that encompass not only a shift in the expressive medium but also a cultural reframing of larger sociopolitical issues.

NOTES

1 Francis Ford Coppola, *The Godfather Notebook* (New York: Regan Arts, 2016), 20.
2 Ibid., 24. My italics.
3 Ibid., 38.

4 Pauline Kael, *Deeper into Movies* (Boston: Little, Brown, 1973), 420.
5 Leo Braudy, 'The Sacraments of Genre: Coppola, DePalma, Scorsese," in *Film Quarterly: Forty Years – a Selection*, ed. Brian Henderson, Ann Martin, and Lee Amazonas (Berkeley, CA: University of California Press, 1999), 209.
6 Fred Gardaphé, 'Italian American Novelists,' in *The Italian American Heritage: A Companion to Literature and Arts*, ed. Pellegrino D'Acierno (New York and London: Garland, 1999), 178.
7 Pellegrino D'Acierno, 'Cinema Paradiso: The Italian American Presence in American Cinema,' in *The Italian American Heritage: A Companion to Literature and Arts*, ed. D'Acierno (New York and London: Garland, 1999), 574.
8 Robert Stam, Richard Porton, and Leo Goldsmith, *Keywords in Subversive Film/Media Aesthetics* (Malden, MA: Wiley Blackwell, 2015), 54.
9 Millicent Marcus, *Filmmaking by the Book: Italian Cinema and Literary Adaptation* (Baltimore, MD: Johns Hopkins University Press, 1993), 24.

DANA RENGA

'In Corleone women are as dangerous as the lupara,' Michael is told by his bodyguard Fabrizio when he locks gazes with a woman (Apollonia) he comes across while traversing the Sicilian countryside. Fabrizio is warning his boss to steer clear of Apollonia, for his advances would bring dishonour to her family and shame to the girl and ultimately provoke her relatives to avenge lost honour. Michael, however, plays his cards well; he wins over the family and gets the girl, whose wrongful death by explosion fuels Michael's quest for vendetta and puts an end to *The Godfather*'s Sicilian episode. Apollonia's death is followed by a fade-out to a scene in New York where Don Vito Corleone negotiates with the heads of the five families the terms for his son's safe return home so that Michael can step in and take Sonny's place as the new godfather-in-training. Apollonia is vitally important to Michael, for she consolidates his 'Italianness' and formally weds him to his father's land and namesake, thus preparing him to fill his father's shoes. Michael's desire to avenge the attempt on his father's life and the murder of his brother and wife is bound up with the loss of Apollonia and the ethnic identity and cult of honour that she engenders. His thirst for vendetta, which is culturally ingrained in him, will never be satisfied.

College educated and with a job, blonde and blue-eyed, frequently wearing bright colours, and outspoken, Kay is the polar opposite of the Mediterranean Apollonia, who is subservient and barely speaks (or when she does speak does so in jumbled English). Her repeated questioning of Michael makes her distinct from other women in *The Godfather*, such as the nameless matriarch 'Mamma Corleone,' who is frequently depicted in the kitchen holding children and the underdeveloped women Sonny sleeps with. Michael's relationship with Kay before the attempt on his father's life is gentle, romantic, and respectful. After Michael declares to his father, who is near death in the hospital, 'I'm with you now,' Kay fades out of view, and is only brought back into the narrative after Michael returns home and tells her he needs her and wants her to marry him. Renate Siebert writes that in the mafia 'a man's first duty is to not be a woman': a mafioso must exorcise feminine qualities, perform virility, and repress emotion.[1] Once he assumes the role of godfather, Michael is stoic, distant, and business-oriented. Kay must fulfil the vital role for Michael of mafia wife and mother, and she is expected to remain silent and to raise her children according to mafia values. The door shut on Kay at the end of the film during Michael's induction as godfather bars her from this key ritual and excludes her from the inner workings of the mafia. Yet the following take frames her solidly within the doorway, which alludes to the paradox of mafia women: they are central to the family as wives and mothers, but, at least traditionally, they must remain silent, subservient, and invisible.

NOTE

1 Renate Siebert, *Secrets of Life and Death* (London and New York: Verso, 1996), 22.

15 *Boardwalk Empire*: Generational conflict between Nucky and Jimmy (HBO/Webphoto)

16 *Mob Wives*: The Mob Wives perform empowerment (Electus/Webphoto)

17 *In the Name of the Law*: Francesco Messana arrested 'in the name of the law' for the murder of Paolino in the town of Capodarso (Lux Film/Webphoto)

18 *Salvatore Giuliano*: 'The only thing certain is that he is dead': Documenting the Bandit's body (Lux Film, Galatea, Vides Cinematografica/Webphoto)

19   *The Leopard*: Tancredi illuminates Sicily's republican destiny for Prince Fabrizio (Titanus/Webphoto)

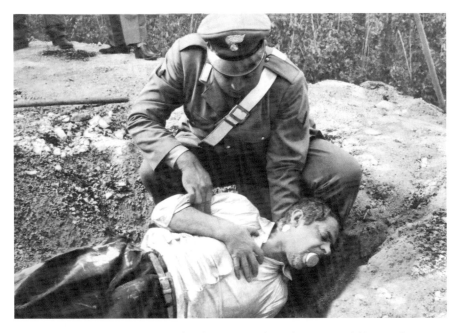

20   *The Day of the Owl*: Parrinieddu pays the ultimate price for violating *omertà* (Corona Cinematografica, Euro International Film (EIA), Les Films Corona, Panda Società per l'Industria Cinematografica/ Webphoto)

21 *The Seduction of Mimi*: Mimi loses his job at the quarry after defying mafia law (Euro International Film (EIA)/Webphoto)

22 *Lucky Luciano*: Lucky Luciano maintains his innocence while charming journalists during a press conference in Naples (Harbor Productions, Les Films de la Boétie, Vides Cinematografica/Webphoto)

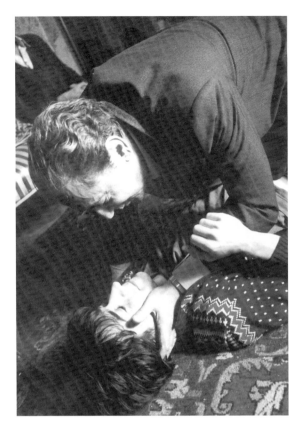

23 *The Hundred Steps*: Luigi implores Peppino Impastato to honour his father and stay out of the way of the Cinisi Mafia (Rai Cinemafiction, Telet, Tutti Film, Ministero per i beni e le attività culturali (MiBAC)/ Webphoto)

24 *Angela*: Angela visits her husband Saro in prison not long before she is exiled from the Family forever (Ministero per i beni e le attività culturali (MiBAC), Movieweb S.p.a., Rita Rusic, Co./Webphoto)

25 *Excellent Cadavers*: One of Letizia Battaglia's photos documenting children 'playing' in the streets of Palermo (Doclab S.r.l., Raitre radiotelevisione italiana/Webphoto)

26 *Gomorrah*: Ciro and Marco emulate Hollywood gangsters in the Neopolitan marshes (Fandango/Webphoto)

27 *Gomorra: la serie*: Genny's (failed) initiation by fire (Cattleya, Fandango, Sky Italia/Webphoto)

28 *Romanzo criminale*: Freddo, Dandi, and Libanese aim to conquer Rome (Cattleya/Webphoto)

29 *Romanzo criminale: la serie*: Freddo, Libanese, and Dandi bond over blood (Cattleya, Sky Italia/ Webphoto)

ALBERTO ZAMBENEDETTI

Since its 1972 release, *The Godfather*'s stature has continued to grow: 'If ever there was a great example of how the best popular movies come out of a merger of commerce and art, *The Godfather* is it,'[1] wrote Pauline Kael. With its hefty running time and its movie star at the head of an ensemble cast, the studio-backed costume drama seemed engineered to become a classic. Its slow pace and ponderous score set it apart from the manic energy that pervaded other contemporary crime films, from *Bonnie and Clyde* (Arthur Penn, 1967) to *Mean Streets*. However, while '[t]here are the born classicists who start with *form*,' there are also 'the born romanticists, who start with an original, untried *matter*' and who continue to refine it until 'the whole effect adjusts itself in clear, orderly, proportionate form; which form, after a very little time, becomes classical in its turn.'[2] In other words, art is elevated to classic stature not by the imitation *of* an established form, but by the effects time has on an artist's experimentation *with* such form: 'It is the addition of strangeness to beauty, that constitutes the romantic character in art.'[3] *The Godfather* does not open with a title card informing us of the time and place, nor does it show the Corleone compound in a wide establishing shot – a disorienting lack of coordinates. Its *strangeness* is a subtle subversion of the rules of continuity filmmaking upon whose foundations the edifice of Classical Hollywood Cinema stands. As in the Gospel of John, *The Godfather*'s universe is conjured up by Puzo's language: the sentence 'I believe in America' is uttered by a heavily accented voice belonging to a minor character, Amerigo Bonasera. Only after these words are heard does the black screen dissolve into his close-up, and he launches into a monologue describing the savagery suffered by his daughter. While the crestfallen undertaker speaks, the camera slowly zooms back, revealing the outline of a figure listening quietly. In the reverse shot, a recalcitrant Don Vito Corleone responds to the plea while playing with a purring kitten. Coppola's shaping of romantic matter into classical, his 'archaic innovation, the creation of the new on the foundations of the old,'[4] begins in the comfort of a dimly lit, elegantly decorated office, where the patriarch explains the strange tenets of an age-old ethical code based on kinship, loyalty, distrust of authorities, honour, and violence.[5]

NOTES

1   Pauline Kael, *Deeper into Movies* (Boston: Little, Brown, 1973), 420.
2   Walter Pater, *Appreciations: With an Essay on Style* (London and New York: Macmillan, 1889), 260.

3 Ibid., 248.
4 Robert Stam, Richard Porton, and Leo Goldsmith, *Keywords in Subversive Film/Media Aesthetics* (Malden, MA: Wiley Blackwell, 2015), 44.
5 For a detailed discussion of the intricacies of this code, see Pellegrino D'Acierno, 'Cinema Paradiso: The Italian American Presence in American Cinema,' in *The Italian American Heritage: A Companion to Literature and Arts*, ed. D'Acierno (New York and London: Garland, 1999), 576–7.

65   *The Godfather*: Scene Analysis – The Baptism/Murder

ALBERTO ZAMBENEDETTI

As established by classics such as *Underworld* (Joseph von Sternberg, 1927), *Little Caesar*, and *The Public Enemy* (William A. Wellman, 1931), the mechanics of the gangster genre require a violent climax from which the protagonist must emerge defeated. *The Godfather* upsets this narrative trope through Coppola's 'Catholic way of regarding the visible world,' which entails 'a specially honed sense of (1) the importance of ritual narratives, (2) the significance of ritual objects, and (3) the conferral of ritual status.'[1] Ostensibly, the technique of cross-cutting between the baptism of Micheal Francis Rizzi and the many murders ordered by his godfather belongs to a tradition in American cinema dating back at least to the horseback rescue by the Ku Klux Klan in D.W. Griffith's *The Birth of a Nation* (1915); the KKK is another organization whose main achievement was the spreading of racial hatred and ethnic violence. The simultaneity of events in *The Godfather* not only articulates the film's narrative discourse but also illustrates the protagonist's a/moral engagement with both the material world and the spiritual one. Coppola implicitly invokes 'the torture scene in *Open City*, set in a room that, with total spatial illogic and psychic logic, is right next door to the main office of the Nazi chief as well as to the clubroom of dissipated pleasures.'[2] By moving between these contiguous environs, Rossellini achieved 'a sacramentalizing of the real,' a cinematic parable that transcends historical record by becoming itself an object of mystical contemplation.[3] *The Godfather*'s synthesis of these two cinematic traditions rests on 'the film's semiotic antinomy,'[4] a comparative architecture based on 'a series of seemingly conflicting signs apparent throughout the film.'[5] Coppola was indeed applying 'the transatlantic gaze,' a dialogic 'framework that surrounds and informs cinematic production in the two countries'[6] (Italy and the United States) and that is informed by the ethnic background of its participants. If 'Puzo's achievement [was] his ability to seduce readers into accepting the Corleone family justice as righteous and rejecting the faceless style of American corporatism,'[7] then Coppola's intuition was to produce a film that rested on this ethical conflict without attempting to find a resolution: Michael Corleone is both a decorated war hero and a cunning mobster; he is both a tender family man and a ruthless killer. Ultimately, he is a new kind of cinematic protagonist, one borne out of an uneasy negotiation of identities that transcend the labels 'Italian' and 'American.'

NOTES

1 Leo Braudy, 'The Sacraments of Genre: Coppola, DePalma, Scorsese,' in *Film Quarterly: Forty Years – a Selection*, ed. Brian Henderson, Ann Martin, and Lee Amazonas (Berkeley, , CA: University of California Press, 1999), 207.
2 Ibid., 206.
3 Ibid., 207.
4 See Anthony Julian Tamburri's essay on *The Godfather* in this volume.
5 Tamburri, *The Godfather*, 95.
6 Mary Ann McDonald Carolan, *The Transatlantic Gaze: Italian Cinema, American Film* (Albany, NY: SUNY Press, 2014), 3.
7 Mary Jo Bona, 'Rich Harvest: An Overview of Italian American Fiction,' in *Teaching Italian American Literature, Film, and Popular Culture*, ed. Edvige Giunta and Kathleen Zamboni McCormick (New York: Modern Language Association of America, 2010), 92.

DANIEL PAUL

The finale of *The Godfather* can be divided into two parts, both of them foregrounding the gendered dynamics of the mafia through Michael's interactions with two women: first his sister Connie, then later his wife Kay. Although these women are crucial to the film's denouement, Michael's ascension to power maintains narrative centrality throughout the closing sequence. Thus, in its final moments, *The Godfather* lays bare that the mafia is, following Renate Siebert's analysis, a 'male only society' that marginalizes women.[1]

As Connie confronts Michael regarding her late husband's death, the camera remains trained on the cold yet calculating gaze of the godfather sitting at his desk – a position coded as one of power in the film's opening sequence – as he quietly endures his sister's tirade. The emotionally charged exchange between Kay and Connie in the foreground stands in stark contrast to the calm, collected, almost emotionless demeanour evinced by Michael in the background. Furthermore, the women are in shallow focus, which positions the new don as the focal point of the spectator's gaze and simultaneously obscures Connie's suffering, as she is pushed to the periphery, both of the frame and of the mafia itself. When the hysterical Connie attempts to move into the male-only space behind Michael's desk, she is immediately grabbed by one of his bodyguards; only after Michael flicks his fingers – an act that again recalls Don Vito's interaction with Bonasera at the film's incipit – is Connie allowed to cross the gender barrier, an act that promptly results in her confinement to a room upstairs.

In one of the film's most iconic moments, Kay is closed out from her husband's office, which reinforces her position as outsider – both as a woman and as a non-Italian. While Kay pours a drink, she is shown in shallow focus, which again calls the viewer's attention to Michael, who is now standing and framed in the open doorway. When Kay looks back towards the office, a point-of-view shot aligns the spectator with her gaze as she witnesses two men kissing Michael's hand and recognizing him as the new godfather. As another man steps to the door and slowly closes it, the spectator remains momentarily positioned with Kay, and we are, like her, shut out of the inner workings of the mafia. However, Kay's permanent banishment is merely temporary for the viewer, as in the subsequent shot the camera is inside framing Kay, who looks on in disappointment. As the edge of the door crosses the screen, Kay gazes forlornly into a world to which she does not belong, and she is cut out – like Connie before her – from the Family Business.

During his sister's wedding, Michael suggests that the violent acts carried out by his family are not part of his identity ('That's my family Kay, not me.') However, in closing Kay out of his office, Michael asserts quite the opposite: 'This is my Family, Kay, not you.'

NOTE

1 Renate Siebert, *Secrets of Life and Death: Women and the Mafia*, trans. Liz Heron (New York: Verso, 1996), 13.

DANA RENGA

Much good work has been done on the allure of the fictional antihero in American serial television, especially since the premiere of *The Sopranos*.[1] The best-known recent American televisual mobster with ties to Italian criminality is undoubtedly Tony Soprano from the six-season blockbuster. The focal character is a mass of contradictions, both visually and emotionally: exceedingly violent yet loving and tender with his wife, children, and select girlfriends; racist and misogynistic but seeking enlightenment through psychotherapy; overweight, crass, and frequently slovenly, yet attractive to beautiful and smart women; a murderer of some of his closest friends and family, for whom he professed (and from whom he received) love, devotion, and loyalty. Such apparently antagonistic qualities mark Tony as a complex man marked by crisis, one of the growing number of morally contradictory characters populating small screens over the last two decades.[2]

The Sopranos marked a watershed in the representation of serial antiheroes. Amanda L. Lotz puts forward that *The Sopranos* advanced the 'template' for future premium programming and offered an important lesson that 'changed television creativity: the protagonist does not have to be a good man' – and, I would add, not even a conventionally good-looking man.[3] Chase stresses that James Gandolfini's physical attributes had nothing to do with his choice to cast him in the leading role. Instead, he always goes 'for the actor. If the actor who came in to read for [the] part had been Cary Grant and it had worked, I probably would've said fine. Let's do that.' He notes that they were blessed 'that James Gandolfini came through that door'.[4] Gandolfini was shocked to get the role, believing that HBO would 'have to hire some good-looking guy, not George Clooney, but some Italian George Clooney'.[5] Gandolfini's landing the part of Tony Soprano opened the floodgates for premium programs to cast actors in central roles with innovative physicalities – think of Bryan Cranston from *Breaking Bad*, and *House of Cards'* Kevin Spacey.

In the American tradition, this recent unconventional physical allure of the antihero can make the viewing process more engaging. This might be because some viewers, maybe many, are not immediately invited to sympathize with these men on the basis of their good looks, which opens up exciting opportunities for creating viewer alignment. At the same time, the unexceptional appearance of a character like Tony Soprano situates him as an American everyman, an ordinary guy who struggles with family, friends, finance, and mental and physical health, concerns also faced by many television viewers. Smith proposes that Tony Soprano is such an 'appealing, attractive murderer' because he is a 'regular guy' who has a 'moral code' and must negotiate the demands two families: both his immediate family and his symbolic mafia family.[6] Quite paradoxically then, a murderous mafioso is also defined by his ordinariness.

NOTES

1 See Alberto N. García, 'Moral Emotions, Antiheroes and the Limits of Allegiance,' in *Emotions in Contemporary TV Series*, ed. Alberto N. García (Basingstoke and New York: Palgrave Macmillan, 2016), 53.

2 For work on morally complex characters, see, Amanda D. Lotz, *Cable Guys: Television and Masculinities in the Twenty-First Century* (New York: NYU Press, 2014); Margrethe Bruun Vaage, *The Antihero in American Television* (New York and Oxford: Routledge, 2015); Jason Mittell, *Complex TV: The Poetics of Contemporary Television Storytelling* (New York: NYU Press, 2015).

3 Lotz, *Cable Guys*, 63.

4 Fresh Air, 'Gandolfini through the Eyes of Those He Worked With,' *Fresh Air*, 20 June 2013, accessed 7 October 2016, http://www.npr.org/2013/06/20/193865792/gandolfini-through-the-eyes-of-those-he-worked-with.

5 Dan Bischoff, *James Gandolfini: The Real Life of the Man Who Made Tony Soprano* (New York: St Martin's Press, 2014), 105.

6 Murray Smith, 'Just What Is It that Makes Tony Soprano Such an Appealing, Attractive Murderer?,' in *Ethics at the Cinema*, ed. Ward Jones and Samantha Vice (Oxford: Oxford University Press, 2011), 73–4.

DOM HOLDAWAY

In the episode 'Nobody Knows Anything,' (1.11) Meadow's denunciation of prostitution being a crime leads Tony Soprano to shift the problem into a family matter: 'I don't think sex should be a punishable offence either. But I do think talking about sex at the breakfast table is a punishable offence.' When Meadow pushes him, saying, 'It's the nineties, parents are supposed to discuss sex with their children,' his response is decisive: 'Yeah, that's where you're wrong. You see, out there it's the 1990s, but in this house it's 1954.'

The divide between the inside and the outside of the house, with its respective acceptances and repressions, encapsulates the tensions and ironies that regulate performances of gender throughout *The Sopranos*. In both of Tony's families, restrictive gender norms are constant and overbearing, to such an extent that the resultant crisis in his own masculinity becomes a driving force for the narrative.[1] Tony's ideal of masculinity is the 'strong, silent type' played by actors like Gary Cooper, as he tells Dr Melfi as early as the pilot, bemoaning the loss of this figure in a world of therapy and emotions. Yet ironically, the mobster's efforts to play this *role* – as much as to enforce the 'good' family behaviour that his cultural and ethnical norms dictate – is what has triggered his need for therapy in the first place.

Dr Melfi's office is one of the spaces where the rigidity of these norms can be broken down: she allows Tony to relive his Freudian dreams of losing his masculinity and failing to maintain the family, as well as his unexpected erotic fantasies. Here he can also break down the cultural and ethnic norms of his family role, so that he can create some emotional distance from his mother, understand his extramarital promiscuity, and articulate the hatred he sometimes feels for his son.

Rather than promoting the representations of gender that destabilize the 'Gary Cooper' monolith, however, *The Sopranos* constantly reminds us of the weight and inescapability of those norms. As the series progresses, Carmela undergoes a psychological liberation that frees her, temporarily, from Tony's patriarchy, yet ultimately this freedom proves false and the traditional family is reconstructed; when Vito Spatafore is outed and forced to flee, he finds a homosexual idyll and a firefighter boyfriend, but his peace is short-lived; and even though Tony learns to express his difficulty with Anthony Junior, this is rooted in his fear that his son is incapable of adhering to gender norms. As such, the series reiterates that, despite the social progress since 1954, the roots of gender repression are deep, and difficult to disinter.[2]

NOTES

1　See Brett Martin, *Difficult Men: Behind the Scenes of a Creative Revolution: From the Sopranos and the Wire to Mad Men and Breaking Bad* (London: Faber & Faber, 2013).
2　See Lynne Hibberd, 'Fucking Vito: Masculinity and Sexuality in *The Sopranos*,' in *The Handbook of Gender, Sexuality and Media*, ed. Karen Ross (Oxford: Wiley & Blackwell, 2012), 174–88.

ALBERTO ZAMBENEDETTI

In *The Sopranos*' opening sequence, Tony travels across four of the six zones that constitute 'what urban planners call a transect, a radial slice from city centre to edge that reveals a range of social and physical habitats.'[1] His ninety-six-second-westward displacement begins with him emerging from the Lincoln Tunnel, the outer limit of New York (the urban 'Core'), leaving behind the city's most iconic architectural markers: the Empire State building, the Statue of Liberty, and the World Trade Center, whose Twin Towers are seen as a gleaming reflection in the car's side mirror (a shot that was removed in the show's fourth season, after the 9/11 attacks). Tony continues on to the New Jersey Turnpike, traversing a landscape dotted with industrial buildings and smokestacks in the vicinity of Newark Airport (signified by an airplane flying overhead) and reaching the outskirts of an urban centre 'constructed from fragments of North Arlington, Harrison, and Kearny'[2] – the transect's 'Center.' One of the mob's dislocated headquarters, Kearny's fictional Satriale's Pork Store, also appears in the sequence – the other being Lodi's equally fictional strip club, Bada Bing! Moving away from the 'Center,' Tony's journey takes him past rows of single-family homes (the 'General'), until he finally arrives at his suburban McMansion in the affluent New Jersey borough of North Caldwell – a zone called the 'Edge.' *The Sopranos*' process of cultural and geographic emplacement begins with this sequence: Tony's homebound drive takes him across areas that function as 'the embodiment of America's environmentally challenged landscape.'[3] A transitional zone between the rural countryside and the urban town, the transect's Edge becomes a larger metaphor for Tony's affiliations: while on the surface the Soprano families (both the nuclear and the criminal) appear successfully integrated in their upper-middle-class American existence, they are in fact morally and legally alien to the community at large. Tony's secluded yet ostentatious home embodies this contradiction: both locus and location, the Sopranos' televisual residence exists only as a combination of exterior location shooting and interior soundstage production, carried out at Long Island City's Silvercup Studios in Queens, New York. Made legible by a process of mediated assembly, the Soprano McMansion is therefore connected to a larger tradition of TV Americans and their studio homes, whose missing fourth walls function as pop variations of Gordon Matta-Clark's anarchitecture – a project that enhanced the visibility of structures by underscoring (or even creating) voids, gaps, and holes: 'The New Jersey of *The Sopranos* is a place after the fall, but there is no indication that its fall has not always been taking place – that there ever could have been an Eden which only subsequently gave way to mass-culture ticky-tackiness.'[4] A garbage-filled, structurally decrepit suburban landscape whose specificity is predicated on the lack of notable landmarks, Sopranoville 'emerges as the metaphoric epicentre of contemporary America,' and its panic-stricken protagonist 'serves as an object lesson in the excesses of free market Capitalism, entrenched criminal interests, and wholesale political mismanagement run amuck.'[5] Adrift in the post-industrial transect, Tony's community finds its sea legs in its transatlantic Italian-ness, an affiliation that is both comforting and confining, protective and exclusionary, empowering and toxic. Ethnically tethered to a landscape where the most prominent features are highways and bridges, structures built to take one elsewhere, Tony Soprano collapses behind the wheel of his aptly named maroon(ed) 1999 Chevy Suburban, crashing it into a bollard – a short vertical post originally found on quays and used for the mooring of ships: 'Communities are always situated – always one place or another – and the particularities of place make for particularities in people.'[6] Economic growth becomes the only measure of success, and in its name the disembedding processes facilitated by global capital become an acceptable trade-in. When all else fails (family, ethnicity, psychiatry), upgrading to a pearl-white 2003 Cadillac Escalade ESV may be the only cure for the death of the American Dream – one that was manufactured in a plant in Silao, Mexico. As Theodore F. MacManus wrote in his famous 1915 advertisement for the Detroit automaker, it is 'The Penalty of Leadership.'

NOTES

1 Carl Abbott, "Jim Rockford or Tony Soprano: Coastal Contrasts in American Suburbia," *Pacific Historical Review* 83, no. 2 (2014): 6.
2 Abbot, 'Jim Rockford or Tony Soprano,' 5.
3 Gary R. Edgerton, *The Sopranos* (Detroit, MI: Wayne State University Press, 2013), 55.
4 Dana Polan, *The Sopranos* (Durham, NC: Duke University Press, 2009), 138.
5 Edgerton, *The Sopranos*, 57–8.
6 H. Peter Steeves, 'Dying in Our Own Arms,' in *The Sopranos and Philosophy: I Kill Therefore I Am*, ed. Richard Greene and Peter Vernezze (Chicago: Open Court, 2004), 113.

DOM HOLDAWAY

David Chase had little hope for the pilot episode of *The Sopranos*. The series appeared to be too risky, with an unusual mob story and an unlikely male lead, not to mention a very high expense for the cable network – the first series was set to cost around $30 million, in part due to the high costs of location shooting in New Jersey.[1] At the time, the writer was in talks with the producers of *The X-Files* to move to a writer/producer position for that series, should the seemingly inevitable happen, and meanwhile he insisted on directing the pilot of *The Sopranos*, in the hope of turning it into a one-off feature and moving permanently from television into the film industry.[2] Instead, the inevitable never happened, and at zero hour, days before the cast's contracts expired, HBO commissioned thirteen episodes for a first season.

It is not difficult to understand what appealed to HBO and to the critics who unanimously praised the series. 'The Sopranos' is incredibly rich and layered, full of the humour, drama, and allegorical imagery that would categorize the following six seasons. It embodied the kind of cinematic quality and complexity that was entirely compatible with HBO's rebranding at that time.[3]

The pilot opens with a long credits sequence, in the course of which a series of brief shots trace Tony's movement from New York City, down the New Jersey Turnpike, then across to the suburbia of North Caldwell, all over a blues soundtrack by Alabama 3. The movement thus inverts the famous opening sequence in Fellini's *La dolce vita* (1960) from the outskirts to the centre of Rome (Chase has spoken on many occasions of his appreciation of Fellini).[4]

The next shot is the now famous image of Tony framed between the legs of a naked statue in Dr Melfi's office. This image is the first of many seeds that Chase sows immediately, which return in the dialogue or photography much later in the narrative – in this case, the shot is reproduced with Carmela between the statue's legs in the third season (3.7, 'Second Opinion'). Thereafter we encounter many other small returning references – from the buried remains of Emil that return to haunt Christopher, to (mistaken) talk of a prophetic hit on Big Pussy, to Carmela's taunt that Tony will go to hell. Tony recalls this in the fifth season; she regrets it in the sixth, at the bedside of a comatose Tony, who has been shot by Junior – another event that is anticipated here, in the pilot's penultimate sequence.

And while the opening shot is a clear and entertaining metaphor for Tony's inability to relate to women and for his problems of repressed sexuality, without a doubt the episode's most significant and memorable symbol is the family of ducks. The departure of the birds causes Tony's first serious panic attack, inspiring Dr Melfi to interpret their presence in his pool as his love for his family. Of course, the constant duality the pilot establishes is that Tony leads not one but two families. The ducks thus make a vital initial contribution to the characterization of Tony: their disappearance represents his fear of losing control – an inability to maintain his family or to contribute adequately to 'the Family' during unstable times. And as revealed by the dream in which is he emasculated by a bird, his gender identity is at play in this, too. In essence, though, the simple happiness that Tony experiences when watching the ducks is a testament to his normality and simplicity – he is a 'sad clown,' as he describes himself to Melfi in the same episode. It is this that makes his character so appealing, no matter how unlikely a protagonist he may once have seemed.

NOTES

1 Peter Biskind, 'An American Family,' *Vanity Fair*, 4 April 2007, accessed 9 July 2017, http://www.vanityfair.com/news/2007/04/sopranos200704.
2 Ziyad Saadi, "'Sopranos' Creator David Chase Discusses the Unknown Facts of the Show and Its Infamously Ambiguous Finale," *IndieWire*, 2 May 2014, accessed 9 July 2017, http://www.indiewire.com/2014/05/sopranos-creator-david-chase-discusses-the-unknown-facts-of-the-show-and-its-infamously-ambiguous-finale-27145.
3 Cf. Mark Laverette, Brian L. Ott, and Cara L. Buckley, eds., *It's Not TV: Watching HBO in the Post-Television Era* (London: Routledge, 2008).
4 For instance in Biskind, 'An American Family,' online.

SEAN O'SULLIVAN

The most consequential eyeline match in the history of American television occurs forty-nine minutes into the fifth episode of the first season of *The Sopranos*. This shot follows one of the most notorious moments in an infamous hour of storytelling, immediately after Tony Soprano has garrotted a former mob informant whom he has discovered accidentally during a college tour with his daughter Meadow. As he wipes his hands, walking away from a brutally realistic scene of revenge, Tony hears sounds above him, slows to a stop, and looks up. The next image, reflecting his visual perspective, is of an array of ducks in flight, arranged in a V that may signal migration. At this point in the series, the presence of the ducks should trouble any viewer of the show, enough to wonder whether it is possible to go on watching *The Sopranos* – or, less hyperbolically, what it *means* to keep watching *The Sopranos* beyond this point.

We have been knee-deep in ducks since the pilot, when Dr Jennifer Melfi diagnosed Tony's melancholy at the disappearance of the birds from his backyard pool as symptomatic of an anxiety about losing his children as they grow up, an anxiety that has triggered the panic attacks that were the initial premise for the narrative. From the start, the show has made plausibility or verisimilitude its primary operational approach. Nothing, however, seems seriously to threaten the basic representational contract of the series – namely, that we are getting a world that operates on the same axes of likelihood as our own. The occurrence of these ducks, at this juncture, is therefore problematic. What are the odds that this species of bird should manifest itself at precisely the moment that Tony has committed a crime whose explanation would shatter the familial connections the ducks supposedly signify? If he tells Meadow what he has done, the bond they have established during this journey to New England will be irrevocably shattered. The ducks manifest what we might deem the heavy-handed design of the show's authors, for they require us to enter the realm of coincidence or the implausible, in a way that benefits the thematic correspondences of the show, but at the cost of the immersive fidelity promised by this story world on a weekly basis.

The solution, or really the explication, of this conundrum occurs a few scenes later, while Tony is waiting in a Bowdoin College hallway during Meadow's interview. On the wall is a quotation from *The Scarlet Letter* – 'No man can wear one face to himself and another to the multitude without finally getting bewildered as to which may be true.' That quotation is typically understood as a comment on Tony's hypocrisy, but that is the least interesting of its many ramifications. As an intertext, the quotation spells out that Tony is himself embarked on a version of *The Scarlet Letter* in the episode – he is the problematic husband Chillingworth, wandering off home base while his wife (Hester/Carmela) gets into sexual hot water with an inflamed priest (Dimmesdale/Father Phil). Beyond the plot parallel, however, there is the very genre of *The Scarlet Letter*. Nathaniel Hawthorne was always at pains to articulate his chosen field as the romance rather than the novel. As he wrote in the preface to *The House of the Seven Gables*: 'The book may be read strictly as a romance, having a great deal more to do with the clouds overhead than with any portion of the actual soil of the County of Essex.'[1] Or, in this case, the ducks overhead. We may have been thinking that *The Sopranos* is a novel – committed to some definable, trustworthy system of connections between the rules of our existence and those of the characters. But the ducks suggest that *The Sopranos* is a romance – one in which interior meaning, the indulgences of art, and the translation of experience into allegory are in fact the lingua franca. The answer, of course, is that from this point forward *The Sopranos* can and will proceed as both novel and romance, choosing between those traditionally opposed modes at whichever points it prefers. That doubled genealogy has prepared the way for the simultaneous precision and scope of the series. And, more narrowly, it has prepared the way for the most consequential missing eyeline match in the history of American television – the one we don't get at the very end of *The Sopranos*, when Tony looks up from the diner booth to see … something we never get. That great refusal – not only of information, but of confining the series to a single explanatory genre – is prepared for in the rural bestiary of Maine.

NOTE

1 Nathaniel Hawthorne, *The Complete Writings of Nathaniel Hawthorne*, vol. 7 (Boston, MA: Houghton, Mifflin, 1900), xxiv.

SEAN O'SULLIVAN

David Chase, the *capo di tutti capi* of *The Sopranos*, directed only two episodes of the series: the pilot and the finale. That restraint, for someone whose career ambitions for art cinema had been frustratingly rerouted to television, only reinforced his ubiquity as a showrunner – one of the first inhabitors of that title to be recognized as, in the twenty-first-century televisual landscape, an artist in the more traditional sense. Perhaps Chase's signature intervention into his own show came in the second season's 'Commendatori,' an episode that, like 'College' before it, allowed the series to leave home base to potentially rediscover itself – only to be brought back bitterly to the familiar. If in 'College' the discovery of the past during the trip came as a surprise, the voyage to Italy of 'Commendatori' is suffused from the start with the always already. The episode's first scene depicts the crew in the offices of the Bada Bing!, about to watch *The Godfather: Part II*, an obsessively canonical tale about which Tony can no longer banter: 'I can't do this again,' he says wearily. By contrast, Paulie is giddy at the opportunity to watch the sacred text through the new technology of DVD, and he eagerly asks Tony to name his favourite scene. The enthusiasm not only of rewatching but also of sharing a storytelling experience that solidifies the contours of ethnic identity meets quickly with the glitches of technology: the DVD fails to load, and Paulie is reduced to hitting the machine fruitlessly with his shoe. Expectation has careened into disappointment – a cautionary tale for all serial narratives.

Disappointment and its darker cousin, failure, are two of the great themes of *The Sopranos*, and that is where Chase comes in. The central tripartite emphasis of 'Commendatori' is on Tony, Paulie, and Chris's trip to Naples to develop and adjust business arrangements with their Camorra counterparts, on their turf. Chris announces that he has 'two definite agendas – hit the topless beaches, and see that fucking crater [Mount Vesuvius].' He spends the entire four days in a heroin haze in his hotel room, an object lesson in waste. Tony seems to have greater success navigating the maze of the Camorra, overcoming and then seeming to relish the shock of discovering a woman, Annalisa Zucca, in charge of the operations, in the wake of so many men imprisoned or assassinated – although that encounter too is laced with misunderstanding and regret. It is Paulie, single-minded in embracing his roots, who registers the most painful bathos, foiled as he is by the dogged insistence that he will find epiphany and transformation in Campania. 'Here they make it real,' he declares after they arrive; but of course the real is not what this ersatz Italian, with his preference for 'macaroni and gravy' and other derivations, can actually deal with. His gregariousness meets constant resistance, nowhere more vividly than at the Bar Neapolis, where he greets the neighbouring table of four men with a cheery 'Commendatori!' – the phrase of unctuous accommodation with which he was greeted at the hotel. The one man of those four who looks over at Paulie is in fact David Chase, in an uncredited cameo. The chilly opacity of his expression, which does not even deign to signal irritation before turning back to his companions, personifies the clinical coldness of *The Sopranos* itself, its commitment to diurnal alienation. The blank stare he delivers to Paulie's jovial bluster is of the real staring at the fake, the serious staring at the trivial, cinema staring down television. Even Paulie can feel the shock waves of that rejection, but he rallies on the return home to Newark, happily reporting that he 'felt right at home' in the old country – a declaration that underscores what may be *The Sopranos*' primary theme: self-deceit.

Tony's disappointment lives in a fancier cultural tax bracket than Paulie's. He has a sex dream about Annalisa, in which he is garbed as a centurion overlooking the Bay of Naples, and in the waking world she drives him to the cave of the Cumaean Sibyl. Tony projects Jennifer Melfi onto both Annalisa and the Sibyl as powerful Italian female erotic objects, although he tries to hide his desire with humour; when reading about the Sibyl's practice of delivering fates to ancient visitors while 'sit[ting] inside the cave inhaling gases,' he jokes, 'I think I dated this broad.' Annalisa responds as blankly to that line as Chase does to Paulie's welcome: sophistication does not care to recognize mere showmanship. The dissatisfactions of those two encounters speak to *The Sopranos*' perpetual anxiety about, and complete commitment to, the possibly doomed effort to lift television above its station.

CATHERINE O'RAWE

Michele Placido's film *Romanzo criminale* showcased to an international audience a new generation of male Italian stars, including Riccardo Scamarcio, Kim Rossi Stuart, Pierfrancesco Favino, Elio Germano, Claudio Santamaria, and the more established Stefano Accorsi, most whom had been working steadily for years prior to *Romanzo criminale*. The ensemble nature of that film was instrumental in foregrounding many of the features of current mainstream Italian cinema production: its emphasis on homosocial bonding, its turning towards the past – particularly the contested period of 1970s terrorism, the *anni di piombo* – and its use of charismatic male performers, often working together repeatedly.

The male ensemble cast in *Romanzo criminale* offers an interesting negotiation between the star performer and the character actor: familiar character actors like Toni Bertorelli, Massimo Popolizio, Antonello Fassari, and Stefano Fresi offer what Ernest Mathijs terms 'referential acting.' This system of acting, which he sees as typical of the ensemble, is 'based on archetypes, exemplary models or cliched stereotypes,' in this case on the well-established types of the gangster genre to which the film pays homage.[1] The 'unnoticeableness' and 'offbeat appearance' of the character actor,[2] who is unburdened by a star persona, intersects interestingly with the principal cast members, who are given a gritty retro glamour, visible even in the casting against type of then-boy-next-door Stefano Accorsi as the corrupt cop Scialoja.

The stars are given moments of 'spectacular acting,' in Paul McDonald's sense: these moments amplify audience 'awareness of the actor as signifier,' thus contributing to the vital 'differentiation [of star] from ensemble.'[3] So we see such acting set pieces as Freddo's (Kim Rossi Stuart) breakdown in the car on the way back from the Bologna bombing, a moment that serves as a turning point in his character's trajectory. A long close-up of his face as he drives is intercut with real footage of the rubble left by the Bologna bombing, and his restrained suffering is presented as an ethical model. To the star performers are attributed physically driven 'concentrated star moments':[4] Scamarcio as Il Nero gets a rock-soundtracked martial arts scene, and Santamaria emerges from his car swaggering to 'Shake Your Booty,' while Favino and Rossi Stuart play out an intense encounter in the scene where Freddo leaves the gang. Placido's penchant for these two-handed confrontations comes to a head in the scene where Scialoja interrogates Freddo about Bologna. The combination of long takes in long shot, with the camera circling around the static Freddo, and the closer two-shot that Freddo physically dominates, offers a neat actorly illustration of the film's view of the toxic collusion between state and criminals.

NOTES

1   Ernest Mathijs, 'Referential Acting and the Ensemble Cast,' *Screen*, 52, no. 1 (2011): 91.
2   Sarah Thomas, '"Marginal Moments of Spectacle": Character Actors, Cult Stardom and Hollywood Cinema,' in *Cult Film Stardom: Offbeat Attractions and Processes of Cultification*, ed. Kate Egan and Sarah Thomas (Basingstoke and New York: Palgrave Macmillan, 2013), 41, 49.
3   Paul McDonald, 'Spectacular Acting,' in *Acting and Performance in Moving Image Culture: Bodies, Screens, Renderings*, ed. Jörg Sternagel, Deborah Levitt, and Dieter Merschl (Bielefeld: Transcript Verlag, 2014), 63.
4   McDonald, 'Spectacular Acting,' 68.

DOM HOLDAWAY

Romanzo criminale is an interesting marker of its time. The story of the Banda della Magliana was first novelized and published by the magistrate-turned-author Giancarlo De Cataldo in 2002, before the film version (released in 2005) and a TV adaptation that ran for two seasons (2008–10). Though not strictly a transmedia story – the series and film are two different adaptations of the novel – the spread of the tale across different media is a testament both to the ongoing public fascination with some of Italy's most notorious gangsters and a snapshot of the changes in the media industry during the years in which that tale was released.

In fact, these three texts – novel, film, TV series – are significantly different from one another, first and foremost due to the different demands the various media impose on the narrative. The film is relatively liberal with its adaptation, following the main thrust of the story while introducing new symbolic elements. This includes the oneiric opening and closing sequences, in which we see the gangsters as 'innocent' boys, and the figure of Il Grana – absent from the book – who is killed by the police. The series is closer to the novel – for example, it begins with an identical incipit of Bufalo in present-day Magliana. It is also structured similarly: Season One narrates Part One, and Season Two covers the second and third parts in slightly fewer episodes. Yet there are differences here, too, such as inserted plot twists (Freddo's death), the expansion or exclusion of characters (e.g., Ranocchia, Conte Ugolino), and the restructuring of the narrative to suit an episodic drama (such as the dramatic shooting of Bufalo at the end of episode 2.3).

As Marta Boni has illustrated, the presence of *Romanzo criminale* in 'off-screen' media attests to an interesting contemporary tendency: the development of an autonomous narrative 'world' built through promotional material that is constantly changed and updated by predominantly digital remixers and fans.[1] An important factor in this process is the historical 'true story' of the Banda della Magliana. The ongoing fascination with these gangsters is evident in the various internet forums that trace the historical roots of the narrative (at present, this includes the Italian Wikipedia page for the series) and in the related films and books that continue to emerge (such as *La verità sta in cielo*, 2016), not to mention in the success of the TV series abroad. These tendencies have made of *Romanzo criminale* an important product that has left a clear mark on the Italian media industry, paving the way for series such as *Gomorra* and the current surge in Italian quality television.[2]

NOTES

1 Marta Boni, *Romanzo criminale: Transmedia and Beyond* (Venice: Edizioni Ca' Foscari, 2013).
2 See Massimo Scaglioni and Luca Barra, eds., *Tutta un'altra fiction. La serialità pay in Italia e nel mondo. Il modello Sky* (Rome: Carocci, 2013); and particularly Aldo Grasso, "Una serie poco italiana: *Romanzo criminale*," 97–99.

DANIELLE HIPKINS

There is something deliciously kitsch about the character of prostitute turned madam Patrizia. She mobilizes all the visual tropes of femininity as sign: as fragmented body (voyeuristic shots of her black lace suspenders) and reassuring phallus (a cigarette seductively dangling from her full red lips, red and white shimmering sheath dresses); as castrating woman (she bites Libanese's finger when he offers to buy her); as bleeding wound (towards the end of the film she is quite literally a 'car crash' figure of drunken abjection); as woman as duplicity (is her name Patrizia or Cinzia?); and as signifier of mystery, interiority, vulnerability, inviting male penetration (the brief porn shot of a woman's looming vagina immediately precedes Scialoja's rifling through her drawers, and shortly thereafter Patrizia becomes the weakest link, his way into the gang). As prostitute, these clichés are further reinforced as she lurches from narrative incarnation as Gold Digger (in her first appearance we see her take money off Dandy no less than four times, money that she then spends on lingerie, allowing Scialoja his attempt to break into the gang's trafficking) to Martyr of the Love Story (this reaches its emotional orgasm of suffering to the yearning crescendo of The Pretenders' 'I Go to Sleep' – only the music tells us she is dangerously in love with Scialoja).[1]

Furthermore, and most significantly, she becomes the object of homosocial exchange that excuses the moral and political ambiguities of 1970s Italy (Scialoja and Dandy displace recognition of their own role as pawns in a larger political picture over her wretched, drunken body). What are we to make of the casting of Anna Mouglalis in this key role as an overdetermined signifier, and what can this tell us about the film's gender representation? On the one hand, this male melodrama works, like its lead character Libanese, 'to craft a homosocial community'.[2] Even the voiceover commentary between author De Cataldo and director Placido uses Mouglalis to oil the wheels of homosocial relations as they joke about her beauty and her breasts. The male characters resonate with Roman authenticity, rooted in their memories of boyhood that bookend the film, replete, as O'Rawe suggests, with 'gender melancholy'.[3] Patrizia, like so many prostitutes, appears instead to come from nowhere, as mere cipher. In fact Mouglalis is French, with a Greek father, hardly a recognizable Italian star, but rather a haughty Mediterranean beauty, her otherworldly glamour juxtaposed with Jasmine Trinca's girl-next-door character of Roberta. Her dubbed voice puts her at one remove from the action; it is sugary and soapy in its modality, expressing a non-accented identity that dislocates her from the discourse of *borgata* authenticity that characterizes the male characters. Yet this points to the rub that remains endlessly fascinating in terms of the alienating narratives that patriarchy creates for women on screen: there is still a flesh-and-blood actor in this performance. What is compelling about Mouglalis's performance of these clichés is that while it projects the detachment and the world-weariness of the cynical Gold Digger whose heart gets broken despite herself, the excesses of this role come to signify more than the role itself. If Patrizia is the ground upon which the men play out their fantasies of power and desire for one another, her boredom with the whole affair collapses into the actress's boredom with her narrative disembodiment. This leaves a post-feminist residue, as Patrizia's ironic distance from the hyperbolic plots of masculinity creates a very contemporary awareness that this retrosexual performance is precisely that: fantasy.

NOTES

1 These three archetypes of prostitution are identified by Russell Campbell in *Marked Women: Prostitutes and Prostitution in the Cinema* (Madison, WI: University of Wisconsin Press, 2006)
2 Dana Renga, '*Romanzo criminale* as Male Melodrama: "It Is in Reality Always too Late,"' in *Italian Political Cinema: Public Life, Imaginary, and Identity in Contemporary Italian Film*, ed. Giancarlo Lombardi and Christian Uva (Bern: Peter Lang, 2016), 377.
3 Catherine O'Rawe, *Stars and Masculinities in Contemporary Italian Cinema* (New York: Palgrave, 2014), 102.

DOM HOLDAWAY

Beginning in the mid-1970s, the action of *Romanzo criminale* concludes at the end of the 1980s, as is confirmed via a diegetic news report on the fall of the Berlin Wall. This period partly overlaps with an extremely tense and violent moment in Italian history: the *anni di piombo*, or 'leaden years.' From the late 1960s to the late 1980s, Italy was afflicted by a series of terrorist attacks, including deadly bombings in Milan and Bologna and the infamous assassinations of policemen, politicians, and journalists. To this day the events are as infamous and traumatic as they are unresolved; false claims of responsibility and political cover-ups have cast an impenetrable shadow over the truths behind this violence.

As the case of the Berlin Wall indicates, the film occasionally uses news footage to signpost historical coordinates. Other examples include the assassination attempt on Pope John Paul II and the 1982 World Cup. This is true of certain significant events of the *anni di piombo*, too, specifically the assassination of Aldo Moro and the bombing of the Bologna railway station (scenes that are analysed elsewhere in this volume). However, the references to terrorism serve as more than temporal markers; they also make a complex contribution to the narrative, insofar as the Banda della Magliana is implicated in these historical events.

Key to the gang's involvement are two mysterious peripheral characters: Carenza, the agent who helps Il Libanese avoid a prison sentence, and his boss, 'Il Vecchio,' both somehow connected to the state and seemingly acting on higher political instructions. To repay their debt, the gang members begin to carry out their orders: for instance, they search for Aldo Moro, and they kill the perpetrator of the Bologna bombing. In each case, however, the Banda never learns the real purpose or aim – its members are mere puppets of a faceless political machine. The moment of Il Nero's death is indicative: he is sent on a mission by Il Dandi to assassinate a Milanese banker on behalf of the Banda's 'friends' – the gangsters intimate that those friends are members of a Masonic lodge, likely a representation of the infamous 'P2' – but the mission backfires when a security guard shoots and mortally wounds Il Nero. Though the assassin calls his victim by a different name ('Signor Danconi'), thereby fictionalizing the account, the turn of events nonetheless recalls the attempted murder of Milanese banker Roberto Rosone and thus partly implicates the Banda in the historical event.

Through this careful semi-fictionalization, *Romanzo criminale* immerses itself in a historical narration of the *anni di piombo*. As O'Rawe has noted, the film employs genre iconography and a lively soundtrack in order to foreground its 'constructed-ness.'[1] Nevertheless, as consciously

partial and *possible* elements of an account that remains deliberately incomplete, this same artifi-
ciality ultimately serves its own political aim: to remind the viewer that the knots of Italian history
remain, to this day, very firmly bound.

NOTE

1 Catherine O'Rawe, 'More More Moro: Music and Montage in *Romanzo Criminale*,' *The Italianist* 29, no. 2
(2009): 214–26.

77 *Romanzo criminale*: Scene Analysis – The Aldo Moro Kidnapping

CATHERINE O'RAWE

The scene in *Romanzo criminale* juxtaposing footage of the March 1978 kidnapping **of** Christian Democrat leader Aldo Moro with the Banda della Magliana's celebration of their control over Rome's drug trade is, at first glance, an example of the retro pleasures typical of the gangster genre. Indeed, the song that plays in the club as the gang members seal their homosocial bond is LaBelle's 'Lady Marmalade,' used to similar effect in De Palma's *Carlito's Way* (1993) to track Al Pacino's character's rise to underworld power.

Yet as I have discussed elsewhere, the incongruity of the juxtaposition between the hedonistic 1970s disco culture and the great tragedy of Italy's *anni di piombo* exposes the complexity of the film's treatment of masculinity and its turn to the 1970s.[1] On one level, the nightclub is merely one of the genre's typical 'transgressive spaces' that 'breach the civil space with the uncivil, the world of law and order with vice and corruption.'[2] The film's retro style – its attention to clothing, hair, music, cars, mise en scène – can be read as pure pastiche, as belonging to the 'retro mode,' critiqued by Fredric Jameson for its 'pseudo-historical depth.'[3] But on another level, the celebrating male gangsters, embracing one another and posing for photos, enact a nostalgia for a type of 1970s vernacular masculinity. If we read the gangster genre as a 'male-addressed costume drama,'[4] it becomes easier to see the connection between the gang's homosocial bonding and the patriarchal crisis of the 1970s represented by the death of the Father (Moro). The iconic Polaroid of Moro in the Red Brigade prison that is intercut with the nightclub scene is itself a reminder of the network of occluded homosocial relations at the heart of Italy's corrupt political system, made further evident in subsequent scenes in which the gang tracks down Moro and is then told by the state to 'forget about it.'

In addition, the violence inflicted upon Moro and his police escort, alluded to in the photo and brief footage of the aftermath of the bloody kidnapping, stands in for the continuum along which violence operated in the 1970s, from the gang's beatings and murders to the revolutionary violence of the left and the state's alliance with right-wing terrorists. As such, the scene draws upon the 'intersection of violence, pain, sexuality and male bonding' at the heart of gangster narratives to interpellate masculinity as the dark heart of Italy's 1970s.[5]

NOTES

1 Catherine O'Rawe, 'More More Moro: Music and Montage in *Romanzo criminale*,' *The Italianist* 29 (2011): 214–26.

2 Ron Wilson, *The Gangster Genre* (New York: Wallflower, 2015), 19.

3 Cited in Esther Sonnet and Peter Stanfield, "'Good Evening Gentlemen; Can I Check Your Hats Please?'": Masculinity, Dress, and the Retro Gangster Cycles of the 1990s,' in *Mob Culture: Hidden Histories of the American Gangster Film*, ed. Lee Greiveson, Esther Sonnet, and Peter Stanfield (Oxford: Berg, 2005), 163–84, 175.

4 Sonnet and Stanfield, "'Good Evening Gentlemen; Can I Check Your Hats Please?," 166.

5 Gaylyn Studlar, 'A Gunsel Is Being Beaten: Gangster Masculinity and the Homoerotics of the Crime Film, 1941–1942,' in *Mob Culture*, ed. Greiveson, Sonnet, and Stanfield, 120–45, 124.

ALAN O'LEARY

Robert Rosenstone, the most influential contemporary writer on cinema and history, has categorized as follows the three types of 'serious' history films. These are the dramatic feature film, the documentary film, and what Rosenstone calls the opposition or innovative historical film, which distinguishes itself from 'mainstream drama' by foregrounding its own construction.[1] The problem with Rosenstone's categorization is twofold. Firstly, it is evaluative rather than descriptive, with Rosenstone's preference plainly being for films of the third type. Second, it can be difficult in practice to distinguish between Rosenstone's three types, something demonstrated by the Bologna station bombing sequence in *Romanzo criminale*.

In this complex sequence, 'il Freddo,' one of the film's gangster protagonists, witnesses the terrible aftermath of the historical bombing of 2 August 1980, when eighty-five people died and more than two hundred were injured. The three-minute sequence mixes time periods and perspectives, intercutting Il Freddo's arrival, the bombing, and his witnessing of the rubble and victims with scenes of him driving and apparently remembering the event. It also shows the retrieval and assassination (by a neo-fascist associate of Il Freddo's criminal gang) of an unidentified character we presume to be the bomber, and it interpolates images from protest marches that took place in Bologna following the bombing. Diegetic sound is initially accompanied by the ambient electronic score employed throughout the film, then by a sombre melody on piano and violin and by fragments of angry speeches from the protest marches. The sequence features a frankly artificial rendition of the explosion itself (the wrong wing of the station is blown up, and an elliptical jump cut just before the explosion insists on the artefactual character of the film being viewed). The sequence also employs upsetting footage from the hours following the explosion, formatted to the film's widescreen aspect ratio, showing the bodies of victims, the rubble, and the clear-up after the bombing. In three brief shots, Kim Rossi Stuart's face and body seem to be superimposed upon this archival footage in a manner that recalls techniques used in *Forrest Gump*. The archival footage may or may not already be familiar to the viewer of *Romanzo criminale* (it is available online and is sometimes shown on Italian television), but the cruder film stock, quite distinct from the saturated or chiaroscuro colour schemes of the rest of the film, will be noticeable to all. In other words, no attempt is made to disguise the insertion of actual material into the 'fiction.' And there is a further layer of complexity: the pictures of Rossi Stuart wandering in the rubble are not, in fact, treated versions of the original footage, but are restaged, filmed, and treated to resemble the archival material.[2]

Romanzo criminale is a genre film, a mainstream dramatic feature; but its foregrounded mixture of fiction, speculation, reconstruction, and documentary archive signals a reflexive inquiry into the means of historical understanding. This description of the Bologna sequence suggests that no sharp or evaluative division can be drawn between Rosenstone's three types of history film.

NOTES

1 Robert Rosenstone, *History on Film/Film on History*, 2nd ed. (Harlow: Longman/Pearson, 2006), 14–19.
2 See the making-of featurette on Warner Home Video DVD release (2005).

ELENA PAST

In *Gomorra*'s dramatic opening scenes, the homosocial spaces of the Camorra crime syndicate are performative and gender-bending. In the hyper-real opening shots, muscular strongmen tan themselves and get manicures in a group grooming outing, until they are massacred by rival clan members. Scenes featuring Totò, the young Camorra recruit, show that part of his initiation ritual involves training in Camorra aesthetics: on a shopping trip with more seasoned *camorristi*, he tries on basketball jerseys and admires himself in a mirror; in another scene, a close-up catches him plucking his eyebrows. The impulsive Marco and Ciro dance and play together in a relationship that is both tragically juvenile and homoerotic.

Missing from *Gomorra*, however, are the homosocial foodscapes of *The Godfather* or *Goodfellas*, places where men cook, eat, and discuss recipes together: in the brutal world of the Camorra, there are no cannoli. Instead, people gather around kitchen tables to package pills for sale on the streets; blenders cut lethal combinations of cocaine or heroin; and ripe peaches are not nourishing, but rather potentially contaminated by dioxins and other contaminants leached from the toxic soil.[1] Rather than reconstruct a traditional if entirely male (and entirely dysfunctional) nuclear family, in *Gomorrah* the Camorra builds a family of neoliberal managers and consumers whose 'upbringing' indoctrinates them into the crime syndicate's market logic. Here, unlike in the mafia *cosca*, which Jane and Peter Schneider describe as 'an exclusively male localized sodality,' women are neither particularly welcome nor categorically excluded. Although men dominate all five of the interlaced story lines, women carry guns, chauffeur people to secessionist meetings, and help traffic drugs. The Camorra's logic of profit excludes no willing partner in crime and in this *Gomorra* reflects the reality of the Neapolitan crime syndicate.[2]

Yet for this reason, two kitchens in the film stand out, offering hospitable, if fleeting, alternatives to Camorra cultures from the margins: domestic space seems to open the possibility of interethnic exchange and female solidarity. One is the fluorescent kitchen of a Chinese factory boss, where the tailor Pasquale is introduced to his hosts' native cuisine and offered a sartorial teaching gig. The other space, more significant when considering gender, is the sun-streaked kitchen in the Vele apartment complex where Maria prepares food and coffee for a crowd of neighbourhood women and children. In this cheerful domestic landscape, the hand-held camerawork, angst-inspiring elsewhere in the film, becomes intimate; the mise en scène is cluttered with refrigerator magnets and overflowing countertops; the soundtrack features laughter and mingled female voices; and the doors are unlocked. However, when Maria's secessionist son exposes her to the brutality of

Camorra retaliation, she begins locking her door, stops inviting people in for coffee, and finally is murdered on her doorstep. The momentary possibility of domestic hospitality is thus swiftly and tragically undermined, revealing that Camorra violence makes no exceptions for age or gender.

NOTES

1 For more on food and dining in Camorra films, see Boylan on 'Toxic Tables' in this volume.
2 For more on gender in the Camorra, see Gabriella Gribaudi, 'Donne di camorra e identità di genere,' 145–54; Anna Maria Zaccaria, 'L'emergenza rosa: Dati e suggestioni sulle donne di camorra,' *Meridiana* 67 (2010): 155–73.

ALBERTO ZAMBENEDETTI

'The World Is Yours,' recites the blimp flying above Tony Montana's luxurious waterfront duplex in Brian De Palma's *Scarface* (1983); the same tag line appears on a flashing billboard advertising 'Cook's Tours' in Howard Hawks's 1932 original. Consonantly with the remake's cultural and spatial relocation, the message is taken to the skies by a Pan Am aircraft – a globalist technological amplification would ring rang hollow following the company's 1991 demise. The gangster genre is predicated on intertextuality and augmentation: Hawks himself had built upon Joseph von Sternberg's *Underworld* (1927), in which the advertisement for 'A.B.C. Investment Co.' states that 'The City Is Yours' – a much more localized goal for the aspiring crime lord. Matteo Garrone's post-9/11 anti-gangster *Gomorra* adds several degrees of (trans)cultural ventriloquism to this formula. Donning the same red Hawaiian shirt as the protagonist, Marco re-enacts scenes from De Palma's film, egged on by an admiring Ciro – both a participant and an intratextual spectator who evaluates his friend's performance. Yet the Neapolitan wannabe gangster's wheezy voice retrieves lines from the Italian version of *Scarface*, in which Pacino's wobbly Cuban accent is replaced by Ferruccio Amendola's richly modulated Roman tenor. The regional realignment produced by the dubbing is 'a form of re-localization, by which (foreign) cultural depictions of ethnic groups are translated, adapted, and modified to fit a new set of (domestic) cultural stereotypes.'[1] In this light, *Gomorra*'s many meta-cinematic references pivot around two complementary discourses: first, they exemplify Genettian transtextuality, a precise narratological framework that includes quotation, plagiarism, and allusion – in this category are the direct references, from Federico Fellini's *La Dolce Vita* (1960) to Martin Scorsese's *Mean Streets* (1973). Second, they foreground Michael Riffaterre's holistic view of intertextuality, whereby 'the reader's perception of the relations between a text and all the other texts that have preceded of followed it'[2] not only accommodates industrial variables like dubbing and international distribution but also rests on reception. In fact, Amendola's voicework connects *Gomorra* to a vast network of signification that includes *The Godfather* trilogy (via Al Pacino) but also Robert De Niro in *Taxi Driver* (Martin Scorsese, 1976) and Brian De Palma's *The Untouchables*. Hollywood is itself a polysemy: as a place, it is both the centre of the American studio system and a villa in Casal di Principe belonging to a Camorra boss who 'wanted the *Scarface* villa, exactly as it was in the movie.'[3] But it is also a porous cultural agent that, historically, has both learned from and contributed to the creation of the gangster lifestyle by providing organized crime with an infectious iconography: 'Camorristi look to the movies to create for themselves a criminal image they often lack.'[4]

NOTES

1 Chiara Francesca Ferrari, *Since When Is Fran Drescher Jewish? Dubbing Stereotypes in the Nanny, the Simpsons, and the Sopranos* (Austin, TX: University of Texas Press, 2010), 3.
2 Robert Stam, Robert Burgoyne, and Sandy Flitterman-Lewis, *New Vocabularies in Film Semiotics: Structuralism, Post-Structuralism, and Beyond* (London: Routledge, 1992), 204.
3 Roberto Saviano, *Gomorrah* (New York: Farrar, Straus and Giroux, 2007), 251.
4 Ibid., 245.

MONICA SEGER

Set in and around the Scampia neighbourhood north of Naples, *Gomorra* only ever skirts the city proper, privileging instead the sub- or even ex-urban realms of housing complexes, abandoned construction sites, open quarries, and more. All of these locations appear neglected and forgotten even when inhabited, leading to a certain 'edgelands' effect – minus much of the nature implicit in that term. They are dirty, with surfaces bare and crumbling, and are filmed in heavily shadowed natural light, and often though not always feature just a few actors at a time. Yet there is something so distinctly urban in feeling about many of these locations: a sense of close proximity to other people despite their lack of visual presence on screen; of living intimately with distinctly unnatural and perhaps even toxic matter; of being confined by cement and never fully escaping the view of the collective. Above all, a feeling of constant surveillance, a sense that others might pop out of the shadows at any time, marks space as somehow urban in *Gomorra*, while also contributing to the film's general narrative of social precarity.

Surveillance is communicated largely through what Pierpaolo Antonello refers to in this volume as Garrone's 'obsessive camerawork' (296), marked by a highly mobile shooting technique as well the director's deft framing of Scampia's blunt architecture. This is no truer than in scenes of the Vele housing project around which much of the film's action occurs. Constructed between 1962 and 1975, the 'Sails of Scampia,' a real-life centre for heavy drug trafficking, form an urban grid above ground. Massive buildings shaped rather like modernist pyramids, the Vele are blockish in the extreme, each floor ringed by an exposed narrow walkway and each building scisioned down the middle by an interior courtyard filled with sharply zigzagged stairwells. They read here as the ultimate panopticon; Garrone's camera is the unobserved yet all-seeing eye that typifies such a structure.

While Garrone often films in close-up on characters, he accents his work with the occasional wide-angle shot of the Vele as a whole, allowing the estate to function as a cinematic character unto itself, a living and perhaps responsible agent for the action it hosts. This is captured well towards the film's end. In a rite of initiation, thirteen-year-old Totò calls his adult neighbour Maria out to her building's interior courtyard and then walks swiftly away as she is gunned down from behind. The camera immediately cuts to a wide-angle shot of the neighbourhood, two Vele buildings in the foreground with other apartment complexes peeking out in the background. Viewers note the many bodies moving in the centre of the frame – those on the walkway where Maria has just been shot but also, more prominently, those leaning over a rooftop balcony a floor or two above. They are small as ants but in constant motion, parallel to a line of cars just barely visible in a far right of the frame. This is *Gomorra*'s urban space, simultaneously vast and miniature and always under view.

ALBERTO ZAMBENEDETTI

If gangster movies have taught us anything, it is that grooming is an inherently unsafe activity for members of a criminal organization. The baptism/murder scene that bookends *The Godfather* contains two deaths staged as a 'barber shop hit,' a sensational and gruesome public execution that occurred as much in real life as it did on the screen. As Dana Renga observed, 'the metacinematic nature of the mafia movie genre and the mafioso's obsession with on-screen mobsters'[1] make this relationship a particularly porous one. For example, in Alberto Lattuada's *Mafioso* an unsuspecting Alberto Sordi is flown especially from Sicily to New York to perform a hit that strongly recalls the spectacular assassination of boss Umberto 'Albert' Anastasio, who was ambushed by two gunmen in the barber shop of Manhattan's Park Central Hotel in 1957. Despite its director's efforts to update the genre, *Gomorra* is no exception to this rule. The film opens with a graphic hit at a tanning parlour, an indication that early-twenty-first-century metrosexuality has infiltrated even the most callous expression of violent masculinity, the gun-toting mobster. Bathed in blue UV light, these manicured criminals possess none of the panache of their pinstriped ancestors, whose blood would have been spilled on reclined leather chairs and hot towels, not on the plastic walls of rented tanning booths. As *Gomorra* makes salient, the ritual may seem the same, but the social and cinematic conditions under which it is performed have radically shifted. When Totò goes shopping with his higher-ups, the young recruit settles for a sleeveless shirt similar to those worn by the elderly mobsters who kill Marco and Ciro in the final scene. Hardly an elegant garment, these shirts are decorated with generic references to foreign sports heroes and teams; they are counterfeited signifiers of a global economy of which organized crime is a driving force, as we learn in the film's postscript. Adolescence awakens in Totò the need to groom, which he channels through his desire to pierce his perfectly tweezed eyebrows, but much as with the tanning parlour dead, his career will consist of a slow rise through the ranks of a 'sweaty, dirty, badly dressed, overweight, unhealthy'[2] gangster underclass whose idea of fashion corresponds to a fake tan and an excessive amount of jewellery. The models are not George Bancroft, Edward G. Robinson, James Cagney, Paul Muni, or Al Pacino as Michael Corleone; in their armed wanderings 'Marco and Ciro act out the famous sequence from De Palma's'[3] 1982 version of *Scarface*, in which Pacino dons a variety of garish attires that exemplify how affluence does not beget taste. Gone are the wide-brim fedoras, tommy guns, and their drum magazines. In their place are beach sandals, tighty-whities, and assault weapons.

NOTES

1 Dana Renga, *Unfinished Business: Screening the Italian Mafia in the New Millennium* (Toronto: University of Toronto Press, 2013), 145.
2 Pierpaolo Antonello, 'Dispatches from Hall: Matteo Garrone's *Gomorrah*,' in *Mafia Movies: A Reader*, ed. Dana Renga (Toronto: University of Toronto Press, 2011), 383.
3 Renga, *Unfinished Business*, 146.

ALBERTO ZAMBENEDETTI

'Now you are a man,' remarks the gunman who initiates young Totò into a life of crime within the Camorra ranks. One shot point-blank to the chest and you are in, provided you can withstand the fear of facing the barrel of a gun while wearing a bulletproof vest. Totò emerges from the cave where the ritual is officiated like Jonah from the belly of the fish, except to spread pain and suffering, not to bring salvation to the people of Nineveh. Naturally, this plunge into physical and moral darkness affects the nature of the boy's daily deliveries: from groceries to drugs to lead, with his friend Maria being the first victim of his coming-of-age. Whether a silent observer or an active agent of the criminal organization, the child is 'a character involved in the drama on screen and, at the same time, a proxy for the viewer,'[1] as Giovanna De Luca argued.

This double function is articulated by a mobile point-of-view shot of Totò entering the cave and approaching the ceremonial vest. Symbolically robed by a figure in silhouette, the boy and the floating camera eye resemble more Plato's slaves than the enlightened prophet. In fact, almost all of Le Vele's inhabitants are caught in the same predicament: kept in the dark by the Camorra's ubiquitous reach, they live facing the back of cave, where only the shadows of reality are visible to them. In this analogy, criminal apprentice Roberto is the freed prisoner whose eyes slowly grow accustomed to seeing the world for what it really is and who rejects the organization's material seductions – a posture Roberto Saviano has taken with his exposé. Unlike the character, the writer returned to the cave via his literature, only to be met with threats of violence, as Socrates had predicted would happen to the enlightened slave attempting to free his peers. In this respect, replacing the Second World War's cataclysmic exceptionality with the quotidian struggle against the Camorra's oppression, Totò's character certainly recalls the many children of neorealist cinema, those 'active participants who have been transformed by traumatic experiences.'[2] Seen thusly, the initiation scene's grimness is balanced between the devastating ending of the Naples episode in Roberto Rossellini's *Paisan* (1946) and the stylized philosophy lessons of Bernardo Bertolucci's *The Conformist* (1970). Dana Renga notes that 'Totò is on the way to passing through the Lacanian mirror stage';[3] if this is true, then the symbolic contraption allowing his apperception is neither the mirror nor the cinematic apparatus, but tattered military equipment fallen off the back of the proverbial truck, perhaps one driven by a child on his way back from a quarry filled with barrels of toxic waste, a byproduct of global capital.

NOTES

1 Giovanna De Luca, 'Seeing Anew: Children in Italian Cinema, 1944 to the Present,' in *The Italian Cinema Book*, ed. Peter Bondanella (London: BFI, 2014), 101.
2 Ibid., 101.
3 Dana Renga, *Unfinished Business: Screening the Italian Mafia in the New Millennium* (Toronto: University of Toronto Press, 2013), 139.

MONICA SEGER

Gomorra's last scene is as brutal as it is mundane in its final reminder that lives are disposable under the Camorra. Set at an abandoned beach resort, it depicts the entrapment and murder of Marco and Ciro ('Sweet Pea'), two cocky *Scarface*-obsessed teens whose plotline resurfaces throughout the episodic film. Brief but shot in real time, the scene serves as a study in contrast. Soft, natural light and pastel colours of the beach at dusk, a score composed almost entirely of ambient noise, and the stoic gazes of all in-scene actors are paired against the frenetic energy of surveillance, as crystallized by an ever-moving camera. The end result is an edgy melancholy, the sense that naive young men like Marco and Ciro – who have just attempted to pull one over on local mob bosses – are doomed from the start.

The scene opens as Marco and Ciro arrive at the beach on a motorcycle, quickly dismounting to hop over a sandy embankment. They move along the top of empty cabanas in the distance, blurry and washed out by sunlight, as the camera focuses on a hidden observer in the foreground, one of many. The boys then peer out from behind a low wall, Ciro on hands and knees and Marco leaning over him with the intimacy of fear. The latter grips his friend's shoulder so tightly that he pulls Ciro's shirt, revealing taught muscle underneath and a palpable vulnerability. The film then moves to its end, alongside Marco and Ciro's lives, as the boys suddenly stumble back and attempt to pull out their guns. Garrone's mobile camera pans to show two full-bellied men in beach attire rushing forward, shooting at close range, and the action is over almost as soon as it begins. The men turn calmly away as the camera makes a wide rotation behind them to finally reveal the ocean in the background and more collaborators approaching one by one. The assailants load the boys' inert bodies into an approaching bulldozer as 'Uncle Vittorio' appears on a roof and congratulates his men on a job well done.

Making a final sweep out towards the ocean, the camera lingers over the horizon line, ever darker in the setting sun, as the bulldozer moves slowly off to screen left, its clanking sound growing louder. Rather than a shot of individual protagonists, viewers are left with an impression of place and culture – business as usual moving steadily forward. The screen cuts to black, but Garrone is not quite done: his closing scene of local brutality is then punctuated, before the credits roll, by a series of statements in plain white text. Presented as fact (though no sources are credited) they link pan-European mob killings with Scampia's drug trade, environmental toxicity, and large-scale global business such as the rebuilding of New York's Twin Towers. With this final blow, viewers move beyond dismay over the local Camorra activities, such as the killing of a boy called 'Sweet Pea,' to horror at the organization's transnational reach.

Filmography

American Mafia Movies

The Black Hand (Wallace McCutcheon, 1906)
The Lure of the Gown (D.W. Griffith, 1908)
In Little Italy, The Cord of Life, At the Alter (D.W. Griffith, 1909)
The Italian Barber (D.W. Griffith, 1910)
The Adventures of Lieutenant Petrosino (Sydney M. Goldin, 1912)
Little Caesar (Mervyn LeRoy, 1931)
The Public Enemy (William A. Wellman, 1931)
Scarface (Howard Hawks, 1932)
Black Hand (Richard Thorpe, 1950)
The Brothers Rico (Phil Karlson, 1957)
The Untouchables (TV Series, 1959–63)
Pay or Die (Richard Wilson, 1960)
The Brotherhood (Martin Ritt, 1968)
The Godfather (Francis Ford Coppola, 1972)
Mean Streets (Martin Scorsese, 1973)
The Godfather: Part II (Francis Ford Coppola, 1974)
Capone (Steve Carver, 1974)
Cotton Club (Francis Ford Coppola, 1984)
Prizzi's Honor (John Huston, 1985)
Wise Guys (Brian De Palma, 1986)
Crime Story (TV Series, 1986–8)
The Untouchables (Brian De Palma, 1987)
The Sicilian (Michael Cimino, 1987)
Things Change (David Mamet, 1988)
Married to the Mob (Jonathan Demme, 1988)
Goodfellas (Martin Scorsese, 1990)
Men of Respect (William Reilly, 1990)
The Godfather: Part III (Francis Ford Coppola, 1990)
My Blue Heaven (Herbert Ross, 1990)
The Freshman (Andrew Bergman, 1990)

Mobsters (Michael Karbelnikoff, 1991)
A Bronx Tale (Robert DeNiro, 1993)
Romeo is Bleeding (Peter Medak, 1993)
Casino (Martin Scorsese, 1995)
The Funeral (Abel Ferrara, 1996)
Bound (Andy and Larry Wachowski, 1996)
The Undertaker's Wedding (John Bradshaw, 1997)
Donnie Brasco (Mike Newell, 1997)
Bella Mafia (TV, David Greene, 1997)
The Last Don (TV Mini-Series, 1997)
Suicide Kings (Peter O'Fallon, 1997)
Jane Austen's Mafia! (Jim Abrahams, 1998)
Mickey Blue Eyes (Kelly Mokin, 1999)
Analyze This (Harold Ramis, 1999)
Dinner Rush (Bob Giraldi, 2000)
Boss of Bosses (TV, Dwight H. Little, 2001)
Friends and Family (Kristen Coury, 2001)
Analyze That (Harold Ramis, 2002)
This Thing of Ours (Danny Provenzano, 2003)
Find Me Guilty (Sydney Lumet, 2006)
The Departed (Martin Scorsese, 2006)
The Sopranos (TV, David Chase, 1999–2007)
Beantown (Timothy Norman, 2007)
Journal of a Contract Killer (Tony Maylam, 2008)
Boardwalk Empire (TV, 2010–14)
Mob Wives (TV, 2011–16)
Eurocrime! The Italian Cop and Gangster Movies That Ruled the '70s (Mike Malloy, 2012)
Killing Them Softly (Andrew Dominik, 2012)
The Family (Luc Bresson, 2013)
Live By Night (Ben Affleck, 2016)
Gotti (Kevin Connolly, 2018)

Italian Mafia Movies

Kri e la mano nera (1913)
Maciste il terrore dei banditi (Luigi Romano Borgnetto and Vicenzo Denizot, 1915)
In nome della legge (Pietro Germi, 1949)
Turri il bandito (Enzo Trapani, 1950)
Processo alla città (Luigi Zampa, 1952),
I mafiosi (Roberto Mauri, 1959)
L'onorata società (Riccardo Pazzaglia, 1961)
Salvatore Giuliano (Francesco Rosi, 1961)
Mafioso (Alberto Lattuada, 1962)
Un uomo da bruciare (Paolo e Vittorio Taviani, 1962)
Le mani sulla città (Francesco Rosi, 1963)

Il gattopardo (Luchino Visconti, 1963)

A ciascuno il suo (Elio Petri, 1967)

Delitto a Posillipo (Renato Parravicini, 1967)

Gente d'onore (Folco Lulli, 1967)

Il giorno della civetta (Damiano Damiani, 1968)

Il sasso in bocca (Giuseppe Ferrara, 1970)

Cose di cosa nostra (Steno, 1971)

Il caso Mattei (Francesco Rosi, 1972)

Mimi metallurgico ferito nell'onore (Lina WertmÜller, 1972)

Lucky Luciano (Francesco Rosi, 1973)

Baciamo le mani (Vittorio Schiraldi, 1973)

L'onorata famiglia: Uccidere è cosa nostra (Tonino Ricci, 1973)

Perché si uccide un magistrato (Damiano Damiani, 1974)

Gente di rispetto (Luigi Zampa, 1975)

Cadaveri eccellenti (Franceso Rosi, 1976)

Il prefetto di ferro (Pasquale Squitieri, 1977)

Corleone (Pasquale Squitieri, 1978)

Da Corleone a Brooklyn (Umberto Lezzi, 1979)

Napoli… la camorra sfida, la città risponde (Alfonso Brescia, 1979)

Tre fratelli (Francesco Rosi, 1981)

Cento giorni a Palermo (Giuseppe Ferrara, 1984)

La piovra (TV series, 1984–2000)

Il pentito (Pasquale Squitieri, 1985)

Pizza Connection (Damiano Damiani, 1985)

Il camorrista (Giuseppe Tornatore, 1986)

Mery per sempre (Marco Risi, 1989)

Dimenticare Palermo (Francesco Rosi, 1990)

Johnny Stecchino (Roberto Benigni, 1991)

La scorta (Ricky Tognazzi, 1993)

Giovanni Falcone (Giuseppe Ferrara, 1993)

Il lungo silenzio (Margarette Von Trotta, 1993)

Palermo-Milano sono andata (Claudio Fragasso, 1995)

Un eroe borghese (Michele Placido, 1995)

Testimone a rischio (Pasquale Pozzessere, 1996)

Un posto al sole (TV, 1996–)

Lo zio di Brooklyn (Daniele Ciprì e Franco Maresco, 1996)

Pianese Nunzio, 14 anni a maggio (Antonio Capuano, 1996)

Diario di una siciliana ribelle (Marco Amenta, 1997)

Tano da morire (Roberta Torre, 1997)

Teatro di guerra (Mario Martone, 1998)

Tu ridi (Paolo and Vittorio Taviani, 1998)

Excellent Cadavers (Ricky Tognazzi, 1999)

Placido Rizzotto (Pasquale Scimeca, 2000)

I cento passi (Marco Tullio Giordana, 2000)

Luna Rossa (Antonio Capuano, 2001)

Donne di mafia (Giuseppe Ferrara, 2001)

I banchieri di dio: Il caso Calvi (Giuseppe Ferrara, 2002)

Angela (Roberta Torre, 2002)

Io non ho paura (Gabriele Salvatores, 2003)

Segreti di stato (Paolo Benvenuti, 2003)

Certi bambini (Antonio and Andrea Frazzi, 2004)

Le conseguenze dell'amore (Paolo Sorrentino, 2004)

La mafia è bianca (Stefano Maria Bianchi and Alberto Nerazzini, 2005)

Alla luce del sole (Roberto Faenza, 2005)

Romanzo criminale (Michele Placido, 2005)

In un altro paese (Marco Turco, 2005)

Il caimano (Nanni Moretti, 2006)

L'onore e il rispetto (TV, 2006–17)

Vedi Napoli e poi muori (Enrico Caria, 2006)

Il fantasma di Corleone (Marco Amenta, 2006)

Milano Palermo Il ritorno (Claudio Fragasso, 2007)

L'ultimo padrino (Marco Risi, 2007)

Oltre la paura: Bruno contro la mafia (Alberto Coletta, 2007)

Fine pena mai: paradiso perduto (Davide Barletti and Lorenzo Conte, 2007)

Il dolce e l'amaro (Andrea Porporati, 2007)

Biùtiful cauntri (Esmeralda Calabria and Andrea D'Ambrosio, 2007)

L'uomo di vetro (Stefano Incerti, 2007)

Era mio fratello (Claudio Bonivento, 2007)

Galantuomini (Edoardo Winspeare, 2008)

Io ricordo (Ruggero Gabbai, 2008)

Gomorra (Matteo Garrone, 2008)

Romanzo Criminale: La Serie (TV, 2008–10)

La siciliana ribelle (Marco Amenta, 2009)

Toxic: Napoli (Santiago Stelley, 2009)

Uomini d'onore (Francesco Sbano, 2009)

La bambina deve prendere aria (Barbara Rossi Prudente, 2009)

Fortapàsc (Marco Risi, 2009)

Tatanka (Giuseppe Gagliardi, 2011)

Campania In-Felix (Ivana Corsale, 2011)

Mozzarella stories (Edoardo DeAngelis, 2011)

Paolo Borsellino – I 57 giorni (Alberto Negrin, 2012)

Sacra corona unita e il pericolo che viene dall'est (Aldo Zappalà, 2012)

Cesare deve morire (Paolo Taviani and Vittorio Taviani, 2012)

Faccia d'angelo (Andrea Porporati, 2012)

Una vita tranquilla (Claudio Cupellini, 2013)

Il clan dei camorristi (TV, 2013)

Salvo (Fabio Grassadonia and Antonio Piazza, 2013)

La mafia uccide solo d'estate (Pierfrancesco Diliberto, 2013)

Anime nere (Francesco Munzi, 2014)

La trattativa (Sabina Guzzanti, 2014)
Gomorra: La Serie (TV, 2014–)
La terra dei santi (Fernando Muraca, 2015)
Lady 'Ndrangheta (Oren Jacoby, 2015)
Era d'estate (Fiorella Infascelli, 2016)
Suburra (Michele Placido, 2015)
Suburra: La Serie (TV, 2017–)
La paranza dei bambini (Claudio Giovannesi, 2019)

Selected Bibliography

Abadinsky, Howard. *Organized Crime*. Belmont, MA: Wadsworth, 2013.

Affron, Mirella. 'The Italian-American in American Films, 1918–1971.' *Italian Americana* 3 (1977): 232–55.

Alba, Richard. *Italian Americans: Into the Twilight of Ethnicity*. Englewood Cliffs, NJ: Prentice Hall, 1985.

Albano, Vittorio. *La Mafia nel cinema siciliano: da In nome della legge a Placido Rizzotto*. Manduria: Barbieri, 2003.

Alexander, Shana. *The Pizza Connection: The Lawyers, Money, Drugs, Mafia*. New York: Weidenfield and Nicolson, 1988.

Allum, Felia. *Camorristi, Politicians, and Businessmen: The Transformation of Organized Crime in Post-War Naples*. Leeds: Northern Universities Press, 2008.

Allum, Felia, and Percy Allum. 'Revisiting Naples: Clientelism and Organized Crime.' *Journal of Modern Italian Studies* 13, no. 3 (2008): 340–65.

Allum, Felia, and Renate Siebert, eds. *Organized Crime and the Challenge to Democracy*. London: Routledge, 2003.

Arlacchi, Pino. *Men of Dishonor: Inside the Sicilian Mafia*. New York: William Morrow, 1993.

– *Mafia Business: The Mafia Ethic and the Spirit of Capitalism*. London: Verso, 1986.

Babini, Luana. 'The Mafia: New Cinematic Perspectives.' In *Italian Cinema: New Directions*, edited by William Hope, 229–50. Bern: Peter Lang, 2005.

Baughman, James L. *Same Time, Same Station: Creating American Television, 1948–1961*. Baltimore, MD: Johns Hopkins University Press, 2007.

Behan, Tom. *See Naples and Die: The Camorra and Organized Crime*. London: I.B. Tauris Publishers, 2002.

Bergreen, Lawrence. *Capone: The Man and the Era*. New York: Simon and Schuster, 1994.

Bernardi, Daniel, ed. *The Birth of Whiteness: Race and the Emergence of U.S. Cinema*. New Brunswick, NJ: Rutgers University Press, 1996.

Bernstein, Lee. *The Greatest Menace: Organized Crime in Cold War America*. Amherst, MA: University of Massachusetts Press, 2002.

Bertellini, Giorgio. *Italy in Early American Cinema*. Bloomington, IN: Indiana University Press, 2010.

Biskind, Peter. *The Godfather Companion*. New York: Harper Perennial, 1990.

Blok, Anton. 'Mafia and Blood Symbolism.' In *Risky Transactions: Trust, Kinship and Ethnicity*, edited by Frank K. Salter, 109–28. New York: Berghahn Books, 2002.

– *Honour and Violence*. Malden, MA: Blackwell Publishers, 2001.

Bolzoni, Francesco, ed. *Francesco Rosi*. Rome: Edizioni Cinecittà Estero, 1990.

Bondanella, Peter. *A History of Italian Cinema*. New York: Continuum, 2009.

– *Hollywood Italians: Dagos, Palookas, Romeos, Wise Guys and Sopranos*. New York: Continuum, 2004.

– *Italian Cinema: From Neorealism to the Present*. New York: Continuum, 2003.

Boni, Marta. *Romanzo Criminale: Transmedia and Beyond*. Venice: Edizioni Ca' Foscari, 2014.

Browne, Nick, ed. *Francis Ford Coppola's the Godfather Trilogy*. Cambridge: Cambridge University Press, 2000.

Brunetta, Gian Piero. *Cent'anni di cinema italiano*. Vol. 2: *Dal 1945 ai giorni nostri*. 4th ed. Bari: Laterza, 2006.

Brunette, Peter, ed. *Martin Scorsese Interviews*. Jackson, MI: University Press of Mississippi, 1999.

Camaiti Hostert, Anna, and Anthony Julian Tamburri, eds. *Screening Ethnicity: Cinematographic Representations of Italian Americans in the United States*. Boca Raton, FL: Bordighera, 2001.

Casella, Paola. *Hollywood Italian: Gli italiani nell'america di celluloide*. Milan: Baldini and Castoldi, 1998.

Casillo, Robert. *Gangster Priest: The Italian American Cinema of Martin Scorsese*. Toronto: University of Toronto Press, 2006.

– 'Moments in Italian-American Cinema: From *Little Caesar* to Coppola and Scorsese.' In *From the Margin: Writings in Italian Americana*, edited by Anthony Julian Tamburri, Paul A. Giordano, and Fred L. Gardaphé, 374–96. West Lafayette, IN: Purdue University Press, 1991.

Cavallero, Jonathan J. *Hollywood's Italian American Filmmakers: Capra, Scorsese, Savoca, Coppola, and Tarantino*. Urbana, IL: University of Illinois Press, 2011.

– 'Gangsters, Fessos, Tricksters, and Sopranos: The Historical Roots of Italian American Stereotype Anxiety.' *Journal of Popular Film and Television* (2004): 50–63.

Chown, Jeffrey. *Hollywood Auteur: Francis Coppola*. New York: Praeger, 1988.

Clarens, Carlos. *Crime Movies: An Illustrated History of the Gangster Genre from D.W. Griffith to Pulp Fiction*. New York: De Capo, 1997.

Cook Kenna, Laura. 'Dangerous Men, Dangerous Media: Constructing Ethnicity, Race, and Media's Impact Through the Gangster Image, 1959–2007.' PhD diss., George Washington University, 2008.

D'Acierno, Pellegrino, ed. *The Italian American Heritage: A Companion to Literature and Arts*. New York: Garland, 1999.

D'Amato, Marina, ed. *La mafia allo specchio: La trasformazione mediatica del mafioso*. Milan: FrancoAngeli, 2013.

Dainotto, Roberto M. *The Mafia: A Cultural History*. London: Reaktion Books, 2015.

Dal Cerro, William. 'Hollywood Versus Italians: Them – 400: Us – 50.' *The Italic Way* 27 (1997): 10–32.

Dash, Mike. *The First Family: Terror, Extortion and the Birth of the American Mafia*. New York: Random House, 2009.

De Stefano, George. *An Offer We Can't Refuse: The Mafia in the Mind of America*. New York: Faber and Faber, 2006.

Dickie, John. *Mafia Republic: Italy's Criminal Curse: Cosa Nostra, Camorra, and 'Ndrangheta from 1946 to the Present*. London: Spectre, 2014.

– *Blood Brotherhoods: The Rise of the Italian Mafias*. London: Sceptre, 2011.

– *Cosa Nostra: A History of the Sicilian Mafia*. New York: Palgrave Macmillan, 2004.

Di Forti, Filippo. *Per una psicoanalisi della mafia*. Verona: Berani, 1982.

Di Giorgi, Silvio. 'The Dream of a New Sicilian Cinema.' *Cineaste: America's Leading Magazine on the Art and Politics of the Cinema* 23, no. 1 (1997): 20–23.

di Lorenzo, Silvia. *La grande madre mafia: psicoanalisi del potere mafioso*. Parma: Pratiche, 1996.

Dino, Alessandra. *La mafia devota: Chiesa, religione, Cosa nostra*. Rome: LaTerza, 2008.

– 'Symbolic Domination and Active Power: Female Roles in Criminal Organizations.' In *Women and the Mafia: Female Roles in Organized Crime Structures,* edited by Giovanni Fiandaca, 67–86. New York: Springer, 2007.

–, ed. *Pentiti: I collaboratori di giustizia, le istituzioni, l'opinione pubblica*. Rome: Donzelli Editore, 2006.

Dougan, Andy. *Martin Scorsese: The Making of His Movies*. New York: Thunder's Mouth Press, 1998.

Duggan, Christopher. *Fascism and the Mafia*. New Haven, CT: Yale University Press, 1989.

– *Sicilian Origins of the Mafia*. Zurich: Centre for Security and Conflict Studies, 1987.

Esposito, Dawn. 'Gloria, Maerose, Irene and Me: Mafia Women and Abject Spectatorship.' *MELUS* 28, no. 3 (2003): 91–109.

– 'Looking at Myself but Seeing the Other: Images of Italian-Americans in the Cinema.' *Italian American Review* 5, no. 1 (1996): 126–35.

Falcone, Giovanni. *Men of Honour: The Truth About the Mafia*. London: Warner, 1992.

Farrell, Joseph. *Understanding the Mafia*. Manchester: Manchester University Press, 1997.

– *Leonardo Sciascia*. Edinburgh: Edinburgh University Press, 1995.

Fazio, Ida. 'The Family, Honour and Gender in Sicily: Models and New Research.' *Modern Italy* 9, no. 2 (November 2004): 263–80.

Fentress, James. *Rebels and Mafiosi: Death in a Sicilian Landscape*. Ithaca, NY: Cornell University Press, 2000.

Ferraro, Thomas J. *Ethnic Passages: Literary Immigrants in Twentieth-Century America*. Chicago: University of Chicago Press, 1993.

Fiandaca, Giovanni, ed. *Women and the Mafia: Female Roles in Organized Crime Structures*. New York: Springer, 2007.

Friedman, Lester, ed. *Unspeakable Images: Ethnicity and the American Cinema*. Urbana, IL: University of Illinois Press, 1991.

Gambetta, Diego. *The Sicilian Mafia: The Business of Private Protection*. Cambridge, MA: Harvard University Press, 1993.

Gambino, Richard. *Blood of My Blood: The Dilemma of the Italian-Americans*. 2nd ed. Toronto: Guernica, 2004.

Gardaphé, Fred. *From Wiseguys to Wise Men: The Gangster and Italian American Masculinities*. London: Routledge, 2006.

– 'Re-Inventing Sicily in Italian American Writing and Film.' *MELUS* 28, no. 3 (2003): 55–71.

Gieri, Manuela. *Contemporary Italian Filmmaking: Strategies of Subversion*. Toronto: University of Toronto Press, 1995.

Glenny, Misha. *McMafia: A Journey Through the Global Criminal Underworld*. New York: Knopf, 2008.

Gribaudi, Gabriella, ed. *Traffici criminali: Camorre, mafie e reti internazionali dell'illegalità*. Turin: Bollati Boringhieri, 2009.

Grieveson, Lee, Esther Sonnet, and Peter Stanfield, eds. *Mob Culture: Hidden Histories of the American Gangster Film*. New Brunswick, NJ: Rutgers University Press, 2005.

Hart, Elizabeth. 'Destabilising Paradise: Men, Women and Mafiosi: Sicilian Stereotypes.' *Journal of Intercultural Studies* 28, no. 2 (2007): 213–26.

Hess, Henner. *Mafia and Mafiosi: Origin, Power and Myth*. Bathurst: Crawford House, 1998.

Holdaway, Dom. 'Boss in Sala: Cultural Legitimacy and Italian Mafia Films.' *Comunicazioni sociali* 3 (2016): 445–54.

Iaccio, Pasquale. *Il Mezzogiorno tra cinema e storia: ricordi e testimonianze*. Naples: Liguori Editore, 2002.

Iannaccaro, Giuliana. "'I'm Going to F***** Kill You": Verbal Censorship in Dubbed Mafia Movies.' In *Enforcing and Eluding Censorship: British and Anglo-Italian Perspectives*, edited by Giovanna Iamartino, 144–66. Newcastle upon Tyne: Cambridge Scholars.

Ingle, Bob, and Sandy McClure. *The Soprano State: New Jersey's Culture of Corruption*. New York: St. Martin's Press, 2008.

Ingrascì, Ombretta. *Donne d'onore: storie di mafia al femminile*. Milan: Mondadori, 2007.

Jacobs, James. *Mobsters, Unions and Feds: The Mafia and the American Labor Movement*. New York: New York University Press, 2006.

Jameson, Fredric. 'Reification and Utopia in Mass Culture.' *Social Text* 1 (Winter 1979): 130–48.

Jamieson, Alison. *The Antimafia: Italy's Fight Against Organized Crime*. London: Macmillan Press, 2000.

– 'Mafiosi and Terrorists: Italian Women in Violent Organizations.' *SAIS Review* 20, no. 2 (2000): 51–64.

Johnson, Robert K. *Francis Ford Coppola*. Boston, MA: Twayne, 1977.

Johnstone, Nick. *Abel Ferrara: The King of New York*. London: Omnibus Press, 1999.

Kelly, Mary Pat. *Martin Scorsese: The First Decade*. New York: Redgrave, 1980.

Kinder, Marsha. 'Violence American Style: The Narrative Orchestration of Violent Attractions.' In *Violence and American Cinema*, edited by J. David Slocum, 63–100. New York: Routledge, 2001.

Klienecht, William. *The New Ethnic Mobs: The Changing Face of Organized Crime in America*. New York: The Free Press, 1996.

Knapp, Lawrence F., ed. *Brian De Palma Interviews*. Jackson, MI: University of Mississippi Press, 2003.

Landy, Marcia. *Italian Cinema: National Film Traditions*. Cambridge: Cambridge University Press, 2000.

Langman, Larry. *American Film Cycles: The Silent Era*. Westport, CT: Greenwood, 1998.

Lavery, David, ed. *Reading the Sopranos: Hit TV from HBO*. New York: I.B. Tauris, 2006.

Lawton, Ben. 'America Through Italian/American Eyes: Dream or Nightmare?' In *From the Margin: Writings in Italian Americana*, edited by Anthony J. Tamburri, Paolo A. Giordano, and Fred L. Gardaphé, 417–49. West Lafayette, IN: Purdue University Press, 2000.

– '*Salvatore Giuliano:* Francesco Rosi's Revolutionary Postmodernism.' In *Poet of Civic Courage: The Films of Francesco Rosi*, edited by Carlo Testa, 8–42. Westport, CT: Praeger, 1996.

LoBrutto, Vincent. *Martin Scorsese: A Biography*. Westport, CT: Praeger, 2006.

Longrigg, Clare. *No Questions Asked: The Secret Life of Women in the Mob*. New York: Hyperion, 2004.

LoVerso, Girolamo, ed. *La Mafia dentro: psicologia e psicopatologia di un fondamentalismo*. Milan: Franco Angeli, 2002.

Lunde, Paul. *Organized Crime: An Inside Guide to the World's Most Successful Industry*. London: Dorling Kindersley, 2004.

Lupo, Salvatore. *History of the Mafia*. Translated by Antony Shugar. New York: Columbia University Press, 2009.

Madeo, Liliana. *Donne di mafia: Vittime, complici e protagoniste*. Milan: Baldoni and Castoldi, 1997.

Marangi, Michele, and Paolo Rossi. *La mafia è cosa nostra: 10 film sull'onorata società*. Turin: Gruppo Abele, 1993.

Marcus, Millicent. 'In Memoriam: The Neorealist Legacy in the Contemporary Sicilian Anti-Mafia Film.' In *Italian Neorealism and Global Cinema*, edited by Laura E. Ruberto and Kristi M. Wilson, 290–306. Detroit, MI: Wayne State University Press, 2007.

– *After Fellini: National Cinema in the Postmodern Age*. Baltimore, MD: Johns Hopkins University Press, 2002.

Masciopinto, Rosa. *Donne d'onore: storie di mafia al femminile*. Palermo: Edizioni della battaglia, 1994.

Mason, Fran. *American Gangster Cinema: From Little Caesar to Pulp Fiction*. New York: Palgrave Macmillan, 2002.

McCarty, John. *Bullets over Hollywood: The American Gangster Picture from the Silents to 'The Sopranos'.* Cambridge: Da Capo Press, 2004.

Messenger, Chris. *The Godfather and American Culture: How the Corleones Became 'Our Gang'.* Albany, NY: State University of New York Press, 2002.

Michalczyk, John. *The Italian Political Filmmakers*. Rutherford: Farleigh Dickinson University Press, 1986.

Milito, Lynda, and Reg Potterton. *Mafia Wife: My Story of Love, Murder, and Madness*. New York: Harper Collins, 2003.

Moe, Nelson. *The View from Vesuvius: Italian Culture and the Southern Question*. Berkeley, CA: University of California Press, 2002.

Morabito, Stefano, ed. *Mafia, 'Ndrangheta, Camorra. Nelle trame del potere parallelo*. Rome: Gangemi Editore, 2005.

Mori, Cesare. *The Last Struggle with the Mafia*. London: Putnam, 1933.

Munby, Jonathan. *Public Enemies, Public Heroes: Screening the Gangster from 'Little Caesar' to 'Touch of Evil'.* Chicago: University of Chicago Press, 1999.

Munn, Michael. *The Hollywood Connection: The True Story of Organized Crime in Hollywood*. London: Robson Books, 1993.

Muscio, Giuliana, ed. *Mediated Ethnicity: New Italian-American Cinema*. New York: John D. Calandra Italian-American Institute, 2010.

Nicholls, Mark. *Scorsese's Men: Melancholia and the Mob*. North Melbourne: Pluto, 2004.

Nochimson, Martha P. *Dying to Belong: Gangster Movies in Hollywood and Hong Kong*. Oxford: Blackwell, 2007.

Orlando, Leoluca. *Fighting the Mafia and Renewing Sicilian Culture*. San Francisco, CA: Encounter Books, 2001.

Oullette, Laurie, ed. *A Companion to Reality TV*. Oxford: Wiley Blackwell, 2014.

Pantaleone, Michele. *Mafia e antimafia*. Naples: T. Pironti, 1992.

Paoli, Letizia. *Mafia Brotherhoods*. Oxford: Oxford University Press, 2003.

Petacco, Arrigo. *Il prefetto di ferro*. Milan: Mondadori, 2004.

Phillips, Gene D. *Godfather: The Intimate Francis Ford Coppola*. Lexington, KY: University of Kentucky Press, 2004.

Phillips, Gene D., and Rodney Hill, eds. *Francis Ford Coppola: Interviews*. Jackson, MI: University Press of Mississippi, 2004.

Pickering-Iazzi, Robin, ed. *The Italian Antimafia, New Media, and the Culture of Legality*. Toronto: University of Toronto Press, 2017.

– *The Mafia in Italian Lives and Literature: Life Sentences and Their Geographies*. Toronto: University of Toronto Press, 2015.

– *Mafia and Outlaw Stories from Italian Life and Literature*. Toronto: University of Toronto Press, 2007.

Pistone, Joseph D. *Donnie Brasco: My Undercover Life in the Mafia*. New York: New American Library, 1988.

Pitkin, Thomas, and Francesco Cordasco. *The Black Hand: A Chapter in Ethnic Crime*. Totowa, NJ: Littlefield Adams, 1977.

Pizzini-Gambetta, Valeria. 'Becoming Visible: Did the Emancipation of Women Reach the Sicilian Mafia?' In *Speaking Out and Silencing: Culture, Society and Politics in Italy in the 1970s*, edited by Ada Cento Bull and Adalgisa Giorgio, 201–11. London: Legenda, 2006.

Principato, Teresa, and Alessandra Dino. *Mafia donna: le vestiali del sacro e dell'onore.* Palermo: Flaccovio, 1997.

Puglisi, Anna. *Donne, mafia e antimafia.* Trapani: DG Editore, 2005.

Raab, Selwyn. *Five Families: The Rise, Decline, and Resurgence of America's Most Powerful Mafia Empires.* New York: St. Martin's Press, 2006.

Rafter, Nicole. *Shoot in the Mirror: Crime Films and Society.* Oxford: Oxford University Press, 2006.

Renga, Dana. *Watching Sympathetic Perpetrators on Italian Television: Gomorrah and Beyond.* New York: Palgrave Macmillan, 2019.

– ed. 'Gomorra: la serie.' *The Italianist 36,* no. 2 (2016): 287–354.

– 'Modern Mob Movies: Twenty Years of Gangsters on the Italian Screen.' In *The Italian Cinema Book,* edited by Peter Bondanella, 238–45. London: Palgrave Macmillan and the British Film Institute, 2014.

– *Unfinished Business: Screening the Italian Mafia in the New Millennium.* Toronto, Buffalo, and London: The University of Toronto Press, 2013.

Renga, Dana, and Allison Cooper, eds. 'Italy's Other Mafias: A Roundtable.' *The Italianist* 33, no. 2 (2013): 190–235.

Reppetto, Thomas. *Bringing Down the Mob: The War Against the American Mafia.* New York: Henry Holt, 2006.

– *American Mafia: A History of Its Rise to Power.* New York: Henry Holt, 2004.

Robb, Peter. *Midnight in Sicily.* Boston, MA: Faber and Faber, 1998.

Rosow, Eugene. *Born to Lose: The Gangster Film in America.* New York: Oxford University Press, 1978.

Russo, Gus. *The Outfit: The Role of Chicago's Underworld in the Shaping of Modern America.* New York: Bloomsbury, 2003.

Ruth, David. *Inventing the Public Enemy: The Gangster in American Culture, 1918–1934.* Chicago: University of Chicago Press, 1996.

Sales, Isaia. *La camorra, le camorre.* Rome: Riuniti, 1988.

Santino, Umberto. *Storia del movimento antimafia.* Rome: Riuniti, 2000.

Saviano, Roberto. '*Gomorrah: A Personal Journey into the Violent International Empire of Naples' Organized Crime System.* Translated by Virginia Jewiss. New York: Farrar, Straus and Giroux, 2007.

– *Gomorra. Viaggio nell'impero economico e nel sogno di dominio della camorra.* Milan: Mondadori, 2006.

Schneider, Jane, ed. *Italy's 'Southern Question': Orientalism in One Country.* Oxford: Berg, 1998.

Schneider, Jane C., and Peter T. Schneider. *Reversible Destiny: Mafia, Anti-Mafia, and the Struggle for Palermo.* Berkeley, CA: University of California Press, 2003.

Schumacher, Michael. *Francis Ford Coppola: A Filmmaker's Life.* New York: Crown, 1999.

Siebert, Renate. *Secrets of Life and Death: Women and the Mafia.* Translated by Liz Heron. London: Verso, 1996.

– 'Women and the Mafia: The Power of Silence and Memory.' In *Gender and Memory,* edited by Luisa Passerini and Paul Thompson, 73–88. New York: Oxford University Press, 1996.

– *La mafia, la morte e il ricordo.* Soveria Manelli: Rubbettino, 1995.

Smith, Murray. 'Just What Is it That Makes Tony Soprano Such an Appealing, Attractive Murderer?' In *Ethics at the Cinema,* edited by Ward Jones and Samantha Vice, 66–90. Oxford: Oxford University Press, 2011.

Sterling, Claire. *Piovra: The Long Reach of the International Sicilian Mafia.* London: Grafton, 1991.

Stille, Alexander. *Excellent Cadavers: The Mafia and the Death of the First Italian Republic.* New York: Pantheon, 1995.

Tamburri, Anthony Julian, Paul A. Giordano, and Fred L. Gardaphé, eds. *From the Margin: Writings in Italian Americana*. West Lafayette, IN: Purdue University Press, 1991.

Thompson, David, and Ian Christie, eds. *Scorsese on Scorsese*. London: Faber and Faber, 1989.

Tucker, Kenneth. *Eliot Ness and the Untouchables: The Historical Reality and the Film and Television Depictions*. Jefferson, NC: McFarland and Company, 2000.

Wood, Mary P. *Italian Cinema*. Oxford: Berg, 2005.

– *Rosi's Cinema Between Literature and Social Themes*. Edinburgh: Italian Cultural Institute, 2001.

Yaquinto, Marilyn. *Pump 'Em Full of Lead: A Look at Gangsters on Film*. New York: Twayne, 1998.

– 'Tough Love: Mamas, Molls, and Mob Wives.' In *Action Chicks: New Images of Tough Women in Popular Culture*, edited by Sharon Innes, 207–29. New York: Palgrave, 2004.

Contributors

Pierpaolo Antonello	The University of Cambridge
Rebecca Bauman	Fashion Institute of Technology
Louis Bayman	University of Southampton
Daniela Bini	University of Texas, Austin
Claudio Bisoni	University of Bologna
Norma Bouchard	San Diego State University
Amy Boylan	The University of New Hampshire
Robert Casillo	University of Miami
Jonathan J. Cavallero	Bates College
Allison Cooper	Bowdoin College
Pellegrino D'Acierno	Hofstra University
Giovanna De Luca	College of Charleston
George De Stefano	Author and Critic
John Dickie	University College London
Piero Garofalo	The University of New Hampshire
Robert Gordon	The University of Cambridge
Thomas Harrison	University of California, Los Angeles
Margherita Heyer-Caput	University of California, Davis
Danielle Hipkins	University of Exeter
Dom Holdaway	Università Cattolica del Sacro Cuor
Fatima Karim	Political Research Analyst
Elizabeth Leake	Columbia University
Giancarlo Lombardi	College of Staten Island and CUNY Graduate Center
Vincenzo Maggitti	University of Stockholm
Millicent Marcus	Yale University
Gaetana Marrone	Princeton University
Chiara Mazzucchelli	University of Central Florida
Nelson Moe	Barnard College, Columbia University
Alan O'Leary	University of Leeds
Catherine O'Rawe	University of Bristol

Michael O'Riley	Colorado College
Sean O'Sullivan	The Ohio State University
Fulvio Orsitto	California State University, Chico
Anna Paparcone	Bucknell University
Elena Past	Wayne State University
Daniel Paul	The Ohio State University
Robin Pickering-Iazzi	University of Wisconsin, Milwaukee
Jacqueline Reich	Fordham University
Dana Renga	The Ohio State University
Franco Ricci	The University of Ottawa
John Paul Russo	University of Miami
Paolo Russo	Oxford Brookes University
Myriam Swennen Ruthenberg	Florida Atlantic University
JoAnne Ruvoli	
Lara Santoro	Drew University
Jane Schneider	CUNY Graduate Center (Emeritus)
Peter Schneider	Fordham University (Emeritus)
Monica Seger	The College of William & Mary
Maddalena Spazzini	Richmond College, Rome
Anthony Julian Tamburri	John D. Calandra Italian American Institute, Queens College/ CUNY
Carlo Testa	University of British Columbia
Laura Wittman	Stanford University
Mary Wood	Birkbeck, University of London (Emeritus)
Alberto Zambenedetti	University of Toronto